The Art of Moral Protest

James M. Jasper

The Art of Moral Protest

Culture, Biography,
and Creativity in
Social Movements

The University of Chicago Press

Chicago and London

James M. Jasper is the author of *Nuclear Politics* and coauthor of *The Animal Rights Crusade*.

The University of Chicago Press, Chicago 60637
The University of Chicago Press, Ltd., London
© 1997 by The University of Chicago
All rights reserved. Published 1997
Printed in the United States of America
06 05 04 03 02 01 00 99 98   5 4 3 2 1

ISBN (cloth): 0-226-39480-8

Library of Congress Cataloging-in-Publication Data

Jasper, James M., 1957–
    The art of moral protest : culture, biography, and creativity in social movements / James M. Jasper.
      p.   cm.
    Includes bibliographical references and index.
    ISBN 0-226-39480-8 (alk. paper)
    1. Protest movements.   2. Dissenters.   I. Title.
HN17.5.J37   1997
303.48'4—dc21
                                              97-8661
                                               CIP

For Sarah

So forcible within my heart I feel
The Bond of Nature draw me to my own,
My own in thee, for what thou art is mine;
Our State cannot be severed, we are one,
One Flesh; to loose thee were to loose my self.

Milton

Contents

Tables

Preface

For a long time, most scholars of protest were skeptical that anything of interest went on inside people's heads. Grievances were always present, and so could not explain the rise and fall of social movements, which were determined by "objective" factors such as resources and political structures. Recently, an explosion of work from a cultural perspective, or demanding a cultural perspective, has yielded insights that cannot be ignored. Too often in this reassessment, though, scholars have reduced culture to a few variables to be added to models alongside more structural (read "objective") factors, without using this new viewpoint to rethink existing findings and theories. For example, are political opportunity structures objectively there, independent of people's interpretations and definitions of them, so that those interpretations can be either accurate or inaccurate? Is rationality a set process, from which culture occasionally causes people to deviate? Are resources independent of what people think about them, and how they decide to use them? Do social networks matter beyond the meanings and affective loyalties they represent?

Culture consists of discrete, measurable items, such as beliefs or rituals, but it is also a filter through which all action occurs. It should not be contrasted with structural factors, because it is fused with them. Cultural sensibilities and processes help define the most "objective" factors as well as subjective ones, but the continual presence of culture need not make it invisible. We can discern its various components and dimensions, isolate it analytically from the resources and political structures it helps to define, and see how it varies across social contexts. It is amenable to rigorous definition, observation, and argumentation.

A concern with mental life leads not only to culture but to individuals, with their complex biographies, personalities, and idiosyncracies. They matter enormously to protest, especially when they found new groups or make key strategic decisions. Sometimes they even protest on their own, outside of organized groups. Then there are the issues of innovation, creativity, and change, which are closely related to culture and biography. Individuals often initiate small changes, many of which become widespread, and it is through cultural learning that they spread. People learn from the interaction between their existing cultural or biographical equipment and new experiences—a preeminently mental process. In paying special attention to individuals and to change, we must also reconsider strategies, which existing paradigms usually reduce to a matter of structure rather than one of conscious choice. People decide what to do, and these decisions have important effects.

Culture is everywhere, but it is not everything. We can only see it clearly by contrasting it with biography, strategy, and resources. At the same time, we cannot understand those other dimensions of protest without defining culture crisply. If culture is defined too broadly, it will encroach on the territory properly left to these other factors. If we ignore culture, as many scholars have, these other variables are forced to do too much work, stretching beyond their natural limits. A critical application of culture should define its limits as well as its strengths.

This book is the latest product of my long-standing concern with culture and morality. When I was in college in the late 1970s, calling myself a marxist was a way to distance myself from conservative political tendencies under Ford and Carter and from the complacent student culture that dominated Harvard. It was a way to express moral outrage over the inequities, waste, and irrationality of American society. But political tendencies such as maoism and leninism and theoretical ones such as althusserian structuralism lacked much humanity. When I moved to Berkeley and Todd Gitlin encouraged me to read E. P. Thompson, John Berger, and Raymond Williams, and then Foucault and Bourdieu, it no longer seemed important to maintain the marxist label in order to be a democrat and humanist. As I discuss in chapter 16, the abstractions of marxism have their share of historical horrors to account for.

Culture and morality are important to me because they make life interesting and meaningful. Culture is unavoidable, but meaningful morality is often hard to come by. To make morality anything but personal choice, though, is a severe challenge for diverse modern societies. Many commentators despair of any shared moral imagination, but they are often reflecting their status as rootless academics, ready to move thousands of miles for a higher salary. Protest movements are a good place to look for collective moral visions, with the good and the bad they entail. In modern society, they are one of the few places where we can see people working out new moral, emotional, and cognitive sensibilities.

In my first book, *Nuclear Politics*, I tried to insert cultural meanings into the heart of a structural analysis of politics and state policymaking. In each of the three countries I studied—the United States, France, and Sweden—politicians had different rhetorical and ideological ammunition for going after each other, different cleavages that defined friend and foe. Yet I found similar bundles of arguments in public debates and bureaucratic policy reports in the three countries. I isolated three such "policy styles"—technological enthusiasm, a cost-benefit style, and moralism—and I argued that the contrasting distributions of these styles (or of the men and women using them) within state structures led the three countries toward different policies after the oil crisis of 1973–74. I was also concerned to show that many of the legal and administrative "structures" often thought to constrain policy formation were as likely to result from policy decisions as to cause them. Yet the balance between artfulness (or agency) and political structure changed drastically during the 1970s, as structures hardened in place. I also had to conclude, with disappointment, that the antinuclear movements in all three countries had little effect on policy outcomes. At most they managed to delay decisions long enough for better information to appear and more rational policies to be laid out. That book discussed antinuclear movements only as one part of a broader story; thus some materials gathered for that project appear here.

In my second book, *The Animal Rights Crusade*, which I coauthored with Dorothy Nelkin, I wanted to pursue more fully the moral dimensions of protest. A movement in which the activists and the beneficiaries aren't even from the same species seemed a good case for examining the moral shocks needed to recruit strangers to a new movement, the strident tone often adopted by those who feel they occupy the moral high ground, and the polarization and mutual demonization that occur in controversies pitting divergent moral visions against each other. But we were reluctant, in a book about a single movement and written for a popular audience, to push our theorizing about morality too far. So, like the antinuclear movement, the animal rights movement appears frequently in *The Art of Moral Protest*.

This book had its share of backers and helpers. The NYU Department of Sociology, where I taught until recently, was a fertile site for thinking about social movements, and the Workshop on Politics, Power, and Protest provided written and verbal critiques of parts of my manuscript. Ed Amenta and Jeff Goodwin were especially good colleagues and commentators. Several students coauthored papers and articles on which several chapters are loosely based, and they and others read additional segments of the manuscript: Mary Bernstein, Nancy Cauthen, Cindy Gordon, Jane Poulsen, and Yvonne Zylan. Jillian Jacobs, Tamara Dumanovsky, and especially Bettina Edelstein did much of the research on consumer boycotts. Tamara Dumanovsky conducted the initial research on the Khmer Rouge. The department's research apprenticeship program provided a structure to polish much of the research, and I thank Gary Ford, Nari Choi, and especially Jordon Peugh for their assistance in checking quotes and citations. Many audiences have responded usefully to my ideas in embryonic form: the Politics and Culture Seminar at the Russell Sage Foundation; the Departments of Sociology at the CUNY Graduate Center, Harvard, the New School for Social Research, Rutgers, Princeton, and Yale; conference attendees from the American Sociological Association, the American Political Science Association, and the Society for Socioeconomics. Bob Alford, a generous friend and incisive critic who knows more about politics than almost anyone, wrote more than thirty single-spaced pages of comments on an early draft. With characteristic energy, Doug McAdam was willing to read two versions for the University of Chicago Press, with the result that the text is more of a dialogue between cultural and political-process perspectives than it once was. Several others also read early drafts, improving it in ways large and small: for this I thank William Gamson, Michael Moody, Kelly Moore, Francesca Polletta, and Sarah Rosenfield.

The NYU administration supported my research by providing a course off in the fall of 1991. Support for the research that went into individual chapters came from the MacArthur Foundation, the Alfred P. Sloan Foundation, the Spencer Foundation, and the National Science Foundation, Ethics and Values Studies, under grant DIR-8820241. I have cannibalized several of my own articles for materials, and for permission to do this I thank the University of California Press, JAI Press, and Sage Publications. They are cited where appropriate in the text.

Many others helped in large and small ways, and I thank Ralph Chipman, Lee Clarke, Stephen Cotgrove, Frank Dobbin, Renée Emunah, Barbara Epstein, Marty Gilens, Irwin Goffman, Kelli Henry, Albert Hirschman, Bob Holt, Robert Max Jackson, Kian-Woon Kwok, Joan Lambe, John Lofland, Valentine Moghadam, James Scaminaci, Neil Smelser, David Starr, Chuck Stephen, Ann Swidler, Evelyn Walters, Davida Weinberg, Harold Wilensky, and Stella Zambarloukos. Doug Mitchell of the University of Chicago Press, aware that man does not live by ideas alone, has provided marvelous sustenance for both body and soul. He is as great a companion as any. His colleagues Matt Howard, Salena Krug, and Billy have also been delightfully helpful. Nick Murray proved to be an excellent copy editor.

Most of all, I would like to thank Sarah Rosenfield, who has made my life complete in every way. As Adam knew, but it took Milton to articulate, she is very much a part of me.

ONE

The Art of Protest

Imagination is the chief instrument of the good . . . art is more moral than moralities. For the latter either are, or tend to become, consecrations of the status quo, reflections of custom, reënforcements of the established order. The moral prophets of humanity have always been poets even though they spoke in free verse or by parable. . . . Art has been the means of keeping alive the sense of purposes that outrun evidence and of meanings that transcend indurated habit.
     —John Dewey, *Art as Experience*

There is a lamppost below my apartment on Bleecker Street that helps me gauge what political causes are popular at any given moment. On 1 May 1991, when I began writing this book, the following announcements covered the metal post:

> WOMEN'S LIBERATION: WHAT WENT WRONG? A Marxist-Leninist group promised to show how the lack of a class analysis had crippled the contemporary women's movement.
>
> CELEBRATION OF RESISTANCE AGAINST THE WAR. While one group attacked one of the most successful movements of recent years, another was celebrating one of the least successful. On 8 May, Margot Kidder, Kurt Vonnegut, William Kunstler and others would denounce the recent war with Iraq at the Wetlands, a politically correct Manhattan club.
>
> NEEDLE EXCHANGE IS AIDS PREVENTION. SHARING NEEDLES SPREADS AIDS. It was unclear whether ACT UP (The AIDS Coalition to Unleash Power) was targeting drug users or city needle policies with this sign.
>
> WOULD YOU KILL FOR AN EDUCATION? This clever but unsigned poster was opposed to military recruiters in high schools.
>
> ABORTION: EVERY WOMAN'S RIGHT. Announcing a pro-choice rally.

Three of the posters protested existing government policies, but two announced events designed to reflect on social movements themselves, showing how contemplative or ingrown such movements can become. The Iraq war poster was specific to 1991; the AIDS poster could have been posted any time since the early 1980s; the others could have appeared at any time in the past twenty-five years. The five posters touched on basic issues of human existence—war and peace, men and women, life and death—about which all of us hold passionate feelings and opinions. They are questions that touch our innermost sense of who we are and why we are, as well as our moral visions about how we should act in the world. Most of our institutions are silent about existential issues like these; protest is one of the few arenas where they are raised and examined.

Several of the posters targeted science and technology—the physical tools we have developed for manipulating the world and achieving our goals. These tools pervade and structure our lives as never before in history, and it is a rare individual who is not ambivalent about them, seeing both their power and their risks. We sense the unprecedented degree to which objective "hard facts" wielded by experts are used to hide or legitimate political and economic power in our society, as elites insist that they are bowing to inevitable forces rather than exercising their own discretion. Ironically, it is our unprecedented technical power over the physical world that heightens our moral dilemmas about how to use that power. The fact that we *can* makes us (or some of us) ask if we *should*. Modern science is also thought to have drained the magic and moral meaning out of the universe; protest is one way to recreate that meaning, to insist that life makes some sense. Corporations and governments create new technologies, products, and laws; protestors help us figure out what we feel and think about them. Moral and technological themes such as these cannot be avoided in public debate, as they are issues which have been defined in part by visible, angry, political movements.

American society is rife with loud, moral protest, and not just in Greenwich Village. In 1991 Operation Rescue flooded the streets of Wichita, Kansas with thousands of anti-abortionists who were willing to be arrested over and over again for blocking the entrances of abortion clinics; George Bush's Justice Department even supported their fight against the federal judge who ordered them not to harass staff and patients. On the west coast, hundreds of environmentalists spent the summer of 1990 camping in the woods north of San Francisco, attending pantheistic rituals, sitting in the sun, sharing philosophies, and chaining themselves to giant redwoods marked for timber. On the east coast in 1980, the Ploughshares Eight—primarily Catholic priests and nuns—broke into a General Electric facility in Pennsylvania, pounded upon two Minuteman missiles with small hammers, and poured their own bright red blood over the cold grey steel of the weapons, juxtaposing the messy frailty of human life with the massive technology of destruction. In front of the United Nations in New York, there is at least one protest almost every day of the year.

Moral protest spans not only state lines, but social class boundaries. Phyllis Schlafly mobilized thousands of lower-middle-class women, perhaps fearful for their own status as homemakers, perhaps outraged by the moral statement of equality and sameness it implied, to fight the Equal Rights Amendment. Thousands of groups have been formed around the United States, many by working-class housewives, to fight local environmental hazards like toxic waste dumps and incinerators or social disruptions like public housing projects and homes for AIDS patients. A college-educated, upper-middle-class population was the primary force behind the movements against nuclear energy and weapons. Even professionals such as lawyers, doctors, and engineers—among the elites of our society—are sometimes swept into large-scale movements expressing dismay, outrage, contempt, or even plain fear. And the very poor, society's true marginals, occasionally join together to protest, overcoming habitual (but learned) paralysis, despair, and cynicism.

Moral protest is no recent fad, no mere child of an affluent society. In the seventeenth and eighteenth centuries, the United States had Bacon's, Shays's, and the Whiskey rebellions. Almost every foreign war and intervention undertaken by the U.S. government has had vociferous critics who took to the streets; in the extremely unpopular War of 1812, for instance, Nantucket Islanders declared their neutrality, while a crowd in Newburyport, Massachusetts forcibly attempted to free British prisoners of war. Ten thousand protestors gathered in New York in 1849 to express their outrage over, of all things, the British nationality and aristocratic tone of a famous Shakespearean actor of the day; twenty-two were killed in the ensuing Astor Place riots. The roots of the trade union movement lie in nineteenth-century outrage over cuts in wages, deterioration of working conditions, and other abuses by employers—in fear and moral indignation, not in calculated efforts at personal gain. Throughout that century, moral reform movements fought against drinking, gambling, breaking the Sabbath, and "licentiousness;" today YMCAs sponsor swimming pools and aerobics classes, but when they were first founded in the 1840s their mission was to help young, single men avoid the temptations of sin. On Christmas day, 1908, the mayor of New York even closed all the city's movie arcades, which, moral reformers insisted, encouraged loose morals and taught new immigrants disrespect for law and order, by means of subversive players such as the Keystone Cops. Diverse movies, plays, books, paintings, and music are regularly condemned, and sometimes purged from stores and libraries, at the urging of groups concerned with creeping immorality.

Although most of this book deals with American moral protest, the United States is hardly unique in giving rise to such political fervor. Islamic fundamentalism, most memorable in Iran in 1978–79 but persistent throughout the Islamic world, has stood as a sweeping condemnation of European imperialism and its accompanying economic and technological institutions. Temperance crusades, for the past century, have been even more popular in Sweden than the United States. Later chapters examine boycotts in nineteenth-century Ireland and the revolution in Cambodia in the 1970s. There is no country in the world forever free from rebellions, religiously based protest, or secular movements to end one or another practice perceived as despicable. Protest is not omnipresent—indeed there is probably far less than there should be—but it is recurrent.

*   *   *

Why do our thoughts about the world lead us so often to want to change it? What moral visions inspire outrage about often-distant practices and institutions? There are, after all, many other ways to respond to what displeases us. We can change our residence to escape many of the ills we detest—relying on exit, rather than voice, as Albert Hirschman once put it. Or we can simply ignore what we dislike, as so many Americans do, concentrating on the pleasures of private life. Commentators complain of apathy, narcissism, and individualism in American society. Some have argued that we lack even a language for discussing the public good as opposed to personal needs and goals. Others have decried a new narcissistic personality type, obsessed with self-identity to the extent that events in the public sphere are reduced to their implications for the self. More sympathetic observers place greater weight on the institutional barriers to voting, party formation, critical perspectives, and social change. All attempt to explain America's supposed lack of political activity.

Such critics manage to ignore the swirl of political activity that nonetheless exists around them. Many Americans are anything but apathetic. Those who choose to engage in politics still face many options short of active protest. In the United States and many other countries (still, alas, a minority of them), citizens can vote for various political representatives. As individuals we contribute money and write letters to politicians. Yet many people feel obliged to step outside these "normal" channels. At that point, they may engage in protest.

Individuals resist or protest what they dislike in many ways. They distance themselves from their organizational roles; they ignore rules they dislike; they criticize and complain; they sabotage their bosses' projects in various degrees; they pilfer supplies. Quiet resistance can grow more public, as when individuals write letters to their legislators or newspapers. Others speak out at public meetings; some send letter bombs. A striking form of individual protest is whistleblowing, an action we shall examine in chapter 6, when individuals make public the transgressions of their employers. There is protest, in other words, even when it is not part of an organized movement. Most scholars have defined this kind of action as outside their interest, preferring to examine full-fledged, coordinated movements. This choice renders invisible all the ways that individual acts of protest do or do not feed into more organized movements. Individual protestors, we shall see, have a variety of relationships to the formal groups most visible in protest movements.

Protestors frequently do organize themselves into groups, collections of which comprise social movements. Social movements are conscious, concerted, and relatively sustained efforts by organized groups of ordinary people (as opposed to, say, political parties, the military, or industrial trade groups) to change some aspect of their society by using extrainstitutional means. Some of these movements have positive agendas and try to build alternative ways of doing things, from communes to neighborhood groups to freedom schools. But most involve protest: explicit criticism of other people, organizations, and the things they believe or do. Rather than simply or directly changing what they dislike—which may not be possible—they also express their contempt and outrage over existing practices.[1]

It is their ability to provide a moral voice that makes protest activities so satisfying. They give us an opportunity to plumb our moral sensibilities and convictions, and to articulate and elaborate them. And it is important to articulate them publicly and collectively, two features which, sociologist Emile Durkheim insisted, deepen the significance and emotional impact of beliefs and feelings. Few other institutions in modern societies provide this kind of forum: schools rarely do; news media claim they're sticking to the facts; normal politics provides extremely constrained choices; even churches, synagogues, and mosques offer social gatherings more often than authentic moral tests.

Moral protest comes in different styles. The standard ones today include large public rallies and marches, occupations of symbolic or strategic sites, provocative verbal and visual rhetoric, and more mainstream lobbying and electioneering. But every group seeks creative variations on these basic tactics. Those opposed to homophobia have sponsored gay and lesbian "kiss-ins" in redneck bars and stamped "Gay Money" on dollar bills to remind us of gay and lesbian buying power. ACT UP holds "Latex Liberation Days," distributing condoms in New York City high schools. Animal rights activists have broken into research laboratories in the middle of the night to "liberate" the labs' "captives;" one group held a "Barf-In" in front of a cosmetics company to show that animal testing made them ill. Jerry Rubin and Abbie Hoffman persuaded anti-war demonstrators to try to levitate the Pentagon by means of the incantations of witches (less plentiful in 1967 than they are today); they failed but attracted amused media coverage. A favorite target, the Pentagon has had its walls splashed with blood, its lawns planted with cardboard tombstones, and its doors woven shut with brightly colored yarn (interested in social and symbolic webs, a later generation of witches chants "We are the flow, we are the ebb/ We are the weavers, we are the web," when they weave over entrances).[2] During the 1968 United Farm Workers' strike, supporters in Toronto took "Don't Eat Grapes" balloons into supermarkets, handed them out to children, and let them float to the ceilings; to the chagrin of store managers who punctured them, the balloons were filled with bright confetti. Human blood, dead fish, live rabbits, effigies of CEOs, and Pinocchio false noses have all been props in protests at the headquarters of large corporations. Even direct mail appeals offer a chance for innovation. One environmental group sent out genuine checks for two cents to attract the attention of each supporter and encourage her to "put in your two cents' worth."

*   *   *

Beyond small innovations like these, moral protest has changed its basic forms over the centuries. Scholars of Western Europe have described the following sequence. From the medieval period until the nineteenth century, peasants either formed religious movements or responded to immediate threats such as grain scarcities and high bread prices, enclosures and other attempts to curtail their traditional rights, and other arbitrary actions by elites. As cities flourished in the early modern period, their residents also took direct action against those they felt were doing wrong, sacking the homes of tax collectors, seizing shipments of grain, or attacking religious minorities. Such actions were local and short-lived, directly targeting those perceived to have erred, and rather directly redressing the perceived wrongs. Around the time of the French Revolution, other forms of protest appeared—boycotts, mass petitions, and urban rebellions—with more general aims. Such tactics, taken up first by members of the bourgeoisie and soon by the emerging industrial working class, gave rise to what I shall call citizenship movements. These efforts were organized by and on behalf of categories of people excluded in some way from full human rights, political participation, or basic economic protections. They were movements demanding full inclusion for these collectivities, including industrial workers, women, and later racial and ethnic minorities. Increasingly national in scope and better organized in a sustained way than peasants had ever been, these movements were part of the expansion of industrial society, incorporating more and more of a society into capitalist labor markets and democratic polities. Because they were making demands of states that were growing more powerful and centralized, they too have tended to grow more formal and bureaucratized over time.

In addition to these pre-industrial and industrial forms of protest, a third kind of social movement—which I shall call post-citizenship—has flourished, composed of people already integrated into their society's political, economic, and educational systems. Because they need not demand basic rights for themselves, they often pursue protections or benefits for others, including on occasion the entire human species. In the nineteenth century, post-citizenship movements often took the form of poor relief or anti-vice crusades; in the last thirty years they have pursued "post-industrial" or "post-material" aims like protection of the environment, peace and disarmament, alternative healing, lifestyle protections, and animal rights—goals which do not especially interest those seeking jobs, equal pay, or the right to vote (none of which appeared on my lamppost). Ambivalence toward modern science and technology, occasionally even outright hostility, are common themes in the recent wave—the "post-industrial" branch of post-citizenship movements. These protestors are especially interested in changing their society's cultural sensibilities. Unlike citizenship movements, which often competed with each other because they had clearly defined constituencies, post-citizenship movements flow easily into each other: the environmental and feminist movements together inspired the antinuclear movement of the 1970s, which in turn gave rise to the disarmament movement of the early 1980s. Many European scholars dubbed these "new social movements" because they contrasted so strikingly with the class-based movements and political parties that had dominated European politics for one hundred years. I prefer the term *post-industrial* because these movements take for granted the complete penetration of industrial society, and seek ways to ameliorate it effects (but they remain a subcategory of post-citizenship movements).

Protest in the United States arrived at post-industrial movements through a trajectory different from Europe's. With plentiful land to be taken from the native Indians, early religious heretics could be expelled rather than burned (witches excepted). Without a traditional peasantry or seigniorial arrangements, there were few bread riots or protest against usurpation of local rights. Americans, many living on frontiers and on farms, were heavily armed, so that—as early as Bacon's Rebellion in 1676—protest regularly took the form of boycotts and armed rebellion against central authority, such as it was. In the nineteenth century, too, the United States was filled with post-citizenship movements concerned with drinking and other sins, health foods, the environment, spirituality, and other "lifestyle" issues sometimes pursued by today's post-industrial movements. Such movements are hardly new in the United States. The labor movement, meanwhile, also differed here. White male workers were granted suffrage early, so that the labor movement concentrated on economic power rather than voting rights. The result was, for complicated reasons, extremely severe repression and the lack of a permanent political party pursuing the interests of the working class. When post-industrial movements grew—here as in Europe—out of the revolutionary efforts of the 1960s, they did not seem so new.[3] They followed a long line of post-citizenship movements.

Even so, most American scholars have taken citizenship movements as their model, as though they had studied Europe's trajectory—as many of them did. Because most students of protest study just one movement, the peculiarities of that movement affect their theories. It is all too easy to overgeneralize from one case, taking as universal many phenomena that vary across movements. The southern civil rights movement, from roughly 1955 to 1965, has provided both intellectual grist and moral inspiration for several generations of American researchers. The labor movement, another classic citizenship movement, has also been heavily studied. As a result, theorists have been slow to recognize what is different about post-citizenship, and especially post-industrial, movements, much less come up with theories to explain why citizenship and post-citizenship movements might look and act differently. In many scholarly models, citizenship movements appear normal, while post-citizenship movements appear so abnormal that they are often not even defined as social movements.

The dividing line between citizenship and post-citizenship movements is not always sharp. Few groups are oppressed in every aspect of their political and economic lives—southern blacks before the 1960s being an exception. Movements for gay, lesbian, and women's rights have partly battled legal discrimination but also tried to rework cultural meanings and tolerance for diverse lifestyles, shading into the concerns of post-citizenship protest. Women, for instance, now have the vote and many other legal rights—they can hardly be called an "excluded" group—but they face disadvantages in private life due to cultural attitudes and lifestyles. Such movements are typically divided between organizations concerned with legal rights and those pursuing cultural change.[4]

Nor are these two the only types of protest movements. There are also "moral panics" over issues like drugs or rock music, nationalist movements aimed at immigrants, and outright armed revolutions, among other types. I use several examples of moral protest in this book, but the main ones are post-industrial movements, including the antinuclear, the animal rights, and the environmental movements. By contrasting these cases with a literature developed for citizenship movements, I can often see generalizations that are true for citizenship movements but not for others—and hopefully explain why. I should be able to see dynamics invisible to those with lenses created to focus on citizenship movements. By comparing different types of movements, and even different movements within the type, we can better see what varies across protest movements and thus avoid overgeneralizations.

* * *

Most academic theories of social movements are not prepared to explain the full range of protest goals and activities, especially those of privileged rather than oppressed citizens. Older theoretical approaches (those developed before the civil rights movement) dismissed moral protest as a crowd dynamic, a sort of irrational frenzy that erupts when people are thrown together in large numbers. The newer ones inspired by citizenship movements often err in the opposite way, seeing all protest as the narrowly rational pursuit of interests, similar in its intent to the more conventional political activities of bureaucratized interest groups. Some even analyze moral protest as the disguised pursuit of material self-interest rather than as an effort to realize a moral vision. Even recent attempts to examine the culture of social movements have mostly focused on cognitive beliefs, overlooking the emotions and moral visions that support them. I shall try to fill some gaps in these research traditions by offering additional concepts and language for understanding moral protest—concepts that highlight its cultural creativity, its serious moral purpose, and its vital contribution to modern societies.

Who are we humans, who protest so much? Most prominently, perhaps, we are symbol-making creatures, who spin webs of meaning around ourselves. We proliferate metaphors and language for describing the world; we elaborate theories, hypotheses, and predictions to satisfy our curiosity; we create symbols to probe deeper and further and to impress ourselves with their beauty; and we tell each other story after story. Into this roiling cognitive activity we mix emotions and moral evaluations, constructing heroes, villains, and comic jesters, anger, envy, admiration, and indignation. We add layer upon layer, creating thoughts about previous thoughts, attaching new moral values to existing ones, working out how to feel about our own feelings. We are aware of our awareness about our meanings—and so on, with infinite complexity. We are constantly learning, revising our views, adapting to new circumstances that we ourselves often create.

A theme throughout this book is what sociologists call cultural "constructionism:" the idea that we humans together create everything that we know and experience, or at least the interpretive frameworks through which we filter all our experience. We build equipment to generate data on which to ground scientific facts. Our institutions constantly promote certain moral beliefs and suppress others. Even most of our emotions are shaped by the understandings and responses of those around us. As the "postmodernists" insist, we have no universal, absolute Truth on which we can construct our beliefs, no firm grounding that we can always take for granted. We have only our own cultural traditions, and the traditions of others. These define our world. Protest too is constructed. No individual or group has goals or interests that are objectively given without any cultural interpretation. In interaction with others, we perceive what our interests (economic, moral, emotional, and other interests) are, and build political goals in accordance with them. We also decide what tactics are appropriate, even what organizational forms fit our moral visions.

This image of humans as communicators and symbol makers, trying to make sense of the world, implies that we often protest because our systems of meaning are at stake, because we have created villains, and villains must be attacked. As Carl Schmitt pointed out, politics is about the creation of friends and foes, two of the most simple, useful—and dangerous—categories for imposing order on the world. An important aspect of this construction of meaning is the creation of moral valuations, which then give us emotional energy for striving to transform our lives and societies. We need to allocate praise and, more importantly, blame. We trust certain groups, individuals, and institutions, and mistrust others. Cultural traditions provide tools and patterns for constructing meaningful lives. Like laws, political structures, or our bank accounts, they enable us to do certain things but prevent us from doing or thinking others. Even when we cannot articulate all our cultural meanings and rules, our actions implicitly depend upon them. We are so deeply embedded in cultural traditions that, even as we transform and attack them, we cannot escape them.

For transform them we do. We are *artful* in accepting, playing upon, bending, or rejecting cultural rules, much as Beethoven absorbed, embodied, and exploded the rules for string quartets. Culture is only one dimension of life that humans are capable of changing: we also invent new technologies, accumulate or redistribute money, change laws and political systems, even reconfigure individual feelings and loyalties. This artful creativity—sociologists refer to it as agency—is present in all social life, not just in protest. But since it is the *raison d'être* of protest movements, it is especially salient there. To understand artfulness, I'll argue, we need to pay attention to the biographical sources of individual variations, for these are the seedbed for innovations.

To understand why and how people organize themselves to protest against things they dislike, we need to know what they care about, how they see their place in the world, what language they use to describe entities such as technologies, corporations, and the state. Naming is a central activity of any movement, for attaching labels to activities and aspects of the world around us helps us change our minds, see new vistas, and rearrange our feelings about others. Some slogans result from endless discussions late into the night, as when Students for a Democratic Society adopted a goal of "participatory democracy." In other cases a slogan catches on first, forcing a group to develop a philosophy to back it up, as the Student Nonviolent Coordinating Committee worked out the idea of "black power" as opposed to civil rights.[5] Others come from publications by philosophers and ideologists, such as the term *speciesism*, which animal liberationist Peter Singer coined to indicate that other species can be oppressed in the same way as certain categories of humans.[6]

When I speak of a group's sense of their place in the world, I mean that in more than a metaphorical sense. We develop routines around ourselves in physical settings, particularly in the place we conceive of as home. All familiar places, but especially our homes, have an emotional charge for us; they carry symbolic meanings which are rarely neutral. Sometimes the charge is negative, as the African-American inner-city neighborhood may connote danger and disorder to the middle-class whites who pass it on elevated freeways while commuting from the suburbs. More often the charge is positive, as it is for those who try to protect cherished neighborhoods by battling garbage dumps, hazardous waste sites, and other facilities. The clash between a good place and a bad threat may heighten the positive and negative affect associated with each. Much if not most protest is reactive, spurred by a sense of threat to one's daily life, including one's physical surroundings—a cultural and biographical dimension that is lost in models of protest as highly purposive, in pursuit of clear rights and forms of inclusion.

In addition to our strong sense of place, we are also caught up in flows of time. Not only do important historical events shape our sense of the world and ourselves, marking political generations in precise ways, but we also have different images of history itself. One dominant image, especially among the middle classes, has been that of a progressive unfolding, but there persists a strong, more pessimistic countercurrent too, one that sees limits or expects collapse. Such sensibilities about the flow of history shape people's sense of political possibilities. An optimistic vision of history as progress often supports faith in technological development and rapid political change, in order to bring about the superior and inevitable next stage. Most moderns—especially, again, the middle classes—also develop personal projects, images of a life cycle with attendant goals that unfold gradually and cumulatively over time. Certain stages of the life cycle are more conducive to political activity than others, yet some people weave political action into the fabric of their entire life tapestries.

Culture, which for now I'll define as shared mental worlds and their physical embodiments, does several things. It provides a collection of discrete beliefs, images, feelings, values, and categories, as well as bundles of these components. It also helps define or "constitute" all social action and the world as we see it. It gives us patterns of acting as well as thinking, judging, and feeling. And it offers many of the building blocks and dynamics of creativity. At the same time, culture isn't everything: it is not physical resources and the money to buy them, nor strategic interactions with other groups and individuals, nor the biographical idiosyncrasies of individuals. Culture helps define resources, strategies, and biographies, but it is not the same thing as they are. These are four autonomous dimensions of protest, each with its own distinct logic. Most traditions for studying protest, I'll argue, have collapsed one or more of these four basic dimensions into the others, sometimes even insisting that protest can be explained by just one dimension.

Our cognitive beliefs, emotional responses, and moral evaluations of the world—the three subcomponents of culture—are inseparable, and together these motivate, rationalize, and channel political action.

Beliefs and feelings emerge from many sources: professional training as an engineer or an economist; hobbies such as gardening or medieval history; rearing one's child or caring for one's elderly parents; interpersonal dynamics that were thwarted or nurtured in childhood. Because everyone has a unique biography, different elements of the surrounding culture come to be embodied in the subjective worlds of individuals (through processes I'll label biographical). The ensemble of one's activities (past and present) makes certain feelings salient, certain beliefs plausible, certain moral principles more important than others. The diversity and sheer number of these sources make it hard to predict the goals and targets of moral protest. Even more, the targets often change during the course of the protest, as participants actively—and collectively—rethink and reframe their beliefs and passions. Social movements are less predictable and stable than many forms of social interaction which occur in formal, even rigid, organizations. They are, as a result, both hard to describe in universally applicable terms and yet an important source of innovation and creativity in modern society.

This view of social life as artful, in which people play on cultural meanings and strategic expectations in a variety of ways, allows us to see many benefits of moral protest.[7] Rather than dismissing protestors as irrational kooks or selfish calculators, we can appreciate their creativity. Much like artists, they are at the cutting edge of society's understandings of itself as it changes. Moral protestors are often sensitive to moral dilemmas the rest of us ignore; they sometimes generate new ways of understanding the complexities of the human condition. Even when we disagree with their positions, they frequently force us to reconsider our own, to think up reasons and rationales, to decide if our intuitions are consonant with our basic values. They extend our moral languages. Such cogitation is an essential human activity. The news media are led to probe (if that is not too generous a word) new places, talk to new people, uncover new experiences. (None of which is to deny that the media and other social institutions at the same time deeply shape protest.) On occasion protestors even inspire practical or technical solutions to social problems, such as tests of new cosmetics that use computers rather than rabbits. In the face of social change, protestors are like the proverbial canaries in the mines, except that they sing out rather than quietly expire.

Protest movements help us articulate formless intuitions of which we are barely aware, bringing them into the light of day so that we can consider them and sometimes act upon them. Not only does this process of formulating our moral beliefs help us get clear about our political goals, but it feels good to make a public statement about what we believe. Protest is like religious ritual: it embodies our moral judgments, so that we can express allegiance to moral visions through our actions. For those who no longer hold to traditional religious practices, protest is one of the few ways to express moral viewpoints. For this reason, the protestor has become an important character type in modern societies.

At first, mine seems like a Romantic, ambitious vision of what protest movements can do, placing them at the center of our moral and intellectual life. I can be hopeful about these effects, though, because of pessimism about others. Total revolutions are not only rare but seem to turn out hellishly. Few protest movements attain even their stated goals, although progressive scholars often delude themselves about this. Nuclear energy was stalemated in the United States, but not by the efforts of the antinuclear movement. The huge peace mobilization of the early 1980s had no discernible influence on weapons policies. Even the civil rights movement, despite major legislative victories, has had disappointing long-term results. My view of protestors as primarily participants in public debates, interested in consciousness as much as policies, is a modest, even disillusioned, perspective.

But this more restricted view of protest allows for normative judgments of how protestors behave. When they undermine public understanding, misrepresenting their goals for instance in order to win, then they are playing this role badly. In the inevitable tension between instrumental success and contributions to public awareness, I favor the latter. This is a relatively arbitrary value call. I fear those who favor winning over honesty, for they can justify this preference only if they are certain that they possess the full truth. I doubt that anyone has the whole truth, but if they do, I want them to persuade me, not impose it on me.

A lens that focuses on culture and creativity may help us judge the goals of social movements as well as their methods. Some movements ignore or deny the value of cultural tradition: the way in which it connects people to their past, to future generations, to each other. Attention to creativity, in addition, may help us criticize movements that are too creative, denying their own cultural debts in an effort to remake society from scratch. Most of all, though, we can censure movements that aim at denying cultural voice and creativity to others, for this is a hideous form of oppression. The Nazis, the Khmer Rouge, and the Taliban of Afghanistan not only aimed at destroying certain cultures, but prevented many people from creating their own culture.

Part one reviews academic theories and conceptual building blocks

for understanding protest. Chapter 2 examines the citizenship paradigms that have dominated research on protest during the twentieth
century; chapter 3 is a broader discussion of the basic dimensions of
protest; chapter 4 presents recent efforts to rediscover culture, partly
by studying post-citizenship movements, especially in their post-
industrial form. Part two probes the multiple impulses that lead individuals to protest, including positive moral utopias, religion, fears of
the unknown, threats to established routines, hatred of other social
groups, professional ethics, and symbolic beliefs. Chapters 5 through
7, respectively, highlight emotional, moral, and cognitive dynamics,
although the main conclusion is that these are inseparable in action.
By concentrating on individual protesters, chapters 5 and 6 remain on
the border of biography and culture, while chapter 7 turns to more
collective cultural processes instigated by movement recruiters. Part
three looks at the internal culture of protest movements: rituals that
sustain the commitment of participants, the many direct pleasures associated with protest activities, the tastes that guide choices among
diverse tactics. I address a range of strategies from consumer boycotts
to site occupations, violence, and the taking of human life. Part four
places protestors in the context of their interactions with others: the
news media and potential supporters in the mobilization of resources
in chapter 12; and the state and other players in strategic games in
chapter 13. I try to show how cultural processes shape both resources
and strategies. In chapter 14 I suggest how culture and the other dimensions of protest work together to explain the growth, strategies,
and effects of protest movements. Finally, in part five, I adopt a more
normative voice. I describe the character type of the protestor, focusing
especially on the meaning protest can give to people's lives. After
pointing to circumstances in which protest can become dangerous
and self-defeating (chapter 16), I discuss why it is nonetheless a vital
activity in modern society, both for protestors and for the rest of us
(chapter 17).

Of the many claims I make about protestors and the scholars who
study them, the main ones are these:

- Protestors are a diverse lot; every one of us cares about something
  deeply enough so that, under the right circumstances, we might join
  a protest movement.

- The central satisfaction of protest is the opportunity to articulate,
  elaborate, alter, or affirm one's moral sensibilities, principles, and allegiances.

- Protest movements have important benefits for modern societies in the way they develop and disseminate new perspectives, especially but not exclusively moral visions.
- Most scholars, by concentrating on citizenship movements and by slighting culture (especially its moral and emotional dimensions), have inadequately understood the causes, unfolding, and effects of modern protest.

Basic Approaches

We already know a lot about the origins, operations, and effects of protest movements, but existing scholarship can be improved upon in several ways. The main paradigms are surprisingly metaphorical, and each favorite conceptual metaphor tends to be extended to cover too much. Concepts turn into entire theories, and practitioners sometimes forget they are using metaphors. In particular, they often forget that their explanatory factors are culturally constructed, not hard, objective facts. My corrective is to identify several basic dimensions of protest which, although they influence each other, cannot be conflated or reduced to each other. Special attention to one of these, culture, not only yields new variables to use in our explanations, but lets us see how the others are constructed and defined through social processes. A sensitivity to another, biography, does the same, as well as allowing us to see that individuals sometimes protest even outside of organized groups and movements.

TWO

The Classical Paradigms

The real voyage of discovery consists not in seeking new landscapes but in having new eyes.
      —Proust

Only recently have students of protest recognized the cultural embeddedness of political action, or appreciated the creativity of protestors in generating tactics, language, organizational forms, and visions of a good society. Most have done neither. At one extreme theorists have demeaned protestors as irrational, altogether outside normal flows of life; at the other they have assumed an extreme form of self-interested rationality that equally divorces protestors from their cultural contexts. In between, mobilization theorists and process theorists have used organizational, political, and historical contexts to understand protest, but have not quite captured the full range of cultural influences, even though these define the rationality of all political action, providing the ultimate criteria for understanding or evaluating protest. In this chapter I examine the century's most influential paradigms of protest, mostly forged to understand citizenship movements.

Theorists of protest have grown more and more aware of the many facets of this complex activity by recognizing additional shaping contexts. New contexts and dimensions have been "discovered" by successive cohorts of scholars, with an explosion of work especially in the past twenty-five years. The cumulative nature of our understanding has been obscured, though, by the tendency of young scholars to carve out niches by attacking established scholars and their paradigms. In part they are driven by the demands of their careers to make a name for themselves. In part the self-image of sociology as a science encourages them to compare and test oversimplified models supposedly representing entire theoretical approaches—a practice John Lofland criticizes as unproductive "theory-bashing."[1] The assumption, drawn from the natural sciences, is that only one model can be right. Either resource mobilization is important or political processes are; either culture and identity drive protest or self-interest does. Every new concept or variable is inflated into an entire theory or approach. The result is often an oscillation between unrealistic extremes, with each generation forgetting the insights of those before it.

Research traditions driven by case studies have further encouraged partial insights with little opportunity for synthesis. To a large extent, nineteenth-century urban revolts gave us crowd theories; the Nazis inspired mass society theories; bureaucratized trade unions contributed rational-choice models; the civil rights and labor movements yielded the strategic models of political process; the post-1960s cultural movements suggested identity theory; religious movements were the paradigm for developing frame analysis. Each research tradition is a metaphorical language highlighting certain elements of protest suggested by its exemplar movement. These languages are not directly comparable but are often compatible. We need to appreciate cultural factors without forgetting the other important dimensions, and my hope is to develop a cultural approach that encourages synthesis of prior paradigms by identifying the dimensions of protest that these frameworks are especially good at explaining. Each has a special aspect of political action that its theorists have thought about and gathered data about—what Robert Alford and Roger Friedland refer to as each paradigm's "home domain."[2] As I explain in chapter 3, I group the different dimensions into resources, strategies, biography, and culture. Although each dimension affects the others, none can be reduced to the others without a loss of understanding. Yet that reduction is what most research traditions have attempted.

I take resources to be physical capacities and technologies, as well as the money that can buy them—a narrower definition than most. They have relatively clear and fixed prices and uses. Strategies are the moves that individuals and groups make in interaction with others, responding to them and anticipating future responses. Both individuals and organizations have strategies. Biography refers to individuals' mental worlds, conscious and unconscious, which for biographical reasons are subsets of items in the broader culture. It also includes personal quirks. Culture is simply (or not so simply, as we will see) the shared aspects of the mental worlds and their physical representations. Parts of culture (goals, emotions, images) are more analytically independent of resources and strategies; others interact with, even help define, these other dimensions (new ideas for strategies, know-how about deploying resources). We will sort out these dimensions by examining them in the metaphors of existing research traditions.

THE CROWD APPROACH

For most of the twentieth century, scholars viewed protest as irregular and irrational; their lens was a "myth of the madding crowd" featuring a crowd mentality outside the range of normal human motivations and experiences. Gustave le Bon set the tone in his 1895 book *The Crowd*, saying of participants: "[T]he fact that they have been transformed into a crowd puts them in possession of a sort of collective mind which makes them feel, think, and act in a manner quite different from that in which each individual of them would feel, think, and act were he in a state of isolation."[3] In particular, crowds were thought to be prone to violence. And other forms of protest—even the most explicitly political—were thought to be built upon basic crowd elements such as rumors, panics, and milling about. Accounts of collective behavior that followed le Bon consisted primarily of psychology, and that of a pejorative type which reduced protest to the release of pent-up frustration. Herbert Blumer, for example, described a contagious "circular reaction": since members of crowds are apprehensive and unsure of what they want, they merely mimic the behavior of those around them rather than formulating coherent projects.[4]

The primary role of social context, in this tradition, was to explain what abnormal situations—such as mass society or the strains of rapid social change—allowed these eruptions of collective frenzy. Neil Smelser emphasized "structural strain" as a necessary condition for collective action, although he risked circularity by defining strains as including tensions between the desires of groups and the conditions in existence. Any effort at change had to be the result of some strain.[5] "Mass society" theorists specified a lack of ties to intermediary groups and institutions as the cause of mass protest, as "people are available for mass behavior when they lack attachments to proximate objects. When people are divorced from their community and work, they are free to reunite in new ways. Furthermore, those who do not possess a variety of relations with their fellows are disposed to seek new and often remote sources of attachment and allegiance."[6] Protest as a normal dimension of life, carried on by healthy people, seemed out of the question. Through "group mind" imagery, culture and strategy were described in biographical and psychological metaphors, but actual psychological dynamics (at the level of individuals) were only occasionally and poorly specified.[7]

Some observers in this tradition were more sympathetic to protestors, transforming irrationality into creativity. Notably, Ralph Turner and Lewis Killian argued that collective behavior is "normal, not pathological or irrational," even though it differs from stable, institutionalized activities. In the face of "uncertainty about reality," members of a crowd interact in ways that create new cognitive, normative, and emotional understandings: "Some shared redefinition of right and wrong in a situation supplies the justification and coordinates the action in collective behavior." As symbolic interactionists, they tied these "emergent norms" to narrow, face-to-face contexts of interaction: "Norms are always connected to conceptions of the situation."[8] If Turner and Killian avoided the worst images of irrationalism, they used interactionist models that grounded social action in an almost momentary context and ignored broader political structures and cultural traditions. Crowds remained a special, unique phenomenon of the moment. The term *collective behavior* implied something less than fully conscious, purposive action. Oddly, Turner and Killian also failed to provide a thorough account of how symbolic meanings are created, negotiated, and deployed. Contagion does occur, but it is not the most interesting aspect of a protest movement, or even of a crowd.[9] Cultural meanings are not created from scratch at a moment's notice; artful protest strategies take longer to emerge than one afternoon's rally or riot.[10]

And yet there are "moments of madness," as Aristide Zolberg called them, when expectations and desires suddenly shift and all things seem possible. Protestors can create an alternative sense of time, in which their actions appear linked to world-historical transformations.[11] These periods are likely to last several days, or weeks, or months, not several hours, and there are many activities, ideas, and sentiments that germinate and develop to prepare these revolutionary moments. Preexisting and widely shared beliefs, feelings, and morals explain the forms this madness takes. Its emergence appears spontaneous primarily to outside observers, who don't know the cultural symbols and traditions that the actions build upon. As James Scott has argued, "If there seems to be an instantaneous mutuality and commonness of purpose, they are surely derived from the hidden transcript [his word for culture]." The open expression of hidden feelings may be necessary for "subordinates [to] fully recognize the extent to which their claims, their dreams, their anger are shared by other subordinates with whom they have not been in direct touch."[12] History seems to move faster at some times than at others; not just species evolution but also political history may be a series of "punctuated equilibria."[13]

The crowd-based tradition often suffered from a lack of direct empirical observation, but it generated several useful insights. In its unfortunate dismissal of protestors as deviants, the paradigm at least allowed for the importance of socially constructed labels, identities, and learning processes—the stuff of deviance research. Ideas were also thought to be important. The paradigm also recognized that certain positions and parts of the social structure, as Smelser argued, are more conducive to protest than others. There are real social problems—oppression, inequality, disruption, brutality—that protestors get angry about; they are not simply pursuing their own interests. New understandings and projects do emerge, even though it may take months rather than hours for a group of protestors to work them out. They do this in ongoing relationships, communication, and activities, not in fleeting encounters, but face-to-face interactions remain important for the construction of shared critiques, goals, and emotions. And, as we shall see, singular events can be important for crystallizing new cultural meanings. The collective behavior school at least dropped the hypothesis of sheer irrationality in favor of an image of sudden creativity; their problem, in the interactionist tradition, was in seeing this artfulness as too immediate, spontaneous, and unrelated to other flows of life. Wedded to psychological imagery, they understated or misread the influence of culture. Most crowd theorists, moreover, concluded that the emotional and creative aspects of protest rendered protestors irrational.

THE RATIONALISTS

In 1965, while crowd imagery still dominated research on protest, economist Mancur Olson, who like all economists believed that humans are rational in precise, measurable ways that do not vary much across different social contexts, argued that individuals, before engaging in collective action, try to estimate their personal costs of participation and their own likely benefits. Rationality, for him, consisted of calculation. He replaced the rich but pejorative psychology of crowds with the simple assumptions of microeconomics, which hardly flatter humans but do make them appear rational—in fact overly so. Olson claimed that rational individuals would not participate in collective action to attain public goods, since they could "free ride," attaining any benefits without having to pay the cost of the pursuit (a single individual's participation rarely affects the outcome). Collective action thus depends on "selective incentives," such as newsletters or union-sponsored life insurance, that go only to those who participate.[14] The term *collective action* implies greater rationality than *collective behavior* had, although it seems to categorize protest movements with trade associations, international treaties, and any number of other formal arrangements.

Several explicit assumptions, drawn from the root metaphor of market exchange, underlie this "rational-choice" tradition: that individuals make knowledgeable choices based on relatively precise calculations concerning the payoffs of various options; that in order to do this humans distinguish between the ends of action (the payoffs) and the means (the costs); that motivations and incentives are sufficiently limited in number to allow calculations and comparisons; and that payoffs are measurable (this usually means that they are measurable in money). Albert Hirschman similarly described this "remarkably parsimonious postulate: that of the self-interested, isolated individual who chooses freely and rationally among alternative courses of action after computing their prospective costs and benefits."[15] Social contexts do not deeply affect choices, as humans in all societies tend to follow the same basic motivations, especially the maximization of wealth. Cultural and institutional contexts are of interest primarily because they provide a distribution of resources and a set of legal constraints and opportunities within which to maneuver. The real focus is on resources and the strategies used to acquire them. Rationality, resources, and interests are usually assumed to be objectively given rather than culturally constructed.

Specifying human motives in addition to the maximization of individual resources transforms the rigorous "strong" model into a looser "weak" one. Philosopher Jon Elster has laid out a typology of other motivations for collective action beyond individual maximization of wealth. We can unthinkingly follow habits and social norms rather than rationally choosing our actions. Or we can act unselfishly because of motives such as altruism (by which we gain pleasure from the pleasure of others) or envy (we gain pleasure from their setbacks). Finally, we can derive satisfaction from the process as well as the outcome of collective action.[16] To further complicate the picture, a protest can be composed of participants driven by different motives, and each protestor may be there for several reasons at once. Motivations quickly proliferate beyond the confines of the spare psychology of calculating models.

In the face of empirical evidence, rationalists have often admitted that humans and organizations "satisfice" rather than maximize: they aim for a certain satisfactory level of profit or resources and sometimes forego opportunities for more. After all, information is costly to obtain, and humans exhibit various biases in how they process it.[17] This wedge of realism renders rationalist models more interesting but less precise. Maximization at least implies (unrealistically, for any empirical application) a single package of strategies, one right answer. But in the realm of satisficing, how much is enough? Only institutional constraints, cultural traditions, and individual biography can provide an answer—and a very complex answer.[18]

Once we have moved from strong to weaker models, we are merely saying that people usually have some idea of what they want, and act to attain it. This is plausible, but we need a better biographical or cultural slant to understand what is considered desirable and rational. Mancur Olson originally criticized this expansion as inelegant and perhaps tautological: "[I]t is not possible definitely to say whether a given individual acted for moral reasons or for other reasons in some particular case. A reliance on moral explanations could thus make the theory untestable." Erotic and other psychological motives, he went on to say, could also be squeezed into his model, but "'affective' groups such as family and friendship groups could normally be studied much more usefully with entirely different sorts of theories, since the analysis used in this study does not shed much light on these groups."[19] But the loss in mathematical rigor, I believe, is compensated for by our ability to understand real-life protestors with their complex motivations. Rationalists rarely even try to explain why people have the preferences they do; for this they need to supplement their models with other frameworks. At least one rationalist, political scientist John Ferejohn, points to culture as the most promising candidate.[20]

Michael Taylor has shown that rationalist models work better in some cultural contexts than in others. He argued that peasants' membership in a strong community makes them more likely to rebel by making it rational for them to do so, on account of normative and interested pressures brought to bear upon them. Trust and credibility, shared beliefs and values, and frequent interactions contribute to collective action, and these can only arise through regular social interactions in particular cultural settings. Echoing Elster, Taylor added that rationalist models are not very useful when participants get pleasure from the activity itself, from altruism, or from expressing themselves through the activity ("the desire to be 'true to one's self,' to act consistently with one's deeply help commitments"). Cultural expectations, feelings, and beliefs determine the extent to which calculating rationality comes into play. By adding factors such as these, theorists have described many ways that protestors overcome or avoid Olson's "free rider" problem, which increasingly seems a problem only within farfetched rationalist models.[21]

One branch of rationalism highlights strategic interaction above all else. Game theories, which set calculating actors in motion maneuvering against each other, seem to assume through their central metaphor of a game that the outcome is open. Indeed their purpose is more normative—showing where actors diverge from calculating rationality—than explanatory. And, strictly speaking, like the other research paradigms, they are primarily frameworks and vocabularies rather than theories. It is precisely because of the number of possible moves that game theories do not get us far in explaining social action. Thomas Schelling points out that even a two-by-two matrix of possible options and corresponding outcomes will yield, when each of the two players rank-orders all the possible outcomes, more than one thousand possible results. If the two players each had three possible choices (in a three-by-three matrix), the outcomes exceed one billion. All before we add a third player, admit the possibility that each player cares about the other's payoffs, allow one player to make her choices contingent on what the others do, or admit imperfections in knowledge and memory.[22] We can admire virtuosic moves, not predict them.

Game theorists try to identify equilibrium points in strategic games, from which none of the players has an incentive to defect. In many cases, the situation is one that none of the players prefers—as game theorists draw on the broader ability of rationalists to plot the unintended consequences of action. The logic of conflict and strategic interaction can work against the intentions of all those involved, an insight that helps to explain frequent situations of stalemate and polarization. But empirical applications of game theory have been more successful in international relations than collective action. The complex strategic interactions among protestors, their allies, opponents, and the state are unlikely to yield a single equilibrium point, or even a small number—except the obvious case of severe state repression. Absent that, there are usually multiple moves open to all the players. In the heat of play, indeed, it may be more important to make *some* move than to delay in order to make the most *rational* move: in other words a rational actor need not always make rational choices.[23]

Another key insight of game theory is that players have expectations about what the others will do. Because the "right" move for each actor depends partly on upsetting the expectations of other players, obvious moves are not always the best ones. Yet sometimes they are. Artful performances depend on biographical sensitivities that elude formulation; if they could be fully articulated, they would no longer be virtuosic or strategically effective. What is more, any game has its thrills—its intrinsic pleasures—so that players often enjoy the playing itself, a motivation normally not allowed within the rationalist confines of game theory. When the payoffs and the play blur, and when players extend the game out of the "thrill of the chase," theoreticians cannot even declare certain moves as right or wrong.[24] In protest, the ends are not always neatly separable from the activity supposed to pursue them; the activity itself is pleasurable. For all these reasons, game theories merely set the players in motion.

By insisting so strongly on the rationality of protestors, theorists in Olson's tradition set up a dubious contrast between rational and irrational that has dogged studies of protest ever since. Is protest rational or irrational? This dichotomy—unsociological in its ignoring of social context—has confused many observers, who feel that the only way to avoid portraying protestors as irrational is to paint them as rational in Olson's calculating way. In the strategic dimension, protestors can make mistakes. But irrationality is not the making of mistakes; it is an inability to learn from them. Rationality consists in improving one's flow of decisions by learning from experience and the environment. Mistakes, as long as they are not fatal, can be part of this process. To question protestors' rationality at the biographical level—another possibility—would be to question their ability to know their own desires or pleasures, and this would require a more elaborate biographical model than any researchers of protest have yet developed. Finally, to question the rationality of protestors' physical resources or cultural traditions (as opposed to how they use them strategically) would make little sense. Protestors can be criticized as mistaken, immoral, or powerless, but rarely as irrational. Yet the fear that they might somehow portray protestors as irrational continues to haunt scholars.

Dennis Chong has done the most to apply rational-choice concepts to a single case of protest, the American civil rights movement. Dismissing strong rational-choice models, he admits that material incentives by themselves can hardly account for much protest activity; besides, if selective material incentives were sufficient to motivate membership, then those who were indifferent or even opposed to a group's goals should also have the same incentive to join![25]

Examining motivations that rationalists usually minimize, such as the expression of feelings, the pleasures of protest, and concern for one's reputation, Chong tries to show that these can be covered by rational-choice models. He argues that "the desires to gain or sustain friendships, to maintain one's social standing, and to avoid ridicule and ostracism are all social goals that constitute selective incentives for individuals to participate in collective action."[26] These are standard "social" goals of weak models, in contrast to the purely material self-interest found in strong models. Chong argues that a good reputation has various personal payoffs: "An esteemed reputation has considerable instrumental value in a society." Yet he also says that one of the best ways to maintain a reputation for altruism and other virtues is actually to become that kind of person: "[I]t may be in my interest to develop genuine (or not consciously calculating) concern for the welfare of others." Rationality becomes, for him, "a delicate combination of thinking as well as feeling."[27] Chong describes how numerous civil rights activists were shamed into various forms of participation, in part because their own reputations were on the line.

Chong shows less than he asserts. His main contribution is to demonstrate that diverse emotional motivations are compatible with self-interested rationality. This is a surprise only to those attracted by rational-choice theory's strict contrast between rationality (based on material incentives) and emotions (most other motivations). If, as he admits, "it is unclear to me how we can disentangle the motivations that impel such people [those who have thoroughly internalized group norms] to behave in the manner they do," then there is no reason to conclude that protestors are more motivated by long-run concern for their own reputations than by genuine altruism or sympathy.[28] People often do what they do because they think it's right, not because they have a long-term interest in cultivating reputations as the kind of people who do what's right (a rather convoluted sequence). To separate individual motives from their social supports like this is possible only within the artificial confines of rational-choice theory; using the theory's own assumptions to test it is bound to confirm it.

Chong claims to bring nonprivate benefits, such as fame, honor, and power, into a rationalist model. He does this by showing that such social goods have rewards, psychic and otherwise, for individuals, and hence can motivate individuals without violating rationalist assumptions. But his ability to translate them into what they mean for individuals does not show that individuals are motivated by purely private rewards, for the rewards of honor and so on are not definable in purely individual terms. A full account of them involves both an individual and a social description, and only a rationalist would be tempted in the first place to doubt that honor and fame motivate people. To show that they are compatible with rationalism opens the door to culture. Without exactly saying so, Chong is suggesting how to incorporate cultural dynamics in rational choice models, as when he says, "the *internalization* of norms through an elaborate social process, which has typically appeared superfluous in a rational choice calculus, may be viewed as a community cost-saving device in the institution of a moral system of rewards and punishment."[29] While trying to collapse culture and biography to strategic action, Chong makes a better case for their compatibility and complementarity.

Models of calculating rationality provide, at best, rough boundary conditions; people will rarely behave in highly irrational ways, and if they do, they may eventually run out of the material resources necessary for sustained strategic action. Even this extreme case sometimes occurs, though, as with martyrs and strong altruists. But even if we accept that the bounds normally operate, calculating models say little about people's actions within them. Rationalists claim to start from individual psychology, but they have reduced it so much they have little to say about it. I too am reluctant to view protestors as irrational, and Olson provided a good corrective to crowd-based models that portrayed them in that light. In his tradition strategic actors have little to strategize about, however, since they are stuck with a psychology too emaciated to carry much explanatory weight. The rationalists have too narrow a view of rationality: they are limited by their own key concept. Rationality should not be equated, as the rationalists would have it, with maximization. Biography and cultural traditions, once they are allowed to thicken rationality, lead far beyond the neat algorithms of game theories and rational choice. They introduce practices too openended to allow us to predict outcomes easily, and intrinsic pleasures too varied to allow us to specify correct moves. They may lead us altogether away from a rational-irrational contrast.

Game theory's focus on the mutual expectations of strategic interaction, especially in conditions when communication is limited, will prove useful when we later examine the logic of strategy. Few other theorists have attended to the strategic dimension of protest as directly as the rationalists. Just as some insights of crowd theories can be revived by placing them in a broader cultural context, so key contributions of the rationalists can be strengthened when we fill them in with cultural and biographical meanings. Game theory will also usefully remind us that the logic of strategic interaction can leave all players in situations they did not desire, such as costly prolonged conflicts, polarization of positions, and protracted stalemates.

THE MOBILIZATION PARADIGM

The second, fatal blow to crowd-based theories came in the 1970s with the new gestalt of "resource mobilization," within which many American students of protest still operate. Most of these theorists came of age in the 1960s with sympathetic views of what social movements might do. Their main contribution was to show that protest was a regular part of politics, that protestors were normal people pursuing reasonable goals, and that available economic resources helped determine what protestors could achieve. Refinements of this tradition have shown, among other things, how activists finance their activities, what tactics tend to be more successful, and what role state structures play in shaping outcomes. Some of this work could be read as a "how-to" guide for activists, addressing the practical exigencies of protest. The urge to protest—precisely what earlier generations had feared and tried to explain—was now taken for granted, on the grounds that all groups in society have interests to advance and defend. "Grievances and disaffection," said one prominent proponent, even as he used contradictory adjectives, "are a fairly permanent and recurring feature of the historical landscape."[30] Conflating objective social conditions with people's perceptions and interpretations of those conditions, these theorists overlooked the cultural meanings that might nurture moral outrage over long-standing conditions or new public policies.

Mobilization theorists are, in a way, rationalists who have built formal organizations and sometimes political and historical context into their models, recognizing that not only individuals, but groups and organizations calculate costs and benefits. John McCarthy and Mayer Zald emphasized the ways that formal organizations, animated by entrepreneurial leaders, accumulate resources for collective action; organizations as well as leaders are rational and primarily materialist in their motivations. Zald and McCarthy have demonstrated a variety of practical constraints on protest, which does not consist of angry individuals but people working in institutional settings. People need time to participate; organizations need money to survive; enough money has even allowed the growth of a large social-movement industry with professionals whose careers are devoted to founding and running protest groups. By offering selective incentives or shifting certain initial costs onto group leaders, formal organizations overcome many of the challenges to collective action that Mancur Olson had posited.[31]

Zald and McCarthy's focus on formal organizations and the resources needed to maintain them has been especially fruitful in generating concrete hypotheses, in addition to a rich language of organizational and monetary metaphors. For instance, financial dependence on direct-mail contributors, or "isolated constituents," implies less stable flows of resources and a heightened concern with advertising. A protest group's own contributors will be a central audience—distinct from targets and beneficiaries—for its action and rhetoric. Competition among social movement organizations for contributions may lead not only to hostility but to specialization, or a segmentation of audiences. Much of the behavior of social-movement organizations can be explained with the language of organizational imperatives—including why some groups grow more conservative.[32]

As one of the dominant paradigms, these models are often unfairly caricatured, because every graduate student of protest sharpens her critical teeth on them. Too often, McCarthy and Zald are transformed into straw men whose explanations relied exclusively on resource distributions. Mobilization, though, is a multifaceted process that also involves strategies and cultural meanings. When we distinguish initial distributions of resources from the strategic activities that can attract (in many cases, create) new resources, resource mobilization can be interpreted as a strategic process of cultural persuasion.

Like the rationalists, mobilization theorists tend to assume instrumental motives of action: groups act for strategic advantage, individuals act in pursuit of their own interests. Some self-interested rationality is usually present, whether for organizations or individuals. Organizational and individual interests are usually assumed to be objectively defined, not culturally constructed. If the irrationalist tradition encouraged an image of angry, frustrated mobs, and the rationalist school one of self-interested, calculating individuals, then the mobilization tradition crafted a picture of purposive, formal organizations. Individuals are capable of calculating, and caring about, the costs and benefits that would accrue not just to them, but to the collectivities and organizations to which they belong. Once we admit this, though, we immediately need to ask what group boundaries and identities they perceive and care about. Mobilization theorists seem to fear that, if we recognize the culturally constructed nature of groups, grievances, and interests, protestors will once again appear irrational.

In rejecting the psychological reduction of the crowd theorists, many mobilization theorists eschew biographical factors altogether, sometimes on the peculiar grounds that these are the domain of another discipline. These theorists often assume that objective self-interest is a sufficient motivating force, which is a reasonable assumption until one faces movements like animal rights that are not based on any perceptible interests of the protestors. Moral and altruistic incentives, at least, must play a role. Cultural and biographical processes help us understand why individuals care about some benefits but not others. And even self-interest is a cultural construction, a perception. It is not always immediately obvious.

The most precise image of resource mobilization involves an entrepreneur or organization conducting activities to extract usable resources from a population; the most clearly defined resource is money. Beyond these easily measured quantities, mobilization perspectives run the risk of becoming tautological, making the entire social world into resources. Even moral support, public opinion, psychological states, and favorable symbolism have been considered resources.[33] In some cases, anything that protestors can use to their advantage comes to be labeled as a resource. Problems arise with this overextension of the label to cover such disparate phenomena. Sometimes, rich strategic or cultural dynamics are reduced so that they are analyzed as though they were static, pre-existing resources. At other times, their complexity is maintained, but the term *resources* no longer makes much sense. The considerable power of the concept can be retained by restricting its use, not applying it wantonly.

Money and meanings operate under different logics. Where money usually has a clear and universal buying power in society, cultural meanings are often local, variable, and contested.[34] Gamson, Fireman, and Rytina usefully insist that resources be countable and transferable, mostly restricting the term to money and the physical objects it can buy: copy machines, bullhorns, corn supplies, a radio station, a factory.[35] Money entails a zero-sum game: more of it in one place means less in another. But enthusiasm and cultural resonance are not zero-sum and can be enhanced without taking resources from other uses. Symbols, like other forms of information, are infinitely reproducible. They are also less easily controlled than physical resources. Through the news media or computer networks, even tiny, poor groups can broadcast symbolic messages, although they don't always control the meanings. Another difference is that meanings and feelings can have a special connection to a particular person, a charismatic leader, and they can disappear when she dies, defects, or is discredited. You can't take money with you when you die, but you can take the feelings and thoughts you arouse in others. Meanings can have similar ties to particular places or settings, as in rituals, and cannot be transferred to other settings as easily as money can. Finally, many cultural practices improve or expand when used, while monetary resources diminish. A protestor becomes a better public speaker through practice. A song or slogan catches on and spreads. Even when protest groups "invest" money to get more money, as in direct-mail campaigns, they are not actually getting a return on that money (as one does on a savings bond). They are deploying rhetoric and symbols to attract new resources; the cultural meanings, disseminated by means of money, cause the payoff just as much as the money does. They are like factors of production: both the means of dissemination and the message are necessary, together creating a product with a return. Artful protest involves diverse practices, not just the expenditure of resources.[36]

Pre-existent organizations and social networks have also been considered resources that mobilizers can exploit, in that they aid recruitment.[37] But they are also the stuff of social life itself, the life forms and social contexts in which people live. When the population or group from which resources are to be extracted comes to be viewed as a resource, the ends of protest have disappeared, and we are left only with the means of extraction. Resources have become everything. Resources and social organization are both important to protest, but they are more powerful concepts when not conflated. Physical resources and McCarthy and Zald's formal organizations, we shall see, are crisper concepts than "social organization," which we'll scrutinize in the next chapter.

Some have almost reduced the culture in social movements to a form of social structure, consisting of interpersonal networks. Anthony Oberschall discusses the importance of "community": the degree to which a collectivity with a grievance is already organized will increase its ability to launch collective action.[38] Charles Tilly emphasizes the importance for collective action of two dimensions of groups: the extent to which potential participants form a category distinct from others, and the extent to which they have interpersonal networks linking them to each other.[39] These Durkheimian factors are similar to the notions of "group" and "grid" of Mary Douglas, who (unlike Tilly) explicitly describes the cultural processes needed to create and define each dimension.[40] Innumerable symbols and rituals lie behind each boundary in a classification, and norms, emotions, and habits reinforce (if they do not create) the ties of networks. The resulting sense of collective solidarity and identity will encourage potential participants to pursue collective as well as individual interests, so that they may participate in protest even in the absence of organizational structure and selective (material) incentives.[41]

Despite its considerable power, much mobilization research is restricted by the rationalist assumptions embodied, often implicitly, within it. In spite of recognizing that groups as well as individuals have interests, the paradigm frequently persists with a narrow set of human motivations, largely centered around the acquisition of money and power, and it normally distinguishes too sharply between the means and the ends of collective action. Ironically the concept of resources is often vaguely specified, perhaps because it is overextended. Missing in this influential tradition are the direct pleasures of protest, the moral visions being pursued, and the emotions accompanying political activities—in other words most of the mental and symbolic worlds of culture and biography. Strategic action is there but not given its full due, because it is conflated with resources.

THE POLITICAL PROCESS APPROACH

Some of the same theorists who articulated mobilization theories have also elaborated approaches to protest with more emphasis on politics and the state, and hence on strategy. Foremost among them is Charles

Tilly, who accepts the importance of material resources but also places mobilization activities in the broad context of urbanization, industrialization, the rise of nation-states, and the development of national markets. He shows how, as the scale of the nation-state and corporations expanded during the past two hundred years, collective action occurred on a larger, more organized scale and hence was able to be proactive rather than defensive and reactive. Most notably, national unions replaced sporadic and local machine-breaking and other forms of resistance.[42] By retaining the rationalist term *collective action*, Tilly is concerned to show the continuities with trade unions, political parties, and other more institutionalized forms of political action. Although known as resource mobilization theorists, Tilly, along with William Gamson and Anthony Oberschall, have focused less on material resources and more on states, strategies, and political mobilization, thus leaving some room for grievances and ideologies and a lot for elite responses.[43] Their focus on political power and the environment that social movements face is a healthy way of linking protestors to other strategic actors in society, recognizing the importance of both resources and strategic choices.

In this "political process" tradition, Sidney Tarrow, Doug McAdam, and others have shown the crucial effect of "political opportunity structures" on the unfolding and outcomes of protest, adding a clear model of political context to organizational and historical ones.[44] McAdam points to three key causal factors behind the emergence of protest: changing opportunities in the political environment, especially state responses to protest; the existing level of organization in the aggrieved community; and the population's assessment of its chances for success (also called the level of insurgent consciousness or cognitive liberation). The process perspective's emphasis on opportunities provided by the state, mostly its occasional slackening of repression, shows how strongly this tradition has been marked by the use of citizenship movements as its exemplars, for these have faced the strongest and most constant repression. Most researchers in this tradition, having studied the labor and civil rights movements, take repression for granted. In McAdam's early definition, social movements are even defined as "those organized efforts, *on the part of excluded groups,* to promote or resist changes in the structure of society that involve recourse to noninstitutional forms of political participation."[45] Assuming he means legally or politically excluded, this is a sure way to focus our attention on protestors' interactions with the state.

Process theorists implicitly tend to contrast outsiders or challengers, who must use extrainstitutional tactics, with insiders or members, who can use institutional tactics. This distinction works for many citizenship movements but not for post-citizenship ones. Even insiders occasionally resort to extrainstitutional protest. Christian Smith, himself sympathetic to process approaches, criticizes this either-or dichotomy: "In fact, the majority of modern social movements possess *moderate* amounts of political and economic resources, enjoy *limited* access to political decision making, employ both disruptive *and* institutionalized means of political influence, mobilize new movement-carrier groups *while simultaneously* collaborating with established political organizations, and vocalize a mix of conciliatory, persuasive, *and* confrontational rhetoric."[46]

If resources are the root metaphor of the mobilization framework, political opportunity structures are the heart of most political process theories—and just as overextended as resources were.[47] Here is Tarrow's recent formulation: "By political opportunity structure, I mean consistent—but not necessarily formal or permanent—dimensions of the political environment that provide incentives for people to undertake collective action by affecting their expectations for success or failure. Theorists of political opportunity structure emphasize the mobilization of resources *external* to the group."[48] Every dimension of protest is packed into this formulation, leaving nothing that is not part of a political opportunity structure. There are political structures which, despite the disclaimer that threatens to obfuscate the concept, are normally formal and "relatively" permanent; it is hard to see what beyond this is meant by "consistent." Culture and biography must be involved if expectations are to be changed. Resources are also here, even if restricted to other people's resources (it is not clear if this is an overextension of the concept of resources, of political opportunity structures, or of both). Tarrow is mostly referring to strategies (how others *use* their resources), even though that is the least apparent dimension in the passage. Finally, we see a familiar hint of circularity in that whatever "provides incentives" for collective action seems to be a political opportunity structure. When there is collective action, there must be a favorable political opportunity structure. When Tarrow specifies four kinds of change in political opportunity structures, only one—expanding access to decision-making power—has a clear element of structure, mixed with some strategic action. The other three—changing political alignments, new allies, and divisions among elites—seem to consist almost entirely of strategic choices and actions consciously made by groups and individuals.

Anything that, in retrospect, helped a movement mobilize or win a victory tends to be labeled a political opportunity structure. In one extreme case, even the grievance that spurred a movement is labeled a political opportunity structure because the movement would not have existed without it![49] Although the process approach corrects game theory by adding rules, resources, and institutions to the strategic mix, the potential focus on strategic interaction tends to be lost in the formulation of opportunities as *structures*—as though they were relatively permanent rather than constantly or potentially in flux. Similarly, although process theorists have elaborated on rules (legal, administrative, and political) as distinguished from (material) resources, they often collapse the two again by using the same label for both. (Rules, in my scheme, would fall under culture.) The term *structure* misleadingly implies relatively fixed entities, so that attention is often diverted away from open-ended strategic interplay. If the point is to highlight strategic political opportunities, adding the word *structure* creates an oxymoron. Culture, resources, and strategy are conflated. We must at least distinguish between fleeting strategic opportunities and relatively fixed aspects of political systems within which strategic maneuvering occurs.[50]

As we did with resources, we can strengthen the concept of political opportunity structure by restricting it, not expanding it. Hanspeter Kriesi proposes confining it to "those aspects of a political system that determine movement development independently of the purposive action of the actors involved." He aims at excluding the strategic dimension in favor of what I would call structure, although he would include not only the political system's formal institutional structure but its "informal procedures and prevailing strategies with regard to challengers, and the configuration of power relevant for the confrontation with the challengers"—two things that strategies consciously aim at changing.[51] State strategies, after all, evolve (often rapidly) in response to movement strategies. I prefer to restrict the term more, applying it to political institutions such as voting systems, constitutional divisions of powers, and so on that change very rarely or slowly. In this sense, "political structure" might be a reasonably autonomous dimension of protest alongside resources and the others—although structures ultimately come out of strategic conflicts.

In process models, culture, like everything else, is subordinated to political structure. In a telling offhand example, Tarrow mentions the Russian Revolution as having opened a political opportunity for revolutionary groups around the world: "If the end of World War I produced more and more energetic movements than the end of World War II, the international incentive of the Bolshevik Revolution had much to do with it."[52] But what kind of incentive was the revolution? It surely inspired capitalist governments to more repression of revolutionary movements, not less; it must have solidified political and economic elites, not divided them. What it did was to inspire revolutionaries as a cultural symbol, in its reassuring message that they were on the side of history. In other words it operated mostly in the realms of culture and biography, not political structure and strategy. Culture and biography rarely achieve full independence in process models. McAdam, for instance, recognizes the importance of cognitive liberation, but in his causal diagram explaining the rise of social movements, cognitive liberation is a function of indigenous organizational strength and expanding political opportunities.[53] Cognitive processes—let alone emotions or moral visions—lose much of their independent theoretical (although not empirical) status. When McAdam argues that "[m]ediating between opportunity and action are people and the subjective meanings they attach to their situations," he implies that there are objectively given opportunities, which potential protestors either see or do not see correctly. There is no room for culture to shape those opportunities, or to spur protest in the absence of "objective" opportunities. Deep structural change ("broad socioeconomic processes") has no causal arrow pointing to it in McAdam's diagram, and it is the only factor whose arrow points to political opportunity structures. Cognitive liberation can either succeed or fail; either way it does not affect political opportunities. Structures seem autonomous, while culture does not.[54]

Cognitive liberation depends on cultural processes, some of which may be independent of strategies and political structures. For people to think that repression has eased, they need to interpret the pieces of information they receive, which may or may not be accurate. As crowd theorists saw, rumors can be as effective in shifting perceptions as sound information—because they are often taken to be sound. Process theorists have had little to say about this interpretive filter, giving the impression that potential protestors respond straightforwardly to objective conditions and probabilities of success.[55] Objective conditions do affect perceptions, but only as one factor among many. The emotional inspiration of events like the Russian Revolution is often central, so much so that people may even protest without thinking that they can win—and perhaps even in the absence of favorable opportunities. Legal scholar and long-time civil rights activist Derrick Bell argues that African-Americans have fought for civil rights to bring dignity and meaning to their own lives, even though many—like Bell—believe that racism and racial oppression will never vanish from the United States. He recounts a conversation with a Mississippi woman during the civil rights movement. When he asked how she had the courage to continue despite life-threatening retaliation, she replied, "I can't speak for everyone, but as for me, I am an old woman. I live to harass white folks." Bell comments, "Mrs. MacDonald didn't say she risked everything because she hoped or expected to win out over the whites who, as she well knew, held all the economic and political power, and the guns as well. Rather, she recognized that—powerless as she was—she had and intended to use courage and determination as a weapon to, in her words, 'harass white folks.' . . . Her goal was defiance, and its harassing effect was likely more potent precisely because she did what she did without expecting to topple her oppressors. Mrs. MacDonald avoided discouragement and defeat because at the point that she determined to resist her oppression, she was triumphant."[56] The Russian Revolution inspired action even at the same time that it decreased the objective odds of success. For many, martyrdom is its own reward.

Because of his civil rights exemplar, McAdam assumes the aggrieved community to be a relatively fixed entity rather than something to be created through cultural processes. A citizenship movement has an unusually close link with some underlying collectivity in whose name it claims to speak, yet even here much work needs to be done to link the movement and the collectivity. McAdam's own rich research shows more room for cognitive and other cultural processes than he provides for in his theoretical framework. Take the much-discussed role of black churches in supporting the civil rights movement.[57] They provided more than opportunities for bloc recruitment into the new movement, according to McAdam, who then describes the rich activities, fervor, and conviction of churchgoers. Protest was in many ways an extension of this churchgoing role. After hinting at all sorts of cognitive, moral, and emotional dynamics, though, McAdam labels them "the degree of prior integration" of the black community, apparently a straightforward matter of "structural" opportunity.[58]

Process theorists have also given us the popular idea of cycles of protest, in which waves of protest alternate with quieter periods. Removal of repression appears crucial: "As opportunities widen and information spreads about the susceptibility of a political system to challenge, not only activists, but ordinary people test the limits of social control."[59] Yet repression is not the whole story: Tarrow says that symbols and frames are also important, as is the creation of mutually supportive protest groups. The idea of clustering may work better for citizenship than for post-citizenship movements, since the former are making parallel demands on the state, which, if it gives in to one group, may have difficulty resisting the others. Perhaps a special family of rhetoric supports citizenship movements and can easily be transferred from, say, the civil rights movement to the women's movement.[60] A series of post-industrial movements have, in contrast, persisted for thirty years, centered around environmentalism, with no obvious changes in state repression. The problem is not that cycles don't exist, but that much of their force comes from cultural factors—skills and know-how, emotional inspiration, raised expectations, shared rhetoric and images—that have been undertheorized. For the paradigmatic citizenship movements on which most process models have been based, repression is so salient that the considerable cultural work these movements do can easily be overlooked.

Mobilization and process theorists have set protest in its historical, organizational, and political contexts. The strategic interplay of multiple actors appeared in these traditions, even when it was theorized as structures. There was also an occasional nod to culture. But in general the willingness to protest has been assumed—reasonably enough in cases of oppressed or excluded groups—so that explaining protest boiled down to explaining opportunities to act. Without extensive attention to culture and biography, it is difficult to distinguish willingness from opportunity, so willingness was dropped as something to be explained. The overly interior focus of crowd traditions, relying on even while misspecifying protestors' psychologies, has been replaced by an almost equally imbalanced concern with the exterior environment. Each of the major paradigms has tended to concentrate on a single powerful metaphor—crowd psychology, strategic rationality, material resources, political opportunities—associated with one dimension of protest, letting other dimensions fall into its shadow.

DESENSITIZING CONCEPTS

Each of the research traditions I've described has its own language, images, examples, and hypotheses, especially suited to understanding one or two dimensions of protest, to which the other dimensions tend to be reduced. The paradigms are impossible to "test" against each other in any way that would prove one better than another, since each is good at different things. I hope to have identified the strengths of each. What is more, I believe that the strengths are often complementary, since the traditions so often focus on different basic dimensions.

Excessive concentration on one aspect of reality and the concept or label that represents it is a perennial risk of the social sciences.[61] We cannot avoid metaphors, yet it is easy to overextend them, especially when we are trying to compensate for past neglect of some aspect of reality. Everything in sight gets redescribed as a resource, or as a political opportunity structure, whether or not the metaphor fits well. Over time, observers of protest have been obsessed with crowds, with emergence, with calculating rationality, with resources, with formal organizations, and with the political structures that activists face. The same thing could happen to culture, which itself already has so many facets. A new word or idea, like a new musical recording, gets used over and over until we are familiar (sometimes too familiar) with it. Often, the next generation attacks it out of overfamiliarity. We can't do without these metaphors, but we need not limit ourselves to a single one. For each metaphor, we can work in its shadow but also outside it, with the grain but also against it. Each metaphor captures one aspect of protest best, distorting others. Lumping things together can be useful, but distinguishing them is also necessary.[62] I hope to show how culture is related to the aspects of protest already heavily scrutinized, not to replace them with it.

It is useful to push a new metaphor as far as possible, generating insights by viewing phenomena through new lenses. But we should not be confused by this. Moral authority and public opinion are not resources in the same way that money is, and we miss a lot if we insist that they are. It is this overextension that explains why the guiding metaphor of a research tradition is often vaguely theorized: it covers too much. In the end rationalists thin out rationality to such a degree that they have little useful to say about it. Mobilization theorists are often surprisingly mute about the dynamics of resources, as process theorists are about political opportunity structures. Even identity, we shall see, remains hazy in the writing of identity theorists. The more work a concept is called upon to do, the less specified it can be. It can desensitize us to other vantage points, other dimensions.

Part of this overextension of new concepts involves creating a new theory on the basis of what is only a new variable. Instead of adding political opportunities to explanations alongside resources and crowd dynamics, a new "approach" develops, and its models are compared with those derived from the other concepts. Arguments are couched in terms of theories, not variables. Another form of overextension involves reifying each new concept into something "hard" and "objective," a solid starting place for an explanation. Crowd dynamics, rationality, interests, resources, and political opportunities have all been defined by their partisans as objective facts, not shaped by social context, not culturally constructed according to the meanings held by social actors. Apparently, the fear is that recognition of the cultural construction of these factors would diminish their importance, transforming them from rock-bottom starting points into things that could themselves be explained. *Yet virtually every one of these major concepts can be analyzed as a cultural product instead of an objective fact.*

Alongside these forms of *theoretical overextension* of concepts is the kind of *empirical overextension* I mentioned in the first chapter: the tendency to make broad statements about movement dynamics on the basis of a single case study or research into a single kind of movement. We should at least leave it as an open question whether, say, citizenship, post-citizenship, religious, and right-wing nationalist movements operate in similar ways. Theoretical and empirical overextension easily reinforce one another. First, one mechanism or dimension may be especially salient in a particular movement—as critiques of technology were in the antinuclear movement or interactions with the state were for the civil rights movement—so that a single concept seems especially important. Then, in the absence of evidence from a variety of movements, it is easy to believe that this effect holds across all movements. For the most part, social movement theory has advanced like this, one new movement and new concept at a time. But this process has its pitfalls.

At the risk of the same kind of overextension, I'll argue that culture is not only an independent dimension alongside resources, biography, and strategies. It can be this, as when it is defined as cognitive grids that encourage or discourage solidarity, or as repertoires of strategic know-how. But because all action involves intention and thought, culture also involves the construction of the other categories: what counts as a resource under what circumstances, what works as a strategy and why, what an individual absorbs through socialization. Neither resources nor strategies are "objective" realities that can be identified outside of their social context, independent of the mental worlds of their users. Even physical resources such as bullhorns or fax machines require familiarity, habits, and messages for effective use. Sometimes culture is a simple causal factor that can be contrasted with other causal factors; at other times (or in other ways) it helps define these other factors too. At some times it is more explicit, at others more implicit, buried in action and the social construction of other categories. There may be a tension between these two aspects, but I hope it's a creative one. The limitation of game theorists, mobilizationists, and process theorists is not that they're wrong, but that they don't look behind the curtain at the origins of the factors they take as independent "givens." This role of culture is the reason, I think, that a cultural perspective is good for helping us to see the autonomy of all four dimensions from each other. And by carefully demarcating the different roles of culture, I hope to avoid the conceptual overextension that has plagued most paradigms.

I am simply redescribing protest movements, suggesting a new language that highlights some aspects of these movements obscured by other approaches. I am not arguing against the older descriptions, especially when they are defined well, and I shall be concerned to show how they relate to the cultural concepts I am about to present. I am offering a new lens, or to put it in trendy language, a new narrative of the growth, functioning, and consequences of social movements. Before I address the dynamics of culture and constructionism, and the research on protest that has begun to take them seriously, I shall examine the basic dimensions of protest in order to see what we lose when we conflate them.

- Scholars of social movements have gradually added more dimensions to our understanding of these complex phenomena.

- Scholars often forget prior discoveries, or overextend their favored metaphor to cover too much.

- New concepts are also frequently inflated into theoretical approaches rather than used to enrich existing ones. Theorists tend to view their favorite concepts as hard and objective rather than socially or culturally interpreted and defined.

- Case studies offer few limits to this metaphorical overextension, allowing an empirical overextension as well.

- Culture differs from other dimensions in that it is a fundamental component in the construction of the other dimensions as well as being its own set of variables.

THREE

Basic Dimensions of Protest

... Facts seize hold of the web
And leave it ash. Still, it is the personal,
Interior life that gives us something to think about.
The rest is only Drama.
  —John Ashbery, "But What Is the Reader to Make of This?"

Having criticized other theorists for conflating autonomous dimensions of protest, I shall try to establish why I think that four dimensions—resources, strategies, culture, and biography—are irreducible, much as they affect one another. And since others will immediately step forward with additional contenders for this list, I shall examine other facets of protest, especially political structures, social networks, and formal organizations. I consider these reducible to my four, even though in some cases it may be useful to think of them as independent. I try to define all these dimensions in table 3.1.

The best way to curtail flights of metaphor is to insist that our concepts have concrete referents in the social world; they must correspond to objects and situations and feelings we can point to with some precision. One strength of my four dimensions is that they correspond roughly to the four worlds toward which, according to Jürgen Habermas, social action is oriented. He has elaborated these worlds in some detail. Resources, as I define them, are the tools through which humans instrumentally change the objective physical world. Biography deals with what Habermas calls "expressive action" related to an inner, subjective self. Strategy and culture are actions and understandings directed toward other people in an interpersonal social world, although strategic action treats others as objects to manipulate, and the communicative action of culture treats them more as subjects with whom to share our understanding.[1] Jeffrey Alexander seconds this last distinction, usefully adding that these are analytic distinctions, in that any action combines the strategic and the communicative: "Every action is both interpretation and strategization; each process ensues at every moment in time."[2] Yet because different audiences for our actions are more or less salient at different times, I think that the mix of strategic and discursive varies in different situations and actions,

Table 3.1 Basic Dimensions of Protest

Dimension	Definition
Autonomous Dimensions	
Resources	Physical technologies and their capacities, or the money to buy these technologies. Related to what Habermas calls the objective, physical world, and to a form of action he dubs "instrumental."
Strategies	The choices made by individuals and organizations in their interactions with other players, especially opponents. Related to the intersubjective world, when others are treated instrumentally, and so to what Habermas calls strategic action.
Culture	Shared understandings (emotional, moral, and cognitive) and their embodiments. Some are shared primarily by protest groups (movement culture), others more broadly. Related to the intersubjective world, when others are treated communicatively, and to Habermas's communicative action.
Biography	Individual constellations of cultural meanings, personalities, sense of self, derived from biographical experiences. Related to the inner, subjective world.
Derivative Dimensions	
Political structure	Relatively fixed aspects of the political system, including constitutions and laws, electoral systems, administrative boundaries.
Social networks	Patterns of interaction, especially communication or cooperation, among individuals or organizations.
Formal organizations	Legal entities with explicit purposes, boundaries, defined roles, flows of resources, and stable interactions with other organizations.

something Alexander seems to recognize when he later discusses the mutual influence of the two components (which can only influence each other if they are distinguishable): "Understanding not only provides the environment for strategization; it profoundly affects the calculation of strategic interest itself. One must immediately add, however, that this interactive effect works both ways: to some degree interpretation is itself a strategic phenomenon. We do not try to 'understand' every impression that enters our consciousness. Considerations of nearness and farness, time, energy, and the extent of possible knowledge all come forcefully into play."[3] Strategy usually involves efforts to transform the social world; culture attempts to understand it. Even if every action has some of each, the logics of the two dimensions differ.

These are analytic dimensions, in that a concrete action involves all four of them, and distinguishing them is an act of the observer. Individuals think and act in a world that is both physical and cultural, and those thoughts and actions—as Alexander says—contain both strategy and culture. We are also enmeshed in networks of other individuals and—in today's world—a myriad of formal organizations.

The purpose of distinguishing the four dimensions is to make as concrete as possible what we mean by different concepts, in order to discourage the overextension of metaphors. When we talk about resources, we know to look at physical capacities and the money to buy them; when we discuss strategies, we look for gamelike responses to others and expectations of how others will respond in turn. When the word *culture* appears, we scurry to find meanings, feelings, and judgments that are shared, usually because they are embodied in texts or images, or reinforced by expectations. Although students of protest rarely mention biography, an interest in it should send them to observations of individuals in order to see how their biographical histories have left them with different selections of cultural meanings and strategic tastes, often summed up in concepts such as personality, self, or personal identity. *Only by distinguishing the different dimensions carefully can we observe how they influence each other.*

RESOURCES AND STRATEGIES

We saw in chapter 2 that the main paradigms of protest have especially elaborated the dimensions of resources and strategies. Although game theories leave room for resources and for a crude psychology, they proclaim the importance of strategy, especially the role of mutual expectations and unintended outcomes. Unfortunately there is little of interest left in strategic choice once the substance of biography and culture is taken away, aside from a few equilibrium traps—which tell us more about the effects of choices than about how the choices are made. By examining the surrounding environment of protest movements, and the many actors in that environment, political process theorists have also concentrated on strategies, with passing nods to resources and to cultural processes such as cognitive liberation. Resource mobilization traditions have been caricatured as concerned primarily with initial resource distributions, although most authors have also attended to mobilization strategies.

Yet resources and mobilization belong to different dimensions of protest. Having resources is one thing; accumulating and using them are another. Availability is a necessary but not sufficient condition for their use. At a simple physical, technological level, a state equipped with tanks, tear gas, helicopters, and automatic weapons is *capable* of more severe repression than one armed with crossbows or muskets. But the decision to use tanks or tear gas is influenced by more than just their availability; it is affected by perceptions about the justice of protestors' claims, of how the news media would respond, of whether political opponents could use these actions to their own advantage. These are cultural and especially strategic considerations. In addition, biographical factors, including personality traits and idiosyncratic emotional responses, affect important decisions such as whether a king flees in the face of a crowd, orders his troops to fire on them, issues concessions, or faces them down. Strategic decisions depend partly on resources—tear gas did not exist in 1789—but also on cultural meanings and biography. But strategic calculations have an additional logic of their own, related to past choices and stances, the responses of others, and expectations of future responses. Strategic interaction is crucially important, the very stuff of protest, but if it is the only lens, then "conflict" replaces "social movements" as the appropriate framework. A purely strategic lens misses much of the "why" of protest.

The logic of strategic interaction, explored in more depth in chapter 13, has two main components. One is the explanation of strategic choices: why players make the decisions they do, how they think about opponents and other audiences. A hefty biographical component affects these choices. So do tastes in tactics, judgments that are partly independent of expected outcomes. The other part of strategy is more structural: people respond to the actions of others in ways that are partly predictable, so that many conflicts follow the same patterns. Outcomes such as polarization, radicalization, and stalemate—as game theorists love to show—are not intended or desired by any of the players. Through the logic of conflict, players can lose much of their own room to maneuver, finding themselves in traps. Some traps are carefully laid by opponents, but others arise out of strategic interaction, much to the surprise of all involved—and sometimes to the disadvantage of all sides. Political opportunities can disappear not only— as process theorists emphasize—because of state decisions but also through a logic of strategic conflict operating behind everyone's back. Strategy involves both individual choices and interactions among many such choices.

Granting autonomy to strategy allows us to appreciate resources more fully, retaining the crisp definition of them as physical technologies and capacities as well as the money to buy them. The zero-sum nature of resources—their countability and transferability, according to Gamson and his colleagues—distinguishes them from many other kinds of advantages protestors seek. Strategies and resources are intimately related, of course: through strategies one accumulates resources, so that the kind and amount of resources a protest group has at any time is a function of prior strategies; and resources are only significant when they are used as part of some broader strategic initiative (even if that strategy only involves the *threatened* use of resources). But the relationship between them varies. Citizenship movements may mobilize their "natural" constituencies with different strategies than post-citizenship movements will use. The two kinds of movements may also differ in their relationship to those outside the movement, in that some group is benefiting, in all likelihood, from the exclusionary practices that citizenship movements are protesting against; thus repression may be quicker and more severe. As a form of property, resources are hemmed in by an extensive web of laws and customs that both restrict access and constrain how resources can be used. Acquiring a physical resource is only the first step towards its application.

In chapter 2, when discussing the overextension of the concept of resource, we saw that cultural meanings and practices operate with a different logic from that of physical resources—even though culture relies on physical embodiments and resources depend on cultural knowledge. Analytically, it is useful not to think of culture or biography as a form of resource.

Resources and strategies differ in their measurability. Strategic choices and programs can be either mistaken or effective. A conclusive judgment about this is possible only in retrospect, for a clever move or reinterpretation can often make a good situation out of a bad one, just as a bad blunder can blow what had seemed an invincible lead. Yet along the way, strategic advantages are real enough, and sudden reversals infrequent enough, for observers to make provisional judgments of who is ahead. Resources are more easily counted and compared, even though spurts of accumulation are also possible with clever strategic action. In any case, advantages in strategic position and resources are more easily assessed, even measured, than cultural and biographical advantages.

Power ultimately rests on resources. Those with more money get their way most of the time. Resources help protect against unexpected attacks, and allow a greater variety and more constant application of strategies. But success is not always determined by power or resources alone. Much protest has been about those with less power winning concessions from those with more—for strategic, cultural, and biographical reasons.

Resources and strategies have been well studied, but a full understanding of either one requires greater attention to culture and biography. Culture helps define the uses of resources and the options available as strategies. Biographical dynamics help to explain the choices made.

CULTURE

My preliminary definition of culture as shared mental equipment and its representations was designed mostly to show how it differed analytically from resources, strategies, and biography. I further insisted on culture's own analytically separable components: cognition, morality, and emotions. We can now make an additional cut into culture, distinguishing different ways it is related to thought and action, and different places to look for it methodologically. Just as debates between different theoretical traditions often collapsed the four distinct dimensions of protest, so disagreements concerning the nature of culture often overlook the fact that it is several things. Arguments unfold over whether culture is subjective or objective, individual or collective, Weberian or Durkheimian, creative or constraining, constitutive or a product, structuring or structured. And just as I have argued for a "both/and" rather than an "either-or" view of protest's dimensions, I'll argue that culture can be observed in many places and ways. Rather than being either individual or collective, for example, it is both.

If we don't distinguish its facets, however, culture can hide more than it reveals. Gary Alan Fine has pointed out the potential vagueness of culture when studied as "an amorphous, indescribable mist which swirls around society's members," the problems being due to "difficulties associated with specifying its content and the population serving as its referent."[4] I suggest that we avoid speaking of "a culture," as though there were a primordial, unitary set of feelings or understandings shared by all or most members of a society. (There may be, in some cases, but it is better not to assume it.) I prefer to speak of separate cultural beliefs, feelings, rituals, symbols, practices, moral visions, and such. How widely shared any of them is should be an empirical question—the answer to which often explains the success or failure of a protest movement. The unitary view of culture is the legacy of older anthropological traditions, French structuralism, parsonian sociology, and marxist analyses of class hegemony. An individual may have a complex, interrelated worldview; a society cannot.[5]

I would distinguish culture along two major dimensions, each of which is correlated with several minor distinctions. First, culture runs the gamut *from implicit to explicit*.[6] The most obvious form of culture consists of explicit chunks, such as ideas, legal identities, moral principles, named emotions, language, as well as the artifacts which express these. But we also operate with metaphors, customs, sensibilities, and assumptions that we cannot fully articulate. As social scientists we try to make all the components explicit (just as many protestors try to do, deriving explicit ideologies from inchoate sensibilities), but most practitioners (real people, that is) are happy to operate with a lot of intuitive common sense. We may have a moral intuition that something is wrong or right without being able to name the principle at stake. It is usually only implicitly that culture helps to define resources and strategies, for instance.

A closely related dimension divides culture into *discrete pieces*, more easily made explicit, versus *bundles or packages* of those components, which are more likely to remain implicit. Discrete ideas and moral values can be packaged together into a worldview or ideology. For example, emotions such as anger or outrage and cognitions such as attributions of blame together form an injustice frame. A related distinction is that culture can be analyzed as a static classification of meanings (usually explicit) or as something that is only visible in action (and hence implicit). This is what philosophers since Wittgenstein have called *knowing that versus knowing how*. We know how to behave at a rally even if we don't have Erving Goffman's ability to formulate the rules we are following. We may have emotions and knowledge that we lack the language to articulate.

The second major cluster of contrasts is between culture as *individual and interior* on the one hand, versus *shared, public, and collective* on the other—"thought in the head, thought in the world," as Clifford Geertz once put it.[7] A commonsense and traditional way to think about culture views it as the intentions, beliefs, values, and such of individuals which motivate, guide, or rationalize their actions. Because of notorious empirical difficulties in linking mental states to actions, many social scientists prefer to define culture exclusively as public statements and artifacts. Only individuals have thoughts, but they express them in media that make them available to others, art being the paradigm case. Symbols can then be studied as structured systems of boundaries and differences with little reference to the subjective state of individuals, allowing students of culture to avoid the thorny problem of trying to probe other people's minds. These theorists hope in this way to sidestep issues of meaning and interpretation. This strategy, according to Eric Rambo and Elaine Chan, "divides culture into text and meaning, establishing text as a universally objective domain of cultural structure, and thereby protecting part of culture from the problem of meaning, protecting the study of culture, that is, from the problem of study-ing a 'phenomenon' that is at the same time interior and collective."[8] This effort ultimately fails, for objective texts still mean something to individuals, shape their ideas and feelings, move them in certain ways.

To me *culture is a duality,* observable either through interviews with individuals or through analysis of public embodiments, with varying kinds of correspondence between the two. Culture links individuals with institutionalized symbols by providing meanings that we can dis-cern both in the consciousness of individuals—the ideas they espouse, the assumptions they reveal in interviews—and in the formal, public events, artifacts, and documents of society. In addition to its public embodiments, in other words, culture is also something that we carry around in our heads. Cultural symbols have meanings (as parts of structures) and they have meaning (for individuals). Culture consists of knowledge, process, and product, as thoughts lead to activities, which create objects. This duality is characteristic of all structures, as Anthony Giddens points out in saying they are "both medium and outcome" of social practices, both structured and structuring.[9] Because of this duality, we can get at culture methodologically either through interviews with individuals or through physical documents and im-ages. Often we can uncover the same meanings from both directions, although we sometimes see variation in how individuals think and feel about the public symbols. Public statements and rituals are compatible with private allegiance, complete cynicism, or many stances in be-tween.

The contrast between public and private is intimately connected to another contrast: culture's *static versus its dynamic face.* As publicly ob-servable artifacts and statements, which together form a discernible structure of meanings with some autonomy from those who use it, culture discourages individual innovation. We cannot say whatever we please or believe whatever we wish and still hope to be understood. Mary Douglas argues, "Culture, in the sense of the public, standardi-sed values of a community, mediates the experience of individuals. It provides in advance some basic categories, a positive pattern in which ideas and values are tidily ordered. And above all, it has authority, since each is induced to assent because of the assent of others. But its public character makes its categories more rigid." We must bend to the cultural structures around us.[10] Yet only partly. We can twist and transform those structures because there is also a subjective and stra-tegic moment to culture. Culture is a set of rules we can use according to our own intentions. We work within certain aspects of the structure to subvert other aspects of it.

Pierre Bourdieu demonstrates how the two sides of culture are inextricably related. He describes culture as a set of available strategies, and likens a cultural product, in his example a marriage, "to a card game, in which the outcome depends partly on the deal, the cards held (their value itself being defined by the rules of the game, characteristic of the social formation in question), and partly on the players' skill."[11] In my terms, there is an initial distribution of resources, followed by the strategic interactions which change that distribution. Culture defines the game and the value of resources, offers discrete moves and skills used in playing it, and still allows room for innovations. The rules, for Bourdieu, are only guidelines, and he criticizes other traditions for reducing people to the role of simply executing or applying fixed rules.[12] Bourdieu's picture contains some structure, but also allows some discretion and creativity. A marriage is a (potentially virtuosic) cultural performance. *There are no fixed rules about when it's best to break the rules.* Because of the duality of culture and other structures, there is room for artistry in social life, especially in protest.

In the similar words of Ann Swidler, "A culture is not a unified system that pushes action in a consistent direction. Rather, it is more like a 'tool kit' or repertoire from which actors select differing pieces for constructing lines of action."[13] Swidler wishes to avoid both subjective and objective concepts of culture by showing how "social processes organize and focus culture's effects on action." She draws on Theodore Caplow's analysis of Christmas gift giving, in which people continue to give gifts, even though they dislike the custom and don't believe it has any meaning, because they believe that it has meaning for others. Swidler concludes, "What governs action in this case, then, is not individuals' internalized beliefs, but their knowledge of what meanings their actions have for others."[14] Yet subjective assessments still matter—in fact there are two layers of meanings: *our* perceptions about *other* people's subjective meanings (and feelings and judgments). Our actions do not simply embody our intentions; they include a strategic element of mutual expectations about other people's responses. It is not clear that Swidler has eliminated the subjective or the objective aspects; rather, she has shown how they interact. Besides, even if culture sometimes operates through mistaken impressions of other's meanings, this does not mean that it never works as internal subjective intentions or as structured, objective constraints.

Swidler addresses another distinction among forms of culture: as goals for action, and as means of attaining them. Attacking parsonian images, she is concerned to show that ultimate ends and values do not guide action. She conceptualizes culture, then, as a repertory of ways of acting, related not only to habits but to skills. Culture becomes a form of strategy.[15] Culture, I would agree, includes models and schemas for action: knowledge that can be put into practice. But why exclude ends as another component of culture? Do humans not have goals, at least some of the time? And if they do, where would they come from but the world of culture, the beliefs, aspirations, and moral visions that we share with others?

Cultural meanings and feelings can be either explicit or implicit; they can be more like means or more like ends. They are publicly embodied yet also lodge in individuals' heads—where they intersect with the realm of biography. I prefer not to exclude any kind of culture that clearly exists and affects action, just so that we can fit it all into a single concept. Narrow conceptual definitions are good, but we may need several of them to cover culture. My hope in the rest of the book is to tease out meanings that are implicit as well as explicit, and to get at them, when possible, through both individuals and public embodiments. As Ralph Waldo Emerson said, "[W]e are symbols, and inhabit symbols." We use culture to constitute ourselves and our worlds; it both constrains and enables us.

It should be clear how intimately culture shapes resources and strategies. We learn how to use resources and to make strategic choices from others and from our own experiences, with a kind of residue that lodges in our minds. Strategizing, in particular, is a matter of sometimes following culturally ingrained rules but at other times bending them, breaking them, playing off them to thwart expectations. As Swidler showed, strategies put culture into action. Contrary to Swidler's argument, culture also provides the goals that we strategize for, the reasons we accumulate resources. On top of this, we shall later see, we attach moral and emotional values to strategies, above and beyond valuing them for their sheer efficacy.

That meanings, feelings, even resources and strategies are "culturally constructed" does not mean that they are arbitrary or infinitely flexible. Socially constructed meanings and practices can exert considerable constraint or provide equal room for creativity. The great story of the human sciences for at least forty years has been the recognition of just how completely everything humans know about the world, everything they do, even all that scientists (both social and natural) do, is socially constructed. That is, all our physical and mental tools are cultural conventions that work in part because people in a group or society agree upon them. Our very perceptions of the external world and of our interior selves are guided by expectations and categories shaped by those around us; we have no direct access to either. The tools and visions thus constructed are culture. Cognitively, emotionally, and morally, we are all deeply embedded in cultural contexts, even defined by them. Concepts such as political opportunity structures, resources, and rationality are not just interpreted through a cultural lens, but are constituted and defined from the start by cultural contexts.

Social constructionism avoids both traditional objectivism—the idea that we can come to understand and grasp "the world" out there in a fairly direct way—as well as utter relativism—the idea that different conceptual systems so constrain our ability to grasp the world that we cannot compare these systems with each other, that our frameworks trap us in different worlds. Once we admit, with the constructionists, that we cannot know with certainty the relationship between our beliefs about the external world and the true state of that world (we suspect that modern science is a pretty accurate picture of nature, but we cannot prove it with certainty), then we can look for the social mechanisms that help sort out better and worse opinions. We can examine the "sifting" function of scientific journals, peer reviews, data gathering, conventions for sampling and statistical analysis, hypotheses and predictions—all of which are ways of judging the validity of claims about reality. We can also judge malfunctions in those "validity mechanisms," as when the prestige of the investigator influences her argument's chance of acceptance, when the interests of the biotechnology industry influence scientific research funding, when political pressures close down laboratories.[16]

Even if emotions, morals, and scientific facts are socially constructed, even if they are not "objectively" out there, independent of human observers, at least in any form that humans can access directly, this does not mean that they are a subjective matter of individual choice. Culture is structured and constraining. I cannot believe just anything I wish. I may say that my cocker spaniel influences the daily vicissitudes of the NASDAQ exchange, but I cannot force even myself to believe it—much less persuade my friends. This claim is a biographical quirk, not a cultural achievement. If I truly come to believe it, rejecting culturally accepted evidence and arguments in discussions with my friends, then I will be dismissed as insane (even though no one else has a better account of NASDAQ prices). Even in small groups or pairs we cannot "negotiate" just any emotion or belief. There are constraints imposed by the distribution of power in society, by organizations with interests in constructing certain emotions, by acceptable kinds of "evidence" filtered from the external world, and by a variety of other institutional and cultural practices. For every environmental group trying to portray single-hull oil tankers as risky, there is a Mobil ad in the *New York Times* reassuring readers about the oil industry.[17]

Each institutional setting has its own criteria for separating valid emotions and beliefs from invalid ones. Scientists persuade one another by means of journal articles, institutional affiliations, and personal reputation. Protest groups too have their characteristic mechanisms for defining appropriate behaviors and emotions. Innumerable validity mechanisms help us construct shared understandings and suppress idiosyncratic ones. We are left with what some observers have labeled the postmodern condition, in which we are so aware of our limited contexts that we refuse any single, overriding narrative as a description of history. There is still extensive validity testing that occurs—something the postmodernists often overlook. That is what institutional and historical contexts provide: cultural criteria for judging one account of the world better than another.[18] There are firm pressures on individuals to believe certain things, feel certain ways, and act according to the rules.

In sum, culture is about meaning and interpretation, whether we get at them through individual minds or external, objectified embodiments. Some parts of culture are discrete entities—rituals, ideas, slogans—easily added to existing models, but others are more implicit, constitutive constructions of action, institutions, and objects. A cultural perspective requires a rethinking of concepts like rationality, resources, interests, and political opportunities. Although scholars of social movements have recently begun to bring culture into their models, the realm of biography has yet to be rediscovered despite its considerable parallels with culture.

BIOGRAPHY

Inside each individual's head are both culture and biography: the implicit and explicit mental constructs that she shares with others are cultural; those she does not share are biographical. But biography also covers the processes by which certain elements of a broader culture are selected for use in an individual's mental and emotional arsenal.[19] Thus the biographical dimension results from the idiosyncratic experiences an individual has lived through, including the interpersonal dynamics, originally rooted in the family, that lead to unconscious mental states and to what is commonly called a personality, a kind of filter that encourages certain ways of feeling, judging, and thinking while discouraging others. This kind of individual diversity means that protestors participate out of different bundles of motivations, interpret leading symbols and rhetoric in slightly different ways, and have varying aspirations for their actions. To understand a movement or event completely, we would need information about these individual stances, but no researcher has time to conduct depth interviews and life histories with more than a handful of participants. We usually stop with those whose views and decisions are most influential, those who are leaders in some formal or informal way, and we only make inferences about the biographical makeup of other participants.

Biography is not all idiosyncrasy, however, but is also wrapped up in psychology and social psychology: predictable dynamics, responses, and learning processes common to many individuals, perhaps sometimes even universal. If I am labeling as biography a level of mental life that is more particular than culture because it is a selection from culture, then psychology usually deals with a level broader than culture, often at a supposedly universal level. All humans have limits on their cognitive processing capacities and so rely on various heuristics to remember things and make decisions; we all have affective bonds to significant others; we respond with emotion to the loss of a loved one; we trust certain people and mistrust others; we learn language at an early age and use it in situating ourselves in the world; we all try to make sense of existential issues of birth, death, and reproduction. The learning of meanings and feelings from one's culture is a universal process, even though cultures differ considerably in the substance of those meanings, and even though within each culture individuals end up with unique bundles. Other social-psychological dynamics are somewhat less universal, including group dynamics, responses to authority, or feelings of shame and pride. Specific sources of shame or attitudes to authority differ across cultures and groups. This area of social psychology borders on culture, especially since culture includes emotional responses and affective bonds. Occasionally I shall refer to psychological processes in this latter sense, by which I mean group reactions or interactions grounded in cultural meanings, and in a few cases I shall even try to discern some potentially universal psychological processes, for example, how we respond to feelings of threat. Mostly, though, my interest in psychology is for the light it sheds on biographical factors.

Personality is the most common concept meant to cover individual idiosyncracies. Actors not only "have" personalities, according to Jeffrey Alexander, in some sense they "are" personalities, for all their actions are filtered through, if not generated by, their internalized dispositions. He continues: "Yet personalities, in turn, represent a selection of objects introjected from social encounters, a selection dictated by the play of organic and developmental needs. Each acting 'I' and his or her personality, moreover, changes decisively at different stages in his or her own life."[20] Despite these transformations, the concept of personality implies at least some continuity across time and in different contexts, characteristic responses, styles, and behaviors that we would have trouble changing. They are bundles of traits and feelings selected from surrounding cultures.

The concept of a self, with connotations that it is relatively conscious and purposive, can partly replace the idea of a personality. My biographical dimension at the individual level is a recognition that there is such a thing as a "self," about which people care deeply. They concern themselves with who they are, what groups they identify with, what others think of them, and how their past, present, and future are linked together into some provisional coherence. They take pride, or sometimes shame, in the kind of person they are, and in the image others have of them. Social psychologist Thomas Scheff goes so far as to argue that shame and pride are the two most important, perhaps universal, motivations in social life, the glue that makes cooperation possible.[21] The self is a deeply moral construct, according to philosopher Charles Taylor, who claims that "[w]e are selves only in that certain issues matter for us. What I am as a self, my identity, is essentially defined by the way things have significance for me."[22] It is this deep moral significance buried in self-identity—which Taylor says is never fully explicit—that protest taps into. Moral self-identity ultimately derives from cultural contexts, but once created it can have considerable autonomy from them. Once again, my discussion of the analytic autonomy of the basic dimensions of protest is meant to allow us to see better how they influence each other empirically.

Even recent attacks on the notion of a self are usually questioning specific concepts of the self, leaving open the possibility that there is some continuity to individual actions and intentions. Qualifying "postmodern" criticism of images of the self as unitary and stable, Jane Flax says, "while I advocate decentered forms of subjectivity, I do not think fragmentation is the only desirable or plausible alternative to a false sense of unity. Fragmentation also entails many risks. In many contexts it is inappropriate, useless, or harmful. People can achieve coherence or long-term stability without claiming or constructing a (false or true) solid core self."[23] Drawing on pragmatism, Norbert Wiley has similarly described a cultural self, which semiotically interprets, creates, and deals with symbols and emotions.[24] He insists that this is not an unrealistically unified self, but rather a "decentered" self. It is externally decentered because it depends so heavily on the social world for its meanings; it is internally decentered because it consists of a "conversation" among different parts of the self, notably an expected or desired future self, a remembered and constructed self from the past, and the present self. As long as individuals have some coherence or stability in their actions and intentions, biography will be an important dimension of protest.

Just as culture involves the interplay between individual meanings and more structured public systems, the same kind of duality can be applied to biography. Labeling this a "discursive" model, Rom Harré and Grant Gillett claim that recent cognitive psychology yields precisely this lesson: "1. Many psychological phenomena are to be interpreted as properties or features of discourse, and that discourse might be public or private. As public, it is behavior; as private, it is thought. 2. Individual and private uses of symbolic systems, which in this view constitute thinking, are derived from interpersonal discursive processes that are the main feature of the human environment. 3. The production of psychological phenomena, such as emotions, decisions, attitudes, personality displays, and so on, in discourse depends upon the skill of the actors, their relative moral standing in the community, and the story lines that unfold."[25] This view highlights the dependence of the biographical dimension on the cultural.

Because individuals carry selections of cultural meanings around in their heads, they can transport them from one context to another, and from one organization to another. Concentrating on the activity of organizations, mobilization and process theorists overlook the individuals who fit poorly into organizations, who move between them, who attend rallies and write letters without belonging to groups. Not all moral protest occurs in protest movements, although it is crucial to ask what makes individual protestors join organized movements. These individuals can transmit ideas and know-how from movement to movement, and their lives can be transformed in ways invisible to scholars concerned with individual social movements as defined by formal organizations. In discussing the "fluidity" of social movements, Joseph Gusfield sees individuals as capable of both "carry-overs" and "carry-ons" between movements, bringing ways of acting and thinking with them to new movements.[26]

In the structural vision of most process theorists, individuals do not matter. Sidney Tarrow sets up a false dichotomy when he declares, "The collective action problem is social, not individual. Movements are produced when political opportunities broaden, when they demonstrate the existence of allies and when they reveal the vulnerability of opponents."[27] In the passive construction "are produced" and the unclear referent of both instances of "they," people seem to have disappeared. But these "social" phenomena can be simultaneously mapped at the level of individuals, and in many cases those individuals' actions and choices matter a great deal. It is better not to define them away at the outset.

The disrepute of psychological theories comes in part from the Freudian content of so many of them, especially in the first half of the twentieth century. Works such as Harold Lasswell's *Psychopathology and Politics* of 1930 were filled with discussions of narcissism, latent homosexuality, oral dependence, and anal retention—often aimed at showing protest participation to be an immature activity.[28] Freudians emphasized processes of ego defense, which Fred Greenstein defines as "the means through which individuals, often without realizing it, adapt their behavior to the need to manage their inner conflicts."[29] These were unsavory images of personalities as unconscious interferences with purposive behavior, as handicaps which, developed if not fixed in childhood, distort perceptions and sometimes prevent direct responses to our environment, through mechanisms such as denial, splitting, or projection.

The Freudian challenge is that unconscious dynamics may prevent us from learning in response to our environment. Alexander too seems to equate personality dynamics with unconscious emotions as he concludes his discussion of personality: "Action occurs within systemic environments, the organization of unconscious emotional needs not the least among them."[30] Yet a post-Freudian ego psychology has increasingly stressed the cognitive strengths and adaptive resources of the ego, which transforms the unrealistic wishes of the id into more socially acceptable desires.[31] In normal adults, these ego dynamics make their actions more rational, not less so, more realistically attuned to their social surroundings. Long-standing affective loyalties and emotional responses to events and information are not, as we shall see in chapter 5, incompatible with rationality. Nor are they sudden eruptions of the psyche, but adaptations to events and information. Most idiosyncrasies of personality are better seen, I believe, as variations in desires and coping, not simple deviations from rationality.

STRUCTURES

There are other contenders for the list of basic dimensions of protest, mostly some form of social, political, or organizational "structure." In particular, political structures, formal organizations, and social networks have been used as starting points in explaining the rise and fall of protest movements. When properly specified, each of these can be useful, but in the long run I believe that they derive from my four dimensions. Part of the problem with such concepts is the way that they are theorized as "structure."

Structure is perhaps the most metaphorical concept we use in the social sciences, for social life is not constructed with walls, floors, roofs, and so on, as the root implies. And yet, according to William Sewell, it is a necessary metaphor. He has cogently argued that structures consist of physical resources and the cultural schemas (know-how, procedures, assumptions) necessary for using them: "Sets of schemas and resources may properly be said to constitute *structures* only when they mutually imply and sustain each other over time." Resources embody the schemas, and in doing so justify them. "Agents are empowered by structures, both by the knowledge of cultural schemas that enables them to mobilize resources and by the access to resources that enables them to enact schemas." [32] Analytically, structures are reducible to culture and resources, but they serve a kind of signaling function for the scholar. When a researcher uses the metaphor of structure, which Sewell says is "less a precise concept than a kind of founding or epistemic metaphor of social scientific—and scientific—discourse," she means that she is taking something as relatively fixed and stable for her current purposes, as a given in order to explain something else. [33] Unfortunately, it is easy to forget that a structure is a sign or metaphor, not a real thing.

In an earlier book, I argued that a reification of structures limits explanations in several ways. We "tend to recognize formal, legal, codified power more readily than the informal power that comes, for example, from skills at persuading people or attracting favorable public opinion." Second, decision makers exercise discretion, and the choices they make depend on biographical and psychological factors as well as their structural positions. Elections, persuasion of the public, and other strategies also matter. In addition, I argued, the goals even of rationalized state bureaucracies do not always follow directly from any structural organizational interest: these stakes are sometimes contested and have to be constructed. Finally, structures change continually in small ways, and occasionally in large ones. They are harder to change than other aspects of the political situation, and thus change less frequently. But they do change. No structure is so primary and fixed as to be immutable for all times—although the image of a structure seems to imply just that. [34]

Process theorists feature political structures prominently in their explanations, making them a basic dimension of protest. Sometimes, es-

pecially in cross-national comparisons, they view them as provision-
ally fixed. Protestors may maneuver within electoral systems but take
for granted governmental systems. In many cases, though, protestors
are out to change precisely those political "structures." Sewell argues
against applying structural metaphors to states, on the ground that
they are so obviously the result of strategizing and power: "State and
political structures are consciously established, maintained, fought
over, and argued about rather than taken for granted as if they were
unchangeable features of the world."[35] That structures do not change,
in the period being considered, is sometimes taken to mean that they
cannot change. With this caveat, though, political structures may occasionally prove a useful tool for seeing constraints on protest movements.

Other process theorists, usually taking a longer view, look precisely
at changes in political structures as opening up opportunities. One
problem, we saw, was that these changes are not themselves explained.
At a more fundamental level, though, structural change is usually
thought to follow its own logic, independent of culture and strategy,
although often linked to resources. Political systems constrain action
because people believe in them and follow the rules, or because powerful institutions and individuals use their resources to enforce compliance. At a logical level, there is little left of political structures when
we account for resources, culture, strategy, and occasionally biography.

A worse candidate for an autonomous dimension in explanations
of protest is "social structure," one of the most common and long-
standing uses of the structure metaphor, which comes perilously close
to tautology. What is social structure but patterns of human interaction? Fine, except that this is often what we are trying to explain. To
explain a social movement, we need to explain why certain individuals
come together at certain times and places to do things together. How
good an explanation is it to say that they have come together before in
other times and places? Our curiosity is pushed back a step: if people
have interacted with each other before, they are likely to again, but
why did they interact the first time? There is something inadequate
about this sort of account. Yet this is roughly what many structural
concepts do, especially the very popular concept of social networks.

The concept of a social network has been widely used in research
on protest, especially as a means for explaining recruitment patterns.
They are a way of operationalizing social structure. One network
scholar, Mario Diani, recently defined social movements as a network,
listing several kinds of ties one finds in a network: "personal ties between individuals who either sympathise for or mobilise in a move-

ment; inter-organisational linkages; informal links between organis-ations created by activists through their multiple memberships and by personal ties between members."[36] So we have personal ties and organizational ties. The vagueness of words like *ties*, *linkages*, and *knowing* someone else is reduced, for organizational ties, by the follow-ing operationalization: "I considered two movement organisations to be in touch if they: (1) jointly promoted specific campaigns; (2) regu-larly exchanged information; (3) shared some core members; (4) had one or more core members with friendship ties to core members of the other organisation."[37] What can we explain through these interactions? What exactly do we know when we discover that protestors are more likely to recruit people they know than people they don't know? Or that two organizations exchange information? Do the network interac-tions tell us much that is interesting by itself? We need to push beyond the network metaphor, most often, to see what resources, rules, cul-tural schemas, and patterns of affect lie behind it. Why this network, rather than another? When can an existing network be used for recruit-ment, and when does a new network arise out of protest itself?

One problem is that the effects of personal networks have often been misrepresented. The effects of political and organizational sources of networks have been underestimated in order to exaggerate some kind of "pre-existing" social organization. It seems to me that most of the people with whom we interact regularly are either *colleagues* or *com-rades* or *friends and family*. Let's take each in turn. *We associate with col-leagues because of the formal organizations that shape our lives, and these or-ganizations do much of the work that gets credited to networks.* In some organizations, our incentives are primarily monetary: we gain re-sources as compensation for our interactions. Other organizations pur-sue political ends; their existence is a conscious strategy. Facets one and two in Diani's case of organizational ties could easily result from conscious decisions by organizations engaged in strategic campaigns, not from a pre-existing bond; if such a tie existed from prior cam-paigns, we need to explain only why it was continued. When Doug McAdam and Ronnelle Paulsen reanalyzed Freedom Summer data, which had previously been used to show that potential volunteers with ties to another volunteer were more likely to show up than those without such ties, they found that this "was merely a proxy" for or-ganizational membership, accompanied by a compatible personal identity.[38]

This is the second qualification of networks as an explanation of mobilization: *Many networks result from conscious, often political, deci-sions: comrades are those we have chosen because we share with them some image of social justice and social change.* In the area of protest, at least, we are often trying to explain this very choice of comrades. The usual image of networks, based on research on citizenship movements, is that they are part of a community that exists prior to and independently of political action, as southern black communities did before the civil rights movement. But other networks, we shall see, develop specifically for political purposes without any independent collective identity behind them. These activist networks, common among post-industrial movements, can help a new movement arise, as shown in chapters 7 and 8. But they can also be developed specifically for a particular cause and not have much life beyond it; in this case explaining a protest movement in terms of the network it creates is especially tautological. Diani found surprisingly few regular contacts in the environmental movement in Milan: organizations were in regular touch with fewer than three other groups; individuals with only 3.5 other environmentalists. Post-industrial movements may emerge or continue without dense pre-existing networks, but this suggests that the pre-existing ties of citizenship movements may also have been exaggerated or misinterpreted. In the absence of controlled comparisons with dense networks that do not issue in organized movements, it is possible to suspect that such ties are common or universal. They may channel recruitment without causing it.

One promising contribution of networks is to show how different organizations might become connected in the first place: how one individual who belongs to both might organize the bloc recruitment of one group to a new cause. Even to understand the loyalties in these bonds, we must often turn to individual traits: the charisma of those in certain key positions in networks, for instance. And it is not clear what the concept of a network adds to our attention to this individual. How are links between formal organizations created and maintained? I think that resources and strategies explain most of these contacts, but ties between individuals explain some of them.

Once we separate out the effects of formal organizations and consciously created ties, it is not clear what is left of networks. They seem reducible to my other basic dimensions. Even the third type, bonds to friends and family, is largely explained on the basis of affect, a combination of culture and biography. Social ties of some sort are present in all social life. Frances Fox Piven and Richard Cloward admit that a minimal level of social organization ("numbers, propinquity, and some communication") is required for protest, but this is found in virtually all human societies: "To be sure, people have to be related to one another; they must have some sense of common identity, some sense of shared definitions of grievances and antagonists, some ability to communicate, and so on. But these requisites do not depend on the dense and enduring lateral relationships posited by the [resource mobilization] school."[39] Piven and Cloward imply that social networks are like oxygen: we would not exist without them, but that very fact makes them suspect as independent explanatory variables in the absence of greater specification.

Networks also benefit from an odd methodological bias: once a mechanism is identified, even small bits of evidence are taken as favoring it. In the heavily studied case of recruitment, should we be impressed if 10 percent of participants are recruited through personal networks? Fifty percent? Ninety percent? A survey of the members of one social movement organization of the 1980s found that "19 percent first heard about Witness for Peace through a religious publication they read and 9 percent through contacts at their church or synagogue." The author takes this as evidence of the importance of networks in recruitment, even though publications are fairly anonymous and available to whoever wants them, leaving only 9 percent recruited through direct personal ties.[40] The very small number of contacts among Diani's environmentalists and environmental organizations is also taken as evidence for the importance of networks.

In all these cases, networks are closely related to one of the other basic dimensions (resources for colleagues, strategies for comrades, and the emotional component of culture for friends and family). It is not always clear what the concept of networks adds, except a methodology for measuring these other dimensions. Like political structure, networks may be derivative but still frequently useful. They may be important primarily for the symbolic and emotional messages transmitted across them, which might find other, more anonymous, media such as direct mail or advertisements if networks were not there.

The most promising aspect of structural influences is probably that of a formal organization, since this is an extremely routinized cluster of resources, laws, rules, and cultural expectations. Most of McCarthy and Zald's imagery involves formal organizations, which arguably could represent an independent dimension. Organizations can, though, be analyzed through my four basic dimensions, in that organizations, established out of prior strategic choices, are both sites for the accumulation of cultural expectations and resources as well as contexts for further strategic choices. Their relative stability comes from cultural expectations as much as from their resources. "Structure" adds little to this. Like other aspects of structure, organizations come and go, and this coming and going is much of what we wish to explain. But because organizations are recognizable entities, about which there is a rich sociological literature, it is often useful to take them as givens for short periods of time. (Distressingly short, for most protest organizations.)

Structural metaphors are plausible because they express the insight that social life does constrain individuals, that there is an enduring quality to institutions and rules. But the reason is that resources, culture, even strategies and biography are relatively enduring and structured. To add another "thing" on top of these is unnecessary. If we want to explain why one institution endures longer than another, we immediately turn to their resources, cultural legitimacy, the strategies and biography of leaders and opponents, and so on. To explain a structure, instead of taking it as a given, we probe its component aspects.

The problem with structural terms is not that they are meaningless, but that they are easily misrepresented. To call something a structure is to foreclose further investigation into it, especially into its variability. In explaining short-term phenomena, we can take many things as given that we could not in explanations of long-term developments. Political structures change infrequently. Resource distributions and cultural meanings also, for some purposes, may change too slowly to matter. But the changes in these dimensions are often exactly what we are interested in. What we should *not* do is to *assume* that political structures, networks, or formal organizations will not change.

ARTFULNESS

The basic and subsidiary dimensions that I have discussed so far can all be studied in a static way, as though time did not matter. Some game theorists even study strategies, the dimension most intimately connected with time, as though they were mechanical steps to a foregone outcome. But each dimension is distorted when viewed statically, and the interactions among the dimensions can easily disappear from sight. We misdescribe strategic opportunities as aspects of political structure; we miss how strategies transform distributions of resources. Culture has little explanatory power if we ignore how it is used and changed; even biography is a dimension that develops and grows rather than remaining fixed from childhood. Over time, more or fewer resources are available to protestors; strategies become less effective as opponents come to expect them; new sensibilities and rhetorics become more plausible; even biographical needs and capacities change—not only across history but across the lives of protest generations. Recognizing history and change can prevent us from reifying one dimension as somehow prior to the others.

One way to think about how all these dimensions change is through the idea of artfulness: people are aware of what they are doing, they make plans and develop projects, and they innovate in trying to achieve their goals. In their characteristic jargon, sociologists often refer to artfulness as "agency" in order to emphasize that individuals are not mere bearers of structures or dupes of culture. They act, albeit within certain limits. They monitor their actions and the outcomes, make adjustments, imagine new goals and possibilities, respond to others. Agency, according to sociologists Mustafa Emirbayer and Ann Mische, is oriented toward the past, in that one selects from elements of habit and tradition, and toward the future, as one experiments and tries to generate new ways of doing, feeling, and thinking. The concept also has a crucial normative element, in that one problematizes past practices, and makes decisions about future efforts; judgment is an active part of human life.[41] Art pulls these dimensions together succinctly, for it consists of experimental efforts to transmute existing traditions into new creations by problematizing elements that have been taken for granted. The resulting projects can be either large or small, extending over a lifetime's work or a month's, and an artist is likely to have several of each kind of project going at the same time. Protestors, just as clearly, rethink existing traditions in order to criticize portions and experiment with alternatives for the future, in both large and small ways. They also offer ways of getting from here to there.

Much of what protestors do can be understood as experiments aimed at working out new ways of living and feeling. Among post-industrial movements, especially, there is considerable attention to equality within the group, to the relationship between leaders and others, to democratic processes for decision making, to potential conflict between morality and instrumental efficiency. Most citizenship movements seek inclusion in existing ways of life, while post-citizenship movements arise precisely out of dissatisfaction with them. Sometimes the experiments are cumbersome and "inefficient" from a purely strategic point of view; an insistence on consensus, for instance, can prevent any action. But from a cultural perspective, these efforts may have important results, opening up our imaginations of what the future could hold. Much of this innovation, scholars like Alberto Melucci and John Lofland have argued, takes place offstage, in apparently quiet periods, as ideas circulate and new forms of living are tried. Only occasionally are these experiments taken up in explicit political programs.

Artfulness appears in all the dimensions of protest, singly or simultaneously. Protestors may fall back on traditional cultural tropes or aspirations in order to construct a new strategy or new uses for old resources. They may promulgate radically new cultural sensibilities through existing resources and strategies. They may strive to transform the psychic needs and feelings of their own members, as the women's movement and the New Age movement do. In some cases, they may pursue change in several dimensions at once, using new strategies that symbolize new cultural aspirations and psychic freedoms or that free them from the tyranny of existing resources. In little ways and big, protestors experiment with novel ways to think, feel, judge, and act. Effective strategizing, especially, relies not only on good timing but on artful innovation and choice.

Biography also has a special connection to artfulness. If time plus innovation equals change, biography and the individual variations it implies are necessary for that innovation. There is a natural selection process by which certain ideas or feelings catch on and spread. New strategies, technologies, and cultural elements usually begin with individuals—perhaps many at once, responding to the same broad social changes. They may then spread among protestors who see their effectiveness or feel their plausibility. Meanings and feelings are then, if successful, taken up by the arts, the news media, and finally other institutions. Artists are especially good at formulating new visions and expressions, while the news media are especially dull at spreading them, reducing them inevitably to lifestyles rather than recognizing them as critiques of major social institutions. Innovation in sensibilities is a complex process involving biography and broader cultural processes, shaped as well by resources and strategies. But it starts, as all culture does, with individuals. In darwinian imagery, we have natural variation across individuals, then some selection process by which the new ways of thinking, feeling, and acting are tested for their plausibility and strategic effect, and finally either rejection or widespread adoption.

Learning indicates a more active, open-ended image of culture that helps us escape an "oversocialized" conception of humans, in which they passively do what their culture directs. People choose among possible beliefs and feelings, although not freely. And they even innovate when existing roles don't fit. Protest is often generated, as Faye Ginsburg has shown in the case of the abortion controversy, when individuals feel uncomfortable with the dominant images offered them. Life crises, she says, "might indicate a lack of fit between a cultural ideal for the life course and individual experience."[42] Even someone's emotions may not fit precisely with society's definitions.[43] Dominant ideas and sensibilities always have gaps and contradictions which give alternatives some leverage and opportunity. The idea of some kind of misfit is especially promising as a way to approach those who go on to develop an ideology opposed to some part of their own society, as we shall see in chapter 9. Biographical factors, often quite subtle, may help explain why some individuals fit more easily into expected roles than others do, why some follow the rules more readily or enthusiastically than others. Only the most important leaders of protest have been favored with extensive biographical attention—Gandhi, Luther, Lenin, Mao—but all participants are affected by similar biographical histories.[44] Such dynamics are important even when they are out of fashion.

NOTHING COMES FIRST

Back when marxists walked the earth, they were fond of insisting that material existence, resources, came first. Different marxist schools meant different things by this: that there was a direct relationship between technological systems and the kind of beliefs people held; that the means of production determined the class structure and that class struggle affected our consciousness; that material production was only determinant "in the last instance" but allowed considerable autonomy to ideas in the meantime; that this last instance only occurred during economic and political crises; or that material and ideal worlds had their separate logics, but there had to be a functional fit between them. Sometimes "coming first" was meant historically: that people existed in their physical form before they communicated and watched television. At other times the priority was a logical one: material existence and interests were simply more important. Today, I think, most theorists recognize that our physical world and our ideas about that world can never be separated; one without the other makes no sense. Neither comes first.

To say or imply that one dimension of protest comes first, in the sense that it is most important, is to foreclose certain paths of research, to predetermine what results one can find. Neither culture nor strategy, nor resources, nor biography comes first. The only way that anything comes first is in the chronological flow of events. Even with historical chronologies, we must remember that resource distributions or cultural meanings at any given time are the result of prior actions and conflicts, the result, in other words, of resources, strategies, culture, and biography—none of which has logical priority over the others. The artfulness of social life guarantees that we can only derive empirical generalizations (and we do, as social scientists, make such generalizations) after the fact; we cannot derive logically what will happen in any situation. Even big processes like urbanization or industrialization are never predetermined.

I recommend these four dimensions as building blocks of protest because an emphasis on their autonomy should help us remember that we cannot know in advance what will be built with those blocks. Over a long enough period, it is all up for grabs. Knowing what comes first, after all, has always been a way of knowing what comes last.

- Although this book deals primarily with cultural aspects of protest, it is useful to keep in mind the irreducible, analytic autonomy of at least four dimensions: culture, biography, strategy, and resources.
- Culture is dual, combining structured, public systems of symbols with more open-ended, individual meanings.
- "Structures" are never as structural, namely unchanging and unchangeable, as they seem. They usually represent clusters of my four basic dimensions.
- Protest's artful side originates in the idiosyncracies that arise in individuals partly because of biographical factors. Each of the basic dimensions is dynamic, not static.
- The relative importance of any of the dimensions cannot be decided in advance; nothing comes first.

FOUR

Cultural Approaches

The inner world cannot be observed with the aid of our sensory organs. Our thoughts, wishes, feelings, and fantasies cannot be seen, smelled, heard, or touched. They have no existence in physical space, and yet they are real, and we can observe them as they occur in time: through introspection in ourselves, and through empathy (i.e., vicarious introspection) in others.
  —Heinz Kohut

Although fortunately it never had to be tested, it seems most likely that the British would have indeed fought on the beaches, landing grounds, streets, and hills—with soda-water bottles too, if it came to that—for Churchill formulated accurately the mood of his countrymen and, formulating it, mobilized it by making it a public possession, a social fact, rather than a set of disconnected, unrealized private emotions.
  —Clifford Geertz

In the past ten years students of social movements have rediscovered the importance of culture. They have begun to write about the social construction of grievances and worldviews. They have described the social-psychological identity formation of activists, often through critiques of rationalist and mobilization approaches. They have refocused their attention on the role of ideas and ideologies in political action. And they have pushed the idea of culture beyond static cognitive grids and into modes of action. European theorists of post-industrial movements, as their works were translated into English in the 1980s, helped to inspire American researchers to rethink their commitments to mobilization and process approaches by rediscovering culture.

Even those theorists most associated with the mobilization paradigm—so often attacked by culturally oriented scholars—have recognized the importance of culture in protest. William Gamson says, "Mobilization potential has, then, a strong cultural component. To understand it, we need to assess not only structural conduciveness but cultural conduciveness."[1] Gamson, whose 1975 book *The Strategy of Social Protest* helped define resource mobilization, now says that the primary blind spots of this perspective were culture and social psychology, claiming, "[I]t is still necessary to understand hearts and minds and emergent processes, not merely bureaucratic ones."[2]

Anthony Oberschall and John McCarthy have also used cultural constructionism in their recent work.[3]

This chapter examines and clarifies some of this recent work, beginning with the European theorists misleadingly labeled "new social movement" scholars. But I also probe the limits of this scholarship. Far more attention has been given to cognition than to morals or especially emotions. The problem of meaning has frequently been sidestepped by emphasizing the "structured" aspects of culture. Worse, cultural concepts such as framing and identity can be just as overextended as the concepts of resources or political opportunity structures. Time and place, two fundamental sets of cultural stances—ways that we place ourselves in the world and in history—also need consideration. So do the symbolic importance—and effects—of events and individuals. Then there are more existential aspects of culture: those moments when we consider what life is all about are good opportunities for protest organizers and ideologists. And in the end, cultural dynamics must be integrated into a view that balances strategy, resources, biography, and culture.

POST-INDUSTRIAL THEORIES

As the concept of mobilization gripped Americans in the 1970s, many European scholars reacted to the same protest movements of the 1960s and after by situating them in a broad vision of the sweep of history. Several discerned an emerging post-industrial society based on the increased importance of knowledge in economic production and a shift of productive activity from the industrial processing of physical materials to the manipulation of symbols, knowledge, and human relations. New political struggles, typified by the student movement, would characterize post-industrial society: struggles over cultural meanings, the quality of leisure activities, and autonomy and democracy, rather than over pieces of the economic pie. Compared to the older workers' movement (and other citizenship movements), the post-industrial movements were less interested in gaining state power or even electing legislative representatives, less oriented toward establishing citizenship rights, and more suspicious of formal, especially hierarchical, organizations. Rather than aiming ultimately at changes in state policy, much of their activity was intended to change the practices and beliefs of members and other segments of the public. Civil disobedience, for example, was intended as exemplary moral action transmitted by means of news coverage. If the labor movement had insisted that the workplace was part of the public rather than the private sphere, and hence open to contestation, then post-industrial movements were going even further, finding political meaning in intimate relations and sources of consciousness. (As I argued in chapter 1, movements like these have been around a long time, but they have flourished especially in the last thirty years.)

Alain Touraine looked for one social movement to emerge out of apparently disparate causes such as feminism, ecology, and peace: a movement that would fight technocracy—governance by technical experts housed in corporations and the state—just as the labor movement had opposed industrial capitalism.[4] Some European theorists asked what protestors wanted, and how their struggles revealed their "identity" as a force for historical change. Others viewed these movements as trying to forge collective identities based on gender, locale, or ethnicity rather than class—foreshadowing what has since come to be called identity politics in the United States. For both reasons, some dub them "identity theorists." More often, they have been referred to as "new social movement theorists," although this term probably exaggerates the differences between citizenship and post-industrial movements (and the newness of the latter, which are only the most recent form that post-citizenship movements have taken).

Alberto Melucci has specified in more detail the cultural processes at work in these movements. They are vehicles for moral utopianism, consisting of "a certain number of moral and totalizing expectations for happiness, justice, and truth."[5] He also argues that movements have not only a mobilization phase (normally studied by scholars) but also a latent period which involves "the daily production of alternative frameworks of meaning, on which the networks themselves are founded and live from day to day. . . . Latency does not mean inactivity. Rather, the potential for resistance or opposition is sewn into the very fabric of daily life."[6] The audience for much activity is not the state, but the members of social movements themselves, or their fellow citizens; how one lives one's life is itself a moral message. In Melucci's imagery, formal organizations are not always the main carriers of protest. Melucci traces movement discussions as protestors try to balance exclusionary practices that build solidarity with inclusionary ones that reach out to the rest of society. He not only recognizes that protestors have more than one audience but also that action aimed at strategic success may differ from that concerned with communication. In a word, he is sensitive to how protestors use culture to craft new visions and identities.

Residual marxist ideas of polarized class conflict and of social evolution remain undigested lumps in Touraine's analysis, and in Jürgen

Habermas's similar account.[7] Both sociologists see contemporary movements as fighting a contemporary ruling class of technocrats. (Process theorists are also influenced by marxist metaphors, and for them too the state has replaced the capitalist class as the usual source of oppression and target of protest.) Touraine and Habermas additionally share an evolutionary confidence that they know what the new social movements should be doing: pursuing universalist communication and protecting private life from colonization by technocrats, for Habermas, and battling technocrats for control over the direction of historical change, for Touraine. Underlying this battle is the evolution of society toward greater capacities for self-steering (whether by technocrats or citizens), combined with correspondingly greater intrusion by those in power into the lives of citizens (in other words the technocrats are winning). Just as marxists criticized workers for false consciousness when they did not embrace the theorists' analyses, so Habermas and Touraine have a clear idea of the battle that social movements should be waging, and they criticize them for making other choices. Their normative enthusiasms occasionally crowd out their explanatory projects.

Post-industrial theorists handle culture better than other major traditions do, highlighting the ability of groups to shape the world around them, but some of them still impose their own meanings on protestors instead of watching how participants create their own meaningful worlds. Touraine sees world-historical actors in recent social movements, but with regard to the movements he has studied through his method of "sociological intervention," he has had difficulties persuading them of their proper historical role. Protestors construct their own projects. Cultural meanings are made and modified to fit many local contexts as well as national and international ones; in every society subcultures clash over their constructions of the world. A theorist is unlikely to persuade them of his own construction from the outside. Touraine might have less faith in the power of protest movements to develop programs for social change, rather than simply responding to the projects of technocratic institutions, if he recognized how open-ended their cultural creativity is. He might also relax his distinction between "defensive" work such as building collective identities and "offensive" activities that have more to do with strategic efforts to control institutions.

With Europeans asking *why* and Americans asking *how*, there seemed to be a complementary division of labor between post-industrial and other approaches, yet the two visions did not exactly add up to a complete picture of protest. The language of resources and political process never linked up with that of cultural and historical identity. The Europeans cared little for empirical studies about how leaders mobilized resources, while the Americans often dismissed issues of the broader significance of protest as speculative philosophy. What might have been fruitful dialogue between the two approaches soon entered the theoretical *cul-de-sac* of trying to decide what was "new" about post-industrial movements.

In another case of overextension, the European theorists were writing about post-industrial movements as well as about the cultural dynamics of movements in general, so they were read as saying that "old" citizenship movements had lacked the rich cultural dynamics of the recent ones. It is tempting to argue that the labor and civil rights movements were based on self-interest in ways that many recent movements are not, but this is a misleading image of those earlier movements. I find it most useful to think of the post-industrial theorists as describing dimensions of all social movements—culture and a little biography—that other schools of thought had overlooked. If these seem more prominent in some recent movements, this is partly a methodological bias. When the labor movement was young, and not dominated by bureaucratic unions, it had much of the rich culture found in recent movements, including efforts to work out a new identity as workers. But our means for studying movements from the nineteenth century may be less effective at uncovering this cultural activity than the participant observation and depth interviews we can use on contemporary movements.

The concept of new social movements gets at several recent developments. One is the increasing presence of television in the last several decades, forcing political efforts to include symbolic statements directed at the viewing public.[8] In addition, the new participants may differ from the older ones: they are more privileged groups with sufficient economic security and citizenship rights for them to care about and pursue "post-materialist" demands such as clean air, democratic workplaces, or multicultural education. The high levels of education of many participants in recent post-industrial movements are likely to encourage attention to ideologies and ideas as well as a high degree of self-awareness on the part of participants.[9] In this, post-industrial movements differ not only from most citizenship movements but also most prior post-citizenship movements.

The impasse between European and American traditions, I believe, arose from the psychological assumptions they had (implicitly) adopted. The crowd schools had admitted only the wilder and more irrational emotions into their schemes: protestors were subject to collective fantasies, or were acting out generational rebelliousness. Rational-choice theorists—by their very name claiming rationality for their own ideal type—had an unrecognizably narrow portrait of human desires, motivations, even rationality. Mobilization adherents did not stray far from rationalist models, despite expanding rationality to include the costs of learning new tactics, calculations concerning group costs and benefits, and the effects of organizational and political contexts. Most mobilization and process theorists, however, simply denied the importance of psychology altogether. Process theorists added some sense of strategy, but had less to say about the construction of the goals the protestors were maneuvering to attain. European theorists, often clinging to marxist images, seemed to describe the psychology and motivation of collective historical actors, not individuals.[10] All these traditions perceived protestors' "real" identity or interests in advance, or saw this identity as momentary; they felt no need to study protestors in the act of constructing their identities and interests for themselves. Culture and biography—complementary dynamics—can usefully supplement each of these other traditions and help them work together.

The work of the post-industrial theorists has encouraged American researchers to take culture seriously. Identities are a product, not a genetic inheritance. Much of the work of a social movement takes place outside formal organizations, and much of it consists of biographical adjustments and creativity. One of the first places these ideas were put to use was in explaining recruitment.

FRAME ALIGNMENT

Of the American efforts to examine culture and social movements, the "frame-alignment" approach deriving from symbolic interactionism has most clearly gelled into a distinct research program. In one interactionist tradition, we saw that Turner and Killian focused so closely on the symbolic creativity of interactions between individuals as to exaggerate the conscious creativity of participants at a micro-level, distorting the balance between acceptance of existing cultural meanings and efforts to change them. In another, quantitative techniques have allowed sociologists to map and group interactions into regular networks. One limit of this latter work is its focus on mechanical interactions—like those of billiard balls—and inattention to symbolic or emotional connections. Although the flow of innovations or information through the networks can be traced, quantitative techniques are less graceful at capturing the actual meanings. People can be thrown together, but what lasts are the ideas, visions, or emotions they give each other or create together. The physical networks are often important, but so are the mental constructs that energize them. Indeed, many of the scholars who pioneered the study of cognitive aspects of social movements had previously done research on interpersonal networks.[11]

Combining mobilization and interactionist approaches, David Snow, Robert Benford, and their collaborators have promoted the recent cultural turn through their work on "frame alignment."[12] In a series of articles, Snow and Benford showed that the cognitive "frames" of social movement organizers and potential participants must be brought into "alignment" regarding a diagnosis of the situation, a prognosis of what should be done, and motivation to do it. They define a collective action frame as an "interpretive schemata that simplifies and condenses the 'world out there' by selectively punctuating and encoding objects, situations, events, experiences, and sequences of actions within one's present or past environment." Frames must link movement perspectives to the broader culture through processes of bridging, amplification, extension, and, ultimately, transformation. Potential participants are more likely to accept frames that fit with their existing beliefs, their sense of empirical credibility, their own life experiences, and the narratives they use to describe their lives. Further, there are underlying "master frames" that can be used by more than one protest movement: they "are to movement-specific collective action frames as paradigms are to finely tuned theories. Master frames are generic; specific collective action frames are derivative."[13]

Frame-alignment theories have remained rather abstract, describing the need for resonance without always exploring its substantive sources. In one article Snow and Benford claim that resonance is enhanced by presenting a range of beliefs in movement rhetoric, but their main example is a movement which extended its references too far: the effort to stop the deployment of cruise and Pershing I missiles in Europe in 1983 began to refer to feminism, Palestinian rights, and other causes, attracting some new recruits but losing other members. It is hard, without looking at pre-existing cultural meanings, to distinguish "not far enough" from "too far." Credibility, or resonance, comes from the compatibility of new arguments with existing expectations. Snow and Benford also argue that the falsifiability of a claim increases its credibility, yet they give an example of a falsifiable claim—nuclear winter as a consequence of nuclear war—which had great cultural resonance but was not well supported when examined closely.[14] At times Snow and Benford seem to desire an "objective" way to judge the power of frames that is not circular or *post hoc*, but this power depends as much on the pre-existing worldviews of potential recruits as on formal aspects of the frames.

Associating frames with their use in recruitment highlights the dynamic way that movements actively formulate cultural meanings, but it sometimes reduces those meanings to recruitment strategies. Movement organizers and participants may forge new meanings, but by appealing to and building on existing ones. Even master frames seem tied to particular strategies in these models. Snow and Benford present the nuclear freeze proposal as an example of a master frame, apparently because it spurred considerable mobilization.[15] Finding evidence of frames that is independent of their use in mobilization would avoid this circularity. Frames resonate with potential recruits precisely because these recruits already have certain visions of the world. Cultural meanings can certainly be shaped and transformed by groups and individuals, but they also already exist "out there," just as language is a pre-existing set of rules that we must, to some extent, adapt to.

Pre-existing beliefs may be more important in some kinds of movements than others. Studying religious movements seems to encourage recognition of cultural dynamics, as with Snow and John Lofland, but when differences between religious and political movements are downplayed (as in a focus on organizational dynamics at the expense of ideas and moral values), religious movements as exemplars may actually hide parts of culture again.[16] Snow's work on religious recruitment may have initially predisposed him to overstate the importance of networks as opposed to the cultural messages transmitted across them, for analyzing religious and political movements in the same way necessarily deemphasizes the cognitive content of movements in favor of organizational and network dynamics. The main article to establish the importance of social networks in recruitment, by Snow, Louis Zurcher, and Sheldon Ekland-Olson, found ten empirical efforts to measure how many participants were recruited through people they knew in the movement.[17] Eight were religious movements, one the March of Dimes (a huge voluntary organization whose relevance to protest movements is not clear), one a study of only thirty-one anti-abortion activists. In addition, the authors added their own evidence from another religious movement and from University of Texas students (apparently undergraduates).

We might expect religious and political movements to differ in their recruitment. Most who join a political movement already have opinions and feelings of their own: they detest abortion or care deeply about animals. They are recruited to a group or movement, not converted wholesale to a new belief system. Frames resonate with potential recruits precisely because they already have certain visions of the world, moral values, political ideologies, and affective attachments. In contrast, it is not clear exactly what pre-existing beliefs might lead one to self-recruit into a religious movement. It seems unlikely that one would have Nichiren Shoshu beliefs without being a member. Here, recruitment does entail conversion. For religious movements, being a member comes close to being an end in itself; for political movements it is also a means—possibly to ends the recruit already values. We need a similar caveat for students. Younger and less experienced, students may be less likely to have explicit beliefs, which they are in the process of forming. For them, recruitment to a movement may entail a conversion in beliefs. If true, this means that we should also be cautious about generalizing from student-based movements. In some cases, framing and recruitment have a lot to do with tapping into pre-existing culture, in other cases less.

The frame-alignment school has done a lot to revive interest in cognitive dynamics as well as to relate them to mobilization. The ideas and ideologies of protest movements have become valid research topics once again. As one of the only ways for students of protest to talk about culture, however, frame alignment has been asked to do too much work, getting overextended so that it could cover almost any form of culture. In the interactionist tradition, beliefs tend to be reduced to their role in local processes of recruitment, and culture is not seen as having much autonomy from strategic action. If we are willing to use some additional concepts to get at culture, then we can restrict framing to the *conscious efforts by groups or recruiters to craft their rhetoric and issues in such a way that they appeal to potential recruits*.[18] Frame alignment highlights the creative potential of culture, but the pre-existing side must also be given its due. Focusing on the interaction between organizers and potential recruits (an important audience for movement rhetoric but not the only one), frame-alignment theories do not adequately address the broader culture outside the social movement or the ongoing culture inside it.

THE BROADER CULTURE

William Gamson has explored the cultural meanings "out there" in American society for building political consciousness, especially in his book *Talking Politics*. In addition to looking at the meanings associated with particular issues (such as nuclear power and affirmative action), he found four widespread pairs of "themes" and "counterthemes" in American culture: regarding technology, the dominant theme was "progress through technology" and the countertheme "harmony with nature"; regarding power, interest-group liberalism versus popular democracy; regarding interpersonal dependence, self-reliance versus mutuality; and regarding nationalism, global responsibility versus America first.[19] Such tropes are part of the repertory of American politics, a kind of language out of which arguments are made. As familiar references—about which people have both positive and negative feelings—*they help explain why certain protest ideologies or frames resonate with their audiences and others do not.* These pairs are rather broad, but they are an example of the cultural interpretation needed in order to establish the pre-existing meanings organizers can appeal to. In discussing media framing of stories on nuclear energy, for example, Gamson traces a struggle between nuclear technology as a part of progress and the technology as runaway, out of human control (the critique that accompanies the countertheme of harmony with nature).

Gamson and others have tried, often building on frame alignment, to take cultural meanings seriously without abandoning the insights of the mobilization and process paradigms. As part of this project, Gamson, Bruce Fireman, and Steven Rytina elaborated the important idea of an "injustice frame," defined as "an interpretation of what is happening that supports the conclusion that an authority system is violating the shared moral principles of the participants. An alternative to a 'legitimating frame,' it provides a reason for noncompliance."[20] An injustice frame can be held with varying degrees of conviction: it can be entertained, considered, or adopted. The authors are explicit about the emotional basis of the frame, the suspicion and hostility that foster it, and the outrage and indignation that define it. In some ways, though, by focusing on interactions with authority, Gamson and his coauthors overlook other aspects of the process of creating an injustice frame: defining the source of the threat, who gets blamed, what the appropriate emotions are, what role authorities should play in rectifying the problem. Citizenship movements typically make their demands directly of state authorities, but not all movements do.

Our broader culture shapes us in many ways. Gamson's research with focus groups reminds us that media discourse is only one source of cognitive understandings, along with personal experience and popular wisdom (including maxims, bible stories, analogies with personal life). Because people already have opinions about many subjects, they can interpret or even reject media framings of events, even though, according to Gamson, the strongest frames are those in which different kinds of knowledge reinforce each other. Gamson and Andre Modigliani see an interaction between individual views and media framing: "[M]edia discourse is part of the process by which individuals construct meaning, and public opinion is part of the process by which journalists and other cultural entrepreneurs develop and crystallize meaning in public discourse."[21]

Yet, over time, media presentations surely mold popular common sense. Through a series of experiments, Shanto Iyengar has contrasted the effects of "episodic" framing (in which the media tell stories as singular cases or events) versus "thematic" framing (when the stories place issues in a broader social context). Episodic framing usually discourages social explanations of and solutions to public problems. In the case of terrorism, for instance, episodic framing "made viewers more likely to consider punitive measures rather than social or political reform as the appropriate treatment."[22] (Unemployment, though, was consistently seen as a social problem, not attributed to individual actions.) Political mobilization is difficult in the face of individual attributions. The media affect our views implicitly through this kind of framing, as well as more explicitly through overt content—and it is not clear which path is more powerful.

If the news media are influential, so are those people who have access to them, who are themselves "newsworthy" either because of institutional position or personal celebrity. Politicians, of course, have this kind of power. In studying the nuclear freeze movement, for instance, David Meyer found that the members of Congress who jumped on the bandwagon around 1982 twisted the freeze idea in many different directions. Compared to highly visible politicians like Senator Edward Kennedy, movement organizers were almost impotent to define the issue.[23] In my own work on civilian nuclear energy, I found that American politicians reframed the debate over safe and cheap energy as one of markets versus government intervention: these ongoing ideological cleavages—the language politicians use for debating and labeling each other—shape our understanding of the world because politicians are newsmakers.[24] David Meyer and Joshua Gamson have examined the utility of celebrities, especially rock and movie stars, for bringing attention to protest demands, although, as with politicians, the risk exists that the celebrities will redefine the issue.[25] Celebrities are a useful window onto a society's cultural understandings, especially its patterns of attention and trust. Newsmakers are those we pay attention to. Innumerable studies of culture, politics, and the media are available for students of protest who wish to understand the pre-existing cultural meanings out there for organizers to work with in their framing efforts.

MOVEMENT CULTURE

Because social-movement scholars usually favor methods like partici-pant observation and case studies, not opinion polls, Iyengar's experi-ments, or Gamson's focus groups, they have studied internal move-ment dynamics more easily than the cultural meanings of the broader society. Some have examined the skills and roles that activists use in political activity. Doug McAdam's work on Freedom Summer in 1964 showed that volunteers developed life routines and skills through their activism that were as important as their beliefs and ideologies in shap-ing their later lives.[26] They adopted what John Lofland calls an "activ-ist" role.[27] In Tilly's concept of "repertoires of collective action," pro-testors know how to do certain things better than others, due to their prior experiences, their daily routines and internal movement organi-zation, selective repression by the authorities, and prevailing standards of rights and justice.[28] Choices of tactics are driven by what works, by what protestors know how to do, and by their moral visions. The cul-tural meanings of the protestors influence all three: even "what works" depends on the protestors' (socially defined) sense of what they're try-ing to do.

Several scholars have looked at the internal processes by which orga-nizers create affective bonds and thus a sense of solidarity among pro-testors. This kind of cultural work is sometimes explicit on the part of group leaders but implicit on the part of rank-and-file. Eric Hirsch described consciousness-raising, feelings of empowerment, and rhe-torical escalation and polarization, all of which increased commitment and levels of participation in Columbia's student movement against apartheid. Barbara Epstein adds feminist spirituality, magical politics, and processes of internal democracy as contributors to the enthusiasm and joy in the post-industrial antinuclear and peace movements of the 1980s. Mary Douglas and Aaron Wildavsky theorized a cognitive po-larization that reinforces group membership by building a strong sense of inside versus outside, of saints within the group versus sinners out-side it, of purity within versus danger and pollution outside. Although these works concentrate on cognitive processes, they inadvertently highlight processes that are also strongly emotional.[29]

John Lofland has also described the internal cultures of protest movements and the contexts from which they grow, beginning with the "youth ghetto" he described in 1968. He has also depicted the joys and other emotions of crowds. In a theoretical essay, he lays out several aspects of movement culture: the elaboration and dramatization of distinctive goals, behavior, and roles; the development of symbolism and emotional expression; and the level of one specific emotion, compassion. Movements and their component groups can differ on all these dimensions. Lofland claims that protest movements, by focusing on what they dislike in society, sometimes fail to develop a positive, joyful culture. This seems an odd idea, in light of the rich antinuclear culture we'll examine in chapter 8, but makes sense in view of the implicit comparison between political and religious movements that runs through much of Lofland's considerable oeuvre. The internal culture of religious movements, he argues, is usually denser and more emotionally satisfying. Throughout his work, Lofland has been concerned to show that culture varies across protest groups in both content and degree.[30]

Culture is not only embodied in action but also operates as a form of motivation and goal. Once we look inside movements, we see that individual protestors have numerous motives for participation, mostly lying between the irrational ones of crowd theories and the calculating ones of mobilization and rational-choice models. They have visions and projects emerging from their cultural contexts that are rational, but not always in a materialist or calculating way. They may express anger and frustration, but in the context of their broader projects, not in momentary fits. They may promote their material interests, but rarely as their only goal. Their purposes in protesting are bound up with many other motives: sexual desire, a sense of fellowship, a response to technocrats' decisions, a working out of personal identity, a need for security, the dynamics of job or family, to name several. To understand what people are doing when they protest, we need to know a lot about their lives outside of protest, and what meanings they carry with them.

At a different level we can view motives, not as pre-existing preferences, but as the rationales that people give when asked to justify their past and future activities—as C. Wright Mills pointed out. Motives are partly normative vocabularies by which people define their situations.[31] They learn to act in certain ways and to talk in corresponding ways, without having to stop and refer to their motivations. They know "how to" act and talk. Their tacit, implicit knowledge, which makes them artful protestors, cannot be neatly broken down into means and ends, motives and payoffs. Metaphors of flows, webs, and networks—linking different kinds of knowledge and of action—may be more appropriate. Once in a movement, participants often "rewrite" their own biographies and reasons for joining, in order to heighten the rhetorical message of the movement. The "narratives of conversion" that members tell frequently sound similar: they report that they joined because of the horrors of nuclear war, not because their friends were joining. Such stories are not simply accounts of the past; they are affirmations of allegiance and identity in the present, a kind of ritual by which people align their own lives with important basic values.[32] Robert Benford points to four common rhetorics that protestors use to justify their action: the severity of the problem, the urgency of a solution, the efficacy of their own efforts, and the propriety of taking action.[33]

Motives also correspond to diverse pleasures in protest. One satisfaction comes from a sense of collective empowerment, and the expression of group solidarity. Another is the thrill and energy derived from rituals and symbols: the myths and folktales participants tell each other, the heroes and villains who emerge, the sacred places and moments in the subculture's history. In addition to developing simple group loyalty, the latter often deploy rhetorical devices linking present conflicts to grand moral themes of good and evil.[34] As Derrick Bell described in the case of Mrs. MacDonald (chapter 2), bearing witness against evil and "doing what's right" are satisfying in and of themselves, lending dignity to one's life even when stated goals are elusive. Participating in important historical events, the kind that are reported on the evening news, is another profound satisfaction. Individual participants may also have erotic motives, pursuing their love lives at the same time as their political goals. Note that every one of these motives is emotional as much as it is cognitive or moral.

Once they are in a movement, political activity often becomes a central component of many people's identity and way of life, so that they barely need to be "mobilized," at least in any active, meaningful sense of the word. Protest activity is a pleasure, not merely a cost, for them. This seems especially true of post-industrial movements, whose members regularly move from one cause to the next. Wini Breines, for example, describes the way in which the New Left tried, in its own organizations, to "create and sustain within the live practice of the movement, relationships and political forms that 'prefigured' and embodied the desired society." The bonds of community were essential: "For new leftists the assertion and discovery of self were linked to meaningful political action. Personal liberation, the escape from loneliness, meaninglessness and manipulation were attained through collective political action. Community was created in the midst of fragmentation and inhumanity, and the self liberated."[35] Created precisely as a moral rejection of instrumental, means-ends calculation, protest movements are often seen by their participants as seamlessly interwoven with their lives. All movements can become communities, ends in themselves, for many participants, although this may be especially true for post-industrial or religious movements.

In rationalist terminology, movement culture helps explain why groups value the costs of participation and the potential rewards the way they do. We can understand why certain groups become what Tilly calls zealots, who highly value the collective gains they pursue compared to their valuation of the costs of that pursuit.[36] Cultural and biographical processes—for example rituals, symbols, and mutual affection that motivate and shape perceptions—help explain this valuation, whereas rationalist and other approaches rarely try to account for these different utilities. In the case of zealots, the material interests of a group do not guide its collective actions in any straightforward way. We cannot assume, with the rationalists, that rationality yields the same (calculable) implications for all individuals, since biography and culture thoroughly shape our evaluations of both costs and benefits, means as well as ends. Spending time in jail as the result of an illegal protest may be a stiff cost for one person, but a moving, even addictive, "peak experience" for another. Among fellow protestors (who may also be family, friends, and lovers), it may be a badge of honor.[37] Costs and benefits issue from the stories protestors tell themselves, the heroes they praise, the moral visions they espouse, and the way they feel about each other and the external world.[38]

Culture even provides our criteria for rational action. Mary Douglas has argued that culture does some of our thinking for us, providing answers to questions that we lack the time to examine ourselves.[39] *Culture not only bounds rationality but defines it. It provides the context and criteria for recognizing and judging rationality, which cannot exist in a pure form outside of social contexts.* Different institutional settings develop their own cultures, with contrasting assumptions about the world and skills for acting in it. Action that is rational in one context may be irrational in another. Martyrdom makes more sense in a setting of ultimate ends than in one of profit maximization. In the rationalist tradition, this ultimate form of altruism is incomprehensible, since it altogether removes the individual from the game. What tactics and goals are rational for a group is clear only when we understand their explicit beliefs and implicit definitions—upon which individual members may not even entirely agree. Cultural traditions provide the raw materials for creating and revising the means and ends of protest—but also for determining the boundary between means and ends.

Once we recognize the multiple satisfactions of protest, "rationality" may be a misleading criterion to apply, for the term is clearest when it means finding efficient means to attain a given end. When the means partly become ends in themselves, it is harder to make judgments of rationality. Some goals may be morally objectionable, even sometimes self-defeating or self-destructive, but it is more difficult to show that they are irrational. Actions too may be mistaken or ineffective for a given end, but that does not necessarily make them irrational. Scholars do not ask if the modern nuclear family is "rational" or not; we also need to ask other questions of protest movements. Put another way, any choice or action has several simultaneous levels on which it can be judged as rational or not, corresponding to the various motives and overlapping institutional settings of the actors. No single judgment of rationality is possible.

Movement culture also includes the skills we have for trying to re-make ourselves and our worlds. For most students of protest, the pref-erences and choices of individuals and organizations—whether based on irrational emotions or rational calculation—lead to collective ac-tion, but they forget that this activity also feeds back to influence those preferences. Some theorists have suggested that collective action changes participants and their tastes. Samuel Bowles and Herbert Gintis discuss a *constitutive* aspect of collective action linked to forms of identity: "[I]ndividuals and groups in general participate not merely to meet preexisting ends, but also to constitute themselves, or to reaf-firm themselves, as persons and groups with particular and desired attributes."[40] Movements help participants craft identities, as we shall see momentarily. In criticizing Charles Tilly, James Rule argues that group interests

> cannot be automatically predicted from the structural positions of various groups, but are defined by the groups experiencing them. When such 'vital interests' emerge, however, the groups concerned are apt to perceive them as matters essential to their own symbolic or literal self-perpetuation. . . . Collective action in support of such interests may be either expressive or instrumental—an end in itself, or a means to some longer-term end. In any particular collective ac-tion, the two are apt to be mixed. . . . Collective actors do calculate costs and benefits of their actions at least enough to avoid over-whelming repression and to seize evident political opportunities. But where collective actions represent ends themselves rather than means to other ends, the sheer fact that an action takes place may make it 'profitable' to the participants.[41]

Claus Offe has similarly distinguished two forms of collective action: straightforward, calculated pursuit of interests, and the internal, interactive work "concerned with a redefinition of what we mean by 'costs' and 'benefits.'"[42] Social movements create goals as well as pursuing them; sometimes they even become goals in themselves. The task, at this point, is to specify how such construction occurs, not simply to assert that it does.

Naming is an important component in the construction of political realities. This involves not only the clever coining of a term—*sexism, black power, speciesism*—but the elaboration of problems, causes, blame, and solutions. The labels we apply constitute our understanding of the world: they direct concern, outrage, and sympathy; they allocate blame, praise, and trust. The naming of one's own group or movement is an important part of creating an identity in whose name the movement justifies its own action. As Jane Jenson argues, "[M]ovements struggle over names and seek recognition of the one they prefer, both within and outside the community. In competing for discursive space, communities are imagining more than their present and future; they also imagine their pasts."[43] Groups and individuals must decide who they are as part of deciding how they should act.

Both explicitly and implicitly, in both ideas and actions, culture helps us define or construct the world around us, or at least that part of the world we can experience in a meaningful way. We interpret our own actions, we have ideas about what we're doing, especially for complex activities such as protest. Culture involves meaning and interpretation. We can't ignore these mental constructions, even when we deal with apparently "objective" phenomena like interests, resources, and rational strategies, all of which are constructed via cultural understandings. We've seen that cultural processes and constructs have been discovered in several places: in recruitment's framing processes, in the broader languages available to protestors, and in the internal processes by which protest groups maintain morale and solidarity. Each case involves different mixes of audiences for cultural meanings: potential recruits, the broader public, and members themselves. Internal versus external culture is an inadequate distinction, however, when we turn to the issue of identity, for there is considerable interaction between them.

THREE KINDS OF IDENTITY

Identity is one of the most trendy yet confusing terms in the current rediscovery of culture, in part because it has been overextended as badly as framing, resources, and political opportunity structures. Sometimes theorized as internal to a movement, sometimes as external, I believe it is both. I see three main categories of identity. *Personal identity,* a sense of who one is, a sense of self, combines attributes (I'm a good person, or tough, or smart), activities and interests (I'm a welder, jogger, or Grateful Dead fan), and identification with collectivities (I'm American, Italian-American, a Southerner, or a member of the V.F.W.). Such identities emerge from the idiosyncratic biographies of individuals, forming part of the biographical dimension of protest, although they borrow broader cultural meanings. Such selves, we saw, are not unitary and fixed, but neither do they change rapidly or unpredictably.

Collective identity consists of perceptions of group distinctiveness, boundaries, and interests, for something closer to a community than a category. The most familiar are caste, class, religion, race or ethnicity, sexual preference, and gender. There are also collective identities based on geography, notably nation, region, and neighborhood. All these collectivities are independent of both individuals and movements. The interaction with personal identity is strong: the sharper a collective identity, the more likely I am to identify with that group as part of my individual identity; and the more individuals who identify with a group, the stronger the group's collective identity. Whereas a personal identity is defined by the perceptions of that individual (albeit influenced by others), collective identities depend on perceptions of both members and nonmembers, often filtered through the mass media. In describing a nation as an imagined political community, Benedict Anderson says, "It is *imagined* because the members of even the smallest nation will never know most of their fellow-members, meet them, of even hear of them, yet in the minds of each lives the image of their communion."[44] Nancy Whittier insists that collective identities "exist only as far as real people agree upon, enact, argue over, and internalize them; group definitions have no life of their own, and they are constantly changing rather than static."[45] But I would add that some identities are more mutable than others. As Frances Svensson describes the impact of such identities, "[T]he group functions as a mechanism for mobilizing the individual to act in general social situations, helps to define needs and desires and the ways to achieve them, and forms the locus of strong affective attachments which figure prominently in self-identity."[46] In other words, groups offer culture. Although political mobilization of a collectivity certainly increases its collective identity, collective identity is possible without that mobilization.

Thus collective identity differs from *movement identity,* which arises when a collection of groups and individuals perceive themselves (and are perceived by others) as a force in explicit pursuit of social change. Although often conflated, collective and movement identities are not the same thing. While a movement may act in the name of a collective identity, such as women or African-Americans, it need not, as in the animal rights or nuclear freeze movements. Citizenship movements are linked to a collectivity defined independently of the movement and typically pursue equity, inclusion, or some benefits for that group. Post-citizenship movements are not linked to a collective identity and tend to speak in the name of all humanity, future generations, or natural laws, usually pursuing noneconomic goals.[47] Some scholars have tried to get at movement identity with the concept of a social movement *community*—a term that I believe conflates social networks and cultural images.[48] Both collective and movement identities can contribute to a personal identity, which normally consists of a complex blend of identifications. *Personal identities exist on the biographical level; collective identities are part of the broader culture; and movement identities arise from the interaction between internal movement culture and the broader culture.*

Movement identities can themselves be broken down into several levels. In addition to identifying with a protest movement as a whole, people can identify with a particular group, perhaps because they founded it (I'll call this *organizational identity*); with using a particular tactic like direct action or being in some wing of a movement, like the radical vanguard (*tactical identity*); or with a broader activist subculture that might nourish several distinct movements (*activist identity*). My hunch is that in post-citizenship movements activist and tactical identities will usually be stronger than organizational ones, and that in citizenship movements the underlying collective identities usually remain stronger than movement identities.

As these various kinds of movement identity show, identities are rarely a primordial ascribed trait, but rather something that individuals and groups must work out. Collective and movement identities are subject to considerable conflict, claims-making, and negotiation.[49] To complicate matters further, part of an individual's identity can come from allegiance to universal moral principles or commitments, such as being a democrat or a Quaker, as well as from more particular, ascribed ones such as being Native American. Citizenship exemplars sometimes hide these complexities of choice. Being black in the United States carries with it a more forceful and constraining collective identity (although even this is not fixed) than being Quaker.

Another complexity is that protestors (and others, for that matter) can hold different attitudes toward their own identities. For some, identity is a deep trait that helps define who they are, an essential part of the self. At the other end of the spectrum there can be considerable distance from an identity, which can be adopted for strategic reasons or as a tentative experiment to see if it "fits." Movement identities, especially, can be tried on and discarded with relative ease.

All three basic forms of identity depend on interactions with others.

Even personal identities must usually be supported by those around one. Collective and movement identities also depend on the recognition of bystanders, opponents, and other actors, especially the mass media.[50] As Todd Gitlin said in the title of his book about how news media shape movement identities in the world of television, "The Whole World Is Watching."[51] Movement identities, we shall see, invigorate members, yet they also frequently scare the movement's opponents into their own countermobilization.

All forms of identity affect movement participation. Individuals must be comfortable that protest activity fits with their conceptions of themselves. If the protest role becomes part of their personal identity, this is a strong incentive for continued participation. Collective identities strongly encourage protest that is in the group's interests. Movement identities too can provide a reassuring sense of efficacy and solidarity. In chapter 8 we shall see that a strong activist identity drew people into protests against nuclear energy. As with all explanatory factors, though, identities should ideally be identified independently rather than inferred from actions. Explanations that identify protestors' personal identities as part of a movement, for example, often employ a circular logic that uses protest to demonstrate identity. With the current dearth of concepts for discussing culture, identity—like framing—is often called on to cover too much.

Frequent tensions between personal, collective, and movement identities emerge due to the constructed character of each, what Joshua Gamson refers to as "their made-up yet necessary character."[52] Many individuals are not comfortable with the collective identities to which movements refer: many African-American women felt ignored by the rest of the early women's movement; bisexuals and cross-dressers by many gay rights groups. Fighting against the very images and stereotypes that strengthen the collective identity on which a movement's own identity is based, many movements are caught in what Martha Minow calls the "dilemma of difference."[53] You both contest and, in mobilizing members, rely upon the same collective identity. This is most obvious for movements protesting against stigmatized collective identities, but if a collective identity had no negative effects, a protest movement would probably not appear in the first place. Citizenship movements may be the best poised for mobilization, for their potential members already have identities imposed on them legally and politically. They can worry less about their reputations, since these reputations are strongly being used against them.

Of the many categories on which collective identities can be based, social scientists generally focus on the more ascribed categories, notably race, class, gender, and—increasingly—sexual orientation, rather than on chosen ones, for it is the ascribed identities which, through stereotyped expectations, the rest of society tends to impose on the groups. As a result, though, one bias of social-movement research has been the assumption that protestors arise out of some already-defined category and collective identity, such as labor or African-Americans, rather than coming together out of shared goals or ideas. The citizenship-movement paradigm reinforces this tendency. Verta Taylor and Nancy Whittier point out that structural positions do not automatically lead to shared consciousness, identity, or action (although in their model structural position may still be a *necessary* condition, and the lesbians whose movement they analyze are definable independently of their activism). Group boundaries must be highlighted, consciousness raised, and internal and external negotiations conducted before political action results.[54]

Despite recent attention to the culture of protest, then, there is a lingering reluctance to abandon the idea that protestors build their consciousness on the basis of solid material and political interests, structurally defined. But this must be an open, empirical question, not an assumption. Not all protest emerges out of clear structural positions, but often simply out of a shared vision. Participants can still craft part of their identity on the basis of their principles or activism, forming a movement identity without demographic or economic undergirding. Being someone who fights for animals, who opposes technocracy, or who believes in god can be a part of one's identity, especially for those whose lives are devoted to their political activities. As we shall see later, identification with a movement (personal identities based on movement identities) is one of the most important cultural creations for successful organizers. Scott Hunt and Robert Benford distinguish several types of "identity talk" that contribute to identification with the movement: associational declarations, stories of disillusionment, tales of atrocities, "personal is political" reports, stories of inspiring individuals, and war stories about one's commitment.[55]

Movement identity is not simply the sum of many individuals' identification with groups or goals, but a sense of that movement as a coherent actor with shared goals and strategies. In this way, identities are closely tied to social networks, which are assumed to support the identities. A feeling that they are part of a big, national movement is often important to participants, and especially to their (fragile) optimism about their eventual success. But this identity is a cultural achievement that does not always depend on personal networks. Abalone Alliance staffers, fighting nuclear energy in California in the

1980s, often referred to the national antinuclear movement, even though they had as few concrete contacts with other groups as Diani's Milan environmentalists did. This sense of identification with a national or international movement, rather than being built on face-to-face experience, is heavily affected by media labels and portrayals. This movement coherence is largely a fiction, as critics of crowd theories have suggested, for movements are composed of diverse groups and individuals with particular goals and interests beyond the shared ones. And yet the feeling of a shared identity is a powerful emotional motivation, a necessary fiction. This is one reason that a collective identity, based on shared structural positions and ascriptive traits, aids mobilization.

Identity is a tricky concept, often a crude label for a collection of other things. When possible, we must try to specify its content. It may include cognitive images of a collective actor, boundaries perceived or drawn among social groups, affective solidarities to certain abstract or concrete groups and individuals, moral intuitions and principles, even tastes or styles of action. At their most powerful, identities fuse these aspects of culture, but then they aren't always at their most powerful. The term *identity* is a recognition that actions are filtered through some sense of self, a kind of residue from past experiences.

Because only individuals feel emotions, hold beliefs, and identify with collectivities, the distinction between movement culture and the broader culture has more to do with the origins of language, identity, emotions, and so on, than with their ongoing location. The processes that generate or sustain meanings inside protest groups differ from those of the national news media and other institutions in the broader society. Yet once created, as the case of identity shows, cultural meanings easily cross institutional boundaries. Both insiders and outsiders contribute to the construction of identities, and of other cultural meanings.

EVENTS AND INDIVIDUALS

Culture brings into focus several aspects of political action not well handled by the major traditions. These include singular events and individuals, the influence of time and place, and even existential moments that help determine the meaning of life. Although most sociologists prefer to analyze statistical aggregates, not singular events, some scholars have turned to protest events as their dependent variable: Why do people come to this particular protest? Process theorists use events as independent factors to explain other phenomena, claiming that protestors take events as an indication of what is likely to befall them should they decide to protest. For some theorists, such an event is a straightforward piece of information, although for others it requires cognitive processing. We have seen this in the work of Tilly, Tarrow, and McAdam. From a cultural vantage point, this is hardly satisfactory.

Culture and biography help us understand why single events can have a big effect on protest by arousing strong emotions, encapsulating hopes and desires, constructing interests, even defining new collective actors on the political stage. Founding events are particularly important because they forever symbolize the regime, form of action, group, movement, or rhetoric that they helped establish. Events can also be moral models that shame others into acting.

According to culturalist William Sewell, Tilly is unable to see the importance of the French Revolution because Tilly believes that only structural changes—urbanization, the growth of the nation-state, the extension of markets—really matter. Particular bread riots, rallies, even big events like revolutions are the result of these deeper forces; they are not themselves a cause of anything. Instead, Sewell and others have shown that the French Revolution extensively transformed the way that the French (and many others) thought about political action (giving us Left versus Right, for example), legal rights (adhering now in individuals rather than corporate bodies), and the state. Sewell argues, "Such regime changes initiate redefinitions of sovereignty, of legitimate forms of political action, and of the nature and identities of legal and social categories in civil society. Regime changes are crucial in the history of collective violence because they significantly reconstitute the bases of collective loyalties and action."[56] This shift away from corporate bodies as the rightful political actors made citizenship movements, based on individual rights, possible.

Events do not have to be as dramatic or long lasting as the French Revolution to change the way we think. Nuclear accidents, court decisions, a successful demonstration or bus boycott, can trigger action in others.[57] These events can positively inspire imitation, or they can negatively create shocks, fears, a sense of threat (chapter 5 examines these negative effects). Events shock us when they sum up our anxieties, allowing us to name what we feel threatened by. The Three Mile Island nuclear accident, dramatically broadcast by the media, crystallized the dread felt by many neighbors of proposed nuclear plants, helping them to focus their indignation. The accident not only changed their cognitive assessment of the chances of accidents, but also helped articulate their emotions and moral objections. Our symbolic universes can change quite suddenly.

In mobilization and process traditions, an event is viewed simply as an additional piece of information, changing rational assessments of chances for success or the costs of repression. It is simply added to all the other bits of information a potential protestor has at her disposal. But this misses the special heuristic function of a prominent event. As cognitive psychologists have shown, certain pieces of information affect us more than others, even when, from a perfectly rational standpoint, they should not. We give extra weight to highly publicized or memorable events, for example. Some events simply encapsulate for us what we feel about an issue, just as a maxim or parable might be an efficient vehicle for a complex moral message. They must be interpreted before they affect either thought or action, but individuals as well as movement organizers are often capable of this interpretation. The special salience of certain events is based partly on how cultural meanings are transmitted and partly on the psychology of information processing, these being sides of the same coin. It was the extreme cognitive orientation of process models, in which events are preeminently indicators of repression, that led Tarrow to misread the impact of the Russian Revolution.

Individuals can take on a symbolic power similar to that of events, leading lives that inspire others, embodying particular ideologies, showing courage or passion or love, surviving (or not surviving) extreme hardships. Martyrs are an obvious example; founders of organizations may also have a kind of aura. Succession can trigger a crisis in an organization when its founder finally gives up power. In strategic interactions, too, an individual leader can accumulate so much symbolic baggage that negotiation can be deadlocked, with the leader's resignation the only way out. For example she might be so associated with a certain position that she cannot abandon it without losing part of her credibility or identity, or associated with a tactic, such as violence, that permanently stigmatizes her. Both biographies and the cultural meanings they respond to come into play in these cases, creating resilient symbols out of individuals.

Not all events or individuals are equally salient, and the symbolic resonance of each can be contested and reshaped. But they are one example of how cultural meanings shape action in ways missed by mainstream traditions.

TIME, PLACE, AND LIFE PASSAGES

Cultures exist in specific times and places, and are partly defined along these dimensions. Just as we are always embedded in culture, we are inevitably situated in places. And our culture gives us a sense of where we are in both time and space. If space is endless and abstract, a place is what we carve out of it, a "conceptual fusion of space and experience" that is crucial to both our identity and our sense of agency.[58] Cultural sociologists use the term *map* loosely in the sense of worldview, but we also apply cultural algorithms to the physical space that we inhabit.

Certain settings and certain situations, not to mention certain musical works, automatically elicit appropriate emotions from those familiar with the culture; emotions are rarely idiosyncratic creations of individuals. The power of symbols arises in part from the times and places—often formalized in rituals—of their use. Much political action plays upon precisely the symbolism of place, as protestors occupy legislatures or picket before courthouses. Caesars are best killed on the steps of capitols. Especially in the age of television, public spaces can be occupied to great effect, and the sites for protest are carefully selected.

Students of collective memory have shown that places are unusually strong carriers of history. Battlefields, buildings, monuments and statues, rivers and forests, regions: all can gain special resonance because they conveniently express how a group or nation constructs its history, what it selects for retention out of all the possible facts and emotions. Some, such as monuments, are designed precisely to express concrete memories; others gain this function through association with events. One can visit, touch, and smell these sites, and somehow be persuaded of the reality of history through the reality of the physical objects and places.

There are more private senses of place as well. Protesters are often motivated to protect special places, perhaps because they help define one's home or because they have a sacred aura setting them apart from daily life. Not all activities have the same moral value, and not all places have equal emotional weight. Positive affect for a place usually depends on a sense of its being our home or neighborhood, but the beauty of a site or its ability to evoke good memories can also help. A sense of home derives from factors such as local relationships with others, shared values and identity, a childhood or family heritage, continuity and familiarity, the ability to personalize the space, and physical structures.[59] Our construction of home is probably like concentric circles, most intense at the center but extending outward to tint neighborhoods and larger regions. Probing a single family's construction of meanings, psychologist Jerome Bruner found a clear contrast between home as safe, forgiving, intimate, and boring, versus the outside world as dangerous, intolerant, tough, and exciting.[60] Emotionally, our sense of place and home shade into our feeling of community, which itself is highly malleable. We have positive feelings toward places we associate with community, or perhaps with beauty or spirituality. The very concept of community, Joseph Gusfield argues, is a utopian measuring rod for evaluating our actual social relations.[61] As a result, places associated with our moral community reinforce our collective identity even as they encourage political outrage when they are threatened.

We orient ourselves in space, dividing it into identifiable places, through our senses, each of which can transmit a visceral feeling of security or threat. Sight is perhaps most important for placing ourselves, and in the chapters to follow we'll see protest spurred by graffiti, by the beauty of the California coastline, by visible pollution. Taste and smell can also arouse us, as when our water develops a bad taste or the air a noxious odor. Sound is conceivable as a source of threat, although it must be a rare one. Touch is a more intimate sense, but anyone who has been violated so closely will surely feel deeply threatened.

There are some relatively objective aspects to the places where we live. Urbanization and industrial capitalism systematically transform the landscape, threatening people's ways of life in a manner that often spurs protest. There is nothing accidental to this pattern, as David Harvey describes: "Capitalism perpetually strives to create a social and physical landscape in its own image and requisite to its own needs at a particular point in time, only just as certainly to undermine, disrupt and even destroy that landscape at a later point in time. The inner contradictions of capitalism are expressed through the restless formation and re-formation of geographical landscapes."[62] Industrial pressures on the landscape may be one way to revive collective-behavior theorists' idea that we could expect protest in certain places, under the impact of social change—an insight lost when protest came to be seen as a normal part of everyone's politics. The spatial distribution of industrial processes and wastes may provide clues to resistance (we'll examine "not in my backyard" movements in the next chapter), even if changes in one's physical surroundings never *automatically* result in protest.

Protestors can also play on special senses of time. They appeal to the sweep of history, or the urgency of the moment. Many movements contain a millennial impulse that concentrates attention on political issues. If you believe the world capable of sudden and drastic transformation, your political tactics may be more revolutionary and less reformist. The French revolutionaries hoped to start history over, resetting their nation's calendar to year one; the Khmer Rouge, always trying to outdo previous revolutions, chose (appropriately, given the horrors of their regime) year zero. Religion has often been the source of a culture's fundamental sense of time, as in Christian millennialism, which envisions a dramatic endpoint to history. A striking example occurred in the United States after the extensive religious revivals of 1831 had converted large numbers of middle-class Americans to millenial beliefs; the decade that followed saw a massive "protest cycle" in temperance, abolition, and moral-reform movements, each based on a sense that sudden, dramatic change was possible in this world—a view impossible under older Calvinist fatalism.[63] Secular revolutions appear to have had similar effects, as national histories also shape our sense of time. Countries that have had one key revolution, such as France and the United States, have a different sense of time's unfolding than countries, such as Germany, where history has seemed more a cycle of great moments and collapses.[64] Such deep implicit images guide our sense of how change occurs, of what is possible for a protest movement.

Culturally defined "situations" are combinations of time, place, and social roles.[65] Regulated by shared norms, situations trigger expectations that we can either follow, thwart, or transform. Rituals are only a highly stylized form of situation, with a heightened sense of place and time; protest activities also have their "situated" expectations. Later chapters will examine home, neighborhood, and pilgrimages as familiar situations.

Death and funerals also form salient situations. If time and place are two influential—but often overlooked—dimensions of culture, helping to define protestors' identities and projects, then so are the existential boundaries of human life. As we saw in the examples that began chapter 1, protestors continually strive to reach beyond their own contexts, raising fundamental questions about life and death and the purpose of a good life. Certain moments in life demand a moral reckoning, explicit affirmations of beliefs and feelings. If they truly hope to move people, protestors must claim special insight into one of those defining moments of human existence.

As Samuel Johnson pointed out, death focuses the attention. It eliminates nonessential concerns from sight. The prospect of one's own death, the death of a loved one, even the death of a stranger (perhaps because she was a young child or because she died in a grisly manner): all these can arouse intense, urgent emotions, can force one to affirm or reconsider basic values, and can motivate political efforts. ACT UP constantly works under the specter of AIDS' final outcome. Many of the Mothers Against Drunk Driving were driven to join or found chapters by the loss of a child, and MADD runs a powerful television advertisement featuring a small girl on a swing, singing; after a few moments, the voice-over tells the viewer on what date she was killed by a drunk driver. The heightened emotions of funerals are promising contexts for political mobilization, as Shakespeare's Mark Antony knew well. For African-American slaves, funerals, usually held at night, provided a sheltered space for expressing their resistance. During the civil rights movement these services helped to build emotional solidarity; after the funeral of a black boy killed in Selma, Mississippi, for instance, a member of the large crowd bitterly recalled, "We wanted to carry Jimmy's body to George Wallace and dump it on the steps of the Capitol."[66] There is no more powerful rhetoric than that of death. "Death," says Michael Blain, "enters the trajectory of political violence as both beginning and conclusion. In the end, it communicates the sense of completeness, totality, consummation, the ultimate, final, and supreme. Total commitment is commitment unto death. The commitment to death liberates the committed from the complacency of ordinary life."[67]

All societies recognize certain moments in human lives as emotionally, morally, and cognitively weighty. Philosopher Peter Winch calls them "limiting notions" that help us define what a good human life is, and he points to death, birth, and sexual relations.[68] Moral systems inevitably have standards for these moments, even though the content of the standards varies considerably. These life passages are a good place to look for protest, since they involve deeply held intuitions and convictions. They tightly weave together our assumptions about how the world works, our standards of how it should work, and our emotions about fulfilled and unfulfilled visions—just the things to which protest organizers appeal. Threats to our understanding and our life passages will lead to moral outrage. Often in ritualized fashion, life passages expose our basic moral views; they use emotions to get at moral understandings, so that both appear in heightened form. Not that moral visions, emotions, and cultural meanings are not operating at other times, but they never operate so explicitly as during life passages.

Life passages are not the only moments when moral protest can be sparked. There are many potential "fateful moments," to use Giddens' term, when individuals make choices that set their lives on long-term trajectories.[69] Societies, too, face such fateful moments, when a celebrated trial, Congressional hearing, war, or other event becomes a lightning rod for the hopes or fears of different groups. Such moments may be either planned or unexpected, but they involve weighty contemplation of one's basic commitments and ambitions. Protest organizers try to jar the public into thinking deeply about their convictions even in the absence of direct confrontations with death, but they are most successful when they link their platforms with the big existential issues we all face. Moral protest helps us understand the value (and values) of our own lives, and to deal with the prospect of our own mortality. Protest movements suggest that we link our life passages with the important moments of our society, receiving a jolt of energy because we feel attached to world-historical processes. They link our private troubles and disruptions with social problems.[70] From existing cultural traditions, they create their own images of humanity's life passages. Like artists, activists create new moral possibilities.

APPLYING CULTURE

Culture is complex. We can analyze it as the pleasures, motives, or goals that lie behind action or view it as the skills, habits, and tastes that form action itself. It is inside individuals, yet outside them. It is within movements, yet outside them. Cultural components cross these boundaries so easily because they are not, foremost, physical things like resources (although they may be embodied physically). They are ideas and enthusiasms and sensitivities. Sometimes they are graciously explicit, but often they are implicit and subtle and difficult to measure, or even to observe clearly. Their methodological challenge, however, does not render them unimportant. In the end, we must be sensitive to what is going on inside people's heads and hearts.

Culturally oriented scholars have had an uneasy relation to other traditions. Some have simply reduced culture to a new variable or two that can be added to an existing sequence of events or processes: a plausible ideology or frame is a kind of resource or political opportunity. The existing theoretical frames remain intact. Others have theorized culture as something new altogether, with no clear relationship to resources or strategies, or worse, as competitive with them— as though a complex tradition like resource mobilization could be dismissed if one could only show that ideas count. New cultural concepts have been placed within or alongside other frameworks, either becoming insufficiently distinct or too distinct. Real integration, recognizing the autonomy of culture and nonculture, but also the interpenetration of the two, has been rare. Culture and resources are not the same, but this does not prevent culture from helping to define what resources are.

For this reason, cultural concepts such as frame alignment or identity have been overused, made to cover diverse phenomena that are better distinguished. The solution to this fuzziness is the same we used for resources and political opportunities: restrict the concepts by coming up with other words for what they are not. Explicit cultural components are not the same as implicit, constitutive cultural definitions. Collective identities are not movement or activist identities. Framing stops when recruitment does. Cognition or morality is not the same as emotions. Moral intuitions aren't even the same thing as moral principles.

The kind of culture that has been rediscovered so far is highly cognitive, with little attention to emotions or moral visions. For example "motivational framing," as Snow and Benford call it, makes motivation sound like a cognitive process with little emotional content. Identity, too, involves deep emotions, but it is often treated simply as a matter of cognitive boundaries. The emotions of protestors are still unsettling to those who study them, as though protest might suddenly seem irrational after all. Emotions, morals, and cognition—embodied in practical know-how—are equally important components of culture.

Since most recent theorists have been concerned to demonstrate the rationality of protestors, does attention to cognitive, moral, biographical, and especially emotional processes undermine models of protestors as rational? In bringing culture and biography back into the analysis of protest movements, we need not rely on the rich but demeaning assumptions of the crowd tradition or the thin, calculating image of economists. People can be reasonable—applying their cultural repertory of morals, meanings, and skills in purposive and creative ways—short of calculating self-interest. Most of the time, normal adults avoid extremes of calculation or self-destruction in their actions. They simultaneously pursue a range of goals with a variety of means, and they constantly generate new goals and means. Collective action, in particular, is a rich breeding ground for new understandings of the world and new patterns for action. Learning—which is difficult for perfectly rational or perfectly irrational beings—lies at the heart of social movements.

Far from being the opposite of rationality, culture, including emotions, defines rationality. By shaping the evaluations of the situation, the preferences of potential protestors, and their repertories of action, culture affects what goals as well as what tactics are rational for individuals and for organizations. Attention to cultural activities can overcome the gap between approaches that analyze protest either as purposive and rational or as expressive and irrational. It helps us to understand the diverse goals of protestors and so to judge better their success or failure. The social constructionism that dominates research on social problems and deviance has still not been fully absorbed by students of social movements, presumably because of their efforts to ground protest in rational and hence, they presume, objective rather than constructed interests.

In addition to the other aspects of culture is its creative moment, the active side of construction in which culture meets artfulness. People work out new sensibilities in response to economic, technological, demographic, and other changes. Groups, interacting with each other, breed patterns of friends and foes. Tactical innovations arise from the interplay of protest groups and their opponents. A gifted speaker invents new frames and images that resonate with varied audiences. And so on. Cultural creativity begins with individual idiosyncracies and spreads from there. The next part of the book works the border of culture and biography in three chapters that examine the diverse dispositions and motives that might open people to the possibility of joining a protest movement, or even lead them to individual acts of protest. They move from emotional (chapter 5) to moral (chapter 6) to cognitive (chapter 7) factors that make people willing to try on the role of protestor. Many of these processes occur without the aid of protest recruiters; others require their shaping hand. Individuals are often defined as outside the purview of social-movement research; I want to put them back.

- Inspired by Europeans, American scholars have recently rediscovered culture as an autonomous dimension of protest, especially its cognitive components. In the rush to understand this cultural dimension, concepts such as framing and identity are threatened by overextension.

- Events and individuals have considerable symbolic effects, both positive and negative, on thought, feeling, and action.

- Cultures are situated in concrete times, places, and institutional arrangements.

- Protestors regularly raise, or try to raise, existential issues about the meaning of human life.

PART TWO

Biography, Culture, and Willingness

Much goes on inside individuals' heads that could lead them into protest. They have long-standing affective ties to people and things as well as shorter-term emotional responses to events and information; moral intuitions and principles derived from religion, professional training, and other experiences; cognitive assumptions and beliefs through which they interpret the world. Depending on how threats are constructed, all these may make individuals open or willing to protest. Some protest as individuals, others seek out existing groups, some found their own groups, but most will simply be open to the arguments of recruiters. In order to understand willingness to protest, we must examine individual biographies and cultural practices and meanings, as well as—in the final stages of the causal chain—the resources and strategies of formal groups. We shall see that emotions, morality, and cognitive beliefs are inseparable in action.

FIVE

Not in Our Backyards: Emotion, Threat, and Blame

'Mid pleasures and palaces though we may roam,
Be it ever so humble, there's no place like home;
A charm from the skies seems to hallow us there,
Which, seek through the world, is ne'er met with elsewhere.
    —J. H. Payne

I drove out to Ian McMillan's ranch in September 1984, following his directions of rights and lefts along unmarked roads through the golden countryside of middle California. His sprawling home sat at the head of a valley cutting down through a high ridge, and the large picture windows of his living room framed the valley and the hills rolling out toward the Pacific Ocean twenty miles away. During our conversation the sun set slowly over those hills, filling the living room with a yellow glow. Although McMillan's age (in his mid-70s) had slowed him, the filled gun rack, the saddles on the porch, and the many broad-brimmed hats in the house showed that this was very much a working farm. At the same time, the brambles and pools of water carefully placed around the house, harboring countless species of birds, reflected McMillan's lifelong membership in the Audubon Society. McMillan's family had been on the same land since the 1870s— a long time in that part of the country.

Tall and stately, McMillan did not move quickly. He didn't need to. He had a powerful presence that bespoke fortitude and honesty. Both traits proved useful in opposing the Diablo Canyon nuclear power plant beginning in the late 1970s. With his hat and height, McMillan was an unmistakable presence at demonstrations, and he participated with his grandson in the two-week encampment and blockade of the plant site. (The plant is on the bay where he first saw the ocean, at the age of ten, when his father drove the family's spring wagon there after the harvest one fall.) He became something of a folk hero to the subculture of protestors against Diablo, many of whom did not live nearby at all, and none of whom had lived there as long as McMillan. "I love this land; I feel part of it, and it's part of me. This is my life here. If there were an accident, the wind would blow in from the ocean, and blow everything right at my ranch." McMillan knew the land around Diablo Canyon, and Diablo Canyon itself. He appreciated its beauty, which he said was not compatible with enormous concrete structures. "Local governments—county commissioners for example—are always for development; more industry means more tax money. But that's not what people want. They want to live their lives, raise their kids." People need a place to live their lives, and that place becomes an intimate part of the lives people construct. Threats to those places trigger complex emotional reactions, combining dread, anxiety, and fear; anger, outrage, and hatred.

McMillan's agricultural roots shaped his image of the land. He spoke of being able to see urban encroachment from his house, slowly nibbling away at the ranches. I wondered if he were speaking in a figurative—or paranoid—manner, since I could not see a single other building, only rolling hills. But the evening was slightly hazy. Farmers should want to preserve farms, he reckoned, although most had instead supported the Diablo plant when it was first proposed in the 1960s. They were more interested in money—in land prices and county tax revenues—than farming. To McMillan the land represented both productivity—in the shape of the cattle scattered over the hills—and preservation—embodied in the birds he and his wife loved.

McMillan's passionate feelings for the land and against the Diablo reactor were obvious in what he said but even more in how he said it. His reasons, polished over eight years of opposition, were mostly rational, even cerebral, and it is impossible to know if he would have given the same ones at the beginning. But the underlying love for the land and its creatures, for a simple agricultural existence, permeated his tone of voice: venomous when speaking of Diablo's owners, and soft, even dreamy, when describing rural pleasures. Words like "love" and "outrageous" dotted his speech, and there was little doubt that these animated his protest. As we'll see again and again, cognitive, moral, and emotional languages blend inextricably together.

McMillan operated on the sizeable border between individual protest and organized protest movement. He began calling neighbors and attending meetings of county commissioners before there were organized protest groups, and once these started organizing events, he attended those too. Besides lending his impressive biographical credentials to their events, however, he did little to sustain the protest groups per se. He did not go to regular meetings or belong to an ongoing affinity group. He was heavily involved in protest, only partly involved in a protest movement.

In the nearby town of San Luis Obispo I met another kind of anti-Diablo protestor, the Mothers for Peace. If McMillan embodied local opposition to industrial projects on the basis of traditional ways of life, the Mothers typified a new kind of protestor that has become common since the late 1970s. These "housewife warriors," feeling their children and homes at risk, have organized to attack hazardous waste sites, nuclear power plants, and any number of other industrial facilities around the country. Many have recently sent their youngest child to elementary school, freeing time for political work. Others still have children keeping them at home, but their flexible schedules allow them to make innumerable telephone calls. Sometimes they have college educations and professional husbands, so that they have enough cultural and political skills to succeed with the media and hold their own in public hearings. Many have moved to small towns and rural areas because of the congestion of cities, and are especially disappointed to face industrial facilities and environmental problems in their new neighborhoods.[1]

The Mothers were hardly unsophisticated when they decided to oppose Diablo Canyon in 1973. The group had formed in 1969 in opposition to the Vietnam war, and it began to study nuclear energy as the war wound down and plans for Diablo Canyon were working their way through official channels. They had activist identities, and some networks derived from that activism. Coming to the nuclear issue with a clear political ideology, the Mothers' real shock came at how they were treated by the Nuclear Regulatory Commission (NRC) at hearings. The Pacific Gas & Electric Company, owner of Diablo Canyon, barely deigned to discredit them, as NRC representatives did not even begin to take them seriously; they were a bunch of housewives challenging testimony by an extensive staff of professional engineers. They and their husbands valiantly and angrily represented themselves at hearings for the first three years, but in 1976 they began to hire lawyers.

They also grew more and more knowledgeable about the hazards of nuclear reactors. As McMillan said of them, "When they get up there you expect them to bake muffins or something, but then they just let you have it. I wouldn't want to be on the other side against them." They are, he says, protecting their babies: "It's like driving around a corner into a family of quail. The mother will flare up and attack the car, do anything to protect her babies, whatever it takes." (The fond stories that protestors tell about each other, creating local folk heroes, help reinforce the kind of internal movement culture we'll examine later, especially in chapter 8.) This is a different kind of emotion from McMillan's love for the land, but equally powerful. They were, literally, mothers, with a passionate interest in protecting their children, their daily lives and routines, almost no matter what it took. And from past experience they knew what it took.

Neither Ian McMillan nor the Mothers for Peace fit popular images of protestors: an aging farmer and a band of middle-class moms. They, like many other people, became protestors suddenly, when a network of large organizations, both public and private, did something that amounted to a "moral shock" for many local residents. Minding their own business, enmeshed in their daily routines, they suddenly saw the possibility that a nuclear accident could render their homes uninhabitable, make their communities ghost towns, and kill their animals, if not their children. Their very homes could lose their reassuring protective ability, the food in their refrigerators could turn against them, contaminated by unseen radiation. Even beyond the fear of radiation sickness and cancer, these people saw a possibility that their entire way of life, rooted in this scenic place, would end.

"Moral shocks" are often the first step toward recruitment into social movements: when an unexpected event or piece of information raises such a sense of outrage in a person that she becomes inclined toward political action, with or without the network of personal contacts emphasized in mobilization and process theories. The triggers may be highly publicized public events such as a nuclear accident or personal experiences such as the death of a child. They may be sudden, like an accident or public announcement, or they may unfold gradually over time, as in the gradual realization by Love Canal's residents that they were living over a toxic waste dump. Most are dramatic and attention-getting, but some are modest, more like the "last straw" that finally spurs action. Similarly, the shock may come from a plan for something new or from new information about something existing, which has already done unseen damage. The information or event helps a person think about her basic values and how the world diverges from them in some important way. Such individuals often search out political organizations themselves, without waiting for recruiters to contact them. These shocks are similar to Edward Walsh's "suddenly imposed grievances," like his case of the accident at the Three Mile Island nuclear power plant, that can spur recruitment.[2] Events can be powerful symbols.

Responses to moral shocks vary greatly. Most people, in most cases, resign themselves to unpleasant changes, certain that governments and corporations do not bend to citizen protest. But others, through complex emotional processes that few researchers have described, channel their fear and anger into righteous indignation and individual or collective political activity. The prospect of unexpected and sudden changes in one's surroundings can arouse feelings of dread and anger. The former can paralyze, the latter can be the basis for mobilization. Activists work hard to create moral outrage and anger, and to provide a target against which these can be vented. One of the Mothers for Peace told me, "Everyone around here is nervous. Especially after the blueprints. [In 1981 an engineer discovered that the plans for the two Diablo reactors had been reversed, with millions of dollars in structural supports done incorrectly.] If they can't even read a diagram right, can they run them safely? But what we've got to do is work on the paralysis. People can sit around thinking 'Oh My God,' or they can go out and fight. We put them into attack mode."

"Attack mode" is a cluster of emotions that activists try hard to cultivate: inchoate anxieties and fears must be transformed into moral indignation and anger toward concrete policies and decision-makers. Patterns of affect—either positive or negative feelings toward people, events, things, and places—exist before the activists go to work. Otherwise there would be no shock. Positive feelings toward one's home and surroundings, coupled with strong negative affect toward a proposal that seems to threaten these, are common raw materials for protest. Activists must weave together a moral, cognitive, and emotional package of attitudes. By framing the problem as, say, "big business" or "instrumentalism," they suggest a moral judgment: disregard or abuse of humans by bureaucracy. The proper emotion shifts from dread to outrage. There is someone to blame.

Suspicion and distrust, even a touch of paranoia, are sentiments that can help people work their discontent into protest by locating a villain. The creation of enemies allows the allocation of blame and encourages concrete demands for redressing grievances. McMillan and the Mothers shared a deep distrust of experts and their assurances. "They lie," insisted one of the Mothers. "They lie right to you, and they wrap it up in fancy-sounding scientific terms. And if they're not lying, they're ignorant, and that makes their arrogance even more obnoxious." This distrust of experts is almost universal in American society, even when it is mixed with appreciation of the benefits of science and technology. As we shall see in chapter 7, there are both left-leaning and right-leaning critiques of expertise, both intuitive and highly articulate ones. All the versions have been finely honed in the past thirty years, as Americans have recognized the dark side of science and technology that accompanies their promise. Today virtually all local resistances can appeal to the intuitions of normal men and women that, given the chance, people in power will do bad things to them. This "critique of instrumentalism" always provides someone to blame.

The language used by McMillan and the Mothers shows how closely tied together are the cognitive, moral, and emotional dimensions of protest. McMillan's love of his land is stirred partly by his understanding of the effects of a Diablo accident. The Mothers' moral outrage (the very term showing a synthesis of morality and feelings) is based on their expectations of what government can and should do to regulate technology. Often, though, the emotions elude articulation, appearing in body language: the passion when McMillan says, "I love this land;" the snarling grimace of the mother describing the patronizing NRC panel. Neither cognition, emotion, nor morality comes first; all are there in equal degrees.

With local "not in my backyard" opposition as an empirical case, this chapter highlights the emotional processes that accompany the cognitive and moral ones in protest. These include the varied responses to perceived threats, from paralyzing dread to anger to outrage over perceived injustice. Behind these responses lie complex affective grids, through which people divide the world into positive and negative places, safe and dangerous neighborhoods, and sinful or saved groups inhabiting them. In this chapter we examine especially how emotions, in this case those attached to places, help shape a sense of threat and of blame, two central constructions necessary for most protest. Things can happen to individuals that make them available or willing to protest, even inspire individual acts of protest, before they join formal groups, so this chapter and the next deal especially with the intersection of culture and biography. (Chapter 8 concentrates on the emotions generated and sustained *within* a social movement.)

THE EMOTIONS OF PROTEST

Our cognitive beliefs about how the world is, our moral vision of how the world should be, and our emotional attachments to that world march in close step. Emotions don't merely accompany our deepest desires and satisfactions, they constitute them, permeating our ideas, identities, and interests. They are, in Randall Collins' words, "the 'glue' of solidarity—and what mobilizes conflict."[3] Anxiety, enthusiasm, or even stronger emotions may be necessary to focus our attention, especially on political issues outside our normal daily routines.[4] In the past fifteen years, sociologists have rediscovered emotions, although they have yet to be integrated into much empirical research outside of social psychology.[5] Several have even begun to theorize emotions as the fundamental motivating force at the heart of social action.[6] Thomas Scheff bemoans the absence of emotions in explanations of political conflict: "Emotions lead only a shadow life these days. Shame, particularly, has dropped out of the discussion, along with other emotions and personal motives. Lust for possessions or power is seen as real; for honor, unreal. . . . [S]ocial scientists, like most others in our civilization, are too ashamed of emotions to give them serious attention as causal elements."[7] Most social scientists mimic the tendency of modern societies to denigrate emotions as the opposite of rationality.

A long tradition of rationalist philosophy, psychology, and commonsense thinking has viewed emotions as natural sensations—"feelings"—originating in the body, beyond the control of those experiencing them. People are said to be "seized by emotion," to be "in the grip" of passions such as jealousy or anger, which are thought to be physical sensations along the lines of vertigo, nausea, or fatigue. The irrefutable bodily symptoms of emotions, whether increased adrenaline or redness in the face, are taken to be the emotions themselves, to which we then attach names. Emotions, in this view, thwart our wiser intentions and prevent rational actions. No doubt this sometimes happens: a southern sheriff who angrily hit peaceful civil rights demonstrators often regretted his impulsiveness—especially when he was captured on film. Ironically, social scientists especially lack any language for describing the visceral aspects of emotions, so that reducing emotions to their bodily symptoms is a way of abandoning any effort to explain them.

But most emotions are part of rational action, not opposed to it. If cognitive processes and moral values are socially constructed, emotions are too.[8] Rather than being a simple set of inner sensations (are the physical sensations that accompany annoyance and indignation, for example, distinguishable?), an emotion is an action or state of mind that makes sense only in particular circumstances. James Averill describes emotions as *transitory social roles,* which he in turn defines as "a socially prescribed set of responses to be followed by a person in a given situation." The rules governing the response consist of "social norms or shared expectations regarding appropriate behavior."[9] Because emotions normally have objects (we are afraid *of something*), they depend partly on cognitive appraisals.

In the constructionist view, emotions are constituted by shared social meanings, not automatic physiological states. Some theorists argue that bodily changes are there, but must be interpreted before they can become emotions; others take the more extreme view that bodies change only in response to situations associated with particular emotions. Evidence of the many cross-cultural differences in emotions seems to support this position. Nonetheless the apparent existence of several universals, such as facial expressions of surprise, anger, and fear, suggests a constructionist model in which, while some or most of any emotion is socially constructed, some natural expression is involved as well.[10] Virtually all efforts to catalogue primary emotions include fear and anger; it is plausible that a handful of primary emotions are less socially constructed than the much larger group of culturally variable secondary emotions.[11] Primary emotions, tied more directly to bodily states, are probably more important in face-to-face settings—of the kind many interactionists study—than in ongoing political processes, where complex secondary emotions such as outrage or pride may be more influential.[12]

This definition ties emotions to morality and cognition in several ways. Emotions involve socially learned beliefs and assumptions open to cognitive persuasion. We can often be talked out of our anger, on the grounds that it is too extreme a response, or that we are misinformed. If emotions are tied to beliefs and contexts, they are also partly open to debate as to whether they are appropriate or not at a given time. Because there are rules governing them, certain emotions can be labeled as deviant.[13] Even our gut-level primary emotions, if they exist, are conditioned by our expectations, which in turn are derived from knowledge about conditions in the world.[14]

Emotions are also tied to moral values, often arising from perceived infractions of moral rules. In the words of Rom Harré, "[T]he study of emotions like envy (and jealousy) will require careful attention to the details of local systems of rights and obligations, of criteria of value and so on. In short, these emotions cannot seriously be studied without attention to the local moral order."[15] One context in which emotions unfold is that of common human narratives, or what de Sousa calls "paradigm scenarios."[16] Just as the death of a friend leads one through several predictable emotional stages, other unexpected and unpleasant events—such as a proposal for a nearby nuclear power plant—may lead to surprise, sadness, anger, then outrage. Robert Solomon even describes the roles that accompany these plots: with anger, you are the judge, and the other person is the defendant; with contempt, you are pure and blameless, while the other person is vile and despicable.[17] Each emotion implies a family of terms to hurl at your opponent. A social movement organizer deploys different language and arouses different emotions in her listeners if she paints her opponents as inherently malevolent rather than well-meaning but ignorant. Emotions are closely connected with the cognitive meanings one constructs about the world, and to the moral valuations accompanying them. Such links are present even when emotions are in conflict with moral and cognitive knowledge.

The complex emotion of compassion, important for many protest movements, further shows the connection between emotion and morality, for it is a frequent spur to moral action. According to philosopher Lawrence Blum, "Compassion is not a simple feeling-state but a complex emotional attitude toward another, characteristically involving imaginative dwelling on the condition of the other person, an active regard for his good, a view of him as a fellow human being, and emotional responses of a certain degree of intensity." Compassion's moral force comes from this sense of shared human solidarity, in contrast to pity, "in which one holds oneself apart from the afflicted person and from their suffering, thinking of it as something that defines that person as fundamentally different from oneself."[18]

Compassion is a relatively stable disposition, not a fleeting response, and it illustrates an important distinction. *Emotions form a continuum from relatively temporary reactions to events and information, at one end, to more stable affective dispositions at the other.* I get angry at a political decision, but I have ongoing affection for a political party. I am shocked by the Chernobyl nuclear accident, but I have a deeper mistrust of nuclear energy. Envy and respect usually fall somewhere in the middle of the continuum, anger and relief at the short-term end. At the long-term end, I have negative and positive feelings (hatred, love, pride) toward individuals, places, and symbols that form part of the background for "transitory social roles" such as anger toward my father or panic over flag burning. The dispositions change, to be sure, but in the short term they help explain my emotional responses. (Short-term responses may either reinforce or undermine the deeper sentiments.) Tamotsu Shibutani theorized religious conversion to be based on the convert's affective loyalties: she would convert if she felt positively toward members of the new group and negatively toward the old.[19] Emotions are generated through the interaction between our environments and our biographical quirks, goals, interests, and affects.[20]

David Heise concentrates on affect as a central component of social life: all actions, actors, and settings have an affective component, involving not only a good-bad dimension, but a potency dimension and a dimension capturing level of activity (lively-quiet).[21] Humans act, according to Heise, in order to confirm their underlying sentiments. If "neighborhood" has positive connotations of safety and quiet, Heise's "affect control theory" would show how a resident would fight to keep her neighborhood that way. Most political activity, no doubt, involves the reference to or creation of positive and negative affects toward groups, policies, and activities.

Trust is a general affect with enormous effects on political life. We have very deep tendencies to trust certain individuals, groups, and institutions but not others, and many of our allegiances and alliances follow from this pattern. Past experience or observation, agreement over goals or values or styles, collective identities, maybe even abstract deductions from principles: all affect whom we trust. *We trust those we agree with, and agree with those we trust.* Generalized trust in the political system, furthermore, affects political behavior, usually dampening protest because of an assumption that the government will fix things without public pressure. (For those who do protest, system trust may encourage use of legal rather than illegal channels.) Its opposite would seem to be a mistrust of experts, bureaucracy, and their instrumental attitudes, a stance that has spread in recent decades.[22]

To complicate this picture further, we don't just have emotions, we have them in certain ways, with a certain style. As the first sociologist of emotions, Max Scheler, put it, "[W]e can 'give ourselves up' to suffering or pit ourselves against it; we can 'endure' suffering, 'tolerate' it, or simply 'suffer'; we can 'enjoy' suffering (algophilia). These phrases signify *styles* of feeling and of willing based on feeling, which are clearly not determined by the mere state of feeling."[23] Taste and tone enter into emotions just as into actions and judgments. As Raymond Williams says, "We are talking about characteristic elements of impulse, restraint, and tone; specifically affective elements of consciousness and relationships; not feeling against thought, but thought as felt and feeling as thought; practical consciousness of a present kind, in a living and interrelating continuity."[24] Part culture and part biography, these styles of feeling no doubt help explain phenomena such as the popularity of a charismatic leader.

Our relationships with other humans, even fleeting ones, are charged with affect and emotions. Those intimates whom we know well are wrapped in a complex web of affects that we can never fully sort out. Sexual desire, fulfilled or merely aroused, affects many of our choices of how to spend our time—or more precisely, with whom. We often have simple feelings even about strangers: attraction or repulsion, for example. Affection or anger toward our parents gives many activities associated with them (even symbolically) a positive or negative affective charge; we may protest in order to shock them or gain their respect, or to replicate some childhood dynamic (not all our emotions are conscious). Admiration for others also influences our choices, as we follow their examples or strive for their approval. We also have emotional attachments to places, and fight fiercely when we feel that certain locales are threatened. Symbols too are never merely cognitive but are enveloped in emotions. Political organizers arouse, manipulate, and help to construct a variety of emotions: anger over various injustices, compassion for certain groups, joy in mass assemblies. Table 5.1 describes some of the emotions that help lead people into protest and protest movements and keep them there.[25]

The specter of irrationality arises when we assume that emotions—conceived as momentary "passions"—lead us to do things we normally would not do or "really" do not want to do. But even the most fleeting emotions are firmly rooted in moral and cognitive beliefs that are more stable. In addition, most emotions, far from subverting our goal attainment, help us define our goals and motivate action toward them. The southern sheriff's rage is a major part of what animates him, even when protestors can manipulate his rage strategically to his disadvantage. His actions may be mistaken, hurting him strategically, but the source of most misguided actions is as likely to be cognitive as emotional.

Anyone not a sociologist would assume that the first step on the road to protest must be anger and discontent. Yet discontent, the linchpin of collective behavior, disappeared in the works of mobilization theorists, not because they assumed everyone was perfectly happy, but because they assumed that everyone was always discontented. Rational, self-interested actors are always looking to improve their status, power, and wealth, not merely to retain what they already have. If every group in society has a continual interest in organizing to promote its goals, then these incentives cannot explain why some groups organize to express their grievances and others do not. John McCarthy and Mayer Zald described "professional" social movements in which resources came first and grievances second; issue entrepreneurs could themselves create grievances.[26] Craig Jenkins and Charles Perrow said that "discontent is ever-present for deprived groups,"—a dubious proposition in itself, but one that leaves open the question of protest by privileged groups like those behind most post-citizenship movements.[27] Such statements miss the extensive emotional work needed to create indignation and outrage. There are many, perennial reasons for discontent, but the discontent must still be constructed out of those situations.

If researchers paid attention to them, I think they would discover a variety of emotions in protest. First, individuals have emotional allegiances and experiences that help propel them into protest. Fear, dread and an accompanying sense of threat are key motives. Grief could also play a role, either following the loss of a loved one or as a more general sense of cultural loss. An alternation between shame and anger drives much political conflict, according to Thomas Scheff, as shame often

Table 5.1 Some Emotions Potentially Relevant to Protest

Types	Possible Effects
Affect	Basic positive or negative feelings toward people or places can trigger sense of threat.
Anger	Can have many sources, and can be channeled in many directions, including both rage and outrage. Can interfere with effective strategies.
Compassion, sympathy, pity	One can imagine the plight of others and develop a desire to help them.
Cynicism, depression	More moods than emotions, they dampen hopes for change.
Enthusiasm, pride	Positive emotions that protest leaders try to encourage: enthusiasm for the movement and cause, pride in the associated collective identity, as in Black Power, gay and lesbian rights.
Envy, resentment	Exaggerated by early crowd theorists, these are emotions that few admit to and which usually lead to actions other than protest; yet they may also appear among protestors.
Fear, dread	These can arise from a sense of threat to one's daily routines or moral beliefs. They can paralyze but also be developed into outrage.
Grief, loss, sorrow	Loss, especially of a loved one, can bring on life passage and raise issues of the meaning of life.
Hatred, hostility, loathing	Powerful step in the creation of outrage and the fixing of blame. Can alter goals from practical results to punishment of opponents.
Joy, hope	One can be attracted by the joys of empowerment, a sense of "flow" in protest and politics, or the anticipation of a better state of affairs in the future.
Love	One can have erotic and other attachments to people already in a movement; love also shapes one's affective map of the world.
Outrage, indignation	These build on other emotions, largely by providing a target or analysis.
Resignation	Like cynicism, can dampen perceived possibility for change.
Shame	Can lead to anger and aggressive reactions.
Suspicion, paranoia	Often lead to indignation and articulation of blame.
Trust, loyalty	Basic positive affects that influence other emotional and cognitive responses, patterns of alliances, and credibility.

triggers aggression.[28] Anger and outrage will almost always play a part, as will pre-existing negative and positive affects toward symbols, places, individuals, and groups. (In chapters 8 and 9, we'll examine the emotions derived from the activity of protest: the collective affection, enthusiasm, joy, even wonder, at possibilities for social change; the pride of revaluing a stigmatized identity; the many pleasures of protest, ranging from erotic attraction to avoidance of boredom.) I turn now to the example of "not in my backyard" movements (NIMBYs) opposed to new facilities proposed near them, as well as related movements, in order to show how complex constructions like threat and blame can develop out of simpler emotions such as fear and dread.

NIMBYS AND OTHER THREATS

In April 1987 three middle-class neighbors set fire to a house that was to hold foster-care babies in Queens, New York. In Ventura, California, another home was torched before it could house a group of mentally handicapped adults. In Passaic County, New Jersey, protestors gathered on Good Friday, 1988, to prevent the state government from moving 120 AIDS patients to a nursing home there. An Ohio farmer has organized a group to stop plans for a large garbage incinerator next to his fields. Thousands of groups have formed throughout the United States to oppose gas pipelines, hazardous waste sites, nuclear power plants, airports, public housing, and facilities for the poor, sick, or disabled. They especially mushroomed in the late 1980s: between 1987 and 1992 the number of community groups working with the National Toxics Campaign grew from 600 to 1,700; in the same four years those in touch with the Citizens' Clearinghouse for Hazardous Waste jumped from under 2,000 to over 7,500.[29] In poor neighborhoods as well as rich, in rural areas as well as urban, local opponents are standing up to developers, large corporations, and federal, state and local governments, often with remarkable success. Some engage in individual acts of protest, sometimes cowardly ones, but many have formed highly organized movements.

There are several reasons why NIMBYs—groups protesting against local threats—are on the rise. Foremost, perhaps, is the increasing distrust of technical authorities. Another is the growth since World War II of an enormous chemicals industry, and the widespread use of hazardous chemicals in many other industries. There has also been a growth of risky technologies, nuclear energy most prominent among them. Intensive media coverage of environmental hazards since the 1960s has raised environmental awareness throughout the advanced

Table 5.2   Types of Perceived Physical Threat

	Ultimate Cause	
	Human	Nature
Immediate embodiment		
Human	Prisons Halfway houses Public housing Some diseases	Some diseases
Environment	Nuclear reactors Incinerators, Hazardous waste sites	Floods, fires, Earthquakes, and other natural disasters

industrial countries. In addition, an increase in government programs, such as public housing and school busing, designed to change the social topography of a community, has also stimulated protest. Finally, in ways that McCarthy and Zald described so well, opponents are increasingly likely to *organize* when they are angry, since national organizations and social movement professionals—a vibrant social movement industry—are available today to advise and help them.

NIMBYs come in many forms. Virtually anything can be seen as threatening, and any perceived threat can become the target of protest. Mobilization usually requires two complex constructions: a sense of threat must be built out of raw emotions like fear, dread, and hate, and some group of people must be blamed for that threat. Different sources of threat will be constructed in different ways, with contrasting implications for protest. As I express it in table 5.2, we culturally construct threats based on both their ultimate causes and their proximate embodiments. We can attribute the ultimate source of the threat to either nature or human action; in either case the threat can be directly embodied in humans or in the inanimate environment. If protest forms around fears of technological risks and unknowns, it also arises out of loathing for groups about whom (protestors think) they know too much. Two additional dimensions not illustrated in table 5.2 are whether the threat already exists or is planned or proposed for the future, and whether the feared outcome is sudden or slow.

Some threats are embodied in technologies, industrial processes, and the built environment. These threats may take the form of sudden catastrophe: risky technologies like nuclear energy raise the possibility that an entire community would be suddenly destroyed—evacuated and abandoned for generations to come. Indeed, Charles Perrow has argued persuasively that very complex technologies, when their sub-processes are tightly "coupled" with each other, inevitably suffer periodic breakdowns of the entire system, as small malfunctions ramify in unpredictable ways throughout the system.[30] Other risks involve or suggest the possibility of slow, chronic damage and more cumulative catastrophes: low-level radiation, chemical contamination, and incinerators may pose long-term health threats that scientists cannot specify precisely or confidently. These effects are increasingly being recognized in the courts as well as by protest movements. For example, in 1989 the Department of Energy agreed to pay a total of $73 million to residents near an Ohio plant producing weapons materials. This was the first time the department had made such a payment; it admitted "emotional distress," although it refused to acknowledge health effects.[31] The NIMBYs that respond to this kind of threat, linked to the environmental movement, are easily seen as a form of post-industrial movement concerned about the quality of local life.

Other threats are directly embodied in humans. Public housing, prisons, homes for the mentally handicapped, and various halfway houses are part of the social as well as the physical environment. In such cases fear and loathing reinforce each other. Rather than arising from instinctual prejudice, however, protest against these threats is similar in some ways to that against environmental threats. Some protestors are concerned with property values, others are morally shocked by their perceptions (accurate or not) of other groups' lifestyles. But there is also sometimes an accompanying sense of physical threat, based on expectations that crime will increase in areas once considered safe. People's physical world may no longer feel secure to them. Most threats that stir local opposition are perceived as physical, grounded in our sense of place. In contrast to movements against technologies or environmental hazards, no one would class movements against group homes as post-industrial, however; in their concern for social control of others, they are closer to "anti-citizenship" movements.

So far I have only discussed physical threats, but economic threats are another important source of protest, more in the tradition of citizenship movements. Layoffs, plant closings, wage cuts, and deskilling threaten standards of living and self-esteem. When labor was still a social movement, much or most of its activity was ignited by this kind of threat. Even though its demands were formulated more cognitively and abstractly as inclusion in political and economic rights, it often took an emotional sense of threat to trigger activism in pursuit of such rights. A large literature has appeared on the reactive, defensive nature of early labor protest and urban revolution, which were often led by artisans facing the extinction of their way of life. Only later, as the labor movement was represented by ongoing unions rather than by protest groups, were there continuing, systematic efforts to improve workers' positions.[32] The civil rights movement, too, was ignited partly by a sense of threat that southern blacks felt as white racist groups spread after the 1954 *Brown vs. Board of Education* decision—the same ruling that process theorists see as a sign of lowered state repression.[33]

In a world of rationalistic protestors, pursuing a well-defined package of citizenship rights or out to increase their resources, a psychological construct like threat has little role, for potential participants are waiting and watching for their opportunities to act. In fact, though, it may take something startling to get people's attention. Craig Calhoun said of revolutions, the ultimate form of many citizenship movements, that they "take place when people who do have something to defend, and do have some social strength, confront social transformations which *threaten* to take all that from them and thus leave them nothing to lose."[34] Common rhetoric about innocent victims and evil opponents is meant to heighten this sense of threat. Although the threats differ, both citizenship and post-citizenship movements respond to and try to create a feeling of threat, and their success depends on it. Emotional responses to perceived threats, though, are only the beginning.

ALLOCATING BLAME

The ability to focus blame is also crucial to protest, and it depends on the perceived ultimate causes and direct embodiments of each threat. Our understanding of and feelings toward a threat differ if its cause is natural or human, if it is embodied in other humans or inanimate technology, if it already exists or is being planned, and—to add another dimension—if we assign someone responsibility for fixing it regardless of what or who caused it. There are both *causal* and *remedial* forms of blame: causing a threat differs from responsibility for fixing it. If people believe that their government should have foreseen or prevented a catastrophe, or should have done more to help afterwards, they may become indignant even without believing that the government actually caused the calamity. The dual meaning of responsibility (as either cause or solution) works to protestors' advantage: organizations can be held responsible for a solution even if they didn't cause the problem.

We usually let nature off the hook. "Acts of god," such as forest fires or floods, discourage the blaming of any group or institution and rarely lead to protest; more often they create a broad solidarity by pitting humans against nature.[35] In fact, "The tasks that survivors engage in are helping, altruistic endeavors that require people to work side by side, in unison, to save lives and property. Such tasks encourage the formation of communal associations, which function to reassert the power of the group over nature by reconstituting routines that reinvest daily life with a sense of permanence and predictability."[36] In some cases, though, survivors are so devastated, thinking there is nothing left to save, that trauma, depression, and lethargy result.[37] In either case, there is no one to blame, so protest is uncommon (see the lower right-hand corner of table 5.2). We frame this kind of event as a misfortune, not an injustice.

When humans can be blamed for causing a threat, outrage is a more common response. Economic changes perceived to result from the arbitrary choices of corporate executives are viewed differently from those seen as the inevitable result of "natural" forces such as the dynamics of markets or international competition. Business has worked hard, and successfully, to paint its unpleasant decisions as responses to such natural laws.[38] Human-made environmental sources differ in the extent to which morally responsible actors can be singled out for blame. For example, air pollution is so diffuse as to seem more like an inevitable force of nature, while nuclear power plants have clear owners, regulators, and neighbors. We could formulate the following prediction: the more clearly defined the proximate source of the threat, the more likely opposition is to form. Human-made waste products and technologies represent a "new species of trouble" not only in being especially deadly but in being made *by* someone, yielding a clear perpetrator to blame.[39] If technological threats are easily tied to conscious choices made by others, causal blame for economic threats is regularly contested.

These boundaries shift over time, often subject to political conflict. In a way, this is the essential business of protest movements, as Ralph Turner recognizes when he argues that "emergent norms arise, provided other conditions are conducive, when the sense of normally acceptable risk is greatly intensified or greatly diminished."[40] Many outcomes that we once accepted as natural catastrophes we now blame humans for, and expect governments to protect us against. Public health threats became the government's business to fix and prevent as scientists learned more about the causes of disease and as public health, vaccination, and sanitation programs were established with the promise of eradicating killers such as cholera, typhoid, smallpox, and tuberculosis. So when AIDS appeared in the 1980s, ACT UP and other protest groups blamed Ronald Reagan for ignoring the epidemic. As president, he was responsible, even if he had no causal blame. Governments also provide meteorological information about hurricanes and floods as well as developing evacuation plans (in the United States the government also insures those who build on flood plains, exacerbating risks).

The boundary between social and natural causes (and responsibility) is politically contentious. Groups like ACT UP try to enlarge the boundary of nature as a cause, in order, paradoxically, to increase social responsibility for a solution. Innocent victims especially deserve aid. AIDS activists search for government agencies or corporations that can be blamed and thus shamed into remedial action. Conservative groups, conversely, want to insist on the social causes of AIDS, which they see as homosexual or promiscuous sex, in order to blame the victims and restrict governmental responsibility for solutions. They are painting AIDS with the moral tincture that has characterized many other diseases, from syphilis to cancer.[41]

Governments, in fact, are all-purpose villains that can be blamed for almost all the kinds of threats I have discussed, even natural disasters. Even when the government is not the cause, it can be blamed for not preventing, predicting, or fixing the problem. In many cases, governments are implicated in the siting of new facilities, either directly, as in the case of public housing, or indirectly through their ability to regulate land use, and so are frequent targets of NIMBYs. Governments are frequent "second-order" targets for blame in the realms of both cause and solution.

Existing and proposed threats may lead to different emotional responses, due to the different relations between cause and solution. Many previously unknown but existing hazards inspire trauma and resignation when they are discovered, especially when those who caused the problem have left the scene or gone out of business. Anger at those causally responsible must be translated into demands for another party (usually a government agency) to find a solution. This diversion of outrage is often hard to accomplish, and protest has an emotional advantage when redress is demanded of those who actually caused the problem. What's more, in the case of slowly unfolding, existing threats, we have more defense mechanisms—denial, resignation—that prevent our recognizing the full extent of a threat.

We can return to Gamson's concept of an injustice frame. He and his coauthors were clear about the primacy of emotions in the adoption of such a frame, since the bonds of authority being questioned in their experiments were primarily affective. Suspicion, hostility, and anger may arise even before blame is allocated through more cognitive processes. They quoted psychologist Robert Zajonc: "Preferences need no inferences. . . . Affective reactions can occur without extensive perceptual and cognitive encoding, are made with greater confidence than cognitive judgments, and can be made sooner."[42] By examining encounters with authorities, Gamson and his collaborators did not need to examine the process by which blame is attached to groups or individuals; in their case the authorities were the natural target, as is the case in most citizenship movements. In other cases blame may be more complex: those responsible for fixing a problem, for instance, may not be those who caused it, as is true of many environmental problems.

Gamson later elaborated on the sources of injustice, saying, "Concreteness in the target, even when it is misplaced and directed away from the real causes of hardship, is a necessary condition for an injustice frame." Of all the emotions, injustice is most closely associated with "the righteous anger that puts fire in the belly and iron in the soul."[43] He then pointed out a recurrent dilemma for protest movements: How are they to balance concrete targets of blame with a structural analysis of the social problem? Protestors may "exaggerate the role of human actors, failing to understand broader structural constraints, and misdirect their anger at easy and inappropriate targets."[44]

The specification of blame is important because it generates villains. We examine the utility of having enemies later, in chapter 16, but it is important to recognize the emotional basis of much political rhetoric. A recent study of pro-choice and anti-abortion newsletters found that they "identify concrete and specific adversaries, characterize enemy action in an entirely negative light, attribute corrupt motives to the foe, and magnify the opponents' power."[45] Such characterizations enhance protestors' outrage and sense of threat. Demonization fuels powerful emotions for protest: hatred, anger, suspicion, and indignation.

Mothers Against Drunk Driving (MADD) has succeeded so well in part because its name formulates both threat and blame. As Joseph Gusfield puts it, "The very name, MADD, presents the symbols that carry an expressive imagery. 'Mothers' puts the issue in a framework of violence against children. 'Against' provides an emotional sense of battles and enemies. 'Drunk drivers' provides an image of the DUI asocially irresponsible and out of self-control. This is the 'killer drunk' who constitutes the villain of the story. MADD has brought to the public arena the emotional and dramatic expression of the public as victim."[46] The analysis of the problem, neatly condensed in a name, tells the public what emotions to feel toward each of the characters in the drunk-driving drama. Injustice frames and other moments in the unfolding of protest are pushed along by the emotions they crystallize.

ONTOLOGICAL SECURITY AND RISK AVERSION

Sensations of a pleasurable nature have nothing inherently compelling about them, whereas unpleasurable ones have it in the highest degree. The latter impel towards change, towards discharge, and that is why we interpret unpleasure as implying a heightening and pleasure as a lowering of energetic cathexis.

—Sigmund Freud

Human fears are complex and poorly understood, but there are a lot of them. Only a careful study of culture and biography could help us predict exactly what groups and individuals would feel threatened by. I suspect that significant changes in one's daily routines, unless they are small and predictable, tend to be unsettling. I even think that this is something close to a universal psychological dynamic. But any change in the environment requires considerable cultural interpretation to be framed as a threat.

Technological fears have been most thoroughly studied. Risk analysis arose in the late 1970s partly to explain why so many local populations opposed new technologies that were to be sited near them, especially nuclear power plants. Through many experiments and surveys of the public, it was found that "lay" estimates about the probabilities of hazards differed from expert ("correct") estimates, and that even when given proper information, the public tended to misuse it. Assessments were biased by people's concentration on prominent, visible examples, especially those covered in the news media; different ways of expressing fatality rates influenced estimates; respondents ignored sample size and were influenced by irrelevant information, such as the wording of questions. Risk experts concluded that the public was both ignorant and irrational.[47]

Yet the more candid researchers realized that these pessimistic findings showed the limits of the tests as much as the irrationality of the test-takers. Tests "need to request knowledge in a form that is compatible with people's customary way of thinking about the topic. To acquit themselves properly in an interview, people must be able to express what they know."[48] While risk experts reduced all hazards to the resulting fatality rates, in order to compare them easily, the public seemed to care more about the potential for destroying an entire community, a way of life. They disliked technologies they perceived to have catastrophic potential, even if this were only a remote chance. They were also more willing to accept risks that were controllable, justly distributed, voluntary, and did not affect future generations.[49] Fairness and predictability mattered most. How people felt about risks was what mattered most to them, not the precise calculation of expected costs and benefits. Culture, including emotions, affected people's preferences.

In the right circumstances, almost anything can be perceived as a threat by someone. Responses to various threats, whether natural, technological or human, may involve similar emotions. Drawing on Alfred Schutz's discussion of the way we commonsensically take the world around us for granted, Anthony Giddens has argued that individual psychological needs and sustained social interaction require "ontological security," defined as "confidence or trust that the natural and social worlds are as they appear to be."[50] Ordinary daily life depends, he argues, on "an *ontological security* expressing an *autonomy of bodily control* within *predictable routines*."[51] Part of this security involves the confidence that the physical environment will not change quickly and unpredictably. The environment may be harmful or threatening, but we know what to expect from it under normal circumstances. Humans will act, when possible, to prevent changes in the environment that could remove this ontological security. This is the reason they are especially opposed to involuntary, uncontrollable, or unknown risks.

The importance of ontological security becomes clear when it is removed. Ethnomethodologists have shown that breaking the presuppositions of the social environment both frustrates people and outrages their sense of justice; even the most seemingly cognitive challenges arouse passionate emotions. Similarly, studies of disasters have shown that destroying physical sources of ontological security—that is, the physical environment—can be devastating if social ties are not strong enough to compensate. Kai Erikson's study of the Buffalo Creek flood victims showed the emotional problems and destruction of social ties—both individual and collective traumas—that resulted from the physical world's turning against them. They "have clearly lost much of their confidence in the workings of nature," partly because death came directly into their homes, tainting the rooms and belongings that were "a part of one's personal world, the natural setting for one's life."[52] The flood victims exhibited "a feeling that one has lost a certain natural immunity to misfortune, a growing conviction, even, that the world is no longer a safe place to be."[53] Their sense of community had been tied up with their physical surroundings, and they no longer had a safe place called home. It is easy to see why so many people fear the possibility of losing these things, even when that possibility is statistically small. Just imagining the catastrophe is enough for it to scare them.[54]

We process different threats in different ways, and Kai Erikson believes there is something especially unsettling about the threat of radiation. The senses cannot grasp it or define it, for it cannot be smelled, heard, or seen. Because of its stealth it could be anywhere at any time. There is no clear end to it, as it works its way into one's body and genes, with unknown future effects. The malevolent forces at work in the universe seem even bigger, more omnipresent, than those feared by flood survivors. Victims feel tainted forever, deep inside themselves. Dread is the emotion inspired by such threats.[55] When radiation can be blamed on human actions, strong indignation usually results.

Evidence from economics hints at a partial tendency to reject changes in the status quo. Some studies have found that people tend to be "risk averse," placing a higher value on situations and utilities that they already have than on gambles which should—with some known probability—yield even better situations. Imagine yourself on an airplane ready to take flight. You're offered a good deal to disembark and wait for a later flight, but refuse. If you were off the plane and had to bid to get a seat on it, you would probably bid much less than you just refused for giving up your seat: you value what you already have and would pay far less for an identical "good" (the seat) if you didn't already possess it. Economists' examples often have a remote, fairy-tale quality, but they get at a truth: We feel entitled to what we have and value it simply because we have it.[56]

There may be an almost universal psychological propensity to dislike prominent changes in one's way of life, unless those changes provide clear benefits. From factory mechanization to nuclear power plants, there has been resistance when distant, impersonal bureaucracies, whom we do not trust, attempt to impose changes on us. Resistance does not arise only from concern with fatality rates, as risk analysts assumed it should, but from affective attachments to places and routines summed up in the concept of home. Much of our ontological security depends on the routines, material possessions, and family members that center around a stable place where we go regularly, especially to sleep. Home is supposed to protect us from threats, so threats to the home are especially unnerving. Not all opposition focuses on possible disasters—like industrial accidents—that are vividly imagined. It often comes instead from the uncertainty of changes, and the possibility of drastic changes in established patterns of interaction. Change itself may threaten our ontological security, whatever the eventual outcomes of the change. There is a horror of the unknown. The future becomes unimaginable, in the sense of unthinkable and in the sense of simply unknown. This kind of dread can motivate local opposition. It is not easily put into a cost-benefit calculation, but it is a reasonable response.[57]

Even small adverse changes can trigger protest. When the University of California decided to enforce an old rule barring the distribution of literature on a small strip of sidewalk where students had grown accustomed to handing out materials, it quickly had the Berkeley Free Speech Movement on its hands.[58] Seemingly trivial and innocuous decisions can take on enormous symbolic weight, as clever activists work them into moral shocks. The symbolic force of an event or individual can never be predicted from its literal effect—the mistake often made by process theorists in analyzing opportunities.

I believe that some sense of threat can be found in the origins of most social movements. This claim, put strongly for polemical purposes, contrasts with reigning images of collective action. In one of his formulations, Charles Tilly argues that collective action has shifted, in recent centuries, from reactive actions based on defense of local rights and communities (rich, cultural, communitarian protest) to proactive projects based on the systematic search for new opportunities for advancement of group position and interests. Bureaucratic trade unions and interest groups systematically look for opportunities. To Tilly, defensive responses to threat are more "emotional" and probably—in today's bureaucratic world—less effective. If the goal of protest is the control of resources, this is no doubt true. But if the goal is psychological security and the assertion of basic worldviews, it may not be. The powerful emotions triggered by threat can be quite effective.[59]

Tilly himself admits that "a given amount of threat tends to generate more collective action than the 'same' amount of opportunity." People tend to "inflate the value of those things they already possess," presumably due to emotional attachments. In addition, according to Tilly, threats are more generalizable. If one interest is threatened, it is easy to imagine that others will be as well. Such predictions only hint at the rich psychological dynamics underlying them.[60]

Progress has been one of the central tropes of the modern world, suggesting ceaseless change for the better. Tilly's groups in proactive pursuit of their interests fit well with this rallying cry. Eternal change has set the agenda of most of our large bureaucracies, both public and private. Yet during the entire two centuries when this ideology of progress has seemed ascendant, protest movements have regularly challenged it. In the last thirty years post-industrial movements have explicitly criticized the idea. In the nineteenth century, workers' movements did so implicitly. With sociologists' rediscovery of moral communities has come research on lower-middle-class and working-class resistance to change. Christopher Lasch wrote a long book celebrating a tradition of limits, in opposition to unending progress; he associates this critique of progress with today's working and lower middle classes.[61]

In the injustice frame described by Gamson and others, the passion for justice is fueled by anger over existing injustice. Turner and Killian say that "The common element in the norms of most, and probably all, movements is the conviction that existing conditions are unjust."[62] Since protest is aimed at what one dislikes, negative emotions have a prominent role, even though they seem furthest from the rational calculations envisioned by the rationalists and others. Jürgen Habermas sees this power of negativism when he argues that many recent social movements arise from the threatened "colonization" of private life by formal organizations.[63] Negative emotions, as Freud saw, are powerful ones. The complex interplay of threat and blame has an enormous emotional component.

Finally, part of ontological security involves what might be termed *dignity,* a serenity and pride that come from confidence in one's place, whether that place is one's social role or physical surroundings. Floods and nuclear accidents destroy that confidence in obvious ways. Economic deprivation can also threaten dignity through sudden changes in daily lifestyle. But dignity can also be disrupted by stigmatized identities, including geographical identities. Are we the kind of people who have a toxic waste dump next door? The kind who will accept public housing that no other neighborhood wants? Will others think us stupid if we support a proposed incinerator? Identities can be threatened with the stigma of all sorts of proposals and facilities.

Many phenomena that scholars point to as crucial in the emergence of a protest movement—injustice frames, cognitive liberation, suddenly imposed grievances, framing—are meant to sound austerely cognitive, but in fact they are fairly dripping with emotions. Grievances sound like some sort of straightforward objective information, but they are only grievances because they upset or outrage people. Injustice frames, like other collective action frames, depend for their force on the emotions they arouse. Likewise the term *cognitive liberation* overlooks the many noncognitive processes in liberating one's vision, including some that have little to do with a careful assessment of the chances of success. If we are not careful, labels can distort what we are seeing.

THE PUSH OF EMOTIONS

Pick up any rich case study of a protest movement, and it will be full of words like *anger, outrage, pride, frustration, joy,* and *fear.* Look in the index, and there will be no entry for *emotion,* or for individual emotions. Nor will there be any discussion of these emotions in the conclusions, the hypotheses, or theoretical chapters. Emotions are there, but we don't think about them. Their very ubiquity may render them invisible, like the air we breath.

Emotions give ideas, ideologies, identities, and even interests their power to motivate. Just as they must respond to cognitive grids and moral visions, movement organizers and participants appeal to and build upon pre-existing affects and emotional responses such as fear, outrage, even love. In their desire to demonstrate the rationality of protest movements, recent researchers seem to have concluded— wrongly—that emotions were inevitably irrational and should be minimized in their models. Emotional dynamics, like morality and cognition, are ubiquitous in social life, and hardly render action irrational.

Many protestors are themselves reluctant to admit the power of emotions, following researchers and the broader society in denigrating emotions as the opposite of rationality. They insist that they are responding to objective conditions in the most logical fashion, drawing conclusions about what must be done. A peace activist in the early 1980s criticizes another group for its emotionality: "I quit the Mobe because their strategy is based on moral outrage. . . . They're just motivated by their anger at the system. And I mean that's justified. I'm angry, too. But I was drawn to the Freeze and remain here because we are motivated by . . . logic and common sense."[64] This person, although admitting that emotions such as outrage draw people into a movement, draws a false dichotomy by then insisting that protestors must transcend their emotions and arrive in the realm of cognition.

Threat and blame—which thoroughly fuse emotion, morals, and cognition—are two crucial building blocks of protest. Different kinds of threats may be surprisingly similar in how they undermine ontological security, but they allow different formulations of blame. We'll see in chapter 12, for instance, that a more universalistic rhetoric can be built against environmental threats than social ones. Responsibility is itself a complex construction, varying in specificity. It is also divisible into causal and remedial forms, and blame is more powerful when the same institutions are responsible in both ways.

Changes in a person's physical surroundings are only one kind of threat that can spur protest. Most of the cases I've examined were responses to proposals for the future, containing uncertainty about what their effects would be: either the effects were genuinely unknown, or there was some probability of an unintended consequence such as an accident. They are *prospective* threats. Fear and hope are emotions that have this forward-looking quality because of the attendant uncertainty. Most emotions, though, are feelings about known situations: amazement, indignation, anger, disgust.[65] Anger that the government has allowed a proposal for a nuclear plant differs from the fears of what the plant will be like. Most threats are of this known kind, and they have been extremely common in the history of protest. Cuts in wages threatened workers' lifestyles and commonly led to strikes in the nineteenth century (when wage cuts were common). Part of the urgency of the civil rights movement came from the fact that young black men were still being killed in the South, and the NAACP was being outlawed in many southern states. There can even be threats to one's sense of moral order, as when others are allowed to get away with flagrant activities that one considers immoral.

So, even though I have primarily used prospective threats from one's environment as a way to discuss the emotional dynamics of protest, there are other sources of powerful shocks and emotions. Explicit moral systems, whether a belief in equal rights, faith in religion, or adherence to professional norms, can generate outrage when violated. For protest to arise, both the moral rules and their violation must be defined as such, and the threat must still lead to blame. In the following chapter I examine the case of "whistleblowers," whose moral rules (usually derived from their professional training) were violated by their employers. Their protest usually began with individual actions, but in many cases they ultimately joined or encouraged organized movements. Like those in this chapter expected to live next to hazards, these individuals were going about their normal lives when something was asked of them that shocked them. They were shocked not only by being asked to ignore their principles but by their treatment when they refused. The example of whistleblowing highlights the moral dimension of protest.

- All social life is riddled with emotions, from simple positive or negative affects to complex constructions such as compassion or indignation. We can distinguish ongoing affective loyalties from more immediate emotional responses to events and information.

- Emotions cannot be separated from cognitive beliefs or moral values; they by no means render action irrational.

- Moral shocks occur when an event or piece of information so upsets someone that she becomes open to the possibility of protest, sometimes even in the absence of active recruitment.
- Attachment to place, grounded partly in the need for ontological security, is a widespread example of an affect that can motivate protest.
- Much protest—more than has been recognized—has at its core a sense of threat, a key component of moral shocks.
- Ostensibly cognitive concepts such as suddenly imposed grievances, cognitive liberation, frame alignment, and injustice frames are infused with emotions, especially negative ones such as fear, threat, and outrage.

SIX

Whistleblowers: Moral Principles in Action

Good men must not obey the laws too well.
— Ralph Waldo Emerson

It's very simple when you get right down to it. You either do what's right or
you do what's wrong. It's black and white. It's very cut and dry. . . . It was a
very personal thing. My conscience told me that it was wrong. You either
believe in your morals or you don't have them. You have a certain faith or
you act on self-interest.
— Bert Berube, whistleblower[1]

From Clayton Street in the upper Haight district, the dark wood of
John Gofman's home is barely visible through the wisteria. Inside, the
shadowy interior contrasts with the brilliant light shining in through
the numerous windows, which frame cascades of pink roses and rich
green foliage and, beyond them, the pastel hills of San Francisco. The
home, its garden, and two decks are spiced with mischievous, whimsi-
cal sculptures—some gargoyles, others dragons—created by Gofman's
sister-in-law. Gofman and his wife have lived in this fairy-tale house
for fifty years.

"I love science," says John Gofman. "It's an extremely worthwhile
method, and I am very hard-nosed about data. You must have confidence in your tools, and science provides some very powerful tools."
Confidence in science allowed Gofman to tell some very powerful
people and institutions in America to go to hell. His data and his tools
provided him with a strong sense of truth that enabled him to resist
pressures from "interests" he felt were distorting and suppressing the
truth. Stubborn, passionate allegiance to his moral principles led him
from a career in science to a career in protest.[2]

With degrees in both medicine and chemistry, Gofman had a long
and distinguished career in science. He helped Glenn Seaborg isolate
plutonium, and he helped discover several other radioactive elements
in the mid-1940s. He refused an invitation to move to Los Alamos during the Manhattan Project because his wife was in medical school in
San Francisco and because he felt that the project's most interesting
scientific work had already been completed. On the faculty at the University of California at Berkeley during the 1950s, he worked on the

relationship between heart disease, cholesterol, and lipoproteins—two decades before the cholesterol panic. As he puts it, "[M]y ability is to look at data and to analyze them, to see patterns. I'm lucky to have been able to do this all my life." Even in periods when he had extensive administrative duties, Gofman tried to work part of each day in his laboratory.

At the end of the 1950s, with pathbreaking work on heart disease done, Gofman's interests shifted to the effects on human health of very small amounts of hazardous elements. In 1962 he cut his teaching by 90 percent and went to set up a lab at the Atomic Energy Commission's new, expanding Lawrence Livermore Laboratory forty miles east of San Francisco. Because he did not trust the AEC to let science run its course without interference, his decision was difficult. A staff of 150 (including 35 scientists) and a budget of three million dollars were less important than assurances from the director of the laboratory that "[i]f they [the AEC] try to prevent you from telling the truth about what you find about radiation, we'll back you and the Regents [of the University of California, which operated the lab for the AEC] will back you, and they'll just have to eat it."[3]

The AEC, Gofman knew, was less interested in the scientific truth about the effects of radiation than in deflecting public criticism, intense because of discoveries then being made about the radiation released during earlier atomic testing. Gofman's own instincts were that this was a serious problem, but at the time he also believed that "you don't interfere with scientific and technological progress unless you have firm evidence; you give them the benefit of the doubt"—a belief which, to say the least, he no longer defends.

Several incidents confirmed Gofman's suspicions about the AEC's intentions, even though his mentor, Glenn Seaborg, now head of the AEC, assured him that "all we want is the truth." Within weeks of setting up his lab at Livermore, Gofman was called to Washington, where he and several others from AEC labs around the country were expected to dissuade a staff scientist from publishing his findings that Utah residents had received radiation doses from bomb tests one hundred times greater than previously announced. Gofman and the others refused, and the man published his results. Alas, Gofman reports, there was little uproar when he did.

Three years later, in 1965, Gofman was asked to evaluate the AEC's Project Plowshares, a giddy proposal to use atomic bombs for civilian construction projects such as a new Panama Canal. When Gofman concluded that this would be "biological insanity," his division at Livermore gained the nickname "the enemy within." The project was abandoned, not because of Gofman's calculations but because of nuclear treaty negotiations that made it awkward for the United States to encourage the proliferation of atomic bombs around the world. The reaction to Gofman's Plowshares report was some grumbling, but no retaliation.

The AEC's response was different with the low-level dose controversy of 1969. That year, *Esquire* published an article titled "The Death of All Children," based on estimates from a physicist named Ernest Sternglass that as many as four hundred thousand American children had died from radiation released during atomic testing. The AEC asked several of the laboratories it supported to refute Sternglass's claims, and Gofman asked a former student and now colleague to evaluate the work. Arthur Tamplin concluded that Sternglass had misread a curve; he thought the figure was around 4,000, not 400,000. Colleagues at Livermore were delighted with Tamplin's refutation, but the AEC disliked his alternative estimate of 4,000 deaths. Officials suggested that he publish his critique of Sternglass in a popular magazine, and his own fatality estimate in a journal for specialists. Gofman and Tamplin refused, and Tamplin published both in the *Bulletin of the Atomic Scientists.*

Gofman and Tamplin began compiling data on people who had had low doses of radiation, curious about whether they were dying at younger ages than they should. They began to question the AEC's claim of a "safe threshold" dose, below which radiation would not affect human health. The two scientists calculated the number of deaths they believed would result each year if all Americans received the maximum "safe dose:" they came up with 16,000 fatalities (which they later raised to 32,000). At this point, the AEC began trying to suppress Tamplin's findings. Rumors were spread that Gofman's and Tamplin's work was incompetent, and Gofman was referred to as an "ex-scientist"—clearly the two slurs that annoy Gofman most even today. The AEC requested that Tamplin get approval for all professional papers he presented; without it he would have to pay his own way to meetings and could not use a Livermore secretary to type his papers. In January 1970 it removed twelve of his thirteen staff members. Two years later, the Commission removed Gofman's funding, and, now notorious, he was unable to get support from other federal agencies. In 1975, at the age of 55, he took early retirement from the University of California. Although he has slowed down somewhat, and no longer has a laboratory, Gofman has had an active "retirement," continuing to write and lecture about the effects of radiation and founding an antinuclear group, the Committee for Nuclear Responsibility.

Because data are scarce, estimating the effects of low levels of radiation exposure is heavily affected by the assumptions one begins with. The best data for this work come from Japanese survivors of Hiroshima and Nagasaki, and children from 1945 are today just in their fifties and sixties. Only now are data becoming available that could show whether they are dying at younger ages than other Japanese of their generation. Gofman and Tamplin argue that cancer cases are roughly proportional to the amount of exposure, that there is no safe threshold. The nuclear establishment believes the opposite. But because the evidence is not conclusive, Gofman is right that no safe threshold has been established.

Gofman continues to believe in science, even as an antinuclear strategy. Although he has spoken to antinuclear groups, he derides some of their tactics: "I wouldn't spend five minutes of my life at an NRC hearing: it's a kangaroo court, and is designed to be just that." Antinuclear groups should put more resources into supporting staff scientists who could argue against nuclear energy on scientific grounds, because, otherwise, "you can scare people, and that's all." The groups must do good science, however: "If antinuclear people produce lousy work, they're going to get a lousy review from me." He mentions one prominent group that decided not to use Gofman's evidence because they had no staffers who could understand it, and he says that many environmental and antinuclear groups were not interested in receiving a free copy of his latest—highly technical—book.

Gofman proudly claims that there has never been a scientific rebuttal of his work on radiation. The problem with science is not its methods, but "bad scientific faith." Those who conduct science often have conflicts of interest, thus following motives other than pursuit of the truth. He is, he admits, "a linear thinker, with faith in rational science, logic, and reasoning. For a given problem, there is an answer, call it M. It exists, and it's not going to change tomorrow." Long experience has confirmed this faith: "I've stuck my neck out again and again based on my reading of the data, and I've usually been right."

According to his critics, Gofman's indignation over his treatment by the AEC settled into a strident self-righteousness. Confident in his scientific findings, he had little patience for those who refused to accept the facts as he saw them. He told *Newsweek*, "The statement that there's some number that's safe is an absolute, unmitigated lie." In response to one critic, he said, "I am really inclined to tell you how idiotic you truly must be to write the brash, insulting letter you have written." And of the AEC: "There is no morality, and there is not a shred of honesty in any one of them."[4] The same faith in science that sustained his dissent gave Gofman the rhetorical style of an Old Testament prophet, crying alone in the wilderness. His protest relied on a powerful blend of emotions (from pride in his science to outrage over the AEC), well-articulated moral principles, and cognitive beliefs (scientific findings and observations about bureaucracy).

Gofman is quick to contrast the search for scientific understanding with the confidence of engineers who believe they already have the answers. He recounts a conversation with one who insisted that engineers could build facilities to process plutonium that would lose only one part in a million, in ten million, or in a billion—whatever was necessary. Nonsense, thought Gofman: "That's the arrogance of engineers—they think they can do anything." In contrast, Gofman insists that he could change his mind in the face of new data, that science must always be critical, questioning, and open to empirical tests.

Here is a man sustained by a clear moral vision, a belief in a set of rules: those of scientific method. Professional ethics can often take on the status of a moral absolute. This faith, along with a personality suspicious of bureaucratic authority, helped Gofman stand up to continual pressures from the AEC. The moral shock he felt when the AEC violated, and asked him to violate, his deepest moral principles generated deep emotions that have not subsided after twenty-five years. Gofman came to protest against nuclear energy and, by virtue of his expertise and moral authority, helped inspire the national movement that formed in the early 1970s. To become a dissenter and then a protestor, an employee needs a strong system of beliefs to say no to the daily routines, to question the normal rules of the game, to stand up to the formidable powers and likely retaliation of employers. Nonetheless, this happens frequently.

MORAL PRINCIPLES

In daily life we are sometimes asked to do things we consider wrong. When we are asked by our boss, backed by a large corporation or government agency, most of us, most of the time, comply. The inertia of our daily routines prevents us from stopping and thinking about what we are asked to do, and fear of retaliation prevents us from acting on our scruples when we do stop and think. Occasionally, however, people do say no, just as John Gofman refused to pervert science despite the wishes of the AEC. These "ethical resisters" (or "whistleblowers," once they take their dissent public) undertake striking acts of individual protest—perhaps the most distinctive form of individual protest we shall examine. In addition many of them go on to provide important energy and inspiration to organized protest movements, often ending up activists themselves. Like the local NIMBY protestors we saw in the last chapter, these employees and former employees feel betrayed by authority. Being asked to do something which, according to their moral principles, is wrong operates as an important moral shock. For some, it is an opportunity to articulate and reaffirm those principles.[5]

Morality is that dimension of culture which draws implications for judgment and action from the emotions and cognitive understandings that people hold. How one pictures the world and how one should act in it are separable only in the "value-free" ideologies of social scientists. If you perceive embryos as "unborn babies," similar to normal humans in the shape of their appendages, awareness of surroundings, and fingerprints, you are likely to condemn abortion as murder. Concrete social practices and beliefs almost inevitably take on emotional and moral weight; you are morally outraged, not merely baffled, by threats to your understandings, as Harold Garfinkel showed in his experiments nearly forty years ago. When their commonsense assumptions about appropriate behavior were violated, the subjects of Garfinkel's experiments responded with "astonishment, bewilderment, shock, anxiety, embarrassment, and anger."[6] Ontological security is cognitive, emotional, but also moral. Protest is pre-eminently about moral vision, for participants make claims about how the world should be, but is not. Often, protest helps the participant realize how the world is and how it should be.

In the modern world, our moral visions often consist of blueprints—utopias—for how a good society would be laid out: what distribution of work and rewards there would be, which kinds of activities would be favored or discouraged, what patterns of decision making would exist. Most moral visions also contain (at least implicit) images of the good life for individuals. These were more prominent in the moral philosophies of ancient Greece and Rome, which saw the good society as that which provided opportunities for good lives. Today we focus more on plans for possible societies, since we have large intellectual and professional strata with the skills and impulses to work out the details. But protest movements give individuals things to do: activities they build into their lives and which add meaning to those lives. At the very least, protest itself becomes part of a good life. The good society and the good life are often rejoined in protestors' moral visions, especially as they develop personal identities as activists.

What kind of satisfaction does morality provide? Not the satisfaction of actually achieving a utopia, but that of striving for one. As Oscar Wilde said, "Any map that does not include the land Utopia is useless." This is the pleasure of setting our own personal conduct on the right course: the intrinsic reward accompanying a life we perceive as moral. In a formulation that could almost define artfulness, Albert Hirschman speaks of this action as a "fusion of (and confusion between) striving and attaining," which in turn rests upon the pleasure of savoring a future event in advance.[7] In morality and art, the striving is partly the goal. Criticizing rationalists, Amitai Etzioni argues that actions based on moral commitments differ fundamentally from those in pursuit of other pleasures. Moral acts, he says, "reflect an imperative, a generalization, and a symmetry when applied to others, and are motivated intrinsically." Morals reflect long-standing commitments and usually persevere under changing circumstances. When our morals conflict with more immediate pleasures, we do not always choose the former, but when we do we experience a deeper, distinct satisfaction.[8]

Less directly, doing the right thing is a way of communicating, to ourselves as well as others, what kind of people we are. To the rationalist, reputation can be a purely instrumental asset that enables us to get what we want. In a less cynical vision, my personal identity is something I craft over time, by making choices large and small. I identify, in varying degrees or styles, with one or more collectivities or sets of principles, and act in ways that display this identification. My sense of personal identity then influences my future choices. Individual biography is important as the accumulation of bits of the surrounding culture and the memory of my own past choices and behaviors. Group memberships typically reinforce these identities. Religious principles are easier to follow if others respond with praise, or if violators are chastised. Professional ethics are harder to forget when they are written down, promulgated, discussed, and taught in courses. Every form of identity—individual, collective, even movement identity—carries certain moral obligations. Indeed, identity is pre-eminently moral. As Charles Taylor puts it, "To know who you are is to be oriented in moral space, a space in which questions arise about what is good or bad, what is worth doing and what not, what has meaning and importance for you and what is trivial and secondary."[9] Identity is never a purely cognitive boundary.

But most protest involves, not necessarily *doing* the right thing, but *saying* what the right thing is. This kind of moral testimony is itself an important practice. One probes one's own psyche and orders one's beliefs and feelings; one articulates the most important ones. One also speaks out alongside others, gaining confidence and enthusiasm from being part of a group. But one also speaks for others, and hopes to encourage them to articulate their own visions. One tries on certain formulations, hoping they will inspire. One offers new language for describing the world, and for acting in it.

Simply put, this chapter is meant to demonstrate that *normal people have moral principles which may open them to the possibility of individual and collective protest under the right (and partly predictable) circumstances.* Like the other components of their cultural systems, morals make people more likely to engage in certain actions. These moral rules are likely to be explicit, so that the dissenter knows when they have been violated and gains confidence from being able to say why something is wrong. Whistleblowing is especially likely to issue in individual acts of protest. Although it is only one example of action based on moral principles, it is an important one for post-industrial movements questioning science, technology, and experts. Many basic moral principles could, if violated, provide a similar moral shock and make someone available for protest. The more explicit those principles are, the more likely an individual is to protest alone; shocks against implicit principles, in contrast, probably require activists to articulate the violation and draw the victims into organized protest.

WHISTLEBLOWERS

When ethical resisters, who have criticized something in their organization, go *public* with their grievances, they become whistleblowers—commonly defined as employees who publicly expose what they consider wrongful practices in their organizations. The rules whistleblowers feel are being broken may be professional (in Gofman's case, scientific progress was being blocked by the suppression of findings), legal (laws are being broken; regulators are being misled), or directly ethical (for example, laboratory animals are being abused; public health is being threatened). In each case the rules have a moral basis. These ethical resisters usually try to correct the situation through internal procedures but, thwarted in their efforts, decide to go public with their knowledge. Their first public statement of their indignation radically transforms their resistance—and often their careers.

The root cause of such dissent is that two sets of rules and expectations, each possibly reasonable on its own, clash. The violation of professional standards is the most common cause of whistleblowing—the result of an almost universal tension between professional judgment and autonomy on the one hand and the needs of large organizations for control and profitability on the other.[10] Sometimes, when the clash is over basic values, "infiltrators," who have moral objections to begin with, join organizations in order to bring suspected abuses to light. Although rare, infiltrators appeared, for example, in the animal rights movement, whose members occasionally took jobs in laboratories to document the conditions of experimental animals.

If dissent first arises out of a clash of rules or expectations, it evolves into whistleblowing through an interaction between individual and workplace characteristics. Scholars have found that employees are more likely to go public with damaging information if they "are committed to the formal goals of their organization or to the successful completion of their project; identify with the organization; and have a strong sense of professional responsibility."[11] In other words, they are *more* committed to the rules than others. Interestingly, loners and other "prickly personalities" appear more likely to withstand the workgroup pressures for conformity that work against whistleblowing—another reason to attend to the biographical dimension of protest. Personalities, as we'll discuss in chapter 9, matter.[12]

Workplaces likely to foster whistleblowing tend to have indirect and complex lines of communication and authority, lack structures designed to accommodate technical dissent, and discourage the expression of doubts by employees. The corporate drive for profit maximization encourages the suppression of dissent that could lead to costly corrective measures; strict timetables and internal competition embedded in the organizational structure give managers and co-workers a stake in silencing dissent. Public protest follows when private protest is thwarted.[13]

Internal dissent can have many motivations, but taking it public is inevitably an act of denunciation of the wrongdoing. Even when done in anger or hurt, it is a consummate moral act of individual protest.

Whistleblowers normally point out discrepancies between the legitimating rhetoric of an organization and an organization's actual behavior—a powerful point for any protestor to make. In diverse modern societies, where disagreements over basic values are common, critics can say few things about an organization that everyone would agree are damning. Catching it in a lie is one. And contradictions between what an organization says and what it does are usually felt to be a kind of lie. This is the specialty of the whistleblower.

Whistleblowers are uniquely credible as witnesses. Organizations have more resources than individuals have to promote their version of reality, yet they are so patently self-interested that most audiences are skeptical of their arguments. In criticizing their employers, whistleblowers have considerable credibility because they are not promoting their own organization's interests. Their stories can be quite powerful, playing on common cultural themes such as the conflict between an honest individual and a corrupt corporation, their efforts to practice their time-honored craft without interference, or the danger of scientific expertise subverted to ignoble ends. The public understands these rhetorical tropes, and readily discerns heroes and villains.

Whistleblowing sometimes leads to changes within a firm or agency. In a survey of eighty-seven whistleblowers, Karen and Donald Soeken found that 20 percent reported positive changes as a result of their actions. "Many of the 20% cited personnel changes: complete management change, personnel practices corrected, persons transferred or replaced or not reappointed, department restructured. Others cited changes in policy, indictments, improved safety, or official investigations by the FBI or NRC." [14] In a few cases, whistleblowing has created public awareness of a social problem, spawning and influencing a public debate over a technology, practice, or industry, or encouraging new regulations and policies. Whistleblowers are a key source of testimony about potential hazards to the public, faulty construction and installation, concealment of risks known to developers, or corruption and payoffs.

If whistleblowers help society by publicizing important and suppressed information, their employers rarely see it that way. The main response to whistleblowing is retaliation, as employers are indignant at these "enemies within." Time after time, whistleblowers are harassed, transferred, and fired. In one case, Alyeska, the company operating the Trans-Alaska pipeline, hired private investigators to search garbage and phone records to identify employees giving tips to outsiders; one of them was fired. [15] Character assassination is another common tactic; the dissenter and her personality—rather than her complaint—become the issue. In New York City, when a teacher complained publicly of corruption in the local school board, her opponents circulated old photos of her in the nude. [16] Of the Soekens' eighty-seven whistleblowers, all but one had experienced some form of retaliation, the most common being harassment from superiors, closer monitoring of their activities, removal of job responsibilities, loss of job, and harassment by peers (each of these was experienced by more than half of their respondents). [17] Retaliation only seems to harden the resolve of dissenters and—when it takes the form of layoffs and blackballing—frees them to pursue their vision of the truth. Their moral visions can withstand terrible attacks. [18]

Whistleblowing is a moral act par excellence. In their extensive study of whistleblowers, Myron and Penina Glazer make this clear: "Only those employees who have a highly developed alternative belief sys-

Table 6.1   Moral Aspirations and Expectations Capable of Being Shocked

Type	Examples
Professional ethics	Expectation of being able to do one's craft well, for example, engineers' expectations that they will be allowed to build safe structures; employees' expectations of following the rules of their firm.
Religious beliefs	Believers' expectations that they will not be forced to disobey principles of their religion.
Community allegiances	Community members' desire not to hurt or threaten their fellow community members or the community's physical setting; citizens' expectations of obeying the law.
Ontological security	Assumption that one's physical surroundings are safe, stable, and trustworthy.
Economic security	Expectation of being able to support and protect one's family.
Political ideologies	Politically based beliefs in right and wrong acts, institutions, and practices, combined with the hope of living out these beliefs.

tem can withstand the intense pressure to conform to the requirements of management."[19] They found three kinds of moral systems that gave whistleblowers this kind of strength. The most common was professional training. Another was religious faith. The third, especially important among blue-collar and clerical workers, was a strong solidarity with one's community, reinforcing concerns about the health and safety of other residents. Strong moral beliefs, of course, still had to be combined with equally strong emotions and, often, personality traits like Gofman's pride and stubbornness. To these three systems we might add political ideologies and the expectations of ontological security discussed in chapter 5. These moral aspirations and expectations appear in table 6.1.

Blowing the whistle is often a life passage in which the dissenter must articulate her moral suppositions and decide what costs she will accept to uphold them. The retaliation and publicity often launch ethical resisters on new career trajectories, in which they spend most of their time pursuing their charges and defending themselves. In many cases dissenters are fired and must actually begin new careers, as Gofman did. Although some whistleblowers can now collect rewards for uncovering fraud against the federal government, most suffer greatly for their actions. When people act so contrary to their material self-interest, we especially need to seek a moral and emotional logic in what they do.

At the beginning, an ethical dissenter often thinks she is acting in the best interests of her firm, which she naively expects to welcome her revelation of errors. She often feels that her boss is mistaken, but that her boss's boss will set things right. When her employer's response is denial and retaliation, she begins to see the wrongdoing as a systematic, common practice, and then starts to criticize the company itself. Even so, a whistleblower may continue to believe that her company is a bad apple in an otherwise sound industry. Yet some are radicalized by their experiences, seeing the problems as endemic to the technology or industry. For them, protest groups become attractive allies.

Among typical whistleblowers, some are more likely than others to perceive the problem they complain of as systemic. Those who have had disappointing experiences with regulators, whom they often approach first, are likely to see the official "solution" to the problem as part of the problem itself. Malcolm Spector and John Kitsuse argue that social-problem claims often continue after an official effort has been made to solve the problem, as "assertions about the inadequacy, inefficacy, or injustice of the procedures may themselves become the conditions around which new social problems activities are organized."[20] This response is especially common among whistleblowers, most of whom believe in the ideals of the system and simply ask it to live up to them. Many are surprised at the inadequacies of a regulatory solution to technological problems.

Infiltrators, in contrast to other whistleblowers, are often affiliated with a protest group before they take a job for the purpose of gathering information that can be used against a company, industry, or practice. Whistleblowing, rather than creating a new "career" for them, is only one part of their political activity. They already have activist or movement identities. They are especially likely to be attacked by their employers, who feel betrayed. The information that infiltrators uncover will be taken up directly by protest groups, as intended. Infiltrators can give a big boost to controversies. The photographs Alex Pacheco took and the conditions he documented in the research laboratory where he did volunteer work in 1981 helped to launch his organization (People for the Ethical Treatment of Animals, now the country's largest animal rights group) and the entire animal rights movement in the United States.

Few whistleblowing cases affect the organizations in which they occur, and fewer still affect public policies, but a small number of influential cases have been important in creating and shaping protest movements in technical and other controversies. As insiders and professionals, it does not take many whistleblowers to create a fuss.

ETHICAL RESISTERS AND SOCIAL MOVEMENTS

Some whistleblowers contact a group that is protesting against their employer or industry. Perhaps not at first, since such groups are often highly critical of the organizations and industry where the whistleblowers work, and of the kinds of projects the whistleblowers have spent their lives pursuing. A naval officer who is upset about a particular incident, for example, is unlikely to enjoy the company of pacifists who condemn the military as a way of life. Nuclear whistleblowers may admit that a particular plant is badly constructed but refuse to condemn nuclear energy altogether as a viable source of electricity. Nonetheless their sense of urgency and their need for an ally often prompt whistleblowers to overcome their ideological differences and contact protest groups, since the latter are open to the whistleblowers' critiques. Once a whistleblowing career develops, protestors become natural allies.

Some protest groups are more receptive to whistleblowers than others. Large, national organizations, such as the Union of Concerned Scientists or Friends of the Earth, have more strategic connections and resources—access to the news media, political contacts, financing—to protect a whistleblower, or at least publicize her case. And if a social movement is large enough and persists over time, these national groups may provide employment for a number of knowledgeable ex-insiders now blackballed by their former industries. In addition, a few protest groups house scientific and technical professionals who speak a language of expertise familiar to technical whistleblowers. These organizations know the importance of a whistleblower's information as well as how to use it effectively, and on occasion they may also provide employment. Finally, a few protest groups are geared specifically toward whistleblowers, such as the Government Accountability Project or the Project on Military Procurement. They have political connections and can cope with the special needs of whistleblowers.

Whistleblowers can occasionally change the rhetoric of protest, grounding it more solidly in the detailed facts that whistleblowers know well, building cognitively upon moral outrage or fears about the unknown. Since many whistleblowers are professionals, often engineers, the language they use most comfortably is a precise, technical one. Ethical resisters who work with or for a protest group increase its technical understanding, provide an additional level of rhetoric for its arsenal, and give it more credibility in the eyes of the public—not to mention John Gofman.

Not only do whistleblowers help protest movements, but the reverse occasionally occurs. The vibrant campaign against the Diablo Canyon nuclear power plant, and especially the presence of the Government Accountability Project, encouraged a number of employees to blow the whistle on construction flaws. Protestors' arguments may cause employees to question their own work, as has happened in the military from time to time.

Wars and preparation for wars have always produced ethical resisters, as most wars involve the breaking of moral rules dear to many. Vietnam generated a disproportionate amount of whistleblowing. In 1971 more than one hundred Vietnam Veterans against the War testified publicly about the war crimes they had witnessed, and a few months later Daniel Ellsberg released the Pentagon Papers to the press. A war planner who had helped write this secret history of American involvement in Vietnam, Ellsberg quickly became a prominent figure in the anti-war movement and has remained active in left-liberal causes since. In the last twenty years, hundreds of employees of the CIA, the military, the weapons laboratories, and other segments of the defense establishment have become whistleblowers.[21] Dozens of them have turned to activism, protesting extensively against their former employers. If blowing the whistle on civilian industries makes someone a "traitor" to her former industry, doing that in the military or defense industry is even worse. Whistleblowers often have such unpleasant, radicalizing experiences that joining the peace movement is an obvious choice.[22]

Ethical resisters made their most important and visible contribution, however, to the movement against civilian nuclear energy. John Gofman and Arthur Tamplin were the first in a series of technical and scientific experts who felt compelled to oppose America's nuclear programs. The nuclear case also demonstrates that, even if relatively few whistleblowers contact or become protestors, these men and women can be vital to a protest movement and the surrounding controversy.

Soon after the Gofman and Tamplin incident in 1969, several engineers at the AEC's Oak Ridge laboratory leaked to the Union of Concerned Scientists information indicating that the emergency core cooling systems then in use in nuclear reactors had failed major tests. These results had been suppressed by the AEC in the interest of licensing new plants promptly. The union published this information, prompting the AEC to hold hearings in 1972, at which the same engineers reluctantly testified. These hearings, lasting more than a year, helped form a network of antinuclear intervenors that became the core of the antinuclear movement. Because it was founded and operated by engineers and scientists, technical whistleblowers seemed to feel comfortable approaching the Union of Concerned Scientists with information.[23] Like John Gofman, these men felt that valid scientific and technical findings were being suppressed in the interest of rapid nuclear commercialization.

John Gofman himself helped to organize and inspire antinuclear groups around the country. In 1971 he founded the Committee for Nuclear Responsibility to promote a moratorium on constructing nuclear reactors. He also traveled to innumerable sites of local opposition to proposed reactors. In 1973 he helped inspire the Mothers for Peace—whom we met in the last chapter—to shift their attention from the Vietnam war to the nearby Diablo Canyon nuclear power plant. In May 1979, six weeks after the Three Mile Island nuclear accident, Gofman visited Pennsylvania. Hundreds heard him speak at Franklin and Marshall College in Lancaster (about twenty-five miles from the accident), and according to sociologist Edward Walsh, "This outside expert would become the single most important influence on the . . . goals and strategies" of the Susquehanna Valley Alliance, one of the region's new antinuclear groups.[24]

Several whistleblowers appeared in 1976, just as the antinuclear movement was beginning to capture national headlines with its turn to direct-action tactics. Three engineers resigned from General Electric because they felt the company was producing a reactor with known flaws, likely to result in a major accident. Two other engineers resigned from the Nuclear Regulatory Commission (successor to the AEC) because they felt they were not being allowed to pursue safety issues. Blackballed from the nuclear industry, disillusioned with regulators' responses, the three GE engineers formed their own consulting company, MHB Technical Associates, often selling their services to citizen intervenor groups.[25] One of the NRC engineers found work with the Union of Concerned Scientists. These resignations were widely reported, and the whistleblowers' seniority in their respective organizations made their critiques hard to dismiss.

Several weeks after they resigned, the three former GE engineers (Dale Bridenbaugh, Richard Hubbard, and Gregory Minor) testified before Congress's Joint Committee on Atomic Energy. The hearings were held expressly to examine their reasons for leaving GE and their claims about the risks of nuclear energy. Even though he insisted that his concerns had developed gradually over many years, Bridenbaugh described one event that shocked him enough to cause him to resign:

"[S]omething that proved to me and made it crystal clear to me that there is no way to make the system work, was a meeting in Bethesda, Maryland. . ."[26] Without exactly specifying what happened, Bridenbaugh described this moral shock in a way he hoped would inspire audience sympathy. The implication was that anyone in his position would have come to the same conclusions.

The engineers denied a blanket opposition to nuclear energy, so that their complaints about the current system could have fuller force. Bridenbaugh said, "I think that there is no basic technological fault with the concept of producing electricity by nuclear power. I think, however, in order to make it safe enough you would probably approach a militaristic kind of system" (p. 28). By addressing specific problems, whistleblowers increase the odds of remedial action. Limited claims often seem more plausible, and their solution more feasible. The engineers were presenting themselves as moderates, not ideologues.

The engineers often complained about the curtailment of information. Said Hubbard, "The public was told by the president of GE and their chief executive that he had this 5-foot-long study about nuclear power. If you picked up that quote you would assume that the study said nuclear power was clean, safe, and economic. I think you ought to ask the people in GE what the report really says" (p. 71). Failures of safety equipment, predictions about accidents, and other negative information were being suppressed. Freedom of speech, like honesty, universalism, and moderation, is a powerful theme. The engineers explicitly laid out the moral values that had led them to protest.

One pronuclear Congressman on the Joint Committee, Mike McCormack (D-Washington), attempted to undermine the engineers' credibility by reframing the issue; he referred to their membership in the Creative Initiative Foundation, a religious group: "There have been serious suggestions made about the resignations by these gentlemen, that they have been pressured into these resignations by this religious group to which they belong, that it has been orchestrated for a public relations effect, and that they are being exploited by the political organization that is running the antinuclear petition in California" (p. 42). McCormack said nothing about the engineers' charges, but addressed only their motives and the uses to which their resignations could be put. (Religious beliefs, reinforcing their professional code of ethics, might well have bolstered the engineers' moral confidence and fortitude.) He attempted to make whistleblowing, not nuclear energy, the issue. The act of protest was the problem, and the protestors, McCormack implied, were kooks.

At this point, all three engineers insisted on the immense personal sacrifices they had made in resigning: "You must understand, Senator, that I worked for the General Electric Company for 22 years and had invested my total professional career in this area (p. 30). . . . I received no compensation whatsoever other than the savings and securities that I had built up over that period of time" (p. 43). Other committee members defended the integrity of the engineers at this point, largely referring to their sacrifices as whistleblowers. Said Senator John Tunney (D-California), "I admire the courage of your convictions, and the fact that you were willing to undertake what I consider to be a considerable sacrifice in order to make your views known. I am very convinced by what you have said" (p. 76). Their material and occupational sacrifices gave them high credibility. They were concerned only with truth and morality.

McCormack later tried another means for undermining the engineers' credibility, saying that there was merely a difference of opinions among experts. This would undercut the outrage and indignation (and hence credibility) that whistleblowing and resignations usually carry with them. He said, "What we are dealing with here is the fact that your judgment is a little bit different than the judgment of others. You are saying for this reason it is not safe, but other competent engineers look at the same problem and would say it is safe" (p. 60). Using a trick from the sociology of knowledge, McCormack was saying that their view was no more "objective" than those of their opponents, so why take it seriously?

The engineers responded in several ways. One was to fall back on their own narrow expertise and experience. Said Hubbard: "We have had our hands on the product for most of our lives. So we are not talking about theory. We are talking about what actually is going on" (p. 79). At other times they insisted that other engineers felt the way they did, but did not come forward because there were few mechanisms to encourage or protect them. At this point the engineers accepted the switch to whistleblowing (or good communication) as the issue, away from nuclear safety. But they never relinquished their strong personal identities as engineers, legitimating their claims whenever possible on the basis of their expert knowledge. This is true for almost all professional whistleblowers, for whom an activist identity, if it develops at all, must be grafted onto a personal identity already dominated by the person's profession—the same principles that gave them the strength to blow the whistle in the first place.

We see in these transcripts a struggle over cultural meanings at the most micro-level. What were the engineers' motives? What were the broader implications for nuclear energy? How valid are religious perspectives? Students of social problems have often examined this kind of "claims-making" in the contest over the construction of reality. This is exactly what social movements engage in, but research into protest has usually ignored these activities. The rhetorical repertories used here are culture in action. Even though most of the engineers' testimony was factual, the discussion returned constantly to their motives, for the underlying context was their dramatic moral act of having resigned their jobs. The facts were placed in a moral and emotional context, not a scientific one.

How effective was the engineers' testimony? The resignations boosted the antinuclear movement, as the very fact of disagreement between engineers (which oddly reassured McCormack) disturbed more and more members of the public. Within months the Joint Committee itself, long seen as a promoter of nuclear energy, was disbanded, due to legislators' increasing skepticism about this energy source. Within several years, a handful of Congressional committee chairs were getting political mileage from attacking the industry. Many factors—involving costs, safety, public opposition—undermined the U.S. nuclear industry, but the resignation and testimony of the GE engineers was one of the most visible acts of protest. Their skeptical claims about nuclear energy soon came to be held by a majority of Americans.

In addition to their contributions to the national antinuclear movement, whistleblowers were prominent in several battles over individual nuclear plants. The Government Accountability Project (GAP), formed in 1977 primarily to aid whistleblowers in national security, took on several civilian nuclear plants as projects; it encouraged whistleblowers, protected them in court, and used their disclosures to try to shut or modify the plants. GAP helped to close two nuclear plants under construction. It also gained internal representation on an oversight committee at the Comanche Peak nuclear plant, although this settlement was controversial because it involved an agreement not to litigate before the NRC licensing board.

Whistleblowers greatly strengthened the rhetorical arsenal of the antinuclear movement. As technical experts, they provided credibility, especially for the movement's technical claims that plants were unsafe. After the hearings over the emergency core cooling system in 1972, antinuclear intervenors shifted their focus from environmental issues such as the warming of lakes or the release of small levels of radiation to safety issues such as the threat of catastrophic accidents. Faulty concrete, bad welds, and other slipshod construction practices became major issues in part because of innumerable whistleblowers who raised them at individual plants. Attention shifted to the general competence of the utilities and the nuclear construction industry. Some whistleblowers brought attention to the flaws of particular sites; others, including the three GE engineers, helped focus criticism on generic design issues and long-term health and safety effects.[27] On top of their substantive complaints, the ethical resisters also revealed the willingness of regulators and the nuclear industry to deceive the public and suppress negative information. Without these disclosures, the antinuclear movement would probably not have sustained itself for ten or more years, much less have had the policy influence (albeit indirect) that it did.

TECHNOCRACY'S VICTIMS

Corporations and states often administer the moral shocks that push men and women into protest, sometimes by siting an offensive facility near their homes, sometimes by asking them to carry out repugnant acts. Both local protestors and internal organizational resisters are typically nonpolitical citizens whose outrage changes their lives. Once they feel the adrenaline of political activity, though, many of them remain active. In the usual case, such protestors feel they are obvious victims, and cry out for redress. Their second moral shock comes when the politicians or state agencies to whom they complain ignore them. They believe—justifiably, in most cases—that their government has reneged on its end of the social contract: to protect its citizens from undue and unfair interference. Their outrage at being brushed off by their own representative government is often as great as their original grievances. Good middle-class citizens, in particular, expect government to be on their side. There are times when doing the right thing and obeying the laws, as Emerson said in the chapter epigraph, are not compatible.

Whistleblowers hold a valuable asset: credibility. Because they are speaking out against their own self-interest, facing the threat of retaliation, their audiences usually conclude that they are concerned with truth and justice. I agree. Most whistleblowers are striking examples of people moved to individual protest by moral principles. What they do is very hard, and they come more and more to define it as "the right thing," a label that sustains them through hard times. They are only one example of morally driven protestors, of course, but their moral stance is highlighted by their frequent suffering for it. Suffering has rhetorical power, so that whistleblowers are a boon to protest movements.

Even more than the expert language and evidence they wield, whistleblowers can boost protest movements through what they are: walking tropes, embodiments of a moral tale about brave humans and ruthless organizations. Like the many artists whose best art is their own lives, whistleblowers' own histories are powerful evidence and symbolism. As individuals, they carry moral, emotional, and cognitive messages. This apotheosis often occurs despite their best intentions, as their experiences are transmitted to multiple audiences over whom they have little control. Their pain and courage are nowhere presented as vividly as in their own bodies.

With the explosion of post-industrial protest groups in the past thirty years, many of them explicitly questioning the practices of science and technology, whistleblowers today often have consultants, lawyers, and organizations they can turn to. But few of them know this when they decide to blow the whistle. Their initial acts of protest are often quite isolated. These are brave people, abandoning their comfortable lives (and many know they are doing this) in order to stand up for their moral values. They improvise in deciding what is offensive, as well as in finding forums for telling their stories. They create new moral lives, identities, and careers for themselves. And uniformly, despite the harassment and deprivation, they never regret it.

In an advanced industrial society, with its complex and risky technologies and its extensive, powerful bureaucracies, the whistleblower who points out problems and infractions of rules plays a difficult but important role. Whistleblowers must stand fast against all the power of their superiors and organizations, against the near certainty of retaliation. Even so, their numbers appear to have increased in the last twenty years, for many of the same reasons that NIMBYs have flourished: an explosion of high-tech industries and jobs; greater "post-industrial" suspicion of complex technologies and the corporations responsible for them; a resulting increase in the willingness of news media to cover technical controversies; and supportive protest groups that legitimate and protect whistleblowers. Most NIMBYs and whistleblowers are part of the spreading post-industrial interrogation of industry and technology.

Whistleblowers' importance has grown with their numbers, for they often provide information about risks and corruption that could not be attained in any other way, information that occasionally helps societies protect public health and safety as well as spurring protest.[28] Recognizing their potential importance, federal legislation in 1986 allowed federal whistleblowers to keep a percentage of monies recovered by the government in cases of fraud brought to light by the whistleblowers. The amounts recovered through the program have been growing since then, totaling roughly one billion dollars.[29] Most whistleblowers, though, have nothing but material disincentives. The main satisfaction of whistleblowing still comes from making strong moral statements, from doing the right thing.

Just as I used NIMBYs to highlight the importance of emotions in social movements, I have found whistleblowers a good example of individuals examining and listening to their moral ideals. Because these principles are a most explicit form of culture, in contrast to the implicit expectations of ontological security we saw violated in the last chapter, whistleblowers are rarely confused about what is wrong. We can also see that their moral rules existed prior to their entry into protest; in other words, the causal connection—moral principles contribute to protest—seems clear. Many individuals hold pre-existing moral principles whose violation propels them into protest. What moral systems can be strong enough to inspire individuals to resist? Religious ones, certainly. The movement against military intervention in Central America in the 1980s, for example, was primarily the creation of people applying their religious beliefs to politics.[30] Professional ethics can also inspire protest, as we have seen, for these can be held with an almost religious fervor. Political and ideological beliefs are another source of moral resistance, as is a desire to protect one's community. Many other people, though, have more intuitive moral sentiments that need to be nurtured and articulated by protest organizers before they take action. Either way, moral visions are as important a part of protest as emotions and cognitive beliefs, and are inseparable from them.

Individuals can engage in protest without (or before) joining organized groups. Even mundane and local activities such as complaining and arguing with superiors are an explicit criticism of existing practices, moving beyond silent forms of resistance such as foot dragging, shoddy workmanship, or even sabotage. Whistleblowing is an especially thoughtful form of individual protest, like the self-immolation of a Buddhist monk or the parcels sent by the Unabomber. Sometimes individual actions precede recruitment into more organized protest movements, but not always. By defining such actions as outside their purview and then ignoring them, mobilization and process theorists cannot even ask when these acts do and do not lead individuals into social movements. Citizenship-inspired images of formal organizations arising out of some predefined natural constituency make such individual acts seem unlikely. Post-industrial sympathizers, with large amounts of formal education, are perhaps more likely to have the explicit moral principles and personal or professional confidence to act individually. Without psychological and biographical tools, we cannot hope to understand such actions.

For two chapters we have mostly examined the biographical and cultural dimensions of protest, since we have focused on individuals' belief systems, affective grids, personality traits, moral shocks, and so on. In doing so we have seen how individuals can carry out their own acts of protest, but also be opened to recruitment to organized protest movements, even sometimes seeking out or founding groups. But biography is intimately connected to the other dimensions of protest. Individuals internalize the professional ethics, religious beliefs, and even stubborn arrogance from the cultural repertories around them. And they interact strategically with others, notably their employers and co-workers. Resources are probably important only after the whistle has been blown, when they affect what happens to the dissenter. If biography and culture are especially prominent in explaining why whistleblowing occurs, then strategy and resources are most relevant in accounting for what happens after that.

In the last chapter and this one, we have seen how individuals, minding their own business, can receive deep moral shocks. These usually come from corporations and state agencies, although they might also derive from personal tragedies such as the death of a loved one. The anger and outrage can often propel people toward protest, even in the absence of past experience or personal ties to protest groups. In shifting our focus now from emotions and morals to cognitive beliefs, we shall see more of the active part that protest groups can play in channeling and elaborating feelings and beliefs; the most outraged individual easily lapses into resignation without organized groups to turn to. Not everyone has explicit moral principles to guide her in the face of moral shocks; most of us have more intuitive moral sensibilities that we need help in elaborating. In some ways moral indignation and emotional feelings are quick and intuitive responses: cognitive understanding is slower and harder. It often crystallizes later.

- Explicit moral beliefs often lead to anger, outrage, hurt, and a moral shock when they are violated. Such emotions can propel even unlikely candidates such as engineers into protest.

- Whistleblowers are a clear example of these ethical dissenters, and the antinuclear movement shows just how influential they can be.

- Professional ethics, religious beliefs, and community solidarity are the main sources of moral principles whose violation leads to whistleblowing.

- Post-industrial challenges to science and technology have made whistleblowing, like NIMBYs, more common.

SEVEN

Recruiting Animal Protectors: Cognitive Dimensions

Literature is the conscience of society. It expresses the social feelings of a period, at the same time as it analyzes them and judges them. Like a seismograph, it registers and amplifies the shocks agitating society—currents of opinion, moods, confused aspirations, discontent, hope.
　　—Micheline Tison-Braun

Imagine yourself living two hundred years ago. If you were a typical citizen of the United States—or any other country—what would you have thought about the many animals you encountered in your daily life? When you needed to go farther than you could walk, horses took you. When they misbehaved, you used your whip or sharp spurs to discipline them. If a man, you probably hunted, sallying forth into the woods to kill a rabbit or pheasant. You cared assiduously for your sheep and pigs, perhaps even kept a young lamb in the kitchen as a pet, but this was mainly to keep them alive until you sliced their throats, cut them up, cooked and ate them. Dogs performed some useful tasks, but cats were little better than the rodents they devoured. Their main utility was at festivals and political demonstrations, where they would be stuffed into sacks and set afire; their terrible caterwauling was impressive. Animal fights were another favorite amusement: dogfights, cockfights, dogs versus badgers, even a dog versus a monkey. Several dogs might be set loose to destroy a pack of rats or torment a bull or bear; "bulldogs" were specifically bred low to the ground to avoid being gored, and with powerful jaws so they could hang on after sinking their teeth into the vulnerable cartilage of a bull's snout.

Animals were everywhere in that age, much more familiar in daily life than today, when the only animals most of us encounter are pets. But there was little need to think about them. They did not have souls. The bible explicitly said that they were under human dominion, which seemed to mean that we could use them however we wished. They did not have feelings, according to most philosophers, who argued that animals writhed and screeched as automatic reactions, not because they felt pain as humans do (exactly what people still say when boiling lobsters). Even if they did feel pain, so what? They were only animals. The occasional poet, priest, or—most often—aristocratic lady who worried about animal suffering was derided as kooky, even insane.

Today, attitudes toward animals are different. Most of us, especially in the advanced industrial countries, would be disturbed—to say the least—by the sight of cats being torched. We could imagine their hideous pain, since we know that their nervous systems are similar to our own. We appreciate many species, further, for the emotions and personalities we perceive in them: loyalty, love, affection, even pride or sloth. And in the last fifty years, we have come to understand the complex thought patterns of nonhuman animals. We have taught a primitive sign language to apes, recorded whales singing to each other, deciphered the elaborate dances of bees. In their physical sensations, emotions, and cognition, at least as we perceive them, animals have edged closer to humans.

It is hard to appreciate how far we are from the attitudes of two hundred years ago. Bull-baiting was banned in Britain and the United States in the nineteenth century, as was cruelty to carriage horses. The humane movement of that period credited animals with feelings, especially the ability to feel pain, but not notable cognitive capacities. They were still the "dumb brute" in need of human protection. We now debate protections that would have been inconceivable to our ancestors, even to those Victorians who belonged to humane societies. How much light and space do laying hens need for their psychological well-being? Is it permissible to develop techniques for human heart surgeries by experimenting on dogs? On dogs taken from pounds? Is it unfair to animals to keep them as pets? Do mice have rights? Mollusks? Beetles? Rattlesnakes? These are all issues, out of dozens, raised quite seriously by the contemporary animal rights movement. Once, this movement would have been unimaginable; today it is affecting how we think about animals and, in part, how we treat them. It has cut into consumer demand for fur coats, transformed the way new products are tested for toxicity, obtained stricter rules for the treatment of laboratory animals, and generally raised public awareness of how humans interact with animals (although activists feel frustrated at how little they have done). The movement's goals would have been unthinkable under an older view of animals.

It would be impossible to understand or explain a protest movement like animal rights without paying close attention to a broad range of intuitions and attitudes toward nature, bureaucracy, technology, and animals. And it is only one of many possible examples. Increased public suspicion toward experts, science, and technology has allowed a whole series of post-industrial movements to blossom during the past thirty years that would have been hard to imagine in other historical periods. New intuitions about the place of humans in the physical world have spawned movements expressing moral visions once thought laughable. Protests against hazardous waste dumps, nuclear power plants, and university laboratories have proliferated. Challenges to genetic engineering, fertilizers, and hydroelectric dams have appeared. Americans, often acting alone, drive steel spikes into ancient redwoods to damage the chainsaws used to fell them. Snail darters and spotted owls are argued to have rights powerful enough to stand up against the interests of large industries. People question their own government's right to develop and deploy new weapons. *Basic sensibilities—part affect, part moral vision, part cognitive beliefs—are the first building blocks of any protest movement.*

In this chapter I concentrate on some of the cognitive aspects of the emergence of a protest movement, including pre-existing beliefs and intuitions that organizers can appeal to even as they attempt to transform them. If the emotions and moral intuitions and rules examined in the last two chapters are important, so is the cognitive articulation that binds them together in definitive form. Moral shocks and other reactions often begin at the "gut level," as moral intuitions trigger emotions; explicit cognitive understandings, such as the attribution of blame, take longer. There is considerable room for the ideological work of movement leaders, who weave together the emotional, moral, and cognitive threads. As examples I shall mostly use the animal rights movement, with occasional references to the antinuclear and anti-abortion movements. Having seen people like Ian McMillan and John Gofman, who undertook much protest as individuals, we can now add the contribution of movement recruiters in artfully formulating feelings and beliefs, appealing to but also transforming existing sensibilities. What Clifford Geertz said of art applies equally to the arguments of protestors: they "generate and regenerate the very subjectivity they pretend only to display."[1]

COGNITIVE UNDERSTANDINGS

Morality and emotions are important parts of the willingness to protest, but political programs and demands for change must ultimately be formulated in cognitive claims about how the world works, not just how it should work or how we feel about its workings. Much of the

Table 7.1 Levels of Cognitive Meanings and Their Embodiments and Supports

Types	Definition	Examples
Goals and proposals	Explicit, specific policy proposals or critiques of existing practices.	Free-ranges for hens; ban on painful experiments; moratorium on nuclear weapons, reactors.
Ideas, ideologies, frames	Explicit, contested packages of proposals and critiques that fit together to highlight certain aspects of the issues.	Rights of animals; nuclear reactors as accident-prone; civil rights for all humans.
Worldviews, master frames, traditions, policy styles, themes	Analyses and underlying images, e.g., of modern society; often shared by several movements.	Capitalism as driven by profits; critique of homocentric view of natural world; animals as innocent sufferers.
Common sense, intuitions, sensibilities	Implicit cultural meanings, images, and feelings, often an incipient worldview, and sometimes widely shared.	Suspicion of experts, capitalism, or instrumentalism; sense of need for harmony with nature; human nature as good.
Condensing symbols	Multireferent, visual or verbal encapsulation of other cultural meanings.	Photo of cat in cage with electrodes planted in skull, or reactor on beautiful coastline.
Plausibility structures	Institutions and practices that make cultural meanings plausible or implausible.	Contact with live animals as pets, not resources; life in modern bureaucratic societies.

Source: Adapted from James Jasper and Jane Poulsen, "Recruiting Strangers and Friends," *Social Problems* 42: 493–512.

point of protest is the articulation of inchoate feelings and moral impulses. We can perceive varying levels of cognitive meanings at work in protest, along a continuum from the most implicit to the most explicit, with inchoate, commonsense intuitions at one end and highly elaborated political platforms or scientific formulations at the other. For convenience I list these concepts in table 7.1, along with the symbols that embody them and the plausibility structures that support them.[2]

At bottom are commonsense assumptions, images, and sensibilities. Often these are widely shared, so that diverse protestors can appeal to them; they may even be common to a nation or international in scope.

On the other hand, they may not be widely shared; their implicit character does not guarantee consensus. They remain inchoate feelings; people often know how they feel ("from the gut") about an issue before they develop reasons for their positions. Their implicit understandings of the world "open" citizens to the possibility of protest, so that explicit movement ideologies make sense when encountered. Many Americans, for example, have intuitions that homosexuality is unnatural, that cities are corrupt, or that children are valuable in and of themselves rather than as economic resources. Local opponents of nuclear power plants, toxic waste dumps, and industrial parks often know only that they don't want one of "those things" near them, developing an ideology of opposition only when they contact a national group. Says one, "I didn't know why I hated it [a nuclear plant] at first; it just scared me I guess. But as I read more about nuclear power and nuc-waste, I found lots of good reasons [for opposing it]—reasons I could tell to other people." These instincts are often expressed in proverbs and maxims, but they can be probed through depth interviews. Poetry or humor often capture them more clearly than sociology.

Social movements rest ultimately on the "sensibilities" of adherents—a word that captures the tight connection between beliefs, morals, and emotions. As the bedrock on which more explicit beliefs are built, these intuitions—"structures of feeling," Raymond Williams called them—help people sort out what they like from what they dislike, what they find plausible from what they find implausible, whom they trust from whom they distrust. As philosopher Charles Taylor puts it, "I come to understand someone when I understand his emotions, his aspirations, what he finds admirable and contemptible in himself and others, what he yearns for, what he loathes, and so on."[3] As in the case of animal protection, these sensibilities, sensitivities, and sentiments affect what issues we find ludicrous, and which ones we might be persuaded to back. Broad historical conditions change them slowly.

As these intuitions develop they need poets and protestors to express them as distinct worldviews, still largely implicit to those who hold them but clear when compared to those of other groups in the same society or to other historical periods. These are the raw materials from which protest organizers try to spin explicit positions, drawing out the implications of what people only vaguely feel and believe. Kristin Luker, for example, described the worldviews of anti-abortion and of pro-choice activists, whose contrasting intuitions involved different formulations about women's careers, family, sexuality, and reproduction.[4] Other examples are the beliefs that animals are innocent sufferers, that technology is out of control, that communists are evil. Similar to what Gamson called themes and counterthemes, and to Snow and Benford's master frames, these visions provide familiar references, tropes, heroes, and histories that can often be adapted by both sides in an argument, and certainly by related protest movements. Post-industrial movements for peace, environmental and animal protection, and against nuclear energy shared many such constructions.

At the most articulated level, we have ideas and ideologies: the more-or-less coherent set of explicit, stated beliefs and values es-poused by a protest movement (or political party, or even some indi-viduals). Often the handiwork of intellectuals who write and lecture, the formulation of ideologies is an important activity for organized protest movements, which need to present coherent programs for their members, potential members, and the public. This activity may help a movement coalesce in the first place, much as Rachel Carson's *Silent Spring* spurred the environmental movement that emerged in the 1960s. Such intellectual work may also redirect the goals of a move-ment, as when intellectuals push a movement's sentiments to their most radical conclusions. This partly happened to the civil rights movement in the mid-1960s.[5] Although these ideas have deep roots in intuitions and worldviews, the same worldview may give rise to sev-eral ideologies; conversely the same ideology may occasionally appeal to those with different worldviews. Snow and Benford's frames are similar to ideologies, their master frames to worldviews. Ideologies are often worldviews with rationales added: the belief that animals have rights *because* they share important traits with humans or that nuclear reactors are dangerous *because* they are complex systems prone to accidents.[6]

In addition to explicit but general programmatic statements, there are also specific proposals or policy goals (a nuclear freeze, the animal welfare act, a ban on abortions, a moratorium on nuclear reactors), which are symbolically and logically linked back to worldviews and even common sense. Surprisingly often, narrowly defined proposals can come to symbolize bigger differences in underlying worldviews.[7]

Proposals, ideas, worldviews, and intuitions normally have natural affinities, and so are found in predictable bundles even when one level is not logically deducible from another or one idea necessarily linked to another. In an earlier book, I used the concept of "policy style" to show how implicit assumptions and explicit problem-solving tech-niques were clustered in recurring families of arguments. For example cost-benefit rhetoric is based on implicit feelings about the importance of efficient resource distributions in modern societies, a worldview elaborated by economists for describing these distributions, and specific algorithms for judging policy choices. I contrasted this with technological enthusiasm, based on physical re-engineering as a problem-solving technique, and with ecological moralism, which derived judgments of right and wrong directly from basic moral values. There were predictable misunderstandings between the three contrasting policy styles.[8]

None of these meanings are static. They change, first, as the broad historical conditions that make them plausible change. Sociologists often use the term *plausibility structure* to get at the economic, political, and other structures and routines that give mental frameworks resonance.[9] The malevolence of the natural world, for example, becomes less credible as it is tamed through urbanization, industrialization, and other accompaniments of modernity. Wolves no longer come out of the woods and kill our sheep; our food no longer depends on good weather (only its price does). But we can also see that few meanings, even at the level of common sense, are shared universally in a society. Those who still work the land, remaining subject to the whims of nature, may still believe in its active malevolence, and be less likely to romanticize its goodness. Ian McMillan notwithstanding, ranchers are unlikely to become environmentalists or animal protectionists. Although it is tempting to think that a society's common sense is more universally shared than its political programs, there is little evidence that this is so.[10] That explicit programs build on implicit meanings seems to indicate the opposite. Explicit proposals and ideas may be more controversial than implicit meanings, however, if only because protest movements make them so by promoting them.

Basic assumptions and worldviews can also be changed, no doubt, by current experiences, both emotional and cognitive, including formal schooling.[11] For example, many of us have intuitions about the world that, upon consideration, turn out to be inconsistent with our other beliefs or practices. As we'll see in more detail in chapter 12, there are individuals, groups, and institutions in any society constantly at work shaping interpretive frames and common sense, not just of the public, but of protest movements themselves.[12] William Gamson and Andre Modigliani, in one case, trace the relationship between the media's framing of nuclear energy and the public's framing, finding in both a shift away from a "progress" package and toward a "runaway" and an ambivalent "devil's bargain" package after Three Mile Island and Chernobyl.[13]

Protest movements have their own internal division of labor, and intellectuals are especially charged with working out these new meanings. It is easy to lose sight of this internal division in images that pit movements against the state or contrast formal organizations with those they represent and mobilize resources from. Some of the most influential intellectuals operate independently, unaffiliated with organized groups. Like whistleblowers, their acts of protest are individual, consisting of their writing. In the early stages of a movement, especially, a clever formulation or accumulation of evidence can be a powerful inspiration to both recruiters and their audiences.[14]

Although I have presented these levels of meaning as though they were purely cognitive, when we see them in action we will recognize that they also carry heavy moral and emotional baggage. Despite considerable research into these meanings in recent years, we are only beginning to understand how they shape protest.

CONDENSING SYMBOLS AND MORAL SHOCKS

The possibility that beliefs can be changed is an opening for protest organizers, who hope to provide experiences that will cause potential recruits to rearrange their beliefs and act on them. In chapter 5 we saw moral shocks to one's physical security and sense of home. Chapter 6 concerned moral shocks in the workplace. Now we'll see shocks that come more abstractly from what one reads, sees, and learns—often due to the efforts of activists. We move from actions that individuals can undertake to the collective protest of organized groups.

There is a complex balance, corresponding to what I called the duality of culture, between organizers' creative efforts and pre-existing cultural meanings. At one end of the spectrum organizers may find existing symbols and labels that resonate widely but can still generate protests (or which resonate well with a small number of potential recruits). More creatively, they may also re-imagine old themes and tropes, adding new connotations to what people already know and understand. Finally, at the most creative extreme, ideologists operate as poets; they define emerging structures of feeling with new terms and images. Sidney Tarrow points to the challenges organizers face in making cultural appeals, since frame alignment "is not always easy, clear or uncontested. First, movement leaders compete with other movements, media agents, and the state for cultural supremacy. These competitors often have immensely powerful cultural resources at their disposal. Second, movements that adapt too well to their societies' cultures lose the force of opposition and alienate their militant supporters. Third, movement participants often have their own 'reading' of events that differ[s] from those of their leaders."[15] Cultural resonance is defiantly subtle, usually amenable only to *post hoc* explanations of why some arguments and frames catch on, while others flop.

Protestors' creativity comes partly from their devising of symbols for expressing the various levels of meaning, often simultaneously. Depending on their place in cultural structures, certain symbols are more powerful than others. Edward Sapir contrasted a "referential symbol," which had relatively straightforward meanings, with a "condensation symbol," which "strikes deeper and deeper roots in the unconscious and diffuses its emotional quality to types of behavior or situations apparently far removed from the original meaning of the symbol."[16] Certain objects and classifications—such as animals, gender, and even "up" and "down"— are simply "good to think with."[17] They attract charged meanings and connotations as readily as metal rods attract lightning or magnets attract metal shavings. Two reasons for their power are that they have emotional depth (Sapir refers to them as "associated with repressed emotional material of great importance to the ego"), and that they resonate with multiple meanings and connotations. Gender, species, technology, nation (and in America, race) suggest boundaries and categories which we all encounter and use to situate ourselves in the world; they mean something to us, just as "home" does.

Animals have been powerful condensing symbols throughout human history. In almost every society humans have projected their concerns onto them, sometimes using animals as symbols of what is nonhuman (as in nature versus culture) and sometimes as what is human (humans are called pigs, dogs, chicks, and much worse). In all societies, they are easy repositories for cultural meanings, ranging from embodiments of the sacred in early cave paintings to images of social order in Mandeville's bees and fears of the wild in medieval images of wolves. Animals have great power and flexibility as condensing symbols, as activists have discovered. Cultures vary in how they view animals, but animals are always there for deep symbolic applications.

Social movement organizers use such condensing symbols to recruit members; strategic action is used to convey the cultural meanings. A rich condensing symbol will attract members (although it might repel others); a weak one will leave them indifferent. The symbols themselves are multireference because they connote different levels of cultural meaning, or different cultural meanings within a single level. A powerful symbol can lend credibility to an explicit argument by connoting the implicit assumptions embedded in worldviews and common sense. The role of symbols can be seen as connotative, evoking associations in an audience, or constitutive, helping to create the audi-

ence's world. To me, symbols do both. Good ones resonate with a potential recruit, at least catching her attention, even though this resonance always depends on what cultural meanings are already
distributed in a society. New meanings must have some fit with existing ones, and both must be compatible with the daily lives of those
holding them.

*The most effective moral shocks are those embodied in, translatable into, and
summed up by powerful condensing symbols.* This is especially true for
recruitment by organized groups. Moral shocks do not arise only from
grievances imposed by employers or authorities; movement organizers
try hard to generate them through their own rhetorical appeals to
strangers—whether by going door-to-door ("canvassing"), setting up
tables in airports and other busy places ("tabling"), or mailing brochures to people's homes ("direct mail").[18] Appeals are also made
through public displays, for example in libraries, lectures open to the
public, and—of course—advertising. The technologies of direct mail,
in particular, have developed into a small industry, as "brokers" buy
and trade lists of potential contributors. The great expense of such
procedures reminds us that resources remain an important factor,
helping to determine how widely such appeals can be broadcast. Although the response rate of strangers to these solicitations is very
low—since most pay no attention or are not sympathetic—there are
far more strangers out there than there are friends, family, and acquaintances. Even low response rates can yield large absolute numbers—
potentially far greater than what social networks can provide.[19]

The persuasive power of rhetoric does not rest only on the content of
what is said, as though political persuasion were an exercise in logical
deduction. There are not only the hidden appeals to implicit emotions
and moral intuitions, there is also a style or tone that independently
attracts attention and justifies action. Robert Benford has described
four elements of this justifying tone: the severity of the problem, the
urgency of finding a solution, the efficacy of collective protest in bringing about that solution, and the propriety of acting. These are aspects
of an argument that have to do with the action context of the argument
more than its simple substance, implying a political project rather than
simply an analysis.[20] Part of this stylistic thrust is emotional, as Pat
Watters recognizes in describing the civil rights movement: "SCLC veterans maintain that it was not the words but the emotional tone Dr.
King expressed that was important. . . . Often in mass meetings, they
say, people who couldn't understand all the words responded to the
tone."[21] The persuasive artistry of rhetoric often lies in what is not said
explicitly: in diction, manners, decorum, sensibility, and other factors

hard to pin down because they only accompany the main argument.[22]

In addition to suggesting action, an important result of protestors' rhetorical appeals is a tendency toward articulation: the development of less explicit meanings into more explicit ones. As Max Weber showed, this is partly what modernity is all about: an expanding division of labor, with ever more specialized institutions and experts whose job is to think about things people did not previously think about. Protest is one of the main mechanisms modern societies have for pondering basic worldviews and morals, for crystallizing inner sensibilities. Most protest movements strive to make us think about our intuitions, to question practices we previously took for granted, to derive ideologies from our intuitions. Let us return to see how this happened with the animal rights movement.

REFIGURING ANIMALS

Our ancestors simply had different intuitions about nonhuman species from those most of us hold today. Their sense (the "common sense" of the time) was that animals were more like grain and lumber than like humans. They were raw materials for us to consume, not creatures with acute physical sensitivities and elaborate mental activities. Thanks in part to modern science, most contemporary Americans see animals as closely related to humans, not only in their evolutionary origins but in their nervous systems. We have considerable sympathy for them—some of us have so much sympathy that we are willing to grant them extensive rights.

In *The Animal Rights Crusade* Dorothy Nelkin and I tried to show how these moral sentiments have changed gradually during the past several hundred years.[23] Most societies in history have had—like our ancestors of two hundred years ago—a dual approach to animals: they kept some as pets, forming emotional bonds with them; but they exploited others as resources, eating them, wearing them, and using them in farming. They saw no contradiction in these attitudes. Only since the urbanization and industrialization of modern Western Europe and America has this dualism been upset, so that meat today comes from the store wrapped in plastic, neatly sliced, with little obvious relationship to living animals, which we mostly encounter as pets.

New ideas about nonhuman species have roots in sixteenth- and seventeenth-century Europe, where there emerged a distinct middle class whose plausibility structures were shaped by towns rather than agriculture. This new commercial milieu accelerated what Norbert Elias called the "civilizing process" through which Europeans learned concern for the sensibilities of others; no longer did they spit on the floor, blow their noses on their sleeves, or eat out of common bowls.[24] One result of this growing awareness of unique individual identities and emotional needs was that children were no longer seen as small adults, but as special beings to be cherished and protected. In a process of "sentimentalization," love and affection rather than economic need came to be the glue holding the family together.[25] In the paintings of the sixteenth and seventeenth centuries, families and interior spaces began to replace the crowd scenes and public places of artists like Peter Breughel.

Pets were incorporated in the tight emotional circle of the new bourgeois family and home, often appearing in family portraits. By the early eighteenth century, many people were giving their pets human names, burying them and writing epitaphs for them, and occasionally leaving them legacies. Except for cart and carriage horses, town dwellers lost more and more instrumental contacts with animals. They hunted less, had fewer fields to plow, and raised fewer animals to slaughter (the last exception being a few backyard chickens, which disappeared from Manhattan only in the mid-twentieth century). Their main contact with animals was now with their pet dogs. As a result they were less likely to see animals primarily as resources, existing to serve economic ends. Animals could now fulfill important emotional needs for humans, providing love and loyalty. In a long process extending from the sixteenth century to the present, compassion and companionship replaced cruelty as the most common feeling about animals.[26] Our deepest intuitions about animals are different today.

Beginning in the eighteenth century, scientific developments also contributed to a revaluation of animals, reshaping not just our sensibilities but our explicit worldviews. Naturalists developed classifications based on similarities between humans and animals. Geologists studied the age of the earth and speculated about the evolution of complex species. The Comte de Buffon and others searched for the missing link between humans and apes. The capstone of this process was Charles Darwin's 1859 publication of Origin of Species (followed by The Descent of Man in 1871), which supported the growing belief that humans and animals were descended from common ancestors, with all the similarities that implied. Darwin later wrote The Expression of the Emotions in Man and Animals to demonstrate the common physiological source of emotions across species, insisting that human mental capacities were superior in degree but not in kind to those of animals.[27]

This rethinking of animals accelerated in nineteenth-century Britain and the United States, spreading across social class boundaries. With nature neutralized for many by industrialization and the growth of cities, reduced to a suburban lawn and garden and a pretty landscape painting, people could romanticize it as innocent and good, ignoring its cruelty and violence. Animals, accordingly, were seen not simply as like humans in their emotional capacities, but as superior. They were never duplicitous or unkind. They were innocent and helpless, perfect objects for compassion.

In recent years, the moral intuitions and worldviews supporting animal protection have, if anything, spread further. Urbanization and industrialization have continued, with only 3 percent of contemporary Americans working in agriculture. Pet ownership has continued to expand, so that 60 percent of American households now have pets. The personification of these animals continues, as people often project onto their animals suspiciously human tastes. They buy their dogs mink stoles, bottled water, and vegetarian, low-cholesterol food. Pets receive orthodonture, plastic surgery, pacemakers, even CAT scans. Humans treat their "companion animals" as full members of the family: talking to them, carrying their photos, celebrating their birthdays, and letting them sleep in their beds.

In an additional twist since the humane movement of the nineteenth century, recent research on animal communication and cognition has filtered into public awareness. Most striking have been efforts to communicate with chimpanzees, who share 98.5 percent of our genes. They can master more than one hundred words in sign language or keyboard symbols, even learning to piece them together in new ways. Lacking a symbol for cucumber, one asks for a "green banana." Another, introduced to fellow chimps for the first time, is unimpressed, dismissing them as "bugs . . . black bugs." Those who have mastered sign language use it to talk to themselves when alone, to other chimps, even to their inanimate toys. They can make the remarkable leap of classifying words. Two of them, when asked to group seventeen nouns as either tools or food, made only one mistake between them. One chimp said that sponges were food—but that chimp regularly gobbled up sponges, used around his compound to soak up spilled soft drinks.[28] We now explicitly appreciate animals for their intelligence as well as their loyalty, and our sympathy has expanded to incorporate "intelligent" species such as whales and dolphins as well as cuddly, loving ones like dogs and cats. Animals are no longer "dumb brutes." Since World War II, scientific advances, buttressed by nature programs on television and articles in *National Geographic*, have increased popular appreciation for the cognitive capacities of other species. People have become more likely to see animals as "like humans," capable of similar feelings and thoughts, and thus holding, perhaps, parallel rights.[29]

With nature shows and scientific findings, we have moved into the more explicit realm of worldviews and ideologies. People can say why they are sympathetic to animals by referring to "objective" scientific facts. They can talk about their contacts with and love for pets, the place of animals in their own lives. They can describe what they think is the relationship between animals and humans: companionship, hierarchy, or domination. It is these worldviews that have changed considerably in the last thirty years.

Few moral sentiments are unanimous in a society. Many have claimed, for instance, that employment in the industrial, manufacturing sector makes economic growth a central value and suggests a vision of the natural world as a set of raw materials to be transformed. Work in the service sector, or work manipulating symbols, leads to aesthetic appreciation of nature and a higher value placed on interpersonal justice—a critique of bureaucracy, a concern for democracy, abhorrence of oppression.[30] This is the "post-industrial" vision. Those who work in agriculture or who hunt, on the other hand, are naturally less likely to sentimentalize animals, more likely to persist in viewing them as resources.[31]

In contemporary societies, people who live with pets but not with other humans should be especially likely to bring animals into their own emotional circle. Sustained contact with their pets will allow them to perceive (or project) a range of emotions, thoughts, and intentions in their "companion animals," which will then appear to have the same complex personalities humans do. (Psychologists have discovered that people who live alone grieve more over the death of a pet, indicating deeper emotional attachments.)[32] Strong claims about the capacities and rights of animals will be more plausible to these people, and images of the suffering of animals will be especially shocking to them. My own surveys of animal rights protestors found them more likely than the average adult American to have pets, and less likely to be living with other humans.[33] Two-thirds of my respondents were unmarried, compared to roughly one-third of adult Americans. Eighty percent of the respondents had pets (as opposed to 61 percent of households nationwide); only 2 percent said that they didn't have pets and had not grown up with them. Their personal experience and resulting moral sensibilities made them especially susceptible to the condensing symbols wielded by animal rights organizers.

Many religious Americans are less open to this personifying of animals because in their worldview—based on strands of the Judaeo-

Christian tradition—animals are explicitly subordinate to humans, available for our purposes. Their views are an updated version of those held by eighteenth-century Americans. Fundamentalist readings of the Book of Genesis give humans "dominion" over the rest of the world, which is apparently to be used to satisfy human needs. Fundamentalist Christians are skeptical of evolutionary theories, which imply family resemblances between humans and other species due to our shared family tree. Most animal rights protestors, in contrast, profess to be atheists and agnostics (fully 65 percent, according to a survey conducted by the movement's leading magazine, *The Animals' Agenda*), open to a master frame implying more equality between species. Carolyn Chute captures some of the religious attitude in her novel, *The Beans of Egypt, Maine*. A child asks her mother,

> "Do chickens and fish go to heaven?"
> "No," I say.
> She whispers, "Why not?"
> "Only man was made in God's image."
> Bonny Loo screws up her face. "You mean NONE of Madeline's chickens are goin' to heaven?" A whisper. Her breath smells like the clean, dark pond.
> "That's right, Bonny Loo."
> "What about fish?"
> "Only people."
> She brushes my face with her fingers as she whispers extra close.
> "People are best, aren't they?"[34]

Women seem more likely than men to have moral intuitions and worldviews amenable to animal rights messages. At least 70 percent of participants, according to my surveys and others, are women. Several reasons are given in personal interviews. Despite their increasing integration into the workforce, women still devote much more time than men to the nurturing activities of childrearing, opening them to appeals that portray animals as innocent victims in need of protection. Sara Ruddick has argued that women's disproportionate role in childrearing gives them a greater degree of "maternal thinking" than men, one reason that they were more likely to participate in the peace movement, another post-industrial cause.[35] The same argument would hold for animal protection, given some overlap between the animal rights and peace movements. Here the causal effect of maternal thinking might be even stronger, due to the symbolic similarities between animal protection and child protection (in the nineteenth century many groups pursued both). In addition, women are less likely to participate in activities which place animals in the role of resources, such as hunting (90 percent of hunters are men), slaughter, and racing. Even women who are not mothers face innumerable mechanisms of gender socialization that encourage traditional nurturing, empathic emotions. Boasted one activist, "Women are taught all their lives to care for others; it's just that no one expected us to apply this to research animals." Finally, some animal rights groups—most prominently Feminists for Animal Rights—work hard to link feminist issues with animal liberation.

Political ideology has also helped prepare the cultural soil for the animal rights movement. Most animal activists hold a left-leaning ideology: 34 percent of my respondents claimed to be liberal, another 31 percent progressive or radical left (*The Animals' Agenda* had almost identical results). Thus animal rights organizers package appeals in left-liberal terms: large corporations abuse animals in their reckless search for profits; consumer culture encourages testing on rabbits in order to invent "one more shade of mascara"; agribusiness deploys ruthless technologies that intensify the suffering of farm animals. Animal rights arguments are framed in ways that appeal to those whose worldviews picture capitalist corporations and markets as sinister, and whose ideologies recommend government regulation.

Such ideologies had been developed, in part, through activism in other protest movements. When asked what other causes they had been involved with, animal rights protestors mentioned peace/disarmament most often, followed by civil rights, human rights, and antiracism, then environmentalism, the women's movement, Vietnam, opposition to U.S. military intervention, and the antinuclear movement. This rich culture of activism is a seedbed for symbols and arguments, the reason that Snow and Benford's "master frames" transcend individual movements.

In addition to these pre-existing sensibilities, worldviews, and political ideologies, it took a handful of memorable labels and condensing symbols to pull the modern animal rights movement together. Philosopher Peter Singer provided a term, *speciesism,* and a book full of striking images and evidence in his 1975 *Animal Liberation.* The book was a gold mine of gruesome photos, examples of dubious animal experiments, and arguments that activists could use in recruitment. It helped the new movement to coalesce, and it became its bible. Other philosophers also contributed important ideas; as Nelkin and I put it, they were midwives to the new movement. Notably, the idea of *rights* for animals, although not found in Singer's utilitarian approach, resonated broadly with American political traditions, becoming an important frame and rallying cry. This was a popular slogan even though, at a philosophical level, it is unclear on what grounds nonhuman species might be granted rights rather than simple protection.

A leader of the New York chapter of Trans-Species Unlimited recognized the conflict between appealing to existing beliefs and trying to change them: "You gotta start where people are. That doesn't mean you can't bring them around to somewhere else. Sometimes you can and sometimes you can't. You gotta go with *them*. . . . It's hard to predict." Trans-Species Unlimited's leaders did not like the concept of rights, thinking it philosophically muddled, but its attraction was enormous, and the organization eventually changed its name to Animal Rights Mobilization! "We also didn't like companion animals, because of [founder George] Cave [who had written an article against pet owning]. But that was the best way to recruit members [by appealing to pet owners]. We did better on other issues . . . like pushing for abolition rather than reform." As with artists and their audiences, organizers and their followers mutually shape and adjust their rhetoric and beliefs.

Demographics, affections, and political beliefs help explain why the appeals of animal rights organizers resonated with the people they did. Those with special emotional attachments to their pets, who lived in urban and suburban areas, who lacked traditional religious worldviews, and who were left-liberal had a special ear for animal protection arguments. Not all, certainly, became animal activists or supporters. Nor was it impossible for someone lacking these traits to become involved. But such plausibility structures and pre-existing beliefs shifted the odds considerably.[36] There was an opening for protest groups to recruit new members and gain sympathy among the broader public. Because different citizens had different inchoate assumptions about the relationship between humans and other species, as they articulated these feelings they often came to contrasting conclusions. Some changed their minds, of course, but most did not. All who engaged in these debates, however, worked to reconcile their intuitions and their expressed ideologies.

As a result of this protest movement, many Americans have developed explicit ideologies about the relationship between humans and other species. They can talk about why animals may or may not have rights, differences in consciousness displayed by mollusks and crustaceans, and alternatives to live-animal testing. Such levels of articulateness about species, relatively new, are due to intellectuals and protestors. Nature writers and television producers, popular philosophers and psychologists, even academics whose ideas are disseminated by activists all help their audiences think through their intuitions about animals.

I have traced several cognitive preconditions to the emergence of the contemporary animal rights movement. Broad sensibilities had to shift, leading to a sentimentalization of animals. Then worldviews had to be articulated: in the nineteenth century this vision included the emotions and suffering of animals; since World War II it has also embraced their cognitive capacities. Even more specifically, philosophers and activists had to craft condensing symbols and arguments to focus these feelings and beliefs. Yet by creating an especially poetic or memorable term, ideologists also restructure popular belief systems. Cultures change constantly, though different parts change at different rates. The sentimentalization of Western culture has taken hundreds of years to dominate our society; the political frame of animal rights spread rapidly among hundreds of thousands of Americans in the 1980s, and resonated with millions more. To tap into deep sensibilities, movement ideologists strive, like poets, to find a language that both expresses and shapes new thoughts and feelings.

SHARED THEMES

Worldview seems to imply a cluster of meanings that fit together into a coherent package, but it is actually made up of a collection of discrete themes, to use Gamson's term, which can be used separately. In other words, there are images and tropes that form a common vocabulary anyone can use. They are like words, out of which whole sentences (arguments) can be constructed. In the United States, rights talk, references to god or to science, and critiques of experts resonate widely, even though they can be used in contrasting ways—even by opponents (as with women's rights versus fetal rights). Research on a society's political culture—what themes and images are used, by whom, how they have changed over time, how they differ from those used in other societies, how they are crafted into familiar arguments—could help students of protest understand better how framing works, when resonance is likely and when not, how language actually works to recruit protestors.

Despite their differences, the animal rights, antinuclear, and even the anti-abortion movements have tapped into similar underlying cultural tropes out there in American society. In particular, these movements often turned to Gamson's theme of "harmony with nature," in contrast to progress through technology. This sensibility linked ambivalence about science and technology, a critique of bureaucracy and "instrumental rationality," and a general suspicion of progress. There is considerable evidence that the "harmony with nature" theme has fared well in the last thirty years. Touraine argues that it undergirds the large

Table 7.2   Selected Values and Beliefs of Antinuclear and Animal Rights Protestors
(Percentage Agreeing/Disagreeing)

Statement	Antinuclear	Animal Rights
Human beings must live in harmony with nature in order to survive.	99 agree 1 disagree	98 1
We are severely abusing the environment.	98 agree 2 disagree	99 1
Humans have the right to modify the natural environment to suit their own needs.	18 agree 71 disagree	11 82
There are limits to growth beyond which our industrialized society cannot expand.	72 agree 11 disagree	68 14
We are in danger of letting technology run away with us.	84 agree 10 disagree	86 8
We are being involved less and less in important decisions that shape our lives.	88 agree 7 disagree	88 6
The benefits of technology outweigh its negative consequences.	20 agree 54 disagree	12 69

Source: From James Jasper and Jane Poulsen, "Recruiting Strangers and Friends,"
Social Problems 42: 493–512.

cluster of post-industrial movements opposed to "technocracy."[37] Many movements rely on cultural images and themes that revolve around a critique of instrumentalism, defined as the reduction of humans and nature to the status of means, and the elevation of tools (bureaucracy, markets, technologies) to that of ends. Fear, anxiety, and outrage against instrumentalism are common in modern societies, and hence make good starting points for many efforts at frame alignment. They are a natural means for raising moral issues.

Such themes at least appear in survey data. In my surveys of antinuclear and animal rights protestors, one cluster of questions dealt with humans' relationship to the environment.[38] There was almost unanimous agreement in both groups with the post-industrial statements, "We are severely abusing the environment," and "Human beings must live in harmony with nature in order to survive." Respondents also disagreed with the statement that "Humans have the right to modify the natural environment for our own ends." A majority in both groups agreed that "[t]here are limits to growth beyond which our industrialized society cannot expand." Table 7.2 presents the statements and responses. Many scholars have isolated these statements as key beliefs in the "new environmental paradigm" held as well by members of environmental movements. Studies comparing samples of the general population with environmentalists have found that these clusters of beliefs distinguish environmental activists from the public, as well as from business and labor leaders.[39] People no doubt join these movements out of such feelings, but the movements also help them forge a language for polishing, rationalizing, and expressing the beliefs.

A related cluster of beliefs portrays technology as out of our control. Both samples strongly agreed that "[w]e are being involved less and less in important decisions that shape our lives," and that "[w]e are in danger of letting technology run away with us." Many implicated government in this lack of control, disagreeing with the statement, "We can trust government to protect the public health and safety." There was similar skepticism about the likely benefits of science and technology. Both clusters of values and beliefs form a key part of the cultural frame supporting the animal rights, antinuclear, environmental, and many other post-industrial movements.[40]

Social movement leaders design visual and verbal rhetoric to make anti-instrumental intuitions into an explicit frame. Related beliefs and fears appear in the literature from the animal rights and antinuclear movements, often less in explicit analyses than in cartoons, graffiti, and editorials. The Abalone Alliance, an opponent of the Diablo Canyon plant alongside the Mothers for Peace, published a newsletter, *It's About Times*, almost monthly from 1979 to 1985. Most front covers had cartoons depicting nuclear technology as a grotesque giant, a rampaging Tyrannosaurus, and a glowing, fiery skeleton. Humans were shown as dead or dying, often being crushed in enormous skeletal hands. The federal government was sometimes shown as an android composed of nuclear missiles, sometimes as Gestapo-like agents. Cartoons and editorials from *It's About Times* defined the threat and allocated blame with themes of a technology out of human control, the destruction of the natural world, and a government in complicity.

Violence, force, and environmental catastrophe also appeared in the animal rights literature. Patrice Greanville, writing in *The Animals' Agenda*, explicitly linked animal rights to broader environmental issues, "For no other cause surpasses political ecology in its affinity with animal liberation." He used language such as "impending catastrophe" and "underlying exploitative logic *based on force, not consent.*"[41] Rather than focusing on a big, ugly industry like nuclear energy, animal activists emphasized the victims, with pictures of cute, furry animals in nooses, cages, and traps. Less explicitly political than the antinuclear movement, in that it focused on threat more than blame, the animal rights movement targeted the government's complicity only rarely. But agencies that fund biomedical research, such as the National Institutes of Health and the National Institute on Drug Abuse, were portrayed as villains. In post-industrial rhetoric, large organizations and their bureaucratic experts are always available for blame.

Almost everyone, these days, attacks experts and their instrumentalism. The anti-abortion movement—despite its very different, right-leaning worldview and ideology—deploys many of the same references. It regularly paints doctors as unfeeling careerists, and science as godless. Human life is portrayed as either under god's control (as it should be) or under experts' control (as it currently is). The private, moral realm of the family is said to be under threat from instrumental, uncaring bureaucrats and professionals. At the same time, some of this movement's enemies—those in favor of legalizing suicide and euthanasia—also criticize the experts in modern society for stripping individual citizens of control over personal decisions.

All these movements paint technocracy as the enemy: large bureaucracies, driven by profits or careerism, insensitive to human needs, wielding complex technologies beyond human control. They desire moral standards and political control over instrumental techniques and rationalities. Because fears and suspicions of large organizations are widespread in American society, at the level of common sense and worldview, movement leaders can plausibly and successfully appeal to them. Very different movements can deploy the same themes to construct a multitude of contrasting ideologies, from post-industrial critiques of capitalism to religious attacks on soulless modernity.

EXPLAINING RECRUITMENT

The purpose of this chapter, along with chapters 5 and 6, has been to show the cultural processes by which people are opened to the possibility of joining a protest movement. Some protest on their own; others actively search out a group to join; still others must await the recruiter's letter, call, or knock. As I have shown in this chapter, people's intuitions and worldviews may be such that recruiters' own rhetoric may administer the necessary moral shock. The final stage in all this is that individuals begin to participate in organized protest movements—perhaps the most studied process in the social-movement literature.

My emphasis on how individuals may be prepared before they encounter a movement's members contrasts with the usual concentration on structural positions conducive to activism. Most scholars who have examined movement recruitment have focused, not on moral shocks and condensing symbols, but on social networks, which are prominent in both mobilization and process theories.[42] Because of their underlying image of formal organizations mobilizing people and resources from a natural constituency, most scholars have oddly separated the origins or emergence of a movement from recruitment into it once it is going. Proximity is usually necessary for cooperative action. Anticipating Karl Marx, Andrew Ure, an early advocate of the factory system, argued that the physical concentration of those with a common grievance is a prerequisite of action: "Manufactures naturally condense a vast population within a narrow circuit; they afford every facility for secret cabal . . . ; they communicate intelligence and energy to the vulgar mind; they supply in their liberal wages the pecuniary sinews of contention."[43] This proximity seems to hold true for workers during industrialization, African-Americans during urbanization, and perhaps students in their "youth ghetto."[44] This concentration, process and mobilization theorists have argued, must be accompanied by social organization.[45]

When we earlier saw the vagueness of conceptions of social networks, I argued that much of their effect was due instead to formal organizations. Aldon Morris found African-American churches, for instance, to be crucial to the emergence of the civil rights movement in providing meeting spaces, financing, and personal contacts.[46] The extreme case is "bloc recruitment," when entire networks, almost always based on organizations, are brought *en masse* into a movement.[47] For example, busloads of Christian fundamentalists visited state legislatures to oppose the ERA, organized and led by their preachers. McAdam and Paulsen were surprised to find that what looked like the effects of personal contacts on recruitment were actually due to organizational memberships and the identities accompanying those memberships.[48] Members of blocs typically share many cultural meanings, so that they are recruited to new issues that can be shown to be logical extensions of prior concerns. Network or organizational memberships often reflect prior choices, sometimes for political purposes, not some kind of primordial bonds (as may exist, sometimes, in the collectivities underlying citizenship movements, with the African-American community as perhaps the extreme example).

It has also been argued that recruits must be "biographically available" for protest, meaning they do not have jobs from which they will be fired or small children at home that they must care for.[49] Such barriers certainly matter. What is odd is that they have been theorized as structural, as though they had an automatic effect regardless of an individual's psychology in shaping such roles into a coherent personal identity. Biographical availability presumably works best in explaining recruitment to activities that might lead to violence or land one in jail for a long time. Once again, these are probably more likely to be found in citizenship than post-citizenship movements.

Another factor found to influence recruitment is prior activism.[50] Those who have been protestors before can more easily become protestors again. They have appropriate cultural skills and awareness of the potential pleasures of protest. They may also continue to have an activist identity. And they have personal networks that derived at one time from political action.[51]

Organizational membership and personal contacts are important, however, because they allow organizers and potential participants to communicate, achieving a common definition of a social problem and a common prescription for solving it. In other words, at the heart of an approach that has been highly structural, focusing on the proximity of bodies, there is a recognition that "the immediate impetus to collective action remains a cognitive one."[52] And an affective one, I would add, since much of the effect of personal networks must depend heavily on the affective ties they represent. Organizational membership, past activism, and personal contacts are important carriers of biographical ties and cultural meanings, but if cultural meanings are so important, can they not persuade people directly, outside of personal interactions—especially in light of the mechanisms described in these three chapters as creating willingness in potential recruits?

To answer such questions it is useful to remind ourselves how such networks differ. Some do fit the pattern found in mobilization and process models: a pre-existing community and collective identity, like those of southern African-Americans, which exists prior to political activity. Others are networks and organizations of comrades, originally developed for political activity in some other, related cause, and held together by an activist identity. But they were voluntary, in ways that being black in America, or a woman, or working-class, is not. Thus organizations founded for antinuclear work could be recruited for protest against nuclear missile deployment. (We shall examine this kind of activist subculture in the following chapter.) Third, a network can develop on the basis of a movement identity, forming just for protest against a single kind of cause, and recruiting people into that network for just that issue. In this case, there are still networks and organizations, but they are the result of successful recruitment, not its cause. If the civil rights movement is an example of the first kind of network, then the movement against Diablo Canyon represents the second, and the animal rights movement is a good example of the third.

In a separate article, Jane Poulsen and I used the animal rights movement to show that personal networks are not the only way to recruit new members.[53] Strangers, after all, join movements, and some movements, including the animal rights and anti-abortion movements, are composed primarily of new recruits. If personal contacts are one means for spreading the messages of a movement, moral shocks administered through more impersonal media are another. Cognitive meanings, emotions, and morals are important in both mechanisms, but more obviously in the recruitment of strangers. It is possible to build movement-specific networks by recruiting strangers.

This difference between recruiting friends through personal networks and strangers through impersonal media was apparent in my animal rights and antinuclear samples. When asked to estimate the importance of a list of factors that might have involved them in their movements, the majority of Diablo protestors listed specific events, previous activism, and family and friends each as very important. (Even the "events" were primarily rallies, protests, and referenda in which the respondents had participated.) Only 7 percent of the respondents said that neither previous activism nor family and friends were important, indicating that social networks helped draw almost all the respondents into the movement. As we shall see in chapter 8, these participants were part of a long-standing activist network. In contrast, 27 percent of the animal rights protestors said that neither previous activism nor family and friends were important. Instead, animal rights respondents heavily chose the "other" category (78 percent) and "reading" (72 percent) as very important in involving them. Most of the responses written in as "other" involved reading, listening, and watching television. Fewer than 10 percent of Diablo respondents mentioned these activities in their "other" category (they were not, alas, provided a "reading" entry). Of the antinuclear protestors, 51 percent rated previous activism as "very important" in involving them in Diablo Canyon, compared to 33 percent of the animal rights sample.[54] The antinuclear activists used pre-existing activist networks in building their movement against Diablo Canyon, but the animal rights organizers had to develop their own network for their cause. Neither group, however, could turn to networks that existed prior to political mobilization in the way that civil rights activists had.

People were recruited by an animal rights literature filled with powerful images designed to shock. Because we think we "know" the feelings of animals, we do not have to be told if an animal in a photograph is happy or unhappy. We believe the evidence to be clear and direct. The visual images used in animal rights recruitment have a simple but effective structure based on good versus evil. There are pictures of happy animals, sometimes in the wild and sometimes in loving homes, living fulfilled lives. Next to them are pictures of unhappy animals:

stabbed bulls; starved dogs; clubbed baby seals; cats with electrodes implanted in their skulls; terrified, neurotic monkeys and apes in cages; white rabbits with inflamed, pus-filled eyes from cosmetics testing. These are presented as innocent victims of an evil force. The contrast between the happy and the victimized animals is carefully orchestrated in movement literature. Animal rights activists deploy photos of animals that look most like human babies: large eyes, large heads, "cuteness." Animals that whimper or cry, spill red blood, and have fur all arouse sympathy because it is easier for viewers to anthropomorphize them.[55] Animals are even portrayed in "family" settings, either happy or nefariously disrupted (the same contrast between good and evil): mother seals next to the carcasses of their babies; baby monkeys stripped from their mothers; baby elephants dying without their parents.

Animal rights protestors testify to the importance of such visual images in drawing them into the movement, explicitly describing the moral shocks that first grabbed their attention. "I had never thought about it much," said one New Jersey activist. "But I went by a table one day and saw these terrifying pictures. *That's* what goes on inside our country's best, most scientific labs? There was a tabby [cat] that looked just like mine, but instead of a skull it had some kind of electrodes planted in its head. I thought about that a little bit, right there on the street, and I brought home all their literature. I decided, that's gotta stop" (personal interview, May 1990). Others report similar epiphanies upon receiving movement literature in the mail, or picking it up at pet adoption clinics.

The shock value of condensing symbols is also clear in anti-abortion recruitment. Fetuses are a strong condensing symbol for the anti-abortion activist, connoting children, birth, motherhood, family values, and life itself. Condit describes the ways that activists build fetuses into condensing symbols.[56] They use the brilliant oxymoron "unborn baby." They distribute small lapel pins shaped like tiny feet. They order their slide presentations to work backwards from babies to embryos, helping the viewer see the latter as human rather than an unrecognizable blob. Like animals for the animal activist, fetuses are innocent victims to the anti-abortionist; the idea of killing one is a sufficient moral affront to draw many new recruits into the anti-abortion movement. Certain beliefs about the world, especially religious ones, make some people more susceptible to fetuses as a condensing symbol than others. So do certain life experiences, such as a large family, a miscarriage, or the death of a newborn. These are "people whose values made pregnancy central to their lives."[57]

As a result, the anti-abortion movement also recruited many strangers in its early stages, before it linked up with fundamentalist churches that provided blocs of participants. Many abortion protestors joined the movement under the shock of *Roe v. Wade* in 1973. Kristin Luker says, "More of the people we interviewed joined the pro-life movement in 1973 than in any other year, before or since; and almost without exception, they reported that they became mobilized to the cause on the very day the decision was handed down."[58] The shock of this decision, based on the fetus and abortion as condensing symbols, was more important than movement activities in recruitment. Two-thirds of the anti-abortion activists in Luker's California sample were self-recruited in this way. Networks first built for a specific cause may, of course, then develop into activist networks recruitable for related causes, just as a movement identity can develop over time into an activist identity.

The antinuclear protestors were more tightly involved in pre-existing activist networks than the animal rights or anti-abortion protestors. Said one anti-Diablo protestor, "I was still more interested in revolution, and nuclear energy seemed a bullshit reformist issue, like environmentalism. But friends convinced me I was wrong, that the issue was capitalism and militarism and social justice. But it wasn't easy." Another commented, "When I first came to Diablo, I was already more interested in working against military intervention in Central America, but I came down because a lot of my friends were going, so it was easy to get a ride." Most of the Diablo protestors already shared an analysis of capitalism and many an analysis of nuclear energy under capitalism; they needed only to be mobilized for this particular issue and demonstration. Friends can take the time to persuade, whereas condensing symbols and moral shocks can lead to sudden conversions. Both involve frame shifts, but through different processes.

The existence of strong activist networks in antinuclear mobilization does not mean that condensing symbols were unnecessary. They were important for attracting new recruits to the network, and for maintaining the emotional allegiance of those in the subculture (as we'll see in the following chapter). Thanks to assiduous efforts by antinuclear activists, nuclear reactors are now effective condensing symbols for many people, due in part to the visual imagery of the huge concrete cooling towers usually attached to them. Various associations are possible. One is their "man-madeness," particularly offensive when they are constructed on beautiful or pristine coastlines and rivers. Another is the radiation they contain, which might in turn connote nuclear weapons. Their man-madeness and their radiation might together yield the further connotation of unnecessary technological complexity. The reactors might be associated with economic growth as a social imperative, or a utility company's search for profits. Their size may connote the centralization of economic production and control. Especially now that major nuclear accidents have been in the media, reactors are reminders of the devastating consequences of accidents.[59] Indeed, the Three Mile Island accident in 1979 was a national moral shock and became a powerful condensing symbol.

The antinuclear cartoons described above contrast tellingly with the photographs from animal rights magazines. The cartoons would not impress strangers who did not already share the cartoonist's frame; they are better at implying the urgency of the issue. The photos in *It's About Times* tended to be of demonstrations, reinforcing existing solidarity; the news, too, was most often of protest events (in the antinuclear but also in related movements). In contrast, the photos so common in animal rights literature and placards are more clearly designed to persuade strangers (especially since certain famous photos are repeated often on posters and brochures). Photos present an aura that "this is the way it is," and these particular ones are well chosen to shock. Susan Sontag once pointed out that photos give us an illusion of unmediated reality, even while they rely on pre-existing conventions and understandings: "A photograph that brings news of some unsuspected zone of misery cannot make a dent in public opinion unless there is an appropriate context of feeling and attitude. . . . Photography implies that we know about the world if we accept it as the camera records it."[60]

Self-recruitment or openness to recruitment, on the basis of moral shocks, is possible because people already have sensibilities and worldviews that can be offended. Outrage is possible even in the absence of personal persuasion. Further research on the psychology of recruits will someday tell us more about these first steps and the complex feelings and beliefs involved. For now it can suffice to contrast recruitment through networks based on independent collective identities, networks derived from prior political activism, and new networks created for emerging causes. Culture and biography are crucial parts of recruitment, something we can see only when we break down the concept of a social network to see what makes it tick.

CHANGING WORLDS

Before changing the world, protestors need to change a variety of mental worlds—their own, to start with, as well as those of potential recruits. Sometimes they only need to appeal to meanings already held, perhaps drawing out their implications. Many labels have been used to get at different aspects of these cognitive meanings, but they all point to the importance of beliefs about the world in generating protest. Protestors are extremely creative in finding new condensing symbols, in rearranging existing sensibilities, worldviews, and ideologies, and in making explicit what many had only intuitively felt. They are doing what Toni Morrison says artists do: "Responding to culture—clarifying, explicating, valorizing, translating, transforming, criticizing ... "[61] Sometimes, too, protestors are simply responding to deeper structural changes, clarifying them as they occur; but often they do much more.

Moral shocks come in many forms. In chapters 5 and 6, I looked at moral shocks administered from the outside by large organizations that did things, or asked employees to do things, that some people perceived as outrageous. In this chapter I have emphasized how movement organizers try to administer shocks through their own rhetoric, as well as the underlying mental constructions they must appeal to. In all cases, the cognitive aspects of moral shocks and other recruitment dynamics are inexplicable without their moral and emotional sides. Injustice frames, for example, are as important for their anger and outrage as for their cognitive understandings.

Chapters 5 through 7 have tried to show what makes individuals open to the arguments of recruiters, even sometimes to protest or to seek out groups on their own. There is a tendency to start explanations of protest with the networks of organizations already composing the movement, ignoring what happens at the level of biography and culture that might make people available and willing. This willingness is especially important for understanding those who first found the groups that later do the recruiting. We cannot simply assume willingness, then explain opportunity. Individual dynamics are hard to get at, but they are no less important for that. It is time, though, to turn to what goes on in movements once they have recruited people. The following four chapters look at movement culture, beginning with an activist subculture full of symbols, rituals, solidarity, and pleasures.

- If they hope to recruit others, protestors must build on existing intuitions, worldviews, and ideas.

- In doing so, however, they have considerable freedom to articulate these feelings creatively in different ways, sometimes transforming them in the process of elaborating them.

- The cultural meanings that are crucial to building a protest movement are transmitted both through personal networks of acquaintances, through formal organizations, and through less personal media to strangers.

- The culture and biography in the heads of potential recruits are as important in explaining recruitment as the strategies and resources actively deployed by protest groups; the two sides are inseparable.
- For a moral shock to lead to protest, it must have an explicit cognitive dimension as well as emotional and moral ones.

PART THREE

Movement Culture

Once an individual is recruited to a group, once a movement has established itself, its internal cultural dynamics differ from those relevant to recruitment. Now the salient questions have to do with why people return to protests, why they remain loyal to protest movements which often demand considerable time, effort, risk, and money, and why they engage in certain activities rather than others. Loyalties and choices are related to the pleasures and satisfactions that participants feel, sometimes reinforced through rituals and symbols. Protestors face many decisions, especially involving tactics, that are affected by the kind of internal culture their movement has developed. Biographical idiosyncracies also affect the pleasures individuals will derive from protest.

EIGHT

Rituals and Emotions at Diablo Canyon: Sustaining Activist Identities

[By the very action of praying] a man excites himself to pray more and to groan more humbly and more fervently. I do not know how it is that, although these motions of the body cannot come to be without a motion of the mind preceding them, when they have been made, visibly and externally, that invisible inner motion which caused them is itself strengthened. And in this manner the disposition of the heart which preceded them in order that they might be made, grows stronger because they are made.
—Augustine, *De cura pro mortuis*

It is 23 September 1981, the autumnal equinox. A small group has hiked into the golden hills surrounding the Diablo Canyon nuclear power plant under construction on the California coast. Far below them, the Diablo blockade is in full swing: a two-week site occupation followed by weeks of jail, which many participants found the most moving experience of their lives. Abalone Alliance staffer Geoff Merideth and his affinity group had wanted to perform some sort of autumnal ritual, but had no idea how. So they contacted another affinity group at the blockade, Matrix, and the two groups have hiked above the reactor. Led by Starhawk, a San Francisco Bay Area feminist and pagan spiritual leader, they create a ritual circle on the hilltop and step into this magical space. With mirrors they direct the rays of the sun down toward the reactor building, and call upon the evil powers within to destroy themselves. Because radiation is one of the few major sources of electricity that do not derive ultimately from the sun, the sun's rays, soft and brilliant in a California September, seem to join in the protest against the massive concrete structures and complex technologies inside. The ritual participants feel the entire beauty and awe of nature cry out against this human effort to play god.

Nuclear reactors require vast amounts of water for cooling, and for this reason are normally built along rivers, lakes, and seashores—sites which, throughout human history, have had a special, sacred aura. The human imagination has peopled them with nymphs and spirits and other *genii loci*. The coast of California has few spots that are not beautiful or special, and Diablo Canyon was the third coastal site where the Pacific Gas and Electric Company had tried to build its nuclear plant. The place where Ian McMillan first saw the ocean, it is set among beautiful rolling hills that turn golden when the grasses dry out during the summer. Whether or not they believed, like Starhawk, in unseen spirits and powers, those who protested against the Diablo nuclear plant were moved in part by the power of the setting. Even for these (primarily) atheists, Diablo Canyon was a sacred site.

Rituals need not be old to be powerful. Starhawk crafted this one for the occasion, tapping into the antinuclear movement's belief system, in which solar energy contrasts sharply with radiation. The exact ways in which the protestors believed in the unseen powers they called upon probably do not matter; the activity was most important. Nor do rituals need to be so explicit and purposive as this one: all sorts of collective routines can serve similar ends. Dancing, singing, camping, getting arrested, even holding meetings: all these can, because done collectively, bind participants together.

Collective rites remind participants of their basic moral commitments, stir up strong emotions, and reinforce a sense of solidarity with the group, a "we-ness." *Rituals are symbolic embodiments, at salient times and places, of the beliefs of a group.* Ritual is, in the words of Jonathan Smith, "a mode of paying attention,"[1] raising the expectations of participants that "this is important, special." They set a time, and place, and activity off from the everyday, so that what occurs there—references to beliefs and myths, assertions of solidarities and group boundaries, altered states of consciousness—increases in importance. Since explicit rituals are usually religious, they define what is sacred, including sacred places such as temples, churches, or shrines. They involve highly condensed and multivocal symbols, hinting at more meanings than could be consciously thought about during the ceremony itself. We also tend to think of rituals as actions that are standard and repeated; even Starhawk's new rite incorporated existing symbolic elements and could conceivably become a standard observance of the autumnal equinox. Not just the repeated character of rituals but their affirmation of basic beliefs seems to connect participants with deep truths about the world, and hence with the past and the future. Ritual is about underlying permanence and order, reinforcing moral and cognitive beliefs through heightened emotions.

In many forms, rituals are vital mechanisms keeping protest movements alive and well. They pull together, in an emotional format, many of a movement's cultural processes. They not only reinforce preexisting feelings, but help construct new ones. Comparing ritual to language, Mary Douglas said, "It can permit knowledge of what would otherwise not be known at all. It does not merely externalize experience, bringing it out into the light of day, but it modifies experience in so expressing it."[2] This is the way, as we saw in chapter 7, that protest leaders both express, crystallize, and transform moral sensibilities.

Rituals also allow creativity: in the actions, in the feelings aroused, in the virtuosity of performance. The special charisma of certain participants may deepen the meaning of a ritual, just as a mass performed by a Pope is special, because this individual embodies the same beliefs the ritual is intended to express. Not least, both rituals and customs provide the raw materials for artful displays. They set up expectations of how everyone will behave—expectations which can be teased, developed, and played with, before they are eventually fulfilled. The maxim that "god is in the details" applies to art works and to rituals. Details allow artfulness, but they also, because of such condensed symbolism, convey meaning. Even tiny intentional deviations from expectations are noticed, sometimes appreciated, sometimes condemned. Rituals, finally, are a crucial component of what we will examine in this chapter: the collective emotions and identities generated within a movement. In the preceding three chapters we analyzed cultural and psychological dynamics that help involve people in protest; now we will look at the culture within ongoing movements.

The Abalone Alliance exemplifies an activist network based on activist identities. It was not grounded in some pre-existing collectivity with its own networks and collective identity, like the civil rights movement, nor was it simply a movement network constructed for one cause, like the animal rights network we examined. The bonds that animated the Abalone protestors had been developed for political action before Diablo Canyon was taken up as an issue, and persisted after it. They show that networks can be both cause and effect of political programs.

COLLECTIVE EMOTIONS

Chapter 5 described the importance of emotions in spurring or opening individuals to political action, concentrating mostly on mechanisms that operated before individuals actually became active. Once a person begins to participate, she is subject to new social processes that help shape her emotions, morals, and cognitions. Her basic intuitions may not change in the course of protest, but more explicit ideas and expressions are likely to, as protestors together think through the implications of their moral visions, work out a language for describing their goals, and set out to accomplish them. Her feelings about her fellow protestors, if not about the surrounding world, are likely to be transformed. Here, many protest movements are at their most creative.

The emotions generated within protest movements contrast with the ones examined earlier, the individual feelings that might make one open to recruitment in the first place. Although both kinds are shaped by their social settings, the initial feelings grow out of existing moral frameworks such as ontological security or professional ethics. The feelings created within protest movements are attempts, often explicit, to elaborate the intuitive visions into ideologies and proposals. The outrage of a farmer living near a proposed site for a nuclear plant is the intuition that the antinuclear movement tries to build into a systematic ideology of opposition. What the farmer sees first as "meddlesome outsiders" develops into "technocracy;" fear develops into outrage. The emotions may be the same, but leaders work to strengthen, reformulate, or reframe them. Sometimes the issue is how one should feel about one's own feelings. Some of this work goes on in recruitment, but it continues within the movement itself, since recruitment and retention rely on many of the same processes.

To take one example, the women's movement of the late 1960s had, as part of its central mission, to create, legitimate, and name women's anger. In thousands of consciousness-raising groups women learned to feel less guilty about their resentment toward husbands, fathers, employers, and others. Indeed, anger was not only considered positive, it was almost a requirement for membership. As Arlie Hochschild wrote of this process, "Social movements for change make 'bad' feelings okay, and they make them useful. Depending on one's point of view, they make bad feelings 'rational.' They also make them visible."[3] According to Verta Taylor and Nancy Whittier, women's groups regularly try to transform negative feelings that many women have due to their structural positions, including depression, fear, and guilt.[4]

I once attended a meeting of an animal rights group at which protestors discussed how they should feel about the scientists, furriers, and others whose activities they disliked. Should they hate them? Pity them for being unenlightened? Try to educate them? One suggestion was to refrain from personal judgments altogether, since it was institutional demands and the structures of modern society that forced people to do these things. This effort at depersonalization failed when someone pointed out that, if evil things were being done, someone had to be doing them. The group retained its villains, and the accompanying outrage, even though the hatred was leavened by some sympathy on the grounds that everyone in modern society is a victim of instrumental bureaucracies. But speeches and placards continued to name names. The effects of such emotions are obvious in the demonization of individual scientists by many animal rights groups. Researchers receive extremely nasty letters and phone messages, expressing aggressive feelings that their sources probably never show elsewhere in their lives. Like the repressive southern sheriff, such letters can backfire when their recipients use them strategically. Those who have received anti-Semitic hate mail, for example, have been happy to share the letters with the press in an effort to tarnish the animal rights movement. In a pattern common in political conflict, each side demonizes the other.

More striking, perhaps, are emotions not just refined but created by participation in the movement, feelings that could not develop in an individual before joining. Many of the emotions generated within a protest movement—call them *reciprocal*—concern people's ongoing feelings toward each other. These are the close, affective ties of friendship, love, and loyalty, but also their negative counterparts such as rivalry, jealousy, and resentment. Together they create what Jeff Goodwin has called the "libidinal economy" of a movement, yielding many of the pleasures of protest, including erotic pleasures. Erotic motivations probably matter more than we realize in explaining participation—as well as explaining its termination when love relationships go sour.[5] Reciprocal emotions also include the complex feelings that leaders and followers feel for each other in many movements, and the extremely important *trust* that members begin to feel toward each other.

Other emotions—call them *shared*—are consciously held by a group at the same time, but they do not have the other group members as their objects. Collectively the group generates or elaborates anger toward outsiders, or outrage over government policies. It trusts certain individuals and institutions and mistrusts others. The power of shared emotions comes from expressing them together, from recognizing and proclaiming that they are shared, so that they become what Max Scheler called a "feeling-in-common."[6] It is this collective expression that helps create movement identities.

Reciprocal and shared emotions, although distinct, reinforce each other. Each measure of shared outrage against a nuclear plant reinforces the reciprocal emotion of fondness for others precisely because they feel the same way. They are like us; they understand. Conversely, mutual affection is one context in which new shared emotions are easily created. Because you are fond of others, you want to adopt their feelings. As I said of individuals, you trust those you agree with, and agree with those you trust. Reciprocal and shared emotions both foster solidarity within a protest group. They are key sources of identification with a movement.

Scale should be a relevant factor in generating collective emotions, since face-to-face interactions differ in groups of ten, fifty, or five hundred people. It would be useful to sort out the emotional dynamics of each kind. There is some related evidence that smaller churches (say, fifty people) are better at generating long-term emotional commitment than larger ones, although revival meetings of thousands can be effective in other ways.[7]

Collective emotions, the reciprocal ones especially, are linked to the pleasures of protest, many of which will be discussed further in the following chapter. Most obvious are the pleasures of being with people one likes, in any number of ways. Other pleasures arise from the joys of collective activities, such as losing oneself in collective motion or song. This can be satisfying even when done with strangers—who of course no longer feel like strangers. The example of the Abalone Alliance shows the conscious cultivation as well as the broad impact of collective emotions.

THE ABALONE ALLIANCE

The Abalone Alliance was formed in 1976 to use "direct action" (illegal activities such as blockades and site occupations) against the Diablo Canyon nuclear plant in San Luis Obispo. Its members worked alongside the Mothers for Peace, local protestors primarily using legal interventions in Nuclear Regulatory Commission (NRC) hearings. Nationally, too, the antinuclear movement adopted direct-action tactics at this time, as local opponents were joined by nonlocals favoring more radical tactics and ideologies. The radicals were impressed by the apparent success of the German antinuclear movement in stopping construction at Whyl by camping at the site and physically blocking work. This was more than normal civil disobedience, the breaking of a law in order to get arrested and thereby make a moral statement. This tactic, in the tradition of peasant sabotage and workers' sit-down strikes, involved direct obstruction. First in Seabrook, New Hampshire, then at other sites around the country, American activists tried similar direct actions. With this wave of new recruits came extensive media coverage and a reassuring sense of their identity as a national antinuclear movement.[8]

The Abalone Alliance held two large rallies in 1977 and 1978, timed to coincide each year with the anniversary of the Hiroshima bombing. Roughly five thousand participated and five hundred were arrested at the 1978 demonstration. The anti-Diablo efforts received a boost from the Three Mile Island accident in March 1979, after which several protest events around the state culminated in a rally of forty thousand at Diablo Canyon. In September 1981, after the plant had received its first license for low-power testing, an Abalone blockade and encampment lasted two weeks and attracted more than two thousand. It was during this direct action that Starhawk developed the ritual described above. Perhaps her magic worked. On the day the blockade was scheduled to end, an engineer for the electric company announced that, due to a misreading of blueprints during construction, extensive retrofits would be necessary. This reconstruction lasted three years, during which many of the alliance's component affinity groups began turning their attention to other issues.

In the summer of 1984 the NRC granted another low-power testing license for one of the two Diablo reactors. After years of protests, site occupations, and construction scandals, it seemed the protestors had finally lost. Yet two weeks later, the first Sunday in August, one thousand of them gathered at the plant gate for an afternoon of speeches and arrests organized by the Abalone Alliance. The afternoon's program, after speeches on Diablo Canyon's history and risks, culminated in a sit-down blockade of the gate by dozens of protestors, most of whom allowed themselves to be arrested while the rest of the crowd cheered. The entire process seemed comfortable to both sides: as one bystander said, "After so many actions, they're just going through a ritual." Almost one hundred were arrested. During this rally a friend and I collected the data used in this chapter and in chapter 7 (and described in the Appendix).

The Abalone Alliance and similar antinuclear groups were part of a subculture of nonviolent direct action that developed in many parts of the United States and Europe in the late 1970s, defined by egalitarian, feminist, pacifist, and ecologist values, and by internal procedures centered on consensus decision making and efforts to create community: the post-industrial movements described by European theorists. This "countercultural network" also shared a willingness to break the law, avoidance of normal political channels as too slow or resistant, rejection of violence against people, a concern with exemplary moral actions (especially civil disobedience) covered by the news media, and criticism of bureaucracy and hierarchy, even in the groups' own internal structure.[9] Drawing especially on feminism and ecology, the culture's ideology entailed personal autonomy, a rejection of oppression (including sexism, racism, and other biases), and a critique of capitalism. There was an anarchist, "small-is-beautiful" suspicion of large organizations, and a left-leaning critique of instrumental rationality. For some post-industrial activists, a market distribution of goods and services was repugnant, while others looked to markets as protection against state bureaucracy. Yet most agreed that markets could not be left completely unregulated.

The favored organizational form of this culture, especially in the United States, was the affinity group: a small number of people (usually ten to fifteen) who supported each other, made decisions together, and carried out direct action as a team. The affinity groups were autonomous units, sometimes even moving intact from one protest movement to another, especially from nuclear energy to the peace movement of the early 1980s; they occasionally linked pre-existing personal networks (some groups were based on common church membership, neighborhood, occupation, or ideology) to activist networks within political movements. More often these were networks of comrades developed out of political loyalties and action. They embodied the reciprocal emotions that arise out of political activities, as group members developed strong attachments to each other.

The names of the Abalone Alliance affinity groups convey messages about their function and mood: The Eyes of the World, Matrix, No Nukes and Hold the Anchovies, Love and Rage, the Solar Spinsters, the Wild and Tackeys, SABOT (Society against Blatant and Obnoxious Technology; also the French root for *sabotage*, referring to the wooden clogs with which nineteenth-century workers jammed new machines). The naming of one's own group—and the organizational identity this proclaims—can be as important as naming the abuse one protests. The light, humorous touch of the Abalone Alliance was combined with a sophisticated social and historical analysis.

Members of this subculture consciously avoided creating the visible leaders that movements of the 1960s had. An affinity-group structure discouraged this (especially with task rotation), and these activists had learned a lesson from, or in, the 1960s. One told me how, as a Yippie, he had learned the dangers of letting "leaders" be created by the media or government (through trials). Abalone staff at the statewide office (four full-time activists who called themselves anarchists and had worked in many movements for social change) rotated jobs, and they were carefully controlled by the alliance of affinity groups, a continual source of friction. This concern for internal democracy rested on an awareness of the emotional needs of the groups, on a desire to build emotional ties between members even when these interfered with efficiency.

The direct-action groups also built solidarity through "decision making by consensus"—also called "feminist process": discussion of an issue was expected to continue until all present agreed, with the proviso that an individual with a strong moral objection could block a group decision. Most organizations in advanced capitalist societies value clarity of argument, supporting evidence of an objective, factual nature, and critical procedures capable of uncovering incorrect positions, regardless of the feelings of the participants. In contrast, feminist process valued participants' feelings and emotions, whether or not lessons could be drawn from them; what someone said had to be taken seriously and not directly attacked as wrong; discourse was constrained by the context of human emotional responses. The ideal of one position being proven against all others was replaced by the incorporation of all perspectives into one position, however unwieldy and inelegant. If this could not be done, no position was taken. This process rarely led to clear, concise positions, which would have risked alienating those who disagreed with them. The truth of participants' feelings was as important as the truth of facts.[10]

What scholarly observers criticized (using strategic criteria of the efficient attainment of external goals) as a reduced ability to achieve stated political goals instead reflected the emotional needs of the movement subculture. In this case, the explicit goal was to build positive affective bonds of solidarity between members and to "prefigure" a social order ruled by consensus, even though this procedure sometimes precluded effective action. The cultural and strategic logics of protest were sometimes in conflict but sometimes not.[11]

The Abalone Alliance devoted considerable time to developing member solidarity. Barbara Epstein described the "monthly conferences at which people shared meals, partied together, and spent nights side by side in sleeping bags on the floor."[12] The local affinity groups had their own regular activities that brought members together. Then the occasional direct actions brought everyone together at Diablo Canyon, in very intense periods of living together. These activities were like rituals, in that people were enacting their deep moral values, in this case centering on participatory democracy: "It was like an overstimulated New England town. Part of what Diablo was about was just that: self-government. We were using a model that we really had faith in. It was our ideology in action."[13]

Strong emotional attachments were reinforced by other cultural processes: spiritual images and inspiration, a folklore about the movement, complete with embroidered stories and heroes, a great deal of singing and dancing and physical contact. California's direct-action movements were held together not just by a shared political analysis and strategy but also by affective bonds and a sense of shared experience, which members in turn reinforced by using direct-action strategies. Said one participant of the 1981 blockade, "This was a town with no discernible leaders; everyone was equal, everyone was walking around hugging each other, there was incredible bonding."[14] Such processes helped to build a strong sense of community among Abalone members, who intentionally crafted solidarity out of shared emotions, moral visions, and beliefs. All social movements rely on cultural processes, but those in the anti-Diablo movement were especially extensive and pervasive, as well as consciously designed, developed, and promoted. The Abalone Alliance richly demonstrates the emotional and other cultural processes that help sustain a protest movement.

Citizenship movements can usually take an underlying collective identity for granted, albeit one constantly or potentially under revision. Post-citizenship movements cannot, and so spend considerable time building and maintaining activist, movement, and organizational identities based on political goals. They had to create the kinds of social networks and accompanying solidarities that civil rights organizers could take for granted. The rituals of the civil rights movement, based in African-American protestantism, were just as culturally rich, but they did not have to be invented in the way Starhawk's was. Having existed for decades, they could be reworked within tighter limits.

SONG AND DANCE ROUTINES

When I first visited the Abalone Alliance staff in their San Francisco office in 1984, I had to wait at the open door while the four of them finished dancing. It was the slow, loose dance style of the 1960s, not the crisp, showy style then popular—more Woodstock than Michael Jackson. It was introspective, therapeutic, and hypnotic. At times, the staff members touched each other and swayed (more or less) in unison. I waited awkwardly, not sure what to do, or what I had stumbled upon. They had just finished a staff meeting, they later explained, and this was their way of reasserting their solidarity, of washing away disagreements and nervous energy that the meeting might have generated.

Singing and dancing are two activities often found in rituals, providing the requisite emotional charge through music, coordinated physical activity, and bodily contact. Since Emile Durkheim first described "collective effervescence," it has been clear that these activities are crucial in creating it, in transporting participants onto another plane, into what they feel is a more ethereal, or at any rate different, reality.[15] The actions themselves strengthen the will that should create them, as Augustine pointed out in his example of prayer. In many ways, singing and dancing (and other forms of coordinated movement, from marches to human chains) are the kernel of truth in crowd theories, the one moment when a large group can attain a certain coordination and unity, can silence the small groups talking among themselves, can concentrate the attention of all. Of course, this coordination can never emerge spontaneously, since participants must know the dances and the lyrics. And it is hard to imagine *all* participants joining in. But Durkheim was pointing to important processes.

Singing can combine the thrill of crowd unison with statements of basic cosmological beliefs, as Aldon Morris discovered in the Christian hymns and spirituals of the civil rights movement. Lyrics such as "Onward Christian Soldiers," "There's a Great Day Coming," and "We Shall Overcome" lent biblical authority to the campaign with specific references to fundamental beliefs and narratives. Deliverance through a great leader—Moses, Jesus, Martin Luther King Jr.—was a reassuring message. Extensive religious training meant that almost all black participants knew the music, loudly generating a feeling of solidarity. Lyrics are a form of shared knowledge that helps one feel like an insider. But the emotions remain foremost. Morris quotes King: "The opening hymn was the old familiar 'Onward Christian Soldiers,' and when that mammoth audience stood to sing, the voices outside (the church building could not accommodate the large gatherings) swelling the chorus in the church, there was a mighty ring like the glad echo of heaven itself.... The enthusiasm of these thousands of people swept everything along like an onrushing tidal wave."[16] It is hard to imagine more powerful emotional materials.

Dance too can express fundamental stances toward the world. Judith Lynne Hanna has described cases when "dance groups became conscious collective efforts to bring about change." In the industrialized countries modern dance was itself partly a rebellion against constricting styles of dress and expectations for women's bodies: "Braless, corsetless, and barefoot, the modern dancer's free style of dress symbolized a host of freedoms and a renewed, diversified self-image."[17] Social attitudes and aspirations are literally embodied in human postures and gestures, so dance firmly expresses moral visions and emotions. Dance is a stylized language that can convey messages as part of a ritual or in a ritualized form on their own. Perhaps most important, dance conveys the unity of a group whose bodily motions are carefully coordinated. It "provokes a sense of personal and group power for performer and observer alike."[18] This is the reason that dance can be vital to building collective solidarity, empowerment, and affection.

To return to the Abalone Alliance, the only segment of the crowd I could not survey in 1984 was the thirty or forty people who spent the day dancing, apparently oblivious to the other protest activities. Like the staffers, they danced with the loose, introverted writhing of the 1960s meant to rearrange one's inner spiritual life more than to impress others. (The remnants of California's counterculture were equally evident in those who built altars and spread flowers and artifacts in the dirt. These respondents reacted suspiciously to the survey, but often spent an hour or more going through its four pages, scribbling commentary on the questions and discussing it with each other. For them, even responding to a questionnaire was not an individual act, but a collective and political one—like so much of their lives.)

Singing and dancing contribute to the euphoric moods that rituals, at their most successful, create. These are affirmations of participants' identities and beliefs, as well as of their power. As Durkheim sensed, collective rituals and gatherings suggest that you are participating in something bigger than you: you are a part of history, or you are morally sanctioned, or you truly belong to a group. The emotions of rituals reinforce cognitive and moral visions as well.[19]

ONE CULTURE OF ACTIVISM

The California direct-action subculture is the kind of activist network that has supported many post-industrial movements. The solidarity of the Abalone Alliance was built on a long history of shared political activities. Foremost, naturally, was their heavy involvement in anti-Diablo and antinuclear work. While 42 percent had traveled 24 miles or less to attend the 1984 protest, 17 percent came 25 to 149 miles, 29 percent came 150 to 250 miles, and 12 percent came more than 250 miles. Protestors had also made large contributions of time: while 54 percent spent less than five hours per month in antinuclear work, 22 percent spent five to nine hours per month, 9 percent ten to nineteen hours, and 15 percent more than twenty hours. Almost everyone also claimed to have contributed money to the movement: only 15 percent had donated nothing in the previous year, 30 percent under twenty dollars, 21 percent twenty to forty-nine dollars, 11 percent fifty to ninety-nine dollars, and 24 percent one hundred or more dollars. Respondents had invested a lot in a campaign that seemed, in 1984, to have failed to attain its most direct objective, shutting Diablo Canyon.

For most respondents, though, antinuclear work was simply the current stage in activist biographies. Many came from cohorts influenced by political movements of the 1960s: 22 percent were under 25 years old; 60 percent were between 25 and 40; 18 percent were over 40. These

Table 8.1   Events Mentioned Most Often as Leading to Antinuclear Activism

28	Three Mile Island accident
14	Previous rallies and demonstrations
8	1981 Diablo blockade
7	Diablo's problems in general
6	Conferences and teach-ins
6	Livermore activities
5	Proximity to the plant
5	Nuclear accidents
4	Anti-war activities
4	Courses
4	Anti-missile activities
4	Seabrook anti-nuclear activities
3	1984 Democratic convention
3	Nuclear Regulatory Commission hearings
3	Other environmental activism

were not—as some have said of the new social movements to explain their interest in personal identity—young people trying to work out their own identities as they came of age. As many studies have shown, those politically active in the 1960s generally remained active later.[20] In the Diablo case, the reason seems to be participation in an ongoing subculture centered around political activity. The projects, skills, mutual support, and reciprocal emotions of this subculture helped activists to avoid "burnout," which some observers believe endemic to political activity.[21] Their ongoing activist identities made them more likely to join the fight against Diablo Canyon.

I asked participants what had brought them to Diablo that day and to antinuclear activism more generally.[22] Events were cited as important most often, even though fewer people specifically wrote in important events than wrote in previous activism. Table 8.1 presents the number of respondents who mentioned each catalyzing event. Events were mentioned, naturally enough, because participants insisted they were reacting directly to phenomena in the world, namely the dangers of nuclear energy. We have seen the symbolic power of events. But few of the entries in table 8.1 are historical events in the sense of the Three Mile Island (TMI) accident; they are not dangers, accidents, or threats from nuclear plants; nor political or regulatory decisions; nor events related to the proliferation of nuclear weapons materials. Instead they

Table 8.2   Previous Activism Mentioned Most Often as Leading to Antinuclear
Activism

37	Anti-war activities
19	Environmentalism
12	Feminism, women's movement, and ERA
11	Nuclear disarmament
9	Civil rights
8	Animal rights
7	Electoral politics
6	Draft resistance
6	Central America
4	Gay rights
4	Greenpeace
3	1981 Diablo blockade
3	Unionism

are antinuclear and related activities in which respondents themselves
took part. The TMI accident heads the list, as a striking media event
and moral shock. But organizers told me TMI was important partly
because there were organizations ready to channel people's anxieties;
likewise, there was a large rally in San Francisco only ten days after
TMI, enticing people into antinuclear work. Overall, activities and
events in which respondents participated were more salient than simple events they saw in the media. TMI was an important moral shock,
but people's own actions were just as important in building movement loyalty.

Respondents also described prior activism, ranging back to the political movements of the 1960s (table 8.2). The anti-war category probably consists mostly of anti-Vietnam activity, since many specified this,
and others were of the right age. Environmentalism and feminism—
said to be at the heart of the direct-action culture—were also important. Only one person mentioned the 1976 antinuclear referendum
in California. The reason may be that many, while active in some cause
at that time, did not come to the antinuclear movement until the late
seventies. In interviews, several protesters said they had to be convinced by friends and fellow activists that the antinuclear movement
was not "hopelessly" middle-class and reformist. Said one, "I was
Maoist then [in 1976] and still hoping for a real revolution. But less
and less. But nuclear energy as a radical cause? Forget it. I wouldn't
have touched it back then. A couple years later, my girlfriend changed

my mind, though. . . . It wasn't easy: she basically threatened to dump me before I took it seriously" (more erotic motivations).

What is an activist identity? One reason that activity in one cause leads to activity in another is a sense of personal and collective efficacy, a feeling that one's participation may actually make a difference—what movement activists call "empowerment." They are explicit about the activities that foster this powerful emotion: sustained, difficult, emotional, even painful collective experiences. Demonstrations and marches work, but jail time works even better. The greatest instance of empowerment in the California direct-action culture was the Diablo blockade of 1981, during which participants camped together, made decisions together, then endured jail together. Almost everyone who participated in the blockade and stayed in the movement speaks of it in the kind of glowing terms usually reserved for religious conversions. And as with religious conversions, some participants rejected this style and left the movement completely, first shaking but ultimately reinforcing the fervor of those who stayed. Several other Diablo occupations had similar effects. This is the reason the "events" of table 8.1 were most often political activities in which respondents had themselves participated, activities that had given them a sense of their own power. As someone commented who joined the movement after the 1981 blockade, "I've always been kind of jealous of the people who went through the blockade. They have an incredible bond that they'll always have."

There are many components to an activist identity: skills and know-how; awareness of the potential pleasures of protest, although also its pitfalls; an articulate political ideology, program, and specific goals; and a network of friends and comrades who support all of this. Network analyses of protest have often been satisfied with pointing out interpersonal ties, without elaborating on the accompanying habits, sense of efficacy, and role expectations that also support political activism. It is impossible to say which comes first: friends and even family are important in drawing one into political activism, but one then develops other contacts within a movement. Once people get involved, the subculture welcomes them, sustaining their participation through affective bonds as well as practical convenience (information about events, shared rides to them). They don't face the same costs and benefits of participation: the benefits increase and the costs decrease, as the following remark indicates: "You get hooked. Plus you meet people who remind you, can give you rides, just make it more fun." Here is a subculture of people who have been politically active, whose friends, family, and acquaintances also are, and who feel that this activism is an important part of their lives. When asked what had kept her going during four years of work on women's issues followed by five years of antinuclear work, one local activist replied, "There's a seamless web of spiritual energy flowing through it. My fellow activists, many of which are also personal friends (in fact most of my friends are pretty active: that helps). . . . Then there's all the stuff I've learned: everything about nuclear energy, but also about organizing. The beautiful thing is that I learned it from people I love, and with people I love. Sometimes literally: I've had three lovers who were also very active."

Activist networks, like most subcultures, are typically based on similarities in age, occupations, social background, and education, and my sample is distinct from the surrounding California population in all these. Marital status reflects lifestyle choices: only 25 percent of respondents said they were living with a spouse (compared to 53 percent of Californians age 15 and older); 22 percent were divorced or separated; 40 percent said never married; 12 percent said they were "living together"; and 0.1 percent were widowed. Not having a family enables one to attend political protest events, but not having a family in turn often reflects—for those in their thirties—conscious decisions. Biographical availability, which appears at first as an objective demographic or structural trait, is partly a political choice. One Abalone Alliance staffer described her household (herself, a male partner, two children, and two other adults) as part family and part affinity group, run by consensus even down to the raising of her ten-year-old son.

Occupations also reflected politics. Respondents tended to have jobs with helping and person-to-person contacts, personal autonomy, and an ability to shape or nurture something—the plant world and inanimate objects as well as people (see table 8.3). There were many gardeners, landscapers, carpenters, and artists alongside teachers, activists, nurses, and secretaries. A "feminist beekeeper" was nurturing in her work, but not in the service sector; she was obviously highly political as well. The counterculture was further represented by occupations such as tempeh maker, plant healer, and squatter. "It's funny," said one gardener, "I gave up law school [after college] to shovel cowshit. But I love it. . . . I work outside, in the sun, and nobody ever bosses me around. I haven't worn a tie in twenty years."[23]

Other job characteristics confirmed that personal autonomy was important to respondents; they were living out the anti-instrumental values we saw in chapter 7. They have avoided large, bureaucratic organizations: 54 percent said they were neither supervised nor in charge of anyone else at work. When asked what size of business or organization they worked for, 22 percent said only themselves (compared to 10 per-

Table 8.3 Antinuclear Respondents' Occupations

59	Students (39 full-time; 20 in combination with another occupation)
29	Teachers
17	Gardeners, landscapers, and horticulturalists
9	Carpenters, woodworkers, and cabinet-makers
8	Activists
7	Artists
7	Waitresses and waiters
6	Nurses
6	Secretaries
6	Engineers, mostly electrical
6	Volunteers
6	House-persons
5	Domestics
5	Social workers
4	Writers
4	College professors
4	Farmers and ranchers
4	Unemployed
4	Electricians
4	Bookkeepers and accountants
4	Journalists
4	Small business owners and operators
3	Retired people
3	Psychological technicians
3	Administrators
3	Lawyers
3	Manual laborers

Two of each of the following: custodians, biologists, video filmmakers, anthropologists, librarians, medical assistants, truckdrivers, salespeople, computer specialists, factory workers, postal clerks, lab technicians, and musicians.

One of each of the following: radio program producer, psychologist, auto mechanic, announcer, fork-lift driver, store manager, principal, program coordinator, marine ecologist, administrative assistant, photographer, tree trimmer, dance teacher, biologist, house painter, marketing manager, media consultant, mechanical designer, roofer, keypunch operator, physician's assistant, medical secretary, civil servant, art dealer, solar installer, counselor, inventor, occupational therapist, computer systems analyst, physicist, scientist, research specialist, builder/boatmaker, purchasing agent, naturalist, kitchen manager, advertiser, telephone operator, massage therapist, hairdresser, chiropractor, interviewer, chemist, ecologist, jeweler, clergyman, child therapist, dilettante, plant healer, squatter, tempeh maker, beekeeper, and student of life.

Note: Some respondents gave more than one occupation; each is listed.

cent of employed Californians who are "self-employed" or employed by their own company, and to only 6 percent of all adult Californians). Only 29 percent said their employers had one hundred or more employees (compared to almost half the national work force), and many of these were government employees such as teachers. One commented: "I'm not a hippie, but I'd drop dead before I worked for a big corporation."

In addition to a certain lifestyle and autonomy at work, respondents' educational levels, unusually high for their occupations and incomes, suggest occupations chosen for inherent pleasures rather than high incomes. Fully 33 percent had completed some graduate work; 23 percent had only finished college; another 32 percent had done some college work; a mere 12 percent had only high school or less. So 56 percent were college graduates, compared to 16 percent of California's adults at the time. Approximately one-fifth of the respondents were students, but one-third of these also listed another occupation (which was probably primary, to guess from most respondents' ages): education was for them a way of life, not a stage of life.

The picture of a single, direct-action subculture is blurred slightly in the survey results by a mixture of local and nonlocal protestors. (This uneasy coalition will be described further in chapter 10.) Not all my respondents belonged to Abalone affinity groups or were part of this activist subculture. Some were curious passersby; others (like the Mothers for Peace, many of whom attended the rally) opposed Diablo Canyon but did not belong to the Abalone Alliance. I believe that most of the casual participants are identifiable because they had traveled shorter distances to the protest; most were locals. In the results below I shall occasionally use contrasts between those who traveled less than twenty-five miles with those who traveled more, in order to strengthen points about the activist subculture represented especially by the nonlocals.

Why did protest against Diablo Canyon persist even after it seemed to have failed with the granting of the license, and after direct-action protest had disappeared from most other contested nuclear plants around the country? The emotional dynamics of the Diablo subculture were strong enough to keep the movement together after its "rational" or instrumental life should have been over. I want to look at three effects of these collective emotions: the symbolic place of Diablo Canyon in California's activist subculture; mobilization and tactical efforts; and individual motives that combine expressive and instrumental goals. Affective allegiance to the subculture influenced each of these.

EMOTIONAL RESONANCE AND MOTIVATION

Protestors had strong loyalties to each other, and to their shared history. Diablo Canyon had a central place in the history and mythology of California's direct-action subculture. Several Abalone staffers told me that activists had a sentimental attachment to Diablo Canyon and would come to it far more readily than to actions elsewhere. This attachment arose out of Diablo's deep resonance for many political activists in California: a collective history, including the creation of many affinity groups; strong emotional and symbolic connotations, supported by a rich culture of heroes and stories; heightened symbolic importance due to the national news media, which portrayed the controversy as representative of nuclear energy's fate; and a beautiful site. The name, meaning Devil, also played into the subculture's rhetoric emphasizing good and evil. "Send the Devil to Hell," said one placard. The Abalone newspaper, as we saw in the last chapter, portrayed Diablo Canyon and nuclear energy as the devil, death, a bloated military bureaucracy, a clown, and a nuclear missile. Just as individuals and events can take on special symbolic salience, so can places.

The visual beauty of Diablo Canyon was crucial to its development as a sacred site, for the expansive vistas helped protestors—or any visitors—appreciate the setting. In explaining why offshore oil drilling was opposed in California but not Louisiana, William Freudenburg and Robert Gramling found an important difference in the fact that the California coastline is clearly visible, while Louisiana's is inaccessible and impenetrable due to the muddy swamps. Ninety percent of California's coastline can be reached by roads, compared to only 12 percent of Louisiana's. The imagination can define and defend a place more neatly when the eyes can see its parameters, especially when to see it is to appreciate it.[24]

Gorgeous weather confirms the special character of a place or an event at that place. It is not only for reasons of turnout that organizers hold rallies in June rather than January. Outdoor events have a special thrill, often a joyful carnival atmosphere. Some protest groups are probably stuck with bad weather; anti-fur demonstrators, for example, must march in November because that's when people buy coats. But who in the animal rights movement chose early April for their annual Lab Animal Day? Someone in California, not New England. When the weather is nice, the whole earth seems to be an ally—an important symbol for environmental and related movements. Like rituals, good weather heightens emotions.

Events can loom large, I have argued, in collective memory, and none more so than founding events. Sometimes these are large founding events like the French Revolution. Others are smaller in scale, like the creation of a protest group. Diablo Canyon had special resonance in part because so many of California's affinity groups had been created for action there, especially for the dramatic 1981 encampment. Places can have charisma just as surely as individuals can.

For religious people, regular church attendance is important, but so is an occasional pilgrimage to an important and perhaps distant shrine. Affinity groups carried on regular local activities, but Diablo Canyon provided the occasion for a pilgrimage to a sacred—and quite beautiful—place. Victor Turner has described the significance of pilgrimages. *Outside normal social structures, pilgrimages to a sacred site involve a loosening of usual bonds, a heightened sense of community, strong emotionality, a sacred time for miracles.* Victor and Edith Turner suggest that "some form of deliberate travel to a far place intimately associated with the deepest, most cherished, axiomatic values of the traveler seems to be a 'cultural universal.' If it is not religiously sanctioned, counseled, or encouraged, it will take other forms."[25] This sense of a sacred site and history is one reason that direct action continued at Diablo while it faded at other sites (Seabrook in New Hampshire might have had a similar magical draw as the inspiration for the American direct-action movement, had not bitter conflict over property destruction destroyed the Clamshell Alliance). Protestors had special emotional motivations to continue.

As cultural constructs, pilgrimages and homes form a striking contrast. "Home," we have seen, offers shelter, security, and comfort. Nothing "happens" there. Home is an important pillar of ontological security, offering (symbolically, although not always in actuality) characteristic emotions. Pilgrimages and their sites, in contrast, are unusual places where things can happen; their emotions are too intense for daily consumption. Home is safe, tolerant, intimate, and rather boring, while the external world is exciting but dangerous and unforgiving. For some, the "real self" is associated with the home; for others with the altered reality of the pilgrimage and other public events.

Local protestors, somewhat less likely to belong to Abalone affinity groups, attached a different importance to Diablo Canyon: it *was* near *their* homes. The motivation to protect their homes was as strong as the Abalone members' desire for a pilgrimage, but by 1984 locals may have already begun the process of resignation apparently necessary for living near an operating nuclear plant.[26] Locals had the fears and anxieties examined in chapter 5: direct emotions, a feeling of threat to their homes, that made them open to protest. The nonlocals had other emotions, partly derived from the pleasures of protest itself. "What's amazing," said one local activist, trying to contrast his motives with those of nonlocals, "is how much these people [from other places] care about Diablo. There's something magical about it for them."

The two families of collective emotions—shared and reciprocal—generated within social movements were here fused. The same emotional experiences, notably the blockade and jail, heightened participants' bonds with each other and helped them construct similar feelings of anger and outrage over Diablo Canyon, the same strange sensation of power and powerlessness. Their affection for each other and shared outrage over Diablo Canyon altered their assessments of the costs and benefits of participation in protest.

EMOTIONS AND RESOURCES

The protestors' emotional bonds and activist identities drastically reduced the resources necessary for mobilizing participants to attend protests. At the suggestion of local affinity groups, for example, the Abalone Alliance office in San Luis Obispo planned the 1984 demonstration. It publicized the event by calling local affinity groups and placing a notice in the Abalone Alliance monthly newspaper *It's About Times*. But the planners report a minimum of effort: "We mostly just had to pick a date, then it was a few hours of phone calls," said one.

What had occurred over the previous eight years to build the newsletter and the network of contacts? The expenditure of time and money by leaders was never great. The Abalone Alliance lacked the tools often important in rationalist and mobilization models: it had no material incentives to reward those who participated (and to withhold from others); it had no coercive sanctions; it represented a minimum of formal statewide organization and leadership. Further, the affinity groups had established the statewide office and continued to control it, not the reverse. The Alliance, as the name indicates, was composed of the local groups; the staff in the statewide offices were simply paid employees. The staff even had to form their own affinity group to participate in Alliance decisions, since individuals could not be members. The Alliance had no formal leader. As with much post-industrial protest, it was an extremely "loosely structured" (decentralized, segmented) movement.[27]

Formal organizations were created by networks of activists, and the organizations attained little autonomy from that subculture. There was important feedback, though: the statewide staff helped the groups co-

ordinate their actions, especially by publishing the newsletter and accumulating information on political and legal developments. It reinforced the solidarity of the subculture. But it may be more useful to
see these organizations as one facet or outgrowth of this cultural network, rather than as purposive extractors and mobilizers of resources.
They are "collectivist organizations," defined by Joyce Rothschild-
Whitt as lacking central authority and hierarchy, using job rotation,
minimizing material incentives, and driven by shared political values
and a sense of community.[28] To use Tönnies' old distinction, they are
more like communities, blurring means and ends, than like purposive
organizations.

"I'll always have time for Diablo Canyon," said one protestor who
had traveled 150 miles from the San Francisco Bay area. "Even when
it's sad and frustrating, it'll be important to me. This is my political
life, and these are my comrades." The trip to Diablo was not a cost,
calculated against some potential payoff. It was part of this man's political life, part of his favored set of routines for doing politics. He went
on to talk about the people he knew there, the people he had driven
down with, and his experiences in previous protests. To me, the best
way to think about this man is not that he confuses costs and benefits,
or that he blurs them, or even (although this is accurate) that he simply
values the benefits more than the costs. There are so many kinds of
costs and especially benefits here that there is no straightforward way
to tally them up and compare them. Going to Diablo has a lot to do
with who this man is, at a level where time and money do not usually
matter. The trip is also a kind of habit, but a moral, thoughtful habit,
not a thoughtless trivial one. Costs may even boost the moral weight
of participation in protest.[29]

Emotional allegiance to fellow protestors affected every aspect of
their protest. For the nonlocals who were the core of the activist subculture, even tactics and organizational structure were chosen partly to
reinforce the subculture. In a survey question about future tactics for
fighting Diablo, locals were more likely to favor (more individualistic)
lobbying and letter-writing, while nonlocals were more in favor of
(more collective) civil disobedience. For the locals, solidarity-building
tactics had less value aside from their ability to stop Diablo Canyon.
(Not that tactics were simply neutral for them, either, but as we'll see
in chapter 10, their tastes were quite different.)

It is peculiar to think of affective ties as some kind of "resource" to
use in mobilization, for they are part of the cultural context that defines
both the goals and benefits of the protest as well as its perceived costs.
Spending a sunny afternoon with a beloved community along the Cali-

Table 8.4   "Most Likely Outcome" of the Anti-Diablo Protest

99	Public-oriented: media coverage, influence public opinion, education, publicity. (36 percent of respondents)
42	Nothing, not much. (15 percent)
40	Express solidarity, movement building: reinforce movement, keep going, mutual support, empowerment, maintain energy, solidarity. (15 percent)
25	Express emotions: show them we're here, show them we're angry; show NRC in a bad light; emotional release; feel good about our activities. (9 percent)
9	Direct: More investigation, delay, shut it down, get license revoked. (3 percent)
3	Encourage workers, whistleblowers to come forward. (1 percent)
2	Miracle. (1 percent)
59	Did not answer. (22 percent)

Note: Due to several multiple answers, percentages sum to 102.

fornia coast is not, it would seem, best analyzed as a cost. Cultural and emotional contexts determine what is a cost and what is a benefit.

GOALS AND EXPECTATIONS

The expectations and goals of protestors were also shaped by their emotional loyalties. My survey asked what respondents thought was the most likely outcome of the day's protest. As Bert Klandermans has argued, expectations are a crucial intervening variable in explaining the rationality of protest participation: what people do depends partly (but not entirely) on what they think can be achieved.[30] Table 8.4 lists the numbers of respondents who gave various answers.

Nine respondents aspired to direct, external goals: having the license revoked, reopening NRC hearings, shutting the reactor. In most rationalist and mobilization approaches, these are the "real," practical goals of protest. One protestor, interviewed later, said, "There's always a chance that some politician in Sacramento will hear us and rethink, or the wife of some NRC guy will be vacationing out here and will get turned on by it all, and go back and talk her husband into having more hearings." These narrow hopes were unlikely to be realized, given that the reactor had just been granted a license, so that to expect this result was almost to engage in a form of magical thinking (in the sense that there is no practical mechanism for attaining the hoped-for result). One woman who canvassed full-time for the Alliance did believe in the possibility of a literal miracle (as did one other respondent): "Remember what happened right after the [1981] blockade? They discovered the reversed blueprints [which delayed construction]. We've got a lot of beautiful energy here today, and that's very, very powerful." Pilgrimages, as the Turners say, are a time of miracles.

Twenty-five respondents seemed satisfied to express emotions without ulterior motives: showing the NRC and the reactor owner their anger, releasing their frustrations, feeling good about their activities. That number climbs to sixty-seven if we include those who expected nothing to happen (it is hard to understand their participation as other than expressive in this way). Said one, "It's a catharsis. I know nothing's going to happen, but I'm angry, and it feels good to be with other people who are angry too. Those bastards haven't paid any attention to us yet, but that doesn't mean we don't matter. We're here and we're mad." Another: "It's too late to stop Diablo. But it feels good to have kind of a last hurrah, to console each other that we're still right, even if nobody's listening." A third: "I wanted to show some sympathy for the poor people who have to live around there." All three protestors mentioned emotional expression, but none saw this as the act of a frustrated individual, as crowd theorists might. They described both the shared and reciprocal emotions of the anti-Diablo movement.

Forty respondents directly mentioned the movement: maintaining its energy, a feeling of empowerment, mutual support, solidarity. "Diablo's just one battle; we'll be fighting the same people and the same ideas in other places. . . . It's important to keep together." Ninety-nine others mentioned outcomes that could either curtail nuclear energy (albeit indirectly) or bolster "the cause" by reaching out to the public: media coverage, public education, public opinion. (Reflecting their activist identities, many understood "the cause" as a broad search for social justice, whatever the fate of nuclear energy itself.) Reinforcing the movement, or "the cause" broadly construed, was the expectation of most respondents.

These expectations fit together more than they appear to at first, casting doubt on any simple contrast between instrumental and expressive, rational and irrational, or cognitive and emotional. "Expressive" responses were given not just by individuals who felt the need to let off steam, but by those who wished to renew their affective ties to others. Hopes of building a broader culture of people concerned for social justice outweighed hopes of directly stopping the reactor. Both goals are practical, but directed toward different audiences and kinds of outcomes. And an "expression" of solidarity with the movement has the instrumental effect of reinforcing it. Even those who said "nothing" often felt they had attended in order to reinforce this subculture. It is equally important for an activist subculture to attract new members and to reinforce the enthusiasm of the old. A trip to Diablo, a big crowd, getting arrested: these added up to a collective ritual that helped to revivify the subculture. Diablo's status as a sacred place in the activist subculture, and protestors' sense of being on a pilgrimage, reinforced this. So even though the demonstration had little chance of stopping Diablo, it may have had significant practical effects (partly intended) on the movement. The man who complained, "They're just going through a ritual" had the analysis right, but he should not have regretted it. Rituals matter.

The responses of locals and nonlocals differed here too. Locals were more likely to expect nothing to happen (23 percent compared to 10 percent of nonlocals), to give expressive responses (17 percent compared to 4 percent of nonlocals); and to have direct aspirations, (6 percent compared to 1 percent). Nonlocals were more likely to give movement-oriented responses (18 percent versus 10 percent). Although these are not large differences, they show the locals (less likely to be part of the activist subculture) as less interested in movement-building and as either more resigned or more interested in simply stopping the plant. The strength of one's allegiance to a subculture affects one's goals for the protest.

PROTEST'S EMOTIONAL INFRASTRUCTURE

The mutual loyalties and shared emotions created within the Abalone Alliance subculture shaped virtually all aspects of the anti-Diablo protest movement. Over the years protestors developed both activist and movement identities, based on their political activities. They defined what they wanted from their protest, but also what they thought was possible. Both the perceived benefits and the perceived costs of protest were determined by the feelings, judgments, and beliefs created partly by the protestors themselves, through their loyalties and feelings of empowerment. The extent to which costs and benefits were allowed to influence decisions, or at what levels, were also affected by these collective emotions. Their shared and reciprocal emotions shaped both their means and their goals, and hence what was rational for them. The collective emotions of protest are crucial for sustaining any movement. If emotion is the glue of solidarity, then movements depend on an emotional infrastructure. As Augustine said, actions are important for reinforcing beliefs. Moral visions are most satisfying when we can express them, embodied in rituals with clear meanings. Singing, danc-ing, and other collective activities are an integral part of protest.

Every social movement has a culture in which activities are inter-woven with the beliefs and feelings that give them meaning. Although I have stressed the emotional side of this internal movement culture, it has been impossible—again—to separate this from the moral and cognitive. The Diablo activists were explicit and open about their re-ciprocal emotional bonds, which they worked hard to build and main-tain. These particular emotions may work better in explaining the con-tinuation of protest than its origin (for which the pre-existing emotions discussed in chapter 5 may be more important). The Diablo protest was unusual in persisting after direct-action protest had disappeared from most other sites. It persisted even when the battle over Diablo seemed (and was) lost, because of the strength of the subculture be-hind the protest, and because of Diablo's unique role as a sacred shrine in that subculture. Protest activity which would seem irrational, if judged by narrowly instrumental criteria, appears rational in the light of the incentives constructed collectively by the participants' subcul-ture. There is nothing irrational about the pursuit of collective goals such as reinforcing the affective bonds of one's community.

All movements create and depend upon emotional bonds between members, but not to the same degree and not with the same result. Diablo Canyon may be an extreme case, as the direct-action wing of the antinuclear movement was more self-conscious in its cultural cre-ativity than most protest movements are. Many post-industrial move-ments try to mimic or recreate rituals like those of religion, which were so helpful to the civil rights movement. But some movements either do not try or do not succeed in creating a rich internal culture; some rely more on direct-mail contributions from strangers who never par-ticipate in a collective activity. And of those that do generate collective emotions, not all are served by them. Erotic attraction can lead couples out of a movement as well as in. The very intensity of emotions can exhaust. Overall, though, I suspect that movements with a vibrant in-ternal culture—and it is hard to predict which ones will manage to create this—are more likely to flourish.

Charisma has typically been analyzed as the property of an individ-ual, but places, events, and groups can inspire the same kind of emo-tional allegiance. Charisma relies on the duality of all culture: feelings, thoughts, and judgments are crystallized in a new or profound way in a person or thing, thereby inspiring affective loyalty. A person can ac-tively formulate or transform cultural sensibilities, while inanimate ob-jects or events can only symbolize them. In either case, it is the cultural meanings of the audience, and the symbolic place of the charismatic person or thing in those meanings, that generates charisma. Like an art work's popularity, it arises from the play between an individual embodiment and the surrounding culture.[31]

This chapter has focused on the satisfactions of protest that derive from highly emotional, often ritualistic, collective activities. These are some of the most striking achievements of a movement, a vibrant culture that gives participants a strong sense of movement identity, and internal movement practices that yield immense solidarity. But there are many pleasures that protest activity offers, including satisfactions that depend on the biographies and personalities of the individuals involved. And the deepest satisfaction, perhaps, is the devotion of one's entire life to a career in pursuit of social change. This can be a source of profound meaning and personal identity. The next chapter returns to the biographical dimension to examine further pleasures that ongoing protest movements have for participants.

- Protest movements generate, consciously or not, a variety of emotional processes that may either encourage or discourage participation.

- Singing, dancing, and other ritualized activities can help create solidarity, joy, and other positive emotions.

- Shared and reciprocal emotions reinforce each other. Physical sites, often because of their beauty or their histories, can be important in movement cultures, and activities there can be sacred pilgrimages.

- The personal networks that form around protest are important partly for the shared and reciprocal emotions that they involve, not simply as flows of information or resources.

- Protestors can care about reinforcing their subculture and networks as much as about their publicly stated, instrumental goals.

NINE

Culture and Biography:
The Pleasures of Protest

Over my head
I see freedom in the air . . .
There must be
A God
Somewhere
        —Civil Rights hymn

. . . that dreary tribe of high-minded women and sandal-wearers and
bearded fruit-juice drinkers who come flocking towards the smell of
"progress" like blue-bottles to a dead cat.
        —George Orwell

When I first met him in 1984, Geoff Merideth struck me as friendly in
a sincere way that indicates fondness and concern for other people,
humorous in a self-deprecating manner that bespeaks self-confidence
tempered by his interest in others, and intelligent in a thoughtful style
that hints at many years of grappling with important social questions.
Rounded and a bit sloppy in his dress, at the age of thirty-six Merideth
sported a pony tail almost to his waist—something he had started long
before such hair became fashionable in the 1980s. Despite working to
find housing for AIDS victims, and spending his life on the cutting
edge of social change, he seemed deeply, perhaps spiritually, relaxed.
He epitomizes many of the post-industrial sensibilities and ideas that
have motivated so many recent protest movements.[1]

Geoff spent his teens on the streets of New York. At the age of thirteen he ran away from his working-class foster parents—an alcoholic
father and physically abusive mother—and went to Greenwich Village. It was September 1968, and he was in for an unusual education.
He was first taken in by members of the Living Theater, and soon
adopted by the Up Against the Wall Motherfuckers. In the next year
"Geoff Motherfucker" became "Geoff Yippie," when he joined the
group with whom he still happily identifies. Like many others in the
spring of 1970, Geoff believed violent revolution to be imminent, and
he armed himself. At the age of fifteen, he was convicted of armed
robbery.

As he sat in the city jail of Dedham, Massachusetts, the prospect of hard prison time (very hard, he knew, for a skinny white kid) sobered him, and he made many promises to all the gods he could think of. At least one must have heard him, for he was released in January 1971 after 101 days in jail. Already the prospects for revolution had soured, and the pressures of state repression had grown. Rumors were circulating that the Justice Department had plans to round up five thousand movement leaders in a sudden sweep. Geoff spent the next three months in a drug rehabilitation center, until he decided that the techniques used there merely switched people's addiction from drugs to the program itself. He went back to high school and managed to graduate only a few months late for his age group.

Merideth then spent a year as a counselor for runaways on the Lower East Side of New York, another year trying to keep a low profile in Buffalo, and three years in New Paltz doing a radio show and developing off-campus housing programs for students at the local campus of the State University of New York. He eventually felt that he had become a bureaucrat, and he began to question his "burrowing from within" strategy. "The better the work you do within an institution, the more it gets used to offset the bad stuff the place does. So the organization can admit, 'Yes, we do things that aren't good, but on the other hand look at all these good things we do.'" Society's institutions, says Geoff, depend on sucking in each new generation of young, energetic people, then grinding them up. "I like to think of what would happen if they stopped doing it, stopped going into the big institutions." In the fall of 1978 he fulfilled an old ambition; he moved to California.

In the San Francisco Bay area, Geoff worked for a disabled rights group from 1979 to 1982 and from 1985 to 1988. In between he fought the Diablo Canyon nuclear power plant as one of the staff of the Abalone Alliance, until, in March 1985, the staff decided to fire themselves rather than devote most of their time to raising funds just to keep the organization alive. After 1988 Geoff spent several months in Germany, then several months as campaign director for the Progressive Way (a left-leaning alternative to the United Way). From November 1989 to August 1991 he looked for work with progressive groups. With 200–300 applicants for each job, he notes, who would hire a straight white male? Geoff toyed with alternative careers, perhaps as a writer, or a private investigator for lawyers working on issues like tenants' and workers' rights. Finally, the Catholic Charities of Oakland hired him to work on housing for AIDS victims. An unlikely match, it would seem, but the post allowed him to do progressive housing work and be paid for it.

Geoff still identifies himself in jest as a yippie, which he defines as someone who "believes in the politics of ecstasy and joy." The yippies always had a pleasant leaven of culture and humor in their politics that prevented them from taking themselves too seriously. When Geoff was in New Paltz playing the bureaucrat, for example, word came that he might be "pied" for this transgression. Although he felt the accusation was unfair, he took the precaution of bringing his own pie to each radio show, consuming it afterward with the staff. Despite the light touch of the counterculture, Geoff realizes that "We'd have been in trouble if we had succeeded with the revolution in 1970. We weren't ready to live in a new society, to be new people. In particular we hadn't dealt with our sexism: the pig within."

Merideth sees the most important developments of the 1970s as the spread of feminism and of collectivism (by which he means ways of acting that prefigure the new society, as we saw in the last chapter). He thinks that the yippies were more open to these new perspectives than marxist-leninist revolutionaries, since "our politics were driven by personal needs and attachments rather than by an ideology." Although he admires many of the marxist-leninist groups with whom he has worked—especially their capacity for hard work—he finds them self-righteous because they believe they have found the scientifically correct analysis, the true laws underlying social life. As a result they can only manipulate people, not listen to them seriously. They, in turn, have accused him of being "Communist in practice, but liberal in theory," a charge that pleases him. "I talk to people; they don't."

Geoff's own life has certainly been driven by "personal needs and attachment." When still with his foster family, he joined a church group fighting racism—not only because his parents objected, but also to get to know the pastor's daughter. His move to Rochester had similar romantic roots, as did his 1989 sojourn in Germany. A satisfying personal life is crucial, he feels, and Geoff's political goal is that everyone be able to live a balanced life. He has pursued politics for three decades because he enjoyed it, and scoffs when asked what he has sacrificed as a result. "For me, helping others is completely selfish. The kind of work I do is also a way I work on myself; I get control over my own life this way. After all, people do what they do because it makes them feel good."

If Geoff came to appreciate feminism in the 1970s, he learned about spirituality during the 1980s, and now labels himself an "anarcho-feminist pagan." Both developments came at just the right time for Geoff, as for thousands of others confused by their experiences in the 1960s. Of feminism, he says, "It saved my life, helped me to overcome a lot of the confusions I had felt when the sixties collapsed." He feels that both feminism and paganism are about control over one's life and one's community. "If I control my own life, I won't want to control you." He had long felt the need for a cosmology to match his secular worldview about politics and society. Here, writ small, were the roots of the participatory democracy that was central to the antinuclear and related protest movements.

Geoff's initiation into paganism came during the 1981 encampment to block the Diablo Canyon nuclear power plant. His affinity group was one of those that, as we saw, performed a rite for the autumnal equinox, hiking into the hills above the reactor and reflecting the sun's light at the building to destroy the evil inside. Three days later, the plant's owner announced that blueprints had been reversed during a late phase of construction and that major delays would be necessary while corrections were made.

For Geoff, pagan magic fills in several pieces of life's big puzzle. In addition to providing a strong sense of community—which most religions do—it emphasizes the divine within each of us ("tapping the inner well within ourselves that goes into the infinite"), suggesting that we not exploit each other for instrumental purposes. It is also a form of empowerment, for it allows us to "change consciousness at will." Most of all, it connects us with each other and with the natural world. The "law of return," like the concept of karma, says that whatever you do will return to you threefold. All action thereby carries a deep moral responsibility combined with joyful self-interest. Paganism harks back, in Geoff's eyes, to early peoples closer to nature, who were decimated—sometimes literally through witchhunts—in the period of the rise of the modern state, Newtonian science, and the industrial revolution. This unfortunate historical development Geoff sees as a logical extension of the Judaeo-Christian tradition, if not of all monotheisms. Geoff now teaches in Starhawk's Reclaiming Collective and at Witchcamps in Vancouver and Upper Michigan each summer.

What has kept Geoff Merideth politically active since 1968? "I've seen glimpses of what it could be like, little moments of true community among autonomous individuals." That vision keeps him striving, along with a mildly cynical sense of humor that prevents him from turning bitter in the face of so little progressive change in the United States. The playful vision that motivates him and others has roots in "feminism, politics, and drugs." Burnout, he feels, is a luxury he has no right to. For he knows that, someday, it can all work. (He was able to insist on this even after ten years of Reagan and Bush presidencies.)

By returning to the biographical dimension and its related psychological dynamics, this chapter continues the discussion of what kinds of satisfaction protest offers its participants. These include the collective emotions of the last chapter, but also the opportunity to give direction to one's life and to fulfill a range of personality dispositions.

Reinforcing what we have seen throughout the book, Geoff Merideth's career shows the diversity of motives that bring people to moral protest and keep them there. Humans hold a dizzying array of sensibilities and sensitivities, inchoate assumptions, utopian fantasies, ego defenses, and explicit beliefs, any of which can be threatened or shocked by new knowledge, requests, and activities. We pursue a variety of pleasures; we try to do what we consider the right thing; but we also tend to fall into routines because they are easy. Our choices and actions are, finally, shaped by an infinite number of personality quirks and character traits. Most protestors are compelled by a combination of motivations, compulsions, and desires, some of them conscious and others not. Simple models of human motivation, whether rationalist or crowd-based, miss the lion's share of reality. So do theories that look for the motivations of entire protest movements rather than those of the individuals who compose them. The biographical dimension of protest cries out for exploration.

Merideth's career as an activist began partly as a rebellion against his foster parents. Many of its vicissitudes were due to erotic pursuits. The life he followed—"chose" implies too much foresight—was also attractive in being, quite simply, fun. His vision of a just and pleasurable society emerged more and more clearly over the years, as Geoff added feminism and then spirituality to the mix. He also accumulated impressive skills at organizing for social change, skills that have allowed him—with a few gaps—to find jobs doing what he loves. Merideth found his way into protest by relative accident, but once there he found more and more reasons to stay. He has moved from group to group and movement to movement, but the draw has always been the many pleasures created by internal movement cultures.

Does it add much to our understanding to say that Geoff has an activist identity? If anyone has one, he certainly does. But once we have specified his goals, pleasures, skills, and sensibilities, at a biographical level, we can see that "activist identity" is primarily a proxy for all these specific characteristics. It can be a useful proxy when we lack the time for multiple interviews with a sample of protestors, but we need to be cautious about reifying it into a separate "thing." One interesting feature of an activist identity, at least in this case, is that it seems a property of an individual, since Geoff takes it with him when he moves to a new city where he has few if any personal networks to support that identity. He develops those ties quickly—but only because he becomes active and meets like-minded individuals. He draws on cultural as well as biographical meanings in maintaining this identity, but not so much on resources or other structural factors.

Students of protest movements know far too little about individuals such as Merideth. Aside from a few biographies of famous revolutionaries, only recently have scholars set out to learn about the lives of individual protestors through "life course" analysis.[2] Merideth is unusual in the number of years he has spent pondering his own life and reasons. Even sustained conversations will not yield such insights from every protestor. As a result we frequently use "identity" as a proxy for the many things we would really like to know.

Literature has often been better than social science at capturing the nuances of human action and displaying them for the reader. In a recent short story, for instance, Joyce Carol Oates describes a high school sophomore named Hope who goes to her state capital to protest the execution of a murderer.[3] Oates situates this incident of protest in the context of the girl's difficult relationship with her uncomprehending father and that of her emerging personal identity at school. She had once prized her friendships with black students, who now—this is the late 1960s—shun her; the condemned is related to one of them. Race, compassion, and awareness of current events become means by which she can distance herself—a brainy, awkward girl—from her brutish father. A single act of moral protest (possibly the only one in her life) crystallizes her emerging intuitions about her own personal identity in opposition to her father's.

Research that focuses on the organizations of protest, as important as these are, loses sight of careers of protest, the personalities of protestors, and the pleasures of protest. Protest becomes a means to an end, not a pleasure or source of identity, with purposive organizations as the main arena for that pursuit. Motivations are reduced to self-interest, in one tradition, to anger or frustration in another. The image of artfulness, in contrast, suggests that protest always combines strategic purpose, pleasures and pains in the doing, and a variety of emotions that both motivate and accompany action. The coherence of Merideth's life does not come from the organizations to which he has belonged.

The contrast between formal organizational rules and the impulses of individuals should not be overdone, though, *because many protest groups are the work of a single individual and reflect that person's idiosyncra-cies.* Probably the majority of local protest groups are tiny, and no mat-ter how many members they have on their mailing list or can mobilize for a rally, they are essentially the work of driven, committed individu-als, who keep the group alive through enormous subsidies of time and often money. To borrow a French verb, this person "animates" the group. A clash between two such strong personalities usually results in two groups. I think it is crucial to understand such individuals, not least because they are often extremely strong and creative. Although organizational needs and dynamics may sometimes explain the actions of individuals, the reverse is also often true.

Individuals, with their idiosyncrasies, neuroses, and mistakes, are troublesome for social science. If each protest movement is composed of individuals with varying biographies, drives, and goals, and if each individual has many motivations, some of them hidden even to herself, what can we say about the roots of protest? Rationalists ignore this challenge through oversimplification of human psychology; mobiliza-tion theorists respond similarly, downplaying the importance of men-tal life altogether. General theories by definition try to exclude the com-plexity of individual variations, or they assume them to be random noise in the system, as rationalists do. We often mistake our abstract theories for reality, a convenient assumption that encourages us to overlook individual psychology, variations, and anomalies. But a good social observer, if only to renew her humility, must look at the individ-uals now and then, to see what motivations and symbols and strategies her models have overlooked. We can search for patterns in the careers and life histories of individual activists. We can compare their moral visions and values with the requirements imposed on them by formal organizations: sometimes organizations serve their purposes; at other times they clash with them.[4] We can contrast individuals' careers of protest with their membership, even leadership, of formal organiza-tions. Tracing individuals might allow us to see many sources and ac-tivities of protest that are not organized by formal groups and leaders, as well as the cultural and biographical materials out of which new organizations arise. We can look for a variety of biographical factors in our explanations, even occasionally draw on theories of psychology and personality.

Some individuals play a more weighty role in history than others, of course, and deserve study for that reason. The personal tastes of prime ministers and generals affect policies and battles—and, presumably, history—more than those of individual peasants and workers. For ex-ample, Karl Marx's bundle of beliefs and tastes—especially his unstable combination of faith in science and insistence on critique—has affected more people than the equally idiosyncratic beliefs of my great-grandmother. Among political scientists and psychologists, biographies of protest leaders have remained popular even while, under the spell of structure and rationalism, sociologists rejected this source of understanding. Rationalism suggests that all normal individuals would act the same way in the same circumstances, so that personality quirks only cause unpredictable deviation from rationality. But the visions of important leaders and theoreticians get taken up as influential truths, if not sacred texts.

THE PLEASURES OF PROTEST

The great secret of morals is love, or a going out of our nature and the identification of ourselves with the beautiful which exists in thought, action, or person, not our own.

—Shelley

Because they are directly connected, the satisfactions that individuals get from their activities will be just as diverse as their biographies. Crowd models overlooked the pleasures of protest because they viewed participants as overwhelmed by anxieties and fears. Rationalist models often reduce protest to the pursuit of economic interests. This is a fundamental motive, to be sure, but these models tend to miss the pleasures along the way to ultimate material (or other) success.

One such pleasure, we saw, is romance. A woman attends a march on Washington because her girlfriend is going, or because she hopes to meet someone there. What greater aphrodisiac than the excitement of so many bodies, the thrill of collective empowerment? As Todd Gitlin has written of the New Left, "The movement, along with the rampant counterculture, was a sexy place to mix. . . . Meetings were sites for eyeplay and byplay and bedplay. Some leaders in effect recruited women in bed—what Marge Piercy in a classic polemic called 'fucking a staff into existence.'"[5] Students for a Democratic Society, Gitlin says, was a circle "made of triangles, consummated or not, constantly forming, collapsing, reforming, overlapping. The sexual intensity matched the political and intellectual; or was it the other way around?"[6]

Sexual forms of what I called reciprocal affection, because they are usually "dyadic," have the potential to crowd out broader loyalty to the group. The flip side of the sexual draw of protest is that these "dyads" often go their own way, withdrawing from extensive public participation into the private pleasures of each other's company. Indeed, this is a notorious problem in protest movements, especially those that demand total commitment. In a creative essay, Jeff Goodwin examines the efforts of the Huk rebels in the Philippines to deal with libidinal desires within their ranks.[7] For ten years following World War II, while the Huks waged war from their camps in the mountains, they faced interminable problems of discipline, which they termed the "sex problem," the "baby problem," and the "family problem." The first of these dealt with horny rebels who had wives back in the cities and wanted new "forest wives." The second had to do with the smaller number of women among the rebels who wished to have babies. The third was the issue of rebels reluctant to leave their spouses and families for the hill camps. Erotic and affective bonds often interfered, it would seem, with revolutionary discipline, and leaders sentenced more than a few rebels to death for transgressions. Although not many protest movements spend years in isolated forests, the same motivations that draw people into activism can easily draw them back out.

If the excitement of a crowd is a means to erotic ends, it is also an end in itself, a rare but unforgettable pleasure. Durkheim described well the feeling of being swept up in something larger and stronger than oneself. It is a kind of joy, like a religious ecstasy, often reinforced through song and dance. We saw this with the anti-Diablo protestors.

Merideth's joy at glimpsing what society could be like is a similar satisfaction: hope and desire combine emotional excitement with cognitive plans and moral visions. Anticipation makes desire different from other emotions. Desire leads to projects for changing the world. Projects can be local and personal or ambitious and global. They can have a greater or lesser chance for success. They tie the present and future tightly together, giving one's life a direction, purpose, and sense of flow. The successive unfolding of a project over time is one of the deepest of pleasures, providing the kind of narrative that Alasdair MacIntyre says humans need for meaning. This is art at its best, and life at its most artful.

MacIntyre tries to get at this deep satisfaction through his concept of a "practice": "[A]ny coherent and complex form of socially established cooperative human activity through which goods internal to that form of activity are realised in the course of trying to achieve those standards of excellence which are appropriate to, and partially definitive of, that form of activity, *with the result that human powers to achieve excellence, and human conceptions of the ends and goods involved, are systematically extended.* Tic-tac-toe is not an example of a practice in this sense, nor is throwing a football with skill; but the game of football is, and so is chess."[8] MacIntyre's favorite game metaphor is chess because it provides extensive room for virtuosic strategies within strict bounds. (The bounds are so rigid and explicit that chess is misleading as a metaphor for social life, even for strategic action.) MacIntyre contrasts practices with instrumental activities that have no inherent value of their own, undertaken purely for their efficiency in attaining some external end (for example money). In a way that eludes rationalist models, we often engage in practices for their intrinsic rewards, the satisfaction of the activity itself, rather than for extrinsic rewards such as remuneration. This is one of the key ways that unpaid protestors regularly differ from the paid state and corporate spokespersons opposed to them.

Culture and practices—closely related concepts—offer any number of intrinsic rewards, from the experience of rich emotions to virtuosic performances of duty. Even within one culture there are many ways to get married, drive a car, smoke a cigarette, or protest government activities. Each of these can be more or less satisfying, in and of itself, regardless of the outcome of arriving at a destination or stopping an official policy. Nevertheless, some activities in modern society have more room for artfulness than others. The production of art itself is perhaps the paradigm as well as the linguistic root, heightened by the immense value we place today on individual creativity. Corporate management is another example. Top executives have maintained considerable freedom to maneuver, revealing their power to shape job descriptions in their organizations. Any functions that could be routinized were spun off to other functionaries. Shoshana Zuboff comments, "[T]he more executive activity was projected downward and materialized in more rationalized processes, the more the executive was freed to indulge in the essence of his or her craft—the artful expression of knowledge in action."[9] Protest—along with art, science, and corporate management—is at one end of the spectrum, providing many opportunities for virtuosic performances and intrinsic satisfactions. It has considerable space for creative potential, especially to the extent that it is driven by moral visions rather than self-interest.

Part of the satisfaction of artful creativity comes from a sense of "flow"—Mihaly Csikszentmihalyi's term for "the state in which people are so involved in an activity that nothing else seems to matter; the experience itself is so enjoyable that people will do it even at great cost, for the sheer sake of doing it."[10] According to Csikszentmihalyi, "Each of us has a picture, however vague, of what we would like to accomplish before we die," and we spin large and small projects as ways of doing it.[11] "Projects," we saw when we discussed artfulness earlier, are important because they make sense of our past and present by pointing them toward some future accomplishment. They provide the lure of practices as defined by MacIntyre, and the excitement of Csikszentmihalyi's concept of flow. Protest activity shares many of the same intrinsic pleasures. The art of persuading others, crafting new organizational forms, renaming parts of the social world, or trying to shape society itself: all these are the pleasures of a craft or practice.

There is a danger accompanying the artfulness of protest, however: rather than being craftpersons, learning slowly through experience, many protestors wish to be architects, working with abstract blueprints, or legislators, making simple decrees from a distance. They lose or deny their own cultural embeddedness, like the marxists Merideth criticized as driven by ideology, not social connections. The concepts of embeddedness and artfulness will yield grounds for evaluating protest movements and criticizing those that ignore their own defining cultural traditions in favor of general theories. Some protestors, we might say, operate with a faulty model of culture, seeing only its creative and not its constraining side. We'll see this when we look at the Khmer Rouge in chapter 16.

Entire lives can be lived in artful ways, ways that allow creativity, discretion, the elaboration and breaking of rules as well as the mere following of them. A few people spend their lives in protest and related activities, which give those lives a sense of dignity and purpose rare in modern society. Like artists or religious leaders who feel a sense of calling, these critics of society often lead immensely satisfying lives through honing their moral voices. Some of the pleasures of protest are trivial and fleeting, but striving for a meaningful life (despite frustrations) is one of what Charles Taylor calls "hypergoods, i.e., goods which not only are incomparably more important than others but provide the standpoint from which these must be weighed, judged, decided about." [12]

Virtually all the pleasures that humans derive from social life are found in protest movements: a sense of community and identity; ongoing companionship and bonds with others; the variety and challenge of conversation, cooperation, and competition. Some of the pleasures are not available in the routines of daily life: the euphoria of crowds, a sense of pushing history forward with one's projects, or simply of making the evening news, of working together with others, of sharing a sense of purpose. And, perhaps most of all, the declaration of moral principles.

One aspect of collective effervescence is *empowerment,* a term activists use to describe the feeling of participants that they can accomplish changes, that they have both individual and collective power. Doug

McAdam gets at something similar with his idea of cognitive liberation: the sudden sense that change is possible, that one no longer has
to put up with oppressive conditions. There is both a cognitive assessment of chances for success and an emotional thrill derived from the
pursuit itself, from the sensation of working together toward a common moral end. And as we have seen, rational calculations that success
is possible may not even be necessary, given the other satisfactions
of protest.

Protest offers more intellectual pleasures as well. The ability and
opportunity to articulate one's basic moral values, I have argued, is
central to protest. Even complaining, Faye Crosby says, is an important
human activity, open to those who are too vulnerable to protest more
actively. Crosby also argues that complaining helps one focus on one's
opponents as complex human beings rather than oversimplified
demons.[13] Complaint and criticism are surely among the most basic of
human traits, as close as we might come to universals of human nature.
Not just collective but also individual acts of protest can have these satisfactions.

This catalogue of the pleasures of protest would suggest that everyone should run out and join up, but in fact there are pains as well.
Some movements simply have fewer of the collective joys and other
pleasures I have described. Others demand considerable sacrifice. Full-
time protestors usually give up health insurance, lucrative careers, and
other material advantages. Many, like the Huks, are asked to give up
some of the pleasures of normal private life. Still others face the stigma
or misunderstanding that greet most efforts to think, feel, or live differently. Some risk their very lives. Most people differ from Geoff Merideth in seeing a trade-off between the pleasures of protest and those
of private life, and most people most of the time choose the latter.
The kinds and degrees of pleasure in protest differ not only across
movements but across individuals. Some feel those pleasures more
strongly than others.

The diverse reasons for protesting range from initial, individualistic
motivations—whistleblowers' outrage over mistreatment, fears of local pollution—to more collective practices of active protest—marches
and rallies, and the pleasures and collective effervescence that result.
With so many potential paths to protest, and so many satisfactions
available once there, it seems that anyone could be drawn into it under
the right cultural, biographical, and structural circumstances. Many
crowd theorists believed this, even though others looked for individual traits like alienation to explain who was prone to participate. Recent researchers have also assumed that, because everyone has inter-

ests, anyone might join a movement to pursue them. I think that almost everyone cares about something deeply enough to engage in protest. And yet there may also be personality traits that increase the odds slightly, that help sustain action through the hard, dull periods as well as the exciting ones.

KOOKS AND STIRRER-UPPERS

"Kooks" . . . "professional stirrer-uppers."
—Congressman Chester Earl Holifield, speaking of antinuclear protestors
in 1969

I interviewed Susan Johnson in Washington at Food for Thought, a haven for the leftie counterculture in an unremittingly bourgeois and bureaucratic city. Most cities have a place like it, mingling several styles of protest: the tie-dyed clothes and long hair of one era, the black clothes, grizzled hair, and masochistic jewelry of another. Folksingers and angry political rockers alternate as the evening's entertainment; at least one hundred political causes are represented by announcements on the bulletin board, an enlarged version of my Bleecker Street lamppost. When Susan arrives, slightly late, she scans the bulletin board—at annoying length—before coming to sit down and introduce herself. Her first words: "You look about the way I expected." Upon request, she specified, "Well, fuzzy." She is not quite rude, but hardly endearing. She has apparently not been endearing, either, to the groups she has participated in, and she recounts the personality clashes she has had in a long series of left and libertarian protest groups.

Susan is hardly the only protestor with an abrasive personality. Like most people, I first encountered followers of Lyndon LaRouche in an airport, when one shouted at me, "Even guys with beards can support nuclear power." In my case, he was wrong. But I was struck by how unconcerned he was with making a favorable impression on others. So sure of the scientific correctness of LaRouche's weird economic analyses, his followers were just waiting for their vindication. They displayed the arrogance of certainty in addition to the irritation of difficult personalities.

It is unfashionable to inquire into the personalities of those who make a career of protest, since the current consensus is that they are no different from you and me. Moral shocks can happen to anyone—at least anyone with a home, a moral system, and feelings about the world. There may also be, as McCarthy and Zald would suggest, the prospect of a job and career in protest. Lois Gibbs received a severe moral shock from the revelations about her Love Canal neighborhood, but she remained active by founding a successful protest group, Citizens' Clearinghouse for Hazardous Waste.[14] Given the material deprivations of most lifelong activists, however, other factors are also at work, possibly including personal obsessions. The crowd tradition looked for pathological aspects of protestors' personalities; the rational choice and mobilization schools responded by insisting on a universal rationality. Yet a more cultural approach casts some doubt on both extremes. Not only are actions constrained—as mobilization theorists recognize—by imperfect knowledge and variations in political structures, but they are also constituted by cultural meanings in complex ways. Personalities are shaped by culture.

Culture provides the raw materials for biography and psychology in a number of ways. Individuals identify with a variety of culturally defined groups. They interpret their own past experiences, including political experiences, through many cultural lenses, including those of the media. And they idiosyncratically blend skills and habits, values and beliefs, intuitions and principles from the cultural repertories that surround them. Even unconscious identifications, perhaps internalized at a young age, reflect one's interpreted surroundings. Fear, anger, and threat—which may be universal psychological responses—vary at least in their content and triggers across cultures.

I wish to make some extremely tentative suggestions about personalities, as a way of pointing out possibilities for research. I raise two possibilities. One is that there is often a perceived "kookiness" to protestors, almost by definition, since they are normally opposed to some of the common, perhaps consensual meanings and styles of a society. This is one reason, I believe, they can play the crucial social role of gaining new perspectives and insights before the rest of us. This kookiness has less to do with personality traits than with sensibilities that diverge from the mainstream. I would like to know more about the origins of these alternative sensibilities.

My second suggestion, equally tentative, has to do with a kind of stubborn rigidity that allows some people to keep a critical distance from the social routines and complacency around them. Whistleblowers often combine a rigid belief in their profession's ethical rules with a loner's ability to withstand social pressures to go along. Studies of rescuers who saved Jews from the Nazis find few ways that these extreme altruists are distinct, except that they are able to cling to moral principles in the face of strong contrary pressures.[15] Stubbornness, sometimes reinforced by arrogance, rebelliousness, or rigid adherence to rules, may nurture protestors.

Michael Walzer has even given us the beginning of a history of a fruitful personality for protest. Part of what the Puritan "saints" invented in the sixteenth century was a new character type, which Walzer believes also animated later, secular revolutions. An "impersonal, ideological discipline" encourages "extraordinary self-assurance and daring."[16] The stubborn strength of the individual conscience, fed by a like-minded group, provides self-control and confidence capable of driving the most revolutionary acts of protest. Rigidity, ideological confidence, and a sense of marginality can be a powerful combination.

Activism is sometimes rooted in personal traits that, under normal circumstances, might seem objectionable. Geoff Merideth was not "well adjusted" as a child; John Gofman was arrogant in his scientific faith. Idiosyncrasies may be important precisely because they lead some people to see the world—or the data—differently, to feel differently, or to act differently. The effect of personality is probably minor, but the truth is that we have no evidence one way or the other. We saw earlier that crowd theorists' and other explorations of the psychology of protestors simply assumed, contrary to any evidence, that they were defective in some way. Since then, mobilization and process theorists have assumed, with just as little evidence, the opposite. No one has done compelling empirical research into the issue.

The possibility remains, therefore, that certain kinds of personalities encourage long-term protest careers, or grow out of such careers. In 1936 George Orwell traveled and worked in the industrial north of England, and wrote *The Road to Wigan Pier* to document the need for, and the roots of, a strong socialist movement. The appalling conditions of workplaces and homes certainly established the need for a socialist redistribution of society's wealth. Orwell was less impressed with those promoting the movement for change, complaining that "there is the horrible—the really disquieting—prevalence of cranks wherever Socialists are gathered together. One sometimes gets the impression that the mere words 'Socialism' and 'Communism' draw towards them with magnetic force every fruit-juice drinker, nudist, sandal-wearer, sex-maniac, Quaker, 'Nature Cure' quack, pacifist, and feminist in England."[17] One of the Left Book Club editors who had sent Orwell on this journalistic errand felt obliged to write a preface intended to soften the sharp remarks in the book. Nonetheless, Orwell had captured a truth about the organizers of many protest movements.

The word *crank* has an unpleasantly acidic flavor, hinting at dyspepsia. We could, at the other extreme, adopt the colorless language of science and speak of "outliers" whose opinions fall in the tail of the distribution for their society. I prefer the term *kooks*, partly because of its cousin, *kookiness*, which many observers (such as Chester Holifield) explicitly attribute to protest movements. These terms are not usually intended as compliments, but I hope they capture the fluidity, expansiveness, and creativity of protest. It is easier to celebrate kookiness than crankiness. We should not be surprised that movements for fundamental change attract those who desire change, even if their goals do not coincide exactly with those of the movement's founders and organizers. If nothing else, they are attracted to their enemy's enemy. As Orwell's epigraph said, there is often a mere desire for progress and a fondness for anyone who speaks in its name.

Protestors are perceived as kooks mostly because they disagree with their society's consensus. This is—naturally—why they wish to change society and its consensus. It is always difficult for new opinions and new points of view to emerge, yet they can provide important social knowledge and opportunities for taking stock of moral sensibilities, as I detail in the final chapter. We hardly need to celebrate "special" opinions—as R. D. Laing, Thomas Szasz, and perhaps Michel Foucault celebrate insanity—to cherish the creativity of social movements. One can never predict in advance which points of view will survive the test of public discourse, which will become common sense, and which will become historical footnotes. But we can welcome their proliferation, for as we saw earlier it is this variation that allows social change when some of the idiosyncracies are adopted by others. According to Frank Kermode, analyzing *The Crying of Lot 49,* "A great deviation is called a sect if shared, paranoia if not."

The apparent kookiness of many protestors comes from their alternative lifestyles. In post-industrial movements especially, people are tying to work out new ways of living, gentler or more ecological practices that are difficult to sustain in a society whose institutions uniformly encourage consumerism. Most citizenship protestors want to be included in the modes of life that already exist rather than work out coherent alternatives, so they may take pains to "look" normal by mainstream definitions. The Nation of Islam's bow ties and short hair hide some rather surprising theological beliefs, for example. In addition, post-citizenship movements are potentially open to anyone who shares their goals and styles (Orwell's cranks cannot be excluded), with no clear underlying collectivity. On the other hand, for those in an excluded group, their citizenship movement may be their only avenue for participation; it will attract those with many different personal styles. Since far more people have conventional styles than do not, the former will probably dominate. So post-citizenship protestors may ap-

pear stranger—refusing meat or leather, wearing long hair or distinctive clothes, avoiding traditional careers and their rewards—than
members of citizenship movements.

Protestors themselves may find reassurance in their kookiness. Animal rights protestors, for example, are fond of quoting John Stuart
Mill: "Every great movement must experience three stages: ridicule,
discussion, adoption."[18] They interpret the ridicule as evidence that
adoption will follow. This happened to the antinuclear protestors derided by Holifield in 1969: within ten years a majority of Americans
shared their doubts about nuclear energy. I think it is common for the
perspectives of protestors to be ridiculed at first, although some never
get beyond that stage. This marginality can be a source of strength in
itself, to those with the right personality. Joseph Smith, founder of the
Mormons, said, "The Lord has constituted me so curiously that I glory
in persecutions" (a lucky trait, in his case). Following this hint, historian R. Laurence Moore has argued that a strong sense of their outsider
status has been a major asset to many American religious groups.[19]
The same could be said for many protest groups. What others would
consider one of the drawbacks of protest, some value positively.

Along with the pleasures of protest can go equally strong pains. As
Joseph Smith learned, these can be physical, sometimes even fatal.
There is disappointment, exhaustion, frustration, and fear. Sometimes
protestors can turn these around, making them a symbol of the importance of their work. The pursuit of "hypergoods" can be simultaneously satisfying at one level, painful at another. They can even be more
satisfying *because* they are painful. Most times, the pains of protest are
eventually too great and drive supporters back to their daily routines.
Military or police action by the state is notoriously effective. Active
criticism of one's society, especially its economic and political leaders,
has costs.

PSYCHOLOGY IN PROTEST

At the most, personality is just one factor that might help lead someone into protest. Turner and Killian have tried to sort out its effects.
"First," they say, "we are probably on safer ground to assume that different kinds of motivations draw people to different kinds of movements than to search further for a generalized movement-prone configuration." I would go further: even a single movement contains
participants who are there for a variety of reasons. They then argue
that "each movement modifies the attitudes and motivations of its
members, so that distinctive attitudes reflect experience in the move-

ment as much as predisposition." A valid point, although attitudes are not quite the same as personality. Turner and Killian then argue that "whatever movement a person joins may serve as a vehicle for the expression of preexisting personal needs, without these needs having been crucial in bringing one to the movement." This is another fine point, except that motivations are so complex and multiple that it is difficult to separate "crucial" ones from others. Finally, they go further than I probably would, in admitting that "some people may have personalities that make them indiscriminately susceptible to participation in social movements."[20] Even those who are more susceptible because of their personalities are never *indiscriminately* susceptible.

Sadly, we have virtually no empirical evidence about the role of personality in protest. Crowd theorists assumed a big role without demonstrating it. Recent theorists have assumed there was little or no role—again without demonstrating it. Evidence on attitudes and values, inadequate enough on its own, does not begin to touch personality factors. If, as most recent theorists believe, individuals are theoretically and methodologically unimportant, then so are personality and psychology.

There is creativity in difference. The joy of protest that Geoff Merideth describes is very like the playful potential of art, which creates another reality for us to "try on." This other world often feels more real than our everyday life, for we can try on our "real" selves there, penetrate to deeper truths and identities normally blocked by our everyday routines. The philosopher Hans-Georg Gadamer described how we are taken up by this vision, losing our everyday, instrumental sense of ourselves as actors. We become different people as we are lost in the world of the art work, just as protestors can be transformed by the worlds they create. Play, to Gadamer, is an engrossing activity that sweeps us up in it, much as dance does; because it has its own rules and realities, we can "lose" ourselves in play, letting go of our usual subjectivity and becoming part of something else. Games and dance do not exist except when played and danced, and for a while we are absorbed by the role of player or dancer. The similarities to Durkheim's description of collective ritual are striking.[21]

Movement culture offers satisfactions to all sorts of people, and movements attract quite a variety. The last chapter examined emotional bonds that strengthened movement and activist identities. This one has examined the diversity of psychological makeups that could find outlets or pleasures in movements, and the variety of those pleasures. Protestors enjoy what they do, and do what they enjoy. Otherwise they quit, when the pains and costs overwhelm them. The next chapter looks more specifically at the tactics of protest, arguing that they too offer pleasures to participants, who choose their tactics in part for their emotional and moral satisfactions rather than simply their efficacy. They demonstrate, in other words, a persistent taste in tactics that is partly independent of their strategic interaction and learning.

- Protest is sustained by innumerable complex motivations, skills, and pleasures—the stuff of an activist identity.
- Pain and deprivation also abound, helping draw people back out of participation.
- Unusual personality traits—including stubbornness and even kookiness—can be a useful, sustaining necessity for long years of protest activity, helping to define what are pleasures and what are pains for protestors.
- Individuals move in and out of formal protest organizations as the latter fit their needs.

TEN

Tastes in Tactics

Taste classifies, and it classifies the classifier. Social subjects, classified by
their classifications, distinguish themselves by the distinctions they make,
between the beautiful and the ugly, the distinguished and the vulgar, in
which their position in the objective classifications is expressed or betrayed.
    —Pierre Bourdieu

When I asked one of the Mothers for Peace about the Abalone Alliance,
she smiled and rolled her eyes. "Well, they have a certain charm to
them," she said, picking her words slowly. "We don't deal with them
more than we have to, 'cause they drive us crazy." But she later admitted, "We're glad they're there, doing their own thing. They've had a
big impact, especially with media coverage." The Mothers for Peace,
we saw, were primarily middle-class and middle-aged local residents
who testified at Nuclear Regulatory Commission hearings and pursued other legal tactics. There was little overlap between their membership and that of the countercultural Abalone Alliance.

Both groups "did their own thing" with energy and sincerity to try
to stop Diablo Canyon. They had distinct "tastes in tactics" that led
them to favor different paths of action, and a clear division of labor
evolved between them. The Mothers pursued legal avenues for dissent,
using the courts and avoiding illegal activities, while the Abalone Alliance sponsored illegal and extralegal actions. Here is a common
feature of protest movements: an uneasy coalition between groups favoring different tactics, often with slightly different moral sensibilities.
The term *movement* often disguises this immense diversity; in many
cases the groups have little to do with each other, even dislike each
other.

Movement identities can form in the absence of many personal or
organizational linkages, based instead on a sense that like-minded others are out there working toward similar goals. The Abalone staff, for
example, had no regular ties to other antinuclear groups; Mario Diani's
rigorous network analysis of the Milan environmental movement
found the average group to have regular contacts with fewer than three
other groups—right there in the same metropolis.[1] Whereas citizenship movements often see national organizations as a sign of strength

and visibility, recent post-citizenship movements usually avoid them. Having seen how, in the 1960s, the news media focused on a few prominent leaders and groups, distorting and eventually undermining the broader New Left and related movements, leaders of post-industrial groups that formed in the 1970s and 1980s took pains to avoid prominent leaders and centralized organizations. They believed in decentralization for society, and they practiced it in their movements. Although most protest movements have diverse groups pursuing diverse tactics, this is especially (and intentionally) so for post-industrial movements.

The Mothers and the Alliance exemplify a common type of coalition, especially in movements against technological or environmental hazards, between people who live near the target of protest and those who do not. The first large wave of orders for nuclear reactors in the United States during the mid-1960s had occasioned scattered protest, usually by those living near the proposed sites, although most reactors were unopposed. In the early 1970s national groups appeared that were concerned, first, with the environmental effects of reactors (the warming of waters, the release of radiation), and second, with the chance of accidents. Debates among experts, and criticism from within the nation's atomic energy laboratories, helped bring public attention to these issues. When energy policy made headlines after the 1973–74 oil crisis, Ralph Nader and others gave the movement a national voice. A movement identity emerged for the first time, renewing and reassuring scattered groups of protestors (who got little else from the national groups). Lobbying Congress was added to testifying at NRC hearings as the main tactics of dissent. It was all quite conventional.

Beginning in 1975 and 1976, the antinuclear movement took a dramatic new turn. Illegal direct action, especially site occupations, spread rapidly to local antinuclear efforts in many parts of the country, starting with the Clamshell Alliance, which opposed the Seabrook plant in New Hampshire. Along with these tactics went explicit training in nonviolence and an organizational structure based on affinity groups. The "alliances" that sprang up—the Abalone Alliance, the Sagebrush Alliance, the Saguaro, the Armadillo—were alliances of affinity groups. These groups spurned the legal interventions of prior antinuclear organizations, preferring instead site occupations, encampments, and large rallies. Some were even willing to sabotage buildings and equipment. All were willing to break the law, sometimes spending days or even weeks in jail. As we saw, the Abalone Alliance was a typical example. Along with new tactics went a new ideology that linked nuclear energy to the unfettered search for profits by large corporations and the complicity of the American government in these activities. It traced the history of civilian nuclear energy to its military origins, conjuring problems of proliferation.

Between them, the new tactics and ideology attracted a new kind of antinuclear activist. Most of those who joined the affinity groups, inspired by what they had heard about the Clamshell Alliance or the success of a similar site occupation in Whyl, Germany, were new to the antinuclear movement. They were younger, further to the Left, more ideological, and less likely to be affected directly by nuclear plants. They had little to do with either the local intervenor groups or the national organizations. Factor analysis of my survey results for Diablo shows that the nonlocals were more interested in small-is-beautiful values, and more suspicious of technology and science. Nonlocals had a broader agenda than simply stopping Diablo Canyon. Indeed, after 1984 the activities of the Abalone Alliance staff expanded to Central America, nuclear weapons, and other issues, while the local protestors in San Luis Obispo remained focused on Diablo.

At one ideal-typical extreme were protestors from around California, with well-developed political positions, often full-time political activists, frequently in nontraditional living arrangements, for whom Diablo was just one more instance of technocracy blindly pursuing technological change, economic growth, or profits. At the other were middle-class local protestors, who were more interested in shutting down Diablo than in global political issues, but had become disillusioned with governmental processes and technology through this and previous experiences.[2] Typically the locals had been working against Diablo before the Three Mile Island (TMI) accident in 1979, while more of the nonlocals began after TMI. Of course, some locals had been drawn into the Abalone counterculture by their opposition to Diablo. But locals versus nonlocals is a good proxy for the two segments of the antinuclear movement.

In my survey, the locals and nonlocals differed in the pattern of "undecided" responses. Since one bias of survey research is that it forces respondents to take stands on questions as presented by the survey, the number of "don't know" responses may indicate the degree to which a group speaks the same language as the surveyor. In this case both locals and nonlocals had definite opinions about nuclear energy and weapons, science and technology, the environment, and economic growth. But on questions concerning business and government and their respective roles, the locals had more "undecided" responses than did nonlocals: typically 25–30 percent as opposed to 10–15 percent.

Table 10.1   Selected Differences between Locals and Nonlocals

	Distance Traveled to Anti-Diablo Demonstration	
	Under 25 miles ($n = 114$)	25 miles or more ($n = 159$)
Political leaning		
Libertarian, conservative, middle-of-the-road	12%	6%
Liberal, progressive	70	51
Anarchist, radical left	17	42
	99%	99%
Political strategy for environmental problems		
Conformist	31%	24%
Reformist	49	39
Radical	21	37
	101%	100%
Importance of previous activism in getting respondent involved		
Very important	39%	65%
Somewhat important	24	15
Not important	37	20
	100%	100%
Importance of friends in getting respondent involved		
Very important	52%	52%
Somewhat important	31	27
Not important	17	21
	100%	100%

The direct-action subculture, in addition to having a more radical political position, was more likely to formulate a response to this kind of political question.

Table 10.1 reports other differences between local and nonlocal respondents. Although both local and nonlocal activists had a history of political activity, it was more formative and forceful for the latter group. Of those who traveled more than twenty-five miles, 65 percent said previous activism was very important in getting them involved in antinuclear activism, as opposed to 39 percent of those who traveled under twenty-five miles. Similarly, 75 percent of those from urban areas said this, as opposed to 45 percent from other locales; 71 percent of "environmental radicals" said this, as opposed to 45 percent of reformists and 37 percent of conformists (definitions were based on how much structural change they thought was necessary for accomplishing environmental goals). On the other hand, there were no significant differences between these categories in the relative influence of friends, the media, and events. Social networks mattered for all categories of respondents, but those networks were more likely to have been formed through and for political activity with the nonlocals, the radicals, and the urbanites—the direct-action wing of the movement. The locals were more likely to have bonds independent of political activity, of the kind normally portrayed in network models. Said one local participant, "We're likely, I think, to know each other through the PTA; the Abalone people seem to live together in group homes, or to be long-time comrades from other causes." An Abalone member said, "They [local protestors] have families, and they'll be killed in an accident. I feel real sorry for them. . . . A lot of us [from San Francisco] are here to fight capitalism and technocracy. We tend to think that's more important— these big issues—but it's pretty abstract compared to worrying about your kids."

The new protestors formed an uneasy alliance with the older ones. The Mothers for Peace continued to pursue electoral strategies and testify at NRC hearings. As individuals, some of the Mothers attended Abalone Alliance events, including the 1981 blockade, but coordination between the organizations proved difficult. The Mothers found Abalone staffers "too flaky." The Mothers for Peace utilized, in contrast to the job rotation favored by direct-action groups, a clear division of labor based on who had enough time, willingness, and expertise to do each task. One of them was critical of the Abalone Alliance: "It sounds great to rotate tasks, but the truth is you build up contacts with the media, expertise and know-how. It's stupid to get someone new just when you've learned the ropes." Less concerned with subculture maintenance, and dealing primarily with the media, lawyers, and NRC officials, the Mothers were uninterested in tactics which devoted so much attention to building subcultural bonds rather than efficient actions and arguments. Abalone members, in turn, found the Mothers' legal interventions ineffective and quixotic. The two groups were happy enough to have allies, but also happy not to have to work closely with each other. A shared sense of movement identity and common purpose fostered mutual respect between the two groups, but it could not make them like each other. Around the country, the local groups remained active when the direct-action groups began to leave the antinuclear movement (often to become active in the burgeoning nuclear freeze movement) in the early 1980s.

In this chapter I continue to explore internal movement culture by asking whether tactics are selected not simply for their efficacy, but also for their symbolic and emotional implications. Are they, in other words, part of a movement's or a group's culture? Or do protestors simply try whatever might work, searching for the most effective means? The Mothers for Peace and the Abalone Alliance, with the same goal of stopping Diablo Canyon, could consistently draw different tactical implications from what was happening. Did each of them have additional, but different, noninstrumental goals beyond simply stopping Diablo? Are tactics oriented exclusively toward audiences outside a protest group, or do they have internal audiences and satisfactions as well? Were the Mothers' tactics, as they claimed, simply the most effective, or did the Mothers have an independent preference for legal routes? Do tastes, in other words, affect strategic and tactical choices?

To explain what protestors do, we must answer three successive questions. First, why do they have the repertory of possible tactics that they do? Of all conceivable forms of protest, why are only certain ones used, or even considered, at a particular point in history for a given society? Being the most structural, this question has received the best treatment, especially from process theorists. Second, given a repertory of possibilities, why do protestors choose the tactical courses they do? Why bombs rather than marches, or marches rather than letter-writing campaigns? Third, once they have chosen a particular tactic, how do they apply it? How do they decide where to plant a bomb, and when, and whether to ignite a second? These details make an enormous psychological difference—often the difference between success and failure. If the choice of tactics is like deciding to take a car rather than a bus or train, strategic decisions include how fast to drive, when to switch lanes, and whether to use the horn. This chapter examines the choice of tactics; chapter 13 will turn to strategic choices in their unfolding. All three explanations involve a mix of internal culture and external strategy.[3]

CHOICES OF TACTICS

How protestors pick their tactics, how they decide what actually to *do*, is a question rarely addressed in research on protest. Crowd theorists dismissed all noninstitutionalized tactics as misguided and irrational, the product of immature minds. In many accounts, protest was a momentary passion, driven by the frenzy of the crowd, emergent norms, alienation from the political system, or generational rebellion. It was a psychological process, the direct result of frustration and anger, having little to do with existing strategic opportunities, and not involving rational choices.

At the opposite extreme, recent observers sympathetic to protestors have occasionally concluded that changes in tactics are rational responses and adaptations to existing conditions and opportunities. When scholars in the mobilization and process traditions began to view protest as rational and purposive, they analyzed tactical choices as a search for effective means to attain independent ends. Tactics themselves were seen as neutral; what mattered to protestors was their efficacy. A frustration model persisted—but with a different definition of frustration. Rather than a psychological and emotional process within individuals that caused them to change their tactical preferences, and possibly to act irrationally, frustration was now a response to blocked political channels. In particular, political process approaches emphasized the state's ability to aid or repress protestors' demands. Once the external environment was fully specified, tactics usually followed straightforwardly.[4]

Herbert Kitschelt captured this view concisely in explaining why the movements against nuclear energy in France and West Germany were more violent than those in Sweden and the United States. His political opportunity structure approach predicted that "when political systems are closed and have considerable capacities to ward off threats to the implementation of policies, movements are likely to adopt *confrontational*, disruptive strategies orchestrated outside established policy channels."[5] Kitschelt presented his explanation in a peculiarly static language, as though the antinuclear movements did not need to try mainstream tactics in order to discover whether or not existing political structures were permeable. He did not discuss the cultural processes by which protestors learn this. It may be trial-and-error by the same people, or it may be efforts by new people. It may reflect contrasting assumptions about tactics and strategies. What is often lost in the mobilization and political process models is the insight that people prefer certain tactics to others, at least partly independently of their effect on outcomes. Protestors care about the outcomes, to be sure, but they also care about the tactics.

This emphasis on state responses as the major determinant of tactical choices usually works better for citizenship movements that make demands directly on the state. Kitschelt's application of the model to a post-citizenship movement remains plausible because the state was so involved in the development and deployment of nuclear reactors. But this involvement varied considerably across issues and across countries. Nuclear energy *was* the state in France, but not in the United States, where private companies built and operated reactors. In the United States antinuclear protestors had more of a choice of audiences and tactics, and more room for variation in tactical tastes. In France tactical choices were more driven, as Kitschelt says, by a strategic rather than a cultural logic.

The emphasis of process theorists on the opportunities and constraints of political structures works better for explaining repertories than the choices and applications within them—but at this level it is almost a truism. In regimes without courts, protestors will not bring lawsuits. They will not pursue electoral strategies under dictatorships lacking elections. In a broad historical perspective, changes in repertories are of interest. Usually, however, the choice of tactics and their application are more influential factors in explaining what protestors do.

For most scholars, the choice of tactics has simply not been an interesting question. Either tactics were psychological, part of the anger and emotional expression of crowds, or they were chosen in a straightforward way to maximize a group's external effectiveness. Either way, they seemed to have little meaning for protestors in and of themselves. In an extensive recent review of the literature on social movements, less than half a page out of thirty-four is devoted to the choice of tactics; the only empirical study cited is William Gamson's *The Strategy of Social Protest*, which actually deals with the effects of varying goals and tactics on success, not how they are themselves selected (the assumption being that effectiveness is the criterion).[6] In McAdam's study of the pace of tactical innovations, these become a function of strategic interaction with opponents, lacking any independent cultural or psychological element. He too is more interested in the effects than the sources of tactical innovation.[7]

Explaining how protestors choose from among available tactics is often reduced to explaining the range of tactics available in the repertory. Charles Tilly directly addresses protestors' "repertoires of collective action": in any society, groups use a surprisingly small number of tactics to pursue their collective ends, given the innumerable activities that have been used throughout history.[8] Protestors know how to do some things but not others; they prefer to do some things rather than others. Tilly lists five factors that shape repertories: "the standards of rights and justice prevailing in the population; the daily routines of the population; the population's internal organization; its accumulated experience with prior collective action; the pattern of repression in the world to which the population belongs."[9] These factors primarily explain the various contents of the existing repertory, although they may also help to explain the selection of tactics from within the repertory. When the concept of a political opportunity structure is added to that of a repertory, explanations tend to show that protestors do what works. Tilly leaves little room for *choice* on the part of protestors, perhaps because for him it is "populations" that accumulate experience, not groups and individuals.

These repertories have a straightforward cognitive component: protesters must be familiar with the practices. But there is an additional moral component: protesters must feel that the activity is good or tasteful as well as efficacious. "Standards of rights and justice" are a highly variable cultural construct that applies to actions as well as goals. And there is an artful, strategic component: protesters do what they are good at, what they can do creatively or freshly. Skill at a technique goes beyond familiarity with it, helping to explain choices made *within* repertories. Repertories and choices within them both depend on cultural learning and strategic virtuosity as well as on structural constraints. With Tilly's model of a repertory, it is hard to explain why groups with the same goals and opportunities so often use such different tactics.

Even in Tilly's complex analysis, tactics remain relatively neutral, the result of extrinsic considerations more than intrinsic, moral preferences. They are primarily shaped by existing knowledge, by relative access to resources, and by assessments of how other actors will respond. This is why all "rational" protestors would pick the same tactics from the repertory. Yet protestors also select tactics partly for their intrinsic value. Sometimes they are simply pleasureful. At other times, they help reinforce affective ties among protestors, so that building the subculture becomes as important as achieving stated goals in the external world—even when there is tension between internal and external goals. Even when we are explaining repertories, but especially when we are explaining choices and applications within them, we must rely on a combination of internal preferences and external, strategic considerations.

Tactics are rarely, if ever, neutral means about which protestors do not care. Tactics represent important routines, emotionally and morally salient in these people's lives. Just as their ideologies do, their activities express protestors' political identities and moral visions. To participate in NRC hearings or to block traffic in the street outside is to say different things about one's personal identity, a movement's identity, attitudes toward governmental authority, and much else. Within the same movement or activist identity, there can be divergent tactical identities: some think of themselves as the kind of people who engage in direct action, others pride themselves on being the radical guard, and still others feel comfortable dealing with professionals or government representatives in formal settings. I would guess that activist identities that transcend movement identities are usually built on identification with tactics. But where do these tactical identities come from?

Pierre Bourdieu has probed the origins of tastes with his concept of "habitus." Although over time he has added many layers of meaning to his definition, habitus is most easily thought of as a disposition to act in certain ways, a flexible "matrix of perceptions, appreciations, and actions" that allow one to improvise in both new and familiar situations.[10] The habitus is just below the surface of explicit consciousness, and a shared habitus is needed for people to understand what their fellows mean and what they are doing in their ordinary practices. Because it operates as a sensibility or intuition, the habitus has a spontaneity that distinguishes it from many other influences on action, such as more explicit rules of morality or rationality. It is an "immanent law . . . laid down in each agent by his earliest upbringing, which is the precondition not only for the co-ordination of practices but also for practices of co-ordination."[11] Far from rigid rules or norms, however, these tastes allow virtuosic playing with and against rules. They suggest certain thoughts, feelings, evaluations, and actions, while discouraging others, yet they allow considerable room to maneuver within these broad channels. Such dispositions are also implicit moral judgments.

Tactical tastes, like most cultural sensibilities, combine morality, emotion, and cognition. Characteristically, only the cognitive dimension has been recognized by scholars. Snow and Benford make a point similar to mine: "Movement tactics are not solely a function of environmental constraints and adaptations, but are also constrained by anchoring master frames."[12] Their general emphasis is on beliefs, but they also mention values (although it is not clear that they are part of the frame, which seems to be purely cognitive). Emotions are absent.

The tactical tastes of Abalone Alliance members grew out of a complex series of factors: what they learned through formal education; their concern to avoid large bureaucracies; their reactions, often negative, to the evolution of the movements of the 1960s; their extensive socialization in the movements of the 1970s; various ideological commitments to social justice; and the self-conscious discussions of democratic procedures that took place within many political groups. Similar factors led the Mothers in a somewhat different direction; as daughters of the professional middle class, many of them expected the world to be controllable through state intervention. Their trust in the system was stretched by Vietnam and Diablo Canyon, but not altogether broken. Tastes in tactics may show some stability over time, in part because they are reinforced by the development of associated skills and beliefs, in part because of positive emotional and moral valuations embodied in deep dispositions. The Mothers never let go of their inclination to follow the rules, even when this strategy worked poorly.

The Mothers grappled with their lack of success. "It was often depressing," said one. "We knew we weren't being taken seriously. . . . But you keep going, you play it out as long as there are hearings to go to, once you've hired the lawyers and started on a path." So tactics can take on a life of their own through inertia and trajectory. Psychologically, sunk costs can loom large. But the Mothers retained more positive assessments despite their disappointments; hearings had not worked yet, but another one might. They also had negative feelings about alternatives. One said, "Me, go sleep in a field?" And another, "It's not like the Abalone people were stopping the plant either."

Such appraisals were somewhat arbitrary, since no one knew what—if anything—would stop Diablo Canyon. Although the Mothers insisted they were doing what would be most effective, they were instead doing what they *perceived* would be most effective—a perception in need of an explanation. The Abalone Alliance and the Mothers each believed their tactics were most likely to succeed—beliefs with emotional and moral bases as much as cognitive. But in both cases, winning was not everything. "Another action [civil disobedience] won't stop Diablo now," an Abalone staffer admitted, "but it's still the right thing to do"—for the sake of her personal identity and dignity, and for the broader subculture. There might also be a variant of ontological security here: it would be unsettling to abandon paths of action so habitually rooted. The result, though, is that success, narrowly defined, is not all that mattered.

Mobilization and process theorists often reduce tactical tastes to structural position. Were the Mothers' tastes shaped by biographical availability, with children at home precluding a weeklong encampment? "We didn't do much illegal about Vietnam either," said one. Their tactical tastes do not seem to have changed much over fifteen years. Besides, many of them *were* biographically available again, with kids who had already left for college. But they stayed with their favorite tactics. Initial socialization into protest can, like memorable events, leave a lasting symbolic imprint. Yet structural incentives and cultural tastes or knowledge are not incompatible. In his study of new recruits who radicalized a Catholic rights group in Northern Ireland, Stephen Beach says, "The working class converts were familiar with a community tradition of violent protest well over a century in age whereas the middle-class students were much less aware of this tradition. The ghetto youths were not afraid of harming their future careers by participating in radical action; they had little to lose."[13] Culture and structure are rarely opposites; they normally reinforce each other.

Resources and a "population's" stock of know-how are, as Tilly says, important for explaining the repertory of tactics open to a protest group. But explaining how they will pick and choose among the tools of this repertory requires more attention to culture, biography, and the art of protest. Even more, how they apply a tactic once they have chosen it demands attention to psychological nuance, including the importance of both internal and external factors. Strategic considerations such as timing and surprise play a key role. Protestors do not simply apply existing repertories; they innovate within them and deploy different combinations at different times. Repertories, tactical choices within them, and strategic applications of tactics are affected by internal movement culture and individual biographies as well as by external opportunities and the moves made by other players.

INTERNAL CONFLICT

Different tactical tastes can lead to conflicts among different groups within the same movement, and conflicts within a single group, just as surely as differing goals can. Competition among social-movement organizations, especially for contributions, was a central insight of mobilization theorists, especially of McCarthy and Zald.[14] Sometimes there is direct competition, as different groups aim at the same audiences: raising funds from the same direct-mail lists, striving for attention from the same news media, attacking the same opponents, and dealing with the same arms of the state. Sometimes competing groups can divide up their audiences, avoiding direct competition: the radicals have their supporters, their own set of opponents, and even state agencies they deal with, while the moderates have their own sets of each.

Tactical tensions often arise between different cohorts of recruits, who arrive with contrasting tastes in tactics. Examples abound. Writing about abolition, temperance, and other reform movements, historian Paul Johnson describes how "[i]n the early 1830s newly converted evangelicals invaded all of these organizations and took most of them over." Driven by a millennial hope for sudden change, they brought a range of new, more radical tactics.[15] The parallel generational and tactical cleavage in the civil rights movement has been analyzed partly as a practical result of "biographical availability": students can afford long afternoons at lunch counters, several days in jail, even a summer in Mississippi. The sit-ins were more than a matter of finding out what worked for which protestors, though. The students were carving out a niche for themselves, with personal and movement identities more radical than those of SCLC's preachers and their wing of the movement. It's not that bus boycotts did not work (they often did); they didn't fit the students' emerging style.

Nancy Whittier has written the most detailed study of these generational cleavages, focusing on the women's movement in Columbus, Ohio from the late 1960s to the early 1980s. The experiences of new recruits differed considerably as the movement changed, so that "[e]ach micro-cohort entered the women's movement at a specific point in its history, engaged in different activities, had a characteristic political culture, and modified feminist collective identity. Each defined the type of people, issues, language, tactics, or organizational structures that 'qualified' as feminist differently. Presentation of self, use of language, and participation in political culture help to identify individuals with their micro-cohorts." Her cultural analysis shows how these different sensibilities caused cleavages in the women's movement and led to changes in tactics. (Her emphasis on the cultural activities of the movement also shows that the women's movement was as much a postindustrial as a citizenship movement.)[16] *Generational cleavages arise because each new cohort is responding not only to problems in the broader society, but also to existing movement activists, their activities, and their identities.* New recruits may be as interested in changing the movements they join as in transforming the rest of society.

As we saw with the Abalone Alliance and the Mothers for Peace, divergent factions often work out a strategically effective division of labor. This often means that they concentrate on different audiences. Moderate groups may focus on the broader public and more radical groups on activists themselves. "In the case of the Austin peace movement," according to Robert Benford, "the moderate SMOs [social-movement organizations] refined the art of problem identification and other framing activity aimed at effecting consensus mobilization. Radical groups, on the other hand, developed a knack for prodding adherents to take action."[17] The efficacy of such a specialization, however, does not mean that it was intended.

The diversity of tastes within a protest movement is not always apparent. A policy goal—equal justice, voting rights—or a condensing symbol—suffering animals—can tie diverse tactical preferences together into what looks like a coherent social movement. But any number of internal dynamics are affected by conflicts between tastes, especially schisms and alliances. Diversity in tactical tastes can destroy protest movements. The Clamshell Alliance is a notorious example, pulled apart by different attitudes toward property destruction, in particular whether to cut fences in order to occupy the Seabrook nuclear site in 1978. This seemingly small issue tapped into a variety of disagreements in the Alliance: "where the line between violence and nonviolence should be drawn, what to do when consensus could not be reached on a major issue, and whether there was any legitimate role for leadership."[18] The Alliance's undoing came partly from trying to keep diverse tactics within the same group, forcing everyone to follow the same line. Schisms are the usual—and often healthy—result. By the time the Alliance spun off a new group for those willing to use wire cutters, though, the dissensus had already soured participants' emotional enthusiasm. The example nonetheless shows that the founding of organizations and the form they take are also a tactical choice reflecting members' tastes.

No matter who the audience, protest groups appeal to it through rhetorical framing. They try to define issues, appeal to underlying values, link to positive and negative affects and symbols, spread new information and points of view. Not all their messages are purveyed by words. Actions and the choice of tactics send all sorts of signals; they tell an outsider as much about a group as its explicit arguments do. Cultural persuasion also takes place through organizational forms, which are themselves a form of tactic.

TASTES IN ORGANIZATIONS

Formal organizations originate in the strategic choices of protestors, who exhibit tastes in organizational form as much as in other tactics. Organizations are never simply the most efficient way to solve some problem; their structures, bylaws, decisions, and practices are partly symbols and myths designed to send messages to various audiences.[19] Businesses, for example, wish to send the message that they are efficient and profitable. Social-movement organizations may also wish to indicate efficacy, for example when asking for support through direct mailings. Other protest organizations, especially when their main audience consists of their own members, may wish to send the message that they are democratic and moral—as we saw with the Abalone Alliance.

The Abalone affinity groups consciously aimed at informal, nonhierarchical forms, and this is one of the most noted characteristics of recent post-industrial movements. Embracing the informalism of "collectivist organizations," they typically have moral visions that include what group procedures are best—whether they should be, for example, democratic or consensus-oriented. A large part of their goal will be to shape their own group so that it conforms to their values. Not all protest groups avoid the creation of formal structures to this degree. They may have moral tastes that simply do not include the functioning of their own groups in significant ways. Procedures may be sacrificed to the greater cause, sometimes as defined by group leaders. Most citizenship movements have tolerated strong leaders; in the early civil rights movement, for example, the authority of the preachers was enormous. In some groups decisions are made by participatory democracy of all members; in others, they are made by a leader or a small group of leaders. Either process could be a part of the group's moral vision. The leader's authority could be seen to come directly from god, for example, whose commandments understandably trump internal group procedures.

A movement that is loosely structured in its formal organization may *require* more solidarity of ideology, beliefs, and moral vision. Luther Gerlach and Virginia Hine point not only to personal ties and ideology but also to "ritual activities" as binding forces available to loosely structured movements.[20] Further refinements are possible along the same continuum. John Lofland has imaginatively labeled a range of different organizational types, from the least to the most organized and demanding of their members: "(1) associations sustained by volunteers; (2) bureaus employing staffers; (3) troups deploying soldiers; (4) communes composed of householders; (5) collectives consisting of workers; (6) utopias populated by utopians."[21] Each presumably corresponds to different individual preferences and local cultures.

Elisabeth Clemens has written about the choice of organizational forms in a very different period from that of the Abalone Alliance: the labor movement of one hundred years ago.[22] Criticizing prior social-movement theory for measuring formal organizations simplistically as either bureaucratic or not, and as either present or absent, she shows that the content of organizational form also affects strategies and allegiances by framing them in much the same way that arguments do. "Fraternal" forms of organizing tended to downplay economic interests and discourage political action; "military" forms, such as Coxey's Army, had broad patriotic resonance in the decades after the Civil War but tended to elicit violent repression; "craft" unions had the notorious consequence of emphasizing economic rather than political gains. Although Clemens is more interested in the consequences of such organizational forms, it is clear that their causes lie in contrasting images of a worker identity, along with contrasting ideas of natural allies. Organizations are a form of tactic, reflecting cognitive frames, moral tastes, and practical know-how. Organizational forms send clear messages about what kind of protestors these are.

If tactical tastes, including organizational tastes, shed light on questions of internal movement dynamics, they also help explain changes in movements over time. When do groups become more bureaucratic? More radical? When do they undergo schisms? Is radicalization of a protest movement the result of frustration among existing members or of new recruits with different tastes in tactics?

CHANGE OVER TIME

Some protest groups grow more radical over time, others more moderate. Entire movements often change in this way, as one kind of group gains more prominence in the media, or seems to be more successful, or as new groups appear that redirect a movement. Such transformations arise out of the competition among groups. The winners put their stamp on the movement's identity, due to their success at gaining financial support, media attention, access to politicians, and alliances with sympathetic organizations from related movements.

The radicalization of protest movements is a problem that has haunted political commentators throughout history. For crowd theorists, most protest appeared too radical, based on irrational passions that made demands and actions unpredictable and dangerous. To more recent theorists, protestors could almost never be irrational, and radicalization followed when other political opportunities were closed off. Like culture more generally, the concept of tactical tastes may provide an alternative to this standoff between overly irrational and overly rational imagery. Rather than an expression of anger or a calculated search for efficient means, the radicalization of a social movement is a complex process combining rational assessments of a range of tactics, moral and affective valuations of those tactics, and the recruitment of new participants with no investment in prior tactics. It is the new recruits who often drive the change in tactics by bringing with them different tastes in tactics. As in other cultural work that movements do, though, there is an interplay between pre-existing tastes and their transformation during protest. The more prior political experience the new recruits have had, in all likelihood, the stronger their tastes in tactics when they join a new movement.

Protest movements may grow more radical in different ways. In the usual model, protestors try a range of tactics to see what works; radical tactics prove more effective and spread throughout a movement. Groups learn from each other. Appeals to authorities often prove disappointing and exacerbate outrage. This pattern is consistent with Kitschelt's political opportunity approach. In a second pattern, a large number of activists build their identities around being on the cutting edge of protest, and they respond to the expansion of their own movement by adopting new, more radical tactics, always a step ahead of the pack. Third, new recruits to a movement bring with them a different (and more radical) taste in tactics than existing protestors exhibit.[23]

New recruits may have different tactical tastes because they negatively assess the efficacy of existing protest groups with their more moderate tactics, or because they have identities bound up with certain tactics (although this is a circular way of saying they prefer certain tactics). For example, the New Left of the 1960s was reacting not only to the problems of bureaucracy and capitalism, but also to the political tactics of the Old Left. Or new recruits may bring different tactical tastes with them from other protest experiences. Tastes in tactics may therefore be associated with protest cohorts, as Whittier shows. This is the reason that, especially among post-industrial movements, tactical innovations spread rapidly from one movement to another. Not only does know-how spread, but protestors positively value the tactics they learn, so that the tactics become partly an end as well as simply a means. Some tactics are enjoyable. An animal rights demonstrator once told me, "I hate writing letters and making calls [to legislators of university administrators]. It's boring, and they don't pay any attention anyway. But—I know this is weird—I love these marches. I get off on shouting at the [fur] stores." Others cling to tactics they don't enjoy at all, like the anti-Diablo protestor who said, "The meetings [of her group] are boring. They go around and around. But they're important for democracy. If you care about people's power you've got to have them." In this case, though, we see a conscious choice based on an explicit ideology more than an inchoate, deep-seated taste. Past activism may be more important in shaping the tactical tastes of participants in many of the post-citizenship movements, who are likely to move from one movement to another, than of those in citizenship movements.

Frances Fox Piven and Richard Cloward suggest an additional reason that new recruits to a movement may be crucial to its adoption of more radical tactics, arguing that over time protestors are made more moderate by cautious leaders and the demands of organizational survival. If this is true, then new groups and new recruits may be relatively free of these pressures. Whatever one thinks of Piven and Cloward's romantic image of natural radicalism, one can agree that the lack of bureaucratic pressures may allow new recruits to pursue other tactical tastes. They are free to innovate.[24]

Protestors develop identities as activists, based on a willingness and ability to carry on certain kinds of activity. The identity of a protestor may be that of someone who attends rallies and marches, or someone who sabotages corporate labs, or someone who constructs bombs. These are quite distinct identities, and there is no reason to think that it is easy to switch from one to another. A taste in tactics persists partly because it shapes one's sense of self.

New recruits found new groups as well as transform old ones when they are dissatisfied with existing activities. They may not like existing groups because of the kind of people they contain (black college students vs. preachers in the SCLC), or because of the tactics they favor. In some cases they can take over the existing groups; in others their creation of new groups is a needed symbol of innovation, change, or radicalism. Sometimes the new groups are so different that a new movement identity forms alongside the old.[25]

Let's look at one of our recurrent examples. The movement to protect domesticated animals had existed in the United States for one hundred years when a more radical "animal rights" movement began to take shape around 1980. Most of the thousands of groups in existence then were local humane societies that helped control excess cat and dog populations and tried to promote kind treatment toward nonhuman species, especially mammals. A few dozen groups were national in scope, and a handful were more inclusive in the species they hoped to protect. These groups can be distinguished by cohort. Several founded in the 1950s, including the Humane Society of the United States, were especially concerned that lost pets not end up in laboratories. Several founded in the 1960s and early 1970s, including Cleveland Amory's Fund for Animals, addressed diverse practices such as trapping, species extinctions, and high school biology classes. In the late 1970s, however, a new network of people concerned with animals began to emerge. They were inspired by the work of the older generation of activists more than they actually cooperated with them. They sharply distinguished themselves from the older movement, abetted by news media happy to declare them "new." Said one activist, "Sympathy wasn't enough. We all knew serious movements had serious ideologies. A lot of us were coming from the Left, and we didn't like the little-old-lady image." This network of individuals gradually grew and resulted in the founding of hundreds of radical animal rights organizations in the early 1980s.

As with the antinuclear movement, these new recruits were younger and further to the left politically than members of the older animal welfare societies had been: a new political generation. Although comparable statistics are not readily available for the two groups, members in both kinds of groups believe in these differences. Said one animal rights activist in 1989, "If you become interested in helping animals today, you join an animal rights group and go to rallies. If you became interested ten years ago, you joined a humane society and helped strays." Previous political experiences had set the tactical tastes of some new animal activists, as a significant minority had been involved in other protest movements. Although the printed testimony of activists traces the intellectual influence of other movements, in interviews they admit to additional sources of tactical tastes: "I started getting arrested in college in the late 70s, and that continued in the freeze movement [in the early 1980s]. . . . So it was no big thing to sit down in the street and get arrested in front of NYU [in a 1989 protest against vivisection]."

With this training, the new animal rights groups proved more aggressive in their tactics than the older, staid humane societies. Beginning in 1979, the Animal Liberation Front conducted a series of secret raids on research laboratories using animals, causing millions of dollars worth of damage and "liberating" hundreds of animals. Other tactics sought publicity, such as the "Barf-In" at the New York headquarters of cosmetics giant L'Oréal, at which protestors pretended to vomit into a large toilet to show that the company's animal testing "made them sick." One protestor returned from a summer on the *Sea Shepherd*, where he learned to confront whalers in tiny boats, and cofounded People for the Ethical Treatment of Animals (PETA), now the world's largest animal rights group. PETA has occupied offices at the National Institutes of Health and regularly acts as a spokes-group for the Animal Liberation Front.

Of course, tactics have multiple audiences, so that strategic concerns also shape tactical choice. A group may itself be disposed toward property destruction yet be aware that the news media, state agencies, and most of the public have a strong distaste for such tactics. Each group tries to show potential supporters—an important audience—that it does more to save animals than its rivals, and the evidence has often been that its activities are more radical. In one example, Trans-Species Unlimited, recognizing that it was losing the national direct-mail competition, changed its name to ARM! (Animal Rights Mobilization), which it printed in a font that looked like spray-painted graffiti. This effort to associate itself with illegal tactics was too late to save the group, but it reflects a common perception among animal rights groups that radicalism attracts members. Older groups, perceiving the same appeal, often adopted more radical rhetoric, using some of the same issues in their fundraising appeals. The older groups radicalized their rhetoric partly because they saw changes in public sentiment, but also because staff members adopted new ideologies. They rarely, however, changed their tactics to mimic those of the new rights groups, preferring to continue their traditional activities.

We have seen several causes of tactical change. One derives from fund-raising needs, with past and future supporters as the central audience. Another relatively instrumental mechanism is a strategic assessment of what is likely to work (including what will surprise one's opponents). Another cause lies in the personal identity needs of participants who take pride in being on the cutting edge of protest, innovating tactically and doing things that other protestors do not. All, though, occur against the backdrop of protestors' own dispositions and tastes. Although I have discussed a case of radicalization, each of these factors can sometimes lead in the opposite direction, toward moderation: some activists retain moderate identities; some potential contributors prefer softer tactics; moderation probably works better when broad sections of the public need to be persuaded.

CHACUN À SON GOÛT

Just as protestors have intuitions and beliefs about what is wrong with society, they have feelings about the appropriate methods for changing what's wrong. Different groups, composed of different kinds of protestors, may cooperate effectively or tolerate each other for strategic reasons, but at another level they may never overcome their "distaste" for one another. Such tastes run deep.

Protestors deploy the tactics that they value, enjoy, feel are appropriate, and have some skill at. Their investment in selected tactics encourages them to believe that these are also the most effective ones. Tactics are never neutral means to an end, but in part reflect an independent preference. We examined one frequent result of these tastes: the process by which protest groups try more radical tactics. Because social movements learn from each other, especially as individuals from one movement join another, tactical innovations have spread across movements over the last thirty years. According to Kevin Everett, marches and rallies are more widely used than they were thirty years ago, showing that broad changes in tactical tastes are possible; even elected officials increasingly participate.[26]

It is the influx of new participants, often founding their own groups as they join, who usually lead movements to adopt new tactics. They have learned these tactics from other campaigns they have been in, but they also assess the strategic effectiveness of existing tactics. They may decide that the tactics being used by existing groups will never work, so they never bother to try them. Artistic tastes change in much the same way: an artist can challenge her audience, but is often simply rejected until a younger generation appreciates her style. Thomas Kuhn made the same point in describing how scientific revolutions depend on fresh young scientists not committed to older paradigms.[27]

Protestors also want to win. They will rarely stick with strategies that are obviously not working (although clear judgments about this are not always possible). They may try to balance internal and external goals, but they rarely let the former dominate completely. This either-or way to think of goals, however, may be wrong. Just as no movements have purely external, instrumental goals, there are no purely neutral tactics and strategies, chosen only for efficacy. All are endowed with meanings. In many cases, the strategic and the cultural dimensions conflict.

The issue of explaining protestors' choice of tactics, I have argued, differs from two closely related issues. One is explaining the broad repertories from which they choose their tactics—an issue addressed in the literature through resources and political opportunities. Another is how they apply those tactics over time: the nuances, the delays and hesitations, the style. These nuanced choices, which have rarely been addressed, are examined in chapter 13, because they depend greatly on the parallel strategic choices being made by other players, especially opponents. Here, I have concentrated on the internal factors that affect tactical choices, in contrast to the emphasis placed on external factors by those who collapse the question of tactical choice to one of repertory. All three issues, in the end, involve factors external to a movement as well as internal ones.

As a final effort to see what movement culture provides for protestors, we turn to consumer boycotts. One form of boycott, local in scope, offers a rich set of activities, opportunities for moral voice in collective settings. A second type, the national boycott, provides much less of this. The two appeal to different audiences, and operate in different ways. Local boycotts work by changing the behavior of large numbers of consumers; national boycotts, lacking a rich collective life, rarely do this. When national boycotts work, it is almost always through the publicity effects of media coverage. The labor and civil rights movements had local boycotts; post-industrial movements deploy national ones. The two types of boycotts target different audiences with different cultural and strategic tools.

- One aspect of movement culture involves tastes in tactics, which are partly independent of efficacy.

- To explain what protestors do, we must explain the available repertory, the selection of tactics from within that repertory, and the subtle choices made in applying those tactics. All three are affected by internal movement culture as well as external constraints and opportunities.

- Many protestors have pre-existing tactical tastes when they are recruited to a movement, often resulting in internal movement divisions and change.

- Organizational form can be viewed as a kind of tactic, and movement cultures often favor certain forms, regardless of their apparent efficacy.

- Clashes between tastes help to explain movement dynamics such as alliances, schisms, and radicalization or moderation over time.

ELEVEN

Direct and Indirect Action:
Boycotts and Moral Voice

My feets is tired but my soul is rested.
    —Mother Pollard, when encouraged to drop out of the Montgomery bus
        boycott because of her advanced age

Charles Cunningham Boycott, born in England in 1832, was immortalized in Ireland almost fifty years later when his name was appropriated for a political tactic of group ostracism. The word soon appeared intact in almost every European language, a useful label for a newly revitalized form of protest. Boycott, at one time a Captain in the English army, had become a landlord in the Irish countryside, helping to impose a squirearchy like Britain's on a country where peasants not only detested the British but claimed extensive implicit rights. It was this battle over land that led to the world's first boycott to be so labeled. In 1873 Boycott leased some land in County Mayo, on the rocky western coast of Ireland, and arranged to serve as agent for the owner's other local properties, his primary function being to collect rents from thirty-eight small tenant farmers. He soon developed a reputation as a mediocre farmer and a curt, petty manager.[1]

Six years later, as part of a growing Home Rule movement, the National Land League of Mayo was formed to promote the interests of local peasants through reform of existing land laws. It grew rapidly during the famine of 1879, remaining strong in County Mayo—20,000 to 30,000 attended one rally—but also extending beyond it. The Land League pursued two strategies: to prevent eviction notices from being served, a strategy which failed, and to discourage other tenants from renting the land made available by evictions. The landlords' power derived, the League understood, from their ability to find new tenants willing to pay unrealistic rents. In a speech in September 1880, the legendary Irish nationalist Charles Stewart Parnell articulated a tactic for dealing with these "landgrabbers":

> When a man takes a farm from which another has been evicted you
> must shun him on the road-side when you meet him, you must shun

him in the streets of the town, you must shun him in the shop, you must shun him in the fair green and in the market place, and even in the place of worship. By leaving him severely alone, by putting him into a moral convent, by isolating him from the rest of his countrymen as if he were a leper of old, you must show him your detestation of the crime he has committed.[2]

Drawing on medieval traditions through which peasant communities had kept their members in line, Parnell announced this tactic as a way for tenant farmers to control one another. But the League innovatively deployed it directly against Captain Boycott.

Several days after Parnell's speech, during a dispute between Boycott and his tenants over rent adjustments due to the previous year's poor harvest, an angry mob marched to Boycott's house and persuaded all his employees, indoors and out, to quit. Soon the local blacksmith, laundress, even postman, refused to provide their services, and shopkeepers refused to sell their wares to the Boycott household. The Boycott family was given extensive police protection, warding off expected violence, but the new tactic was much more effective. Supplies had to be brought by boat from some distance; the Boycotts had to care for their own extensive household and livestock.

The new word was coined, but remained purely local for several weeks, until the London newspapers began to pick up the story. Captain Boycott himself wrote an indignant letter to the *Times* detailing his treatment, and a correspondent for the *Daily News*, sent to the area to cover other instances of unrest, wrote a column about Boycott's situation. Other coverage followed, and Boycott became something of a cause in England, with a movement developing to raise funds on his behalf. British troops were also sent to protect the Boycott family, who within weeks were escorted away from the property, leaving for England on 1 December. The first modern "boycott" was a great success, and the tactic was adopted almost immediately throughout Ireland. The word was even more successful, spreading throughout the world.

No opportunities, structural or strategic, had changed in the peasants' environment to create this new form of action. They had simply thought up a new tactic that took Boycott and the authorities by surprise. The broader Land League movement too was responding to the physical threat of a deteriorating economy and high rents, not changes in the level of British repression. The boycott, although its form can be explained through the weak legal position and limited resources of the peasants, was born when a small local group revived a lost cultural tradition in their search for effective strategies.

The modern boycott emerged as a "weapon of the weak," to use

James Scott's term for forms of resistance employed by oppressed groups who cannot easily organize because of constant, close scrutiny. Violent repression, as process theorists would be quick to point out, is the background condition. Slaves and peasants can rarely manage revolutions, but they resist their subordination through regular pilfering, poaching, sabotage, and slow, ineffective work. They can do some of these even under the watchful eyes of their overseers, and others surreptitiously. Because in many cases they are not actively and explicitly resisting orders, they are not subject to punishment. They are also protected by their anonymity and by the reluctance of authorities to publicize the activities for fear of exacerbating and popularizing them.[3] *The Irish peasants and shopkeepers would have been decimated by British troops had they violently attacked Charles Boycott, but no peasant girl could be forced to work as his maid. The funds raised on Boycott's behalf made little difference if no help could be hired with them.*

This passive resistance proved effective. It depended on a tightly knit community in agreement over moral expectations, goals, and outrage, with a rich cultural life as well as the ability to punish those who broke the boycott. Collective identity and movement identity were virtually the same. In such a setting a boycott could be a highly satisfying way of expressing solidarity with the rest of the community against someone who had broken significant moral rules. The tactic is primarily reactive, since communities most easily recoil against threats to their ways of life, but it can have a large impact. The moral solidarity and the personal contacts necessary to reinforce or enforce it are inseparable.

Other boycotts, we'll see, are not rooted in local cultures, but involve national media appeals to anonymous individuals. This difference will help us compare movements with a strong pre-existing culture and those without one. Both can succeed, but in different ways. To engage significant numbers of people usually requires the emotions of cultural solidarity, which even national boycotts try to mimic. Without face-to-face cultural communities, national (and occasionally international) boycotts succeed, when they do succeed, because of symbolic meanings broadcast through the mass media. If I am right that protest is primarily about exercising moral voice, then collective events and rituals are better at this than a quiet, individual decision in the aisle of a supermarket. One involves direct action, the other indirect action, in the same sense that the moral statement is not explicit. Local boycotts are thus capable of more intensive mobilization.

If we saw in the last chapter that the same goal can be pursued through different tactics, we shall now see that the same tactic can have different meanings for those who use it. For a local face-to-face community, united by a collective or movement identity, a boycott is usually a visible, physical expression of solidarity. Almost like a ritual, it involves the placement of one's body: on the sidewalk not the bus, in one store rather than another, working for one farmer instead of another. In national boycotts no one is watching, and the act of protest typically entails pulling one can from a shelf rather than another. The expression of solidarity is with a "virtual" community composed of like-minded people around the country, not with those one knows personally. Although post-citizenship and post-industrial movements sometimes issue in the kind of activist community we saw with Diablo Canyon, more often they consist of this more abstract, symbolic form of solidarity. This can be satisfying, but not to the same degree as a rousing community effort.

FROM MAYO TO MONTGOMERY

The local form of boycott arrived in the United States in 1882, when Irish workers—recent immigrants aware of the Land League's success—shunned several of their fellows who returned to work during a strike.[4] Their union president threatened to publish the strikebreakers' names in New York and Ireland, and encouraged their friends and neighbors to avoid all contacts with them. Labor unions quickly applied the strategy to hundreds of manufacturers thought to be unfair to their workforce. The American Federation of Labor kept a list of unfair employers, many of whom were singled out for boycotting. Boycotts avoided the devastating costs of strikes, although they were also used in many cases to reinforce strikes. They were especially effective in cities, such as New York, with a high degree of working-class consciousness and cohesion, and against those companies which marketed goods—from cigars to starch to beer—to the working class in limited, local markets. Active working-class culture, comprising both politics and consumption patterns, made boycotts a popular strategy. In the rough labor relations of the time, violence and intimidation reinforced the boycotts. Because unions had no legal rights and faced considerable violent repression, they needed this weapon of the weak.[5]

America's most famous boycotts, though, were those against racially segregated transportation systems in the South. These have a long history. During Reconstruction there were protests against newly segregated horsecars, and at least one boycott, in Savannah. Later, between 1891 and 1906, African-Americans boycotted segregated streetcars in virtually every southern state. The sense of threat and moral shock motivating the protests arose from the wave of Jim Crow segregation laws attacking the rights and dignity of southern blacks. One newspaper wrote of the "mingled disgust and bewilderment" felt by southern blacks accustomed to unrestricted travel since Reconstruction.[6] Streetcar companies were themselves usually opposed to the new restrictions, seeing them as expensive. As often happens in rising protest movements, the earliest boycotts—in the 1890s—were more successful than those after 1901, as segregationist forces redoubled their ultimately successful efforts.

When the civil rights movement arose in the 1950s—partly in reaction to a wave of racist violence and the frequent outlawing of the National Association for the Advancement of Colored People—segregated buses were one of its first targets. In Baton Rouge, civil rights groups moving beyond the legal tactics of the NAACP organized a bus boycott in 1953 when white drivers refused to honor a new city code abolishing whites-only seats in favor of a system—hardly very progressive—in which blacks filled the bus from the back and whites from the front. The boycott lasted several weeks and crippled the bus line, costing it $1,600 a day. A compromise was reached in which only the first two side seats were reserved for whites and the rear bench for blacks. It was not integration, but civil rights activists could claim a victory. Black leaders throughout the South noticed.[7]

The most famous civil rights bus boycott was launched in Montgomery, Alabama in 1955. The city had been the site of battles over segregation at the turn of the century, and several incidents—when blacks refused to sit in the backs of buses—had occurred in the years before 1955. On 1 December of that year, seventy-five years to the day after Charles Boycott had left Ireland, seamstress and NAACP secretary Rosa Parks was arrested when she refused to yield her seat to a white man after the white section had filled up (she was in a section reserved exclusively for neither race). Events unfolded quickly that night.[8]

E. D. Nixon, an official with the Brotherhood of Sleeping Car Porters, and Clifford Durr, a patrician white lawyer, after posting bond for Parks, conferred at her family home. They decided that this was the case they had been waiting for: Parks was soft-spoken, well-mannered, and dignified enough, they felt, to impress white juries; yet she was tough. During that night, a Thursday, Jo Ann Robinson, an English teacher at Alabama State and member of the Women's Political Council in Montgomery, recruited several friends to mimeograph 35,000 announcements urging blacks to stay off the buses the following Monday as a gesture of solidarity with Parks. Nixon phoned Montgomery's black political leaders, fifty of whom attended a meeting the following day to discuss tactics. They too agreed on a Monday boycott, and scheduled a public meeting for Monday night at a large Baptist church. On Sunday, the city's black preachers—and one white one—urged their congregations to honor the boycott. Blacks did, almost without exception. The city's size of 120,000 people (45,000 of them black) made coordination challenging, but not impossible.

The boycott was accompanied and supported by other forms of protest, which I call "companion tactics." Protestors usually employ a variety of tactics; what is unusual is that campaigns are usually called boycotts even when boycotting is only one tactic among many. When Parks was convicted and fined $14 dollars on Monday morning, a supportive crowd of five hundred rallied, with no prodding from leaflets or leaders, at the courthouse. That evening ten thousand appeared at the church for the seven o'clock meeting, filling not only the church but several acres of streets and lots nearby, where they listened to loudspeakers. Chosen that day to head the new Montgomery Improvement Association (MIA), and stirred by the excitement of the events, Martin Luther King Jr. soared to oratorical heights he had not previously reached in his young career (he was only twenty-six).

The boycott extended past Monday, and past that week, and into 1956, and the nightly meetings also continued, with extensive songs and sermons and testimony from participants. Individuals were praised for their special efforts, including an ancient woman known as Mother Pollard, who insisted on honoring the boycott despite her age and pain. Some evenings saw a sequence of meetings at different churches. As Aldon Morris has shown, the extensive array of religious images and activities—emotional prayers and songs, Bible stories, lessons, and analogies—were crucial to the emergence of the civil rights movement.[9] As rich companion tactics, they created virtually unanimous black support for bus boycotts.

As all effective moral protest does, the boycott elicited a response from the other side, in this case from Montgomery's white establishment; the city council and the MIA traded tactical innovations and responses for the twelve months of the boycott.[10] When the police commissioner threatened to arrest black taxi drivers who were charging less than the minimum legal fare, the MIA started an extensive carpool system and even (when its cause became national news and contributions flowed in) purchased several new cars. Then a story was planted in the newspapers that the boycott had ended through negotiations, but this ploy was discovered a day early and defused through Sunday sermons and extensive legwork. In January, traffic tickets for false charges were issued against carpool drivers. On 26 January, King's arrest for allegedly driving 30 mph in a 25-mph zone drew a large crowd to the jail and renewed attendance at a series of seven successive mass meetings that night. Later, a grand jury issued indictments against boycott leaders, who then turned the event into a triumph by arriving at the courthouse at the head of large crowds, helping to ease the stigma and fear of jail. These arrests brought no fewer than thirty-five reporters from around the country to Montgomery, stoking the excitement of the mass meetings with their cameras; the number grew to one hundred for King's trial, which was conducted alone as a test case (he lost and was fined $500).

The city, in negotiations with the MIA, became less and less flexible, refusing to budge even though the bus company was going broke. The parent company in Chicago claimed that the boycott was 99 percent effective among black riders, and it imposed an emergency fare hike on the remaining white riders. A separate lawsuit had been filed challenging Montgomery's segregated bus systems, and on 4 June 1956, three federal judges ruled that the city's bus segregation was unconstitutional, boosting the morale of the boycotters as well as eliciting donations from around the country (amounting to well over $100,000). Montgomery city officials responded by requesting a state injunction banning the MIA carpool as an unlicensed municipal transportation system. On 13 November, the day the injunction was granted, the U.S. Supreme Court declared bus segregation unconstitutional. During the five weeks before the decision could be implemented, but with the injunction against them still in effect, Montgomery's African-Americans gave a final tiring but triumphant performance: they walked to work each day. Here was one more virtuosic moral act.

In addition to official repression, a wave of violence against the boycotters terrified them but strengthened their sense of themselves as a moral community under threat. In addition to shots fired into homes from passing cars, bombs went off in four black Baptist churches and the homes of three boycott leaders. Two KKK members were tried but not convicted. When the boycott got under way, membership in the Alabama White Citizens' Council skyrocketed; even Montgomery's three city commissioners joined. The vicious response by whites only raised the stakes of the boycott. The protestors and their opponents were watched closely, so that all their actions had power far beyond their own pains and pleasures. Their victory would be a victory for people they didn't even know in places they hadn't heard of. The "benefits" of a victory, they knew, were literally incalculable.

This repression shows that in Montgomery, the boycott was still a weapon of the weak, chosen by those under considerable pressure and surveillance. Their main strength was in their moral community, which relied on considerable consensus about injustice and the need for action, and striking emotional solidarity. The threat and reality of repression was an assault, not just on prominent activists, but on that whole community. And, as we have seen, threat can be a powerful motivation. That black people were being punished for activism in the name of the whole community further fused collective and movement identities. The vicious white repression of black protest, revitalized after 1954, casts some doubt on process models that would emphasize lessening of state repression as the key to movement emergence. The *Brown* decision of 1954 was an inspirational symbolic message to African-Americans, not an indicator of less actual repression. Lynchings may have subsided since the 1920s, but civil rights activism was still a dangerous, frequently fatal, business. Like the benefits, the potential costs were beyond measure.

Civil rights boycotts occurred at a crucial time in the evolution of moral protest in the United States. They were a forceful and direct tactic in comparison to the NAACP's court challenges, which were conducted by lawyers and provided little opportunity for other blacks to express their solidarity and outrage. Within a few years boycotts were themselves eclipsed by more radical tactics, as new, younger cohorts joined the civil rights movement and invented other forms of moral protest. Other protest movements, inspired by civil rights, went through a similar evolution in tactics. But in the mid-1950s, consumer boycotts were a satisfying way to express moral outrage, at least when accompanied by marches, songs, and mass meetings. These companion tactics were crucial in crystallizing solidarity in the African-American community, creating confident and experienced political leaders, and drawing national attention to the southern civil rights movement. Boycotts were a refusal, a silence; they needed to be accompanied by tactics that permitted the loud expression of outrage and moral vision. In tight communities like that of Montgomery's blacks, New York's working class, or Mayo's peasants, this articulation was easy, and compliance with the boycott was nearly complete as a result. For these citizenship movements, boycotts were a powerful opportunity for collective voice. Neither the voice, the solidarity, nor the compliance would be so strong in the national boycotts about to appear.

GRAPES AND FARMWORKERS

Boycotts were soon deployed on very different terrain, partly as a result of the consumer protection movement of the 1960s. Over the past thirty years, hundreds of boycotts have been launched against manufacturers in the United States, involving thousands of common consumer goods. Any number of causes have been pursued this way, ranging from post-industrial issues having to do with environmental degradation, the treatment of animals, and cultural images of women to moral panics over television violence. As national, if not international, campaigns, they operated differently from local boycotts such as Montgomery's, posing greater difficulties for organizing the companion tactics needed to maintain and express moral outrage. These were no longer exclusively weapons of the weak deployed in local settings by those with limited political options in pursuit of political inclusion. One of the earliest and most prominent of these new national boycotts was against grapes; it began as a local effort by a weak, solidaristic community but was soon forced to expand, pioneering the new kind of boycott.

The United Farm Workers of California (UFWOC) actually organized two sets of grape boycotts—one against wine grapes, the other against table grapes—as a means to pressure California farmers into recognizing and negotiating with the union. Founded as the National Farm Workers Association by César Chávez in 1962, the UFWOC used a combination of strikes and boycotts to win wide recognition first in the wine-grape industry. The key was three successful boycotts in 1965 and 1966 aimed at specific companies with nationally known brand names. The first was against Schenley, producer of Cutty Sark, Ancient Age, Cresta Blanca, and other wines and liquors; the second targeted DiGiorgio, whose main product was actually Treesweet orange juice; the third went after Perelli-Minetti, the maker of Tribuno Vermouth. In each case the union concentrated on the Los Angeles market, and each time the manufacturer gave in quickly, before the boycott had a chance to cut into consumer demand. Making products that were indistinguishable from those of competitors except in their carefully cultivated public image, these companies could not risk damage to their reputations. By 1967 the union had signed contracts with nine of the largest wine-grape growers, covering five thousand workers. It then turned its attention to table-grape growers.[11]

In contrast to brand-name liquors, table grapes are sold without identifying labels, making it difficult to boycott a particular grower. So when the UFWOC launched a strike and boycott against the Giumarra Vineyards Corporation (the country's largest table-grape grower) in late 1967, the company began shipping grapes under one hundred different labels. At the beginning of 1968 the union decided to boycott the entire California table-grape industry, a new and unusual boycott strategy. In May 1969 it extended this boycott to Arizona growers, who were also refusing to negotiate with the union. These two states accounted for virtually all domestic table-grape production.

Because the workers were on strike, they were available in large numbers to travel across the country to organize the new boycott efforts. By 1970 they were at work in thirty-one major cities in the United States and Canada, and had volunteer committees in more than two hundred other cities. Boycott organizers, sent to a city with little money, had to raise funds, recruit volunteer help, form a support coalition of prominent citizens, publicly represent the UFWOC, deal with local union and church officials, plan and execute a boycott, publicize it, and negotiate with chain stores. Accustomed to harvesting fruits and vegetables, these farmworkers had to develop many new skills quickly. In each city two or three of them had to create protest movements from scratch. They had artfulness forced on them.

Despite all odds, the farmworkers managed to make grapes into a potent cultural symbol. The boycott became a prominent media issue primarily because it came to represent important cleavages in national politics, pitting Richard Nixon and the military and corporate worlds against labor, the anti-war movement, liberals, and the Left. The symbolic associations appeared during the 1968 presidential campaign, when Ronald Reagan and Richard Nixon opened a Republican party rally in Fresno by eating grapes. Hubert Humphrey and Eugene McCarthy both endorsed the boycott and referred to it in their campaign speeches. The Defense Department purchased almost ten million pounds of grapes in 1969, 40 percent more than the year before—despite a decrease in military personnel in Viet Nam.[12] When the UFWOC claimed that Nixon and the Pentagon were intentionally helping grape growers, the "grapes of war" issue brought new support from anti-war groups.

As a result of these rich connotations, the farmworkers were able to establish a broad coalition of supporters, including not just the major trade unions, but church, civic, student, environmental, anti-war, and consumer groups. Civil rights and consumer groups endorsing the boycott included the Urban League, the NAACP, the Southern Christian Leadership Conference, the Mexican-American G. I. Forum, the Consumer Federation of America, and the National Consumers League. Dozens of mayors, senators, and congressional representatives announced their support. The farmworkers and their grapes were an effective multivocal condensing symbol, with organizations supporting the boycott for a variety of reasons. Unions saw it as a labor dispute, focusing on the right to organize. Clergy were attracted by the emphasis on nonviolence and social justice. Civil rights activists were concerned with the struggle of Chicano and Filipino workers for economic equality. Consumer and environmental groups were alarmed about pesticides. Others saw the boycott as a way to fight worker poverty. The National Farmers Organization and the National Farmers' Union, representing small farmers, endorsed the boycott as a crusade against agribusiness.

The boycott succeeded in cutting consumer demand for grapes. By the end of the 1969 growing season, grape shipments to major urban markets were down as much as 40 percent, and wholesale prices for Thompson seedless grapes were down as much as 30 percent. Media attention was important, as grape sales declined even in cities without a formal boycott organization: from 1966 to 1968, for example, grape shipments to San Antonio and Salt Lake City fell by 19 percent and 21 percent respectively. Yet sales went up in some cities, especially in the South. The biggest drops in sales were in heavily unionized cities such as New York (with sales down 28 percent from 1966 to 1969), Detroit (down 30 percent), Boston (41 percent), and Chicago (43 percent). Because judges quickly ended the unions' (highly effective) secondary boycotts, unions were important primarily in providing space, publicity, picketers, and morale.[13]

In the spring of 1970, facilitated by a committee of the National Conference of Catholic Bishops, three large growers signed contracts recognizing the union, granting a wage increase, eliminating the use of certain pesticides, and introducing grievance procedures. Another provision called for union-picked grape boxes to be stamped with the UFWOC label, not visible to consumers but allowing handlers and truckers to know the grapes' origins. Soon 85 percent of the industry had recognized the union. The five-year strike and two-and-one-half year boycott ended.

The grape boycott seems unique among national consumer boycotts in having a demonstrable and acknowledged—by both sides—effect on consumer demand. In no other national boycott have I been able to find such clear evidence of a similar impact. How did the farmworkers do it? How did they persuade so many people to change their buying habits?

It took considerable work at cultural framing to make grapes relevant to so many existing organizations, but once this happened there were resources and personal networks there to aid the farmworkers. On top of this, the farmworkers and their supporters artfully constructed a range of new tactics, applying the general concept of a boycott in new ways. They conducted what amounted to a series of local boycotts, concentrating on particular cities, on particular chains in them, and on particular stores belonging to those chains. In that way, organizers did not need to rely merely on the goodwill of individual shoppers, but could use the personal and more intensive tactics normally available only to truly local boycotts in sympathetic and tightly knit communities. A variety of companion tactics contributed to this sense of local movement identity.

Boycotters picketed individual stores. Turning away a small fraction of shoppers at a store was sufficient to worry managers, because this small percentage cut into the slim profit margin on which chains operate. Many who were not supporters of the boycott would not shop at a picketed establishment because of the (real or imagined) hassle, intimidation, or potential for danger. Once one store stopped selling grapes, the picket would continue until all stores in the chain stopped selling grapes. Because chains would often return grapes to the shelves a few days after responding to the picket, supporters were assigned to check stores regularly.

Another companion tactic was to encourage boycott supporters to mail postcards to stores saying they would not shop there until they stopped handling grapes. Rather than a private, personal refusal of a purchase, the postcards allowed an explicit, sometimes angry, denunciation. They allowed sympathizers to articulate their moral outrage.

Boycott organizations also sponsored special collective events. For example, the UFWOC called an International Boycott Day, for which each boycott committee was asked to plan a special activity, such as a demonstration. Other creative activities used to break the tedium of picket lines included a tour of migrant labor camps in Maryland for the press, politicians, and unionists. The Boston boycott committee had a "Boston Grape Party." In Toronto, boycotters entered several stores with "Don't Eat Grapes" balloons, many of which were given to children and some of which floated up to the high ceilings. The balloons also contained brightly colored confetti, creating a mess for those store officials who angrily popped them.[14]

Like other national and international boycotts, however, the main companion tactic was to gain media coverage. In February 1968, early in the boycott, César Chávez went on a twenty-five-day hunger strike, calling it penance for the dissension and talk of violence within the union. His fast increased morale by creating an image of a "saintly martyr" sacrificing for the workers. Priests organized nightly masses around the fast, using it as a way to rebuild morale and strengthen movement identity for local workers. Many workers and their families who were practicing Catholics responded with strong religious emo-

tions. A large cross was erected, to which believers attached holy images and pictures; many came to the nightly masses on their knees.
Eventually the fast even won over unionists who had initially been
offended by the religious imagery. The fast also brought extensive media attention to the strike and boycott. When grape growers from Giumarra asked a local judge to bring Chávez into court for defying an
injunction on picketing the previous fall, the courthouse walkway was
lined for his arrival with rows of silently kneeling farmworkers. Surprised by the media attention, the growers asked the judge to dismiss
the charges. Presidential candidate Robert Kennedy attended the mass
at which Chávez ended his fast.

Despite the success of the boycott in cutting consumer demand for
table grapes, the effort nonetheless reveals the peculiar impotence of
national boycotts. Union recognition was followed by years of bitter,
unyielding negotiations, and a continuing series of other boycotts of
grapes and lettuce. Labor struggles never cease, whereas a boycott
must achieve a single, binding decision (such as the banning of a particular product or a new law) in order to succeed. Despite its ability to
cut consumer demand temporarily, the table-grape boycott had little
long-run effect. Even today, the UFW is sponsoring another grape boycott on the same issues.

NATIONAL BOYCOTTS AND MORAL OUTRAGE

Now that national boycotts are common, we have all been urged to
boycott one consumer product or another. There have been consumer
boycotts against Beefaroni, Dinty Moore stew, Sani-Flush, Minute
Maid orange juice, Right Guard deodorant, Jiffy Pop popcorn, and
Preparation H, to protest the activities of their parent companies (Nes-
tlé, American Home Products, Coca-Cola, Gillette, and Hormel). Buying one brand of deodorant rather than another is an easy way to reg-
ister moral protest. But do national boycotts like these work? Is
switching brands a satisfying way to express moral outrage? Who can
even remember what company produces Sani-Flush?

Potentially, we do many things when we buy a product. A purchase
can have many dimensions, including a statement about what kind of
person you are, an expression of solidarity with the producers (say, of
Nicaraguan coffee), or loyalty to a company ("I never drive anything
but Fords"). It is this kind of satisfaction that boycott activists offer:
purchasers can feel they are making a political statement in buying
one hot dog rather than another, or scouring their toilets with baking
soda rather than a specialized commercial product. Protest organiza-

tions call upon consumers to insert a political or moral element into their purchasing decisions, rather than being driven by purely utilitarian concerns such as price and quality. In a way, protestors want us to be better-informed consumers, and they pay the cost of gathering information, a cost that would be enormous for individuals who had to do it independently. Consumers are asked to consider the "externalities"—such as pollution, sexism, poor labor policies, the deaths of infants in the Third World—that do not appear in product prices because manufactures have pushed them off onto other members of society. This awareness is especially appealing to those with postindustrial sentiments, including a concern with a moral lifestyle and a critique of blind consumerism. The creativity of boycott organizers is to offer a new forum for expressing dissent, a new—and relatively easy—opportunity to make a moral statement. Here are plentiful opportunities for individual acts of protest. Consumer decisions can express a moral stance.

But they never do so very articulately or forcefully. *A silent choice, made alone, in the aisle of a crowded supermarket, is a poor way to sustain a sense of injustice and indignation.* To the extent that it becomes habitual to buy one brand of coffee rather than another, this form of political protest becomes a relatively thoughtless routine. And to the same extent, it no longer provides much conscious moral satisfaction. Expressions of moral outrage are most satisfying when they are done with others, when they explicitly describe the reasons for action, and when they name the villains. Probably the mildest strategy for moral protest, consumer boycotts by themselves seem too mild, an inappropriate way to express moral positions. As such, though, they might be a conduit for individual acts of protest to feed into collective participation.

Consumer boycotts, of which there are more than two hundred currently active in the United States, engage large numbers of people only when they are combined with other tactics that are more emotionally expressive. Tamara Dumanovsky, Bettina Edelstein, and I gathered data on fifty-five boycotts started in the early 1980s.[15] We found that fifty-two of them used companion tactics, the most popular being rallies (or marches) and picket lines. Most combined rallies, picket lines, and letter-writing, with some adding civil disobedience and advertisements. Even today's national consumer boycotts are typically part of a broader protest movement with a range of tactics; boycotts are almost never the only prong of a strategic campaign.

Because of their companion tactics, boycotts can attain their goals even without reducing consumer demand for the targeted product. They work when corporate decision makers are embarrassed, when they *expect* (rightly or wrongly) an economic impact, or when they fear even more restrictive government regulations. The long-running tuna boycott, for example, persuaded Star-Kist and other companies to buy tuna caught with dolphin-safe methods only when Congress began debating a law requiring can labels to say that the existing processes killed dolphins. Cosmetics companies abandoned live animal testing because they feared a loss of consumers, not because they had any evidence of it. The companion tactics generate bad publicity, not economic loss. The mere announcement of a boycott has more effect than the boycott itself.[16] Most effective is a series of press conferences by disparate groups, each in turn announcing its support for the boycott. When they succeed, national boycotts usually work through political voice, not consumer exit. In today's world, the news media are a vital conduit for political messages.

Companion tactics have two functions: to maintain moral outrage and give it a voice, and to bring media attention and bad publicity to the targets. The former is crucial to moral protest movements; the latter is sufficient for bureaucratic interest groups without memberships. There are different audiences for the two kinds of actions. One or the other, if not both, are necessary for boycotts to succeed. It is the companion tactics that give protestors something positive to do, in addition to the negative refusal of a purchase; participants can articulate and express their moral visions. In liberal democracies, most protest movements need not rely on weapons of the weak, and normally favor stronger stuff: marches and site occupations, civil disobedience and sabotage. They thrive by telling their stories, shouting and singing out, even acting out their anger—the things we saw with the Abalone Alliance.

Boycotts work better when they give people an opportunity to do things together than when they ask individual consumers to make private decisions. These indirect actions are apparently not satisfying enough. Relying either on local communities and activities or on companion tactics, boycotts need to provide mechanisms for collective moral voice. The shared understandings and emotions of movement culture are crucial for sustaining protest. Individual feelings and views may help make someone susceptible to recruitment, and capable of some individual protest, but few continue without the many pleasures found in protest itself. With this contrast between two types of boycott, we end our discussion of the culture within protest movements. It is time to look at protest in its broader cultural context.

Positive collective emotions and tactical pleasures can sustain protest, just as negative emotions and pains can hurt it, but social movements do not exist in political or cultural vacuums. There are many audiences for protestors' actions and statements. There are cultural institutions and moral gatekeepers, notably the media, who shape the popular understandings that protestors must build on and appeal to. Then there is a range of potential sympathizers and supporters who might be persuaded to join or send money to protest groups. Finally, other organizations and individuals respond to the protest, shaping the political context in which protestors operate. In the case of state repression of movements, this "context" can quickly snuff out a movement. If movements have important internal dynamics, they are also strategic actors, playing a complex, often dangerous, set of games with other actors around them. Resources and strategies are crucial dimensions of protest movements, already well studied by many scholars. What remains is to show how culturally and biographically embedded they are, as well as how all these dimensions interact. In the next chapter, we'll see that the mobilization of resources depends greatly on cultural processes, especially the rhetorical persuasion of others and images in the news media. The chapter after that will show that strategies too—and hence success and failure—are also partly influenced by culture. Chapter 14 will then try to bring the dimensions together.

- Boycotts began as weapons of the weak for highly oppressed, tight moral communities of the kind that usually animate citizenship movements.
- When they became national, they lost the moral consensus, community compliance mechanisms, and some of the companion tactics that had helped local boycotts.
- Boycotts are nonetheless a way of encouraging individual protest, which may eventually feed into more collective protest.
- Consumer boycotts attract more participants when they provide outlets for articulating moral visions than when they simply ask for changes in purchases.
- Local boycotts and the companion tactics of national ones provide the collective-voice mechanisms that seem especially satisfying to participants.

PART FOUR

Protest and the Broader Culture

Protest movements do not arise or operate in a vacuum. If individuals were our main unit of analysis in part 2 and movements in part 3, it is time now to look at protestors' relationship to the rest of their society. The broader environment includes many actors, including states, opponents, allies, the news media, and the public. The two most prominent interactions that protest groups have with their environment are the mobilization of resources from it and their efforts to attain their goals. Both entail considerable cultural persuasion of diverse, often contrasting, audiences. Strategic efforts, in addition, depend greatly on biographical and psychological variations among key individuals on every side of the battle.

TWELVE

Culture and Resources:
The Arts of Persuasion

Nos numerus sumus et fruges consumere nati.
— Horace, *Epistles*

For rhetoric he could not ope
His mouth, but out there flew a trope . . .
For all a rhetorician's rules
Teach nothing but to name his tools.
— Samuel Butler

The Montgomery bus boycott of 1955–56 lasted twelve hard months. In addition to maintaining morale for that period through its many companion tactics, the Montgomery Improvement Association (MIA) had to find the resources to get supporters to work during the boycott. It first relied on black taxi drivers, who drove at heavily discounted fares. When the police commissioner threatened to arrest drivers for charging less than the minimum legal fare, the MIA started an extensive carpool system. The city responded with false charges against boycott leaders, who turned this setback into a triumph by drawing one hundred reporters from around the country to Montgomery, gaining invaluable publicity. After this, as its cause became national news and contributions flowed in, the MIA purchased several cars of its own. When city officials gained a state injunction banning the carpool as an unlicensed municipal transportation system, Montgomery's blacks used their feet as their last resource, walking to work during the final five weeks of the boycott.

The boycotters mobilized new resources, new alternatives to public buses, in response to each move by the city: the taxi network, then the carpools (first supporters' cars, then ones the MIA purchased), and finally walking. They had little money to start with, but were able to overcome this weakness through fund-raising and using inexpensive transportation. They invented alternatives. In part they mobilized outside financial support, in part they relied on their own fortitude and resourcefulness. Walking was an option available from the start, but the MIA could use it only because of the exuberance, optimism, and

desperation generated by months of protest. To mobilize new resources, it persuaded both members and outsiders of the justice of the
cause and the potential efficacy of the boycott.

As this case shows, protestors interact with a variety of groups and
individuals in the society around them. Process theorists are right to
point to the environment as a key influence on social movements, although, ironically, by labeling courts, politicians, allies, supporters, the
police, and so many other actors as the "environment," those same
theorists run the risk of reducing them to fixed structures rather than
conscious actors making choices, responding to protestors. These other
players have their own resources, strategies, culture, and biographies,
that make them parallel in many ways to protestors. In this part of the
book, I place protest movements in this broader context. In particular,
it is easy to analyze resources and strategies as defined by the interaction between a movement and the rest of society.

WHERE RESOURCES COME FROM

I argued earlier that physical resources and cultural meanings are analytically distinct, operating with different logics. Now I hope to show
that these two entities, while mutually irreducible, heavily affect each
other. (In the next chapter I'll attempt the same for culture and strategic
action.) Not only do resources depend on cultural interpretations for
their force, but the strategic mobilization of new resources is primarily
a function of cultural persuasion. Pre-existing resources usually matter
less than those aggregated during a protest, a process heavily dependent on cognitive, emotional, and strategic dynamics.

As twenty-five years of research have shown, resources are crucial
in explaining protest activities and outcomes. How much money a
group can deploy limits what tactics it chooses and how well it per-
forms them, including its ability to broadcast its message to new audiences. Most protest groups, for example, cannot afford to place full-
page ads in the *New York Times* or even local newspapers. Access to a
mimeograph or photocopy machine may be necessary for publicizing
certain events. When limited to money and what it can buy, the concept
of resources has a nice rigor and measurability. We saw that problems
arise when the concept is expanded to cover other facets of political
or social life. Such disparate entities as laws, public attitudes, social
networks, group identities, and daily routines all get lumped together
as though they had similar dynamics and effects. To revive the power
of the concept, we need to restrict its use, not confound it with strategies or cultural meanings.

Other problems arise when resource distributions are viewed as largely predetermined or fixed, rather than as something to be mobilized and transformed. Initial distributions, especially if we narrow resources to money and what it buys, are important but never final. The point of many protest tactics is to gather new resources, as the Montgomery boycotters did. Much of what is explained by resources might be better explained through the lens of strategic decisions: how to raise funds, what alliances to make, how to attract favorable media attention, how to demonstrate the urgency of the issue. The resources a protest group controls primarily depend on its strategies, on the "mobilization" in resource mobilization. The best resource-mobilization research has always focused on strategic action, but the assumption, drawn from citizenship movements, that protest organizations have "natural" constituencies whose interests they pursue leads to the expectation that the wealth of its constituency determines the resources a group can mobilize. Every protest group knows that rich people have more money, and it targets them as benefactors when possible. Fund-raising, though, is a cultural process of trying to create interest, sympathy, and support among people who can contribute. Financial backing is never automatic, even for those movements that do speak in the name of a clear collective identity.

With the Diablo protesters in chapter 8, we saw how the reciprocal emotions built over several years operated as a kind of functional substitute for financial resources in motivating participation. To label these as resources, I think, misleadingly reduces much of the interpersonal relations involved to a kind of investment by movement leaders. All participants embraced and nourished collective emotions, as much for the direct enjoyment as for some subsequent payoff.

A final confusion concerns the causal mechanisms by which resources affect outcomes. Many resources are lumpy, so that they are superfluous past a minimal level. In calling this the "threshold hypothesis," Gamson, Fireman, and Rytina point out, "If one has a good megaphone to address a crowd with, what good are 20 more?"[1] *The effects of resources lie in their use,* and the contribution from a second megaphone is limited. In addition, resources sometimes interfere with effective action, as with a trade union that discourages disruptive wild-cat strikes out of concern for its own organizational maintenance.[2] In this case, the logic of resource accumulation and protection may contradict the logic of emotional and moral outrage—and perhaps that of effective strategic action. An organization's credibility and public sympathy are undermined by accusations of being rich, big, and powerful. More is not always better. Whether or not it is depends on how protestors view, feel about, and deploy their resources.

Because resources are a form of property, there is a vast web of laws and customs governing their ownership and use. Land, most obviously, has been hemmed in by a variety of restrictions—which the land-use battles of today's NIMBYs are trying to expand. Money, too, although seemingly neutral, is surrounded by rules of possession and use, including rules of trusteeships, nonprofit organizations, and political contributions. Even physical objects such as telephones are regulated. The considerable resources of the state, such as surveillance or eavesdropping mechanisms, are supposedly covered by rules of law. So even physical objects are culturally shaped, not only through knowledge about how to use them but also rules for that use.

We can make parallel arguments about political structures, for those who would treat them as an independent dimension. Political systems are made up of laws and other rules: about institutional procedures and boundaries, about taxing and spending, about voting procedures, about legal and illegal forms of dissent. Most rules and laws are like traditions, depending heavily on how they are interpreted. Laws, even the U.S. Constitution, appear at first to be permanent and fixed, but on closer examination we see that they shift subtly over time under the impact of changing public perceptions, judicial reinterpretations, and political action. Even the more fixed rules—electoral systems, constitutions—are a combination of physical resources and schemas for their use. Administrative structures are also *relatively* fixed, in that they are harder to change than many other aspects of the situation, and thus they change less frequently. But they do change, and protest strategies are often aimed precisely at changing them. The constraining power of these rules is easily exaggerated, leaving us with an image of protest groups facing the state and its rules, with few other players in between or around them. Likewise the rules can be seen as overly fixed rather than open to interpretation and change. Some political process models make both errors. The rules of the game are precisely what many protesters are trying to change, especially those who seek participation in a political system. In other examples, too, protestors challenge laws and administrative rules in courts, pursue other legislative changes, and constantly promote reinterpretations of existing rules and laws. Strategies and culture are as important to this process as resources.

We see some reification of resources in debates over the extent to which resources and organization must exist within a protesting population versus the extent to which this group must attract resources from outside itself—an especially important question for the local protest groups we saw in chapter 5. Mobilization theorists have argued that outsiders, especially elites, provide important, perhaps essential, services and resources to protestors.[3] In his study of the southern civil rights movement, Aldon Morris criticized these theorists for their emphasis on the public attention and financial resources provided by northern whites, the news media, and the federal government.[4] Morris alternatively detailed the importance of indigenous cultural resources, leadership, and even financial support from within the black community. Yet he detailed the financial support coming from northern blacks and urban blacks, not the poor, rural, southern blacks most helped by the civil rights movement. Morris emphasized the contributions of some outsiders rather than others, in the process showing that the boundary between insider and outsider was itself unclear, shifting, and actively constructed.

The debate over outside resources is misleading in that it normally assumes a clear, fixed boundary between the (affected, potentially active) beneficiary group and those outside it, whereas activists constantly strive to expand the number of people who feel affected by the grievances being addressed. This is true even for citizenship movements. Southern blacks in the 1950s did not simply appeal for charity; they persuaded northern blacks, and many white Americans, that the issue of civil rights was important to them too. They spread a sense of outrage and anger, increasing levels of discontent and thus the resources available for civil rights work. This *grievance extension* is especially important, if difficult, for local protestors opposed to a single facility such as a nuclear reactor, yet almost all protest groups must do it. It is a form of persuasion and framing. The extreme case may be the animal rights movement, in which grievances are promoted among those who don't even belong to the same species as the beneficiaries, but other charitable movements also appeal to those without direct personal interests at stake.

Rhetoric—which as a discipline traditionally dealt with the relationship between speaker and audience—is the main tool with which activists "create" or collect new grievances, resources, and constituents in this way. They must persuade expanding circles of people that they too are affected by some condition—at least in their ideal interests if not in their material ones. Organizers can then draw on additional resources and pre-existing organizations. I have argued elsewhere that most participants in public debates search for irrefutable bedrock principles and images—what Kenneth Burke called "god terms"—to clinch their arguments, relying on religion and science as two prominent sources.[5] Even small and apparently local groups regularly attempt to broaden their appeal in this way. Whether or not they successfully mobilize resources and people depends in part on their rhetoric: how persuasive it is, how broad an impact it claims for the problem it

Table 12.1   Audiences and Corresponding Goals of Protest

Audience	Desired Outcome
Opponents	Directly change behavior, through persuasion or intimidation; barring that, goad into blunders, undermine credibility for sake of other audiences.
State agencies	Change laws, policies, regulatory practices, administrative rules. (Different parts of the state represent many different audiences.)
Courts	Have adverse laws and rules declared illegal.
News media	Gain public discussion, awareness of issue; reshape common sense; gain access to bystander public.
Professional groups	Change norms, standards; attract supportive statements.
Bystander public	Attain awareness, change sensibilities, attract sympathy, support, and financial contributions.
Other protest groups	Attract potential allies, resources, strategic support.
Movement itself	Personal transformation, especially in consciousness; reinforce fervor for continued activism.

addresses, how it fits with the audience's existing beliefs. Can it find a god term or other theme that is widely honored?

Because protestors appeal to many different audiences, it is difficult to generalize about effective rhetorics. Table 12.1 lists some key audiences and what protest groups might like to get from them. It is easy to see that appeals fine-tuned for one group may backfire with another—a frequent problem since audiences are not easily segregated. Different constructions of threat, blame, and injustice may be required for different audiences. "Rhetoric" has been a popular way for students of protest to examine cultural meanings, placing them in the context of strategic interactions between the senders of messages and their audiences.

Audiences differ even within each of these categories. Movement participants, for instance, have a variety of goals, allegiances, solidarities, and tastes in tactics. A common difference pits radicals against moderates. Herbert Haines has studied the effects, sometimes positive and sometimes negative, of radical flanks on movement success. Because of the variety of audiences out there for protest, these effects can be positive and negative at the same time: "Each audience and target group has its own interests, its own range of ideologies, and its own set of constraints within which it must operate. It is quite possible, even probable, that simultaneous opposing radical flank effects may occur."[6] Many such complicated effects are due to differences among the audiences for protest.

The interactions between resources and culture are several. The use of resources requires cultural know-how, and attracting new resources depends heavily on moral, emotional, and cognitive persuasion. The broader cultural context is also important for the use and mobilization of resources. Their use depends on the laws and traditions of a society, and on previous strategic battles over these. And the cultural persuasion involved in mobilization operates partly through the filter of the mass media. Resources, in turn, affect culture in familiar ways: wealth offers the ability to use direct mail rather than depending on news coverage to spread the message; it allows the hiring of clever marketing experts; and it provides support for intellectuals who can develop new images, arguments, and scientific evidence. There is constant interplay between cultural messages and physical media.

GLOBALIZING RHETORIC

We can examine processes of persuasion by returning to the kinds of local groups explored earlier. Rhetorical extension is a considerable challenge for local groups fighting a facility or plan, since the solidaristic rhetoric that attracts fellow locals may have little appeal to audiences outside the community. It is more difficult to persuade nonlocals that they too should feel affected in some way. Nor is globalization an unmixed blessing. Locals need allies, and are tempted to craft their goals and tactics to appeal to nonlocals, but they do not want their own concerns to be diluted or submerged by the goals and tactical tastes of outsiders. Different frames may appeal to locals and nonlocals. Building a movement (among locals) and achieving its goals (with nonlocals) often conflict because of this difference in audiences. Selecting strategies to send the right cultural messages to each audience can be very complex.

The rhetorics available to NIMBYs differ considerably in how broadly they might appeal to outsiders. *Particularistic rhetoric* opposes the facility, plan, or proposal at this one site, but nowhere else. In many cases this is the only rhetoric available. An example might include opposition to an airport: the protestors don't oppose airports in general, but merely don't want one near them; this single airport proposal is what mobilized them, and they have no broader strategy to oppose others. *Universalistic rhetoric*, at the opposite extreme, would oppose any instance of the proposed thing, no matter where it was. Most antinuclear arguments, even those made by local groups, take this form, since there is so much persuasive ammunition available. In between is a *semi-universalistic rhetoric* that opposes siting the thing in certain kinds of places, including the one currently being proposed. For example, some might oppose having hazardous waste sites in densely populated areas but not in desolate ones, or they may fight pornography outlets in residential neighborhoods but not in an inner-city tenderloin.

A fourth oppositional rhetoric, referring to the validity of decision-making procedures rather than the direct merits of the target, can sometimes avoid the suspicion of special-interest pleading, even while pointing to the special injustice done to local populations. Many local protestors believe that institutions of the state will promptly eliminate sources of threat when informed of them. In most cases they learn otherwise. Out of a sense of betrayal they often develop an additional rhetoric that concentrates on abuses of power, lack of official accountability, or cozy relations between business and the state. As social-problems scholars Malcolm Spector and John Kitsuse say, "As a consequence, assertions about the inadequacy, inefficacy, or injustice of the procedures may themselves become the conditions around which new social problems activities [especially protest] are organized."[7] More universal than particular, this *procedural rhetoric* is often quite powerful. It is one common way that local protestors develop more global rhetorics and strategies.[8]

Citizenship movements demanding rights face parallel choices of rhetoric. They can pursue the same rights for all humans, at one extreme, or just for their own group, at the other. In between, they can argue for the rights of groups like theirs: for all ethnic and racial minorities, say, but not for women. Their critiques can also address biases in governmental procedures, although for citizenship groups this is usually the main form of discrimination they face to begin with. Post-citizenship protestors, in contrast, may initially expect the state to address their grievance, adopting procedural rhetoric when rebuffed. Many movements face this dilemma between particularistic appeals that build solidarity within a tight community and universal appeals to outsiders: this is the dilemma of difference we saw in chapter 4.

A *globalization of rhetoric*—moving from local to global arguments—should help many groups to dodge the charge of self-interest and to recruit outsiders to their cause. If there exist semi-universal or universal arguments to condemn a project, protestors will presumably rely on them when they need to appeal to outsiders or nonlocals—as they frequently do, since most local protests are against large corporations or government agencies, whose final decisions are made far from the local impacts. Among NIMBYs it should be exceptional for protestors to retain a local or particularistic rhetoric. However, they might do this when it could help maintain solidarity among locals who feel especially aggrieved and unjustly treated, just as citizenship movements need to reinforce underlying collective identities. For example, environmental activists can argue that their community has suffered more than its share of "public bads," as in the case of Circleville, Ohio, which contains six industrial plants with severe emissions and landfill problems and two sites designated for the Superfund by the Environmental Protection Agency. Activists need not oppose all polluting factories in order to nurture outrage against Circleville's having yet another one, an argument that shades into procedural rhetoric.

Aware that local rhetoric will rarely yield the results they want, local environmental protesters strongly reject the label "NIMBY." This denial is part of the globalization process. An Alabama activist says, "I was a NIMBY to begin with. But I've realized that I don't want them to dig it up and move it somewhere else. We've changed our attitude. We're gathering information on this landfill and we're sharing it with people all over the United States. We've stopped being NIMBY's and become NIABY's (Not in Anybody's Back Yard).[9]

Successful rhetorics attract not only individual recruits but also organizational allies, an important way that culture is connected to strategy and resources. Local protestors may try to attach themselves to nonlocal organizations that can provide political access, respectability, and resources. Cynthia Gordon and I have called these *linking organizations*, which give credibility to protestors' universalist rhetorical aspirations; indeed they may actively encourage or force the local protestors to globalize their rhetoric.[10] They can show local interests to be part of a more general pattern, or provide a broader sense of distributive justice. Local environmental groups can find national organizations to help them; neighborhood protection groups can find city- or state-wide groups with similar agendas. Potential linking organizations are especially common in cities, where there are already many existing political organizations. New protest groups encounter a dense population of other groups with which they may wish to form links (or cannot avoid linking with). We again see that, through the right framing and strategizing, new networks can be formed for political action.

The risk of linking organizations is that they may suppress or reinterpret protestors' original concerns. As Spector and Kitsuse point out, "By entering into a coalition with others, a group may gain numbers, prestige, institutional authority, or other advantages. But group members may find that these advantages are purchased at the cost of diffusion of their issue and involvement in other issues in which they have little interest. Their own troubles may be considered only a part of the larger problem by their allies, and thus be given a low priority." Spector and Kitsuse connect this organizational problem with the corresponding rhetorical and ideological one: "Large organizations may provide sophisticated ideologies that make a complaint more forceful, although a general ideology may be a disadvantage in making visible a specific claim."[11] Blame is dissipated as the source of threat broadens.

How large an area protestors see as their affected "neighborhood" is difficult to predict in advance. It will vary according to factors such as population density, political and natural boundaries, and the nature of the issue. These are important, though, as raw materials with which activists frame appeals to new audiences, and as determinants of how well those appeals resonate. Success at mobilization partially depends on how large an area activists can make feel part of the same affected area, just as rights activists must make outsiders feel that other people's rights also matter to them.

INCINERATION AND INTEGRATION

Two Brooklyn cases—Canarsians fighting racial integration and opponents of a proposed garbage incinerator—show how local groups attempt to broaden their appeal and tap into additional resources. In the mid-1980s the New York city government announced plans for a large incinerator at the Brooklyn Navy Yard, a site abandoned by the Navy in an industrial area full of warehouses, but only five blocks from a dense residential district. It would burn three thousand tons of garbage each day from around the city, producing one thousand tons of ash as well as steam and electricity. First approved by the city's Board of Estimate in 1984, the plan was on hold for thirteen years while the State Department of Environmental Conservation held hearings and reviewed available data in order to decide whether to grant permits. Cynthia Gordon and I began following the controversy in 1989.[12]

Two local organizations have actively fought the incinerator plan. The Williamsburg Association for Safety and Health (WAS&H) had been formed in 1983 but quickly came to focus on the incinerator plan when it was announced in 1984. With fifteen hundred members, WAS&H has strong community roots. It is chaired by David Niederman, a Hasidic rabbi who lives ten blocks from the proposed site; by the late 1980s he was spending fifteen hours a week on the incinerator issue. Niederman's religious position helped tie WAS&H into the local community, an instance of a charismatic individual linking two networks together. This area of Brooklyn has a reputation for strong community groups and an active public life, due largely to the strength of Hasidic religious institutions. Politics and religion had long reinforced each other. WAS&H raised $500,000 toward legal fees, but it balanced its legal strategy with community consciousness raising and lobbying.

In 1988 another group, Brooklyn Recyclers Against Garbage Incineration (BRAGI), was formed, largely through the efforts of Ora Yemini and her husband. Yemini had been a direct-mail member of Greenpeace, sending in her contributions and reading the literature sent to her. One article discussed the hazards of incinerators, and mentioned that NYP-IRG (the New York Public Interest Research Group), was working against proposals to build incinerators in New York City. Yemini called NYPIRG, and was soon accompanying NYPIRG and WAS&H to Albany to lobby against the proposals. Niederman suggested that she start a group: she only needed letterhead stationery for everyone to assume she had a membership. She would gain credibility, if not clout. She could create the illusion of supporters and resources. Like so many other protest groups, this organization was essentially an individual.

Incinerator opponents explicitly described their issue in universalist terms. In an interview, Ora Yemini told us, "The incineration problem or any environmental problem is really a national and global problem. So this just gives us an opportunity to organize locally because there's a local threat. But our approach is not just a local concern; it's a concern generally." And Nicole Meyers of the Brooklyn Greens, also involved, said, "The NIMBY thing is a way to discredit concerns about the environment by passing them off as self-interest. The incinerator is not just a local issue. It has grave consequences for everyone." Finally, Leslie Park from Work on Waste (WOW) claimed, "Pollution knows no boundaries. We are involved in this to save our planet. It's a global issue." These protestors easily and insistently adopted the global rhetoric of environmentalism. None of their rhetoric was particularistic or even semi-universal; none referred to the injustice of siting the incinerator in the Navy Yard, for example.

For this environmental issue, the globalization of rhetoric was convincing, in part because of the organizational credibility behind it. There were several linking organizations that were national, such as Greenpeace and the Sierra Club, several that were local chapters of national groups or networks, like NYPIRG, and several that were state-level organizations. WOW-New York State was a coalition of almost fifty groups opposed to garbage incineration and promoting recycling; it helped coordinate lobbying in Albany to defeat this and other incinerator proposals. Founded in 1987, its function was to provide information and share tactics with local groups. So BRAGI and WAS&H worked closely with an extensive network of environmental groups ranging from other local ones to national ones. Few events or decisions were undertaken by one group acting alone.

These linking organizations had been opposed to the Navy Yard incinerator before the local groups contacted them, having independently discovered the issue as part of their general opposition to waste incineration. For example, WOW had noticed funding for incineration in the state budget and, along with NYPIRG, started a "No Money to Burn" campaign. So BRAGI and WAS&H were able to find larger organizations that already shared their goals. There was less danger of co-optation than there would have been in trying to convince existing organizations of the importance of a new issue.

With organizational linking came a broadening of issues and strategies. BRAGI was soon working on a program to recycle plastics, pushing legislation to ban plastics in New York restaurants, and lobbying for various other kinds of recycling. With a universalist rhetoric, it would have been difficult for Yemeni not to expand her range of issues. Incineration and recycling are clear alternatives to each other; an effective way to fight one is to promote the other. Similarly, WAS&H broadened its causes so that it was no longer a single-issue group, but an ongoing neighborhood organization working on housing, crime, and a variety of local issues. In contrast to BRAGI, which adopted regional and national environmental groups as linking organizations, WAS&H linked with the United Jewish Organizations of Williamsburg, taking a local, trans-issue turn rather than a nonlocal, environmental one. Both paths offered ways to globalize the groups' rhetoric.

In 1989 Barry Commoner provided the protestors with valuable ammunition when he published an op-ed piece in the *New York Times* about the Navy Yard proposal and incineration in general.[13] Using the example of New York City, Commoner argued the merits of recycling as a substitute for incineration. Here was a respected, even famous, scientist and writer linking the particular proposal to general problems with incineration. His authoritative use of facts and figures lent an objective aura to the piece.

So far, incinerator opponents have prevented any construction at the Brooklyn Navy Yard. Local elected officials have opposed the plan, but city-wide politicians have had mixed views. Mayors Ed Koch and Rudolph Giuliani supported incineration, while mayor David Dinkins called for a moratorium while studies of recycling were completed. The Dinkins administration lifted the moratorium in 1991, but did not move to site the three incinerators it concluded were necessary. More important, the Navy Yard incinerator did not receive the necessary permits from the Federal Environmental Protection Agency or the state Department of Environmental Conservation until 1994, and no work has begun yet. Through these delays, protestors have allowed the national environmental movement to generate information about the risks of incineration, including possible toxins in the ash, and thus to increase public doubts.[14] The eventual outcome is uncertain.

Incinerator opponents gained outside support, both financial and rhetorical, from national and regional environmental groups. In these groups, they had linking organizations attuned to their own goals, through whom they could tap into a universalist rhetoric backed by increasing amounts of scientific data. In different ways, BRAGI and WAS&H were able to shed the NIMBY stigma by expanding their rhetoric and issues. In the end, though, they relied heavily on their ability to use the city's and state's regulatory systems to delay the incinerator project, rather than getting clear statements of support from politicians—a sign that strategic maneuvering is still partly autonomous from the cultural persuasion necessary for mobilizing a movement.

This globalization works well with environmental issues, in part because of the many linking organizations, but also partly because of the cultural resonances of this family of grievances. The presence of helpful linking organizations and the cultural meanings go hand in hand. Even before their resources allowed them to gather evidence against incineration, environmental organizations gave cognitive and affective credibility to anti-incineration arguments by lending them their own symbolic legitimacy as respected national players.

We can compare the incinerator opponents with residents of Canarsie who protested against the African-Americans who were beginning to live and go to school there in the mid-1970s, based on Jonathan Rieder's book *Canarsie*. The residents of this eastern Brooklyn neighborhood, mostly descendants of the Italians and Jews targeted in similar moral panics earlier in the century, bitterly fought the encroachment of African-Americans through public housing and school integration. Primarily middle class, although sometimes just barely, many Canarsians had moved there to escape economically deteriorating neighborhoods and to have a piece of land for gardens; most could not afford another move farther into the suburbs. Their precarious hold on middle-class status possibly led them to be especially anxious in looking for signs of inferior status in the lifestyles of others.[15]

Rieder describes the combination of threats that Canarsians felt as increasing numbers of African-American faces appeared in and around their neighborhood. Part of their concern was for their property values, heightened by the fact that many had few resources other than their homes. Other concerns had to do with physical safety; they perceived (correctly, Rieder seems to indicate) that certain parts of Canarsie had become less safe; and they worried about their children's exposure to violence at school. Rieder quotes one progressive Jewish woman: "Most Canarsians are against busing. They're afraid their property values will decline, but they're also afraid their kids will be killed in the hallways."[16] This sense of physical threat was accompanied by emotions of the kind described in chapter 5.

Rieder's main emphasis, however, is on the moral threat the white Canarsians felt from a lifestyle which they perceived as chaotic and morally lax. Their images of African-Americans derived less from personal experiences than from observations of the ghettos they drove past between Canarsie and Manhattan, and the public housing projects being built in neighboring Brownsville: "The ultimate message of graffiti was that the public sphere was full of unseen dangers and no longer belonged to the law-abiding. Canarsians reached their judgment about the people of the ghetto by reading such palpable signs. The slums of Brownsville give it an unruly appearance. Canarsie is neat and trim, a grid of repetition, the landscape of order. When whites looked north across Linden Boulevard, the chaos transfixed them." The result was that "race was a kind of shorthand for an array of social, cultural, and economic deprivals," so that policies of integration, especially in the local schools, touched off a vicious not-in-my-backyard response. Perceptions of moral chaos were rooted partly in misunderstanding of the other group; the superficiality of contacts allowed the panickers to inflate their targets into folk devils.[17]

Beliefs about their new neighbors fed Canarsians' moral uneasiness and sense of threat, triggering a range of familiar emotions: fear, first and foremost, followed by anger, outrage, and contempt. They also felt themselves to be innocent victims of insensitive politicians and bureaucrats as well as of criminals. Around them they perceived attacks on their basic values of discipline, hard work, and permanent families. A permissive society as a whole threatened them, but they responded to black ghettoes as an especially flagrant symbol of moral breakdown. The strength of this anger, and the violent behavior that resulted, discredited the protest to outsiders by presenting it as gut-level racism. Portrayed as racists in the news media, Canarsians felt a certain degree of shame that probably further fueled their anger. Their construction of blame, moreover, was caught between cause (the moral qualities of their new neighbors) and responsibility (the government should do something) without achieving stability or clarity.

Physical violence was one response to integration, especially among young Italian men, who organized vigilante groups and had fistfights with blacks. Jewish Canarsians, in contrast, helped launch an organized political response. Rieder sums up the cultural traditions behind each strategy: "Italians rely on the family to settle grudges; Jews accept the state's monopoly on violence."[18] Canarsie's Jews, typically with a liberal or progressive family heritage, remained loyal to local Democrats, while many Italians turned Republican during the 1970s. Jews turned to the local political club, the Jefferson Democratic Club, for help. An old-style political machine headed by both Jews and Italians, with three thousand dues-paying members, the club had a progressive tradition of support for civil liberties. Other Canarsians took strong and even extralegal measures against integration, including not simply personal violence but intimidating crowds, a boycott of the integrated schools, and an electoral challenge to the machine's state assemblyman. Although the electoral challenge came surprisingly close to victory, none of these tactics gained much sympathy from politicians and policymakers outside Canarsie.

In turning to New York City politicians, an audience tied to other ethnic and racial groups in the city and unable to condone racist language, the Canarsians were using the wrong rhetoric for their audience. This was bad fortune, since there were many conservative politicians around the country using the same code words as the local demagogues who "inflamed popular fears about crime, turning 'law and order' into a talisman. The adept orator could speak the unspeakable with a wink, leaving little doubt that he was talking about 'niggers.'"[19] For ten years national politicians and the news media had crafted such language and images. More and more since 1964, conservative politicians have played to white racial anxieties and racist sentiments, especially in presidential elections, transforming Democratic support for civil rights and racial equality into a political liability.[20] The Canarsians had considerable rhetorical ammunition at their disposal, but it was more useful for inflaming neighbors than finding allies among city politicians.

The Jefferson Democratic Club, therefore, proved a poor linking organization for Canarsie protestors, since it was tied to broader political interests that could not appear linked to racism. The club had the clout to meet many of the protestors' demands, but instead it suppressed them. It did not support the school boycott or other extralegal tactics. Rieder says of the club's effect, "Institutional arrangements may silence some kinds of speech and broadcast others. The Jewish leaders who controlled Canarsie politics, and their Jewish and Italian allies in the interlocked network of civic institutions, worked to keep racial invective from spilling over into public conversation. . . . Tightly coupled to a borough organization that spanned black and Hispanic assembly districts, the club was not an autonomous unit free to go its own way."[21] External constraints on the club reinforced the predilections of the club's leaders, who were more cosmopolitan and liberal than the average supporter. The club's considerable resources prevented the electoral challenge from succeeding; on election day the club had twenty-three buses at its disposal, provided by trade unions, to take voters to the polls. Linking organizations offer resources, but only if local demands do not undermine other important organizational goals.

The Canarsians were unable to exploit any of the main strategies open to local protestors. They could find no nonlocal elites to help them; they were unable to link their cause rhetorically with broader issues (except procedural rhetoric criticizing city government for insensitivity to local communities); they had no veto control they could exercise, in part because the school integration and public housing had already been done. And their linking organization, instead of furthering their goals, curtailed and suppressed them. The Canarsians remained local in strategy, recruitment, and ideology, building no bridge for outsiders to help their cause. And their cause was one that few New York politicians were willing to support, so the Canarsians' efforts at cultural persuasion failed.

Did the Canarsians' fears differ from those of the incinerator opponents? Were their appeals less compelling? Did they have fewer resources? Or were they less adept strategically? Yes, on all counts. What is interesting is how the different dimensions were entwined. The Canarsians' resource mobilization and strategic maneuvering were limited because their fears and rhetorical appeals were less globalized, and perhaps less globalizable. They could not achieve rhetorical links with helpful allies. Their lack of credible linking organizations further undermined their rhetorical claims.

Opponents of the incinerator, like other NIMBYs, tried hard to use a nonlocal set of issues, rhetoric, and ideology. All of them saw NIMBY as a pejorative label—as it is usually intended. For an audience of distant strangers, rhetoric is more compelling when it appeals to some set of universal principles, be they instrumental ones like costs and benefits or moral ones like social justice. Despite similar attempts, the incinerator opponents managed to find a more compelling universalist rhetoric, as polished by environmentalists. There were arguments and evidence against incinerators and for recycling as an alternative. The existence of national environmental groups with regional offices provided organizational muscle and visibility to back up the universalist rhetoric.

The Canarsians barely tried to globalize their rhetoric, and their linking organization proved unsympathetic to their concerns. Even so, these local protestors complained about government policies favoring integration more than they attacked directly the individuals they disliked. (Although here Jewish and Italian responses typically differed.) The incinerator opponents raised questions of governmental, procedural fairness in their campaigns too. Given widespread anti-instrumental sentiments, large bureaucracies make good targets.

In chapter 5, I contrasted environmental and social sources of local threat. Environmental sources seem to lend themselves naturally to universalistic rhetoric, since anyone would be affected if the same technology were placed nearby. Concern about environmental problems is widespread, so that the "affected community" can be described more broadly. In contrast, social sources of threat necessarily pit one group against another, so that protestors are unlikely to find a general rhetoric they can use. (Fortunately in contemporary American society, rhetorics of racism are rarely made explicit in public, except in veiled form, although privately they may be common.) Environmental threats typically transcend existing political boundaries and social cleavages (class, ethnicity, gender), whereas social threats are often based precisely on these cleavages. There is also more explicit argumentation available for opposing environmental and technological threats. People may respond more immediately and emotionally to social sources of threat, and more ideologically and articulately to environmental ones.

The kind of information environmental protestors have at their disposal is also more cumulative than that available to protestors against social threats. National environmental organizations gather scientific data on the effects of technologies such as incinerators, which they publish in smoothly written pamphlets. In the ten years that the Navy Yard protestors have delayed the incinerator, environmental scientists have learned a great deal about incinerators. Writers like Commoner and groups like NYPIRG serve up the details in powerful editorials and brochures. A powerful rhetorical machine has been at work, supported by the news media.

THE UBIQUITOUS MEDIA

Protestors' efforts to mobilize people and resources depend, naturally enough, on what cultural understandings are out there to appeal to.

The beliefs, emotions, and morals of individuals—misleadingly aggregated as "public opinion"—continually interact with a variety of other formulations alongside those of protestors. Politicians, newspaper reporters and editors, schoolteachers, preachers, police officials, and many others, along with their institutions, are actively involved, often in conscious competition with the claims of protest groups. There are regular and frequent struggles over common sense, and without them we would have trouble perceiving the active construction of cultural meanings. Even the mental worlds of protestors cannot escape these influences.

The most obvious shapers of cultural sensibilities are the media, which are also the main channel through which protestors broadcast their messages and movement identity. To mobilization and process theorists, the media are essential conduits for outside support; to new-social-movement theorists they spread cultural meanings from and to protestors. A large literature has described the forces shaping what the media present to the public, including audience expectations, journalistic norms, information sources, the tastes of editors and executives, censorship by owners and advertisers, and the technical constraints of each medium. A memorable visual or sound bite, for example, will make a story more "newsworthy."[22]

Others who manage to influence cultural meanings—even while they are shaped by them—can usually do so because they have access to the news media: they are newsmakers. These may be police officials who make statements, funders of social research, politicians who hold public hearings, or professional groups that call press conferences. As we saw in chapter 4, they may simply be celebrities interested in an issue. Each group or individual has a stake or an interest in publicizing some problem: increased funding for police, research, or social workers; official government condemnation of those who violate one's moral sensibilities; extra publicity for a politician's agenda (or embarrassment of her foes); the satisfaction of doing good. As individuals or organizational representatives, they are newsworthy.

Moral panics—sudden hysteria about an activity accompanied by rapid mobilization and calls for suppression—are a dramatic instance when various actors vie to shape public impressions of a social problem, often resulting in the creation of new protest groups.[23] Canarsie was one example of a local panic that never grew, in part because the news media did not directly follow suit; but it contributed to a broader national panic over integration and race relations. Political conflict, cultural meanings, and psychological anxieties help explain the occurrence and the choice of victims of moral panics. For example Philip

Jenkins studied a cluster of British panics from the late 1970s and 1980s which linked issues of sexual violence, child abuse, murder, and ritual satanism.[24] According to him, feminists promoted images of men as regularly, perhaps inherently, violent toward women and children. Ironically, feminism allied with a conservative backlash against "permissiveness" that reasserted the importance of the family, children, and heterosexuality. Supporting this perspective were widespread law-and-order concerns, and a Thatcher government anxious to justify censorship and other repressive acts. The religious right, Jenkins found, was also growing rapidly. Finally, a recent increase in immigration had led to fears about British culture and identity, drugs, and the deterioration of inner cities. In many details, the same description applies to the United States of the period, which, according to Jenkins, pioneered most of the moral panics he describes.

The idea of a "folk devil," an evil wrongdoer who can be blamed for many social ills, spurs the sense of threat that drives moral mobilizations. In Jenkins' cases, specific enemies were occasionally identified and condemned, such as gay men, foreigners, satanists, and elite criminal networks. Despite the lack of any evidence, widespread cultural stereotypes implicated all these. In most cases a group is all too readily identified and targeted, usually a group already disadvantaged by its society's political and economic institutions or cultural biases. Blame can be founded on far-fetched cultural beliefs with little objective evidence.

Because symbolic resonance is difficult to create from scratch, the news media and other moral mobilizers must appeal to the common-sense understandings of their audiences. They need to frame their appeals in ways that resonate with the beliefs and experiences of those they hope to persuade and recruit. Each panic, like other claims made through the media about public issues, elaborates and extends symbols from past panics; this gradual layering increases the plausibility and threatening nature of each panic, no matter how little hard evidence there may be for it. The successive panics may grow increasingly far-fetched, yet even as one panic dies down or is discredited, its symbolic resonances survive, providing raw material for future cultural mobilizations.

Yet moral mobilizations and other public claims don't merely resonate with existing cultural beliefs; they help to construct and transform them. When we examined cognitive dynamics in chapter 7, we concentrated on the broad social processes affecting the common sense of individuals and on the active framing by protest organizers, but there are other institutions and individuals actively trying to shape our sensibilities. Our moral and cognitive common sense is constantly being influenced by preachers, politicians, the media, and others who have access to an audience. Bombarded with media images, instructed by politicians or religious leaders, citizens alter their intuitions and beliefs. They focus on different risks, perceive new dangers, mobilize over new grievances. Analysis of media coverage helps us understand why some political frames have more resonance than others. Panics occur when moral outrage is aroused and focused on specific targets perceived as threatening. They are merely an acute form of what goes on all the time, making it easier to see the kind of shaping that moral gatekeepers constantly do.[25]

Although William Gamson argued that the media are only one source of information, they are an important one, especially for collective and movement identity. The news media influence the attribution of blame, which we saw in chapter 5 was crucial to protest. What Iyengar called "episodic framing" makes viewers less likely to blame public officials or to hold them responsible for a solution—in other words, it discourages protest. Gamson points out that "if people simply relied on the media, it would be difficult to find any coherent frame at all, let alone an injustice frame. The metanarrative is frequently about the self-reforming nature of the system, operating to get rid of the rotten apples that the news media have exposed. If moral indignation is stimulated by fingering the bad guys, it is quickly and safely assuaged by their removal."[26] Alternative frames, pre-existing or fostered by protestors, are necessary for blame to stick at a systemic level. In this clash of cultural interpretations, however, the media are heavyweight contenders.

In addition to shaping public perceptions of the kinds of problems that protest movements are addressing, the news media also affect the movement's own identity. There would be no "movement identity" without ratification from the media, which are especially important for providing a sense of a national phenomenon—which no individual or group could easily acquire for itself. Todd Gitlin showed the extent to which the movement identity of the New Left was partly shared by those inside the movement and those outside it, in both cases due to the news media.[27]

The news media shape our common sense, various definitions of identity, and the messages spokespersons can broadcast. Protest groups have other media at their disposal: direct mail, canvassing, tabling, as well as advertisements in established media. Sometimes, they can craft their own impressions for the public. The news media, by virtue of their reach, nonetheless remain an important part of the broader cultural landscape for protest groups, who work hard to get an issue on the media's agenda and affect its framing once it is there.[28]

PUTTING RESOURCES INTO ACTION

For incinerator opponents, adopting more global rhetoric led to more global strategy and recruitment as well, for the issue attracted groups and individuals already active in the environmental movement. In fact the rhetoric and ideology have a direct parallel, if not an embodiment, in the organizations. Local organizations can sustain particularistic rhetoric, but not global ideologies—at least not convincingly. Observers will always suspect that the universalistic ideology has been adopted merely out of convenience. But national organizations operate naturally with universalistic rhetorics and ideologies, and they can convince people that what seems like a local concern is actually a global one. For movements based on collective identities, there is a parallel question of whether groups should be restricted to members of that community or open to all.

Incinerator opponents found linking organizations that were allies working in parallel, avoiding the co-optation that could come from larger groups with other agendas. In contrast, the Jefferson Democratic Club was quite unsympathetic to the Canarsians. We may be able to discern two kinds of linking organization. In one case the nonlocal organizations are already looking for local allies, either because they wish to oppose all local instances of a threat, or because they have already decided a local siting case is important. Some of these organizations—like the Citizens' Clearinghouse for Hazardous Waste—may even have been founded to support local groups. A second kind of linking organization is a local, pre-existing group founded to wield political power on a range of issues. It may be sympathetic to the new issue or it may not (as with Canarsie's Jefferson Democratic Club), but the new issue is unlikely to get its full attention. For all movements, the choice of allies entails risks of dilution.

One similarity between the incinerator and integration cases is the source of the proposals—in city bureaucracies. In both, protestors' rhetoric could focus on bureaucratic decision making that was insensitive to the needs of local citizens, an external force "imposing" yet another burden. Protestors could attack instrumentalism with a procedural rhetoric. This strategy has been especially effective for the incinerator opponents, for the environmental movement has polished its critique of instrumentalism for two decades. It has spread an image of government and business collusion in pursuit of short-term profits at the expense of the quality of life of the public, an image of negative "externalities" shoved onto the public to lower business costs. Local neighborhoods feel the city government is an outsider, so protestors can stoke local resentment. New proposals become symbols of existing suspicions, cleavages, and tensions in political life, based on what organizations and individuals are backing them: they become associated with coalitions of friends or enemies.[29] If a city bureaucracy is seen as an "outsider," it is likely to meet more opposition than private citizens would. Blame is an easy, natural construction in such cases.

Both protests could refer to property values as part of the adverse effects of the proposals, but the incinerator opposition publicly avoided this theme. Property values are a primarily local concern; as a stated rationale, they would undermine the attempt to globalize the issues. Yet in private conversations, they are sometimes mentioned. Always a worry for owners, property values are rarely raised when local opponents are trying to globalize their ideology. But when a global ideology is unavailable or unconvincing, property values may be adduced as a semi-universalistic rhetoric: sites should not be used when property owners would be penalized arbitrarily. The Canarsians mentioned property values continuously and centrally, perhaps in lieu of more convincing global rhetoric.

The Canarsians were unable to stop integration, partly because of their inability to globalize their rhetoric and find other supporters. The other protestors have succeeded in blocking the incinerator, largely through delay tactics like court battles and demands for better environmental impact reports. Their ultimate success will depend on their strategizing in the courts and with politicians.

The thing to remember about rules is that they can be changed; about resources, that they can be mobilized. Sometimes they are part of the fixed context; at others they are the very point of strategic action. The process by which protestors appeal to others—either decision makers or potential allies and supporters—necessarily involves language, meanings, and resonance. They must persuade allies of a common purpose. They must inspire outrage in potential contributors. They must speak a language that decision makers understand. These interactions involve resources and strategy permeated with emotions and meanings.

At the same time, cultural resonance is hardly a simple matter of adding up intuitions, so that the more people you can persuade, the more likely you are to win. Some people have more power than others;

it's more important to persuade a federal court judge than a neighbor. We need to grasp the epidemiology of cultural meanings: to understand what groups, professions, political parties tend to share which intuitions, motivations, and goals. In *Nuclear Politics* I examined how several prominent worldviews—cost-benefit approaches, technological enthusiasm, and ecological moralism—were distributed within state agencies and protest groups. *It is how cultural symbols, moral values, and biographical responses are distributed in political and organizational structures that matters in explaining political and policy outcomes.* In the case of the Canarsians, for instance, some national leaders would have been more sympathetic to their outrage than the New York Democrats they had to appeal to. We need both strategy and culture; one without the other is misleading.

Much recent cultural work on social movements has used mobilization models as convenient straw men, often assuming that either resources or cultural meanings affect protest, but not both. Or not both at the same time. Instead, resources are used to promulgate ideologies and injustice frames, and cultural meanings and rhetorics shape the accumulation of resources. In promoting one's vision of the world, in making claims about social problems, resources and organizations are the vehicles that deliver the cultural freight, with strategies in the driver's seat. Sociologists need to learn how resources, strategies, and meanings interact.

In the incinerator case, local protest consisted of a network of organizations working together (more or less effectively) to influence state and regulatory organizations. Even though a sense of threat and dread spurred the formation of protest groups, the political battles quickly came to look like other political controversies in an organizational society. Local opponents raised money, lobbied officials, filed lawsuits. They often succeeded in adopting a convincing global rhetoric and ideology. They also found linking organizations that could connect them with other, nonlocal organizations. And they tried to exert some veto power, or at least delaying power, over the proposals. The Canarsians, facing a policy already in place, failed even at this (opponents of *proposals* for public housing have, in contrast, often succeeded in blocking them). In the end, protestors have to play politics, even though resources and cultural meanings are an important part of this game. We have already seen other actors trying to shape cultural meanings; they are also trying to help or hinder protest groups directly. It is to these strategic games that we now turn, for strategy runs through both culture and resources.

- Strong emotions and motivations can often overcome a lack of resources, partially through the recognition of new possibilities in assets and practices.

- Rhetorical persuasion is the central means for mobilizing new resources.

- Networks of organizational allies—linking organizations—are helpful or not partly because they transmit, block, reframe, or give credibility to rhetorical claims.

- Protestors attract outside participants and supporters partly by globalizing their rhetoric to make it seem as sweeping as possible rather than particularistic and contingent. The news media are an unavoidable filter through which most cultural messages must flow.

THIRTEEN

Culture and Strategy: States, Audiences, and Success

Il faut noter, Que les jeux d'enfants ne sont pas jeux; et les faut juger en eux, comme leurs plus sérieuses actions.
  —Montaigne

Everything depended upon the White response. If it proved inadequate, White could quite easily have lost control of the board. . . . If Black 69 was diabolically aggressive, White 70 was a brilliant holding play. Onoda, among others, was speechless with admiration. The Master stood firm and averted a crisis. He retreated a pace and forestalled disaster. A magnificent play, it cannot have been easy to make. Black had charged into a headlong assault, and with this one play White had turned it back. Black had made gains, and yet it seemed that White, casting away the dressings from his wounds, had emerged with greater lightness and freedom of action.
  —Yasunari Kawabata, *The Master of Go*

Fifty miles north of San Francisco, Bodega Head is a rocky promontory sticking out into the Pacific Ocean. The area abounds in spring wild-flowers, and combines sandy beaches with dramatic bluffs. In June 1961, after three years of planning and engineering studies, the Pacific Gas and Electric Company announced that it would buy the site to build a nuclear power plant to service rapidly growing Marin and Sonoma counties. The reactor would be the world's largest yet, and it was nationally hailed as an important step toward nuclear energy's eventual commercialization. The glamour of nuclear fission was yet untarnished, and there was little opposition anywhere in the country. America's largest private utility began negotiations with local property owners, and within months it easily received the necessary permissions from the county commissioners and the state Public Utilities Commission.[1]

Thirty-five years ago, few commercial reactors aroused public protest. Not so Bodega Head. A small number of local residents—including one who had refused to sell her property and had seen it condemned for use by the utility anyway—protested the seizure of land for power generation. More surprisingly, they were joined by a small coalition of environmental groups, including the Sierra Club, aroused by the beauty of the site. Staid PG&E engineers, accustomed to dealing only with other engineers, found themselves facing colorful demonstrations, anti-Bodega bumper stickers, and a popular radio song critical of their company. Protest groups raised a variety of issues, from heat pollution to the milk supply to radiation release into the air, but they eventually focused on what seemed most promising for blocking construction: the proximity of the San Andreas fault, and the presence of a smaller fault line directly under the reactor site. In this instance, semi-universalistic arguments against siting reactors near faults were more effective than a universal opposition to all nuclear plants.

As protestors invented new tactics and complaints, the proponents of the reactor also responded with creative strategies. At one point, for example, the county board of supervisors rezoned the reactor site as "agricultural," making it an area in which public utilities are allowed to build without land-use permits or public hearings. Special reports and design modifications were made to counter the earthquake fears. State and local agencies supported PG&E, and several levels of legal courts decided in its favor (partly on the dubious grounds that PG&E had already sunk so much money into the project). The federal Atomic Energy Commission was not so confident, however, and its staff were sending PG&E mixed signals. Because of this, the electric company, already looking at alternative sites, withdrew its plans for the Bodega reactor. In the end, PG&E chose a site several hundred miles to the south: the rolling hills and coastline of a then-obscure place called Diablo Canyon.

In 1964 a handful of peaceful protestors managed to stop mighty PG&E's plans for a reactor at Bodega Head. Twenty years later one of the most extensive, noisy, and long-running antinuclear protests failed to prevent the opening of the reactors at Diablo Canyon. The anti-Diablo protestors, moreover, had a large national movement supporting them, public opinion in their favor, numerous scientific and technical experts who had testified to the dangers of nuclear energy, and the embarrassment of PG&E's reversed blueprints during construction. Is there no connection between the size of a protest movement and its impact? Why did the tiny effort succeed while the large one failed? Do mobilization and success require different explanations?

This contrasting pair of cases is not unique. Antinuclear groups stopped several planned nuclear reactors in the 1960s—places like Bodega Head, Cayuga Lake, Malibu, Lloyd Harbor, Nippomo Dunes—before a national antinuclear movement emerged. These groups succeeded because electric utilities felt that if one site was controversial, they could find another. Once the national movement gelled in the early 1970s, however, antinuclear groups were unable to stop the construction of reactors, as utilities universally mobilized to fight back.[2] In this case, the surprising relationship between movement size and its effect was this: the larger the antinuclear movement grew, the less successful it was at stopping individual plants. As it became national, the movement adopted universalistic arguments against all reactors, not just specific sites, leaving no room for compromise or negotiation. The emergence of a national movement identity energized protestors but also frightened, shocked, and aroused their opponents to action: the nuclear industry felt the same kind of moral shock we have seen for protestors.

One lesson of this contrast is how tricky definitions of success are. This issue has always bedeviled students of protest. Success can take many forms, with no clear relationship between them. Success at mobilizing a movement, in particular, seems unrelated to success at attaining stated goals. A large movement may be more likely to transform public opinion, and this may in turn encourage policy changes—but such effects are tenuous and largely undemonstrated. The peace movement of the 1980s was one of the largest in American history, but it had almost no impact on government policies. And how are a movement's goals related to each other? Could the antinuclear movement have won by stopping individual plants, or did abandonment of the most dubious proposals merely polish the image of those remaining? In the last chapter we saw how many different audiences protest groups play to, and they have contrasting goals (and corresponding possibilities for success) for each of them.

Another lesson is that the responses of those organizations targeted by protestors make an enormous difference to the success of the protest. Protestors develop their strategies in direct interaction with the choices of their opponents, not in isolation. Not only does each side respond to the other, but protest groups learn from other protesters; opponents learn from other opponents. Then there are other players— friends, foes, and bystanders—who also respond, and must be responded to. One could almost define movements and countermovements as the spread of new tactics, as groups learn from and imitate each other. In the jargon of organizational theories, there is "mimetic isomorphism."[3] The "environment" of a movement does not consist of stable structures but of conscious decision makers shaping cultural meanings, mobilizing resources, and doing what they can to win.

As I have argued, strategic choices and interactions are a dimension of protest logically independent of other basic dimensions. The mutual expectations and games of strategic action are efforts at winning, and some moves are more successful than others. There are regularities, a logic, to conflict that is partly independent of resources, biography, and cultural meanings. Finding the right alliances, inventing tactics that surprise one's opponents, or forcing one's foe into a publicly recognized error all have an impact, whatever one's taste in tactics. Similarly, your own tastes, beliefs, and emotions can help you or trip you up strategically. Strategic choices depend so much on the interactions between various players that we need a "conflict" lens to relate social movements to the broader strategic field. The apparatus developed to explain movement emergence—frame alignment, identity, resource mobilization, moral shocks—*helps us surprisingly little in accounting for success; we must switch to a different vocabulary, of tactical innovation, vulnerabilities, blunders, credibility, and rules.*

But strategies are only partly independent of resources, biography, and culture, since all these dimensions affect each other. Tactics and strategies carry moral, emotional, and cognitive meanings and values; they are part of the know-how that comprises culture. Strategies depend on the expectations of others and on interpretations of prior moves and intentions. I hope to demonstrate both the creativity of putting together strategic campaigns that outwit one's opponents, and the relationship of these campaigns to cultural meanings and processes.

In chapter 10 I distinguished between explanations of what protestors do (choices of tactics), of what they *can* do (available repertories), and of what they do *now* (applications of tactics). Strategic considerations—taking into account what other players have just done, what they expect us to do, how bystanders are likely to react, and so on—help explain all three. They are the external factors that exist alongside the internal movement factors (members' goals, identities, tastes, biographies). The interplay of internal and external defines learning, as players on both sides test and promote their preferences and assumptions against those of other players. Strategy and learning add dynamism, change, and creativity to our image of protest movements.

STRATEGIC LEARNING

Explicit theorizing about strategic choice and interaction has been rare in social-movement research. Mobilization imagery focuses more on competition among social-movement organizations, as well as their extraction of resources from constituents. Considerable attention to resources makes the interaction between most protestors and their opponents less interesting, since the opponents usually have greater resources and so win in the long run. But what is often interesting is how those with few resources manage to attain certain goals despite their handicap—precisely through strategy and culture.[4] Political process language pays more attention to strategic interactions, especially with the state. But the image of a political opportunity structure often renders protestors' opponents part of the landscape more than conscious players.[5] The threat of state repression always looms, sufficient to crush almost any protest movement, but the more interesting questions include when and why repression occurs, when and why the state acts as a unitary player, and what the audiences are for the state's actions.

State agents, as we saw in chapter 12, are hardly the only players. One's own supporters, for purposes of organizational maintenance, are perhaps the most influential audience for the leaders of a protest group. And of course, one's opponents, whose behavior is ultimately the issue, are an important audience for all but the most ingrown protest movement. The news media form their own impressions, framing each issue in various ways before broadcasting it to the general public. "Public opinion" is a slippery factor, important mostly because players on all sides of a controversy think it is and hence play to it. Movements differ considerably in their main interactions. The state is most central for citizenship movements, as they demand legal and political rights. Post-citizenship movements are as likely to engage their own members and the broader culture. Different audiences require different strategies and tactics.

The main literatures on strategy come out of the study of international war and economic competition. Theories of war are not especially helpful for us, since contestants in a war aim at a level of success beyond the hope of most protest groups. One theoretical school, associated with Clausewitz, sees strategy as the pairing of your own strength with your opponent's weakness, in order to attain complete dominance—an unrealistic goal for protestors in nations with civil societies. Clausewitz believed in the importance of numerical superiority, so destroying or disarming the opponent's forces on the battlefield was the main goal. Another paradigm, associated with Sun Tze, concentrates on deception as a means of vanquishing foes. Deception assumes that one's opponent is so untrustworthy or evil that fair dealing is unnecessary—a fine assumption for most wars, in which one's domestic audience shares the low estimation of the opponent. But in most civil conflicts, no matter how a protest group and its opponents may demonize each other, deception easily boomerangs, becoming a deadly blunder.

Public opinion and many state agencies react unfavorably to evidence of deception, as we'll see. Nuclear weapons have inspired another tradition of strategic theorizing, often based on a complete or nearly complete lack of communication between the sides. This poor communication often characterizes the interaction between protestors and their opponents, but they at least communicate indirectly through the media and other intermediaries. In addition, the nuclear-war paradigm is limited because, like Clausewitzean war, the goal is assumed to be the destruction of the other side rather than more limited changes in its behavior.

Military principles of strategy fall largely into two categories: maintain your own freedom to maneuver, and reduce that of your opponent. The former includes many truisms of rational action. The latter includes advice such as taking advantage of divisions among your opponent's forces and cutting your opponent's lines of communication. Military historian Liddel Hart once summed up the "concentrated essence of strategy and tactics" as follows: on the positive side, "Adjust your end to your means. . . . Keep your object always in mind. . . . Choose the line (or course) of least expectation. . . . Exploit the line of least resistance. . . . Take a line of operation which offers alternative objectives. . . . Ensure that both plan and dispositions are flexible— adaptable to circumstances." On the negative side, "Do not throw your weight into a stroke whilst your opponent is on guard. . . . Do not renew an attack along the same line (or in the same form) after it has once failed." Confuse and dislocate your opponent, and exploit any advantages you have from doing this. "Windows of opportunity" open and close suddenly, so one must be prepared to use them. Beyond the truisms, the point is to maintain flexibility and surprise your opponent. Resources certainly sustain maneuverability, and the interplay of culture and biography explain some of the ability to surprise the other side. In addition, traits of individual leaders such as boldness or determination can help.[6]

Saul Alinsky, who unlike academics wrote for community organizers, discussed strategic choice in similar terms. A legendary organizer from the 1930s until his death in 1972, Alinsky formulated several rules of tactics:

> Power is not only what you have but what the enemy thinks you have. . . . Never go outside the experience of your people. . . . Whenever possible go outside the experience of your enemy [in other words, surprise them]. . . . Make the enemy live up to their own book of rules. . . . Ridicule is man's most potent weapon. . . . A good tactic is one that your people enjoy. . . . A tactic that drags on too long be-

comes a drag. . . . Keep the pressure on. . . . The threat is usually more terrifying than the thing itself [this, like the first one, means that expectations and interpretations matter enormously]. . . . The major premise for tactics is the development of operations that will maintain a constant pressure upon the opposition. . . . If you push a negative hard and deep enough it will break through into its counterside [meaning the other side will blunder]. . . . The price of a successful attack is a constructive alternative [be ready with concrete suggestions should the other side ask for them]. . . . Pick the target, freeze it, personalize it, and polarize it [be specific about constructing and allocating blame].[7]

Like all good strategic guidelines, these leave considerable room for creativity and intuition on the part of practitioners. Since surprise is important to both Alinsky and Hart, timing becomes a crucial aspect of strategy.

Game theory, like the models of economic competition that helped inspire it, explains endpoints more than decisions. The maximization efforts of game theory are partly compatible with the organizational focus of mobilization approaches, especially if conflicts are recognized as ongoing games with multiple rounds of play. But the ongoing play, combined with multiple actors, outstrips the simple models of game theory rather quickly. Game theories at least set the players in motion and define different kinds of games—seventy-eight of them in the simplest case of two actors each with two options—with colorful names like chicken, the assurance game, or the prisoner's dilemma.[8] Some real-life situations actually fit one or another of the games, especially two-country conflicts. There is a kernel of truth to the rationalists' framework, despite the silly theories so often constructed on it. The rationalists' atrophied image of human motivation may be misguided, but not the description of strategic games in which each move is made with elaborate expectations about how the other players will respond. Thomas Schelling's useful distinction between zero-sum games of pure conflict, coordination games of cooperation and trust, and mixed-motive games, which combine elements of each, can be mapped onto different audiences and interactants: protest groups mostly have zero-sum interactions with their targets, cooperative ones with allies and members, and mixed-motive games with other audiences.[9] Game theory can describe some strategic interactions, even if it rarely can predict the outcomes. Recall Bourdieu's discussion of how people don't merely follow rules, but stretch and elaborate on them in unexpected ways.

Most efforts to categorize protest strategies have relied on some contrast between conflict and cooperation. One common typology distinguishes tactics involving protest and persuasion (such as demonstrations, teach-ins, and petitions), noncooperation (boycotts, strikes, civil disobedience), and active intervention (sit-ins, direct action, sabotage). A finer one lists six types of strategy from most to least cooperative: educative, conversionist, bargaining, separatist, disruptive, and revolutionary. Different choices are made for different audiences, depending on how friendly they are expected to be.[10]

On top of these different approaches to interaction, there are situations, to give game theory its due, when all players have a limited ability to maneuver. There are stalemates unintended by any of the players. These may result from a form of polarization, from the making of extreme threats, or simply from extended conflict in which both sides come to detest each other so much that the trust necessary for negotiation cannot be restored. Anthony Oberschall declares, "Because protracted conflict keeps creating derivative issues, factionalizes opponents, destroys trust, invites outside intervention, and brings to power hard-liners and extremists, the conclusion from my analysis is that the chances of conciliation diminish with the duration of the conflict."[11] Culture and psychology help explain how groups fall into these traps, to be sure, but strategic interaction also plays an independent role. Other stalemates, however, are precisely what one side intended, as incinerators or nuclear plants do not get built. Strategy is based on timing, and delay is one of the most important strategies.

Strategy, as "a pattern in a stream of decisions or actions,"[12] permeates the actions of protest groups, even before they interact with opponents. Thus observers speak of "recruitment strategies," through which recruiters interact with potential supporters. I avoid such usages when the main purpose is communication and cooperation within the group or potential group. I prefer to restrict the term to interactions with outsiders, the main purpose of which is more instrumental manipulation. Communication can be part of this strategy, but in this case it is usually a means to some other end. In strategic interaction, the means/ends distinction, so favored by rationalists, operates. In other words, alongside the *discursive* function of protest movements is a *strategic* function, and the two are often in conflict. Thus we avoid the danger of reducing everything to strategy.

Timing is subtly crucial to many strategies. In some cases an immediate reaction is the most effective one, before a sudden window of opportunity closes again. In others delay is an enormous advantage, especially if it lulls one's opponents into complacency. Strategies that rely on surprise of any kind require perfect timing. Giving others little time to think keeps them off balance. Responses to the actions of others mean or imply different things depending on how quickly they are forthcoming. One sends signals about one's own feelings and intentions through the timing of actions as well as though the actions themselves.

Strategies interact with resources, biography, and culture in many ways during a protest campaign. The initial distribution of resources and pre-existing cultural meanings are part of the starting point for the interactions between protestors, their opponents, the state, and others. Plentiful resources may help protestors promulgate cultural meanings and consider a wider range of strategies. Effective strategies can in turn accumulate more resources and further disseminate favorable cultural meanings. Or one's own resources can be rendered obsolete by a shift in tactics by opponents. To take advantage of opponents' blunders and vulnerabilities, protestors must define them that way, convince people that an activity is wrong, and respond effectively. Culture not only helps shape the definition and distribution of resources, it also sets limits to strategic repertories through know-how, tactical tastes and identities, virtuosity, and learning processes. In the heat of strategic interaction, furthermore, psychological traits of decision makers (derived from biography) are vitally important, as any student of warfare knows.

Learning, in all its biographical and cultural complexity, is the heart of strategy. Since strategic success involves rapid responses to the actions of opponents and other players, it depends on the ability to learn from one's own mistakes or, even better, from those of others. This rapidly changing game context poses difficulties and opportunities. Speaking of formal organizations, Richard Scott says it is "difficult . . . for organizational systems to learn anything useful, given a rapidly changing environment, selective attention and inattention processes, enactment processes, inertia, cognitive limits, and ambiguity of feedback."[13] The same uncertainties and challenges provide political actors with opportunities for virtuosity and surprise in complex conflicts. The same factors that make conflict unpredictable increase the importance of the players' artful skills. Culture shapes the broad repertory of available moves, but biography and psychology help explain the creativity and brilliance (or stupidity and pathology) of individual decision makers.

In his chronicle of the civil rights movement, Pat Watters gives an example of the subtle complexity of strategic choices, although in this case the strategy was directed partly at fellow protestors. Dr. Martin Luther King Jr. had come to Albany, Georgia to preach one night only.

In the ecstasy and fervor of that meeting, just after the crowd had sung "We Shall Overcome," the young doctor who was supposed to give a short benediction to end the meeting suddenly called for a large march the following morning. King could hardly leave that night, as he had planned. Instead he stayed to lead the march, was arrested, and thus became committed to the Albany Movement, bringing needed media attention. The local physician had made a quick tactical decision (although it may have only seemed spontaneous to everyone else) aimed not only at the local authorities but also at Dr. King. Planned or unplanned, it was a virtuosic move.[14]

Like the other dimensions of protest, the concept of strategy can be overextended. Protestors can be seen as pure strategists with no raw materials to work on: no cultural meanings to respond to, no beliefs or moral visions they are pursuing, no biographical quirks or passions, no tactical tastes to satisfy. Game theories often make this reduction. Political process approaches sometimes do, mostly by making protestors into pure strategic actors without cultural traditions or moral values, who hope only to win. Doug McAdam's "cognitive liberation," for example, is primarily an assessment that success is possible, not a reworking of goals or hopes.

CONDITIONS AND CHOICES

All parties to a conflict make strategic choices in response to existing conditions and the strategic choices of others. Each side tries to take advantage of its own strengths and its opponents' weaknesses. Preeminent among existing conditions are, of course, the distributions of resources and of cultural meanings. One's choices are also shaped by the play, and can have positive or negative consequences depending on how other players respond. Few moves are "game stoppers" that allow a final tally of successes and failures (although state repression is often a game stopper); at most stages in an ongoing conflict, only a provisional scoring is possible. Table 13.1 presents a schematic typology of existing conditions and strategic choices. I reserve the terms *strength* and *vulnerability* for pre-existing conditions (even if they are only brought to light during the controversy), and use *blunder* and *virtuosic move* for actions taken in response to other players' strategies. Both vulnerabilities and blunders can occur at the level of the entire organization—for example, in its official response to controversy—or at the sublevel of the project or activity under attack—for example, a particular research experiment or laboratory. Although the line separating pre-existing conditions from choices results mostly from one's

Table 13.1   Conditions and Choices That Affect Conflicts

	Conditions	Choices
Negative	*Vulnerabilities:* proposed destruction of popular site; lack of obvious public benefits; environmental impact; criticism by external experts; reputation for sloppy management, unsafe practices, previous controversies; weak financial position; internal cleavages or frictions; failure to perform according to organization's own stated standards or goals	*Blunders:* deception, arrogance by spokespersons or other officials; brutal repression of peaceful protest; inability to communicate with the public or news media
Positive	*Strengths:* reverse of the above; strong finances, credibility, and so on.	*Virtuosic Moves:* ability to portray oneself sympathetically; taking opponents by surprise; maintenance of pre-existing strengths

arbitrary choice of starting point (and of course choices once made become conditions), the demarcation between positive and negative is the result of considerable struggle. Your opponents work hard to make your choices into blunders and your conditions into vulnerabilities. You work against this. Some of these efforts are harder than others: it is difficult—although never impossible—to put a positive spin on public lies that have been revealed, or on unprovoked violence. In general, though, as good trial lawyers know, clever strategies can make vulnerabilities into strengths and vice versa.

In a separate article, trying to highlight the strategic interplay between protestors and their opponents, Jane Poulsen and I examined blunders and vulnerabilities.[15] Certain characteristics or practices of targeted organizations usually make them vulnerable to attacks by protestors. Edward Walsh analyzed the "target vulnerabilities" of General Public Utilities (GPU)—the owner of the Three Mile Island nuclear reactor—during the battle over cleanup and restart of the twin, undamaged reactor.[16] Even after the 1979 accident, GPU's credibility was further undermined when a lawsuit, which the utility itself had filed against the reactor makers, inadvertently revealed GPU's own improper management and falsification of operating data, cheating by reactor operators in examinations for promotions, and leaking steam tubes at the undamaged Unit 1 reactor. Several engineers also charged that the cleanup was not proceeding in a safe manner. These vulnerabilities influenced public opinion, regulators, and elected officials. Vulnerabilities can consist of weak or unstable resources, adverse cultural meanings or public attitudes, internal strategic conflicts, or failure to perform according to publicly stated standards.

Protestors understandably seek targets with project vulnerabilities. National antinuclear organizations cultivated the Diablo Canyon reactor as a symbol of nuclear energy, because it was near an earthquake fault and had extreme cost overruns. Animal activists focus on experiments using cats and dogs because, given public tastes in pets, they evoke more outrage than research using rats. Once an organization is spotlighted by protest, its activities are closely watched, and problems unconnected with the controversy can be uncovered. Its general reputation for competence and credibility can be undermined, indirectly providing fuel for its critics. As process and mobilization theorists have seen so well, disagreements between elites may yield an institutional vulnerability by isolating the target from potential supporters.

Protest groups have symmetric vulnerabilities. The most common are the lack of financial resources for sustained activity, and the pursuit of goals not widely appreciated by the public. But a reputation for dishonesty, intimidation, or violence might also undermine the group, as would internal factions or a leader with a reputation for dubious morals. As soon as we go beyond resources that can be purchased in markets, the effects of all these factors depend on the audience. Macho posturing—the Black Panthers come to mind—might get a group in trouble with the police but attract new recruits. Dramatic actions might gain Greenpeace additional contributions from sympathizers, but repel the broader public. Every action or statement has multiple audiences that need to be balanced carefully. Vulnerabilities often arise when actions and statements intended for one audience (supporters, say) are fed to other audiences with different sensibilities (such as the public). Vulnerabilities must usually be interpreted and exploited by opponents to have an effect.

In addition to pre-existing (and relatively passive) vulnerabilities, protestors and targeted organizations actively deploy, in the course of battle, a range of strategies and tactics that may be either wise or mistaken. Each side attempts to goad opponents into mistakes, reduce its own pre-existing vulnerabilities, and avoid blunders. Many vulnerabilities are revealed during this interaction; they can be seen as "accidents" revealing intentions and power structures that institutions often try to hide.[17] A strategic blunder can weaken an organization's reputation for competence, honesty, or benevolence. A classic case is Eugene "Bull" Connor's ferocious attacks on peaceful civil rights demonstrators in Birmingham, Alabama; transmitted through the news media, they created national sympathy for the demonstrators. More generally, Steven Barkan found that southern communities which responded to civil rights protest with violence were less successful at defeating it than those using legal means.[18] Impassioned emotional responses by individuals (driven by biography and psychology) can become blunders for their group or movement (in the strategic dimension). Blunders become new issues to be added to the original causes for protest. The "game," and often the audiences, may shift from the original grievance to issues of fairness or procedure.[19] As Alinsky put it, "The real action is in the enemy's reaction. The enemy properly goaded and guided in his reaction will be your major strength."[20]

Blunders, like vulnerabilities, are not objectively given but must be defined as mistakes or problems. We can borrow from Erving Goffman's description of the work that goes into individual statuses. "A status, a position, a social place is not a material thing, to be possessed and then displayed; it is a pattern of appropriate conduct, coherent, embellished, and well articulated. Performed with ease or clumsiness, awareness or not, guile or good faith, it is none the less something that must be enacted and portrayed, something that must be realized."[21] Actions must be portrayed and accepted as blunders in order to have the effect of blunders.

Blunders and vulnerabilities commonly result from the exposure of a contradiction. An organization or group acts contrary to its own explicit statements, purposes, or rules, or against its implicit rules, such as the professional ethics of employees.[22] This "immanent" critique is not the only kind, though. An organization may be shown to be out of sync with the ethical expectations of the broader society—for instance, that police do not let dogs attack schoolchildren. Such norms are not always clear, and much of the activity of protesters and their opponents is aimed at defining them in advantageous ways.

Credibility, often portrayed vaguely as a resource, is a complex result of institutional affiliations, group memberships, and past actions. The main reason we attribute credibility to an individual or institution is that we have observed and been reassured by their past behavior. Yet past experience is not the only influence on our expectations. All humans employ stereotypes to judge credibility: one might, for instance, systematically doubt corporate PR representatives, trust environmental groups, and give the benefit of the doubt to members of oppressed racial or ethnic groups. These judgments are affective and moral as much as cognitive. An individual's affiliations and characteristics often substitute for a complete track record of her own actions. In addition, credibility is a feature of an entire organization or individual, so that its loss in one area taints others. To quote Goffman again, as the pre-eminent scholar of impression management, "[A] false impression maintained by an individual in any one of his routines may be a threat to the whole relationship or role of which the routine is only one part, for a discreditable disclosure in one area of an individual's activity will throw doubt on the many areas of activity in which he may have nothing to conceal."[23]

Yet, as philosopher Sissela Bok has shown, lies can occasionally be justified. One might lie to one's enemies, who are "hostile and capable of coercion through force, threats of force, or deception." They "have forfeited the ordinary right of being dealt with fairly."[24] Lying to them is justified because defeating such foes is all-important, as in war. Such a strategy overlooks or rejects other possible audiences for one's actions and statements, audiences who are likely to frown on deception. As Bok puts it, "[T]hose who lie to enemies out of a conviction that justice allows it fail to take into account the effects of the lies on themselves as agents, on others who may be affected, and on general trust."[25] Hot struggles ensue over which of these effects a public lie will have.

By themselves, few actions are indubitable blunders, and few practices are unquestionable vulnerabilities. Mostly, these are raw materials that are further framed and interpreted. Protestors must persuade the public that an accident or a decision was a mistake, just as corporations blame accidents on individuals, on "human error," leaving their technologies and organizations blameless. Even mistakes are constructed.

CONFLICT AS CULTURAL LEARNING

Just as protesters learn from each other, so their opponents share words, images, and tactics—often more explicitly than protesters do. Whether an organization attacked by protestors reacts effectively or poorly frequently depends on the experiences of similar organizations that have been attacked or which perceive themselves at risk of attack. When a critical mass of organizations feel threatened, they may organize a countermovement. Existing professional or trade associations can serve as countermovement organizations, giving aid to targeted individuals and institutions, coordinating their responses, providing resources, and sharing information about effective strategies and tactics. Counterorganizations help their affiliates hide pre-existing vulnerabilities and avoid blunders; on their own they frequently search for the vulnerabilities (especially in public opinion) of protest groups.

Doug McAdam suggests that social-movement success depends on whether the movement or its opponents mobilize more rapidly and effectively, and on each side's tactical inventiveness.[26] William Gamson argues that counterorganization is more immediate if a social movement explicitly names its target. Others believe that social-movement successes spur countermobilization, unless they are "crushing victories."[27] This leads to a frequent pattern in which a movement wins some surprising early victories that it cannot repeat when it grows larger. For example, the early successes of the pro-ERA movement aroused a broad backlash, because the issue "provided a link with fundamentalist churches" and "mobilized a group, traditional homemakers, that had lost status over the two previous decades and was feeling the psychological effects of the loss."[28] The pro-choice movement, too, according to Suzanne Staggenborg, "achieved its most spectacular victory—the legalization of abortion in 1973—before pro-choice forces became very well organized or powerful."[29] In these cases, like that of the antinuclear movement (and, we'll see, the animal rights movement), the development of a movement identity out of scattered protest provided the moral shock, threat, and focus of blame to spur the targets of protest into mobilizing in response, reducing movement victories.

"Countermovements" have often been treated as distinct from other social movements. Sometimes they are organized by large institutions or industries under threat, lacking much grassroots flavor. Their funding, as a result, is typically stronger and more stable. They are often designed to attack protest groups, as with lawsuits, a practice so common it has its own acronym, SLAPP, for strategic lawsuits against public participation.[30] Other countermovements are efforts to undo the effects of previous social movements, as with the backlash against women's rights, in which case they operate like any other protest against existing conditions. In either case, from the analysis of the conflict as a whole, movements and countermovements are generally symmetrical.

Movements and countermovements contest each other's interpretations and frames. We can return to whistleblowing to see the cultural framing at stake in strategic competition, for here we see a contest over what the controversy is all about. Commonly, the organizations and industries attacked by whistleblowers respond by framing the act of whistleblowing itself as a problem that is due to aberrant or "troubled" persons, rather than to a troubled industry or society.[31] This counter-claim paints whistleblowers as disgruntled employees with a psychological propensity to complain, as alarmists with their own political agendas, or as publicity seekers. The whistleblower's own biography becomes contested terrain. Personalizing social problems is a common institutional tactic, as Joseph Gusfield says in a related context: "If the condition is perceived as that of individual illness or deficiency, then there can be a social technology, a form of knowledge and skill, that can be effectively learned. That knowledge is the mandate for a profession's license to 'own' [its] social problem."[32] This framing deflects blame from industries, as when the poor judgment of individuals, not unsafe automobiles or the lack of public transportation, is blamed for drunk-driving fatalities. Industries always blame problems on human error, not their own technologies.

The whistleblower naturally rejects the "troubled person" frame, for example, reinterpreting the employer's hostility as further evidence of the corruption of the system, so that retaliation becomes an additional grievance against the whistleblower's (often former) employer. Yet a whistleblower partly accepts the refocusing on whistleblowing as the issue when she criticizes not only the original abuse but her treatment after pointing out the abuse. The focus is then on the practice of whistleblowing and its handling rather than on the practice the whistleblower first criticized. If the debate shifts from the original complaint to the treatment of the whistleblower, the testimony of an earnest individual about the abuse she received from her supervisors can still be stirring and convincing, for she can portray herself sympathetically as a "blameless victim."[33] Some of the whistleblower's most emotionally powerful rhetoric, in fact, describes the retaliation she receives.

In a very different setting, Rick Fantasia and Eric Hirsch provide an interesting example of a cultural object—Algerian women's veils—whose meaning was reworked as part of the strategic interaction between a revolutionary movement and its colonial opponents. Because the French tried to "Westernize" Algerian women by discouraging the veil, it naturally grew into a symbol of resistance: "Whether women would be veiled or unveiled was not determined on an abstract ideological scale (in terms of neither revolutionary ideology nor Islamic law) but was made as a series of strategic decisions that were determined as much by the actions of the opponent as by the movement itself."[34] Cultural meanings and practices become strategic weapons.

Just as the Algerian liberation movement became more Islamic because of state actions, so many movement identities are reshaped during strategic interaction with their opponents. In a constant symbolic struggle, the members of each side try to convey to the public an image of their opponents as well as of themselves. And each side takes steps to emphasize how it differs from its opponents—as Marx recognized when he argued that class consciousness arises out of class conflict. *You know who you are because you know who you are not.* Strategies affect the meanings, interests, identities, and even the goals of protestors themselves.

Over time the complex interplay among movement and countermovement groups often settles into rigid patterns, as each side learns what it can about favorable moves, innovates or fends off opponents' innovations, then settles into a standard repertory of tactics (often shaped by a tension between tactical tastes and strategic needs for innovation). Animosities and paranoia build during long conflicts, often to the extent that they interfere with strategic action. For example, according to conflict theorist Morton Deutsch, "The claim to inherent superiority (whether it be of legitimacy, morality, authority, ability, knowledge, or relevance) by one or another side in a conflict makes it less likely that a conflict will be resolved cooperatively."[35] There are situations in which negotiation and compromise, although the best strategy, are precluded by emotions and symbolic meanings. Punishing one's opponents becomes a new goal partly displacing the original ones. As Deutsch warns, "Destructive conflict is characterized by a tendency to expand and escalate. As a result, such conflict often becomes independent of its initiating causes and is likely to continue after these have become irrelevant or have been forgotten."[36] These are the equilibrium traps that game theorists love. In some cases only a new generation of leaders can break the stalemate.

Movements and countermovements are networks for strategic and tactical creativity. One learns from allies, but also through interactions with opponents. Small innovations, especially in the application of tactics, spread. This is *cultural* learning because the results are changes in shared ways of thinking and acting. Unstable and changing situations force groups to adapt, even when they innovate within a small range of tactical tastes or moral values. As we saw in chapter 10, though, small steps may inspire the formation of new groups willing to take larger steps.

CATS, MONKEYS, AND OSTRICHES

A pair of cases from the animal rights conflict will help us see how organizations learn strategies from each other.[37] In 1987, in response to pressure from an animal rights group named Trans-Species Unlimited, a researcher at the Cornell Medical School in Manhattan returned her federal funding for a long-running cat experiment on drug addiction. From 1988 to 1990 the same group, using the same tactics, failed in its efforts to stop drug-addiction experiments on monkeys at New York University. Both campaigns attacked institutions located in Manhattan and experiments involving higher-order mammals—cats and monkeys—for which there is widespread public sympathy.

The animal rights movement was at its peak size and visibility in the late 1980s. New groups had formed, especially from 1981 to 1985, partly inspired by several notorious challenges to animal experiments, including a 1981 case in Silver Spring that resulted in the indictment of the principal investigator and a 1984 case in which grisly videotapes were taken from a trauma research lab at the University of Pennsylvania. In the years after 1985, several hundred thousand people joined these new groups. Trans-Species Unlimited (TSU) was founded in 1981 in Eastern Pennsylvania, and its largely autonomous New York City chapter grew to be its largest. Each November it held a march down Fifth Avenue on "Fur-Free Friday"—usually led by Bob ("For fur, the price is never right") Barker. Each spring it targeted a local scientific research project, and in 1987 it selected one at the Cornell Medical College (located in Manhattan, not the main campus in Ithaca).

The Cornell experiments, funded by the National Institute on Drug Abuse (NIDA), examined the effects of barbiturates on cats by means of electrodes implanted in the animals' skulls. A pharmacology professor had been conducting this work since 1973 on around two hundred cats. Animal activists often target drug-addiction research, on the grounds that the money should go to help real human addicts instead. The use of a popular species made the project vulnerable to public opinion. On the other hand, the experiments had the full support of the funding agency and the medical school administration—there were no obvious institutional vulnerabilities.

The campaign began with a protest outside the school on 24 April 1987, World Day for Laboratory Animals. Roughly 350 people demonstrated, and 56 were arrested for civil disobedience. TSU benefited from the growing animal rights activism not only through the publicity surrounding World Day for Laboratory Animals, but also by networking with 65 other organizations to generate phone calls and letters of protest. NIDA received over 10,000 written protests, and 80 Congressional offices made inquiries. Several scientists—involved in the national animal rights movement as counterexperts—drafted a critique of the experiments, arguing that because the cat was a poor model for human barbiturate dependence, the research had no relevance for treating addicts.

Cornell officials made several surprising moves that added up to a fatal blunder. In August they met with TSU President George Cave and science advisor Murray Cohen (adviser to many animal rights groups around the country). According to Cave, the officials said that the "experiments were over," and that the renewal grant, approved in May, would not be used. He cited a letter, drafted by a Cornell committee and sent to legislators and the media with the signature of the associate dean for sponsored programs at the medical school. While defending the pharmacologist's research, the letter ambiguously said, "The research . . . that required the use of the cat model has essentially been completed." TSU claimed victory.

Two months later the researcher applied to NIDA for a renewal grant to continue the cat studies and develop an experimental model using rats. The proposal, cosigned by the dean who had sent out the earlier letter, was funded. When TSU learned of this, it renewed its letter-writing campaign, insisting that Cornell had lied. The school was paralyzed. Personally harassed, with little support from Cornell, the researcher returned the grant money in September 1988. Cornell officials said that this was done to preserve "institutional credibility" and also that it was the investigator's own personal decision. The university itself temporarily funded her research, which turned to rats as experimental models.

This was the most prominent scientific experiment (and one of the only ones) stopped by the animal rights movement. It may also have been the last. The case was a strong moral shock for the research community, which was just becoming aware of the "movement identity" of animal rights advocates. Angry scientists around the country wrote to Cornell, arguing that the university had a responsibility to protect researchers from "extremists," and that Cornell's decision was a "disastrous precedent." Even NIDA attacked the university's "ostrich-like stance" and hinted that the decision might affect future funding. The fact that a major private university had stopped an ongoing research project galvanized the biomedical community. New organizations were founded to defend the use of animals in research. Professional associations began discussing tactics for countering the animal rights movement and counseling research institutions to take unyielding positions. This activity was accelerated by the Cornell case. Driven by a sense of threat, a vigorous countermovement rapidly formed to fight the animal rights movement.

Believing it had already won the Cornell campaign, TSU targeted the New York University medical school in the spring of 1988. The experiments in this case involved macaque monkeys (like cats, a popular species), which were taught to inhale toluene, a common industrial solvent used in glues and paints. The purpose was to understand the effects of toluene in early stages of use, since children and teens occasionally sniff toluene for pleasure. Also supported by NIDA, a professor of environmental medicine was conducting the experiments forty miles north of NYU's Manhattan campus.

TSU's campaign against NYU resembled the Cornell protest, with pickets in front of the NYU library and administration building, and extensive letter writing to legislators and NYU officials. In April 1988 (when the survey described in chapter 7 was conducted) and again in April 1989, nearly 1,000 demonstrators participated, compared to 350 in the 1987 Cornell protest. TSU did not even try to talk with NYU administrators as it had in the Cornell campaign.

TSU had little effect on NYU's programs. Although leaders claimed some success because the campaign mobilized new supporters and attracted media coverage, the experiments were not changed in any significant way (beyond tighter security measures). TSU put little effort into organizing the second (1989) rally. After their failure to influence NYU in 1988, many TSU members turned their attention to other animal issues, and the TSU meeting just before the 1989 NYU protest gave more time to furs than to the NYU action. In April 1990 there was no protest against NYU. TSU's campaign was effectively over.[38]

From the start, NYU's response to the campaign was aggressively "proactive." The principal investigator was sent off for intensive public relations training so that he could more smoothly face the media, although professional public relations officers took over most tasks of interacting with the news media. The day before each protest, in a virtuosic move, NYU held a press conference to praise both the targeted experiments and scientific research in general. In 1988 this meeting centered on a sick eight-year-old and his mother, both with down-home Kentucky accents. The boy was a victim of a blood vessel tumor that trapped white cells and prevented blood coagulation, and scientists claimed he would not be alive except for procedures developed through animal experimentation. He and his mother proclaimed their love for animals, but also their gratitude that some animals were sacrificed to save people. Most of the news coverage of the next day's protest included sympathetic clips from this conference.

In the battle over public opinion NYU had found an emotional appeal to match that of furry animals caged and victimized, and its reaction reduced the vulnerability of the project. It could contest protestors' framing of NYU as a heartless bureaucracy guilty of instrumental rationality.

NYU's tactics came to be recognized as the most effective response to animal rights attacks. Around the country, slick PR officials replaced scientists as spokespersons, accompanied by normal Americans (especially children) who had been helped by biomedical research. Only especially charismatic scientists, well coached, were now allowed in front of television cameras. An association named incurably ill for Animal Research (iiFAR) provided extremely dedicated and powerful speakers. Scientists were humanized, portrayed as kindly family doctors or the next-door neighbor. Animal rights activists could be portrayed as a misguided or even misanthropic radical fringe, who were secretly taking over existing animal protection societies with large endowments. Again and again, poignant emotional appeals accompanied hardball efforts to undermine the credibility of one's opponents. Each side portrayed the other as rich, malevolent, and powerful, a blameworthy threat.

Funding agencies were another audience for NYU's actions. NYU was well aware that NIDA, the funding agency for both the Cornell and the NYU experiments, had disapproved of Cornell's capitulation. Moreover, the scientific response and the counterorganization following the Cornell case had strengthened the resistance of other universities to animal rights protests. The message was clear to NYU, which ignored the demonstrators and courted funders and the public. NYU officials worked out their strategy after observing the Cornell incident and dozens of similar controversies around the country. Trade associations and professional groups, through telephone networks, newsletters, and meetings, spread information about effective responses to protestors.

Cornell and NYU may be seen as endpoints in a continuum from defensive and reactive to positive and proactive responses, and research institutions drew lessons from these and similar experiences. As state and national organizations of scientists spread information about tactics, targeted institutions became increasingly likely to adopt the proactive response that had worked for NYU. The result was even fewer victories for animal rights campaigns. The stronger the movement identity for animal rights, the greater the perceived threat, moral shock, and outrage in the research community, leading in turn to more determined resistance.

CULTURAL STRATEGIES

The outcomes of these two controversies differed partly because of Cornell's blunder, its apparent prevarication, but TSU had to frame this as a blunder, insisting on its outrageousness. When the campaign began, Cornell's position seemed strong, and TSU viewed it that way. The targeted research had practical applications, even though it involved a popular species. Cornell is a private research university more dependent on government funding and alumni support than the goodwill of the general public. The funding agency had no desire to stop the experiments; in fact it strongly favored their continuation. But the medical school made strategic mistakes in dealing with the protestors. Its public relations representatives were relatively inactive, instead of trying to shape public impressions. Perhaps they thought that the protestors would go away if palliated with vague promises, or that they were too weak to force Cornell to stick to its apparent promise, or that they simply would not know if the experiment continued. Having made verbal and written assurances implying the research would end, Cornell could be shamed into keeping them. In a series of direct and indirect contacts, TSU kept Cornell off balance.

Although its project used appealing animals, NYU managed to minimize its vulnerabilities and blunders. It worked to maintain its strong position by trying to defuse media attention through its own emotional appeals. A nine-person public relations office at the NYU medical school, with long experience in animal controversies (NYU had been attacked by other animal rights groups in 1979 and 1986), made a difference. Beyond that, the university tried to avoid misleading public statements. It sent the targeted researcher to a media training school, in order to avoid embarrassments in the form of misstatements at press conferences. TSU found few existing vulnerabilities, and could trigger no blunders.

The contrasting responses of Cornell and NYU, only a year apart, reflected a change in the rapidly unfolding animal rights controversy, for the audiences and strategies of protest groups and their targets often change as conflicts mature. As public awareness and media coverage grow, both sides tend to seek favorable public opinion. By 1988 the protestors and NYU representatives were unwilling to talk to each other, although NYU had negotiated with other demonstrators as recently as 1986. Instead, both sides believed themselves part of a symbolic battle for the uncommitted public.

For the animal rights movement, the growth of a national controversy encouraged this expansive strategy. A national network, movement identity, and the spread of organizational know-how and tactical innovation helped animal rights organizations mobilize members and accumulate funds. Photographs and videotapes taken from laboratories were widely distributed and proved to be effective recruiting devices. However, expansion of the controversy also spurred counter-mobilization by scientists. The emergence of a movement identity for animal activists heightened the scientists' sense of threat and provided someone to blame. Targeted research groups began to amass resources, share tactical information and expertise, and develop strategic sophistication with which to counterattack. The victory against Cornell was a moral shock that demanded attention. The subsequent counterorganization successfully showed future targets how to avoid blunders in resisting animal rights campaigns. No fewer than nineteen state-level groups were established in the late 1980s to defend biomedical research by sharing information about tactics. The head of the Alcohol, Drug Abuse, and Mental Health Administration, Frederick Goodwin, decided to attend NYU's 1989 press conference himself, announcing, "They succeeded at Cornell. They got the higher levels of the university to worry about contributions from alumni. They got bad publicity. So the researcher gave up the grant; taxpayers' money was wasted. And this really got the attention of the scientific community. I don't think they're going to pull that off again. I don't think NYU is going to do that. I don't think Cornell would do that again. I think we all learned a very tough lesson."

What happened in the animal rights controversy paralleled developments in nuclear energy. Early protestors were occasionally able to catch their targets off guard and win local victories. As the conflicts spread nationally, countermovements developed, and resistance hardened. The most effective tactics spread on both sides, thereby becoming predictable and less effective. The two industries' resources and political clout enabled them, eventually, to fend off most direct attacks. And yet the way Americans think about nuclear energy and about animals was broadly, and perhaps permanently, transformed. Other movement goals came to the fore.

AUDIENCES, STRATEGIES, GOALS

Protestors, we saw, have varying goals: changes in corporate or state policy, transformations of public sentiments, the personal growth of protestors themselves. They hold multiple goals simultaneously, their goals change over time, and individual protestors may have diverse goals within a movement. Every action and statement has several different audiences, from whom protestors hope for different outcomes. A group may want its financial supporters to recognize its effectiveness, state officials to see its capacity for disruption, and members of the public to observe efforts at compromise. Recall table 12.1, which listed several possible audiences and the goals protestors may have with regard to them.

Protestors would like to reach different audiences by different means, thus controlling the messages that each receives. More public statements have a different tone and intent than more intimate ones.[39] A group might especially like to have a backstage for candid internal discussions among participants who have proven their loyalty. Such efforts often fail, because of informants or the media, so that the same statements and actions are transmitted to multiple audiences. Opponents are always looking for contradictions between the messages broadcast to different audiences, permitting accusations of bad faith. The animal rights movement, for instance, was accused of arguing for reform in public but "really" wanting abolition—as though it were dishonest to moderate one's demands in public debates. This is one reason that, within a movement, different groups often cultivate different audiences: moderates lobby Congress, while radicals carry on direct actions that appeal to hard-core supporters. Yet in most cases they must appeal to the same members of the public for financial support.

Although rhetoric is traditionally about the relationship between speaker and audience, political analysts rarely study its dynamics. Not only the public statements, but also the actions of protestors are designed to send messages to various audiences, including the protestors themselves. Insisting that action and texts can be read in similar ways, Kenneth Burke argued that identification with an action or actor was crucial to successful rhetoric, just as Snow and Benford talk about resonance.[40] But audiences can have a variety of responses to the same message: fear, admiration, envy, outrage, intimidation. It is useful although difficult to sort out the audiences and messages, intended and unintended, in protest actions, but that is necessary for understanding the full strategic game.

Multiple goals allow trade-offs. Strategic metaphors of wars and games tend to downplay the negotiation and communication that occur (sometimes indirectly) in most political conflicts. A recent effort to focus social-movement research on strategic interaction is the "bargaining perspective" of Paul Burstein, Rachel Einwohner, and Jocelyn Hollander, which has affinities with game theory in the assumption that "participation is rational . . . only if [it] can lead to success." For this expectation to be reasonable, "social movements must succeed fairly often, and their achievements must depend at least partly on factors subject to participants' control."[41] Bargaining is a form of strategic interaction in which concessions are rewarded; whether this happens depends on surrounding political structures and the goals of the various actors (especially the state). When a group pursues many goals, failure in some arenas can be balanced by success in others.

We can now see how success in specific campaigns can hurt longer-term success for a protest movement as a whole. In the absence of state repression, a movement may attain early gains.[42] But these may in turn inspire even more rapid and energetic countermobilization. Then, as the controversy matures, protest groups may attend more to convincing the broader public about their cause than to specific short-term goals. For instance, future success for the animal rights movement may come through federal regulations and policies, not from stopping individual experiments. Scientific institutions have reduced their vulnerabilities by improving the conditions of laboratory animals. Such successes (tighter federal regulations, institutional animal care and use committees) may prevent the animal rights movement from attaining more sweeping goals such as the abolition of certain categories of experiments or (as sought by some) of all live-animal experiments. In this case, the movement simply has partly contradictory goals (reform versus abolition). Audiences shift with strategies. Yet it remains an open question whether mild success dampens a movement's fervor or encourages even more radical demands.

Additional research is necessary to uncover more complex relationships between different forms of social-movement success. Perhaps some kinds of early victories do not lead to countermobilization, for example, decisive ones or imperceptible ones.[43] Some kinds of blunders may be especially difficult for a countermovement to suppress, for example, when institutional responses are multiple and decentralized or when elites themselves are divided over the proper response.

In the 1970s, mobilization explanations of movement success typically concentrated on the characteristics, resources, and strategies of social-movement organizations and their supporters. Mobilization was itself a kind of success, and was thought to lead to others. Political process approaches shifted attention to state institutions, with their power to tax and spend, and to use violence to repress protest. Because protestors were viewed as insurgents demanding access to the polity, the state was naturally their pre-eminent opponent. In other cases, the state was important because it set the ground rules for protest and conflict. Others simply assumed that movement goals ultimately involved changes in state policies. Images of the state as perpetrator, rulemaker, or problem-solver imply different goals and tactics on the part of protestors, but many models assume the state is all three (as it is for citizenship movements).

The common assumption that the state is "simultaneously target, sponsor, and antagonist for social movements as well as the organizer of the political system and the arbiter of victory" has led to the truism that more disruptive movements are more likely to attain their goals.[44] Riots were to the civil rights movement what sit-down strikes were to the labor movement. The state must intervene, either firmly repressing a movement or granting concessions. This argument works well for the citizenship movements most studied by process theorists, but perhaps not as well for the many recent movements aimed at public awareness or cultural change, media sympathy or agenda-setting, and participant self-transformation. The target and opponent of many protest movements is not the state, but other actors in civil society. For these movements, which are not automatically repressed by the state, a small amount of action can yield substantial results. An incipient movement can be very successful. In the cases we have seen, one reason for the early success was that audiences were still limited: one electric utility rather than the whole industry; state regulators rather than the U.S. Congress or the president; and few members of the public or the news media. With the whole biomedical community watching it, NYU took a tougher stance than Cornell had. The balance between challenging the political status quo and appealing to widespread cultural sensibilities may tip in different directions for different movements and groups.

The question of success is challenging, I have said, because each protest movement pursues several goals at the same time. Even state-oriented objectives may vary. Burstein and his coauthors discern six types of policy effects: access to legislators and policymakers, agenda-setting for legislators, intended policies, implementation or enforcement of those policies, achievement of the intended impact, and structural changes to the political system. Although they see these as representing increasing degrees of success, different strategies may be appropriate for each.[45] Even within the state, audiences vary somewhat according to each of these goals.

Other goals do not involve the state much at all. The anti-Diablo protestors, we saw, were concerned with maintaining their subculture as well as with shutting down the reactor. Most movements leave behind some broader impact on activist identities and cultures.[46] Many battles also have wider symbolic importance; the Cornell campaign transformed the national animal rights movement and the scientists' countermovement. If different forms of success imply different audiences for protest, even movements that fail to attain their stated goals can affect their society's recognition and framing of important issues. The local victories that dried up for the antinuclear and animal rights movements may have been less significant, finally, than the shifts in public sensibilities. The strategic arena, audience, and rhetoric shifted as the public became more attentive to the issues of nuclear energy and animal protection. At the same time, those early victories were memorable symbolic events that helped shape public awareness of the controversy and what it meant.

Different forms of success have different explanations. Above all, what makes for successful mobilization of a movement sometimes has little to do with what helps that movement attain its goals. Resources, strategies, biography, and culture, in various mixtures, help explain all forms of success. Resources are perhaps most important for influencing the courts and state agencies, and least important for changing movement members. Strategies may be most important in interactions with opponents, and perhaps potential allies. Culture probably has its greatest causal effect in determining whether a movement's own members, the bystander public, and perhaps the media are moved in desired ways. Biography helps explain the responses of key decision makers. But all four are at work in all the arenas.

Social-movement scholars regularly search for policy effects of the movements they study, but settle for institutionalization as a form of success. Almost no social movements fully attain their stated goals; few enough manage to survive as organizations. Yet even organizational failure can hide considerable cultural influence.[47] Most scholars bemoan this as second-best, but I see diffuse cultural impacts as an important goal, one of the most important contributions of protest movements. I would guess that citizenship movements more easily change legal statuses than cultural stereotypes (one of the lessons of the civil rights movement), while post-citizenship movements are more concerned with, and better at, changing cultural sensibilities.

ARTFUL STRATEGIES

Tactical and strategic choices are complex, learned actions, and so they have a deep cultural side. Not only are they conditioned by emotions, cognitions, and moral visions, but the choices made are cultural repertories in action. Virtuosi have sufficient command of their local political cultures that they can play with or against the grain of traditions, sometimes fulfilling and other times dashing expectations. And strategic and tactical innovations spread like any other new idea or piece of information.

If there were no cultural content or context of strategies, game theorists might be able to plot conflicts with greater accuracy. But with some exceptions (polarized standoffs are often equilibria), the game is too complex for much prediction. Most game theorists concentrate on endpoints, without saying much about how players get there, especially subtleties of timing in their unfolding moves. The learning and innovation, attention to multiple audiences, and varied goals of protestors and their opponents add such layers of complexity that we can describe but not predict most strategic interactions. After all, virtuosity consists of coming up with unexpected moves. *As in a chess game, it is sometimes impossible to identify key moves until later. And the importance of many moves depends on whether the players can then capitalize on them.* Alinsky underlined the open-ended nature of strategic choice: "[T]actics are not the product of careful cold reason . . . they do not follow a table of organization or plan of attack. Accident, unpredictable reactions to your own actions, necessity, and improvisation dictate the direction and nature of tactics."[48] And as I said earlier, there is no rule for breaking the rules. Artfulness is crucial here, for people make choices, and those choices matter.

Protestors and their targets think hard about the effects of their initiatives and responses on their opponents as well as on other audiences such as state agencies or the public. If the police think that modest concessions will defuse protest, they may make them. If they think that stonewalling and repression will arouse a public backlash of sympathy for protestors, they will avoid those responses. This is the truth of game theories: each move is made with an eye to the expectations and subsequent reactions of all the other players.

Among other things, protestors want to win, and so strategic choices toward that end are partly independent of other dimensions of protest. They are rooted in the unpredictable dynamics of conflict among many players. Yet in spite of the importance of strategic games, we saw that tactics are never mere neutral means to achieving one's ends. They have value in and of themselves: they can help build solidarity among protestors, prefigure the desired society, offer a variety of pleasures and satisfactions, and represent important moral values such as democracy. Choices reflect movement culture, leader biographies, and available resources as well as purely strategic judgments. Once again, the dimensions of protest intimately affect one another. Having examined the connections of protest movements to the broader society, first in the form of resources, then strategies and success, we can now try to summarize the interactions among the basic dimensions of protest when we are trying to understand movement emergence, strategy, and effects.

- Explanations of movement success must turn to the strategic language of interactive conflict.

- Each side tries to find vulnerabilities in the other, and goad the other into blunders; but vulnerabilities and blunders need to be framed and manipulated as such.
- Protestors' words and deeds are designed for varied audiences, with different goals for each. The state is only one audience, and not even a unified one.
- Strategy, although partly independent of culture, biography, and resources, is closely affected by them.

FOURTEEN

Toward a Balanced Approach

Between the idea
And the reality
Between the motion
And the act
Falls the Shadow.
— T. S. Eliot

Having shown many ways that culture interacts with biography, resources, and strategies, I turn now to a brief effort at synthesis. How
can these four basic dimensions be used together to explain the rise
and fall of protest movements? I hope only to suggest why, at different
phases of research, it might be helpful to look at one dimension or
another, or at intersections between them. I try to avoid assumptions
about logical weight or priority. One easy way to see different configu-
rations of the basic factors explaining protest is to continue the contrast
that has run throughout the book so far between movements for full
citizenship and what I have termed post-citizenship movements. We
have seen that most scholars have examined one type of protest movement, in the process developing theories especially suited to that kind
of movement. By recognizing different kinds of movements, we can
begin to observe what factors make them different. Just as I have
looked at cultural and related processes in movement emergence, in
internal choices and dynamics, and in the external context and effects
of protest movements, I return to these three phases as a way of presenting the questions scholars regularly ask about social movements.

EMERGENCE AND RECRUITMENT

Why does a protest movement arise when it does, and not ten or one
hundred years earlier or later? Some factors are broad, accounting for
now versus one hundred years ago; others are more proximate, explaining why now instead of one or five years earlier. In chapter 7, I
emphasized the broad cultural sensibilities toward animals that allowed the animal-rights movement to arise in the 1980s but not the
1780s. Certain beliefs and feelings about the natural world, consumer

culture, and modern science were important prerequisites, as were emotions such as compassion or sympathy, unease over the treatment of species considered similar to humans, and so on. We should be able to point to the moral intuitions and principles that are being shocked, the identities and practices felt to be threatened. Certain concerns have become possible that were once unimaginable.

In an equally long perspective, there have been historical changes in the resources and strategic capacities to organize protest movements. Charles Tilly has done a great deal to describe how greater residential density, the rise of ever larger cities, and the appearance of factories and other workplaces with vast numbers of workers have all made it easier for people to organize themselves when they wish. Formal procedures for democratic participation have spread across nations and across decision-making arenas. In the decades following the French Revolution, according to William Sewell, new forms of association developed, organized especially around the pursuit of economic interests and so singularly suitable for citizenship movements—a good example of how structural and cultural arrangements go hand in hand.[1] Alongside such efforts and images went the media that transmitted the new ideas and helped construct the new interests. Sidney Tarrow emphasizes the "print revolution" of the late eighteenth and early nineteenth centuries.[2] To explain movements since World War II, one would place equal emphasis on television as a transmitter of political information and cultural sensibilities. More recently computers have aided the inexpensive spread of information. On top of all this, as McCarthy and Zald have explained in their work, has been expanding per capita wealth, so that more and more people have discretionary resources to devote to protest.

Such structures and resources explain the capacity to organize, but say little about what specific movements will be organized—presumably on the assumption that excluded groups have "natural," usually economic, interests. New technological and financial resources and denser community ties are related to culture not only directly through the messages they transmit but indirectly through the altered groupings, identities, and senses of purpose they help inform. Ownership and control of the media, along with control of other resources, influence struggles over such constructions, as do past strategic conflicts.

In addition to general historical shifts, we need to look for more concrete threats, injustice frames, and constructions of blame, whether purveyed by initial activists, the media, or other individuals, as proximate causes. It is these that determine the specific grievances, rhetorical formulations, goals, and identities around which protest will coagulate. Biography and culture can help us understand the interpretive work behind such moments. Events with symbolic implications that go far beyond merely signaling the likelihood of repression are the most common form of moral shock, for they are widely reported and interpreted by the media as well as by individuals. They speak to sensibilities that may have spread but not fully crystallized, hitherto inchoate structures of feeling that they can come to symbolize. Strategic action already enters here, for these triggering events typically result from decisions or other actions on the part of the state, opponents, or other political players. Sometimes movement organizers can even trigger moral shocks through their own appeals. How potential protestors interpret the event or rhetoric will determine whether they help precipitate a movement. We only began, in chapter 5, to explore the psychological and biographical dimensions of threat and blame. Like events, but more consciously, individuals can connote desires and feelings; they can found groups or become charismatic leaders. Biographical traits, for instance special sensitivity to audiences, can help explain whether they do this.

Those traditions based on citizenship movements as exemplars take a somewhat different view, with less emphasis on cultural interpretation, assuming that members of disadvantaged groups are always looking for ways to improve their status. As a result, the key factors allowing the emergence of an active liberation movement have to do with changes in repression and the likelihood of success. What is more, movements of the oppressed, as the term implies, must fight against some level of active disadvantage. Because their disadvantage represents someone else's advantage, protestors are likely to run into resistance from the start. Although the underlying sensibilities, interests, and collective identities of such groups must be constructed over time, they are often taken as given for short time periods. In contrast, postcitizenship movements must typically create their own movement identities and activist networks. This means they can often take their opponents by surprise, even create opponents through their own activity.

Behind these differences among movements lie contrasting combinations of, and interactions between, cultural and other factors. To summarize previous discussions, potential leaders and other protestors must perceive an injustice as well as some opportunity for publicizing and perhaps redressing it. Once the broad cultural prerequisites are in place—once a cause is imaginable—we can search for those individuals most likely to be sensitive to an issue. Here we need both cultural and biographical factors. Cultural meanings are unequally distributed, so there may be particular occupations, regions, sexual preferences, religions, or other practices that predispose some to notice and care more about an issue than others. Cowboys and fishermen would not be the first to care about animal rights, although they might care about animal preservation. We must search for elective affinities between daily practices, cultural meanings, and social issues. Having identified categories of potential sympathizers, biography—properly specified—might help tell us why some of these people notice an issue and others do not, as we examine the selection processes by which certain cultural sensibilities are adopted and others rejected. Psychology is likely to be especially important in accounting for the actions of the first activists for a cause, who began their work before there was a protest movement, before there was a network of like-minded individuals. Threats and moral shocks can only be understood through culture and biography.

Individual acts of protest, more than collective ones, probably require attention to biography, whether that action is setting oneself on fire or seeking out and joining a protest group. We must know the moral principles and intuitions these people respond to. But then we must also set them in a more structural context, just as, for example, some organizational settings are more conducive to whistleblowing than others. Some see an individual action as a reasonable strategy more readily than others do, and it would be helpful at least to gather information about conducive personalities. Even strategic perceptions and choices arise from individual predispositions as well as from the expected actions of others, resource distributions, and past interactions. Few scholars have examined such actions, but they are one path to protest. What is more, such individuals and their actions can, like events, take on a symbolic power that helps inspire others by their example. Their cultural effects can be wildly disproportionate to their numbers.

Other dimensions come into play when we turn to the question of whether the sensitized individuals can pull together a protest movement. Resources, most obviously, play a role at this point, for technical capacities are crucial to spreading a message. Strategic calculations about success are also relevant, in that few are willing to die for their cause, especially when their deaths will have no effect. But such calculations are variable, not automatic as many political process theorists would have it. Whether or not an individual is willing to die for her cause depends on cultural meanings, psychological propensities, as well as a strategic assessment of her death's likely effect. Singular events, such as a Buddhist monk's self-immolation, can have enormous effects if they capture the right cultural sensibilities. It would be useful to develop ways of measuring the symbolic power of events, which is so different from the power of resources. Dimensions of this symbolic power include how many people are familiar with an event, the strength of emotional responses to it, and its ability to symbolize moral and cognitive meanings.

Opportunities, both structural and strategic, are necessary for a protest movement to appear; there must be something to do, after all. Political structures must offer some means of popular input or expression. In the shorter term, special strategic moments appear, if protestors can take advantage of them. Structural opportunities still require cultural schemas and a belief in their feasibility—an aspect of cognitive liberation—before they can be used. Strategic openings require this but also depend on the psychology of leaders, who have considerable discretion in how they respond. Opportunities, even key turning points, are only recognized as such in retrospect, if protestors manage to take advantage of them. Strategic choice probably becomes more and more prominent in explanations as movements emerge, take organized forms, and engage with a variety of other players.

Both initial organizers and later recruits must believe that their action will make some kind of difference to themselves or others, even if it only adds to their personal dignity. Whether they also need to believe it will have a broader effect on policies and attitudes will depend on what that action means to them. In some cases it will be a more strategic choice, in others a deep part of their self-definition. Doug McAdam has identified three structural roots of this cognitive liberation: a political structure that is not entirely closed to protestors; strategic opportunities to act within that structure; and indigenous organizations with some resources. These affect perceptions of threats and opportunities, but so, independently, do culture and biography. Framing processes inhabit the border of culture, biography, and strategy, for they show recruiters trying to read the minds of potential recruits.

Some citizenship models encourage us to think about recruitment as though it were separate from the origins of a movement, since the underlying image is of leaders trying to extract commitments from a "natural" population of potential followers. How and when individuals join an existing movement is one of the major questions that social-movement scholars have addressed. Yes, social networks can aid recruitment, differentiating joiners from nonjoiners, but we must be sensitive to *how* they do this, distinguishing primarily affective ties of friends and family from more strategic bonds to colleagues or comrades. We must be sensitive to the effects of formal organizations, with their resources, strategies, and cultural rules, as well as to the effects of strategies intentionally designed to establish networks. We can watch recruiters reframing their messages to reach both intimates and strangers, we can look for organizational boundaries and identities, and we can be sensitive to existing identities of various sorts. In the end, individuals understand and judge claims through complex cultural and biographical filters. Structural factors like organizations and networks are either a proxy for this kind of process or the context in which it occurs.

As I argued earlier, messages and their paths of transmission—whether personal networks or more anonymous media—are equally important for recruitment. The media are physical resources, to which some groups have more access than others, although this access can change over time. The networks also have a relative stability, even though they are forged like all structures out of past strategic interactions, culture, resources, and biography. Like formal organizations, they tend to outlast strategies, so that they can help explain why certain cultural messages are broadcast, and to whom. Then the interaction between cultural expectations, individual biographical dynamics, and the affective juice maintaining personal networks will help explain why some individuals respond to recruiters' messages, and others do not. It is unrealistic to hope for data on many rank-and-file individuals at the level of detail that would allow us to sort out the effects of cultural meanings from individual psychological traits, for we usually rely on surveys that can barely probe the crudest cultural meanings, much less biographical subtleties. Networks have been emphasized, in part, because they are easy to measure. Life histories—and I have tried to summarize several as vignettes in earlier chapters—offer a time-consuming but informative way to see how much of recruitment depends on personal idiosyncracies. If we could get adequate biographical and psychological evidence, we could even test whether stubbornness, empathy, arrogance, or some other trait might improve the odds of an individual's joining or remaining in protest.

Once again, post-citizenship movements may differ from inclusionary movements. With the latter, there is a natural collectivity associated with the potential movement, from which most recruitment occurs. The potential beneficiaries of the movement share, to some degree, an identity and personal networks, and so they are recruited through these mechanisms. Occasionally the same thing can occur with post-citizenship movements, so that the animal rights movement could recruit pet owners through animal shelters and veterinarians' offices, and the antinuclear movement could recruit those most at risk from nuclear plants through neighborhood networks. But this kind of movement primarily recruits like-minded people, something hard to predict from demographics or networks alone. Since organizers cannot assume shared interests among those they approach, they must rely more on cultural appeals in order to sort out sympathizers from others. For some movements, shared moral visions may do part of the work that personal bonds do in others. In both cases, though, recruitment relies on cultural framing.

It is easy to overstate the differences between citizenship and post-citizenship movements, which must in any case be left to empirical research. In both cases organizers may plausibly insist that there is a strong or natural collective identity supporting their movement, so that their constituencies have grievances that appear objective (even if that constituency is the entire human species). But it usually takes a lot of cultural work to make them appear objective or natural—even for many citizenship movements and certainly for post-citizenship movements. Identities must be imagined, articulated, deployed, applied, reframed, and revised over and over, if not for the sake of the collectivity itself then certainly for the outsiders who will respond. As we saw, there are many individuals and institutions vying to shape collective identities and interests, many of them with greater resources than protest organizers have. This competition begins in the earliest stages of a movement and continues throughout its existence.

Identities themselves must be disentangled with care. Only with the collective identities of pre-existing communities can we even hope to find any legal or cultural status independent of movement activity. We have also seen activist identities (and networks) designed explicitly for political work, movement identities that reinforce action for a single cause, as well as tactical and organizational identities. In a way, then, identities are simply a label for talking about shared moral visions, beliefs, feelings, and preferred ways of acting, and it is usually preferable to talk about these cultural units directly. We can see identities when people talk specifically about what they share with others; we should not infer them from shared feelings, judgments, or even actions.

Creating a social movement is pre-eminently a matter of interpretation and persuasion: people must articulate emerging sensibilities, judgments, and tastes, work through the implications of these, and inspire others to join them. Resources help to spread the message, and strategic action may be necessary for capturing the attention of new audiences. And opponents, especially the state, must be kept at bay.

All these dimensions change over short time periods and over long ones. The unexplored terrain of biography may also help us to explain differences in individual responses to any given message. Because emergence and especially recruitment involve finding or building a single audience—those sympathetic to the cause—strategizing is probably less complex than it will later become. The willingness to act and opportunities to act are not the same, even though process theorists, by emphasizing the external environment, tend to collapse them. In part 2 I tried to show that willingness had many biographical and cultural roots, leaving opportunities open for more structural and strategic explanations.

TACTICS AND STRATEGIES

Once a protest movement has taken root, its constituent groups must decide what to do beyond continuing to recruit new members and gather funds. We saw that there are many audiences for a group's actions, which must be carefully sorted out, but one basic contrast is between activities aimed at members versus those aimed at others outside the group. Desired effects on group members include shared and reciprocal emotions, a movement or related identity, and other forms of motivation and enthusiasm. These will normally make it easier to launch collective protest oriented toward outsiders. Other internal goals might include personal transformations or the establishment of organizational structures, perhaps egalitarian ones, that prefigure the future. These goals might actually conflict with externally oriented ones. Awareness of the variety of audiences at least allows us to see when they conflict.

Post-citizenship movements may do more internal work, since they usually do not rely on a pre-existing collective identity. Citizenship movements, perhaps, can get on with external business sooner, or more directly. The women's movement, for example, has long been divided into a pragmatic branch, especially concerned with economic equality and fairly instrumental in its activities, and a radical feminist branch more interested in personal and cultural transformation, more of a post-citizenship movement.[3] The same is true of the gay and lesbian rights movements. It is the more culturally oriented wing of each movement that has been plagued by debates over identities: What does it mean to be feminist, or queer? Who is and who is not? A tendency toward self-destruction has arisen from these internal conflicts despite the rituals and strong affective ties working in the other direction.

Movement identities are never the result of simple choices by leaders or the rank-and-file, as though one could choose identities by fiat. They are heavily influenced by broader political contexts of the kind emphasized by process theorists, albeit through a discursive filter. As Nancy Whittier says, "Activists discuss their experiences, events in the outside world, their successes and failures, and construct collective identities that make sense of the demands of their social context, both within and outside movement organizations; in this way, social structure affects collective identity."[4] Strategic successes and failures shape cultural images and individual psychology and so help explain identities and tactical tastes, just as these in turn help account for protestors' strategic choices.

In addition to various internal choices, then, external tactics and strategies must also be developed, and here strategic logics are both more central and more complex than they were for movement emergence. Here structural and strategic opportunities are probably paramount. Although resources constrain options and cultural tastes shape desires and feelings about actions, the heat of the strategic moment can escape both. Protestors want to win, and opportunities for advantage open and close with such rapidity that quick choices must be made. These will depend not only on the opportunities themselves, but on individual propensities and artful creativity, on cultural habits, values, and meanings, and on resources. Most notably, greater resources allow tactics not available to those with fewer technical capacities, just as contrasting political structures open avenues for different sorts of strategies, as Kitschelt, McAdam, and others have shown. Antinuclear protestors do not testify at public hearings if there are no public hearings.

Explaining the available *repertory* of tactics, heavily influenced by political structures, is one thing. It is another to explain the choices of actions *within* this repertory, or the slight variations, innovations, and timing in their *application*. All three are affected by factors internal to the movement and factors from the outside, emanating from the actions of other players in a conflict. The choices made in applying a tactic are especially subtle, and they depend more on psychology and strategic logics than on political structure. The biographical dimension is important because of the central role of leaders, whether they are formal or implicit leaders. Not only the ability to innovate, but selecting the best move, making it at just the right time, and the symbolic resonance we label charisma: all these things come from very subtle aspects of individuals. Movements flourish when they have leaders with these traits, and flounder when they do not. This holds true even though movements can themselves often create charismatic leaders, as

Aldon Morris has argued, and even though many movements avoid granting formal powers to these leaders. For understanding strategies and tactics, psychological information about these key people is well worth the research investment, in ways it may not be for large numbers of rank-and-file participants.

Strategic choices lead to responses from others. Among the multiple audiences and players, which is the most important will depend on the priorities protestors give to their various goals. The state will often, especially for citizenship movements, be the most important audience and player, in which case violence and disruption, while risky, may have big payoffs. The national state, with its broad and deep apparatuses, shapes strategies at a very basic level, as process theorists have recognized so well. Its decisions and nondecisions are the targets of many actions, just as its legal imprimatur helps to establish protest groups through recognitions such as tax-exempt status. In other cases there may be audiences and opponents of equal or greater importance. Strategies against opponents typically try to reduce their resources, constrain their maneuverability in using them, discredit them in front of other audiences, force them into unpopular actions or statements, and generally paint them as evil, dangerous, or dishonest. Strategies for bystander audiences are more likely to involve persuasion and the creation of a favorable public image or identity.

Organizational forms are, like arguments and actions, a kind of message. But they are also a cluster of resources and rules that allow certain kinds of tactics and discourage others. Centralized organizations can act differently, and more quickly, than decentralized ones. What to do about the organization—how to keep it going, for instance—requires strategic and tactical choices that are often as important as the choice of protest tactics. These choices depend partly on resources and strategic calculations, but also on cultural goals, skills, and connotations, and on even more ineffable psychologies of leaders and others.

Identifying different tastes in tactics allows us to begin analyzing conflicts within protest movements. Different groups compete to frame issues and goals, one of the most common conflicts being that between more radical versus more moderate goals and tactics. At the same time, they compete for resources that are important for maintaining the organization and pursuing many of its tactics. In fact, the framing of issues, when the intended audience is potential supporters, is a major part of the competition for resources. When the audience for this framing is bystanders, opponents, or the state, the intention probably has more to do with outcomes and goals. Strategic success and cultural resonance both affect what groups attract the most members, media attention, or resources, just as these factors will help shape a group's success and resonance. Furthermore, cultural influence and other forms of success do not always go together, since they involve different audiences.

If the emergence of a movement has a lot to do with motivation and willingness, with cultural meanings and psychological mechanisms such as threats, then the actions of protest groups, once established, may have more to do with the play of strategic interaction. Audiences multiply, and so do the possible options. Tactical tastes and biographical traits such as daring and a sense of timing are relevant. So are levels of resources, but even here strategic action can change what is available. Here, the effect of cultural persuasion is often indirect as it influences these other factors.

MOVEMENT EFFECTS

The factors that explain a movement's success often circle back, especially in traditions that emphasize resources and structures, to the same ones that account for a movement's emergence. The more resources and political capacities a collectivity has, the more likely it is to form a social movement to pursue its interests, and the more likely it is to succeed. The same things that remove repression enough to allow the movement to mobilize will allow it to make gains, in part because—especially for citizenship movements—the group's mobilization and recognition are themselves a victory. When William Gamson studied movement success in 1975, he defined recognition of an organization as one form of success, along with securing benefits for the group it represented.[5] When the state is both arena and opponent, as for most citizenship movements, this conflation is reasonable. Legal recognition is precisely what many groups are after.

Because the state is charged with keeping order, disruption and violence are a direct challenge to it, which it must meet with either concessions or repression. This is the essence of the process approach, forged from citizenship exemplars. The animal rights movement, in contrast, is not going to lure consumers into giving up meat though destructive break-ins at slaughterhouses. Some audiences are better intimidated, others persuaded. Just as strategies and tactics can be aimed at a variety of audiences, so can desired effects, each of which must be explained separately. These audiences must be identified in terms of their cultural visions as well as their institutional settings. We must understand a movement's effects on an audience's beliefs, feelings, and intentions, but we must also examine the audience's capacities for action on the basis of a changed perspective. Their resources and structural positions matter greatly. It is better to persuade a prime minister than your next-door neighbor.

Strategic choices, backed by whatever resources are available, will of course help explain movement outcomes. Protestors' cultural and biographical equipment help explain the choices they make, but the effects of those choices will depend on how others respond, which in turn involves the resources, strategies, biographies, and cultural perspectives of others. In the long run, a lack of resources limits maneuverability. In the short run, however, events occur, information appears, and opponents blunder, yielding sudden opportunities to gain advantages. Laws blocked for years can suddenly be passed; donations triple; news frames turn favorable overnight; dictators abdicate. Rules and structures can be changed with breathtaking suddenness, changing the playing field for all future protest.

Outcomes in different arenas no doubt require different explanations. Many appeals to the state—legislative lobbying, expert testimony and evidence, and lawsuits—require enormous resources, although even here the outcomes do not always favor those with the most resources. Clever strategies are possibly most important in explaining the outcomes of interactions with opponents, but those opponents' own responses still matter. To reach the bystander public, strategies must be crafted to gain favorable media attention, or resources must be spent to reach people more directly through advertisements or direct mail. Changing public sensibilities and ideas, which may be the longest-enduring effect of many protest movements, may require the fewest resources and the most cultural resonance.

In the long run, different forms of success may or may not be correlated. Change enough people's opinions, and politicians may eventually pass favorable legislation. But will the law be implemented fully, changing the behavior of those it is meant to control? Antidiscrimination laws may be passed that ban certain actions but leave public attitudes unchanged. Resentment may even be the stuff of an organized backlash against the laws, as we have seen all too frequently in recent decades. Sometimes politicians are easier to persuade than employers, sometimes the opposite.

A CONCEPTUAL TOOL KIT

For any question we might wish to ask about protest, all the basic dimensions are likely to come into play. As analytic dimensions, they are all always present. But they will be present in differing ways and degrees, and they will interact in different ways in different movements. I do not want to assume away any of them at any stage in the life of a protest movement, but I think it is fair to point out places that a dimension is likely to be especially important. I have tried to lay out some theoretical expectations about those places. Most of all, I hope to have provided a tool kit of concepts (not just my four dimensions, but various psychological mechanisms, many cultural constructs, internal movement processes, strategic dilemmas and choices, to name a few) from which researchers can choose those that apply.

There are also methodological constraints on which dimensions will appear in our explanations. Quantitative approaches may give special attention to resources, the most measurable dimension. Historical approaches might recommend closer attention to political structures and the strategic interactions by which they are created and transformed. Ethnographic and participant research allow attention to biography, in contrast to surveys, which permit little more than a crude reckoning of explicit beliefs. As always in sociology, the more research techniques we can use, the more we are likely to see.

I have emphasized culture, biography, and artfulness in protest, on the grounds that these are especially unfamiliar to most of us. But a cultural approach is not a monolithic blanket to lay down on all aspects of a movement. For a given movement, we might find that culture is especially interesting for explaining emergence and less so for success. Biographies might shed light on the strategic choices of one group and not another. The cultural impact of a movement may interest us even though we don't find that cultural rituals sustained protestors in any significant way. I have not presented a unitary theory, to be tested against others, but a conceptual vocabulary, some parts of which may prove useful.

With this brief effort at synthesis, we have come to the end of our explanatory trail. In the final three chapters we will follow a normative path, using biography, culture, and artfulness to assess some of the benefits and risks of protest. We can explain what movements do, but should we like it?

PART FIVE

A Normative View

We have retraced the history of protest research, first concentrating on the individuals who interested the crowd theorists and the rationalists so much, then turning to social movements, which mobilization theorists typically took as their unit of analysis, and finally setting both of these in the context of their broader environment, which is the favorite lens of process theorists. At every step we have seen how biographical variations and cultural meanings interact with strategic choices and resource distributions to affect why and how protestors act, and to what effect. The last step is to evaluate these activities, to ask what is good and bad, safe and risky, admirable and despicable, about protest, not only for those involved but for all the rest of us in modern societies. Most scholars shy away from such issues as emphatically as they deny the importance of emotions in social life—which only means that normative questions are addressed in distorted and surreptitious ways.

FIFTEEN

Lives Worth Living

Much madness is divinest sense
To a discerning eye,
Much sense the starkest madness.
　　—Emily Dickinson

In the final three chapters I adopt a more normative voice, trying to judge protest movements by their effects on individuals and society. In this chapter I scrutinize what protest offers to its participants: what kinds of practices, satisfactions, and lives. In chapter 16 I turn to some of the risks of protest movements, especially the possibility that they may shift from communication to manipulation, no longer offering moral possibilities to inspire others but attempting to impose their visions through one or another form of force. In the final chapter I return to the benefits of protest movements, looking at their important contribution to self-understanding and social learning in modern societies.

Scholars of protest have frequently been evaluative in their writing, but their judgments have generally remained implicit. The concern to defend the rationality of protestors reflects this. Most study movements they admire and support, although the researchers who study movements they dislike are every bit as obvious in their moral judgments. Few scholars examine movements they like *and* movements they dislike, and those who study only one kind spin different theories according to whether or not they are favorably disposed toward their subject matter. Models derived from favored movements feature purposive rationality on the basis of unproblematic goals, while those derived from disliked movements are more likely to try to explain the beliefs and emotions of participants. I am separating out my evaluations, which I hope are also improved by the inclusion of an extended study of a "bad" movement.

My evaluations draw on several ideas put forward by philosophers. Through his concept of *practices,* Alasdair MacIntyre has tried to describe activities in such a way that evaluative criteria are built into them. If you can identify the function or internal satisfaction of a practice, then you can evaluate whether, in any concrete case, the accompanying human virtues—character traits and dispositions that aid the practices—have been attained. (His virtues are similar to Bourdieu's "habitus.") In MacIntyre's example of a sea captain, the definition of the role implies a normative criterion: how safely you can pilot a ship. MacIntyre claims that honesty, justice, and courage are virtues in all practices.[1] But to prove that a practice is actually morally valuable, MacIntyre also needs to show that the practice contributes to a good life for those who pursue it and that their lives and practices fit into their societies in beneficial ways. One could be a virtuous torturer, carrying out this activity well, yet the entire practice has negative consequences for society. This chapter examines the role of protest in individual lives, and the next two place it in the context of society as a whole. In this way I hope to identify the peculiar virtues of protest, so that we can have criteria for evaluating it.

To get at the virtues unique to protest, I assume that *communication and moral understanding are important human and social needs that protest helps us achieve*. Jürgen Habermas has devoted his career to the proposition that communication is the defining feature of human nature and social life, residing even in the structure of our languages.[2] Richard Rorty, arriving at similar political commitments from a different philosophical tradition, distinguishes systematic from edifying philosophers, who try to "help their readers, or society as a whole, break free from outworn vocabularies and attitudes, rather than to provide 'grounding' for the intuitions and customs of the present."[3] Rorty's edifying philosophers are skeptical of accepted truths, methods, and (he might add) institutions. Fighting systematic philosophers' pretensions to complete truth, edifiers "are reactive and offer satires, parodies, aphorisms. They know their work loses its point when the period they were reacting against is over. They are *intentionally* peripheral. . . . Edifying philosophy is not only abnormal but reactive, having sense only as a protest against attempts to close off conversation."[4] The virtues of protest, albeit more engaged with policies, are similar to Rorty's edifying endeavor, in elaborating a response to and criticism of current ways of living and thinking. As we'll see in chapter 16, protestors are less virtuous when they try to install their own systems, abandoning efforts at communication and treating others in a purely instrumental or strategic way, as objects to manipulate.

The first context in which to judge practices, though, is their place in the lives of individuals. As MacIntyre puts it, "[W]ithout an overriding conception of the *telos* of a whole human life, conceived as a unity, our conception of certain individual virtues has to remain partial and incomplete."[5] MacIntyre insists that humans face two fundamental moral questions: What is the good for me, and what is the good for humankind? And he asserts that "it is the systematic asking of these two questions and the attempt to answer them in deed as well as in word which provide the moral life with its unity."[6] This is a good description of the lives of many protestors, whose activities are a fundamental part of the narratives they construct to justify and make sense of their lives. Most protestors make their activism an important part of their lives; some go as far as Geoff Merideth and make it the center of their life narratives. This is another way of saying that protest is an important identity for them.

Individuals can have different relationships to their own protest activities. Only a few devote their lives to protest. At the other extreme, those who are drawn to an issue through a sudden moral shock may withdraw again once the threat is removed or made to seem unassailable. For NIMBYs, protest can be an important but brief part of their lives. Many members of citizenship movements might be in between: it might take them a long time to gain the recognition they seek, but they can turn to other pursuits when they do. For whatever period and with whatever intensity they are involved, protestors nonetheless share certain traits and images. They can be judged by the same criteria.

Modern society has many character "types." The manager, the therapist, and the artist, to take MacIntyre's favorite examples, are all familiar to us, not only in what they do but in what kind of people they are. MacIntyre calls them "characters" because we think we know a lot about their moral views, their personalities, and their styles of action; we understand their roles in narratives, especially stories of their own lives. What is more, their characters and personalities are fused with their professional activities in ways that make them "moral representatives of their culture." By expressing a kind of cultural and moral ideal, "the character morally legitimates a mode of social existence."[7] The artist struggles to express something of her inner self; the manager pursues organizational goals by instrumentally reducing the human and nonhuman worlds to means to his own bureaucratic ends; the therapist helps individuals realize their inner potential in much the same way that the manager helps organizations realize their goals. These three tropes express moral visions that are widespread in today's advanced industrial societies. As identities, the three characters go far beyond mere occupations.

The protestor is also a recognizable character type, caricatured as naive, admired as compassionate, dismissed as kooky. Most Americans have little sympathy for protestors—until they themselves are thrust into that role. The news media continue to portray most protestors unfavorably—as eccentric and rude—even when they give a sympathetic hearing to the protestors' issues. (As we saw in chapter 12, protestors struggle with the media over movement identity as well as over the movement's goals.) Although large numbers of Americans have participated in or contributed to one cause or another, politicians and the media—the only remaining crowd theorists—have a stake in portraying noninstitutional politics as frightening and weird. This character type, more a symbol than an accurate description, is more contested than most.

The dismissive attitude often, ironically, includes the idea that protestors are not genuine, or are self-interested. I doubt that anything could be less true. The majority of full-time, long-term activists have made enormous personal sacrifices, hold deep moral convictions, and can articulate well-thought-out positions. Susan Johnson had a hope that was touching in its modesty: "If I could make $20,000 some year, just one year, I could buy a car. But that's not the most important thing. I would say the main deprivation of having the kinds of jobs I do is that I never have any health coverage." Geoff Merideth may insist that he has made no sacrifice, but he has certainly traded material comforts for other pleasures. Social change does not pay well.

The character type of the protestor often stands in contrast to the formal organizations through which protest usually unfolds. Geoff Merideth and Susan Johnson have spent their lives in protest, but both feel ambivalent about formal organizations. Neither has founded one, or belonged to one for very long. Their lives of protest have a different logic, a different narrative. They have tried to construct satisfying lives in a world where most people take small jobs in large organizations. Many protestors move among and through organizations only as necessary, joining, founding, and leaving them.

Entire lives can be artful creations, as protestors try to fit their convictions into their daily routines. They epitomize Socrates' call for "the examined life." Protestors often find new ways of living, new modes of applying moral visions in everyday life. As a character type, protestors have their accompanying "virtues": a moral awareness and articulateness, participation in public controversies and the shaping of the future, description of alternative possible moral worlds, and engagement in purposive, freely chosen collective projects. If we want to judge the benefits of protest, we can start with MacIntyre's idea that each practice has accompanying virtues. Protest offers many virtues to its practitioners, giving meaning to their lives. Their moral sensitivity, often painful but also deeply satisfying, is precious to them as well as being their greatest gift to the rest of us.

For some protestors, their activism makes sense only in the broader context of their entire lives and life work. Perhaps they forge new ways of life because they lack the material comforts that make one complacent. As Heinz Kohut said of creative individuals, "The great in art and the truly pioneeringly creative in science seem to have preserved the capacity to experience reality, at least temporarily, with less of the buffering structures that protect the average adult: from traumatization—but also from creativeness and discovery."[8] Many protestors lack these buffers. "Difference," as I have said, may be crucial to creativity. Karl Deutsch argued that solutions to pressing political problems were "more likely to be found by some deviant members of the community—persons whose memories, habits, or viewpoints may differ significantly from those of most other groups in their community or culture and who may have fewer habits and interests to sacrifice in identifying themselves with new ideas and new patterns of behavior."[9] In many cases their ideas are more likely to be accepted than the protestors are.

Here is the key to innovation and social change: this biographical variation in feelings and visions on the part of individuals is followed by a kind of natural selection in which some spread but most do not. Individual differences are the beginning of this process. Even though most idiosyncratic ideas or sensibilities are not attractive to others, the more there are from which to choose, the more likely we are to find some that do have wide appeal.

If artists and long-term protestors are similar in their thoughtful creativity and material deprivation, the underlying reason is a sense of moral and personal calling to their work, the fusion of social and individual fulfillment. Over time, one's work and one's character blend. An observer of the theater once wrote of "the drive or fanaticism or whatever of the person who has made his choice, and will eschew anything else—money, the elite identification of a university degree, even health—to develop the talent he hopes he has."[10] What is unusual about a moral character type is that developing one's own skills is seen as a generous, not a selfish act, a contribution to the good of society. This is a supremely middle-class ideal, but a persuasive and attractive one.

The same traits we use to identify good protestors should help us to judge bad ones. Some protestors are not making honest or courageous efforts to work out their moral principles. Some are paid by large corporations or state agencies to pose as protestors—either quite literally as spies or less directly as organizers of countermovements. Those who organize protest primarily in order to get a salary are not living up to the virtues of this practice, although those who receive a salary inci dentally may. Those who misrepresent themselves in order to manipulate others also violate protest's virtues.

We saw that part of MacIntyre's argument about practices and virtues was that they had to make sense in the context of an individual's life, and we have seen many ways in which protest does this. But the argument remains incomplete until we have placed these lives in the even broader context of society and its roles, traditions, and social identities. Not just any goal or sensibility can make moral sense of a life; it must have some relationship to the goals of those around one. We cannot say that a person is doing right simply because she is virtuously (or virtuosically) engaged in her practices. What, to take the usual counterexample, about the virtuous Nazi, doing a good job at a bad practice? For a practice to be good, we must examine its effects on the entire society of which it is part. Chapter 16 examines cases in which this broader effect of a "successful" protest movement is bad; chapter 17 looks at examples in which it is positive.

To distinguish good from bad effects of protest, I shall argue that some protestors encourage others to acquire the same virtues that the protestors enjoy: moral voice, participation, a probing of one's deepest sensibilities. They contribute to information flows, self-understanding, and communication.[11] Other protestors, concerned only with winning and not with understanding, discourage these virtues in others, strategically reducing nonprotestors to means rather than ends. Deception, manipulation, and control are the result. Pure strategy wins out over cultural communication. The "selection process" by which protestors' ideas and judgments are considered and either accepted or rejected can be a good one, consisting of persuasion and example, or a bad one, consisting of violence and imposition.

I believe that the dangers of protest are more likely to be realized when protestors gain significant power. They lose their position as marginal critics, which can be a frustrating position but allows a truer voice. The most extreme case is a revolutionary seizure of power, for revolutionaries are protestors who have armed themselves and managed to gain control of the state. This is especially a possibility for citizenship movements, which see the state as their main target and audience. Geoff Merideth was glad that the revolution failed in the United States in 1970. In Cambodia five years later a revolution succeeded, giving total power to the critics. The Khmer Rouge are an extreme example, but they show many things that can go wrong when protestors shift from outsiders to insiders, from Rorty's edifying, hermeneutic stance to a systematic one, from moral criticism to political power.

- For some, protest is a way of life, a defining aspect of their identity. Their very lives can be thoughtful efforts to work out the meaning of "the good life."

- Human life requires some artfulness of all of us, yet some activities, including protest, encourage practitioners to be more artful than others do.

- Because the protestor is a modern character type, and protest a practice, there are attendant virtues that can help us judge good and bad performances.

- These virtues include honesty, justice, courage, moral articulateness, and the description of alternative possible moral universes. Good protestors encourage moral self-understanding in others.

SIXTEEN

The Risks of Protest

And when the time for the breaking
of the law is here, be sure it is to take place in the matrix
of our everyday thoughts and fantasies, our wonderment
at how we got from there to here.
  —John Ashbery, "Flow Chart"

The history of thought and culture is, as Hegel showed with great brilliance,
a changing pattern of great liberating ideas which turn inevitably into suffo-
cating straightjackets.
  —Isaiah Berlin

On 17 April 1975, the Khmer Rouge captured and immediately evacuated Phnom Penh, beginning a genocide during their four-year rule
that killed at least one million (out of seven million) Cambodians. The
deaths were due to an explicit program of execution as well as to the
combination of starvation, disease, and exhaustion from forced labor
and evacuation marches. Phnom Penh was emptied in only three days,
and other Cambodian cities were equally devastated. Citizens were
pushed haphazardly into the countryside in all directions.

The Khmer Rouge transformed their society in every imaginable
way. They relocated urban dwellers to the countryside in the name of
national self-sufficiency based on agricultural production, abolition of
private property, and economic and social collectivization. They abol-
ished money and land ownership, confiscated personal property, en-
forced numbing work schedules and strict dress codes (black clothing,
no jewelry), took young people from their families and assigned them
to dormitories. And, most notoriously, they systematically extermi-
nated certain categories of people. The Khmer Rouge divided the
population of Democratic Kampuchea, as the country was renamed,
into the "old" and the "new" people. The "old" people were composed
primarily of peasants, inherently linked to the "pure" Khmer culture
of Cambodia's history. The "new" people were typically those who,
living in the cities, had been tainted with the corruption of capitalism
and other foreign influences; they were considered parasitic, living off
the peasantry. They were singled out for smaller rations, abuse, and
often death. At the extreme, there are stories of revolutionary teens

ordered to kill their own parents. Those who obeyed did so on the grounds that these were not their parents, a role now assumed by the Khmer Rouge organization, and that their erstwhile parents were instead "enemies."[1]

Khmer Rouge policies, rooted in an ideological program and selective reinterpretation of Khmer history developed since the 1950s, were an effort to remake Cambodian society according to an abstract blueprint colored by Khmer national character. Young party leaders, often teachers, had returned from Paris universities to articulate a proudly Cambodian form of marxism. According to Pol Pot, in a seemingly contradictory formula, "The culture of Democratic Kampuchea is . . . a new culture based on national traits, national tradition, and progressive qualities. From the national tradition, we select and pick only progressive qualities which can serve our revolutionary movement, and abolish reactionary and regressive characteristics."[2] If the revolution was unleashing the true nature of the Khmer people, the regime could accept no material or ideological contamination from abroad, and the Khmer Rouge developed a viciously paranoid xenophobia.

Collectivization was presented as a return to the cultural heritage of Khmer society, as exemplified by the Khmer empire of the twelfth and thirteenth centuries, when slave labor built the Angkor temples and an extensive system of canals and dikes. Angkor was reconstructed as a seminal national event, evidence of the collective capacities of ordinary people when united under strong leadership.[3] This image of a "golden age" was itself a considerable construction, since the Angkor period stretched, in most accounts, from 802 to 1431, comprising enormous swings in economic activity and royal power (ranging from only a few hundred followers to an extensive empire).[4]

At the same time that they harked back to a pure earlier epoch, the Khmer Rouge also insisted they were starting anew, throwing off layers of foreign contamination. They combined the rhetorical power of a past golden age with that of a future utopia, linking the two. Part of the process of remaking the world involved relabeling it. Like the French Revolutionaries, they started the calendar over, although beginning oddly at Year Zero rather than Year One. As in all regime changes, places such as streets were renamed.[5] The Khmer Rouge tried to disengage themselves thoroughly from hundreds of years of Cambodian culture, even down to time and place.

The new four-year plan (the Khmer Rouge were determined to move faster than previous socialist revolutions with their five-year plans!) was grounded in an abstract ideology removed from the realities of everyday life. Its language consistently disregarded the objective conditions, capacities, and resources of Cambodia, in favor of the vague will of the people as the motor of change. Collectivization, by un-leashing the power of the old people, would ensure the "political con-sciousness" necessary for success. For instance, after detailing formi-dable obstacles such as the recent war and the lack of technology or capital, the plan lightly dismissed potential difficulties in obtaining desired rice yields: "[T]here are no particular figures that present us important problems. The important issue is that we must do the Plan. . . . Political method, therefore, constitutes the determining fac-tor. . . . Even though there are obstacles, even though our enemies claw at us, we believe in our clear analysis. The problem requires us to be united. What is important about the plan is not its numbers, but the ideology behind it, and the notion that we must all unite together."[6]

The plan detailed, region by region, expected agricultural produc-tion and output, with no reference to the past productive capacities of the land. It established goals for rice production throughout the entire nation of three tons per hectare. As David Chandler says, this target "meant not only more than doubling the *average* rice yield in the 1960s, but doubling the yield *at once*."[7] Mechanisms and incentives were ig-nored, except the odd promise that all Cambodians would have dessert daily by 1980.[8]

The contrast between old and new people shaped practical aspects of the economic plan, sometimes in the face of strong contrary evi-dence. If the old people were peasants, agriculture would have to be the foundation of socialism. A strong agricultural base would ensure independence and self-sufficiency, and modernization and industrial-ization could develop from this base. The Khmer Rouge refused to use the knowledge and skills of the contaminated, formerly urban popula-tion: "[W]e don't use old workers, because if we used old workers without carefully selecting and purifying them first, there would be many complications, politically, which would lead to more difficulties for us."[9] Even the skills for piloting helicopters evidently changed with the establishment of Democratic Kampuchea: "In military matters, people who pilot our helicopters can't read a great deal. But by culti-vating good political consciousness, we all can learn swiftly and we can exceed the Plan's requirements. Formerly to be a pilot required a high school education—twelve to fourteen years. Nowadays, it's clear that political consciousness is the decisive factor. It shows us our line is correct."[10]

Despite absorbing the ideology and goals of marxist-leninist thought, the Khmer Rouge denied its influence and ignored previous efforts to apply it. Or rather they rejected previous revolutions as riddled with mistakes. They stressed the uniqueness of their revolution, in comparison to the Soviet and Chinese models, even changing the official founding date of the Communist Party of Kampuchea from 1951 to 1960 to deny the influence of Vietnamese communism on its early formation. They repudiated any outside assistance or influence; their revolution was purely Cambodian.

Most prominently, though, the Khmer Rouge borrowed the language and ideals of China's Great Leap Forward and Cultural Revolution. Like the Khmer Rouge, Mao had focused on establishing communes featuring collective ownership, military discipline, sex-segregated dormitories, avoidance of foreign technology and expertise, and the "re-education" of urban Chinese professionals through forced labor in the villages. Mao relied on very young people, often taken from the poorest regions of the country, and he searched constantly for enemies of the revolution in all privileged strata. These included city dwellers, the educated, even those peasants slightly better off than their fellows. Underlying the strategy in both China and Cambodia was "a voluntarist belief that human consciousness and the moral qualities of men are the decisive factors in determining the course of history, a populist belief that true revolutionary creativity resides among the peasant masses."[11] Political will could remake society and even, with enough pressure, transform individual motivations. Cultural contexts could be remade at will.

Khmer Rouge leaders adopted Mao's tactics, yet recognized that he had failed. They analyzed this failure as the result of resistance on several fronts: rich peasants who fought collectivization, an emergent intellectual elite within the party, and the difficulties of forcing communal production on the cities. Through a faster and more sweeping transition, the Khmer Rouge believed they could outmaneuver these internal enemies. They hoped to surpass China with a "Super Great Leap." Norodom Sihanouk recounts a meeting between Khmer leaders and China's Zhou Enlai, at which the latter warned to go slowly rather than attempting a Great Leap Forward as China had done. The Khmer leaders smiled, he writes, "an incredulous and superior smile," later telling Sihanouk, "Our country's place in history will be assured. . . . We will be the first nation to create a completely communist society without wasting time on intermediate steps."[12] By thoroughly extirpating all enemies of the revolution, the Khmer Rouge, adopting Mao's goals, would succeed where Mao had failed. The Chinese experience was relevant only as a negative example, for the Khmer Rouge deduced the proper strategy directly from their basic ideology.

The Khmer Rouge interpretation of marxist-leninist thought was shaped by Cambodian culture, history, and demographics, even though the Khmer Rouge were highly selective in the lessons they drew from these. The cities were indeed sites of foreign influence, as a large proportion of the population of Phnom Penh was ethnically Chinese or Vietnamese. All the cities had grown rapidly under French rule (1863–1954), partly due to the colonial schools and administrative apparatus. This urban, French regime had used educational credentials in selecting its functionaries, thereby subverting traditional ties of family and locality. Sihanouk had further Westernized the built environment of Phnom Penh, razing older shantytowns; he had banned traditional peasant garb and carts from parts of the city. This exacerbated the country-city cleavage in Cambodian culture.

The moral boundaries established in the marxist-leninist language of class were reinforced by a moralistic approach to lifestyles, reflecting a concern for Khmer purity embodied in the old people. According to an official Khmer Rouge description, "Upon entering Phnom Penh and other cities, the brother and sister combatants of the revolutionary army . . . were taken aback by the overwhelming unspeakable sight of long-haired men and youngsters wearing bizarre clothes making themselves undistinguishable from the fair sex. . . . Social entertaining, the tempo and rhythm of music and so forth were all based on U.S. imperialistic patterns. Our people's traditionally clean, sound characteristics and essence were completely absent and abandoned, replaced by imperialistic pornographic, shameless, perverted, and fanatic traits."[13] Western influences, symbolized by students' long hair and implying various sorts of moral laxity, were ambivalently dubbed "civilay," or civilized, in direct contrast to the wild forests—themselves seen as a place of healing and regeneration.[14]

Cities were considered an insurmountable obstacle to Kampuchean socialism, since they were linked not only to foreign influences but to private property, developed markets, and morally lax lifestyles. One commentator has suggested that the condemnation of cities was reinforced by a literal interpretation of "bourgeoisie" as "those who live in cities."[15] Yet the Kampuchean condemnation of urban moral chaos is not so different from the American protestants who have launched moral panics against immigrants and the inner-city poor since the mid-nineteenth century.[16] The moral contrast between city and country recurs in many of the world's cultures, and François Ponchaud finds in Khmer literature the theme of forests as "the home of hermits and a place of regeneration. . . . The killings of corrupt and irredeemable elements in the forest were a prelude to the birth of a moral and more properly ordered society."[17] These were enticing cultural images, at the same time cognitive, moral, and emotional.

The theme of purity versus corruption dominated not only the contrast between countryside and city, but also the superiority of youth over their elders, who could not adapt to the new regime except through coercion. For their revolutionary cadres, the Khmer Rouge recruited the youth from among the "old people," many as young as ten or twelve years old. They were assumed to be less contaminated by the corruption of pre-revolutionary Cambodia, and the Khmer Rouge perceived an almost inherent Khmer character that would emerge in the absence of contamination. As a result, few questioned the wisdom of having twelve-year-olds in charge of villages, since—in an ironic linguistic twist—they were drawn from among the "old people."

The combination of marxist-leninist language, ideas about a Khmer essence, cultural imagery common in Cambodian history, and an ability to abstract from concrete realities yielded a watertight, unfalsifiable ideology. It implied, among other things, overlapping categories of enemies, whom the Khmer Rouge set out to destroy. Enemies were created out of those who had opposed the Khmer Rouge, those who might attempt to subvert the revolution in the future, and those so corrupted by foreign influence that they had lost their essential Khmer qualities. Unless they actively opposed the regime, however, these enemies could only be recognized by means of signs, including age, urban residence, and class background. These signs became proof of guilt, as these categories became the important, essential characteristics of human beings in terms of Khmer Rouge ideology.

Like the external, international enemies with whom they were associated, new people could not be reformed or re-educated. They were too deeply contaminated, like the cities where they had lived. Even when new people were relocated to the countryside to work as laborers alongside the old people, they retained the stigma of "new." Oldness and newness were even partly heritable: "Their children and grandchildren have better qualities. . . . and they have better elements than their parents. If the parents have one hundred oppressive elements, their children have only fifty. If we allow them to get mixed in the movement for a time, we can use them as a tactical force in our favor."[18] The elaborate classification of social class divided the population into ten categories of varying moral worth. Despite its supposedly objective, essential quality, the boundaries of this classification changed over time, often moving people suddenly from privileged to suspect categories, for example, if one's parents were reclassified.[19]

The enemy consisted not only of groups (the Cham, the Vietnamese, the "new" people), but of individuals (many party members), and of ideas (individualism, authoritarianism, mandarinism, and subjectivism). In this paranoid categorization, the enemy could be anywhere, taking many forms. Further, the enemy had slowly rooted itself in Khmer society, trying to change the nature and character of that society. Rooted in the individual psychology of individual leaders, especially Pol Pot, paranoia was evident in early party documents: "[T]here will still be enemies in ten years, twenty years, thirty years into the future." Throughout the years of Khmer Rouge control, the cadres searched for enemies (both individual and conceptual) within the party. Individualism was one of the dangerous ideas in the countryside, and there were references to problems of "family-ism, sibling-ism, relation-ism" within the party. The enemy was also "a sickness inside the Party, . . . we search for the microbes within the Party without success. They are buried. . . . They will be pushed out by the true nature of socialist revolution."[20]

An overpowering movement identity, created through two decades of struggle, much of it in isolated jungle camps, was used to construct all other social identities. Anyone not a member of the Khmer Rouge—and a "good" member at that—might end up in some category of enemy. Some of these other identities were rooted in traditional Cambodian culture; others derived directly from Khmer Rouge ideology. Some were genuine collective identities, which the members themselves might recognize, while others were arbitrary legal impositions. But they were equally life-threatening.

The effect of labeling enemies was to dehumanize them. According to Pol Pot, "These counterrevolutionary elements which betray and try to sabotage the revolution are not to be regarded as being our people. They are to be regarded as enemies of Democratic Cambodia, of the Cambodian revolution, and of the Cambodian people."[21] Enemies were defined as "not our people"—and perhaps not people at all. As a result, the new people and other perceived enemies of the regime were the primary victims of violence.

The image of the "enemy around every corner" did not emerge merely as a tactic to suppress opposition, nor was it simply a method of instilling fear, terror, and distrust in the party itself. Although it served these purposes, the idea of the enemy did not arise from a purely strategic logic. Both the conception of the enemy and the resulting legitimation of violence were rooted in the marxist-leninist ideology of the Khmer Rouge and their particular view of Cambodian history and culture. Their cognitive and moral distinctions had developed long before they had the power to act on them. Systematic violence of this sort would not have been possible without some dehumanization of its victims, but the boundaries drawn were hardly accidental. They were planted deep in Cambodian culture, or at least that part of it which the Khmer Rouge saw through their ideological lens. Of course, strategic interaction played a role: once you start denouncing people as enemies, they have a way of becoming enemies.

How did such a murderous moral vision seize hold of sophisticated, Paris-educated intellectuals? And why have so many other protestors and revolutionary movements turned to extermination as a strategy (from the Red Brigades to the Oklahoma City bomber)? Such excesses taint, in the eyes of many, all systematic efforts at social change. As Isaiah Berlin said, even well-intentioned reformers sometimes see their liberating ideas turn to straightjackets. I believe that two cognitive conditions especially encourage murder as a political tactic. *First, abstract visions of the world, especially totalizing visions, allow the reduction of men, women, and children to the status of mere functions, aspects of social structure. Stripping people of their flesh and blood, secondly, allows one to establish a sweeping, dehumanized category of subhuman enemies, and enemies, once created, require repression.* Protestors, in such cases, lose touch with most of their own cultural traditions and social webs. (The only cultural tradition they retain, indeed, is that of their abstract ideology.) Once other people are reduced to means, they can be treated in purely instrumental fashion.

In many theoretical traditions, revolutions are the ultimate outcome of successful protest movements. As indicated in the title of Tilly's book, *From Mobilization to Revolution*, the best way for excluded groups to attain their goals is often to seize or overhaul the state through armed rebellion. Viewed in a purely strategic way, especially for citizenship movements, revolutions are the ultimate victory. On the other hand, in my vision of protest as (partly) communicative action, revolutions are typically disasters, for revolutionaries can treat not only opponents but all of society instrumentally as objects to be manipulated rather than cultural subjects to be reasoned with. Strategies of extermination are the extreme form of instrumental tactics which revolutionary protest movements often employ once they gain power. Playing a useful hermeneutic role as outside critics, they are often less adept or subtle when in control. Those revolutionaries who favor treating others as means, tricking or coercing rather than debating them, are given greater scope for this. Rigidity and certainty, combined with the creation of enemies, even in milder forms than the Khmer Rouge exhibited, can encourage this reduction. Protest movements can be strategic and manipulative before they gain power; control of the state simply gives them greater means for this kind of action.

We have seen milder forms of the tension between strategic and communicative action, a dilemma for all protest movements. And we have seen frequent cases of moral certainty that sustain protesters like John Gofman, a certainty that sometimes pushes protesters in the strategic, instrumental direction. As Maurice Isserman has written of a group of American trotskyites, "Within the SP [Socialist Party] the Shachtmanites continued to function as a small, disciplined cadre, operating in secrecy, persuaded that they alone possessed the truth, at once harsh and unscrupulous and self-righteous in their attitudes, oriented solely toward the struggle for power and the manipulation of power once gained."[22] This is a common temptation, which the Khmer Rouge pushed to the extreme.

THE VIOLENCE OF ABSTRACTIONS

Experience is never limited, and it is never complete; it is an immense sensibility, a kind of huge spider-web of the finest silken threads suspended in the chamber of consciousness, and catching every air-borne particle in its tissue.
—Henry James

Many observers have divided moral visions into two types, roughly what Max Weber called the "ethic of ultimate ends" and the "ethic of responsibility." *Abstract systems* tend to be deductive from a few basic, general principles. They claim to be universal and absolute, covering all cases regardless of social context. Religions, especially those concerned with salvation in an afterlife, have been the classic source of these moral visions, sometimes resulting in chiliastic movements expecting an imminent end to the world. Henry James's web of experience—in this world—holds few lessons for those who take their directives from another, spiritual world. Abstract systems, because they claim to unfold from basic principles with mathematical rigor, may be resistant, even impervious, to contradictory evidence from experiences in everyday life or politics. They are rigidly fixed on basic principles.

Another kind of moral system is highly sensitive to the nuances of specific time and place, that is, to cultural context. These *embedded systems* more readily perceive ambiguities, anomalies, and exceptions to the rules, when normal rules don't apply. They recognize the messy complexity of moral life; they can see tragic dilemmas in which there is no single right answer. Proponents ground their positions in their understandings of complex cultural traditions. Flexibility, openness, and nuance characterize such visions.[23]

The hubris of those with abstract visions is to think they can actually start over and rebuild the world from scratch, ignoring existing cultures. The abstract vision combines—most strikingly with the Khmer

Rouge—a premodern belief in social essences with an ultramodern hope that society can be remade at will. The risk of those with embedded visions, on the other hand, is to despair of ever changing or improving our lives, of criticizing or transforming our explicit rules. Embedded systems often lead to such a strong respect for tradition that political change is rejected; tradition can become an absolute authority much like the principles of the abstract systems (although, of course, the "traditions" of most traditionalists are partly their own invention, often far from the actual practices of previous generations).[24] But those who recognize life's complexity do not always give up on protest and change; they may simply see some limits on them. Because cultural change builds on existing meanings, the latter can be ignored only at one's peril. Shared cultural meanings allow protestors to communicate with others, not just manipulate them strategically. Yet considerable change in those meanings is possible—somewhere between total transformation and complete resistance to change.

Since much of this book has dealt with cultural change, I think we can outline both its possibilities and its pathologies. We have seen protest leaders open up moral vistas by articulating existing structures of feeling and yet also by coaxing their audiences into new understandings. Plausibility structures limit how fast these sensibilities change, and these sensibilities in turn limit the worldviews and ideologies constructed on them. Abstract blueprints ignore much of this complex cultural life, which is why they must often be imposed by force. Even when they are popular with many people, as Hitler was, those who would remake their societies from scratch must ignore large segments of culture and history.

Moral and cognitive grids that are streamlined and abstract tend to portray societies as *totalities*. They see the components of social life as tightly interconnected rather than as relatively autonomous. The most compelling contemporary example, marxism, characteristically sees legal, political, moral, and other systems as tightly coupled with the economy. There must be a functional fit between economic relations and other aspects of society.[25] Religious grids, instead, might see the devil's work or god's grace as underlying every component of society. Such images of totality have enormous implications for social change. If all practices are coupled, then changing one is possible only if all are changed. Any revolution must be a *total revolution*. There may also be a tone of conspiracy and paranoia, as power is seen as emanating from a center and pervading all the rest of society.

In contrast, if practices and institutions have some autonomy from each other, or at least could attain some autonomy, then each can be changed on its own, with some chance that it will not revert before others are changed. Change can be piecemeal rather than complete. There can be local powers. This view seems to encourage negotiation and compromise, since you can lose some battles without feeling this to be a total defeat. You may win the next battle. There is no ultimate, conclusive contest between good and evil.[26]

Like social systems, individuals too can be seen as changing either suddenly or gradually. To adopt an abstract moral system may require a sudden conversion, as the convert grasps the simple underlying logic of the system and accepts the rest on faith. People may come to embedded moralities more gradually, based on piecemeal accumulation of evidence through the test of experience rather than on a sudden epiphany.

By promising ultimate truth, abstracted worldviews hold out the hope of purity, an escape from ambiguity, compromise, and pollution. As Mary Douglas puts it, "The final paradox of the search for purity is that it is an attempt to force experience into logical categories of non-contradiction. But experience is not amenable, and those who make the attempt find themselves led into contradiction."[27] Jean-Paul Sartre, describing anti-Semites, similarly argued that they have no wish to acquire ideas: "[T]hey want them to be innate; since they are afraid of reasoning, they want to adopt a mode of life in which reasoning and research play but a subordinate role, in which one never seeks but that which one has already found, in which one never becomes other than what one already was. . . . Nothing but a strong emotional bias can give instant certitude, it alone can hold reasoning within limits, it alone can remain impervious to experience and last an entire lifetime."[28] The pure world of the abstract system, with all the beauty of mathematical perfection, is attractive because it fends off the challenges of messy experience. This appeal, make no mistake, is universal, even if most of us manage to resist it.

Those in the grip of a totalizing ideology reduce themselves as well as others to a facet of that ideology. One's movement identity takes over the self, crowding out other potential identities (as a son or daughter, for example) as well as any possible distance from that single identity. An identity should contribute to one's sense of self, not displace it.[29]

With the Khmer Rouge, we saw all these tendencies in stark form. They hoped for a sweeping, sudden transformation of every aspect of society, the result of a dramatic battle between themselves and the enemies of the revolution. Leaving any practice or institution untouched would allow it to fester with enemies and eventually to undo the revolution. Their paranoid vision was watertight, impervious to experience which did not already have a place in the system. Their obsession with purity led them to describe the enemies as "microbes," invisible, pervasive, and deeply rooted in party and society. In this vision they followed a long line of marxists whose reified conceptions of economic determination have, according to Derek Sayer, "placed enormous restrictions on human emancipation in this century, when embodied in the planning strategies (and very material apparatuses) of ruling parties in post-revolutionary societies. Marx spoke of the violence of things; the violence of abstractions can be equally devastating."[30] Twelve-year-olds were no longer sons or cousins, friends or lovers; they had "become" revolutionaries.

But the Khmer Rouge are hardly unique in reducing the complex world around them to a simple ideological model. In another notorious case, for instance, the Italian Red Brigades insisted that world capitalism had already reduced international bankers and NATO generals to cardboard figures; they had become their function in the world order. They could be eliminated, because they were capitalists and militarists, not real human beings.

Robert Jay Lifton documented a similar process among physicians involved in Nazi concentration camps. He described the complex mechanisms by which they came to justify their actions. In addition to psychological processes such as the splitting off of their "Auschwitz Self" from the rest of their identities, he mentioned ideological factors such as the willingness to blame Jews for Germany's troubles, making them "arch enemies of Germany."[31] The nation was itself reduced to an abstract essence, threatened by its enemies and in need of sacred renewal and purification, through blood sacrifice if necessary. One's identity as a German, as the Nazis defined it, crowded out other possible roles. As the embodiment of this "holy, divine Reich," the Führer, and not the doctors, was responsible for all that happened in the camps. Yet "even the Führer could be painted as 'helpless': because the Jew's evil forced the Führer to act or make war on him."[32] Here was a multipurpose enemy: "Jews—or the concept of 'the Jew'—were equated with every form of death-associated degeneracy and decomposition, including homosexuality, urban confusion, liberalism, capitalism, and Marxism."[33]

It is not simple to explain the appearance or the hold of either abstract or embedded visions. All of us some of the time, and some of us all of the time, need the certainty of simple, unquestioned beliefs. In some ways they provide part of the ontological certainty described in chapter 5. Higher education should discourage absolute visions, but the Red Brigades and Nazi doctors show that it is not fully effective as a prophylactic. Individual biography might contribute some explanatory power, except that entire groups get swept up into murderously abstract ideologies. Some social structures might lead to absolutist thinking: Mary Douglas claims that small, voluntary groups need this to maintain the morale of their members. At the end of the day, however, none of these factors, singly or together, are entirely persuasive.

A better analysis might emphasize the utility of simplifying ideologies for political leaders who are trying to mobilize people—whether they are running a modern state or attacking it.[34] Citizens and supporters must be jolted with powerful emotions that motivate them to act outside their daily routines, giving them the energy to march off to war or stand up to government tanks. Abstraction, simplicity, and totality become powerful rhetorical tropes, rendering political ideologies more compelling and memorable. Abstraction is a kind of condensing process to create symbolic references with broad connotations. Complexities are stripped away, down to an ideology's underlying god term. As we have seen, rhetoric and mobilization are inextricable, and they are linked via the adrenaline of emotion.

Life is an intricate interplay between our mental grids and our experiences, with each imposing itself on the other. Learning is the mutual adjustment whereby the two constantly interact and are transformed. Abstract ideologies threaten this balance, leading us to cling to our beliefs in the face of contrary evidence, and even to impose our beliefs on the resistant reality around us. Here, finally, is irrationality: an inability to respond realistically to the changing realities around us. Rigid worldviews rip us out of the "huge spider-web" of which Henry James spoke, and thereby distort our connections to the life around us. Rather than trying to change the fabric of social life from within, many ideologues wish to ignore the web and start over from scratch. This image of total revolution has proven a powerful mobilizing trope, if a dangerous one.

MAKING ENEMIES

[Y]ou have great works to do, the planting of a new heaven and a new earth among us, and great works have great enemies.
—Stephen Marshall, English Puritan preacher and member of parliament
in the 1640s

Nowhere is the danger of abstract ideologies more apparent than when they divide the world into friends and enemies, good people and bad.

Like the description of the world through a simplifying ideological lens, the labeling of enemies is both a powerful mobilizing mechanism and a dangerous weapon easily abused. No other cultural meanings so clearly fuse moral and emotional reactions with cognitive ones: enemies are not simply part of a neutral set of cognitive beliefs; they are people who are morally wrong, whom one should despise.

Earlier we saw how the identification of opponents and a formulation of blame could transform anxious frustration into purposive outrage. Injustice frames depend on a belief that others are shaping the world in ways the potential protestor dislikes. Once this negative affective charge is established, we now see, it can be hard to control.[35] Prolonged strategic conflicts, for example, can focus attention on the opponent rather than the grievance, with sustained outrage leading to deep and permanent hatred. If opponents are not simply other players in political games, but are instead reduced to positions in an abstract, totalizing ideology, then they can be destroyed. The dangerous traits attributed to one's enemies come to overwhelm the enemies' other human qualities. Abstract worldviews encourage essentialist thinking— bankers are "essentially" functionaries of international capitalism; urban dwellers are essentially enemies of Kampuchean socialism— which in turn often renders enemies unreformable. If they are inherently corrupt or counterrevolutionary, re-education may be impossible.

In a classic work, Carl Schmitt argued that one of the key functions of politics is to help us align ourselves with our friends and distance ourselves from our enemies. "The political," he wrote, "is the most intense and extreme antagonism, and every concrete antagonism becomes that much more political the closer it approaches the most extreme point, that of the friend-enemy grouping." And later, "Every religious, moral, economic, ethical, or other antithesis transforms into a political one if it is sufficiently strong to group human beings effectively according to friend and enemy."[36] Friends and enemies are one important dimension along which humans build their emotional, moral, and cognitive worlds. This distinction may be as ubiquitous in the cultural construction of reality as contrasts such as male versus female or culture versus nature seem to be. Such binary oppositions are apparently convenient to think with, powerful tools for imposing order on the complex world around us. When perceived enemies can be visually identified—as foreigners, or a minority ethnic group, for instance—they can serve as a resonant condensing symbol.

Much political life—not just protest—is driven by efforts to sort out "us" and "them," to express various solidarities. Phyllis Schlafly and others organized a backlash against feminism by appealing to an image of homemakers as somehow not "that kind" of woman, turning the women's movement's own identity against it. For many social movements, public opinion is more favorable toward the movement's issues than toward its activists, who are often seen as kooky and "different." People develop opinions partly as a response to the messenger rather than the message. Polls of public attitudes, whatever else they are, are often occasions for respondents to align themselves with either the government or its critics.[37] Even partisan electoral politics helps adherents to reinforce their identities in opposition to others. I have argued elsewhere that any political or policy issue provides a chance to show what kind of person you are, and what kind you are not, to confirm your partisan allegiances.[38] The establishment or reinforcement of collective identities and solidarities is a prominent aspect of political action. What is unusual—though, unfortunately, not rare enough—is the dehumanization of one's foes to the point that extermination seems reasonable.

When enemies are embedded in abstracted worldviews they are subject to what Erik Erikson called "pseudo-speciation:" they are treated as though they were another species, exhibiting more differences from the rest of humanity than similarities to it. To Erikson this psychological tendency to draw strong group boundaries is possibly universal; only occasionally does it become lethal: "[I]n times of threatening change and sudden upheaval the ideal of being the foremost species must be reinforced by fanatic fear and hate of other pseudo-species."[39] Under many circumstances, I would add, mobilization is furthered by fear and hate. Other pseudo-species stand outside the universe of moral obligation. They need not be treated "humanely." Although certain ideologues reduce others to essentialized categories of enemies, they don't do this in a vacuum. Even though they may deny their own cultural contexts or try to start anew, they are nonetheless influenced by their culture. We can predict the cultural raw materials with which they construct enemies.

NATURAL BOUNDARIES?

If protest movements exhibit a tendency to search for enemies, what groups and categories do they choose as targets? Why did the Khmer Rouge look backward to the old people rather than forward to new people? Why did American moral panics in the nineteenth century focus on foreigners in the northeastern cities? How does Jesse Helms mobilize support by attacking Robert Mapplethorpe and the National Endowment for the Arts? Why one group rather than another? The simple answer is that cultures identify certain places in the social structure as dangerous. Even abstract ideologies are molded by broader cultural meanings, as when the marxist-leninist thouhgt of the Khmer Rouge was used to condemn the long-haired students of the cities, contaminated by foreign influences. Threats emanate from those who are different in salient ways.

Mary Douglas once argued that cultural boundaries and classifications highlight the dangers of elements (anomalies, ambiguities, fuzzy grey areas) that do not fit neatly.[40] "Order," which contains cognitive, emotional, and moral elements, generates "disorder" in the form of what has no place. Thus, in Douglas's famous example, Hebrew dietary laws defined as unclean those creatures that did not fit smoothly into a division of the world into earth, waters, and firmament—and the behaviors and shapes appropriate to each. Shellfish live in water but do not swim; animals that "swarm" on the earth are not walking, as is appropriate to earthly locomotion. Classifications also cover people: some occupy ambiguous or poorly defined structural positions, and often face terrible accusations as a result.

What is striking is how often the same places and categories of people are seen and felt as threatening. Foreigners, for example, no matter how long they or their ancestors have lived in a country. And those at the bottom of the economic ladder, whether the working class, the unemployed, or the poor. For many, including the Nazis, the Khmer Rouge, American reformers of the nineteenth century, and Jesse Helms, cities and those who live in them are dangerous. Again and again, these form the building blocks out of which threats and enemies are constructed. Certain cultural distinctions, it seems, are easier to work with than others. As Douglas suggested, we can discern dangerous parts of culturally interpreted social structures.

Social sources of threat are often predictable because they are rooted in social structures and social change. One source involves the realities of *social hierarchies,* which are based on economic distinctions in most modern societies, and status or religious distinctions in many others (although these too typically have an economic basis). These boundaries become natural places to look for salient moral differences that a group can use in defining its enemies. Because differential access to economic or spiritual resources rests upon contrasting daily activities, moral distinctions are ultimately related to concrete daily practices, no matter how much autonomous development they undergo. The urban poor, for example, cannot always afford to live respectable middle-class lives. Lifestyles are proxies for, even help define, social status.

Social change also differentiates people, hitting certain groups before others. Cities are often the seedbeds for demographic, political, economic, technological, and cultural changes. It is migrants, many or most of them foreigners, who are often the vanguard of these changes. And it is frequently the poor who are the first victims. Economic and other transformations threaten ontological security, as do those who embody them. Neither stratification nor change automatically generates perceived threats or mobilization, contrary to several of the strain theorists in the crowd tradition. But these theorists were right that certain parts of society are more likely to generate protest than others, depending on how a culture maps itself.

To see the effects of social change, take an example that historians have studied extensively in recent years, the witchcraft accusations of early modern Europe and the United States—certainly one of the nastiest moral panics ever—in which one hundred thousand condemned witches were put to death between roughly 1450 and 1750. A disproportionate number of those accused and convicted were old, single women who lacked a solid economic livelihood. Already marginal, they subsisted—barely—by begging, stealing, doing odd jobs, and often selling magical potions. Further, as modernizing processes cut individuals loose from communal ties, these women were losing the few moral and economic claims they had on those around them. They had no clear place in the emerging order of industrial capitalism and nation-states. Accusing them of witchcraft was a way for the economically successful to renounce their responsibilities altogether, to deny any community with the losers. Such accusations, of outright malevolence and evil, are merely an extreme exemplar that later moral panics could mimic all too well.[41]

Cities have often been the sites of perceived corruption, as societies were colonized, industrialized, or brought into the orbit of the capitalist world system. As in the case of Phnom Penh, cities were the footholds of foreign influence and imperialism, as well as decadent places where loose morals of all kinds occurred. Not coincidentally, they were also the administrative centers of imperial powers and their corrupt puppets. They contained impurities of all kinds, as people and things jumbled together with little apparent order. In most cases cities really were the site of transformations in social structure, political order, and economic practices. They were indeed dangerous places.

It is no accident that foreigners, cities, and industrializing sectors represent "dangerous" or "polluted" areas of society against which revolutionary animus can be constructed, for these are the cutting edge of the capitalist world system. Revolutions, notoriously, occur during the early stages of modernization, with the attendant demographic boom, urbanization, state-building, and economic transformation (national markets, industrialization).[42] Revolutionary masses may understand these threats in a more or a less sophisticated or accurate way, but they have gotten the sources right. (Of course, many revolutions are urban-based, and so deploy a somewhat different set of friends and foes.[43] The Iranian revolutionaries, themselves based in cities, could hardly demonize cities in the same way that the Khmer Rouge, living in the countryside, could.) For such structural changes to become threatening, though, they must be given a cultural cloak.

Foreigners and their practices are another important symbolic building block. They arrive with many differences that can be essentialized: styles of dress, drinking habits, physiognomic traits, languages, and occupational skills. Their presence is often the result of imperial conquest or economic colonialism. Sometimes they are perceived as competitors for desired jobs.[44] Again, some cultural work is required to make immigrants appear dangerous. The Khmer Rouge had to deploy anti-urban and anti-imperialist traditions combined with elements of marxism. In the contemporary United States, anti-immigrant rhetoric not only appeals to racism but associates immigrants with other long-standing American obsessions such as drugs, crime, and welfare dependence.[45]

The dangers of foreign contamination easily become concentrated symbolically in heads of state. Revolutions often unfold against domestic leaders seen as corrupted by foreign influence, such as Lon Nol in Cambodia, Nicaragua's Somoza, and the Shah of Iran. These rulers were linked not only to Western influence, resources, and corruption, but specifically to the United States, the most potent contemporary symbol of capitalist economic power and imperialist military might. The influence of the West on these symbolic boundaries was complex, since many of the ideologues in both the Cambodian and Iranian revolutions had studied in France. In part they were reacting to what they had seen there, in part they were using abstractions they had learned there. The violation of national boundaries is a universally powerful cultural theme in the modern world, and virtually all revolutions use nationalist language. The "nation" is a powerful collective identity capable of inspiring massive mobilization.[46]

Because youth pose a challenge for every society—they must somehow be socialized into adult traditions and understandings—they are also a common threat. They are most likely to spark a moral panic: rock music, premarital sex, motorbikes, and drugs have all inspired cultural mobilization because they were read as signs of youthful rebellion. Youth are less likely to be subject to full-fledged revolutionary campaigns, since a society cannot really eliminate its own young people. If they belong to a particular class or other category, though, they might be expendable. The United States' stigmatization of young black men as dangerous and criminal comes close to this.

Categories of people are not the only cultural meanings that determine who will be singled out as an enemy. Another prominent building block—the contrast between old and new—relies on a culture's sense of time and history. Although many moral systems favor new over old ("new socialist man"), the Khmer Rouge also, simultaneously, harked back to an older, supposedly more pure period in their national history: the Khmer society of the Angkor period. Many Iranian revolutionaries also looked back to a pure Islamic period of Persian history. In neither case was the utopian past the earliest possible period that could have been referenced, but one selected for rhetorical convenience and symbolic resonance. Utopian pasts can foreshadow utopian futures, as well as highlighting supposedly essential traits of a nation. Some moral visions resonate with images of past societies, others with images of societies that have never been embodied.

Protest movements, especially revolutionary ones, necessarily look forward to a better future, even when its image resembles some Golden Past. This expectation will usually be linked to a metanarrative, which comes in two common forms: history as a fall from grace, or history as the march of progress. Although the history of ideas of progress in the modern world is complex, I believe that many abstract visions rest on the idea that history comes in stages, punctuated by rapid transformations. Faith that each stage is an unavoidable improvement over the previous one yields confidence in quick and sweeping revolutions. These visions typically foresee a final stage, when history ceases and there is heaven on earth.

But these positive, utopian images are normally coupled with—even overwhelmed by—negative, critical images. The Cambodian and other revolutions demonstrate a "power of negative thinking." The castigation of evil, isolating and attacking enemies, may be more powerful for forging political alliances than for developing positive policies, plans, and ideologies. It seems easier to forge consensus around an analysis of what is wrong with current policies than around directions for the future. As William James once said, explaining religious rejections of this world, "the sense of our present wrongness" is more powerful than any positive ideal of the alternative. This is the sense of threat we explored earlier in more moderate forms. Extreme perceptions of threat are often linked to a belief in total revolution. If one's enemies are so powerful and so evil, then destroying them has to lead to a vast and sudden improvement. When the existence of evil actors comes to be the central explanation of what is wrong with the present society, there is little need to think about other changes that should be made after the revolution. Removal of the cancer will transform all institutions.

MORAL MONOPOLIES

Fraternity, liberty and equality isolated from communal life are hopeless abstractions. Their separate assertion leads to mushy sentimentalism or else to extravagant and fanatical violence which in the end defeats its own aims.
—John Dewey

Enemies and essences are powerful mobilizing images. Essentialism provides a sense of inevitability and certainty; enemies are the perfect threat, inspiring emotions like fear, anger, and hatred. Both appeal to common moral intuitions by simplifying the world into neat slogans for mobilization. Yet the same rhetorical power can eat away at its own moorings, suggesting abstract utopias far from the moral sentiments that first inspired them. Knowing in advance how the world works—how history unfolds, who is on the side of progress or justice, which traits define people's essences—short-circuits our ability to learn anything new. Cultural frameworks provide answers, but they also provide the means for asking questions and pursuing new answers. They allow questioning, learning, and growth.

Any abstract grid for understanding the world runs the risk of being taken too seriously. Its proponents become guilty of what Alfred North Whitehead called "misplaced concreteness," when simplified labels and models of reality are taken to be reality. (This is a danger for social scientists and their conceptual frameworks as well as for protestors and their ideologies.) The more abstract the system is, the more it reduces human beings to categories and essential functions. Nor is there any reason to communicate with people whose positions and essences one knows in advance. Abstract and totalizing systems allow one to believe one has *the* truth. This possession is a powerful spur to action, even sweeping action. The human beings who are being acted *upon,* who resist because they lack access to the truth, must be overcome. Their ignorance, resistance, and evil are bound up together. The familiar arrogance of those who have special access to the truth may fall short of the murderous program of the Khmer Rouge, as with many protestors who speak for those they are trying to help. Both cases involve a disregard for the hopes and preferences of other individuals and groups, for their human complexities. They reveal a preference for the strategic moment of protest over its discursive one. As Geoff Merideth said of marxist-leninists, "I talk to people; they don't."

The actions of the Khmer Rouge could hardly be more different from those of the post-citizenship movements of the United States and Western Europe, even though Khmer Rouge rule coincided with the height of the direct-action antinuclear movement in the late 1970s. Because citizenship movements focus on state power, seizing the state has occasionally seemed a reasonable strategy for them, a strategy that post-citizenship, and especially post-industrial, movements usually reject as misguided and dangerous. But this difference is primarily one of power; the Khmer Rouge were able to impose their vision because they won control of the state. Even protest groups that do not aim at seizing the state can try to manipulate rather than persuade. One can share many post-industrial values, especially a critique of technocracy, but still lack that central concern with nonviolence, democracy, dialogue, and participation. The temptation to know "the truth" is strong even here. The Unabomber's manifesto, after all, sounded in many places like a post-industrial treatise. His main difference was strategic.

My interest in complex symbolic processes, in people's embeddedness within cultural networks, leads me to reject abstract visions. No one is essentially a tool of the capitalist state, a torturer for a dictator, or an enemy of the people (even though many people allow themselves to be reduced in this way). We have complex, overlapping identities that we construct ourselves, in collaboration with those around us. No single identity ever exhausts the self. Cultural constructionism has two edges: it gives hope to protestors because it means that we can change the world and our identities; but it also shows that we cannot change the world completely, from scratch, ignoring the complex layers of meaning and human bonds that already exist. This is true of artistic as well as political movements; as Mary Midgley says, "The romantic ideal of a totally fresh start, of a 'modern' movement owing nothing to any predecessors—a popular idea at the beginning of the 20th century—is, if taken literally, something of a fantasy. . . . Without a pre-existing framework of shared tradition, all words and notes would be indistinguishable and unmeaning noises. This is a general point about meaning. Where no patterns of expectations have been formed, nothing signifies and nothing surprises."[47] A constructionist view helps us avoid the perils of both objectivism (the idea that world is completely out of control) and relativism (we can do or believe whatever we wish).

We have examined extreme forms of a common problem: when protest becomes a form of expertise. This happens when protestors believe that only certain people have access to the truth, or that a restricted number have the specialized skills to carry out tactics. The rest of us become masses to be manipulated, a public whose opinions are to be probed, potential sources of funds. Protest becomes a virtuoso performance of the few, with the rest of us as audiences. We are politically deskilled, even when we support the actions of the virtuosi. The Khmer Rouge are a deadly example of this. Perhaps Greenpeace, with millions of contributors funding a small number of brave souls who suspend themselves from bridges and place their bodies in the paths of whaling vessels, is a mild example. In between, many anti-abortion protestors typically have unquestioned religious views which justify their efforts, not to persuade others, but simply to block them from having abortions. These three cases, odd to compare, share a confidence that some people have privileged access to moral action, perhaps even moral knowledge. Certain that they know the *substance* of morality, they can overlook the *process* of morality: the discourse, life passages, innovation, and learning by which we can continually interrogate ourselves about our moral sensibilities.

But expertise assumes some kind of professional standards for judging who is an expert. The only criteria available to protestors are those of ideological correctness or special skills such as bomb building. When they adopt such criteria, protestors have given up on democracy, which by definition cannot be handed over to experts. People need to plumb their own hearts, express their own values. Protest movements make their vital contribution to modern society in helping us to do this. Some people are more morally creative than others, but their creativity, like that of artists, consists in showing us the way, in expressing our own visions and actions, not in creating those visions for us. When moralists are put in charge, they cease being moralists. Strategy replaces persuasion and example.

Just as many artists lose their connections to common artistic traditions, so that no one understands their work, so many protestors and revolutionaries ignore or renounce their ties to other humans—with more devastating consequences than for the anomic artist. The best art plays along the border between the known and the unknown, expanding the horizons of what we can recognize; when artists ignore the familiar altogether and try to start from scratch, they lose their potential audience. They can, like extreme revolutionary protestors, lose connection with Ashbery's "matrix of our everyday thoughts and fantasies." Like some priestly caste, they believe that only their actions can save the rest of us.

MacIntyre suggests that we judge practices by their effects on the rest of society. By their own instrumental standards, the Khmer Rouge were as successful as a social movement can be, seizing the state and imposing—for a while—their grim utopia on Cambodia. But from the perspective of most other Cambodians, their rule was a disaster. They changed people physically, not morally. They coerced rather than persuaded. They ignored most of what I described as the attendant virtues of protest. In the terms of Kantian liberalism, they treated people as means, not ends. No one can consent to such treatment, since anyone reduced to the status of a thing rather than recognized as a subject is not capable of agreement or disagreement. Any form of deception violates this principle of consent. Few moral systems today would defend this kind of instrumental reduction.

Fortunately, it is a rare protestor who turns to murder. It is even rarer for a group to gain the military power necessary for a genocidal program. Having seen some risks of radical protest, we can turn to the more common benefits. The very creativity that can spin out of control provides, in moderate doses, an important way for humans to cope with economic, technological, and other kinds of social change. Protest movements can occasionally discourage learning, but they often foster it. We cannot define with certainty the line between dangerous and helpful creativity, for our values vary in modern societies. My attentiveness to cultural context leads me away from abstracted visions; others are attracted to these. Yet if my analysis of culture is accurate, it suggests some limits—both practical and moral—to political change. It also implies, we shall see, that protest is absolutely necessary in modern societies.

- Moral systems run the gamut from more abstract to more embedded in cultural traditions.
- When abstract systems reduce people to their essences and create categories of enemies, they can turn deadly.
- Cultures perceive certain parts of society as dangerous, such as the bottoms of hierarchies, the grey areas outside hierarchies, and the sites of social change.
- City dwellers, foreigners, the poor, and the young are often perceived and stigmatized as dangerous groups.
- Protest movements can be judged by how they treat humans: as conscious subjects, or as pawns to be manipulated.

SEVENTEEN

The Necessity of Protest

All great truths begin as blasphemies.
   —George Bernard Shaw

Despite its risks, modern protest can benefit both participants and so-ciety. It provides individuals with a rare chance to probe their moral intuitions and articulate or alter their principles. Collectively and pub-licly one can take a stand, define one's identity, cry out against injustice. Protest can be a tremendously satisfying part of a modern life; it can even become the defining activity of one's identity. For many, the cre-ativity of protest provides the experience of sheer joy, the play of a utopian vision.

Protest has potential value for modern society beyond the satisfac-tions of protestors themselves. Results include practical information about current problems and techniques for doing things better. At a deeper level, protest can inspire us all, even nonparticipants, to probe our intuitions and question our actions. This in turn is a key compo-nent of democracy, which depends on a conversation between compet-ing moral positions but also on the fullest elaboration of each of them. *My judgment of protest as a practice is based on the liberal assumption that individuals should have the ability to craft their lives artfully, as well as they can, and this means having at their disposal a wide range of possible models as inspiration.* Charles Taylor calls this "a freedom by which men are capable of conceiving alternatives and arriving at a definition of what they really want, as well as discerning what commands their adherence or their allegiance."[1] Diversity is important because, Will Kymlicka says, "everyone has an interest in having an adequate range of options when forming their aims and ambitions, and even those who experi-ment with or leave behind the conventional ways of life in society draw none the less on the social stock of meanings and beliefs in developing their alternative life-styles."[2]

Like artists and intellectuals, protestors are key articulators of these alternatives; their sheer number enhances awareness of choice, at least when they aim to persuade through example rather than manipulate through deception. To do their job well, all these characters need a certain critical distance from their own society; it helps for them to be slightly kooky outsiders. Criticism, Foucault once said, is a matter of making facile gestures difficult. If intellectuals can thus challenge us to serious, thoughtful actions and positions, so, at their best, can protest movements. In contrast, fundamentalists—in religion, art, or protest— hope to narrow our life choices, to limit our ability to shape our own goals and projects or to take a thoughtful stand. They are more inter- ested in the strategic moment of protest than the discursive one, for they believe in a fundamental truth that does not depend on per- suasion.

One gift of protestors is that they create controversy, and controversy is important because it leads to the weighing and testing of perspec- tives and values. People must decide if their opinions on an issue are consonant with their basic values. Just as modern science is driven by the institutionalized clash between scientists who disagree and chal- lenge each other, so society learns through similar conflicts between moral positions. Diverse modern societies can never achieve consensus over basic moral positions; at best we can hope for some mutual com- munication and appreciation across the moral divides. Protest move- ments and controversies, when they are allowed to flower, can help us do this.

Recall the impact of whistleblowers, for example. They make important information public, overcoming a devastating but univer- sal organizational problem: the organizations developing a technol- ogy or carrying on some process know the most about it, at a very de- tailed level, but they're most unable and unwilling to view it critically. Whistleblowers are a way to tap into failed test results, corrupted deci- sions, information about bad welds, and doctored cost figures. One major challenge in bureaucracy is to get adequate information to those who need it in making decisions, despite the many obstacles (corpo- rate secrecy, currying favor with superiors, industry's undue influence on regulators) to doing so. In some cases, major faults have been known to insiders who have kept them secret from both the public and regulators. Private acts of protest have occasionally made these risks known. Only then is informed public evaluation possible.

The antinuclear movement shows how protestors can also help transform public attitudes. As I have argued elsewhere, at the height of the controversy, when nuclear energy became an issue that one was expected to have an opinion about, people shifted their thinking so that their opinions lined up with their basic worldviews. Those suspi- cious of complex technologies, government regulators, and large cor- porations grew more skeptical of nuclear energy during the 1970s. After the controversy, some resignation set in, just as complacency had dominated before it. Only when debates were active did large numbers of the public "rationalize" their opinions on the basis of fundamental values.[3]

As we saw in the last chapter, not all protestors try to foster understanding. Many are happy to trick people if that furthers their goals, even to despise others if there is some payoff for that hatred (as pseudo-speciation of opponents may increase solidarity within one's own group). Thus Randall Terry told his followers in Operation Rescue, "I want you to just let a wave of intolerance wash over you. I want you to let a wave of hatred wash over you. Yes, hate is good."[4] Instead of taking seriously other people's efforts at autonomy and moral articulation, protestors like Terry wish to short-circuit these efforts. *For fundamentalists, democratic processes such as the exploration and articulation of one's moral vision have no value in themselves; they matter only if a person makes the right choice.* Concentrating solely on the product at the expense of the process, this instrumentalism vitiates what I take to be the practice of moral protest and its attendant virtues. There are plenty of bad as well as good protest movements.

HOW SOCIETY LEARNS

Every manner of learning goes on in a society, from the most specific (inventions of new products, research findings, books, a fresh image in a poem, a new recipe, political slogan, or philosophical analysis of sexism) to the most general (a new religion, shifts in basic values or assumptions, a new institution, effective mobilization by political movements). Most innovations, developed in laboratories, corporations, or state agencies, are presented to the rest of us as inevitable facts. How we are to feel about them, although shaped by advertising, schools, and other mechanisms, is mostly left to us. Protestors often help us sort out our responses. Post-citizenship movements, especially the post-industrial branch, are often a response to technological innovations, but even citizenship movements must change basic attitudes if they are to succeed over the long term. Legal rights are never enough. Moral panics and nationalist movements, two other types of protest, are also responses to social change.

We have moral intuitions, but someone needs to articulate these inchoate urges and sensibilities, develop them into explicit beliefs, programs, and ideologies. In doing this, protest organizers are very much like artists, putting into concrete form new ways of seeing and judging the world, new ways of feeling and thinking about it. They are not exactly creating moral sensibilities, at least not from scratch, since they're appealing to popular, pre-existing sensitivities. But they are helping to constitute and to shape exactly what these sensibilities imply, by collectively discussing and rationalizing statements and goals on the basis of the more intuitive feelings. Like artists, they are offering us visions to "try on" so we can see what fits. As Ezra Pound said of artists, protestors are "the antennae of the race." This may be a world of play, in Gadamer's sense, but it's a very serious one.

One of the biggest developments of the past thirty years is the post-industrial vision of nature found in environmentalism, the antinuclear movement, and the animal rights movement, much feminism, even New Age religions. The idea that humans are simply one component—albeit one severely out of kilter—in a broader, ecological system is a radical alternative to traditional, monotheistic views. Robert Paehlke has argued that it is the first new ideology since socialism arose in the nineteenth century.[5] This is a post-Christian vision of nature as more whole, based on a root metaphor of a web of connections. These moral sentiments have been used to elaborate a critique of domination and intervention, which has often been formulated as a critique of technocracy, and which has then become a full-blown theory of participatory democracy. This elaborate program, familiar to all of us, has been built gradually on top of the initial moral intuitions. The original impulses, the inchoate sentiments, grew out of changing social conditions: the rise of a professional middle class, with power based on higher education, and with a belief that the world is essentially rationally organized or organizable as a total system; a desertion of organized religion, especially outside the United States, but also by certain middle-class segments within it; and perhaps a general loosening of the more heavy-handed, direct mechanisms of authority. Waves of protest have refined the implications of these emerging moral sentiments into a new way of understanding the world—and also of acting in the world. Various kinds of practical, even technological, results have come from this new perspective. I'll mention a few examples of new knowledge from the antinuclear, environmental, and animal rights movements.

Antinuclear movements, in a variety of countries, brought pressure to bear on regulators to tighten standards, even though they didn't usually create the engineering knowledge behind the new standards. Their main function was to bring greater rationality to decision making, as gatherers, compilers, of information. Delay itself, in the United States especially, brought greater cost-benefit skepticism to nuclear policy, allowing greater scrutiny of costs. So the movement allowed new, emerging information to be used. It also helped to spread this information. This was not just a random dissemination of information, but a *strategic placement of knowledge* in the hands of those who could use it.

Protest movements can provide an *infrastructure* for critical information—contacts with the news media, financial support, some legal protection, perhaps political shelter. This infrastructure rarely matches that on the other side, but it's important for sustaining any public debate. Such resources are important, though, because of the ideas and feelings they help to convey. The main effect of the antinuclear movement on social knowledge was the dissemination of information and the increased rationality of discussions due to a clash of points of view. There was less effect on actual scientific and technical research, which is understandable given the high cost of reactor research.

The environmental movement has actually encouraged and enabled new scientific findings. In some cases it has funded scientists, in others it has inspired them. One of the main scientific avenues stimulated by the environmental movement, often undertaken by individual scientists sympathetic to the movement's ideas, is the development of benign, renewable substances to replace harmful ones. Fuel is the most obvious: sewage, wood chips, hydrogen, and any kind of biomass can be burned to good effect. But there are others: hungry microbes have been developed to replace chemical pesticides; medicines are derived from rain-forest plants and animals; efforts are being made to derive plasticlike materials from plants (this is, after all, what cellophane is); a clay powder has been produced that absorbs radioactive wastes from water; microscopic glass beads are used to coagulate oil spills; bacteria are deployed to clean up all sorts of pollution.

In addition to new products, there is a revival of folk knowledge in the use of already-existing substances that are environmentally friendly: adobe and other natural building materials are coming back into fashion. There's the environmentalist's friend, baking soda, which activists insist can be used as toothpaste, deodorant, and scouring powder. Certain plants have been found to remove heavy metals from contaminated soil. Or take the case of International Wildlife Research, a group that spent $18 million saving a few hundred otters after the Exxon Valdez oil spill. Their work cost about $50,000 per otter, but they gained considerable understanding of exactly how oil kills otters, and how they might survive—knowledge that can be used in future spills. Finally, there are the thousands of volunteers who have traveled around the world to help scientists gather information about the environment, about endangered species, about climate patterns. They pay their own way, and help out on the assumption that the more we know about the environment, the better we can help it.

The animal rights movement has also directly affected scientific research. In attacking the use of live animals in cosmetics testing, activists demanded that the big cosmetics companies contribute a certain amount of money to research on alternatives. This quickly amounted to several million dollars, enough to start institutes at Johns Hopkins and Rockefeller Universities devoted to alternative methods of toxicity testing. There has been considerable progress in alternatives such as computer modeling, data banks on known toxic compounds, the use of simpler species rather than more complex ones, the use of egg embryos, the development of live cell and even tissue cultures. More obviously, the movement has helped to invent ways of treating animals more humanely—better conditions for factory farms, more healthful regimens for laboratory animals. The animal rights movement is one example of protesters *forcing corporations to be more rational*—even by the companies' own standards. It turns out that non-live-animal testing is less costly and in many cases more accurate than older tests. Similarly, whale researchers developed alarms to scare whales away from Newfoundland fishing nets, not only sparing their lives but saving fishermen one million dollars a year in damaged equipment. Protest and science have forced these organizations to make themselves more efficient.

There are other examples of the scientific effects of protest. Phil Brown has described "popular epidemiology," in which citizens gather their own data on cases of leukemia and other diseases, seeing patterns of risk that experts overlook. Precisely because they expect dangers and risks that the experts don't, activists can go out and find new patterns of diseases. Shocked by their own or a loved one's illness, initially dismissed as kooky—worried about unseen threats—these protestors mapped the world in a new way, quite literally laying out maps and looking for patterns of disease. Physicians are simply not equipped to see certain kinds of environmental effects. They "are largely untrained in environmental and occupational health matters, and even when they observe environmentally caused disease, they are unlikely to blame the disease on the environment."[6] In the case that Brown and Edwin Mikkelson studied in Woburn, Massachusetts, epidemiological research would never have been undertaken, for lack of interest or resources, without community involvement. This case is hardly unique: "Popular participation brought to the national spotlight such phenomena as DES, Agent Orange, asbestos, pesticides, unnecessary hysterectomies, abuse of sterilization, black lung disease, and brown lung disease."[7]

Post-industrial movements are especially likely to have a strong critique of science or technology, and so to have ideas about how to do these differently. Would the same range of practical implications characterize other types of movements? Even the labor movement is interested in technologies of the workplace, looking not only for safety and health but also practices that affect the autonomy and satisfaction of workers (assembly lines vs. job teams and rotation). European unions have done more than their American counterparts to encourage new labor practices. The workers' movement is interested in the practical implications of its moral vision. Civil rights groups, similarly, have taken on issues such as sickle-cell research and the notorious Tuskegee syphilis experiments. In the end, though, citizenship movements are more interested in political change and moral inclusion, and are more likely to change our sensibilities at this level. New forms of knowledge vary, in both type and extent, across protest movements.

The American antiabortion movement is a very different example. It's a movement I disagree with, and one that seems wholly against certain technologies, rather than interested in coming up with alternatives. Its fundamentalist confidence that it knows the truth makes it more interested in manipulation than dialogue. Its moral vision is based on its own version of a critique of experts and of instrumental reasoning, but it links this to faith in god and god's will. So it has led to an elaboration of a certain tradition of moral thinking about the extension of rights, about the relationship between doctors and their patients, about the extreme individualism of American political discourse. At the practical, technical level, its effects are less extensive: perhaps an elaboration and certainly a dissemination of techniques for natural family planning, and perhaps the development of networks for adoptions. These could be important for those who use them. Most of all, though, it has forced us all to think about abortion, to ask ourselves what a good birth control regime would be, what the status of the fetus is when life begins. These are important questions, even when we roundly reject Operation Rescue's answers (not to mention their deceptive or coercive tactics).[8]

We don't have to assume that social movements are right, or somehow privileged, in order to argue that they help citizens think through their moral and cognitive positions. Confronting a movement you disagree with can help you articulate your own position. Social knowledge is not advanced by privileged actors or institutions, somehow outside the biases and interests of existing society, but by the clash of perspectives, by the debate and the counterarguments. It's the proliferation of viewpoints that helps us sort out better claims from worse ones, or moral claims that are consonant with our basic values from those that are not. The existence of alternative viewpoints advances our knowledge.

We should not exaggerate the effects of protest movements. They may develop new ways of thinking and acting, as I have described, but this does not mean that their innovations will be universally adopted. Corporations and governments have considerable power to resist, and protest movements can rarely force them to change. Even the civil rights movement, one of the most successful protests in American history, after its legal victories in the mid-1960s, has had disappointingly little effect on the lives of poor African Americans. Citizenship movements must change cultural attitudes, not just laws. It is not easy to change either one.[9]

Even so, if modern citizens are to articulate their moral visions, rather than simply their technical practices or cognitive beliefs, protest movements appear crucial. After all, there are a variety of institutions designed to increase our technical and cognitive abilities—universities and other research institutions, government agencies, even corporations partly do this. But how many institutions are devoted to our moral thinking? Precious few, especially with the widespread loss of religious faith in many advanced industrial nations. Even schools are primarily concerned with cognitive issues, not explicitly moral ones (efforts by the Christian Right notwithstanding). The news media, too, have an ideology of positivist objectivity, and try not to articulate moral positions. Schools and the media certainly inculcate moral values—but usually implicitly, in such a way that their audiences are not able to decide for themselves what morals to embrace. Protest movements are a key way that modern citizens can articulate their moral visions for themselves.

This is the reason that scholars have made so much over the concept of a "public sphere" in recent years, mostly bemoaning its demise. Protest movements are most beneficial in liberal societies with institutions that protect a clash of opinions, so that the movements' "moral voice" function is most developed. They are at their worst when such guarantees are absent, even when protestors themselves are the ones who have gained power and removed them. Again, final judgments of protest movements depend on their broadest social effects.

Social movements are also a fundamental means by which practices as well as beliefs are rationalized. They spread information, breaking down roadblocks laid by those with power; they suggest cheaper technologies to corporations caught in inertia; they ask regulators to follow their own mandates. Almost as a by-product of morality and rationality functions, protest movements also create and disseminate more technical knowledge. To oversimplify: with technical knowledge, social movements play more the role of disseminators rather than creators; with moral knowledge, they play more the role of creators. But the two kinds of knowledge feed off each other. The post-industrial view of nature is not merely cognitive, nor is it merely a new moral vision. It's a practical way of living in the world. Worldview assumptions about nature have direct implications for technologies that transform nature. People have projects in the world, so that their moral visions and cognitive beliefs provide emotional motivation and practical guidance about what to do, how to carry on. These recent movements' image of nature is a context for living and acting, not simply a mental grid.

The modern environmental vision, in particular, is based on extensive rational intervention. Even though it sometimes presents itself as noninterventionist, its primarily middle-class roots encourage considerable intervention of a very practical sort. Indeed, what environmentalism is often about, as a movement, is increasing the rationality and scope of our practical, scientific control over the natural world. The underlying moral vision—essentially, that the natural world is sacred, has spiritual value in its own right—is fused with but often overwhelmed by the middle-class impulse toward control and intervention.

Different groups within a movement may elaborate and promote different parts of its vision. *Some specialize in the logic of the moral vision, radicalizing it, taking it to its logical extreme. Others specialize in techniques and practical action.* Some movements get divided between purists and pragmatists, or *fundis* and *realos,* because the fundis insist on the primacy of the pure moral vision, despite practical obstacles, while the realos want to know how to act. In some cases the radicals make the moral vision into a simplified, abstract system, giving too much credence to their own model. But as the real poets of a movement, the radicals who live out their visions to the fullest are an important inspiration and starting point for self-reflection.

Protest movements work at the edge of a society's understanding of itself and its surroundings. Like artists, they take inchoate intuitions and put flesh on them, formulating and elaborating them so that they can be debated. Without them, we would have only the inventions of corporations and state agencies, products and technologies created to enhance efficiency or profitability. In order to understand these innovations, we need "moral innovators" too: the artists, religious figures, and protestors who help us understand what we feel about new technologies. It is no accident that these three modern character types frequently overlap, as in artist-activists or religious activists. All three provide social learning, as their formulations enter the public discourse.

Among its satisfactions, protest creates a separate world for its participants, in which they do things they can't do in the quotidian world, establish modes of interaction, gain a taste of a just society, or simply dream. This is quite like art. Sartre describes the experience of leaving a play or concert only to feel "the nauseating disgust that characterizes the consciousness of reality."[10] Wolfgang Iser similarly alludes to the sense of flow in art when he says that the return to everyday reality "is always to a reality from which we had been drawn away by the image-building process. . . . The significance of this process lies in the fact that image-building eliminates the subject-object division essential for all perception, so that when we 'awaken' to the real world, this division seems all the more accentuated."[11] In this prefigurative, artful way, much protest carves out a small world of its own.

The articulation of moral beliefs is the most prominent contribution of the protestor, since there are relatively few sources of these in modern urban societies. Protest quickly gets at the deepest moral questions: how should we live our lives; what are our moral responsibilities, and to whom? We are asked to look anew at moral categories such as fetuses, nonhuman species, even such "pseudo-species" as counter-revolutionaries, racial minorities, or foreigners. Whether or not we agree with their answers, protestors encourage us to shake down our belief systems, interrogating our own intuitions in order to rationalize our own beliefs, principles, even feelings. Of course, when we all have stopped changing our minds, this discursive function dries up.

Protestors are not simply moral innovators, they also transform tactics and organizational forms. Countercultural groups like the Abalone Alliance thought out the political implications of formal organizations, searching for democratic mechanisms in line with their basic moral commitments. Tactical innovations abound, from boycotts to New Age rites to Operation Rescue's military operations and human chains in blocking abortion clinics. Like organizational forms, tactics are never neutral means, but express new moral understandings of appropriate political action.

Self-transformation, finally, is a frequent goal and result of protest. The most extreme version is the man or woman whose identity and career become bound up with protest activities; she becomes that character type ridiculed by George Orwell and others, but who is important for the well-being of modern societies. Short of such complete identification with the role, though, protest movements suggest ways for all of us to live. Morality, after all, is not simply about our obligations to each other. It is also about the good life, about how each of us should live. Socrates saw this more clearly than modern philosophers, but protestors pick up quickly on people's groping efforts to figure out how to live their lives.

I have mentioned several movements—the environmental, animal rights, and antinuclear—that have grappled with how humans should understand their place in the natural world without the guidance of traditional religion. Influenced, ironically, by advances in modern science that undermine religious stories of the natural world, these protestors are working out how we should live in a socially constructed world. Should we control our own deaths? Should we extend our moral concern to plants and animals? What is the value of ecological balance? What is the purpose of new technologies? Protestors, like artists and religious leaders, can help us find answers to basic questions. Indeed my own moral position, articulated in these last three chapters, is inspired by recent post-industrial movements.

POLITICAL IMPLICATIONS

My cultural view yields a potential means for evaluating political activity. Some programs ignore human embeddedness, pursuing instead an abstract agenda that would remake the social world from scratch. Those dangerous utopias range from egalitarian communism to the radical free market of Milton Friedman. Others assume that humans exist in a web of social bonds and meanings, and demand a coherence from those meanings or a tightening of certain bonds. Some discourage moral thoughtfulness; others encourage it. To be judged as a form of moral voice, protest must be examined in terms of the virtues it encourages, the ways it fits into the lives of individuals, and the role it plays in society as a whole.

The embedded, artful view of social life also carries several implications for the practice of social research. The anticultural "view from nowhere" that once dominated the philosophy of social science implied that we should strive for general, universal laws of human behavior, and the best methodological model for this pursuit seemed to be the mathematical precision of physics and chemistry. The cultural approach implies that we can be most certain about our local knowledge, not our general knowledge, for we cannot know in what contexts our findings will apply. This application, when it works, can only evolve out of dialogue with those from other cultural settings.

Rather than deriving spare axioms, we might think of our task as the proliferation of conceptual tools that we can apply as needed.[12]

The order of priority in social research might be reversed. In the model of general science, we are supposed to begin with hypotheses, venture into the empirical world to gather data that might test them in some way, and then return to our theoretical world to rearrange our models. For this reason, grand theory and extensive data gathering are two sides of a single positivist coin, as C. Wright Mills showed. The starting point and the endpoint are in the world of theory, not in the world of social problems and particular puzzles.

In contrast to theory building and testing, the human sciences today are more and more involved in concept proliferation. This could, in the old view, be merely one aspect of theory building: the creation of useful language. But in my cultural view it is one of the end products of research. New concepts are like new tools, which we can apply in new situations. By themselves they add to our social-scientific repertory, and give us more tools to choose from in trying to understand any social phenomenon. Albert Hirschman's concepts of exit, voice, and loyalty, for instance, have helped countless researchers make sense of human activities. They expanded our horizons, helped us see new mechanisms and motivations, without precluding any of the concepts we had previously used. *Whereas the positivist urge is to minimize the explanatory factors we see at work, the cultural urge is to increase them, to concentrate on mechanisms, not grand theories.*[13] I offer the concepts in this book as building blocks, as tools researchers may find useful in some cases but not others, and not as universal theories to be tested.

By concentrating on marxist traditions, Ernesto Laclau and Chantal Mouffe have cogently attacked the possibility of general theories of political action. Recognizing that protest arises from diverse groups and pursues varied ends, rather than from predictable economic interest and positions, they argue that no group of protestors is any deeper or more historically significant than any other. Protest groups themselves, through a variety of internal mechanisms, work out what they want and how they will try to get it. Only attention to protestors' cultural meanings will encourage us to take them seriously as strategic actors, to encourage their participation in democratic conversations.[14]

Those who lack political rights or economic subsistence may give these priority when they organize to protest. Recognition of the essential equality of all humans, and of the basic individual rights this implied, was an enormous advance over an aristocratic hierarchy of differences in the early modern Western world. This universalism was a central inspiration for greater personal autonomy and political democracy, two moral goods that have spread rapidly throughout the world—at least in part because of their natural appeal to so many groups of people. In a theoretical reflection of these citizenship movements, mobilization and process theorists announced that protestors were political actors just as purposive, if not more so, than the well-behaved, civic-minded voter who occasionally wrote to her legislators. Mass marches and civil disobedience could be good for democracy, allowing new voices to be heard and making rigid organizations more accountable. Treating protestors as rational actors not so different from profit-maximizing businesses was a more sympathetic view than treating them as impulsive crowds.

Yet the rationalist language of resource flows and utility maximization encourages the observer to state groups' preferences for them. It suggests that we know what they should want, or what they really want, regardless of what they think or say they want. It is not only marxists who attribute false consciousness to those who do not follow the theorists' descriptions and prescriptions. Even citizenship movements must work at constructing their interests and goals.

The cultural approach is intended to give the voice back to the protestors we study. We can watch them working out their interests, grappling with their sensibilities, struggling over the language they use and the visions they pursue. No one can do these things for them; no one can predict where they will arrive in their deliberations. Our scholarly appreciation of their cognitive, emotional, and moral struggles can only help us cherish what protest movements can offer to society and their members. If my view of protestors' creativity is too romantic for some, there are also the critical standards for judging protestors that I have tried to develop. If, as I have argued, protest is centrally about moral voice, we can criticize movements that undermine the communication and soul-searching that sustain this. We can praise the movements that take democracy seriously.

I can celebrate protest and its accomplishments in part because I have a modest vision of what they are capable of. I was never part of a movement that thought it could change the world. I don't believe in sudden, total transformations, which are neither possible nor good. The Cambodian case is as close as we can come to a new society, and it hardly inspires me. Seeing social movements as a source of vision and voice, rather than the vanguard of a new world, I am not bothered by the fact that they accomplish so few of their stated goals. These goals are often overdrawn; the importance of protestors, I think, lies more in their moral visions than their practical accomplishments. They are more like poets than engineers.

Appendix on Evidence

Because cultural feelings and meanings have both a public, collective face and a private, individual one, it is important to get at them through a variety of methods. Since the early 1980s I have interviewed over one hundred protestors to get at their visions of the world, spending several hours with most, several days with others, and revisiting some years later. Most of these were antinuclear protestors, interviewed originally for *Nuclear Politics,* or animal rights activists, interviewed for *The Animal Rights Crusade.*

The extent of my longer interviews makes each of them a kind of life history rather than a standard depth interview. In several cases I have written vignettes, based on these life histories, that open chapters. Because of the considerable detail, anonymity would not have worked very well. In other cases, when I quote from interviews, I do not name my respondents. And because the dates of my interviews rarely matter, I do not give these. Most of the Diablo Canyon activists were interviewed around the time of the demonstration I surveyed in August 1984. I spoke with other antinuclear activists in 1985 and 1986, including many Europeans, but these results inform this book only in a general way. Most of the animal protectionists were interviewed in 1989 and 1990; most lived in New York or the San Francisco Bay area, although some were from Washington and Boston. In both movements, I talked to those whose names I had seen in print or to whom I was referred by others in their movement. They were not meant to be a representative sample, but an influential one. They were usually the ones choosing strategies, not following them. Around 1990 I also placed advertisements in several political magazines, asking to interview activists. The responses led to a couple of dozen additional interviews with protestors from a wide variety of causes. In several additional projects I sent students into the field; they participated in studies of the anti-abortion movement, local environmental and land-use actions, and whistleblowers, although I do not quote from these interviews unless the student and I together visited someone.

I have tried to write about individuals frequently in the book because I think they represent a different slice into protest than we get when we emphasize formal organizations, protest events, or news coverage (things more easily counted). Individuals move in and out of organizations, attend some events but not others, share some official group views but not others. Some have long-term careers as participants in many movements and groups, suggesting a different way of thinking about motives, pleasures, and choices in protest, complementing more structural information. And depth interviews are the only way, I imagine, to get at biography and strategic choice.

At the opposite end of the spectrum, I have used publicly available documents and symbols primarily to get at movement ideas and feelings. These are more refined materials that protestors deploy in strategic ways, often to outsiders or potential supporters. What is surprising, perhaps, is how often the same meanings or feelings appear here as in the more private interviews, suggesting either that there is not much divergence between protestors' strategic and communicative impulses or that they are carefully strategic in what they say to me. Some of each may be true, although I consider myself a sufficiently good interviewer to get at genuinely intimate feelings at least some of the time—and to recognize when I am not doing this. As all interviewers know, of course, people rewrite their own histories, so that retrospective interviews often get at how individuals feel they "must" or "should" have thought or felt at a certain moment rather than how they "actually" did. That is why it is helpful to get at the same meanings through the more "embodied" culture of public symbols and photos and statements made at the time.

Those who are skeptical about retrospective interviews usually dismiss interviewing as a valid research tool altogether, abandoning the interpretive search for meaning and typically excising mental constructions from their models. I think the burden of proof should be on them to show how interview findings are distorted, so that we can adjust for the biases. Meanings may be hard to get at, but that does not mean they don't exist, much less that they have no effect.

I have also spent some time as a participant observer, especially in meetings, marches, and rallies of the animal rights movement. Since group members are the main audience for internal meetings, I expect that there is less posturing for strategic reasons. Conversations with and observations of fellow participants would seem an especially good opportunity for intimate evidence. I do not see this kind of evidence as more accurate or honest than other forms, but simply as aimed at a different audience, namely fellow participants rather than the media, state agencies, or the public. For the animal rights movement, most of my direct participation was with a now-defunct group named Trans-Species Unlimited, which had a large New York chapter that sponsored the New York demonstration that we surveyed in 1988. It was the main group attacking both Cornell and New York University in the late 1980s (described in chapter 13).

Surveys are my fourth source of evidence. They are a blunt way of getting at cultural meanings, biographical traits, or strategic choices, but necessary for examining distributions of those meanings and how these are correlated with other social characteristics. I collected similar data at three protests organized by social-movement groups: an August 1984 demonstration of almost one thousand people at the gates of the Diablo Canyon nuclear power plant in California, an April 1988 rally of roughly one thousand people protesting an experiment using monkeys at New York University (sponsored by Trans-Species Unlimited), and a rally of a hundred people opposed to animal experimentation at the University of California at Berkeley, also in April 1988. For Diablo Canyon, 136 surveys were completed at the protest, and 137 were mailed in later. In New York, 270 surveys were completed at the protest. At Berkeley, 35 surveys were mailed in. Thus at all three events, roughly one-third of the demonstrators completed surveys. I distributed them alone at Berkeley; a friend helped me at Diablo Canyon; and several of my NYU students helped out in New York. In each case the questionnaires were distributed evenly to all parts of each crowd. Although by this method we could not obtain truly representative samples, I feel this procedure yielded no obvious biases. Although certain questions were tailored to the particular protest and cause, most questions about demographics, cultural beliefs, political activism, and recruitment into protest were identical in the three surveys. The Berkeley animal rights protest occurred on a weekday, limiting the kinds of people who could attend. The other two events were on weekends. The three featured similar activities. Each began with speeches (Berkeley and Diablo Canyon) or chanting and picketing (New York), lasting one hour at Berkeley, two at New York, and three at Diablo Canyon. Then small groups of protestors began offering themselves for arrest by blocking roads or entrances; in New York and at Diablo Canyon roughly one hundred people were quietly arrested. The Berkeley protest had been billed as a direct-action event rather than a rally: participants spent most of the day moving around the large campus chanting in front of buildings where animal research was conducted. Because all three protests included both legal and illegal activities, there is no reason to believe the three appealed to different kinds of protestors with different tastes in tactics.

Participants at three events are not necessarily representative of the two movements to which they belonged. But useful internal diversity, at least in the movement against Diablo Canyon, appeared in my sample. I have checked my results against whatever data were available from national samples. I have also paid additional attention to organizations, magazines, and individuals with a clear national reach, for if there is any coherence to a national movement, they are the ones who create it. Because this is not a book about a particular movement or set of movements, certain issues of whether my data and interviews are representative seem irrelevant. It does not matter whether all anti-nuclear protestors are like the anti-Diablo activists I surveyed, or whether all local boycotts are like the Montgomery bus boycott. I am trying to point up particular mechanisms and dynamics which appear in many movements, but not all, and in varying forms and varying degrees. Trans-Species is not a typical animal rights group—if such a thing exists—but it is hardly unique. The traits most relevant to my use of it—its strategic choices, the responses it elicited, its members' views and networks—are shared not only with certain other animal rights groups but with many groups in other movements. Much of my argument depends on differences among movements and among groups within the same movement, especially when I show that many theorists have made sweeping claims on the basis of a single type of protest movement.

A second data set, described in chapter 11, was created from telephone interviews concerning boycotts from the early 1980s, although few of these findings are reported.

Historical materials, mostly secondary sources, were the basis for case studies of the Khmer Rouge and several of the boycotts analyzed. The formality of the Khmer Rouge documents and reports suffices for my description of their abstract ideology, although I cannot get at the accompanying emotions or—for anyone beyond Pol Pot—biographical details. These materials also limit me to examining the later stages of protest creativity, when something is tried and works, rather than the early suggestions and groping efforts.

Different research techniques have natural affinities with different theoretical approaches. You cannot go out into the field and interview participants if you are studying strikes in the nineteenth century. You need not if you expect political structures to determine all strategic choices. If you believe that social movements consist of formal organizations, that is what you will study, and the only individuals you will see are the leaders of those organizations. If you see strategic choice as a form of interaction, then you must study opponents as well as protestors. If you believe that outcomes result from resource distributions, you will trace financial flows. Increasingly, scholars are recognizing the importance of disparate factors and dimensions. As a result we need diverse techniques in order to understand protest. This is especially true if we hope to understand the complex effects of culture, biography, and creativity.

Notes

1. Some definitions: As I say in the text, I believe that most social movements are also protest movements, one exception being certain kinds of religious movements which aim only at transforming members and attracting converts rather than protesting some broader issue (as many other religious movements nonetheless do). What is more, all protest movements have some moral dimension (although its salience varies across movements). Moral protest, though, involves not only the activities of such organized movements, but also of individuals working toward the same end. An isolated individual with idiosyncratic goals or tactics—the Unabomber for instance—is engaged in moral protest without being part of a protest movement. Other individuals, who work alongside protest groups with parallel aims, I would consider part of the protest movement—in contrast to those researchers who emphasize formal organizations as the components of movements. Part of my goal is to show the varying relationships between individuals and formal groups—between protestors and their movements. Most scholars define individual protest as outside their purview, making it impossible to test its impact on organized protest.

2. See Starhawk, *Dreaming the Dark: Magic, Sex, and Politics* (Boston: Beacon Press, 1988), pp. 168–69. This chant was used by members of Women's Pentagon West while they wove shut the doors of San Francisco's Bohemian Club.

3. I do not define post-industrial movements as "new" social movements or as those movements peculiar to "post-industrial society," but as the recent wave of post-citizenship movements concerned with democratic control, especially of science, technology, and nature.

4. Joshua Gamson, for example, analyzes ACT UP as a post-industrial movement, concerned with the media, cultural imagery, and the practice of science, rather than with voting and legal disadvantages: "Silence, Death, and the Invisible Enemy: AIDS Activism and Social Movement 'Newness,'" *Social Problems* 36 (1989): 351–367.

5. Francesca A. Polletta, "Strategy and Identity in 1960s Black Protest: Activism of the Student Nonviolent Coordinating Committee, 1960–1967" Ph.D. diss., New Haven: Yale University, 1994).

6. Peter Singer, *Animal Liberation* (New York: New York Review of Books, 1975).

7. "Protest as art" is a metaphor with a philosophical tradition behind it. In *Art as Experience* John Dewey argued that art had, in addition to its imaginative aspect, a critical and moral component. Both art and criticism were supposed to evaluate a society's beliefs and feelings "with respect to the good." See also Dewey, *Experience and Nature* (La Salle, Ill.: Open Court, 1929), p. 330 nn.

2. THE CLASSICAL PARADIGMS

1. John Lofland, "Theory-Bashing and Answer-Improving in the Study of Social Movements," *American Sociologist* 24 (1993): 37–58.

2. Robert R. Alford and Roger Friedland, *Powers of Theory: Capitalism, the State, and Democracy* (Cambridge: Cambridge University Press, 1985). They say that the "home domain of each theoretical perspective [they are concerned with traditions in political sociology] comprises a particular level of analysis, world view, and method" (p. 15).

3. Gustave le Bon, *The Crowd: A Study of the Popular Mind* ([1895] New York: Viking, 1960). For similar works, see Sigmund Freud, *Group Psychology and the Analysis of the Ego* (London: International Psychoanalytical Press, 1921), and Robert E. Park, *The Crowd and the Public* ([1904] Chicago: University of Chicago Press, 1982). Clark McPhail coined the phrase used for his title, *The Myth of the Madding Crowd* (New York: Aldine de Gruyter, 1991). For analysis of this tradition, see McPhail's book; Serge Moscovici, *L'Age des Foules* (Paris: Fayard, 1981); Susanna Barrows, *Distorting Mirrors: Visions of the Crowd in Late Nineteenth-Century France* (New Haven: Yale University Press, 1981); and Jaap van Ginneken, *Crowds, Psychology, and Politics, 1871–1899* (New York: Cambridge University Press, 1991). For a recent effort to take crowd dynamics seriously, see Charles Lindholm, *Charisma* (Oxford: Blackwell, 1990).

4. Herbert G. Blumer, "Collective Behavior," in Robert E. Park, *ed., An Outline of the Principles of Sociology* (New York, Barnes and Noble, 1939). McPhail (*The Myth of the Madding Crowd*, chap. 2) points out another tradition of research on crowds (including psychologists Floyd Allport and Neal Miller and sociologist John Dollard) that also viewed them as irrational, but thought that participants came to them with innate drives or frustrations that *predisposed* them to violent activities.

5. Neil J. Smelser, *Theory of Collective Behavior* (New York: Free Press, 1962), chap. 3.

6. William Kornhauser, *The Politics of Mass Society* (New York: Free Press, 1959), p. 60.

7. For a creative attempt to specify the individual psychology behind the group outcomes, see Thomas J. Scheff, *Microsociology: Discourse, Emotion, and Social Structure* (Chicago: University of Chicago Press, 1990) and especially *Bloody Revenge: Emotions, Nationalism, and War* (Boulder, Colo.: Westview Press, 1994).

8. Ralph H. Turner and Lewis M. Killian, *Collective Behavior*, 3d ed. (Englewood-Cliffs, N.J.: Prentice Hall, 1987), pp. 7–8. Also see J. M. Weller and

E. L. Quarantelli, "Neglected Characteristics of Collective Behavior," *American Journal of Sociology* 79 (1974): 665–683.

9. Recently several psychologists have found that emotions can be contagious, not only through empathy and other symbolic interaction with others, but also in an uncontrollable, almost physical way that escapes awareness: a "tendency to automatically mimic and synchronize facial expressions, vocalizations, postures, and movements with those of another person and, consequently, to converge emotionally." Elaine Hatfield, John T. Cacciopo, and Richard L. Rapson, "Emotional Contagion," in M. S. Clark, *Review of Personality and Social Psychology* 14 (1992): 153–154. Also see Ellen S. Sullins, "Emotional Contagion Revisited: Effects of Social Comparison and Expressive Style on Mood Convergence," *Personality and Social Psychology Bulletin* 17 (1991): 166–174; and Elaine Hatfield, John T. Cacciopo, and Richard L. Rapson, *Emotional Contagion* (Cambridge: Cambridge University Press, 1994).

10. Rick Fantasia's *Cultures of Solidarity: Consciousness, Action, and Contemporary American Workers* (Berkeley: University of California Press, 1988) exemplifies the strengths and limits of this approach. He marvelously captures strike action as it develops on the shop floor, but does less to link it with broader beliefs and traditions outside the factory. Consciousness, in his model, arises only from the direct interaction of two social classes, with no obvious effects from pre-existing beliefs, emotions, moral visions, or practices. Like Turner and Killian, he asserts the importance of culture without specifying the mechanisms through which it works, or even defining it clearly (at times it seems conflated with social structure).

11. Georges Gurvitch calls this "explosive time," when the past and present seem to dissolve into mere preparation for a future that is in the process of being created: *The Spectrum of Social Time* (Dordrecht: D. Reidel, 1964). Also see Aristide R. Zolberg, "Moments of Madness," *Politics and Society* 2 (1972): 183–207.

12. James C. Scott, *Domination and the Arts of Resistance: Hidden Transcripts* (New Haven: Yale University Press, 1990), p. 223.

13. Many paleontologists have begun to view evolution as a series of static equilibria, punctuated by occasional shifts caused by the sudden emergence of new species. This view contrasts with more traditional views of evolution as a continual, gradual transformation of species. See Stephen Jay Gould and Niles Eldredge, "Punctuated Equilibria: An Alternative to Phyletic Gradualism," in Thomas J. M. Schopf, ed., *Models in Paleobiology* (San Francisco: Freeman, Cooper, and Co., 1972), "Punctuated Equilibria: The Tempo and Mode of Evolution Reconsidered," *Paleobiology* 3 (1977): 115–151; and Niles Eldredge, *Time Frames: The Rethinking of Darwinian Evolution and the Theory of Punctuated Equilibria* (New York: Simon and Schuster, 1985).

14. Mancur Olson Jr., *The Logic of Collective Action: Public Goods and the Theory of Groups* (Cambridge: Harvard University Press, 1965). Other important theoretical works include Russell Hardin, *Collective Action* (Baltimore: Johns Hopkins University Press, 1982) and Michael Taylor, *The Possibility of Cooperation* (Cambridge: Cambridge University Press, 1987). Empirical applications in-

clude Gordon Tullock, "The Paradox of Revolution," *Public Choice* 11 (1971): 89–99; Morris Silver, "Political Revolution and Repression: An Economic Approach," *Public Choice* 17 (1974): 63–71; and—the most interesting—Karl-Dieter Opp, *The Rationality of Political Protest: A Comparative Analysis of Rational Choice Theory* (Boulder, Colo.: Westview Press, 1989).

15. Albert O. Hirschman, "Against Parsimony: Three Easy Ways of Complicating Some Categories of Economic Discourse," in Hirschman, *Rival Views of Market Society and Other Recent Essays* (New York: Viking, 1986), p. 142. For other critiques of rational-choice approaches to political action, see Alessandro Pizzorno, "Some Other Kinds of Otherness: A Critique of 'Rational Choice' Theories," in Alejandro Foxley, Michael S. McPherson, and Guillermo O'Donnell, eds., *Development, Democracy, and the Art of Trespassing: Essays in Honor of Albert O. Hirschman* (Notre Dame, Ind.: University of Notre Dame Press, 1986); Myra Marx Ferree, "The Political Context of Rationality," in Aldon D. Morris and Carol McClurg Mueller, eds., *Frontiers in Social Movement Theory* (New Haven: Yale University Press, 1992); and Donald P. Green and Ian Shapiro, *Pathologies of Rational Choice Theory: A Critique of Applications in Political Science* (New Haven: Yale University Press, 1994).

16. Jon Elster, *The Cement of Society: A Study of Social Order* (Cambridge: Cambridge University Press, 1989).

17. There is no "rational" way to decide when to stop searching for more information, since we usually don't know how beneficial the new information will be until we have it; nor is it clear that we take full advantage of the information we do have. Cognitive psychologists have studied the malfunctions of human decision making, such as overconfidence in our own estimates, generalizing from small samples, a focus on salient or easily imagined cases, and a misunderstanding of probability. See Daniel Kahneman, Paul Slovic, and Amos Tversky, eds., *Judgment under Uncertainty: Heuristics and Biases* (Cambridge: Cambridge University Press, 1982).

18. On the need for culture in rational-choice models, see Gary Ford and James M. Jasper, "Culture and Rational Choice," (paper presented at the American Sociological Association annual meetings, Washington, D.C., August 1995).

19. Olson, *Logic of Collective Action*, pp. 61, 62.

20. John Ferejohn, "Rationality and Interpretation: Parliamentary Elections in Early Stuart England," in Kristen Renwick Monroe, ed., *The Economic Approach to Politics: A Critical Reassessment of the Theory of Rational Action* (New York: HarperCollins, 1991).

21. Michael Taylor, "Rationality and Revolutionary Collective Action," in Michael Taylor, ed., *Rationality and Revolution* (Cambridge: Cambridge University Press, 1988). Mark I. Lichbach describes two dozen solutions, most of them based on common beliefs, mutual agreements, and authority, in "Rethinking Rationality and Rebellion," *Rationality and Society* 6 (1994): 8–39. The most thorough reformulation and presentation of solutions is Gerald Marwell and Pamela Oliver, *The Critical Mass in Collective Action: A Micro-Social Theory* (Cambridge: Cambridge University Press, 1993). As they put it (p. 7), "[I]t is our

impression that the major predictors of participation are the level of *subjective* interest in the collective good, solidary ties to other collective actors, and personal satisfaction or moral rectitude from feeling that one is accomplishing good—all cultural factors." For a reformulation of their model, see Michael W. Macy, "Learning Theory and the Logic of Critical Mass," *American Sociological Review* 55 (1990): 809–826.

22. Thomas C. Schelling, "What Is Game Theory?" in *Choice and Consequence: Perspectives on an Errant Economist* (Cambridge: Harvard University Press, 1984), p. 222. Because of complexities such as these, Anatol Rapoport argues that game theory is a normative branch of mathematics, not an explanatory branch of social science: "Game Theory Defined," *Rationality and Society* 4(1992): 74–82. For further debates on game theory, mostly questioning its applicability to actual empirical cases, see this special issue of *Rationality and Society* 4(1).

23. Jon Elster makes this point in the introduction to Jon Elster, ed., *Rational Choice* (New York: New York University Press, 1986), p. 19.

24. In some cases, Albert O. Hirschman says, "the benefit of collective action for an individual is not the difference between the hoped-for result and the effort furnished by him or her, but the *sum* of these two magnitudes." See *Shifting Involvements: Private Interest and Public Action* (Princeton, Princeton University Press, 1982), p. 86.

25. Dennis Chong, *Collective Action and the Civil Rights Movement* (Chicago: University of Chicago Press, 1991), p. 32.

26. Chong, *Collective Action*, pp. 34–35.

27. Chong, pp. 72, 52, 54.

28. Chong, p. 68.

29. Chong, p. 69.

30. Anthony Oberschall, "Theories of Social Conflict," in Ralph Turner, James Coleman, and Renée C. Fox, eds., *Annual Review of Sociology* 4 (1978): 298. Classics that defined the mobilization perspective in a very short period include Anthony Oberschall, *Social Conflict and Social Movements* (Englewood Cliffs, N.J.: Prentice-Hall, 1973); William A. Gamson, *The Strategy of Social Protest* (Homewood, Ill.: Dorsey Press, 1975); John D. McCarthy and Mayer N. Zald, "Resource Mobilization and Social Movements: A Partial Theory," *American Journal of Sociology* 82 (1977): 1212–1241; J. Craig Jenkins and Charles Perrow, "Insurgency of the Powerless: Farm Worker Movements (1946–1972)," *American Sociological Review* 42 (1977): 249–268; and Charles Tilly, *From Mobilization to Revolution* (Reading, Mass.: Addison-Wesley, 1978). For a review, see J. Craig Jenkins, "Resource Mobilization Theory and the Study of Social Movements," *Annual Review of Sociology* 9 (1983): 527–553. Theories are easier to classify than theorists, and several of these theorists also helped to develop other approaches discussed later.

31. For McCarthy and Zald's early formulation, see *The Trend of Social Movements in America: Professionalization and Resource Mobilization* (Morristown, N.J.: General Learning Press, 1973); for their most cited, "Resource Mobilization and Social Movements: A Partial Theory." These and other of their articles have

been collected in Mayer N. Zald and John D. McCarthy, eds., *Social Movements in an Organizational Society* (New Brunswick, N.J.: Transaction, 1987).

32. See Mayer N. Zald and Roberta Ash, "Social Movement Organizations: Growth, Decay, and Change," in Zald and McCarthy, *Social Movements in an Organizational Society;* Frances Fox Piven and Richard A. Cloward, *Poor People's Movements: Why They Succeed, How They Fail* (New York: Vintage, 1977).

33. Anthony Oberschall includes nonmaterial resources such as "authority, moral commitment, trust, friendship, skills, habits of industry, and so on": *Social Conflict and Social Movements,* p. 28. Louis Zurcher and David Snow argue that symbols are resources in "Collective Behavior: Social Movements," in Ralph H. Turner and Morris Rosenberg, eds., *Social Psychology: Sociological Perspectives* (New York: Basic Books, 1981), p. 470. Gi-Wook Shin analyzes the importance of "raised consciousness" as a resource in "The Historical Analysis of Collective Action: The Korean Peasant Uprisings of 1946," *American Journal of Sociology* 99 (1994): 1596–1624.

34. Viviana Zelizer has shown that money is not as universal a medium as economists would have us believe; it has many special, restricted uses. Relative to cultural beliefs and emotions, though, money is still quite universal in most circumstances; when money has special meanings, they are due to its cultural context. See Viviana A. Zelizer, *The Social Meaning of Money* (New York: Basic Books, 1994). Rhys H. Williams analyzes "cultural resources," on the premise that they are like other resources, but he spends more time discussing how they differ; see "Constructing the Public Good," *Social Problems* 42 (1995): 124–144.

35. William A. Gamson, Bruce Fireman, and Steven Rytina, *Encounters with Unjust Authority* (Homewood, Ill.: Dorsey Press, 1982), p. 83.

36. Hirschman points out that many key motivations of collective action, such as benevolence and civic spirit, are not precisely resources: "[T]hey atrophy when not adequately practiced and appealed to by the ruling socioeconomic regime, yet will once again make themselves scarce when preached and relied on to excess" ("Against Parsimony," p. 157). What Hirschman calls the overuse of these sentiments, however, may instead be their distortion or abuse.

37. Oberschall, *Social Conflict and Social Movements,* is the classic statement.

38. Oberschall, *Social Conflict and Social Movements,* and "Loosely Structured Collective Conflict: A Theory and an Application," *Research in Social Movements, Conflicts, and Change* 3 (1980): 45–68.

39. Tilly, *From Mobilization to Revolution,* pp. 62–69.

40. Mary Douglas, "Cultural Bias," in *In the Active Voice* (London: Routledge and Kegan Paul, 1984); Mary Douglas and Aaron Wildavsky, *Risk and Culture: An Essay on the Selection of Technological and Environmental Dangers* (Berkeley: University of California Press, 1982).

41. Bruce Fireman and William A. Gamson, "Utilitarian Logic in the Resource Mobilization Perspective," in Mayer N. Zald and John D. McCarthy, eds., *The Dynamics of Social Movements: Resource Mobilization, Social Control, and Tactics* (Cambridge, Mass: Winthrop, 1979).

42. Some of the high points in Tilly's enormous oeuvre include Charles Tilly, *The Vendée* (Cambridge: Harvard University Press, 1964); Edward Shorter and Charles Tilly, *Strikes in France 1830–1968* (Cambridge: Cambridge University Press, 1974); Charles Tilly, Louise Tilly, and Richard Tilly, *The Rebellious Century, 1830–1930* (Cambridge: Harvard University Press, 1975); Charles Tilly, *From Mobilization to Revolution* (Reading, Mass.: Addison-Wesley, 1978); Charles Tilly, *The Contentious French: Four Centuries of Popular Struggle* (Cambridge: Harvard University Press, 1986); Charles Tilly, *European Revolutions, 1492–1992* (Oxford: Blackwell, 1993); and Charles Tilly, *Popular Contention in Great Britain, 1758–1834* (Cambridge: Harvard University Press, 1995).

43. See Michael Lipsky, "Protest as a Political Resource," *American Political Science Review* 62 (1968): 1144–1158; J. Craig Jenkins and Charles Perrow, "Insurgency of the Powerless"; William Gamson, *The Strategy of Social Protest*; Anthony Oberschall, *Social Conflict and Social Movements* and *Social Movements: Ideologies, Interests, and Identities* (New Brunswick, N.J.: Transaction, 1993); Charles Perrow, "The Sixties Observed," in Zald and McCarthy, eds., *The Dynamics of Social Movements*; and J. Craig Jenkins and Craig Eckert, "Elite Patronage and the Channeling of Social Protest," *American Sociological Review* 51 (1986): 812–829.

44. See Doug McAdam, *Political Process and the Development of Black Insurgency, 1930–1970* (Chicago: University of Chicago Press, 1982). Herbert Kitschelt demonstrates the reductionist risk of "political process" models, explaining all the actions of social movements as responses to existing state structures in "Political Opportunity Structures and Political Protest: Anti-Nuclear Movements in Four Democracies," *British Journal of Political Science* 16 (1986):57–85. A small sampling of the interesting work that has been done in this school includes Edwin Amenta and Yvonne Zylan, "It Happened Here: Political Opportunity, the New Institutionalism, and the Townsend Movement," *American Sociological Review* 56 (1991): 250–265; Edwin Amenta, Bruce C. Carruthers, and Yvonne Zylan, "A Hero for the Aged? The Townsend Movement, the Political Mediation Model, and U.S. Old-Age Policy, 1934–1950," *American Journal of Sociology* 98 (1992): 308–339; Hanspeter Kriesi, Ruud Koopmans, Jan Willem Duyvendak, and Marco G. Guigni, "New Social Movements and Political Opportunities in Western Europe," *European Journal of Political Research* 22 (1992): 219–244; Christian Joppke, *Mobilizing Against Nuclear Energy: A Comparison of Germany and the United States* (Berkeley: University of California Press, 1993). Whether or not they represent a distinct tradition (a mere question of labels and turf), I see political process models of the 1980s as a direct evolution from the resource mobilization formulations of the 1970s. A good general formulation of this perspective, and an effort to link it to cultural and other recent developments, is Sidney Tarrow, *Power in Movement: Social Movements, Collective Action, and Politics* (Cambridge: Cambridge University Press, 1994).

45. My italics. In this formulation, apparently, only pre-existing collectivities can form social movements. McAdam definitionally excludes much of what is

commonly considered protest, including post-citizenship movements composed of those with full citizenship rights. See Doug McAdam, *Political Process and the Development of Black Insurgency, 1930–1970*, p. 25.

46. Christian Smith, *Resisting Reagan: The U.S. Central America Peace Movement* (Chicago: University of Chicago Press, 1996), pp. 130–31.

47. Peter K. Eisinger apparently first used the phrase *political opportunity structure* in "The Conditions of Protest Behavior in American Cities," *American Political Science Review* 67 (1973): 11–28; Sidney Tarrow elaborated on it in "Struggling to Reform: Social Movement and Policy Change During Cycles of Protest," occasional paper no. 15 (Ithaca, N.Y.: Cornell University Western Societies Program, 1983).

48. Tarrow, *Power in Movement*, p. 85.

49. In an otherwise excellent book on the movement against U.S. intervention in Central America, Christian Smith labels "President Reagan's obsessive preoccupation with Central America" as one of the political opportunities explaining the movement's appearance, and Bush's retreat from Reagan's policies as the closing of an opportunity that helps explain the movement's demise: *Resisting Reagan*, pp. 378–79.

50. William A. Gamson and David S. Meyer make a similar distinction between stable and volatile opportunities, but they then categorize opportunities *a priori* without fully recognizing that any element of structure can change rather quickly under the right conditions. See "Framing Political Opportunity," in Doug McAdam, John D. McCarthy, and Mayer N. Zald, eds., *Comparative Perspectives on Social Movements: Political Opportunities, Mobilizing Structures, and Cultural Framings* (Cambridge: Cambridge University Press, 1996). "Environment" is another way of saying political opportunity structure, but it runs the same conflationary risk, since it can refer either to relatively fixed political structures or to a rapidly changing strategic environment. Like "structure," it downplays the active strategizing of opponents and other players.

51. Hanspeter Kriesi, "The Political Opportunity Structure of New Social Movements: Its Impact on Their Mobilization," in J. Craig Jenkins and Bert Klandermans, eds., *The Politics of Social Protest: Comparative Perspectives on States and Social Movements* (Minneapolis: University of Minnesota Press, 1995), p. 168.

52. Tarrow, *Power in Movement*, p. 84.

53. McAdam, *Political Process*, p. 51.

54. McAdam (p. 48) goes on to say that cognitive liberation "is not independent of the [other] two factors." William H. Sewell Jr. criticizes Tilly on similar grounds, for giving causal priority to deep structural shifts: "[T]he argument frequently takes on a teleological quality, largely because the asserted causes— capitalist development and state centralization—occur offstage, outside of Tilly's texts, where they are essentially assumed as ever present and ever rising forces, a kind of eternal yeast." See Sewell, "Three Temporalities: Toward an Eventful Sociology," in Terrence J. McDonald, ed., *The Historic Turn in the Human Sciences* (Ann Arbor: University of Michigan Press, 1996), p. 254.

55. Bert Klandermans elaborates on this rational expectation in "Mobiliza-

tion and Participation: Social-Psychological Expansions of Resource Mobilization Theory," *American Sociological Review* 49 (1984): 583–600.

56. Derrick Bell, *Faces at the Bottom of the Well: The Permanence of Racism* (New York: Basic Books, 1992), p. xvi.

57. Aldon D. Morris, *The Origins of the Civil Rights Movement: Black Communities Organizing for Change* (New York: Free Press, 1984).

58. McAdam, *Political Process*, pp. 128–130.

59. Tarrow, *Power in Movement*, p. 24.

60. Sara Evans, among others, argues that the abolition movement inspired the first wave of the women's movement in the nineteenth century and that the civil rights movement inspired the second wave in the 1960s: *Personal Politics: The Roots of Women's Liberation in the Civil Rights Movement and the New Left* (New York: Alfred A. Knopf, 1979).

61. For an interesting discussion of perils such as "conceptual stretching," see Giovanni Sartori, "Conceptual Misinformation in Comparative Politics," *American Political Science Review* 66 (1970): 1033–1053. Kenneth Burke warns that metaphors are often taken to be reality: *Permanence and Change: An Anatomy of Purpose*, 3d ed. (Berkeley: University of California Press, 1954), part 2.

62. Eviatar Zerubavel argues that "lumping" things into one category and "splitting" them into different categories are each necessary or useful at different times; see *The Fine Line: Making Distinctions in Everyday Life* (New York: Free Press, 1991).

3. BASIC DIMENSIONS OF PROTEST

1. Jürgen Habermas, *The Theory of Communicative Action*, vol. 1, *Reason and the Rationalization of Society* (Boston: Beacon Press, 1984).

2. Jeffrey C. Alexander, *Action and Its Environments: Toward a New Synthesis* (New York: Columbia University Press, 1988), p. 312.

3. Alexander, *Action and Its Environments*, p. 315.

4. Gary Alan Fine, "Small Groups and Culture Creation: The Idioculture of Little League Baseball Teams," *American Sociological Review* 44 (1979), p. 733.

5. Margaret S. Archer oddly associates this holistic view with an "artistic" view of culture, in that the interpretation of art involves grasping an overall pattern: *Culture and Agency: The Place of Culture in Social Theory* (Cambridge: Cambridge University Press, 1988). But individuals create and interpret art by switching among specifics, and between specific works and more general meanings. Some individuals have holistic visions; society never does. I follow Talcott Parsons in dividing culture into cognition, morality, and emotion, without his sense that they represent a common culture.

6. Robert Wuthnow and Marsha Witten distinguish cultural research by whether it views culture as an implicit feature of social life or an explicit social construction, and whether it concentrates on the social context that causes culture or the content of what is created: "New Directions in the Study of Culture," *Annual Review of Sociology* 14 (1988): 49–67.

7. Clifford Geertz, *Local Knowledge: Further Essays in Interpretive Anthropology* (New York: Basic Books, 1983), p. 14.

8. Eric Rambo and Elaine Chan, "Text, Structure, and Action in Cultural Sociology," *Theory and Society* 19 (1990): 635.

9. Anthony Giddens, *The Constitution of Society: Outline of the Theory of Structuration* (Berkeley: University of California Press, 1984), p. 25.

10. Mary Douglas, *Purity and Danger: An Analysis of the Concepts of Pollution and Taboo* (London: Routledge and Kegan Paul, 1966), pp. 38–39.

11. Pierre Bourdieu, *Outline of a Theory of Practice* (Cambridge: Cambridge University Press, 1977), p. 58.

12. There are two kinds of rules behind this criticism. One kind *constitutes* an activity: if you break certain rules during a chess game—moving a rook diagonally, for example—you are no longer playing chess. Bourdieu's kind is more of an *empirical regularity* which can be stretched or broken: wedding dresses usually look a certain way, but a provocative new design does not invalidate the wedding ceremony. Although theorists are obsessed with it, the metaphor of chess is a misleading way to think about most social life. For a critique of models of culture as the application of rules, even implicit ones, see Clifford D. Shearing and Richard V. Ericson, "Culture as Figurative Action," *British Journal of Sociology* 42 (1991): 481–506. They emphasize "knowing how" over "knowing that."

13. Ann Swidler, "Culture in Action: Symbols and Strategies," *American Sociological Review* 51 (1986): 277.

14. Ann Swidler, "Cultural Power and Social Movements," in Johnston and Klandermans, eds., *Social Movements and Culture*, pp. 32 and 33. See Theodore Caplow, "Christmas Gifts and Kin Networks," *American Sociological Review* 47 (1982): 383–392; and "Rule Enforcement without Visible Means: Christmas Gift Giving in Middletown," *American Journal of Sociology* 89 (1984): 1306–1323.

15. Swidler, "Culture in Action."

16. Much of the new constructionism grew out of the sociology of science. For instance, Bruno Latour and Steven Woolgar describe the processes by which some "statements" are accepted as facts about the world, and others are not. Statements go through many stages of acceptance, and often fall from grace even though they have been accepted as fact at some point. Scientists use their full resources—including financial backing, personal prestige, and institutional affiliations—to persuade others to accept their claims as facts. See *Laboratory Life: The Social Construction of Scientific Facts* (Beverly Hills: Sage Publications, 1979).

17. Arlie Hochschild usefully criticizes much of the literature on emotions for ignoring the structural context in favor of direct interpersonal negotiations in *The Managed Heart* (Berkeley: University of California Press, 1983), Appendix A.

18. None of this implies that validity mechanisms cannot be criticized, or that they always work as intended. Criteria from one institution are often imposed on another, as when journalists are censored by corporate owners. In fact this is an exemplary case: because of the dominance of large corporations

in the contemporary world, profitability criteria are often used in institutions—hospitals, schools, criminal justice—where they were once absent and probably do not belong. See Michael Walzer, *Spheres of Justice: A Defense of Pluralism and Equality* (New York: Basic Books, 1983). Whatever our normative judgments, the point is that a variety of validity mechanisms shape our visions in systematic ways; to resist or criticize them requires considerable cognitive work.

19. I use the word *biography* to refer to what goes on inside the heads of individuals, especially the individual idiosyncracies that result from different life experiences. Some of this is certainly "psychological," but I shall point to "psychological" dynamics that are far from idiosyncratic and may in some cases be universal, such as the learning of language or emotional responses to threat.

20. Alexander, *Action and Its Environments*, p. 323.

21. Thomas J. Scheff, *Microsociology: Discourse, Emotion, and Social Structure* (Chicago: University of Chicago Press, 1990).

22. Charles Taylor, *Sources of the Self: The Making of the Modern Identity* (Cambridge: Harvard University Press, 1989), p. 34.

23. Jane Flax, *Disputed Subjects: Essays on Psychoanalysis, Politics, and Philosophy* (New York: Routledge, 1993), p. 102.

24. Norbert Wiley, *The Semiotic Self* (Chicago: University of Chicago Press, 1994). A related volume is Judith A. Howard and Peter L. Callero, eds., *The Self-Society Dynamic: Cognition, Emotion, and Action* (Cambridge: Cambridge University Press, 1991).

25. Rom Harré and Grant Gillett, *The Discursive Mind* (Thousand Oaks, Calif.: Sage Publications, 1994), p. 27.

26. Joseph R. Gusfield, "Social Movements and Social Change: Perspectives of Linearity and Fluidity," *Research in Social Movements, Conflict, and Change* 4 (1981), p. 324. Gusfield was one of the few scholars to recognize, as early as the 1960s, the importance of cultural processes in social movements: see his *Symbolic Crusade: Status Politics and the American Temperance Movement* (Urbana, Ill.: University of Illinois Press, 1963), and *The Culture of Public Problems: Drinking-Driving and the Symbolic Order* (Chicago: University of Chicago Press, 1981).

27. Tarrow, *Power in Movement*, p. 23.

28. Harold D. Lasswell, *Psychopathology and Politics* (Chicago: University of Chicago Press, 1930).

29. Fred I. Greenstein, *Personality and Politics: Problems of Evidence, Inference, and Conceptualization* (Princeton: Princeton University Press, 1987), p. 3.

30. Alexander, *Action and Its Environments*, p. 326.

31. For two examples of this shift, see Robert E. Lane, *Political Life: Why People Get Involved in Politics* (Glencoe, Ill.: Free Press, 1959); and *Political Ideology: Why the American Common Man Believes What He Does* (New York: Free Press of Glencoe, 1962). As early as 1955 George A. Kelly formulated a theory of personality that de-emphasized inner drives in favor of the idea that humans actively engaged their environments, formulating constructs or hypothe-

ses about the external world: *The Psychology of Personal Constructs* (New York: W. W. Norton, 1955). More recently, Guy E. Swanson defended ego defenses as a reasonable form of adaptation in normal adults in *Ego Defenses and the Legitimation of Behavior* (Cambridge: Cambridge University Press, 1988), and George E. Vaillant similarly described the adaptive powers of the ego in *The Wisdom of the Ego: Sources of Resilience in Adult Life* (Cambridge: Harvard University Press, 1993).

32. William H. Sewell Jr., "A Theory of Structure: Duality, Agency, and Transformation," *American Journal of Sociology* 98 (1992): 13 and 27.

33. Sewell, "A Theory of Structure," p. 2.

34. See James M. Jasper, *Nuclear Politics* (Princeton: Princeton University Press, 1990), pp. 8–9.

35. Sewell, "A Theory of Structure," p. 24.

36. Mario Diani, *Green Networks: A Structural Analysis of the Italian Environmental Movement* (Edinburgh: Edinburgh University Press, 1995), p. 5. Other examples of network approaches to social movements include David Knoke and James R. Wood, *Organized for Action: Commitment in Voluntary Associations* (New Brunswick, N.J.: Rutgers University Press, 1981); Edward O. Laumann and David Knoke, *The Organizational State: Social Choice in National Policy Domains* (Madison: University of Wisconsin Press, 1987); and David Knoke, *Political Networks: The Structural Perspective* (Cambridge: Cambridge University Press, 1990). For a critique, see Mustafa Emirbayer and Jeff Goodwin, "Network Analysis, Culture, and the Problem of Agency," *American Journal of Sociology* 99 (1994): 1411–1454.

37. Diani, *Green Networks,* p. 201.

38. Doug McAdam and Ronnelle Paulsen, "Specifying the Relationship between Social Ties and Activism," *American Journal of Sociology* 99 (1993): 662.

39. Frances Fox Piven and Richard A. Cloward, "Normalizing Collective Protest," in Aldon D. Morris and Carol McClurg Mueller, eds., *Frontiers in Social Movement Theory* (New Haven: Yale University Press, 1992), p. 310.

40. Christian Smith, *Resisting Reagan,* p. 117.

41. Mustafa Emirbayer and Ann Mische, "What Is Agency?" unpublished paper, 1995. Agency and culture are often conflated, perhaps because structure/agency and structure/culture are common contrasts among sociologists. But agency can be brought to bear on culture (which is itself structured), resources, strategies, and even biography. See Sharon Hays, "Structure and Agency and the Sticky Problem of Culture," *Sociological Theory* 12(1994): 57–72.

42. Faye D. Ginsburg, *Contested Lives: The Abortion Debate in an American Community* (Berkeley: University of California Press, 1989), p. 138.

43. On the occasional misfit between external expectations about emotions and internal feelings, see Carol Zisowitz Stearns and Peter N. Stearns, *Anger: The Struggle for Emotional Control in America's History* (Chicago: University of Chicago Press, 1986).

44. For example, see Erik H. Erikson, *Young Man Luther: A Study in Psychoanalysis and History* (New York: W. W. Norton, 1958); *Gandhi's Truth: On the Origins of Militant Nonviolence* (New York: W. W. Norton, 1969); Robert Jay Lifton,

Revolutionary Immortality: Mao Tse-tung and the Chinese Cultural Revolution (New York: Random House, 1968); Robert C. Tucker, *Stalin as Revolutionary, 1879–1919: A Study in History and Personality* (New York: W. W. Norton, 1973); and John E. Mack, *A Prince of Our Disorder: The Life of T. E. Lawrence* (Boston: Little, Brown, 1976). Closer to home, see William Lanouette, with Bela Silard, *Genius in the Shadows: A Biography of Leo Szilard: The Man Behind the Bomb* (New York: C. Scribner's Sons, 1992). For a reflective piece on psychobiographies, see H. N. Hirsch, "Clio on the Couch," *World Politics* 32 (1980): 406–424.

4. CULTURAL APPROACHES

1. William Gamson, "Political Discourse and Collective Action," *International Social Movement Research* 1 (1988): 220.

2. William Gamson, "Introduction," in Mayer N. Zald and John D. McCarthy, *Social Movements in an Organizational Society* (New Brunswick, N.J.: Transaction, 1987), p. 7. Also see William Gamson, "The Social Psychology of Collective Action," in Morris and Mueller, eds., *Frontiers in Social Movement Theory.*

3. See Anthony Oberschall, *Social Movements: Ideologies, Interests, and Identities* (New Brunswick, N.J.: Transaction Publishers, 1993); John D. McCarthy, "Activists, Authorities, and Media Framing of Drunk Driving," in Enrique Laraña, Hank Johnston, and Joseph R. Gusfield, eds., *New Social Movements: From Ideology to Identity* (Philadelphia: Temple University Press, 1994).

4. Touraine has articulated his general theoretical positions in *The Post-Industrial Society: Tomorrow's Social History: Classes, Conflicts and Culture in the Programmed Society* (New York: Random House, 1971), *The Self-Production of Society* (Chicago: University of Chicago Press, 1977), *The Voice and the Eye: An Analysis of Social Movements* (Cambridge: Cambridge University Press, 1981), *Return of the Actor: Social Theory in Postindustrial Society* (Minneapolis: University of Minnesota Press, 1988), and *Critique of Modernity* (Cambridge, Mass.: Blackwell, 1995). He has written about specific movements, using his method of "sociological intervention," by which he gathers selected participants (usually representing different components) from the movement and leads them through a series of discussions in which he hopes they will eventually embrace his theories of their "true" mission: for example, Alain Touraine, Zsuzsa Hegedüs, François Dubet, and Michel Wieviorka, *Anti-Nuclear Protest: The Opposition to Nuclear Energy in France* (Cambridge, Cambridge University Press, 1983); Alain Touraine, François Dubet, Michel Wieviorka, and Jan Strzelecki, *Solidarity: Poland 1980–81* (Cambridge, Cambridge University Press, 1983); Alain Touraine, Michel Wieviorka, and François Dubet, *The Workers' Movement* (Cambridge, Cambridge University Press, 1987).

5. Alberto Melucci, *Nomads of the Present: Social Movements and Individual Needs in Contemporary Society* (Philadelphia, Temple University Press, 1989), p. 82. Also see his "The New Social Movements: A Theoretical Approach," *Social Science Information* 19 (1980): 199–226; "The Symbolic Challenge of Contemporary Movements," *Social Research* 52 (1985): 789–816; "Getting Involved: Identity and Mobilization in Social Movements," *International Social Movement Re-*

search 1 (1988): 329–348; "The Process of Collective Identity," in Hank Johnston and Bert Klandermans, eds., *Social Movements and Culture* (Minneapolis: University of Minnesota Press, 1995); "The New Social Movements Revisited: Reflections on a Sociological Misunderstanding," in Louis Maheu, *Social Movements and Social Classes: The Future of Collective Action* (London: Sage Publications, 1995); and *Challenging Codes: Collective Action in the Information Age* (Cambridge: Cambridge University Press, 1996). In addition to Touraine and Melucci, works that helped define the post-industrial perspective on protest include Jean L. Cohen, "Strategy or Identity: New Theoretical Paradigms and Contemporary Social Movements," *Social Research* 52 (1985): 663–716; Klaus Eder, "The 'New Social Movements': Moral Crusades, Political Pressure Groups, or Social Movements?" *Social Research* 52 (1985): 869–890; Claus Offe, "New Social Movements: Challenging the Boundaries of Institutional Politics," *Social Research* 52 (1985): 817–868; Alessandro Pizzorno, "Political Exchange and Collective Identity in Industrial Conflict," in Colin Crouch and Alessandro Pizzorno, eds., *The Resurgence of Class Conflict in Western Europe Since 1968* (New York: Holmes and Meier, 1978). For overviews, see Alan Scott, *Ideology and the New Social Movements* (London: Unwin Hyman, 1990), and Rosa Proietto, "New Social Movements: Issues for Sociology," *Social Science Information* 34 (1995): 355–388.

6. Melucci, *Nomads of the Present,* pp. 70–71.

7. Jürgen Habermas, *The Theory of Communicative Action,* vol. 2, *Lifeworld and System: A Critique of Functionalist Reason* (Boston: Beacon Press, 1987), pp. 391–396.

8. The interplay of media and movements can be complex, as Todd Gitlin shows in *The Whole World Is Watching: Mass Media in the Making and Unmaking of the New Left* (Berkeley: University of California Press, 1980).

9. Charles Tilly, revealing a hard-nosed American emphasis on tactics, insists there is little new about the so-called new social movements. Movements such as feminism, environmentalism, and the antinuclear and student movements employ much the same tactics as the labor movement. But if modern collective action differs from premodern because political and economic institutions have changed, as Tilly argues, then small changes in these institutions should also lead to small changes in contemporary movements. Have mass-media technologies (especially television) had no effect? The globalization of markets? Tilly admits that the "orientations" of many participants may be changing; he also points to the importance of media coverage, which encourages the occupation of symbolic places and an orientation toward third parties (states and publics). See Tilly, "Social Movements, Old and New," *Research in Social Movements, Conflicts, and Change* 10 (1988): 1–18. Ronald Inglehart pioneered the study of "post-materialist values" in *The Silent Revolution: Changing Values and Political Styles among Western Publics* (Princeton, N.J.: Princeton University Press, 1977).

10. Ernesto Laclau and Chantal Mouffe attack marxist, especially leninist, traditions for specifying in advance who the revolutionary actors would be,

and ignoring actual processes by which humans create identities and launch resistance: "[T]here are no surfaces which are privileged *a priori* for the emergence of antagonisms, nor are there discursive regions which the programme of a radical democracy should exclude *a priori* as possible spheres of struggle"; see *Hegemony and Socialist Strategy: Towards a Radical Democratic Politics* (London: Verso, 1985), p. 192.

11. See John Lofland and Rodney Stark, "Becoming a World Saver: A Theory of Conversion to a Deviant Perspective," *American Sociological Review* 30 (1965): 863–74. In applying this model, David Snow and C. L. Phillips found that affective bonds and social interaction were key in explaining movement recruitment: "The Lofland-Stark Conversion Model: A Critical Reassessment," *Social Problems* 27 (1980): 430–37. On the general importance of personal connections in recruitment, see David A. Snow, Louis A. Zurcher Jr., and Sheldon Ekland-Olson, "Social Networks and Social Movements: A Microstructural Approach to Differential Recruitment," *American Sociological Review* 45 (1980): 787–801.

12. See David A. Snow, E. Burke Rochford Jr., Steven K. Worden, and Robert D. Benford, "Frame Alignment Processes, Micromobilization, and Movement Participation," *American Sociological Review* 51 (1986): 464–481; David A. Snow and Robert D. Benford, "Ideology, Frame Resonance, and Participant Mobilization," *International Social Movement Research* 1 (1988): 197–217; Snow and Benford, "Master Frames and Cycles of Protest," in Morris and Mueller, eds., *Frontiers in Social Movement Theory*; Robert D. Benford and Scott A. Hunt, "Dramaturgy and Social Movements: The Social Construction and Communication of Power," *Sociological Inquiry* 62 (1992): 36–55.

13. Snow and Benford, "Master Frames and Cycles of Protest," pp. 137, 138, respectively. Two dimensions of master frames are being conflated here: the generality of their content and their usability by multiple movements. These are no doubt correlated, but not perfectly. In emphasizing this deducibility of frames from master frames, Snow and Benford are searching for logical characteristics of frames that would explain their resonance with potential recruits, but the pre-existing cultural visions of those recruits are just as important. Generality alone does not explain resonance.

14. Snow and Benford, "Ideology, Frame Resonance, and Participant Mobilization," p. 208.

15. Snow and Benford, "Master Frames and Cycles of Protest," p. 143.

16. John Lofland, *Protest: Studies of Collective Behavior and Social Movements* (New Brunswick, N.J.: Transaction Publishers, 1985). Lofland describes the emotions of collective action, the many pleasures of crowds, the internal culture of social movements, and many other topics I address in this book. The cultural richness of his work on protest may derive from his research on deviance as well as on religion.

17. Snow, Zurcher, and Ekland-Olson, "Social Networks and Social Movements."

18. Writing together, McAdam, McCarthy, and Zald favor restricting the concept of framing to its use in recruitment, even though they offer no con-

cepts to get at other aspects of culture: "Introduction," in *Comparative Perspectives on Social Movements: Political Opportunities, Mobilizing Structures, and Cultural Framings* (Cambridge: Cambridge University Press, 1996), p. 6.

19. William A. Gamson, *Talking Politics* (Cambridge: Cambridge University Press, 1992), pp. 136–142.

20. William A. Gamson, Bruce Fireman, and Steven Rytina, *Encounters with Unjust Authority* (Homewood, Ill.: Dorsey Press, 1982), p. 123.

21. William A. Gamson and Andre Modigliani, "Media Discourse and Public Opinion on Nuclear Power: A Constructionist Approach," *American Journal of Sociology* 95 (1989): 2.

22. Shanto Iyengar, *Is Anyone Responsible? How Television Frames Political Issues* (Chicago: University of Chicago Press, 1991), p. 45.

23. David S. Meyer, *A Winter of Discontent: The Nuclear Freeze and American Politics* (New York: Praeger Publishers, 1990).

24. See my "Three Nuclear Energy Controversies," in Dorothy Nelkin, ed., *Controversy: Politics of Technical Decisions* (Newbury Park, Calif.: Sage Publications, 1992), as well as *Nuclear Politics*. I show that French, American, and Swedish partisan cleavages differ, and that debates over nuclear energy were framed differently in these countries as a result.

25. David S. Meyer and Joshua Gamson, "The Challenge of Cultural Elites: Celebrities and Social Movements," *Sociological Inquiry* 65 (1995): 181–206. On celebrity more generally, see Joshua Gamson, *Claims to Fame: Celebrity in Contemporary America* (Berkeley: University of California Press, 1994).

26. Doug McAdam, *Freedom Summer* (New York: Oxford University Press, 1988).

27. John Lofland, *Doomsday Cult* (Englewood Cliffs, N.J.: Prentice-Hall, 1966).

28. Tilly, *From Mobilization to Revolution*, p. 156.

29. Eric L. Hirsch, "The Creation of Political Solidarity in Social Movement Organizations," *Sociological Quarterly* 27 (1986): 373–87, and "Sacrifice for the Cause: Group Processes, Recruitment, and Commitment in a Student Social Movement," *American Sociological Review* 55 (1990): 243–254; Barbara Epstein, *Political Protest and Cultural Revolution: Nonviolent Direct Action in the 1970s and 1980s* (Berkeley: University of California Press, 1991); Mary Douglas and Aaron Wildavsky, *Risk and Culture: An Essay on the Selection of Technological and Environmental Dangers* (Berkeley: University of California Press, 1982). Wini Breines examines similar internal processes in *Community and Organization in the New Left: 1962–1968. The Great Refusal* (South Hadley, Mass.: J. F. Bergin, 1982).

30. Many of Lofland's important essays are collected in *Protest*, especially chaps. 2, 3, and 9. See also his "Charting Degrees of Movement Culture: Tasks of the Cultural Cartographer," in Hank Johnston and Bert Klandermans, eds., *Social Movements and Culture* (Minneapolis: University of Minnesota Press, 1995). Related works in religion and deviance include John Lofland, *Doomsday Cult* (Englewood Cliffs, N.J.: Prentice-Hall, 1966); John Lofland with Lyn H. Lofland, *Deviance and Identity* (Englewood Cliffs, N.J.: Prentice-Hall, 1969);

John Lofland and Michael Fink, *Symbolic Sit-Ins: Protest Occupations at the California Capitol* (Lanham, Md.: University Press of America, 1982); and John Lofland, *Polite Protestors: The American Peace Movement of the 1980s* (Syracuse, N. Y.: Syracuse University Press, 1993).

31. See Kenneth Burke, *Permanence and Change: An Anatomy of Purpose*, 3d ed. ([1934] Berkeley: University of California Press, 1954), chap. 2; C. Wright Mills, "Situated Actions and Vocabularies of Motive," *American Sociological Review* 5 (1940): 904–913. Burke's and Mills' rejection of motives as inner springs of action can be overdone, for motives of this kind (the commonsense use of the word) can sometimes be glimpsed in people's broader worldviews. I accept the argument, though, that pre-existing impulses hardly exhaust an explanation of action, and that they are, in practice, difficult to separate from the flows of action they are meant to explain.

32. This "performative" aspect of conversion stories is the subject of Peter G. Stromberg's *Language and Self-Transformation: A Study of the Christian Conversion Narrative* (Cambridge: Cambridge University Press, 1993).

33. Robert D. Benford, "'You Could Be the Hundredth Monkey': Collective Action Frames and Vocabularies of Motive within the Nuclear Disarmament Movement," *Sociological Quarterly* 34 (1993): 195–216.

34. I examine rhetorical styles in "The Politics of Abstractions: Instrumental and Moralist Rhetorics in Public Debate," *Social Research* 59 (1992): 315–344. See also Douglas and Wildavsky *Risk and Culture;* Michael Blain, "Fighting Words: What We Can Learn from Hitler's Hyperbole," *Symbolic Interaction* 11 (1988): 257–276; and Marsha L. Vanderford, "Vilification and Social Movements: A Case Study of Pro-Life and Pro-Choice Rhetoric," *Quarterly Journal of Speech* 75 (1989): 166–172.

35. Breines, *Community and Organization in the New Left*, pp. 6, 44–45.

36. Tilly, *From Mobilization to Revolution*, p. 88.

37. A common critique of rationalist models has been that the supposed costs of protest, especially jail time, are also partly benefits, since they can be satisfying and exciting collective experiences. Certain political activities seem to blur the distinction between means and ends necessary for precise calculations. Rationalist Dennis Chong replies that protestors do distinguish costs and benefits, adducing as evidence the fact that employees of protest organizations care about their salaries (even when they accept low ones to work for groups they like!) and that Gandhi worried what would happen to his legal practice while he was in jail. None of this is surprising, and Chong may have constructed a straw-man opponent. His examples show people consciously giving up considerable material rewards in order to pursue justice. Unlike most rationalists, he recognizes the variability of how people value costs and benefits, but like them he has little to say about why this varies. His own example nonetheless shows the cultural persuasion behind the variation: "Some leaders, notably Martin Luther King Jr., were more effective than others at making the rank and file come to prefer in their hearts (to adopt as their *real* preferences, in other words) the option of staying in jail by refusing bail. King possessed an extraordinary capacity to make his followers focus on the

pleasures rather than the travails of their struggle to achieve racial equality." Ignoring the metaphysical challenge of identifying "real" preferences (a quick way for Chong to make his models unfalsifiable), we see that the most interesting issue is why protestors value the costs and benefits as they do, not that they are aware that some things are costs and others benefits. Chong not only contradicts his own claim (that protestors think about the costs of their actions) but also makes rationalist models into a tautology when he insists that jail time and certain other costs are actually benefits because they increase a protestor's standing among her peers: *Collective Action and the Civil Rights Movement* (Chicago: University of Chicago Press, 1991), p. 87.

38. Ernest G. Bormann discusses the importance for group solidarity of creating heroes in "Fantasy and Rhetorical Vision: The Rhetorical Criticism of Social Reality," *Quarterly Journal of Speech* 58 (1972): 396–407.

39. Mary Douglas, *How Institutions Think* (Syracuse, N.Y.: Syracuse University Press, 1986); Douglas and Wildavsky, *Risk and Culture.* Frank Dobbin brilliantly demonstrates, through cross-national comparisons, that "rationality" is a cultural construction in *Forging Industrial Policy: The United States, Britain, and France in the Railway Age* (Cambridge: Cambridge University Press, 1994).

40. Samuel Bowles and Herbert Gintis, *Democracy and Capitalism: Property, Community, and the Contradictions of Modern Social Thought* (New York: Basic Books, 1986), p. 138.

41. James B. Rule, *Theories of Civil Violence* (Berkeley: University of California Press, 1988), p. 198.

42. Claus Offe, "Two Logics of Collective Action," in *Disorganized Capitalism: Contemporary Transformations of Work and Politics* (Cambridge: MIT University Press, 1985), p. 204.

43. Jane Jenson, "What's in a Name? Nationalist Movements and Public Discourse," in Johnston and Klandermans, eds., *Social Movements and Culture,* p. 107.

44. Benedict Anderson, *Imagined Communities,* rev. ed. (London: Verso Books, 1991), p. 6.

45. Nancy Whittier, *Feminist Generations: The Persistence of the Radical Women's Movement* (Philadelphia: Temple University Press, 1995), p. 15. She later describes "how members defined themselves, as women and as feminists" (p. 57). To me, defining themselves as women created a collective identity, as "feminists" was a movement identity. But movements help construct both kinds. Gender is a tricky collective identity, for men and women rarely live separate enough lives to feel they belong to different communities. A heterosexual couple, for instance, perceive some conflicts of interests, especially within the household, but also some shared interests *as* a household.

46. Frances Svensson, "Liberal Democracy and Group Rights: The Legacy of Individualism and Its Impact on American Indian Tribes," *Political Studies* 27 (1979): 436.

47. A confusion arose in the protest literature because the so-called new social-movements theorists are also frequently labeled "identity" theorists. But one trait of the new social movements is that, with partial exceptions such as

the women's movement or the gay and lesbian rights movements, they are not linked to collective identities. They are about personal identity, and often movement identity, not collective identity.

48. In a now-familiar pattern of conflation, *community* can refer to personal interactions, affective bonds, a sense of group identity and boundaries, and a form of acting together. Its utility is nonetheless obvious in Steven M. Buechler, *Women's Movements in the United States: Woman Suffrage, Equal Rights, and Beyond* (New Brunswick, N.J.: Rutgers University Press, 1990); and Paul Lichterman, "Piecing Together Multicultural Community: Cultural Differences in Community Building Among Grass-Roots Environmentalists," *Social Problems* 42 (1995): 513–534.

49. See Scott A. Hunt, "Social Movement Organizations and Collective Identities: A Constructionist Approach to Collective Identity Claims-Making," unpublished paper, no date.

50. Hank Johnston, Enrique Laraña, and Joseph R. Gusfield distinguish "public identity" from collective and individual identities, as though the latter two were unaffected by what others think. Insiders and outsiders may contest the content of an identity, but I don't think this warrants a separate type. Their typology also makes the usual conflation of movement and collective identities, no doubt because so much research has been on movements linked to clear underlying collective identities, notably citizenship movements. See their "Identities, Grievances, and New Social Movements," in Laraña, Johnston, and Gusfield, eds., *New Social Movements.*

51. Gitlin, *The Whole World Is Watching.*

52. Joshua Gamson, "Must Identity Movements Self-Destruct? A Queer Dilemma," *Social Problems* 42 (1995): 390.

53. Martha Minow, *Making All the Difference: Inclusion, Exclusion, and American Law* (Ithaca, N.Y.: Cornell University Press, 1980).

54. Verta Taylor and Nancy E. Whittier, "Collective Identity in Social Movement Communities: Lesbian Feminist Mobilization," in Morris and Mueller, *Frontiers in Social Movement Theory;* and "Analytical Approaches to Social Movement Culture: The Culture of the Women's Movement," in Johnston and Klandermans, *Social Movements and Culture.*

55. Scott A. Hunt and Robert D. Benford, "Identity Talk in the Peace and Justice Movement," *Journal of Contemporary Ethnography* 22 (1994): 488–517.

56. William H. Sewell Jr., "Collective Violence and Collective Loyalties in France: Why the French Revolution Made a Difference," *Politics and Society* 18 (1990): 534. For similar interpretations of the artfulness of the French Revolution, displacing earlier marxist interpretations which, like Tilly's, emphasized deeper social forces of which the revolution was a surface aftershock, see François Furet, *Interpreting the French Revolution* (Cambridge: Cambridge University Press, 1981); Lynn Hunt, *Politics, Culture, and Class in the French Revolution* (Berkeley: University of California Press, 1984); Mona Ozouf, *Festivals and the French Revolution* (Cambridge: Harvard University Press, 1988); and Keith Michael Baker, *Inventing the French Revolution* (Cambridge: Cambridge University Press, 1990).

406 Notes to Pages 91–96

57. David Waddington, Karen Jones, and Chas Critcher demonstrate the importance of triggering events in *Flashpoints: Studies in Disorder* (London: Routledge, 1989). As they comment, however, "What converts an incident into a flashpoint is not so much its inherent characteristics as the way the incident is interpreted at the time" (p. 157). Rick Fantasia shows just how complex this process can be in *Cultures of Solidarity* (Berkeley: University of California Press, 1988).

58. J. Nicholas Entrikin, *The Betweenness of Place: Towards a Geography of Modernity* (Baltimore: Johns Hopkins University Press, 1991), p. 6.

59. D. Geoffrey Hayward, "The Meanings of Home," *Human Ecology Forum* 13 (1982): 2–6. Other sociological works on the meaning of home include Irwin Altman and Carol Werner, *Home Environments* (New York: Plenum, 1985); Anne Buttimer, "Home, Reach, and the Sense of Place," in Anne Buttimer and David Seamon, eds., *The Human Experience of Space and Place* (New York: St. Martin's Press, 1980); Lee Cuba and David M. Hummon, "A Place to Call Home: Identification with Dwelling, Community, and Region," *Sociological Quarterly* 34 (1993): 111–131; Marc Fried, "Grieving for a Lost Home," in Leonard Duhl, ed., *The Urban Condition: People and Policy in the Metropolis* (New York: Basic Books, 1963); Graham D. Rowles, "Place and Personal Identity in Old Age: Observations from Appalachia," *Journal of Environmental Psychology* 3 (1983): 299–313.

60. Jerome Bruner, *Acts of Meaning* (Cambridge: Harvard University Press, 1990), pp. 132–36.

61. Joseph R. Gusfield, *Community: A Critical Response* (New York: Harper and Row, 1975).

62. David Harvey, "The Geopolitics of Capitalism," in Derek Gregory and John Urry, eds., *Social Relations and Spatial Structures* (New York: St. Martin's Press, 1985), p. 150.

63. See Gilbert Hobbs Barnes, *The Anti-Slavery Impulse, 1830–1844* (New York: Harcourt, Brace and World, 1933); Paul E. Johnson, *A Shopkeeper's Millenium: Society and Revivals in Rochester, New York, 1815–1837* (New York: Hill and Wang, 1978).

64. No one has captured Germany's peculiar sense of history better than Hans-Jürgen Syberberg, in films such as *Ludwig II* and *Our Hitler.*

65. See Joshua A. Fishman, *The Sociology of Language* (Rowley, Mass.: Newbury House, 1972), p. 39.

66. Interviewed on the *Eyes on the Prize* television series (PBS, 1986), episode 6. "I have organized NAACP chapters after a funeral," Vernon Jordan once said (quoted in Pat Watters, *Down to Now* [New York: Pantheon, 1971], p. 46.). Kim S. Law and Edward J. Walsh analyze a protest group founded because of a death in "The Interaction of Grievances and Structures in Social Movement Analysis: The Case of JUST," *Sociological Quarterly* 24 (1983): 123–136.

67. Michael Blain, "The Role of Death in Political Conflict," *Psychoanalytic Review* 63 (1976): 259–60.

68. Peter Winch, "Understanding a Primitive Society," in Bryan R. Wilson, ed., *Rationality* (Oxford: Basil Blackwell, 1970), pp. 107–111. Kathryn Pyne Ad-

delson, in a discussion of unwanted pregnancies, refers to the girls' "moral passages" as they consider in depth the implications of their choices; see "Moral Passages," in Eva Feder Kittay and Diana T. Meyers, eds., *Women and Moral Theory* (Totowa, N.J.: Rowman and Littlefield, 1987).

69. Anthony Giddens, *Modernity and Self-Identity: Self and Society in the Late Modern Age* (Stanford: Stanford University Press, 1991), pp. 112–14.

70. The contrast between personal troubles and social problems is, of course, C. Wright Mills's: *The Sociological Imagination* (New York: Oxford University Press, 1959). Similarly, Georg Lukács claimed that the power of the great realist novels of the nineteenth century was their ability to tie biographies of individuals to the historical destinies and transformations of nations. For example, see his *The Historical Novel* ([1937] Boston: Beacon Press, 1963); and *Studies in European Realism* (New York: Grosset and Dunlap, 1964).

5. NOT IN OUR BACKYARDS

1. A large number of recent social movements have relied heavily upon homemakers with considerable flexibility in their time—who are biographically available, mobilization theorists would say. In his research on Mothers Against Drunk Driving, John McCarthy found that "the typical chapter officer is a woman, who either does not work outside of the home or works part-time. Often she is married with school-age children at home." John D. McCarthy, "Activists, Authorities, and Media Framing of Drunk Driving," in Laraña, Johnston, and Gusfield, *New Social Movements,* p. 145. Richard Madsen describes two such activists—on opposite sides of Southern California land-use debates—in "Contentless Consensus: The Political Discourse of a Segmented Society," in Alan Wolfe, ed., *America at Century's End* (Berkeley: University of California Press, 1991). Many of these homemakers, unlike the Mothers for Peace, have to develop activist and movement identities from scratch.

2. Edward J. Walsh, "Resource Mobilization and Citizen Protest in Communities Around Three Mile Island," *Social Problems* 29 (1981): 1–21. Ruud Koopmans and Jan Willem Duyvendak, however, show that it is the strategic activity of protest groups that ultimately determines how widely a new grievance is interpreted as such, reasonably rejecting the idea that events have some "objective" meaning for observers. What they miss, setting up a false contrast between culture and strategy by assuming that individuals don't do their own interpretation, is that both events and activists' framing of them are filtered through existing cultural patterns of feeling, judging, and thinking. See their "The Political Construction of the Nuclear Energy Issue and Its Impact on the Mobilization of Anti-Nuclear Movements in Western Europe," *Social Problems* 42 (1995): 235–251.

3. Randall Collins, "Stratification, Emotional Energy, and the Transient Emotions," in Theodore D. Kemper, ed., *Research Agendas in the Sociology of Emotions* (Albany: SUNY Press, 1990), p. 28.

4. Anxiety and enthusiasm apparently stimulate voters to follow a presidential campaign more closely and to learn more about the candidates. According

to George E. Marcus and Michael B. Mackuen, "threat powerfully motivates citizens to learn about politics. . . . emotionality aids, rather than disrupts, political reasoning and enhances, rather than diminishes, the quality of democratic life; see "Anxiety, Enthusiasm, and the Vote: The Emotional Underpinnings of Learning and Involvement During Presidential Campaigns," *American Political Science Review* 87 (1993): 672.

5. The American Sociological Association established a section on the Sociology of the Emotions in 1986. Nonetheless, Anthony Giddens, usually an astute observer of trends, had no entry for emotions in his 1991 *Introduction to Sociology* (New York: W. W. Norton).

6. See, for example, Randall Collins, "The Rationality of Avoiding Choice," *Rationality and Society* 5 (1993): 58–67. Gary Alan Fine and Kent Sandstrom have argued that ideologies depend as much or more on emotions as on cognitions: "Ideology in Action: A Pragmatic Approach to a Contested Concept," *Sociological Theory* 11 (1993): 21–38.

7. Thomas J. Scheff, *Bloody Revenge: Emotions, Nationalism, and War* (Boulder, Colo.: Westview Press, 1994), p. 65.

8. A collection of articles that explicitly argue the constructionist position appears in Rom Harré, ed., *The Social Construction of Emotions* (Oxford: Basil Blackwell, 1986). Other useful works include Francesca M. Cancian, *Love in America: Gender and Self-Development* (Cambridge: Cambridge University Press, 1987); Norman K. Denzin, *On Understanding Emotion* (San Francisco: Jossey-Bass Publishers, 1984); Ronald de Sousa, *The Rationality of Emotion* (Cambridge: MIT Press, 1987); Nico H. Frijda, *The Emotions* (Cambridge: Cambridge University Press, 1986); Arlie Russell Hochschild, "The Sociology of Feeling and Emotion: Selected Possibilities," in Marcia Millman and Rosabeth Moss Kanter, eds., *Another Voice: Feminist Perspectives on Social Life and Social Science* (Garden City N.Y.: Anchor Books, 1975); Arlie Hochschild "Emotion Work, Feeling Rules, and Social Structure," *American Journal of Sociology* 85 (1979): 551–575; Lyn H. Lofland, "The Social Shaping of Emotion: The Case of Grief," *Symbolic Interaction* 8 (1985): 171–190; Catherine A. Lutz, *Unnatural Emotions: Everyday Sentiments on a Micronesian Atoll and Their Challenge to Western Theory* (Chicago: University of Chicago Press, 1988); Justin Oakley, *Morality and the Emotions* (London: Routledge, 1992); Amélie Oksenberg Rorty, ed., *Explaining Emotions* (Berkeley: University of California Press, 1980); Stanley Schacter and Jerome Singer, "Cognitive, Social, and Physiological Determinants of Emotional States," *Psychological Review* 69 (1962): 379–399; Susan Shott, "Emotion and Social Life: A Symbolic Interactionist Analysis," *American Journal of Sociology* 84 (1979): 1317–1334; and Robert C. Solomon, *The Passions* (New York: Doubleday-Anchor, 1976). Overviews include Thomas J. Scheff, "Toward Integration in the Social Psychology of Emotions," *Annual Review of Sociology* 9 (1983): 333–354; and Peggy A. Thoits, "The Sociology of Emotions," *Annual Review of Sociology* 15 (1989): 317–342.

9. James R. Averill, "A Constructivist View of Emotion," in Robert Plutchik and Henry Kellerman, eds., *Emotion: Theory, Research, and Experience*, vol. 1, *Theories of Emotion* (New York: Academic Press, 1980), p. 308.

10. Claire Armon-Jones, "The Thesis of Constructionism," in Rom Harré, ed., *The Social Construction of Emotions*. Peggy Thoits distinguishes a strong version of constructionism—there are no basic, universal emotions—from a weaker version—basic emotions may exist but explain very little; see "The Sociology of Emotions," p. 320.

11. Theodore D. Kemper, "How Many Emotions Are There? Wedding the Social and the Autonomic Components," *American Journal of Sociology* 93 (1987): 263–289.

12. Like so much of the constructionist program, this view of emotions is indebted to Wittgenstein's critique of private language and knowledge. Inner feelings are recognizable when they are expressed in a shared, public language. The form of expression is, for Wittgenstein, the emotion itself: "Do I know then that he is joyful because he tells me he feels his laughter, feels and hears his jubilation—or because he laughs and is jubilant? . . . the words 'I am happy' are a bit of the behavior of joy." In many cases, our actions constitute our emotions, which are otherwise inexplicable. Language, action, and emotion are woven tightly together. See Ludwig Wittgenstein, *Remarks on the Philosophy of Psychology*, vol. 1 (Oxford: Basil Blackwell, 1980), p. 151.

13. On deviant emotions, see Peggy A. Thoits, "Self-Labeling Processes in Mental Illness: The Role of Emotional Deviance," *American Journal of Sociology* 92 (1985): 221–249; and "Emotional Deviance: Research Agendas," in Kemper, ed., *Research Agendas in the Sociology of Emotions*.

14. Hochschild, *The Managed Heart*, pp. 219–221.

15. Rom Harré, "An Outline of the Social Constructionist Viewpoint," in Harré, ed., *The Social Construction of Emotions*, p. 6.

16. de Sousa, *The Rationality of Emotion*.

17. Robert C. Solomon, *The Passions* (New York: Doubleday, 1976).

18. Lawrence Blum, "Compassion," in Rorty, ed., *Explaining Emotions*, pp. 509 and 512, respectively. Candace Clark also discusses sympathy in "Sympathy Biography and Sympathy Margin," *American Journal of Sociology* 93 (1987): 290–321. Despite recognizing that "factors such as age, social class, sex, and type of problem are also important" (p. 291), she shares the limits of most work on emotions by concentrating more on direct interpersonal sympathy exchanges.

19. Tamotsu Shibutani, "Reference Groups as Perspectives," *American Journal of Sociology* 60 (1955): 562–569.

20. Psychologist Richard S. Lazarus elaborates on this view of emotions as arising from a person's appraisals of her situation in *Emotion and Adaptation* (New York: Oxford University Press, 1991).

21. David R. Heise, *Understanding Events: Affect and the Construction of Social Action* (Cambridge: Cambridge University Press, 1979), and "Affect Control Theory: Concepts and Model," in Lynn Smith-Lovin and David R. Heise, eds., *Analyzing Social Interaction: Advances in Control Theory* (New York: Gordon and Breach, 1988). Emotions are an amorphous category that merges with moods, sentiments, affects, and feelings, as well as with personality and character traits. The latter two tend to be dispositions to act and react in certain ways,

perhaps entailing clusters of emotions. Moods are less tied to external objects and situations, and more to internal chemical states such as that thought to cause depression. Sentiments are persistent emotions broadly applied to an idea or person(s), such as parental love, national loyalty, or a nostalgic view of nature. Feelings are bodily symptoms often conflated, in the nonconstruction-ist view, with emotions. Affects are simply positive or negative evaluations of a person, group, place, activity, object, or idea. Some psychologists categorize emotions according to whether they carry positive or negative affect; see Kurt W. Fischer, Phillip R. Shaver, and Peter Carnochan, "How Emotions Develop and How They Organize Development," *Cognition and Emotion* 4 (1990): 81–127.

22. On system trust, see M. J. Rosenberg, "Cognitive Structure and Attitudi-nal Affect," *Journal of Abnormal Social Psychology* 53 (1956): 367–372; Alan Marsh, *Protest and Political Consciousness* (Beverly Hills, Calif.: Sage Publications, 1977); and Samuel H. Barnes, et al., *Political Action: Mass Participation in Five Western Democracies* (Beverly Hills, Calif.: Sage Publications, 1979).

23. Max Scheler, *On Feeling, Knowing, and Valuing* (Chicago: University of Chicago Press, 1992), p. 83.

24. Raymond Williams, *Marxism and Literature* (Oxford: Oxford University Press, 1977), p. 132.

25. A. F. Davies discusses many of the emotions found in political action in *Skills, Outlooks, and Passions: A Psychoanalytic Contribution to the Study of Politics* (Cambridge: Cambridge University Press, 1980), chap. 9.

26. John D. McCarthy and Mayer N. Zald, "The Trend of Social Movements in America," in *Social Movements in an Organizational Society: Collected Essays*.

27. J. Craig Jenkins and Charles Perrow, "Insurgency of the Powerless," *American Sociological Review* 42 (1977): 251.

28. Scheff, *Bloody Revenge.*

29. For these figures, and further discussion of NIMBYs, see Cynthia Gor-don and James M. Jasper, "Overcoming the 'NIMBY' Label: Rhetorical and Organizational Links for Local Protestors," *Research in Social Movements, Con-flicts, and Change* 19 (1996): 159–181. General works on the NIMBY phenome-non include Nicholas Freudenberg, *Not in Our Backyards! Community Action for Health and the Environment* (New York: Monthly Review Press, 1984); Laurie Graham and Richard Hogan, "Social Class and Tactics: Neighborhood Opposi-tion to Group Homes," *Sociological Quarterly* 31 (1990): 513–529; Denis J. Brion, *Essential Industry and the NIMBY Phenomenon* (New York: Quorum Books, 1991); Charles Piller, *The Fail-Safe Society: Community Defiance and the End of American Technological Optimism* (New York: Basic Books, 1991); Andrew Szasz, *EcoPopulism: Toxic Waste and the Movement for Environmental Justice* (Minneapo-lis: University of Minnesota Press, 1994); Barry G. Rabe, *Beyond NIMBY: Haz-ardous Waste Siting in Canada and the United States* (Washington, D.C.: The Brookings Institution, 1994); and Edward J. Walsh, Rex Warland, and D. Clay-ton Smith, *The Environmental Justice Movement: Eight Grassroots Challenges to Modern Incinerator Projects* (Pennsylvania State University Press, forthcoming).

30. Charles Perrow, *Normal Accidents: Living with High-Risk Technologies* (New York: Basic Books, 1984).

31. Matthew L. Wald, "Energy Department to Pay $73 Million to Settle Uranium Case in Ohio," *New York Times*, 1 July 1989. Kai Erikson has described the social and psychological effects of such disasters in *A New Species of Trouble: The Human Experience of Modern Disasters* (New York: W. W. Norton, 1994). Let's just say that communities have good reason to fear such traumas.

32. See George F. E. Rudé, *The Crowd and the French Revolution* (New York: Oxford University Press, 1959), chap. 13; Jeremy Brecher, *Strike!* (Boston: South End Press, 1972); Charles Tilly and Lynn H. Lees, "The People of June, 1848," in Roger Price, ed., *Revolution and Reaction: 1848 and the Second French Republic* (New York: Barnes and Noble, 1975); William H. Sewell Jr., *Work and Revolution in France: The Language of Labor from the Old Regime to 1848* (Cambridge: Cambridge University Press, 1980); Mark Traugott, "Determinants of Political Organization: Class and Organization in the Parisian Insurrection of June 1848," *American Journal of Sociology* 86 (1980): 32–49; Craig Jackson Calhoun, *The Question of Class Struggle: Social Foundations of Popular Radicalism during the Industrial Revolution* (Chicago: University of Chicago Press, 1982) and "The Radicalism of Tradition: Community Strength or Venerable Disguise and Borrowed Language?" *American Journal of Sociology* 88 (1983): 886–914; David Thelen, *Paths of Resistance: Tradition and Dignity in Industrializing Missouri* (New York: Clarendon Press, 1986); Carol Conell and Kim Voss, "Formal Organization and the Fate of Social Movements: Craft Association and Class Alliance in the Knights of Labor," *American Sociological Review* 55 (1990): 255–269.

33. The *Brown* decision is parallel to Tarrow's example of the Russian Revolution: process theorists tend to view them as signs of lessened state repression, whereas their real impact seems to me to have been their symbolic and emotional inspiration. If anything, both led to greater repression by panicking elites of the protest movements inspired by them. Part of the impetus to civil rights organizing was a response to white racist threats. As Pat Watters points out, "Now racism, opposition to the momentous school desegregation decision, was the issue in political campaigns across the South that summer of 1954 and overall, the quality of elected leadership, never very high, worsened" (*Down to Now*, p. 43). The complex emotional and psychological dynamics of how people respond to threats, which sometimes increase and sometimes decrease activism, is underemphasized in process accounts.

34. Calhoun, "The Radicalism of Tradition," p. 911; his emphasis.

35. Stephen R. Couch and J. Stephen Kroll-Smith, "The Chronic Technical Disaster: Toward a Social Scientific Perspective," *Social Science Quarterly* 66 (1985): 564–575.

36. J. Stephen Kroll-Smith and Stephen R. Couch, *The Real Disaster Is Above Ground: A Mine Fire and Social Conflict* (Lexington, Ky.: University of Kentucky Press, 1990), p. 165. They later back off from their distinction between natural and technical disasters, on the grounds that what is important is "how people interpret and experience the changes in those environments": Kroll-Smith and Couch, "What Is a Disaster? An Ecological-Symbolic Approach to Resolving the Definitional Debate," *International Journal of Mass Emergencies and Disasters* 9 (1991): 361. But most people, like Kroll-Smith and Couch in 1990, use a natu-

ral/technical distinction of some (albeit of a cultural, not fixed) sort, and allocate blame differently in the two cases. Erving Goffman distinguished natural and social frameworks, arguing that in the latter, "individuals figure differently. They are defined as self-determined agencies, legally competent to act and morally responsible for doing so properly." See *Frame Analysis: An Essay on the Organization of Experience* (Cambridge: Harvard University Press, 1974), p. 188.

37. Erikson, *A New Species of Trouble.*

38. Political elites also insist that their policies are responses to ineluctable forces, reflecting no discretion on their part. For an example, see my "Rational Reconstructions of Energy Choices in France," in James F. Short Jr. and Lee Clarke, *Organizations, Uncertainties, and Risk* (Boulder, Colo.: Westview Press, 1992).

39. Erikson, *A New Species of Trouble.* See also Edward J. Walsh, "New Dimensions of Social Movement: The High-Level Waste-Siting Controversy," *Sociological Forum* 3 (1988): 586–605; Edward Walsh, Rex Warland, and D. Clayton Smith, "Backyards, NIMBYs, and Incinerator Sitings: Implications for Social Movement Theory," *Social Problems* 40 (1993): 25–38.

40. Ralph H. Turner, "The Moral Issue in Collective Behavior and Collective Action," *Mobilization* 1 (1996): 9.

41. On the tendency to view diseases through a moralizing lens, see Susan Sontag's study of tuberculosis and cancer: *Illness as Metaphor* (New York: Farrar, Straus and Giroux, 1978).

42. Robert B. Zajonc, "Feeling and Thinking: Preferences Need No Inferences," *American Psychologist* 35 (1980): 151. Quoted in William A. Gamson, Bruce Fireman, and Steven Rytina, *Encounters with Unjust Authority* (Homewood, Ill.: Dorsey Press, 1982), p. 123.

43. William A. Gamson, *Talking Politics* (Cambridge: Cambridge University Press, 1992), p. 32.

44. Gamson, *Talking Politics*, p. 33.

45. Marsha L. Vanderford, "Vilification and Social Movements: A Case Study of Pro-Life and Pro-Choice Rhetoric," *Quarterly Journal of Speech* 75 (1989): 174. Also see Michael Blain, "Rhetorical Practice in an Anti-Nuclear Weapons Campaign," *Peace and Change* 16 (1991): 355–378.

46. Joseph R. Gusfield, *Contested Meanings: The Construction of Alcohol Problems* (Madison: University of Wisconsin Press, 1996), p. 311.

47. On the various biases in lay estimates of risks (although it turns out that experts exhibit biases as well), see Daniel Kahneman, Paul Slovic, and Amos Tversky, eds., *Judgment under Uncertainty: Heuristics and Biases* (Cambridge: Cambridge University Press, 1982).

48. Baruch Fischhoff and Don MacGregor, "Judged Lethality: How Much People Seem to Know Depends Upon How They Are Asked," *Risk Analysis* 3 (1983): 229.

49. Paul Slovic, Baruch Fischhoff, and Sarah Lichtenstein, "Facts and Fears: Understanding Perceived Risk," in Richard C. Schwing and Walter A. Albers Jr., eds., *Societal Risk Assessment: How Safe Is Safe Enough?* (New York: Plenum, 1980).

50. Giddens, *The Constitution of Society*, p. 375.

51. Giddens, *The Constitution of Society*, p. 50.

52. Kai T. Erikson, *Everything in Its Path: Destruction of Community in the Buffalo Creek Flood* (New York: Simon and Schuster, 1976), pp. 179, 176, respectively. For another case of a town turned deadly, see Phil Brown and Edwin J. Mikkelsen, *No Safe Place: Toxic Waste, Leukemia, and Community Action* (Berkeley: University of California Press, 1990).

53. Erikson, *Everything in Its Path*, p. 234.

54. In many cases, social ties prevent long-lasting emotional effects of disasters, and other factors mediate the effects: see E. L. Quarantelli, "Consequences of Disasters for Mental Health: Conflicting Views," Preliminary Paper 62, Disaster Research Center (1979), and Susan D. Solomon, Elizabeth M. Smith, Lee N. Robins, and Ruth L. Fischbach, "Social Involvement as a Mediator of Disaster-Induced Stress," *Journal of Applied Social Psychology* 17 (1987): 1092–1112. Despite the diversity of actual effects, the anticipated possibilities may be similar. People may oppose a project if they can imagine a disaster scenario, whatever the objective likelihood of that scenario.

55. See, especially, Erikson, *A New Species of Trouble*, chap. 4.

56. For economists, the assumption behind risk aversion is the diminishing marginal utility of money: the dollar that you already have is worth slightly more than an additional dollar would be. The argument is plausible even though the empirical evidence is mixed.

57. How widespread is the propensity to oppose changes in one's environment? Cynthia Gordon and I conducted a simple survey of undergraduates with the intention of finding out who were most likely to oppose the siting of a hypothetical industrial facility near their homes (or the homes of their parents). We showed respondents a series of slides of a generic (although composite) industrial plant, sometimes with and sometimes without a slide of a nuclear plant's control room. We expected students to be more opposed if they saw the control room and also believed that technology is "out of control," if they held environmentalist values and beliefs, if they grew up in the suburbs and so might have a greater sense of the benevolence of their surroundings than city kids, and if they anticipated careers outside business and engineering. This research effort failed, because attitudes toward the proposed industrial plant tended to be *uniformly negative*, no matter what slides students were shown.

The scenes portrayed in the slides showed no smokestacks or visible pollution, no heavy flows of traffic. The only exterior scenes portrayed complex piping and an attractive building with a fountain in front. (These were, after all, public relations slides provided by several U.S. corporations.) We thought that the slide portraying a control room would make students anxious, but its presence or absence had no effect on attitudes toward the proposed plant. Despite the innocuous slides, 72 percent of the respondents would oppose a similar plant within a mile of their homes, and 55 percent would oppose it within five miles. When asked to mark on a scale how close the plant could be for them to feel comfortable, only 14 percent marked something within ten miles, only 45 percent within fifty miles. The other 55 percent wanted it even farther away. While few in the real world would actively fight an industrial plant fifty miles away, these survey responses seem to show a deep suspicion of all industrial plants. And why not? With nothing to gain, why take the risk?

Most respondents, though, opposed the plant even when they believed it was not risky. Most said they did not think they knew what kind of plant it was. But even among the respondents who did think they knew, and thought it was "not risky," most would oppose it. Later in the survey they were given a list of seven kinds of plants and told it was one of them. Those who thought it was a baby food or water purification plant were still opposed. So even industrial plants with no obvious risks were "not worth the risk."

We asked a range of questions concerning environmental values, dealing with the importance of economic growth, whether technology was getting out of control, whether experts could be trusted, and how humans should fit into the environment. Those who agreed or strongly agreed that "technology is running away with us" were more likely to oppose the plant (76 percent) than those who disagreed or disagreed strongly (58 percent). For other beliefs, such as "Humans must live in harmony with nature in order to survive," and "There are limits to growth beyond which our industrialized society cannot expand," there was no significant difference in the number of students who would oppose the plant. Despite the range of answers to these questions, the majority of students in every category would oppose the plant, rather than favoring it or not caring. These values and beliefs are strongly held by antinuclear, animal rights, and environmental activists, but apparently they do not strongly distinguish those with a NIMBY potential from those without it. Likewise, out in the real world, people have been drawn into local opposition whether they had prior environmental values or not.

The students who took our survey opposed a plant they knew virtually nothing about, whether or not they suspected it posed some health risk. While our data are merely suggestive, I think they show a widespread tendency to resist changes in the physical environment that could have unknown effects. In the absence of clear benefits, there is no reason to favor or accept a proposed facility. Something more is needed to trigger active opposition, but the propensity to view changes in the vicinity of one's home as threatening is an important precondition.

Even though much of contemporary psychology is based on it, research based on the responses of 18-year-olds placed in artificial settings is tentative at best. These findings do not suggest that these young people would actually organize a protest group, but they seem to demonstrate some caution about new industrial facilities. There is a long tradition of scholars who insist that the United States is a country of risk-takers. Such a blanket statement may need to be revised. In certain situations, at least, we may be quick to express cautious emotions.

58. Max Heirich analyzes the eventual impact of this small decision in *The Spiral of Conflict: Berkeley, 1964* (New York: Columbia University Press, 1971).

59. See Tilly, *From Mobilization to Revolution,* chap. 5. Process theorists like Tilly emphasize the positive opportunities that *allow* people to pursue collec-

tive action, and not the sense of threat that might make them *willing* to. They seem to believe that feeling threatened is a less rational process than seeking out new opportunities. Ironically, they often admit that a sense of threat motivates protestors' *opponents:* "[T]he degree of perceived threat conveyed by a movement's actions and tactics is a powerful determinant of other groups' responses to the movement"; see Doug McAdam, "The Framing Function of Movement Tactics: Strategic Dramaturgy in the American Civil Rights Movement," in McAdam, McCarthy, and Zald, eds., *Comparative Perspectives on Social Movements* (Cambridge: Cambridge University Press, 1996), p. 341.

This may be a case of citizenship exemplars leading to incorrect generalizations about the extent to which a group is just waiting for a chance to pursue its interests. If there were ever a group aware of its outrageous treatment, it would be southern African-Americans of the 1950s. They already had a strong cultural construction of blame, so that moral shocks may have been less crucial to their cognitive analysis of their plight. But even they needed emotional shocks and threats like the death of Emmett Till to spur them to action.

60. Charles Tilly, *From Mobilization to Revolution* (Reading, Mass.: Addison-Wesley, 1978), pp. 134–135.

61. Christopher Lasch, *The True and Only Heaven: Progress and Its Critics* (New York: W. W. Norton, 1991).

62. Ralph H. Turner and Lewis M. Killian, *Collective Behavior,* 3d ed. (Englewood Cliffs, N.J.: Prentice-Hall, 1987), p. 242.

63. Habermas argues, "The new conflicts arise along the seams between system and lifeworld." *The Theory of Communicative Action,* vol. 2, *Lifeworld and System: A Critique of Functionalist Reason* (Boston: Beacon Press, 1987), p. 395.

64. Quoted in Robert D. Benford, "Frame Disputes within the Nuclear Disarmament Movement," *Social Forces* 71 (1993): 690.

65. Robert M. Gordon distinguishes the "epistemic" emotions that look toward future uncertainties from "factive" ones that respond to known conditions in *The Structure of Emotions: Investigations in Cognitive Philosophy* (Cambridge: Cambridge University Press, 1987).

6. WHISTLEBLOWERS

1. Quoted in Myron Glazer and Penina Glazer, *The Whistleblowers: Exposing Corruption in Government and Industry* (New York: Basic Books, 1989), pp. 98, 101.

2. Unless otherwise noted, quotations are from an interview I had with Gofman in May 1991. His story was polished; what he told me in the first part of the interview was almost identical to what had been published ten years earlier in Leslie J. Freeman, *Nuclear Witnesses: Insiders Speak Out* (New York: W. W. Norton, 1981).

3. Quoted in Freeman, *Nuclear Witnesses,* p. 89.

4. All three quotations come from J. Samuel Walker, *Containing the Atom: Nuclear Regulation in a Changing Environment, 1963–1971* (Berkeley: University of California Press, 1992), p. 348.

5. Myron Glazer and Penina Glazer use the term *ethical resisters* in *The Whistleblowers*. Other sources include Robert J. Baum, ed., *Ethical Problems in Engineering*, vol. 2, *Cases* (Troy, New York: Rensselaer Polytechnic, 1980); Frederick Elliston, John Keenan, Paula Lockhart, and Jane van Schaick, *Whistleblowing Research: Methodological and Moral Issues* (New York: Praeger Press, 1985); J. Vernon Jensen, "Ethical Tension Points in Whistleblowing," *Journal of Business Ethics* 6 (1987): 321–328; Marcia A. Parmerlee, Janet P. Near, and Tamila C. Jensen, "Correlates of Whistle-Blowers' Perceptions of Organizational Retaliation," *Administrative Science Quarterly* 27 (1982): 17–34; Robert Perrucci, Robert M. Anderson, Dan E. Schendel, and Leon E. Trachtman, "Whistle-Blowing: Professionals' Resistance to Organizational Authority," *Social Problems* 28 (1980): 149–164; Alan F. Westin, ed., *Whistle Blowing! Loyalty and Dissent in the Corporation* (New York: McGraw-Hill, 1981). Parts of this chapter draw on Mary Bernstein and James M. Jasper, "Whistleblowers as Claims-Makers in Technological Controversies," *Social Science Information* 35 (1996): 565–589.

6. Harold Garfinkel, *Studies in Ethnomethodology* (Englewood Cliffs, N.J.: Prentice-Hall, 1967).

7. Albert O. Hirschman, "Against Parsimony," p. 150.

8. Amitai Etzioni, *The Moral Dimension: Toward a New Economics* (New York: Free Press, 1988), pp. 41–42. Etzioni, addressing the limits of rationalist models in the face of moral preferences, says, "Choices that are relatively heavily 'loaded' with moral considerations, including many economic choices, are expected to be unusually difficult to reverse (i.e., they are asymmetrical), to be very 'lumpy'(or highly discontinuous), and to reveal a high 'notch-effect' (a resistance to pass a threshold, that makes behavior sticky before it is passed; the reluctance is greatly diminished or lost once passage is completed)" (p. 76). Along these lines, Jon Elster contrasts moral altruism (helping others because it is our moral duty) and psychological altruism (helping others because it makes us feel good). See Elster, *The Cement of Society* (Cambridge: Cambridge University Press, 1989), p. 47.

9. Charles Taylor, *Sources of the Self* (Cambridge: Harvard University Press, 1989), p. 28.

10. On this tension, see Talcott Parsons, "The Professions and Social Structure," *Social Forces* 17 (1939): 457–467; W. Richard Scott, "Professionals in Bureaucracies—Areas of Conflict," in Howard M. Vollmer and Donald L. Mills, eds., *Professionalization* (Englewood Cliffs, N.J.: Prentice-Hall, 1966); Richard H. Hall, "Professionalization and Bureaucracy," in Richard H. Hall, ed., *The Formal Organization* (New York: Basic Books, 1972); and Peter F. Meiksins and James M. Watson, "Professional Autonomy and Organization Constraint: The Case of Engineers," *Sociological Quarterly* 30 (1989): 561–585.

11. Elliston et al., *Whistleblowing Research*, p. 26. Yet when identification with the goals of the organization leads to "lofty executive ambitions," these may dampen whistleblowing; see Andrew Hacker, "Loyalty—and the Whistle Blower," *Across the Board* 15 (1978): 67.

12. As usual, the full complexity of human motivation is best left to fiction, and Tim Parks has painted a nuanced portrait of a whistleblower in his excel-

lent novel *Shear* (New York: Grove Press, 1993). The main character himself is unsure whether he is acting to break the monotony of a soured marriage, to fulfill his sense of duty, or because his girlfriend had shamed him into acting with integrity. Here is the difference between fiction and social science, however: Parks' complex portrait, while plausible, is not representative of most whistleblowers, whose sense of duty seems to outweigh other motivations.

13. See Elliston et al., *Whistleblowing Research;* Perrucci et al., "Whistle-Blowing;" and Westin, *Whistle Blowing!*

14. Karen L. Soeken and Donald R. Soeken, "A Survey of Whistleblowers: Their Stressors and Coping Strategies," unpublished paper (Laurel, Maryland, 1987), p. 9.

15. See Richard Mauer, "Pipeline Company, Stung by Critic, Goes After Whistle-Blowers," *New York Times,* 23 September 1991. There are hundreds of documented cases of whistleblowers harassed, smeared, or fired by their employers. For a sampling, see Ralph Nader, Peter J. Petkas, and Kate Blackwell, eds., *Whistle Blowing: The Report of the Conference on Professional Responsibility* (New York: Grossman, 1972); Charles Peters and Taylor Branch, *Blowing the Whistle: Dissent in the Public Interest* (New York: Praeger, 1972); Leslie J. Freeman, *Nuclear Witnesses: Insiders Speak Out* (New York: W. W. Norton, 1981); Brian Martin, "Nuclear Suppression," *Science and Public Policy* 13 (1986): 312–320; Brian Martin, C. M. Ann Baker, Clyde Manwell, and Cedric Pugh, eds., *Intellectual Suppression: Australian Case Histories, Analysis, and Responses* (North Ryde, Australia: Angus and Robertson, 1986). Marcia Parmerlee and her collaborators found that retaliation was more likely against employees highly valued by their employers because of age, education, or experience. They are presumably more credible and hence, from the employer's perspective, more of a threat. Employers' sense of betrayal is also greater when senior employees blow the whistle. See Parmerlee et al., "Correlates of Whistle-Blowers' Perceptions of Organizational Retaliation."

16. "Wise Guys. Smearing the Whistle Blowers," *New York Observer,* 23 March 1992.

17. Soeken and Soeken, "A Survey of Whistleblowers."

18. They can also withstand bribes. Although sticks are more common than carrots, the United Technologies Corporation apparently offered an executive whistleblower one million dollars in severance pay in a fraud case being investigated by the Justice Department. Of course, the executive collected over $20 million when the Justice Department agreed to a $150 million settlement with the company. See "Report of $1 Million Offer to Whistle-Blower to Keep Quiet," *New York Times,* 27 June 1994.

19. Glazer and Glazer, *The Whistleblowers,* p. 97.

20. Malcolm Spector and John I. Kitsuse, *Constructing Social Problems* (New York: Aldine de Gruyter, 1987), pp. 151–152.

21. Take the CIA alone. In *In Search of Enemies: A CIA Story* (New York: W. W. Norton, 1978), John Stockwell writes of learning "the full, shocking truth about my employers," and of his futile efforts to promote reforms from within the agency. For similar exposés, see Philip Agee, *Inside the Company: CIA Diary*

(New York: Stonehill, 1975); Frank Snepp, *Decent Interval: An Insider's Account of Saigon's Indecent End* (New York: Random House, 1977); and Victor Marchetti and John D. Marks, *The CIA and the Cult of Intelligence* (New York: Knopf, 1980).

22. In *Breaking Ranks* (Philadelphia: New Society Publishers, 1989), Melissa Everett has written the stories of ten of these defense whistleblowers. Their original impulses had the same causes as those of other whistleblowers, but their treatment commonly seems to have been even worse.

23. Daniel Ford, *The Cult of the Atom: The Secret Papers of the Atomic Energy Commission* (New York: Simon and Schuster, 1982).

24. Edward J. Walsh, *Democracy in the Shadows: Citizen Mobilization in the Wake of the Accident at Three Mile Island* (New York: Greenwood Press, 1988), p. 84.

25. Recently, for example, MHB wrote a report for the Union of Concerned Scientists on the risks of advanced reactor designs: *Advanced Reactor Designs* (Washington, D. C.: Union of Concerned Scientists, 1990).

26. United States Congress, "Investigation of Charges Relating to Nuclear Reactor Safety: Hearings before the Joint Committee on Atomic Energy, 94th Congress, Second Session, February 18 to March 4, 1976" (Washington, D.C.: Government Printing Office, 1976), p. 29. Subsequent quotations from this hearing are cited parenthetically by page number in the text.

27. On the prevalence of environmental issues in earlier nuclear opposition, see Dorothy Nelkin, *Nuclear Power and Its Critics: The Cayuga Lake Controversy* (Ithaca: N. Y., Cornell University Press, 1971), and on the evolution of issues and the general history of the U.S. antinuclear movement, see Jasper, *Nuclear Politics,* chaps. 7, 11.

28. Examples of whistleblowers as important conduits of information abound. The National Aeronautics and Space Administration was severely shaken, not just by the Challenger accident, but by the whistleblowers who revealed that they had warned against the fatal launch. See Diane Vaughan, "Autonomy, Interdependence, and Social Control: NASA and the Space Shuttle Challenger," *Administrative Science Quarterly* 35 (1990): 225–257, and *The Challenger Launch Decision: Risky Technology, Culture, and Deviance at NASA* (Chicago: University of Chicago Press, 1996). Other whistleblowers remain anonymous, but pass copies of incriminating memos to the press, as with Ford's calculations about the Pinto fuel tank (see Mark Dowie, "Pinto Madness," pp. 167–174 in Robert J. Baum, ed., *Ethical Problems in Engineering,* vol. 2, *Cases* [Troy, N.Y.: Center for the Study of the Human Dimensions of Science and Technology, Rensselaer Polytechnic, 1980]) or Hooker Chemical's worries about ground pollution (see Baum, *Ethical Problems in Engineering,* pp. 28–34). In this early stage in the recognition of a social problem, the news media are usually key contacts for whistleblowers.

29. See John Holusha, "A Whistle-Blower Is Awarded $22.5 Million," *New York Times,* 1 April 1994.

30. Christian Smith documents the salience of religion in this movement in *Resisting Reagan.* On religion as a source of protest more generally, see Christian S. Smith, ed., *Disruptive Religion: The Force of Faith in Social Movement Activism* (New York: Routledge, 1996).

7. RECRUITING ANIMAL PROTECTORS

1. Clifford Geertz, *The Interpretation of Cultures* (New York: Basic Books, 1973), p. 451.

2. Parts of this chapter, including table 7.1, are adapted from James M. Jasper and Jane D. Poulsen, "Recruiting Strangers and Friends: Moral Shocks and Social Networks in Animal Rights and Anti-Nuclear Protests," *Social Problems* 42 (1995): 493–512.

3. Charles Taylor, "Understanding and Ethnocentricity," in *Philosophy and the Human Sciences* (Cambridge: Cambridge University Press, 1985), p. 119.

4. Kristin Luker, *Abortion and the Politics of Motherhood* (Berkeley: University of California Press, 1984).

5. Herbert H. Haines, *Black Radicals and the Civil Rights Mainstream, 1954–1970* (Knoxville: University of Tennessee Press, 1988).

6. Movement ideologies are frequently studied, although most traditions have applied a healthy skepticism to public statements. Inspired partly by marxist ideas of false consciousness (one of the more dangerous concepts around), mobilization researchers have searched for the "real" interests—professional power, class position, status—being pursued under cover of noble rhetoric. This instrumental assumption misunderstands the cultural embeddedness of practices just as much as the opposite assumption, that ideologies are straightforward programs for action. Ways of talking are themselves complex practices, with many simultaneous motives and audiences. It is time to rescue the term *ideology* from its common usage, especially by marxists, as the opposite of scientific claims (as when the analyst has the truth, but her opponents have ideologies). We all operate with bundles—more or less coherent—of explicit, programmatic beliefs.

7. To take an example from political sociology rather than protest, in the late 1980s three of Sweden's major parties found themselves hotly disagreeing over whether Sweden should have eleven, twelve, or thirteen nuclear reactors. This trivial difference symbolized vastly different underlying attitudes toward nuclear energy and ultimately brought down a government. See my *Nuclear Politics*, chap. 12.

8. Jasper, *Nuclear Politics*, especially chap. 2.

9. See Peter L. Berger and Thomas Luckmann, *The Social Construction of Reality* (New York: Doubleday, 1966), and Peter L. Berger, *A Rumor of Angels: Modern Society and the Rediscovery of the Supernatural* (Garden City, N.Y.: Doubleday, 1970). I find the term *plausibility structure* overly ambitious, since it applies both to existing beliefs and to the daily practices that support them. In *A Rumor of Angels*, Berger says, "When we add up all these factors—social definitions of reality, social relations that take these for granted, as well as the supporting therapies and legitimations—we have the total plausibility structure of the conception in question" (pp. 35–6). Past and present experiences shape mental grids, which in turn filter new information and claims about the world. Both experiences and beliefs determine what we find plausible, but it is useful to distinguish them, not conflate them.

10. For a compelling argument that there is no common culture or dominant

ideology shared by different segments of society, see Nicholas Abercrombie, Stephen Hill, and Bryan S. Turner, *The Dominant Ideology Thesis* (London: George Allen and Unwin, 1980). Also see Michael Mann, "The Social Cohesion of Liberal Democracy," *American Sociological Review* 35 (1970): 423–439.

11. For differing pictures of how education is correlated with political attitudes, see Seymour Martin Lipset, *Political Man: The Social Bases of Politics* (Garden City, N.J.: Anchor, 1960); Herbert H. Hyman and Charles Wright, *Education's Lasting Influence on Values* (Chicago: University of Chicago Press, 1979); Mary R. Jackman and Michael J. Muha, "Education and Intergroup Attitudes: Moral Enlightenment, Superficial Democratic Commitment, or Ideological Refinement?" *American Sociological Review* 49 (1984): 751–769; and Jo Phelan, Bruce G. Link, Ann Stueve, and Robert E. Moore, "Education, Social Liberalism, and Economic Conservatism: Attitudes Toward Homeless People," *American Sociological Review* 60 (1995): 126–140.

12. Todd Gitlin, in *The Whole World Is Watching* (Berkeley: University of California Press, 1980) showed how the news media even changed protestors' understandings of their own movements in the 1960s.

13. William A. Gamson and Andre Modigliani, "Media Discourse and Public Opinion on Nuclear Power: A Constructionist Approach," *American Journal of Sociology* 95 (1989): 1–37.

14. A recent work on the cognitive dimensions of social movements that emphasizes the role of intellectuals is Ron Eyerman and Andrew Jamison, *Social Movements: A Cognitive Approach* (University Park: Pennsylvania State University Press, 1991).

15. Tarrow, *Power in Movement: Social Movements, Collective Action, and Politics* (Cambridge: Cambridge University Press, 1994), p. 123

16. Edward Sapir, "Symbolism," *Encyclopedia of the Social Sciences*, vol. 14 (1935): 493–4.

17. On the universal contrast between up and down, high and low, see Barry Schwartz, *Vertical Classification: A Study in Structuralism and the Sociology of Knowledge* (Chicago: University of Chicago Press, 1981). Anthropological classics on symbols and classifications include Claude Lévi-Strauss, *Structural Anthropology* ([1958] New York: Basic Books, 1963), and *The Savage Mind* ([1962] George Weidenfeld and Nicolson, 1966); Mary Douglas, *Purity and Danger: An Analysis of the Concepts of Pollution and Taboo* (London: Routledge and Kegan Paul, 1966), *Natural Symbols: Explorations in Cosmology* (London: Barrie and Jenkins, 1973); Victor Turner, *The Forest of Symbols: Aspects of Ndembu Ritual* (Ithaca, N.Y.: Cornell University Press, 1967); and Clifford Geertz, *The Interpretation of Cultures* (New York: Basic Books, 1973).

18. John Lofland distinguishes between "embodied" and "disembodied" contacts, but in either case recruiters must catch the attention of strangers through striking visual or verbal rhetoric: John Lofland, *Doomsday Cult* (Englewood Cliffs, N.J.: Prentice-Hall, 1966).

19. Because mobilization and process theorists emphasize social networks, it is hard for them to acknowledge the importance of cultural meanings transmitted more anonymously. For example, John McCarthy described the pro-

choice movement as lacking social networks it could use in recruitment. Because of this "social infrastructural deficit," the movement had to use symbolic appeals to reach its supportive "sentiment pool" through direct-mail technologies. See John D. McCarthy, "Pro-Life and Pro-Choice Mobilization: Infrastructure Deficits and New Technologies," in Zald and McCarthy, *Social Movements in an Organizational Society*. Because McCarthy analyzes the pro-choice case in terms of the social networks that are *missing*, he does not fully explore the cultural work that direct-mail groups need to do, or why some direct-mail appeals work and others do not. Despite their "deficit" qualities, however, direct-mail appeals have proliferated, casting some doubt on the importance of pre-existing networks as absolutely necessary for movement activity. Direct mail appeals not only take advantage of moral shocks such as Supreme Court decisions (each anti-abortion decision floods pro-choice groups with members and contributions: the National Abortion Rights Action League increased its membership by 75 percent in the six months following the Supreme Court's 1989 *Webster* decision), but they try to create their own through their rhetoric and visual images. Most appeals try to create a sense of crisis, shock, and outrage.

20. Benford, "'You Could Be the Hundredth Monkey,'" pp. 195–216.

21. Watters, *Down to Now*, p. 217.

22. See Robert Hariman, *Political Style: The Artistry of Power* (Chicago: University of Chicago Press, 1995).

23. James M. Jasper and Dorothy Nelkin, *The Animal Rights Crusade: The Growth of a Moral Protest* (New York: Free Press, 1992). I have focused on the role of ideas in animal protection movements in "Sentiments, Ideas, and Animals: Rights Talk and Animal Protection," in Stuart Bruchey, Peter Coclanis, and Joel Colton, eds., *Ideas in Social Movements* (New York: Columbia University Press, forthcoming).

24. On the civilizing process in Western history, see Norbert Elias, *The History of Manners*, vol. 1 of *The Civilizing Process* ([1939] New York: Pantheon, 1978); Philippe Ariès, *Centuries of Childhood* (New York: Vintage, 1962); Yi-Fu Tuan, *Segmented Worlds and Self* (Minneapolis: University of Minnesota Press, 1982). Increased awareness of individual feelings led both to more refined table manners and to a greater need for privacy. Servants who once had slept in the same room with their masters were now put in another wing or floor of the house; children were given their own rooms.

25. See Edward Shorter, *The Making of the Modern Family* (New York: Basic Books, 1975), and Viviana A. Zelizer, *Pricing the Priceless Child: The Changing Social Value of Children* (New York: Basic Books, 1985).

26. Historical works on uses of and attitudes toward domesticated animals in Western Europe include James Turner, *Reckoning with the Beast: Animals, Pain, and Humanity in the Victorian Mind* (Baltimore: Johns Hopkins University Press, 1980); Keith Thomas, *Man and the Natural World* (New York: Pantheon, 1983); Yi-Fu Tuan, *Dominance and Affection: The Making of Pets* (New Haven: Yale University Press, 1984); James Serpell, *In the Company of Animals* (New York: Basil Blackwell, 1986); Harriet Ritvo, *The Animal Estate* (Cambridge: Harvard Univer-

sity Press, 1987); and Joyce E. Salisbury, *The Beast Within: Animals in the Middle Ages* (New York: Routledge, 1994).

27. Charles Darwin, *The Descent of Man and Selection in Relation to Sex* ([1871] Princeton, N.J.: Princeton University Press, 1981), and *The Expression of the Emotions in Man and Animals* (New York: D. Appleton, 1896); see also George Louis Leclerc, Comte de Buffon, *Natural History, General and Particular* (London: T. Cadell and W. Davies, 1812).

28. Deborah Blum, *The Monkey Wars* (New York: Oxford University Press, 1994), p. 19.

29. Popular works on animal intelligence include Blum, *The Monkey Wars;* Dorothy L. Cheney and Robert M. Seyfarth, *How Monkeys See the World* (Chicago: University of Chicago Press, 1990); Donald R. Griffin, *Animal Thinking* (Cambridge: Harvard University Press, 1984), and *Animal Minds* (Chicago: University of Chicago Press, 1992); R. J. Hoage and Larry Goldman, eds., *Animal Intelligence* (Washington, D.C.: Smithsonian Institution Press, 1986); Eugene Linden, *Apes, Men, and Language* (New York: Saturday Review Press, 1974), and *Silent Partners: The Legacy of the Ape Language Experiments* (New York: Times Books, 1986); and Stephen F. Walker, *Animal Thought* (London: Routledge and Kegan Paul, 1983). Douglas Keith Candland, in *Feral Children and Clever Animals: Reflections on Human Nature* (New York: Oxford University Press, 1993), sees the effort to communicate with other species as an important part of our nature as humans.

30. See Ronald Inglehart, *The Silent Revolution* (Princeton, N.J.: Princeton University Press, 1977); Stephen Cotgrove and Andrew Duff, "Environmentalism, Middle-Class Radicalism, and Politics," *Sociological Review,* new series, 28 (1980): 333–351.

31. Stephen R. Kellert has documented the distribution of different views toward animals; see "American Attitudes Toward and Knowledge of Animals: An Update," *International Journal for the Study of Animal Problems* 1 (1980): 87–119; (with Miriam O. Westervelt), "Historical Trends in American Animal Use and Perception," *International Journal for the Study of Animal Problems* 4 (1983): 133–146; "Perceptions of Animals in America," in R. J. Hoage, ed., *Perceptions of Animals in American Culture* (Washington, D.C.: Smithsonian Institution Press, 1989); and *The Value of Life: Biological Diversity and Human Society* (Washington, D.C.: Island Press, 1995). Only 7 percent of Americans still hunt: on the cultural implications of hunting, see Jan E. Dizard, *Going Wild: Hunting, Animal Rights, and the Contested Meaning of Nature* (Amherst, Mass.: University of Massachusetts Press, 1994).

32. John Archer and Gillian Winchester, "Bereavement Following Death of a Pet," *British Journal of Psychology* 85 (1994): 259–271.

33. For details about these surveys, see the appendix.

34. Carolyn Chute, *The Beans of Egypt, Maine* (New York: Ticknor and Fields, 1985), p. 177; by permission of Ticknor and Fields.

35. Sara Ruddick, *Maternal Thinking: Toward a Politics of Peace* (Boston: Beacon Press, 1989).

36. Scholars who favor structural analyses argue that many may share the goals of a movement, or the plausibility structures behind the goals, but only

a few of them actually join. They point to an interesting study by Bert Klandermans and Dirk Oegema of Dutch peace mobilization, in which they interviewed citizens before and after a large demonstration. They found that 74 percent agreed with the goals of the event, but of these, only 4 percent attended. First, beliefs certainly differentiated the 26 percent who disagreed with the 74 percent who agreed. Second, as with most social-movement research, this finding generalizes from a single case, possibly unusual in the degree of agreement with its goals. Parallel research into a cause that only 5 percent of citizens supported, in contrast, might do a better job of predicting nonattenders. Third, Klandermans and Oegema studied attendance at a single event rather than all forms of peace protest; even the most dedicated protestor does not attend everything. Fourth, a limitation of surveys like this one (and of most studies that find little relationship between attitudes and behavior) is the crude measures of cultural meanings they include, which rarely get at more than superficial cognitive agreement with a protest's goals. It is no accident that scholars who use surveys rarely see links between meanings and actions, while those who do depth interviews and life histories almost always do. See Bert Klandermans and Dirk Oegema, "Potentials, Networks, Motivations, and Barriers: Steps towards Participation in Social Movements," *American Sociological Review* 52 (1987): 519–531.

37. Despite its concern with cultural meanings and lifestyles, I would not class the anti-abortion movement as "post-industrial" on account of its heavily religious ideology. But it certainly is a post-citizenship movement. For more on post-industrial movements, see Alain Touraine, *The Voice and the Eye* (Cambridge: Cambridge University Press, 1981), among his many other works. Ronald Inglehart (*The Silent Revolution* [Princeton: Princeton University Press, 1977]) and the extensive research inspired by him have made post-materialist values the center of their analysis of left-leaning politics since the 1960s. For a sampling, see Russell J. Dalton, Scott Flanagan, and Paul Allen Beck, eds., *Electoral Change in Advanced Industrial Countries: Realignment or Dealignment?* (Princeton: Princeton University Press, 1984); Scott C. Flanagan, "Changing Values in Industrial Societies Revisited: Towards a Resolution of the Values Debate," *American Political Science Review* 81 (1987): 1303–1319; and Ronald Inglehart, *Culture Shift in Advanced Industrial Society* (Princeton: Princeton University Press, 1990). In *The Fail-Safe Society: Community Defiance and the End of American Technological Optimism* (New York: Basic Books, 1991), Charles Piller documents the pervasive suspicion of and resistance to new technologies in the contemporary United States.

38. Most of my items were taken from Riley E. Dunlap and Kent D. Van Liere, "The 'New Environmental Paradigm': A Proposed Instrument and Preliminary Results," *Journal of Environmental Education* 9 (1978): 10–19.

39. For similar survey results, see Stephen Cotgrove, *Catastrophe or Cornucopia: The Environment, Politics, and the Future* (Chichester and New York: John Wiley and Sons, 1982); Dunlap and Van Liere, "The 'New Environmental Paradigm'"; and Lester W. Milbrath, *Environmentalists: Vanguard for a New Society* (Albany: State University of New York Press, 1984).

40. These survey responses confirm previous research. Anthony E. Ladd,

Thomas C. Hood, and Kent D. Van Liere, in "Ideological Themes in the Anti-nuclear Movement: Consensus and Diversity," *Sociological Inquiry* 53 (1983): 252–272, and James Scaminaci III and Riley E. Dunlap, in "No Nukes! A Comparison of Participants in Two National Antinuclear Demonstrations," *Sociological Inquiry* 56 (1986): 272–282, found values and beliefs similar to those reported here. Susan Sperling encountered strong environmental values among the animal rights protestors she interviewed for *Animal Liberators: Research and Morality* (Berkeley: University of California Press, 1988).

41. The quotations, respectively, are from Patrice Greanville, "The Greening of Animal Rights," *The Animals' Agenda* 7, no. 7 (1988): 36; and "In the Name of Humanity," *The Animals' Agenda* 7, no. 1 (1988): 36.

42. That social networks explain who is recruited is considered one of the soundest findings in social-movement research. The literature review that established this was David A. Snow, Louis A. Zurcher Jr., and Sheldon Ekland-Olson, "Social Networks and Social Movements: A Microstructural Approach to Differential Recruitment," *American Sociological Review* 45 (1980): 787–801; but see also their "Further Thoughts on Social Networks and Movement Recruitment," *Sociology* 17 (1983): 112–120.

43. Quoted in E. P. Thompson, *The Making of the English Working Class* ([1963] New York: Vintage, 1966), p. 361.

44. For workers, see Edward Shorter and Charles Tilly, *Strikes in France, 1830–1968* (Cambridge: Cambridge University Press, 1974); for African-Americans, Doug McAdam, *Political Process and the Development of Black Insurgency, 1930–1970* (Chicago: University of Chicago Press, 1982); on students, John Lofland, "The Youth Ghetto," in *Protest* (New Brunswick, N.J.: Transaction Publishers, 1985).

45. See Oberschall, *Social Conflict and Social Movements*; Snow et al., "Social Networks and Social Movements."

46. Morris, *The Origins of the Civil Rights Movement*.

47. Anthony Oberschall described bloc recruitment in *Social Conflict and Social Movements*.

48. Doug McAdam and Ronnelle Paulsen, "Specifying the Relationship between Social Ties and Activism," *American Journal of Sociology* 99 (1993): 640–667. Jo Freeman also emphasizes the role of organizational networks in "The Origins of the Women's Liberation Movement," *American Journal of Sociology* 78 (1973): 792–811.

49. See John D. McCarthy and Mayer N. Zald, "The Trend of Social Movements in America," in Zald and McCarthy, *Social Movements in an Organizational Society*; and Doug McAdam, "Recruitment to High-Risk Activism: The Case of Freedom Summer," *American Journal of Sociology* 92 (1986): 64–90.

50. See Max Heirich, *The Spiral of Conflict: Berkeley, 1964* (New York: Columbia University Press, 1971); William A. Gamson, Bruce Fireman, and Steven Rytina. *Encounters with Unjust Authority* (Homewood, Ill.: Dorsey Press, 1982) ; and Doug McAdam, *Freedom Summer* (New York: Oxford University Press, 1988).

51. My discussion is meant to address the main factors that explain recruit-

ment, not to list every variable that any theorist has mentioned. John Lofland has done something close to the latter, arriving at a list of sixteen factors. He labels one group individual causes (biological factors, deeper motivation, self-concept, belief and socialization, active seeking, benefit calculation/rational choice, and experimentation). But under structural causes he includes not only macro-structure (political opportunity structures), organizational membership, prior activism, and prior contact/network, but also—what he calls both structural and situational variables—suddenly imposed grievances, situational stress, biographical availability, coercive persuasion, and affective bonds. To me this last group appears to be an overextension of the structure metaphor to cover mechanisms that depend especially heavily on cultural and biographical interpretation. See his thorough *Social Movement Organizations: Guide to Research on Insurgent Realities* (New York: Walter de Gruyter, 1996), chap. 8.

52. Doug McAdam, John D. McCarthy, and Mayer N. Zald, "Social Movements," in Neil J. Smelser, ed., *Handbook of Sociology* (Beverly Hills: Sage Publications, 1988), p. 713.

53. Jasper and Poulsen, "Recruiting Strangers and Friends."

54. In his interviews with members of a local North Carolina animal rights group, Julian McAllister Groves similarly found that 25 percent had heard of the group first through their direct-mail memberships in national groups, 25 percent through the group's own literature, distributed especially at tables, and 20 percent through advertisements and newspaper articles about the group. This is a movement with considerable recruitment of strangers. See his "Animal Rights and Animal Research" (Ph.D. diss., Chapel Hill, N.C.: University of North Carolina, 1992). In unpublished research based on a survey of participants at a rally against the death penalty in New York, Jeff Goodwin found that only 40 percent of his respondents had heard about the rally through personal contacts; 36 percent had seen a poster; 23 percent had just been walking by.

55. Gordon M. Burghardt and Harold A. Herzog Jr., "Beyond Conspecifics: Is Brer Rabbit Our Brother?" *BioScience* 30 (1980): 763–768.

56. Celeste Michelle Condit, *Decoding Abortion Rhetoric: Communicating Social Change* (Urbana: University of Illinois Press, 1990), chap. 5.

57. Kristin Luker, *Abortion and the Politics of Motherhood,* p. 145.

58. Luker, *Abortion,* p. 137.

59. Several studies have probed the complex interweaving of the meanings of atomic bombs and reactors: Colette Guedeney and Gérard Mendel, *L'Angoisse Atomique et les Centrales Nucléaires* (Paris: Payot, 1973); Paul S. Boyer, *By the Bomb's Early Light: American Thought and Culture at the Dawn of the Atomic Age* (New York: Pantheon, 1985); Spencer R. Weart, *Nuclear Fear: A History of Images* (Cambridge: Harvard University Press, 1988); Françoise Zonabend, *The Nuclear Peninsula* (Cambridge: Cambridge University Press, 1993).

60. Susan Sontag, *On Photography* (New York: Farrar, Straus, Giroux, 1977), pp. 17, 23.

61. Toni Morrison, *Playing in the Dark: Whiteness and the Literary Imagination* (Cambridge: Harvard University Press, 1992), p. 49.

8. RITUALS AND EMOTIONS AT DIABLO CANYON

1. Jonathan Z. Smith, *To Take Place: Toward Theory in Ritual* (Chicago: University of Chicago Press, 1987), p. 103. Smith blames modern Christian theology for the contemporary tendency to see ritual as "empty," after writers such as Zwingli and Loyola insisted on the importance of the Eucharist as symbolic and internal, so that an inner space replaced the ritual importance of physical places. The physical actions, then, became hollow compared to the interior, mental, and spiritual ones. On top of this is the tendency for contemporary intellectuals to underestimate the power of religion. Yet for participants, rituals are still gripping.

2. Douglas, *Purity and Danger,* p. 64. Anthropological classics on ritual include Mary Douglas, *Natural Symbols: Explorations in Cosmology,* 2d ed. (London: Barrie and Jenkins, 1973); Clifford Geertz, *Negara: The Theatre State in Nineteenth-Century Bali* (Princeton: Princeton University Press, 1980); and Victor Turner, *The Ritual Process: Structure and Anti-Structure,* (Ithaca, N.Y.: Cornell University Press, 1969). Also see Joseph R. Gusfield, *The Culture of Public Problems: Drinking-Driving and the Symbolic Order* (Chicago: University of Chicago Press, 1981), and David I. Kertzer, *Ritual, Politics, and Power* (New Haven: Yale University Press, 1988). Most scholars who study cultural meanings are nonetheless still more likely to analyze them as static cognitive systems than as embodied in ritualized action. For an application related to protest, see Robert D. Benford and Lester R. Kurtz, "Performing the Nuclear Ceremony: The Arms Race as a Ritual," *Journal of Applied Behavioral Science* 23 (1987): 463–482.

3. Hochschild, "The Sociology of Feeling and Emotion," p. 298.

4. Verta Taylor and Nancy Whittier, "Analytical Approaches to Social Movement Culture: The Culture of the Women's Movement," in Johnston and Klandermans, *Social Movements and Culture.*

5. See Jeff Goodwin, "The Libidinal Constitution of a High-Risk Social Movement: Affectual Ties and Solidarity in the Huk Rebellion," *American Sociological Review,* 62 (1997): 53–69.

6. Max Scheler, *On Feeling, Knowing, and Valuing* (Chicago: University of Chicago Press, 1992), p. 54. Shared emotions correspond roughly to Durkheim's conception of mechanical solidarity, and reciprocal emotions to his more differentiated organic solidarity.

7. Roger Finke and Rodney Stark don't test the issue of scale directly, but they do point out that tiny rural churches can flourish even while large urban and suburban churches stagnate. See *The Churching of America 1776–1990: Winners and Losers in Our Religious Economy* (New Brunswick, N.J.: Rutgers University Press, 1992), chap. 6.

8. I discuss the formation of the American antinuclear movement in *Nuclear Politics* (Princeton: Princeton University Press, 1990), chap. 7. Also see Christian Joppke, *Mobilizing Against Nuclear Energy* (Berkeley: University of California Press, 1993).

9. Especially through the efforts of the new-social-movement theorists, this network has been studied more thoroughly for Europe than the United States:

In addition to the works cited in chapter 4, see Hanspeter Kriesi, "Local Mobilization for the People's Social Petition of the Dutch Peace Movement," *International Social Movement Research* 1 (1988): 41–81. On the United States, see Steven E. Barkan, "Strategic, Tactical, and Organizational Dilemmas of the Protest Movement Against Nuclear Power," *Social Problems* 27 (1979): 19–37; Barbara Epstein, "The Culture of Direct Action: Livermore Action Group and the Peace Movement," *Socialist Review* 82/83 (1985): 31–61; and *Political Protest and Cultural Revolution* (Berkeley: University of California Press, 1991). Harry C. Boyte surveys a slightly broader range of protest movements in *The Backyard Revolution: Understanding the New Citizen Movement* (Philadelphia: Temple University Press, 1980). David S. Meyer and Nancy Whittier examine the effects of the women's movement on the peace movement in "Social Movement Spillover," *Social Problems* 41 (1994): 277–298.

10. A group of feminist scholars has dubbed these two procedures as "separated" and "connected" ways of knowing: Mary Feld Belenky, Blythe McVicker Clinchy, Nancy Rule Goldberger, and Jill Mattuck Tarule, *Women's Ways of Knowing: The Development of Self, Voice, and Mind* (New York: Basic Books, 1986). Both are "procedural" forms of knowing, as opposed to received knowledge and subjective knowledge. "Constructed knowledge," these writers hope, is an integration of all these forms.

11. Several observers have noticed the tension between effective action and internal solidarity: Wini Breines, *Community and Organization in the New Left: 1962–1968* (South Hadley, Mass.: J. F. Bergin Publishers, 1982); Barkan, "Strategic, Tactical and Organizational Dilemmas of the Protest Movement Against Nuclear Power"; Gary L. Downey, "Ideology and the Clamshell Identity: Organizational Dilemmas in the Anti-Nuclear Power Movement," *Social Problems* 33 (1986): 357–373.

12. Epstein, *Political Protest*, p. 99.

13. Quoted in Epstein, *Political Protest*, p. 112.

14. In Epstein, *Political Protest*, p. 111.

15. Durkheim, one source of inspiration for crowd theories, said that song and dance might be necessary to sustain the collective effervescence of crowds: "And since a collective sentiment cannot express itself collectively except on the condition of observing a certain order permitting co-operation and movements in unison, these gestures and cries naturally tend to become rhythmic and regular; hence come songs and dances" (*The Elementary Forms of the Religious Life* [New York: Free Press, 1965], p. 247). William H. McNeill makes a sweeping argument for the emotional power of coordinated movement (marching, drilling, and the like, as well as dancing) in *Keeping Together in Time: Dance and Drill in Human History* (Cambridge: Harvard University Press, 1995).

16. Aldon D. Morris, *The Origins of the Civil Rights Movement* (New York: Free Press, 1984), p. 47. Throughout his book Morris refers to the rich Bible stories and songs that the movement borrowed from black churches. Film footage of the movement, some of it used in the *Eyes on the Prize* video series, also captures the power of song. Pat Watters recounts many of the songs and their importance in *Down to Now* (New York: Pantheon, 1971).

17. Judith Lynne Hanna, "Dance, Protest, and Women's 'Wars': Cases from Nigeria and the United States," in Guida West and Rhoda Lois Blumberg, eds., *Women and Social Protest* (New York: Oxford University Press, 1990), pp. 335 and 343, respectively.

18. Judith Lynne Hanna, *To Dance Is Human: A Theory of Nonverbal Communication* (Austin: University of Texas Press, 1979), p. 128. Of course, like all media, dance can convey a variety of messages. Maurice Bloch argues that ritualized dance can be used to narrow the possible messages, reducing a group's ability to challenge existing structures: "Symbols, Song, Dance, and Features of Articulation: Is Religion an Extreme Form of Traditional Authority?" *Archives Européenes de Sociologie* 15 (1974): 55–81.

19. John Lofland describes these feelings in "Crowd Joys," in Lofland, *Protest*. Another good study of collective euphoria, alternating with a sense of crisis, is Benjamin Zablocki, *The Joyful Community: An Account of the Bruderhof, a Communal Movement Now in Its Third Generation* (Baltimore: Penguin, 1971).

20. Political "generations" have often stood as a proxy for shared cultural meanings and actions. The concept is most often associated with Karl Mannheim: "The Problem of Generations," in Paul Kecskemeti, ed., *Essays on the Sociology of Knowledge* ([1928] London: Routledge and Kegan Paul, 1952). There is a large literature concerning the impact of political activities on the generations who came of age in the 1960s: see James M. Fendrich and Alison T. Tarleau, "Marching to a Different Drummer: Occupational and Political Correlates of Former Student Activists," *Social Forces* 52 (1973): 245–253; James M. Fendrich, "Keeping the Faith or Pursuing the Good Life: A Study in the Consequences of Participation in the Civil Rights Movement," *American Sociological Review* 42 (1977): 144–157; M. Kent Jennings, "Residues of a Movement: The Aging of the American Protest Generation," *American Political Science Review* 81 (1987): 367–382; Gerald Marwell, Michael T. Aiken, and N.J. Demerath III, "The Persistence of Political Attitudes Among 1960s Civil Rights Activists," *Public Opinion Quarterly* 51 (1987): 359–375; Jack Whalen and Richard Flacks, "Echoes of Rebellion: The Liberated Generation Grows Up," *Journal of Political and Military Sociology* 12 (1984): 61–78; James Max Fendrich and Kenneth L. Lovoy, "Back to the Future: Adult Political Behavior of Former Student Activists," *American Sociological Review* 53 (1988): 780–784; Doug McAdam, *Freedom Summer* (New York: Oxford University Press, 1988). More generally, see Anthony Esler, "'The Truest Community': Social Generations as Collective Mentalities," *Journal of Political and Military Sociology* 12 (1984): 99–112; and David Knoke, "Conceptual and Measurement Aspects in the Study of Political Generations," *Journal of Political and Military Sociology* 12 (1984): 191–201. Howard Schuman and Jacqueline Scott ground such generations in the salient events from each cohort's late adolescence and early adulthood in "Generations and Collective Memory," *American Sociological Review* 54 (1989): 359–381. A good recent work, breaking generations down into fine micro-cohorts, is Nancy Whittier, *Feminist Generations: The Persistence of the Radical Women's Movement* (Philadelphia: Temple University Press, 1995). A more general treatment of generations is David I. Kertzer, "Generation as a Sociological Problem," *Annual Review of Sociology* 9 (1983): 125–149.

21. Albert O. Hirschman sums up this view in *Shifting Involvements: Private Interest and Public Action* (Princeton, N.J.: Princeton University Press, 1982).

22. The exact wording was, "How important were each of the following in getting you active in anti-nuclear activity?" They could answer "Very Important," "Somewhat Important," or "Not Important," to each of the following: Friends, News Media, Previous Activism in other causes, Specific Events, and Other. For the last three categories, there were blank lines for them to specify what activism, events, or other factors.

23. These examples show why empirical efforts to link post-industrial movements to a "new middle class" (educated, affluent, and outside the for-profit sector) have usually failed. Participants want satisfying work, with autonomy and certain craft-like traits, even if that means gardening as well as teaching. They are not simply from the "service sector" or any other easily identifiable class segment. See Steven Cotgrove and Andrew Duff, "Environmentalism, Middle-Class Radicalism, and Politics," *Sociological Review* 28 (1980): 333–351; Hanspeter Kriesi, "New Social Movements and the New Class in the Netherlands," *American Journal of Sociology* 94 (1989): 1078–1116.

24. See William R. Freudenburg and Robert Gramling, *Oil in Troubled Waters: Perception, Politics, and the Battle Over Offshore Drilling* (Albany: State University of New York Press, 1994), p. 83.

25. Victor Turner and Edith Turner, *Image and Pilgrimage in Christian Culture: Anthropological Perspectives* (New York: Columbia University Press, 1978), p. 241; also Victor Turner, "Pilgrimages as Social Processes," in *Dramas, Fields, and Metaphors: Symbolic Action in Human Society* (Ithaca, N.Y.: Cornell University Press, 1974).

26. Researchers have discovered that local opposition often turns to support as soon as a plant starts operation, or when operation is imminent: Gérard Duménil, "Energie Nucléaire et Opinion Publique," in Francis Fagnani and Alexandre Nicholon, *Nucléopolis* (Grenoble: Presses Universitaires de Grenoble, 1979); Joop van der Pligt, J. Richard Eiser, and Russell Spears, "Attitudes Toward Nuclear Energy: Familiarity and Salience," *Environment and Behavior* 18 (1986): 75–93; and Joop van der Pligt, *Nuclear Energy and the Public* (Oxford: Basil Blackwell, 1992), chap. 4.

27. Luther P. Gerlach and Virginia H. Hine, *People, Power, and Change: Movements of Social Transformation* (New York: Bobbs-Merrill, 1970); Anthony Oberschall, "Loosely Structured Collective Conflict: A Theory and an Application," *Research in Social Movements, Conflicts, and Change* 3 (1980): 45–68.

28. Joyce Rothschild-Whitt, "The Collectivist Organization: An Alternative to Rational-Bureaucratic Models," *American Sociological Review* 44 (1979): 509–527. Also see Joyce Rothschild and J. Allen Whitt, *The Cooperative Workplace: Potentials and Dilemmas of Organizational Democracy and Participation* (Cambridge: Cambridge University Press, 1986).

29. Christian Smith gets at something similar when he says that activists he surveyed "did not really experience the 'costs' of their activism as costs." Those who had spent more time thinking about the personal costs, Smith found, were actually more dedicated to the cause. See *Resisting Reagan,* pp. 192–193.

30. Bert Klandermans, "Mobilization and Participation: Social-Psychological Expansions of Resource Mobilization Theory," *American Sociological Review* 49 (1984): 583–600. Like McAdam's concept of cognitive liberation, however, Klandermans's expectations are calculations of the likelihood of success and estimates of each participant's contribution to that likelihood. He downplays other reasons for participating, as well as the cultural, biographical, and strategic factors that shape expectations.

31. Patricia L. Wasielewski examines the interactional sources of charisma in "The Emotional Basis of Charisma," *Symbolic Interaction* 8 (1985): 207–222.

9. CULTURE AND BIOGRAPHY

1. Although I first met Merideth when studying the Abalone Alliance in the summer of 1984, most of the information presented here comes from a lengthy interview in May, 1991.

2. Italian sociologist Donatella della Porta praises life-history research because it allows the subject to tell her own story through a long series of conversations, as opposed not only to surveys but even to depth interviews in which the interviewer asks questions. Attention to the entire life context is especially helpful for getting at complex emotional and cognitive motivations. See her "Life Histories in the Analysis of Social Movement Activists," in Mario Diani and Ron Eyerman, eds., *Studying Collective Action* (London: Sage, 1992).

3. Joyce Carol Oates, "Capital Punishment," in *Heat and Other Stories* (New York: Dutton, 1991).

4. Elisabeth S. Clemens and Patrick Ledger show how individuals can foster social change by taking advantage of institutional contradictions; they do not simply adapt to organizational constraints: "Organizational Culture and Careers of Activism in the Woman Suffrage Movement, 1870–1920," unpublished paper, 1994.

5. Todd Gitlin, *The Sixties: Years of Hope, Days of Rage* (New York: Bantam Books, 1987), p. 371.

6. Gitlin, *The Sixties,* p. 108.

7. Jeff Goodwin, "The Libidinal Constitution of a High-Risk Social Movement: Affectual Ties and Solidarity in the Huk Rebellion," *American Sociological Review,* 62 (1997): 53–69. Also see Philip Slater, "On Social Regression," *American Sociological Review* 28 (1963): 339–364.

8. Alasdair MacIntyre, *After Virtue: A Study in Moral Theory* (Notre Dame, Ind.: University of Notre Dame Press, 1981), p. 175; my italics.

9. Shoshana Zuboff, *In the Age of the Smart Machine: The Future of Work and Power* (New York: Basic Books, 1988), p. 108.

10. Mihaly Csikszentmihalyi, *Flow: The Psychology of Optimal Experience* (New York: Harper and Row, 1990), p. 4.

11. Csikszentmihalyi, p. 9.

12. Charles Taylor, *Sources of the Self: The Making of Modern Identity* (Cambridge, Mass.: Harvard University Press, 1989), p. 63.

13. Faye J. Crosby, "Why Complain?" *Journal of Social Issues* 49 (1993): 169–184.

14. See Lois Marie Gibbs, as told to Murray Levine, *Love Canal: My Story* (Albany: State University of New York Press, 1982); Adeline Gordon Levine, *Love Canal: Science, Politics, and People* (Lexington, Mass.: D.C. Heath, 1982).

15. Philip P. Hallie, *Lest Innocent Blood Be Shed: The Story of the Village of Le Chambon and How Goodness Happened There* (New York: Harper and Row, 1979); Nechama Tec, *When Light Pierced the Darkness: Christian Rescue of Jews in Nazi-Occupied Poland* (New York: Oxford University Press, 1986); Kristin R. Monroe, Michael C. Barton, and Ute Klingemann, "Altruism and the Theory of Rational Action: An Analysis of Rescuers of Jews in Nazi Europe," in Kristin Renwick Monroe, ed., *The Economic Approach to Politics: A Critical Reassessment of the Theory of Rational Action* (New York: HarperCollins, 1991); Eva Fogelmann, *Conscience and Courage: Rescuers of Jews During the Holocaust* (New York: Anchor, 1994). Other studies of rescuers have pointed to different personality traits, including a willingness to take the lead from a moral leader such as a priest (Samuel P. Oliner and Pearl M. Oliner, *The Altruistic Personality: Rescuers of Jews in Nazi Europe* [New York: Free Press, 1988]) and a vivid awareness of a common humanity (Kristen Renwick Monroe, *The Heart of Altruism: Perceptions of a Common Humanity* [Princeton: Princeton University Press, 1996]).

16. Michael Walzer, *The Revolution of the Saints: A Study in the Origins of Radical Politics* (Cambridge: Harvard University Press, 1965), p. 317.

17. George Orwell, *The Road to Wigan Pier* ([1937] New York: Harcourt Brace Jovanovich, 1958), p. 174.

18. Quoted at the beginning of Tom Regan, *The Case for Animal Rights* (Berkeley: University of California Press, 1983), p. vi.

19. R. Laurence Moore, *Religious Outsiders and the Making of Americans* (New York: Oxford University Press, 1986).

20. Ralph H. Turner and Lewis M. Killian, *Collective Behavior,* 3d ed., pp. 336–337.

21. Hans-Georg Gadamer, *Truth and Method* ([1960] New York: Crossroad Publishing, 1982).

10. TASTES IN TACTICS

1. Mario Diani, *Green Networks* (Edinburgh: Edinburgh University Press, 1995).

2. Alain Touraine and his research group discovered similar splits—even open conflict—between locals (often housewives) and nonlocals in the French antinuclear conflict: Alain Touraine, Zsuzsa Hegedüs, François Dubet, and Michel Wieviorka, *Anti- Nuclear Protest* (Cambridge: Cambridge University Press, 1983). In many regions with a similar alliance, the relationship between locals and the direct-action subculture is tense but symbiotic: see Edward J. Walsh, *Democracy in the Shadows* (New York: Greenwood Press, 1988). The latter often appear when organizing has been started by the locals, or when there seems

to be the potential for such organizing, as in Walsh's case after the Three Mile Island accident in 1979.

3. Although it is customary to think of strategies as broader than tactics, I define strategy as interactions among players aimed at gaining advantages. Strategic choices can be small (most are) or large (including decisions to switch tactics), but they are always taken with an eye to other players, and in response to them. Explanations of repertories, tactical choices, and the applications of tactics are all affected both by external strategic considerations and internal movement culture, not to mention psychological and biographical dynamics.

4. In explaining why the radical and moderate wings of the women's movement adopted different tactics, Jo Freeman is an exception to this "environmental" emphasis. She lists values, past experiences, a constituency's reference group, expectations concerning responses, and relations with opponents as factors, but instead of theorizing these as cultural, strategic, and open-ended, she describes them as structural constraints. See Jo Freeman, "A Model for Analyzing the Strategic Options of Social Movement Organizations," in Jo Freeman, ed., *Social Movements of the Sixties and Seventies* (New York: Longman, 1983).

5. Herbert P. Kitschelt, "Political Opportunity Structures and Political Protest: Anti-Nuclear Movements in Four Democracies," *British Journal of Political Science* 16 (1986): 66.

6. Doug McAdam, John D. McCarthy, and Mayer N. Zald, "Social Movements," in Neil J. Smelser, *Handbook of Sociology* (Newbury Park, Calif.: Sage Publications, 1988), p. 726.

7. Doug McAdam, "Tactical Innovation and the Pace of Insurgency," *American Sociological Review* 48 (1983): 735–754.

8. Charles Tilly, *From Mobilization to Revolution* (Reading, Mass.: Addison-Wesley, 1978), chap. 5.

9. Tilly, *From Mobilization to Revolution*, p. 156.

10. Pierre Bourdieu, *Outline of a Theory of Practice* (Cambridge: Cambridge University Press, 1977), p. 83. In *Distinction: A Social Critique of the Judgment of Taste* (Cambridge: Harvard University Press, 1984), Bourdieu links habitus more explicitly with taste.

11. Bourdieu, *Outline of a Theory of Practice*, p. 81.

12. Snow and Benford, "Master Frames and Cycles of Protest," p. 146.

13. Stephen W. Beach, "Social Movement Radicalization: The Case of the People's Democracy in Northern Ireland," *Sociological Quarterly* 18 (1977): 312.

14. For McCarthy and Zald's most recent effort to sort out these audiences, see John D. McCarthy, Jackie Smith, and Mayer N. Zald, "Accessing Public, Media, Electoral, and Governmental Agendas," in McAdam, McCarthy, and Zald, eds., *Comparative Perspectives on Social Movements*.

15. Paul E. Johnson, *A Shopkeeper's Millennium: Society and Revivals in Rochester, New York, 1815–1837* (New York: Hill and Wang, 1978), p. 6.

16. Whittier, *Feminist Generations,* p. 56. Whittier points out (p. 83) that mobilization and process approaches, by focusing on external opportunities and levels of active mobilization, miss the cultural identities that are forged and continue to affect individuals, possibly for the rest of their lives.

17. Robert D. Benford, "Frame Disputes within the Nuclear Disarmament Movement," *Social Forces* 71 (1993): 697. Although it is clear that the Austin groups differed in their tactical preferences as much as they did ideologically, Benford tends to describe the differences as ideological ones, apparently with the tactical disagreements following from them.

18. Epstein, *Political Protest*, p. 75.

19. A small industry of sociologists has elaborated on this "neo-institutional" insight: for example, John W. Meyer and Brian Rowan, "Institutionalized Organizations: Formal Structure as Myth and Ceremony," *American Journal of Sociology* 83 (1977): 340–363; John W. Meyer, "The Effects of Education as an Institution," *American Journal of Sociology* 83 (1977): 53–77; John W. Meyer and W. Richard Scott, with B. Rowan and T. Deal, *Organizational Environments: Ritual and Rationality* (Beverly Hills: Sage Publications, 1983); Paul J. DiMaggio and Walter W. Powell, "The Iron Cage Revisited: Institutional Isomorphism and Collective Rationality in Organizational Fields," *American Sociological Review* 48 (1983): 147–160; Lynne G. Zucker, "Institutional Theories of Organizations," *Annual Review of Sociology* 13 (1987): 443–464; Walter W. Powell and Paul J. DiMaggio, eds., *The New Institutionalism in Organizational Analysis* (Chicago: University of Chicago Press, 1991); and Frank Dobbin, *Forging Industrial Policy: The United States, Britain, and France in the Railway Age* (New York: Cambridge University Press, 1994).

20. Gerlach and Hine, *People, Power, and Change*, p. 57. Also see Bruce Fireman and William A. Gamson, "Utilitarian Logic in the Resource Mobilization Perspective," in Mayer N. Zald and John D. McCarthy, eds., *The Dynamics of Social Movements* (Cambridge, Mass.: Winthrop, 1979).

21. John Lofland, "Social Movement Locals: Modal Member Structures," in Lofland, *Protest*, p. 204.

22. Elisabeth S. Clemens, "Organizational Form as Frame: Collective Identity and Political Strategy in the American Labor Movement, 1880–1920," in McAdam, McCarthy, and N. Zald, eds., *Comparative Perspectives on Social Movements*.

23. There are at least two dimensions of radicalization. *Ideological* radicalization entails the adoption of more sweeping, extensive goals. *Tactical* radicalization involves the use of tactics that either are less widely accepted in a society or that require a greater commitment on the part of participants. Here I am primarily concerned with tactical radicalization, although part of my explanation involves the effect of ideological radicalization on tactical. In chapter 16 I look at ideological radicalization more closely.

24. Frances Fox Piven and Richard A. Cloward, *Poor People's Movements* (New York: Pantheon, 1977).

25. Each instance of radicalization can be labeled either as an evolution within a particular protest movement or as the emergence of a new one. Thus the black nationalist movement is sometimes distinguished from the civil rights movement; the direct action movement from the local antinuclear movement; the rescue from the anti-abortion movement; the animal rights from the animal protection movement. The new groups usually adopt a new label and movement identity to prove themselves more radical than the older groups.

26. Kevin Everett, "The Growing Legitimacy of Protest in the United States, 1961–1983," (paper presented at the American Sociological Association annual meeting, Miami, Florida, 1993).

27. Thomas S. Kuhn, *The Structure of Scientific Revolutions* (Chicago: University of Chicago Press, 1962.

11. DIRECT AND INDIRECT ACTION

1. My account follows Joyce Marlow's thorough *Captain Boycott and the Irish* (New York: Saturday Review Press, 1973). Also see Thomas N. Brown, *Irish-American Nationalism, 1870–1890* (Philadelphia: Lippincott, 1966), and T. H. Corfe, "The Troubles of Captain Boycott," *History Today* 14 (November, 1964): 758–764, and (December, 1964): 854–862.

2. Quoted in Marlow, *Captain Boycott and the Irish*, p. 134.

3. James C. Scott, *Weapons of the Weak: Everyday Forms of Peasant Resistance* (New Haven: Yale University Press, 1985).

4. Colonial America, of course, had notorious "nonimportation" agreements against British goods. The Boston Tea Party was, strictly speaking, active destruction, but it was done in support of a boycott—it was what I call a companion tactic. See Richard Brown, *Revolutionary Politics in Massachusetts* (Cambridge: Harvard University Press, 1970). The tactic then seems to have faded. When revived one hundred years later, it was used primarily by the labor movement.

5. Michael Allen Gordon describes the migration of Irish-style boycotts to the United States in "Studies in Irish and Irish-American Thought and Behavior in Gilded Age New York City," (Ph.D. diss., University of Rochester, 1977), especially chap. 6.

6. Quoted in August Meier and Elliott Rudwick, "The Boycott Movement Against Jim Crow Streetcars in the South, 1900–1906," *The Journal of American History* 55 (1969): 761.

7. Aldon D. Morris discusses the origins of civil rights boycotts in *The Origins of the Civil Rights Movement* (New York: Free Press, 1984), chap. 2.

8. Taylor Branch gives a thorough account of the Montgomery boycott in *Parting the Waters: America in the King Years, 1954–1963* (New York: Simon and Schuster, 1988), chaps. 4, 5. Other discussions include Morris, *Origins of the Civil Rights Movement*, chap. 3; and Preston Valien, "The Montgomery Bus Protest as a Social Movement," in Jitsuichi Masuoka and Preston Valien, eds., *Race Relations: Problems and Theory* (Chapel Hill: University of North Carolina Press, 1961).

9. Working in the mobilization tradition, however, Morris gives more attention to the financial and social networks the churches provided. Morris, *Origins of the Civil Rights Movement*.

10. Doug McAdam has described the back-and-forth of protest in "Tactical Innovation and the Pace of Insurgency," *American Sociological Review* 48 (1983): 735–754. Jane Poulsen and I have also shown the influence of actions taken by those targeted by social movements, in "Fighting Back: Vulnerabilities, Blun-

ders, and Countermobilization by the Targets in Three Animal Rights Campaigns," *Sociological Forum* 8 (1993): 639–657. I examine this further in chapter 13.

11. On the UFWOC's struggles, see J. Craig Jenkins, *The Politics of Insurgency: The Farm Worker Movement in the 1960s* (New York: Columbia University Press, 1985); Jerald Barry Brown, "The United Farm Workers Grape Strike and Boycott, 1965–1970" (Ph.D. diss., Ithaca: Cornell University, 1972); Mark Day, *Forty Acres: César Chávez and the Farm Workers* (New York: Praeger, 1971); and John Gregory Dunne, *Delano: The Story of the California Grape Strike* (New York: Farrar, Straus and Giroux, 1967).

12. Brown, "The United Farm Workers Grape Strike and Boycott," p. 139.

13. Brown, "Grape Strike," pp. 212–215.

14. Brown, "Grape Strike," p. 209.

15. We first compiled a list of all the boycotts we could discover that had been started from 1981 to 1986. Using a variety of sources, especially the *National Boycott News*, we put together a list of almost one hundred. Through telephone interviews Bettina Edelstein was able to track down systematic information on 55 of these.

16. One study of the impact of boycotts on stock prices found the greatest effect at the time of the initial announcement, with little effect from the ending of a boycott. It is expectations or fears of a boycott's impact that leads corporations to change. See Dan L. Worrell, Wallace N. Davidson III, and Abuzar El-Jelly, "Do Boycotts and Divestitures Work? A Stock Market Based Test." Unpublished manuscript, 1993.

12. CULTURE AND RESOURCES: THE ARTS OF PERSUASION

1. William A. Gamson, Bruce Fireman, and Steven Rytina, *Encounters with Unjust Authority* (Homewood, Ill.: Dorsey Press, 1982), p. 88.

2. Frances Fox Piven and Richard A. Cloward make this sort of argument in *Poor People's Movements* (New York: Pantheon, 1977). Jeremy Brecher finds the same dynamic with depressing regularity in United States history in *Strike!* (Boston: South End Press, 1972).

3. Michael Lipsky, "Protest as a Political Resource," *American Political Science Review* 62 (1968): 1114–1158; Anthony Oberschall, *Social Conflict and Social Movements* (Englewood Cliffs, N.J.: Prentice-Hall, 1973); J. Craig Jenkins and Charles Perrow, "Insurgency of the Powerless," *American Sociological Review* 42 (1977): 249–268.

4. Morris, *Origins of the Civil Rights Movement*, pp. 280–286. See also Clarence Y. H. Lo, "Communities of Challengers in Social Movement Theory," and Frances Fox Piven and Richard A. Cloward, "Normalizing Collective Protest," in Morris and Mueller, eds., *Frontiers in Social Movement Theory.*

5. See James M. Jasper, "The Politics of Abstractions: Instrumental and Moralist Rhetorics in Public Debate," *Social Research* 59 (1992): 315–344; Scott Sanders and James M. Jasper, "Civil Politics in the Animal Rights Conflict: God

Terms versus Casuistry in Cambridge, Massachusetts," *Science, Technology & Human Values* 19 (1994): 169–188.

6. Herbert H. Haines, *Black Radicals and the Civil Rights Mainstream, 1954– 1970* (Knoxville: University of Tennessee Press, 1988), p. 10.

7. Malcolm Spector and John I. Kitsuse, *Constructing Social Problems* (New York: Aldine de Gruyter, 1987), p. 151.

8. Celene Krauss gives a detailed portrait of one protestor radicalized through outrage over governmental lack of responsiveness: "Community Struggles and the Shaping of Democratic Consciousness," *Sociological Forum* 4 (1989): 227–239.

9. Quoted in Karen Stults, "Women Movers: Reflections on a Movement by Some of Its Leaders," *Everyone's Backyard* 7 (1989), p. 1. Published by the Citizens Clearinghouse for Hazardous Waste, Arlington, Virginia.

10. See Cynthia Gordon and James M. Jasper, "Overcoming the 'NIMBY' Label: Rhetorical and Organizational Links for Local Protestors," *Research in Social Movements, Conflicts, and Change* 19 (1996): 159–181.

11. Spector and Kitsuse, *Constructing Social Problems*, p. 145.

12. The incinerator case is taken from Gordon and Jasper, "Overcoming the 'NIMBY' Label."

13. Barry Commoner, "Don't Let City Garbage Go Up in Smoke," *New York Times,* 29 January 1989.

14. On the anti-incinerator movement, see Edward J. Walsh, Rex Warland, and D. Clayton Smith, *The Environmental Justice Movement: Eight Grassroots Challenges to Modern Incinerator Projects* (University Park: Pennsylvania State University Press, forthcoming).

15. See Jonathan Rieder, *Canarsie: The Jews and Italians of Brooklyn against Liberalism* (Cambridge: Harvard University Press, 1985). Beginning with Hofstadter, the dominant interpretation of lifestyle politics has been that one group, losing economic position, clings to its lifestyle status all the more stridently. See Joseph R. Gusfield, *Symbolic Crusade* (Urbana: University of Illinois Press, 1963). In *Distinction: A Social Critique of the Judgment of Taste* (Cambridge, Mass.: Harvard University Press, 1984), Pierre Bourdieu analyzed the middle-class strata of shopkeepers and clerks as inherently anxious about their own status. Seymour Martin Lipset and Earl Raab suggested that some groups have a large symbolic investment in the past, based on some past group identity which has declined in symbolic importance in the society at large. They reassert this former status by attacking newcomers with different customs. See Lipset and Raab, *The Politics of Unreason: Right-Wing Extremism in America, 1790–1977,* 2d ed. (Chicago: University of Chicago Press, 1978).

16. Rieder, *Canarsie*, p. 72.

17. Rieder, pp. 61, 93.

18. Rieder, p. 43.

19. Rieder, p. 67.

20. On this process, see Thomas Byrne Edsall with Mary D. Edsall, *Chain Reaction: The Impact of Race, Rights, and Taxes on American Politics* (New York:

W. W. Norton, 1991); Stephan Lesher, *George Wallace: American Populist* (Reading, Mass.: Addison-Wesley, 1993); and Dan T. Carter, *The Politics of Rage: George Wallace, the Origins of the New Conservatism, and the Transformation of American Politics* (New York: Simon and Schuster, 1995).

21. Rieder, *Canarsie*, p. 236.

22. For a small sampling of works on the news media, see Michael Schudson, *Discovering the News: A Social History of American Newspapers* (New York: Basic Books, 1978); Herbert J. Gans, *Deciding What's News: A Study of CBS Evening News, NBC Nightly News, Newsweek, and Time* (New York: Random House, 1979); Harvey Molotch, "Media and Movements," in Mayer N. Zald and John D. McCarthy, eds., *The Dynamics of Social Movements* (Cambridge, Mass.: Winthrop, 1979); Todd Gitlin, *The Whole World Is Watching* (Berkeley: University of California Press, 1980); Richard B. Kielbowicz and Clifford Scherer, "The Role of the Press in the Dynamics of Social Movements," *Research in Social Movements, Conflict, and Change* 9 (1986): 71–96; Mitchell Stephens, *A History of News* (New York: Penguin Books, 1988); Ben H. Bagdikian, *The Media Monopoly*, 3d ed. (Boston: Beacon Press, 1990); Charlotte Ryan, *Prime Time Activism: Media Strategies for Grassroots Organizing* (Boston: South End Press, 1991); and William A. Gamson and Gadi Wolfsfeld, "Movements and Media as Interacting Systems," *Annals of the American Academy of Political and Social Science* 528 (1993): 114–125.

23. This kind of "moral panic" has been studied by students of deviance more often than scholars of social movements, presumably because the term *panic* implies a disproportionate (perhaps irrational) response to some threat. But panickers are subject to the same processes we saw in chapter 5 in other groups who perceived threats, physical or human.

Stanley Cohen described a moral panic: "A condition, episode, person or group of persons emerges to become defined as a threat to societal values and interests; its nature is presented in a stylized and stereotypical fashion by the mass media; the moral barricades are manned by editors, bishops, politicians and other right-thinking people; socially accredited experts pronounce their diagnoses and solutions; ways of coping are evolved or (more often) resorted to. . . . Sometimes the panic passes over and is forgotten, except in folklore and collective memory; at other times it has more serious and long-lasting repercussions and might produce such changes as those in legal and social policy or even in the way the society conceives itself." See Stanley Cohen, *Folk Devils and Moral Panics: The Creation of the Mods and the Rockers* (New York: St. Martin's Press, 1972), p. 9.

Other classics on moral panics include Kai T. Erikson, *Wayward Puritans: A Study in the Sociology of Deviance* (New York: Wiley, 1966); Joseph R. Gusfield, *Symbolic Crusade* (Urbana: University of Illinois Press, 1963); Troy S. Duster, *The Legislation of Morality: Law, Drugs, and Moral Judgment* (New York: Free Press, 1970); Stuart Hall, with Chas Critcher, Tony Jefferson, John Clarke, and Brian Roberts, *Policing the Crisis: Mugging, the State, and Law and Order* (London: Macmillan, 1978); and Jerome L. Himmelstein, *The Strange Career of Marijuana*

(Westport, Conn.: Greenwood Press, 1983). The literature on moral panics has grown rapidly in recent years, as the newly rejuvenated Christian right in the United States has promoted censorship in the arts and education and concern over sex, drugs, and other activities. For a sampling, see Linda Martin and Kerry Segrave, *Anti-Rock: The Opposition to Rock 'n' Roll* (Hamden, Conn.: Archon, 1988); Craig Reinarman and Harry Gene Levine, "Crack in Context: Politics and Media in the Making of a Drug Scare," *Contemporary Drug Problems* 16 (1989): 535–577; Nachman Ben-Yehuda, *The Politics and Morality of Deviance: Moral Panics, Drug Abuse, Deviant Science, and Reversed Discrimination* (Albany: SUNY Press, 1990); Donna A. Demac, *Liberty Denied: The Current Rise of Censorship in America* (New Brunswick, N.J.: Rutgers University Press, 1990); and Deena Weinstein, *Heavy Metal: A Cultural Sociology* (New York: Lexington Books, 1991). For overviews of the scholarly literature, see Nachman Ben-Yehuda, "The Sociology of Moral Panics: Toward a New Synthesis," *Sociological Quarterly* 27 (1986): 495–513; Erich Goode and Nachman Ben-Yehuda, "Moral Panics: Culture, Politics, and Social Construction," *Annual Review of Sociology* 20 (1994): 149–171, and *Moral Panics: The Social Construction of Deviance* (Cambridge, Mass.: Blackwell, 1994).

24. Philip Jenkins, *Intimate Enemies: Moral Panics in Contemporary Great Britain* (New York: Aldine de Gruyter, 1992).

25. At this point a nod to Antonio Gramsci is inevitable. Many protest movements battle what he called "cultural hegemony"—the processes by which those in power shape the feelings and beliefs of those who might otherwise wish to rebel. But most moral panics reinforce rather than challenge hegemonic beliefs. Indeed some moral panics construct other protestors as folk devils, as with the organized backlash against the family-destroying "liberated woman."

26. Gamson, *Talking Politics*, p. 35.

27. Gitlin, *The Whole World Is Watching*.

28. John D. McCarthy, in a study of local chapters of Mothers Against Drunk Driving, found that "the mere presence of a group had a strong and significant impact on whether the issue received media coverage during the year." See "Activists, Authorities, and Media Framing of Drunk Driving," in Laraña, Johnston, and Gusfield, eds., *New Social Movements*, p. 149.

29. I show how, in national arenas, issues are transformed by existing political cleavages in James M. Jasper, "Three Nuclear Energy Controversies," in Dorothy Nelkin, *Controversy: Politics of Technical Decisions* (Beverly Hills: Sage Publications, 1992). For a case of the same ideological twisting in city politics, see James M. Jasper and Scott Sanders, "Big Institutions in Local Politics: American Universities, the Public, and Animal Protection Efforts," *Social Science Information* 34 (1995): 491–509.

13. CULTURE AND STRATEGY: STATES, AUDIENCES, AND SUCCESS

1. The story of Bodega Head is told in Lynton K. Caldwell, Lynton R. Hayes, and Isabel M. MacWhirter, *Citizens and the Environment: Case Studies in Popular*

Action (Bloomington: Indiana University Press, 1976), pp. 195–204, and Richard L. Meehan, *The Atom and the Fault: Experts, Earthquakes, and Nuclear Power* (Cambridge: MIT Press, 1984), chap. 1.

2. Over one hundred plants were canceled in the 1970s and 1980s, but for reasons other than public protest. See my *Nuclear Politics,* chaps. 7, 11.

3. DiMaggio and Powell, "The Iron Cage Revisited."

4. To be sure, many early mobilization theorists were explicitly concerned with strategic interaction. Michael Lipsky was interested in disruption as a substitute for resources: see "Protest as a Political Resource." Anthony Oberschall used a conflict framework as much as a movement framework in *Social Conflict and Social Movements.* Strategic alliances were crucial in Jenkins and Perrow, "Insurgency of the Powerless." On the other hand, William Gamson's classic, *The Strategy of Social Protest,* is about the effects of various strategies, but because of its correlational method it presents an oddly static view of strategy and says little about where strategies come from.

5. In his explanation of tactical innovation, Doug McAdam stresses interaction between protestors and their opponents, but he does not actually show how the interactions occurred or decisions were made: see his "Tactical Innovation and the Pace of Insurgency." One work that does describe this interaction is Max Heirich's *The Spiral of Conflict.*

6. B. H. Liddell Hart, *Strategy,* 2d ed. (New York: Praeger Publishers, 1967), pp. 348–349.

7. Saul D. Alinsky, *Rules for Radicals: A Pragmatic Primer for Realistic Radicals* (New York: Random House, 1971), pp. 127–130. On Alinsky as a brilliant strategist, see Robert Bailey Jr., *Radicals in Urban Politics: The Alinsky Approach* (Chicago: University of Chicago Press, 1974), and P. David Finks, *The Radical Vision of Saul Alinsky* (Ramsey, N.J.: Paulist Press, 1984).

8. Anatol Rapoport and Melvin Guyer, "A Taxonomy of 2 x 2 Games," *General Systems: Yearbook of the Society for General Systems Research* 11 (1966): 203–214.

9. Thomas C. Schelling, *The Strategy of Conflict* (Cambridge: Harvard University Press, 1960).

10. John Lofland presents both typologies in *Social Movement Organizations,* chap. 9.

11. Anthony Oberschall, *Social Movements: Ideologies, Interests, and Identities* (New Brunswick, N.J.: Transaction Publishers, 1993), p 104.

12. Henry Mintzberg and Alexandra McHugh, "Strategy Formation in an Adhocracy," *Administrative Science Quarterly,* 30 (1985): 160–197.

13. W. Richard Scott, *Organizations: Rational, Natural, and Open Systems,* 2d ed. (Englewood Cliffs, N.J.: Prentice-Hall, 1987), p. 282.

14. Pat Watters, *Down to Now,* chap. 1.

15. James M. Jasper and Jane Poulsen, "Fighting Back," *Sociological Forum* 8 (1993): 639–657.

16. Edward J. Walsh, "The Role of Target Vulnerabilities in High-Technology Protest Movements: The Nuclear Establishment at Three Mile Island," *Sociological Forum* 1 (1986): 199–218.

17. See Harvey Molotch, "Oil in Santa Barbara and Power in America," *Sociological Inquiry* 40 (1970): 131–144.

18. Steven E. Barkan, "Legal Control of the Southern Civil Rights Movement," *American Journal of Sociology* 49 (1984): 552–565.

19. For a game-theoretic perspective on blunders, see Dennis Chong, *Collective Action and the Civil Rights Movement*, pp. 62–63, 137–139.

20. Alinsky, *Rules for Radicals*, p. 136.

21. Erving Goffman, *The Presentation of Self in Everyday Life* (Garden City, N.Y.: Anchor Books, 1959), p. 75.

22. Jürgen Habermas, of course, argues that speech itself implicitly contains promises that the speaker is sincere, aims at saying something true, and is saying something appropriate in the circumstances. Statements can be criticized for failing to meet any of these criteria, and successful critiques can make blunders out of public statements.

23. Goffman, *The Presentation of Self in Everyday Life*, p. 64–65. I have described battles between protestors and their opponents over credibility in several articles: Jasper and Poulsen, "Fighting Back;" Sanders and Jasper, "Civil Politics in the Animal Rights Conflict"; Jasper and Sanders, "Big Institutions in Local Politics."

24. Sissela Bok, *Lying: Moral Choice in Public and Private Life* (New York: Random House, 1978), pp. 141–142 and 143, respectively.

25. Bok, p. 146.

26. McAdam, "Tactical Innovation and the Pace of Insurgency," p. 736.

27. William A. Gamson, *The Strategy of Social Protest;* Mayer N. Zald and Bert Useem, "Movement and Countermovement Interaction: Mobilization, Tactics, and State Involvement," in Zald and McCarthy, eds., *Social Movements in an Organizational Society,* p. 254; and Tahi L. Mottl, "The Analysis of Countermovements," *Social Problems,* 27 (1980): 624.

28. Jane J. Mansbridge, *Why We Lost the ERA* (Chicago: University of Chicago Press, 1986), pp. 5–6.

29. Suzanne Staggenborg, *The Pro-Choice Movement: Organization and Activism in the Abortion Conflict* (New York: Oxford University Press, 1991), p. 3.

30. George W. Pring and Penelope Canan, *SLAPPS: Getting Sued for Speaking Out* (Philadelphia: Temple University Press, 1996).

31. Patricia Morgan, "The State as Mediator: Alcohol Problem Management in the Postwar Period," *Contemporary Drug Problems* 9 (1980): 107–140.

32. Joseph R. Gusfield, "Constructing the Ownership of Social Problems: Fun and Profit in the Welfare State," *Social Problems* 36 (1989), p. 433.

33. Joel Best, "Rhetoric in Claims-Making: Constructing the Missing Children Problem," *Social Problems* 34 (1987), p. 110.

34. Rick Fantasia and Eric L. Hirsch, "Culture in Rebellion: The Appropriation and Transformation of the Veil in the Algerian Revolution," in Johnston and Klandermans, eds., *Social Movements and Culture,* 158–159.

35. Morton Deutsch, *The Resolution of Conflict: Constructive and Destructive Processes* (New Haven: Yale University Press, 1973), p. 123.

36. Deutsch, *The Resolution of Conflict*, p. 351.

37. The animal rights cases presented in this chapter are taken from Jasper and Poulsen, "Fighting Back."

38. TSU underwent internal splits at this time, and it eventually collapsed. Other animal rights groups demonstrated at NYU in April 1991, attracting almost three hundred protestors, but their focus was not these experiments. Demonstrations since then have been even smaller.

39. Hank Johnston discusses different speech settings in "A Methodology for Frame Analysis: From Discourse to Cognitive Schema," in Johnston and Klandermans, eds., *Social Movements and Culture*. In a classic analysis of politics and culture, Murray Edelman showed that state decisions often send symbolic messages to the broader public at odds with the real economic effects on industry: *The Symbolic Uses of Politics* (Urbana: University of Illinois Press, 1964). He continued this line of inquiry in *Political Language: Words That Succeed and Policies That Fail* (New York: Academic Press, 1977) and *Constructing the Political Spectacle* (Chicago: University of Chicago Press, 1988).

40. Kenneth Burke, *A Rhetoric of Motives* (New York: Prentice-Hall, 1950).

41. Paul Burstein, Rachel L. Einwohner, and Jocelyn A. Hollander, "The Success of Political Movements: A Bargaining Perspective," in J. Craig Jenkins and Bert Klandermans, eds., *The Politics of Social Protest: Comparative Perspectives on States and Social Movements* (Minneapolis: University of Minnesota Press, 1995), p. 275.

42. In "Fighting Back," Jane Poulsen and I contrasted this "early wins" pattern with an "early losses" pattern, which Charles Tilly posits as normal for movements in their early stages. He assumes a little mobilization will automatically elicit state repression, actually hurting the movement until it grows large enough to overcome that repression. I think his model, like so many process theories, is inspired by citizenship movements, especially labor but also civil rights, that do face considerable automatic repression by the state. This is not true for post-citizenship movements, which thus often have early wins.

43. Zald and Useem, "Movement and Countermovement Interaction."

44. J. Craig Jenkins and Bert Klandermans, "The Politics of Social Protest," in Jenkins and Klandermans, eds., *The Politics of Social Protest*, p. 3.

45. Burstein, Einwohner, and Hollander, "The Success of Political Movements," p. 284

46. On how the women's movement affected the peace movement, for example, see David S. Meyer and Nancy Whittier, "Social Movement Spillover," *Social Problems* 41 (1994): 277–298. The effects included tactical innovations, ideological frames, and organizational structures.

47. In a case that Paul DiMaggio reports, the "little theater" movement in the early decades of the twentieth century failed organizationally, but laid the intellectual groundwork for a revamping of American theater two decades later along high-art lines. See his "Cultural Boundaries and Structural Change: The Extension of the High Culture Model to Theater, Opera, and the Dance, 1900–1940," in Michèle Lamont and Marcel Fournier, eds., *Cultivating Differ-*

ences: Symbolic Boundaries and the Making of Inequality (Chicago: University of Chicago Press, 1992).

48. Alinsky, *Rules for Radicals*, p. 165.

14. TOWARD A BALANCED APPROACH

1. William H. Sewell Jr., *Work and Revolution in France* (Cambridge: Cambridge University Press, 1980); "Collective Violence and Collective Loyalties in France," *Politics and Society* 18:527–552.

2. Tarrow, *Power in Movement*, part 1.

3. Of this radical branch, Nancy Whittier has written, "[C]ultural events and institutions existed all along in the radical feminist movement, and participants saw culture as political in the early years as well as after 1980." *Feminist Generations*, p. 52. As the women's movement shows, my distinction between citizenship and post-citizenship movements is hardly rigid, but movements can pursue and attain legal rights without successfully transforming cultural stereotypes, informal inequalities (as in the family), characteristic emotions, or constructions of self-identity.

4. Whittier, *Feminist Generations*, p. 58.

5. Gamson, *The Strategy of Social Protest.*

15. LIVES WORTH LIVING

1. MacIntyre, *After Virtue*, p. 178. There is a leap in his argument here, for there is no reason to assume that all practices will require the same virtues. But the three he mentions are almost certainly virtues for protest.

2. One need not be persuaded by Habermas's efforts to "ground" his commitments to democracy and autonomy in the very nature of language, in order to admit that human nature has much to do with symbols, expression, criticism, and communication. For a good argument that the "semiotic" self is part of universal human nature, see Norbert Wiley, *The Semiotic Self* (Chicago: University of Chicago Press, 1994).

3. Richard Rorty, *Philosophy and the Mirror of Nature* (Princeton, N.J.: Princeton University Press, 1979), p. 12. He mentions Kierkegaard, Nietzsche, the later Wittgenstein, and the later Heidegger as examples. One might add Michel Foucault, who is often criticized for constantly attacking existing systems of thought and action without developing his own positive alternative values.

4. Rorty, *Philosophy and the Mirror of Nature*, pp. 369, 377.

5. MacIntyre, *After Virtue*, p. 188.

6. MacIntyre, p. 203.

7. MacIntyre, pp. 26–29.

8. Heinz Kohut, *The Search for the Self*, edited by Paul Ornstein (Madison, Wisc.: International Universities Press, 1978), p. 273. Douglas B. Emery links this creativity to political activity in "Self, Creativity, Political Resistance," *Political Psychology* 14 (1993): 347–362.

9. Karl Wolfgang Deutsch, *The Nerves of Government: Models of Political Communication and Control* (New York: Free Press of Glencoe, 1963), p. 174.

10. Quoted in Joseph Wesley Zeigler, *Regional Theatre: The Revolutionary Stage* (Minneapolis: University of Minnesota Press, 1973), p. 8.

11. Helping people find their moral voice can take many forms. Many post-citizenship movements do it through participation in group discussions in addition to externally oriented protest. But others (including many citizenship groups) are hierarchical, so that members find their voices in unison with others, and often as embodied in the group's leader. Martin Luther King Jr. did not organize egalitarian affinity groups, but many civil rights protestors, and not just religious ones, found their moral voice through him and in him.

16. THE RISKS OF PROTEST

1. François Ponchaud, "Social Change in the Vortex of Revolution," in Karl D. Jackson, ed., *Cambodia 1975–1978: Rendezvous with Death* (Princeton: Princeton University Press, 1989), p. 165. Other general sources for this chapter include David P. Chandler, *The Tragedy of Cambodian History: Politics, War, and Revolution Since 1945* (New Haven: Yale University Press, 1991); *Brother Number One: A Political Biography of Pol Pot* (Boulder, Colo.: Westview, 1992); David P. Chandler, Ben Kiernan, and Chanthou Boua, eds., *Pol Pot Plans the Future: Confidential Leadership Documents from Democratic Kampuchea, 1976–1977* (New Haven: Yale University Southeast Asia Studies, 1988); Elizabeth Becker, *When the War Was Over: The Voices of Cambodia's Revolution and Its People* (New York: Simon and Schuster, 1986); David P. Chandler and Ben Kiernan, eds., *Revolution and Its Aftermath in Kampuchea: Eight Essays* (New Haven: Yale University Southeast Asian Studies, 1983).

2. Quoted in David P. Chandler, "Seeing Red: Perceptions of Cambodian History in Democratic Kampuchea," in Chandler and Kiernan, eds., *Revolution and Its Aftermath in Kampuchea*, p. 34.

3. See David P. Chandler, "Seeing Red," p. 35; Chandler, Kiernan, and Boua, *Pol Pot Plans the Future*, introduction to Document IV.

4. On the complexities of this period, see David P. Chandler, *A History of Cambodia*, 2d ed. (Boulder, Colo.: Westview Press, 1992), chaps. 3–4.

5. Slavenka Drakulić describes a street in Zagreb once named after King Zvonimir. After World War II it became Red Army Street; when Yugoslavia broke with the Soviet Union in 1948 it became the Street of Socialist Revolution. It's now once again King Zvonimir Street. See "Nazis Among Us," *New York Review of Books,* 27 May 1993, p. 21.

6. Chandler, Kiernan, and Boua, *Pol Pot Plans*, pp. 128–131.

7. Chandler, Kiernan, and Boua, p. 37. Italics in original.

8. Chandler, *A History of Cambodia*, p. 215.

9. Chandler, Kiernan, and Boua, p. 47.

10. Chandler, Kiernan, and Boua, p. 160.

11. Michael Vickery, *Cambodia: 1975–1982* (Boston: South End Press, 1984), p. 273.

12. Norodom Sihanouk, *War and Hope: The Case for Cambodia* (New York: Pantheon, 1980), p. 86.

13. Quoted in Karl D. Jackson, "The Ideology of Total Revolution," in Jackson, ed., *Cambodia 1975–1978* (Princeton: Princeton University Press, 1989), p. 44.

14. François Ponchaud, "Social Change in the Vortex of Revolution," in Jackson, *Cambodia 1975–1978*, p. 160.

15. Charles Burton, quoted in Frank Chalk and Kurt Jonassohn, *The History and Sociology of Genocide: Analyses and Case Studies* (New Haven: Yale University Press, 1990), p. 402.

16. In writing about these moral panics, historian Paul Boyer attributes them, in part, to the same kind of abstracted thinking of which the Khmer Rouge were guilty: "The stock phrases used by these reformers to describe the urban masses—'vicious,' 'abandoned,' 'debased'—convey by their very conventionality the extent to which firsthand knowledge of actual human beings was being replaced by abstractions." See Boyer, *Urban Masses and Moral Order in America, 1820–1920* (Cambridge: Harvard University Press, 1978), p. 56

17. Ponchaud, "Social Change in the Vortex of Revolution," p. 161. Raymond Williams, in *The Country and the City* (New York: Oxford University Press, 1973), traces the importance of this distinction in Western literature, and Robert Pogue Harrison examines the forest-civilization contrast in *Forests: The Shadow of Civilization* (Chicago: University of Chicago Press, 1992); also see Roderick Nash, *Wilderness and the American Mind*, 3d ed. (New Haven: Yale University Press, 1982), and Max Oelschlager, *The Idea of Wilderness from Prehistory to the Age of Ecology* (New Haven: Yale University Press, 1991).

18. Chandler, Kiernan, and Boua, *Pol Pot Plans*, p. 224.

19. Timothy Carney, "The Unexpected Victory," in Jackson, *Cambodia 1975–1978*, p. 28.

20. Chandler, Kiernan, and Boua, *Pol Pot Plans*, pp. 15, 176, and 183, respectively.

21. Quoted in Karl D. Jackson, "The Ideology of Total Revolution," in Jackson, *Cambodia 1975–1978*, p. 56.

22. Maurice Isserman, *If I Had a Hammer . . . The Death of the Old Left and the Birth of the New Left* (New York: Basic Books, 1987), p. 75.

23. Academics, whose professional identity is tied to having "flexible minds," have regularly distinguished flexible from rigid worldviews (even though their own fondness for abstraction has often encouraged inflexibility). Max Weber distinguished the ethic of ultimate ends from the ethic of responsibility; Karl Popper, Milton Rokeach, and others, distinguished the closed from the open mind. Recently Eviatar Zerubavel contrasted the rigid mind with the fuzzy mind, which resists all distinctions and boundaries; he argued for a flexible mind with "the ability to be both rigid and fuzzy. Flexible people notice structures yet feel comfortable destroying them from time to time. Analytically focused at some times, they are quite sensitive to context at others." *The Fine Line*, p. 120. Nuances differ, but the parallel distinctions are usually meant to encourage openness to new ideas and evidence, to what Henry James called experience.

In a way, Kant's categorical imperative exemplifies the ideal of a single rule ideally applicable to all regardless of their social context; Lawrence Kohlberg's scheme of moral development places this kind of vision at the pinnacle of moral development. Kohlberg emphasizes humans' ability to create their own moral systems, but ignores the social contexts of the systems thus created. In *In a Different Voice: Psychological Theory and Women's Development* (Cambridge: Harvard University Press, 1982), Carol Gilligan criticizes Kohlberg and the Kantian tradition for celebrating this abstraction. Arguing that this is a male orientation, she counters with a feminine/feminist attention to local context and nuance, involving an application of more detailed rules, with more sensitivity to context.

24. On the malleability of traditions, even their wholesale fabrication, see Edward Shils, *Tradition* (Chicago: University of Chicago Press, 1981); and Eric Hobsbawm and Terence Ranger, eds., *The Invention of Tradition* (Cambridge: Cambridge University Press, 1983).

25. The most compelling exegesis of marxism's functionalism is G. A. Cohen's *Karl Marx's Theory of History: A Defense* (Princeton: Princeton University Press, 1978). Marxist Derek Sayer attacks this approach, which he admits dominates marxism, in *The Violence of Abstraction: The Analytic Foundations of Historical Materialism* (Oxford: Basil Blackwell, 1987). Martin Jay has traced the history of the concept of totality, especially in Western marxism, in *Marxism and Totality: The Adventures of a Concept from Lukács to Habermas* (Berkeley: University of California Press, 1984). See also Jon Elster, *Making Sense of Marx* (Cambridge: Cambridge University Press, 1985), and Sunil Khilnani, *Arguing Revolution: The Intellectual Left in Postwar France* (New Haven: Yale University Press, 1993).

Other abstract social-scientific programs have had harmful effects when applied in the real world, including modernization theory (itself a reaction to marxism, but with equally rigid ideas of the stages of development) and recent free-market ideology (on the revolutionary spirit of these economistic approaches, see Alan Wolfe, *Whose Keeper? Social Science and Moral Obligation* [Berkeley: University of California Press, 1989]).

One classic critique of such efforts is Karl Popper's *The Open Society and Its Enemies* ([1945] London: Routledge and Kegan Paul, 1974). Popper criticizes "utopian engineering," which "recommends the reconstruction of society as a whole, i.e., very sweeping changes whose practical consequences are hard to calculate, owing to our limited experience" (vol. 1, p. 161).

26. On the philosophical sources of this image of total revolution, see Bernard Yack, *The Longing for Total Revolution: Philosophical Sources of Social Discontent from Rousseau to Marx and Nietzsche* (Princeton: Princeton University Press, 1986), and the work of Jacob Leib Talmon, especially *The Origins of Totalitarian Democracy* (London: Secker and Warburg, 1952) and *Romanticism and Revolt* (New York: Harcourt, Brace and World, 1967). For a long time, analyses and critiques of revolutionary ideologies were vitiated by their strident anti-communism.

27. Douglas, *Purity and Danger*, p. 162.

28. Jean-Paul Sartre, *Portrait of the Anti-Semite* (New York: Partisan Review, 1946), p. 9.

29. See Norbert Wiley, *The Semiotic Self*, pp. 36–37.

30. Sayer, *The Violence of Abstraction*, p. 144.

31. Robert Jay Lifton, *The Nazi Doctors: Medical Killing and the Psychology of Genocide* (New York: Basic Books, 1986), p. 438.

32. Lifton, *Nazi Doctors*, p. 451.

33. Lifton, *Nazi Doctors*, p. 477.

34. Modern states similarly mobilize people, especially for wars. John W. Dower, for example, describes the American government's use of racist propaganda to stir up hatred of the Japanese during World War II in *War Without Mercy: Race and Power in the Pacific War* (New York: Pantheon, 1986). Michael Blain analyzes Hitler's rhetoric to show modern war requires the social integration that follows from the construction of enemies in "Fighting Words."

35. For example, in writing letters of protest to Jewish researchers and apologists for research, several animal rights activists attacked their Jewish heritage rather than their use of animals. This ad hominem hatred was certainly contrary to the instincts and wishes of movement leaders, who were well aware that their opponents could use such evidence to discredit the movement (indeed, one pro-research journalist has spent years trying to collect such letters). Hatred is a dangerous tool.

36. Carl Schmitt, *The Concept of the Political* (New Brunswick, N.J.: Rutgers University Press, 1976), pp. 29, 37, respectively.

37. Pierre Bourdieu, "L'Opinion Publique N'Existe Pas," in *Questions de Sociologie* (Paris: Les Editions de Minuit, 1984).

38. Jasper, "Three Nuclear Controversies."

39. Erik H. Erikson, *Gandhi's Truth: On the Origins of Militant Nonviolence* (New York: W. W. Norton, 1969), p. 432.

40. Douglas, *Purity and Danger*.

41. Witch hunting is a complex phenomenon that has been given many explanations. But most have to do with the victims' lack of a place in the new order, whether that place is defined in terms of market relations, Christian beliefs, or citizenship and obedience to the rising nation state. See Jeffrey Russell, *A History of Witchcraft, Sorcerers, Heretics, and Pagans* (London: Thames and Hudson, 1980) for figures on victims. Also Nachman Ben-Yehuda, "The European Witch Craze of the Fourteenth to Seventeenth Centuries: A Sociologist's Perspective," *American Journal of Sociology* 86 (1980): 1–31; Christina Larner, *Witchcraft and Religion: The Politics of Popular Belief* (New York: Basil Blackwell, 1984); Alan Macfarlane, *Witchcraft in Tudor and Stuart England: A Regional and Comparative Study* (London: Routledge, 1970); Keith Thomas, *Religion and the Decline of Magic* (New York: Scribner's, 1971); and Norman Cohn, *Europe's Inner Demons: An Enquiry Inspired by the Great Witch-hunt* (New York: Basic Books, 1975).

Looking at an earlier period, R. I. Moore linked the systematic persecution of heretics, Jews, lepers, and various other groups to the institution-building and consolidation of power by secular and clerical elites. In other words, persecution and witchcraft accusations were a means by which holders of new institutional positions took power away from those who had traditionally held it.

See R. I. Moore, *The Formation of a Persecuting Society: Power and Deviance in Western Europe, 950–1250* (Oxford: Basil Blackwell, 1987), and Edward Peters, *The Magician, the Witch, and the Law* (Philadelphia: University of Pennsylvania Press, 1978).

42. The literature on modern revolutions is vast, although Charles Tilly is one of the few to link them to other processes of protest. Michael Mann argues that most revolutions are responses to the initial wave of industrialization, since the newly proletarianized workers can remember alternatives: see *Consciousness and Action Among the Western Working Class* (London: Macmillan, 1973). For a demographic twist, see Jack A. Goldstone, *Revolution and Rebellion in the Early Modern World* (Berkeley: University of California Press, 1991). Immanuel Wallerstein analyzes the French Revolution as a response to the world capitalist system, as French monarchs struggled to compete with England: *The Modern World System, III: The Second Era of Great Expansion of the Capitalist World-Economy, 1730–1840s* (New York: Academic Press, 1989).

43. Farideh Farhi even characterizes the Iranian and Nicaraguan revolutions in terms of their urban base in *States and Urban-Based Revolutions: Iran and Nicaragua* (Urbana: University of Illinois Press, 1990).

44. Susan Olzak, *The Dynamics of Ethnic Competition and Conflict* (Stanford: Stanford University Press, 1992).

45. A recent example, where the racism is hardly even disguised, is Peter Brimelow's *Alien Nation: Common Sense about America's Immigration Disaster* (New York: Random House, 1995).

46. Among the many recent books on nationalism, see Ernest Gellner, *Nations and Nationalism* (Oxford: Blackwell, 1983); Anthony D. Smith, *Theories of Nationalism*, 2d ed. (New York: Holmes and Meier, 1983), *The Ethnic Origins of Nations* (Oxford: Blackwell, 1986), and *National Identity* (London: Penguin, 1991); Anthony D. Smith, ed., *Ethnicity and Nationalism* (New York: E. J. Brill, 1992); E. J. Hobsbawm, *Nations and Nationalism Since 1780: Programme, Myth, Reality* (Cambridge: Cambridge University Press, 1990); Benedict Anderson, *Imagined Communities*, rev. ed. (London: New Left Books, 1991); Rogers Brubaker, *Citizenship and Nationhood in France and Germany* (Cambridge: Harvard University Press, 1992); and for a review, see Craig Calhoun, "Nationalism and Ethnicity," *Annual Review of Sociology* 19 (1993): 211–239.

47. Mary Midgley, *Can't We Make Moral Judgements?* (New York: St. Martin's Press, 1991), pp. 44–45.

17. THE NECESSITY OF PROTEST

1. Charles Taylor, *Philosophy and the Human Sciences* (Cambridge: Cambridge University Press, 1985), p. 204.

2. Will Kymlicka, *Liberalism, Community, and Culture* (Oxford: Oxford University Press, 1989), p. 81.

3. By resignation I mean that people tended to follow their government's *de facto* policies: in France large majorities came to favor nuclear energy; in the United States equal majorities opposed it; in Sweden they remained ambiva-

lent. See my article, "The Political Life Cycle of Technological Controversies," *Social Forces* 67 (1988): 357–377.

4. Quoted in *The New Republic*, 1 August 1994, p. 7.

5. Robert C. Paehlke, *Environmentalism and the Future of Progressive Politics* (New Haven: Yale University Press, 1989).

6. Phil Brown and Edwin J. Mikkelson, *No Safe Place* (Berkeley: University of California Press, 1990), pp. 132–3.

7. Brown and Mikkelson, p. 133. For an excellent study of the effects of protest on science, both good and bad, see Steven Epstein, *Impure Science: AIDS, Activism, and the Politics of Knowledge* (Berkeley: University of California Press, 1996).

8. Abortion is such an intimate procedure, for many women a life passage, that women are likely to think about it carefully even in the absence of controversy. This is especially the case for women who have illegal abortions, for whom the consequences could be fatal. For them, the anti-abortion movement is only coercive, not communicative.

9. For a study that explicitly examines the cultural effect of a protest movement, in this case British abolitionism at the end of the eighteenth century, see Leo d'Anjou, *Social Movements and Cultural Change: The First Abolition Campaign Revisited* (New York: Walter de Gruyter, 1996).

10. Jean-Paul Sartre, *The Psychology of Imagination* (London: Methuen, 1972), p. 225.

11. Wolfgang Iser, *The Act of Reading: A Theory of Aesthetic Response* (Baltimore: Johns Hopkins University Press, 1978), p. 140.

12. Many feminists have adopted this perspective, heralding a "feminist methodology" especially attuned to context, even though they are primarily restating the insights of a long, interpretive, interactionist tradition.

13. Jon Elster, *Nuts and Bolts for the Social Sciences* (Cambridge: Cambridge University Press, 1989).

14. In *Hegemony and Socialist Strategy* (London: Verso, 1985), Laclau and Mouffe, alas, adopt a narrow form of cultural analysis, discourse analysis, which tends to treat arguments in isolation from their institutional and other social contexts. The only value they can offer is radical democracy, but they cannot say much about the institutional supports for it. And by making all discourses appear incommensurable, they give little opportunity for dialogue across perspectives. For criticism, see Alan Scott, *Ideology and the New Social Movements* (London: Unwin Hyman, 1990), chap. 4.

Bibliography

Abercrombie, Nicholas, Stephen Hill, and Bryan S. Turner. 1980. *The Dominant Ideology Thesis*. London: George Allen and Unwin.

Addelson, Kathryn Pyne. 1987. "Moral Passages." In Eva Feder Kittay and Diana T. Meyers, eds., *Women and Moral Theory*. Totowa, N.J.: Rowman and Littlefield.

Agee, Philip. 1975. *Inside the Company: CIA Diary*. New York: Stonehill.

Alexander, Jeffrey C. 1988. *Action and Its Environments: Toward a New Synthesis*. New York: Columbia University Press.

Alford, Robert R., and Roger Friedland. 1985. *Powers of Theory: Capitalism, the State, and Democracy*. Cambridge: Cambridge University Press.

Alinsky, Saul D. 1971. *Rules for Radicals: A Pragmatic Primer for Realistic Radicals*. New York: Random House.

Altman, Irwin, and Carol Werner. 1985. *Home Environments*. New York: Plenum.

Amenta, Edwin, Bruce C. Carruthers, and Yvonne Zylan. 1992. "A Hero for the Aged? The Townsend Movement, the Political Mediation Model, and U.S. Old-Age Policy, 1934–1950." *American Journal of Sociology* 98: 308–339.

Amenta, Edwin, and Yvonne Zylan. 1991. "It Happened Here: Political Opportunity, the New Institutionalism, and the Townsend Movement." *American Sociological Review* 56: 250–265.

Anderson, Benedict. 1991. *Imagined Communities*. Rev. ed. London: Verso Books.

Archer, John, and Gillian Winchester. 1994. "Bereavement Following Death of a Pet." *British Journal of Psychology* 85: 259–271.

Archer, Margaret S. 1988. *Culture and Agency: The Place of Culture in Social Theory*. Cambridge: Cambridge University Press.

Ariès, Philippe. 1962. *Centuries of Childhood*. New York: Vintage.

Armon-Jones, Claire. 1986. "The Thesis of Constructionism." In Rom Harré, ed., *The Social Construction of Emotions*. Oxford: Basil Blackwell.

Averill, James. 1980. "A Constructivist View of Emotion." In Robert Plutchik and Henry Kellerman, eds., *Emotion: Theory, Research, and Experience*. Vol. 1. *Theories of Emotion*. New York: Academic Press.

Bagdikian, Ben H. 1990. *The Media Monopoly*. 3d ed. Boston: Beacon Press.

Bailey, Robert Jr. 1974. *Radicals in Urban Politics: The Alinsky Approach*. Chicago: University of Chicago Press.

Baker, Keith Michael. 1990. *Inventing the French Revolution*. Cambridge: Cambridge University Press.

Barkan, Steven E. 1979. "Strategic, Tactical, and Organizational Dilemmas of the Protest Movement Against Nuclear Power." *Social Problems* 27 (1): 19–37.

———. 1984. "Legal Control of the Southern Civil Rights Movement." *American Sociological Review* 49: 552–565.

Barnes, Gilbert Hobbs. 1933. *The Anti-Slavery Impulse, 1830–1844*. New York: Harcourt, Brace, and World.

Barnes, Samuel H., Max Kaase, Klaus R. Allerbeck, Barbara G. Farah, Felix Heunks, Ronald Inglehart, M. Kent Jennings, Hans D. Klingemann, Alan Marsh, and Leopold Rosenmayr. 1979. *Political Action: Mass Participation in Five Western Democracies*. Beverly Hills, Calif.: Sage Publications.

Barrows, Susanna. 1981. *Distorting Mirrors: Visions of the Crowd in Late Nineteenth-Century France*. New Haven: Yale University Press.

Baum, Robert J., ed. 1980. *Ethical Problems in Engineering*. Vol. 2. *Cases*. Troy, New York: The Center for the Study of the Human Dimensions of Science and Technology, Rensselaer Polytechnic.

Beach, Stephen W. 1977. "Social Movement Radicalization: The Case of the People's Democracy in Northern Ireland." *Sociological Quarterly* 18: 305–318.

Becker, Elizabeth. 1986. *When the War Was Over: The Voices of Cambodia's Revolution and Its People*. New York: Simon and Schuster.

Belenky, Mary Feld, Blythe McVicker Clinchy, Nancy Rule Goldberger, and Jill Mattuck Tarule. 1986. *Women's Ways of Knowing: The Development of Self, Voice, and Mind*. New York: Basic Books.

Bell, Derrick. 1992. *Faces at the Bottom of the Well: The Permanence of Racism*. New York: Basic Books.

Benford, Robert D. 1993. "Frame Disputes within the Nuclear Disarmament Movement." *Social Forces* 71: 677–701

———. 1993. "'You Could Be the Hundredth Monkey': Collective Action Frames and Vocabularies of Motive within the Nuclear Disarmament Movement." *Sociological Quarterly* 34: 195–216.

Benford, Robert D., and Scott A. Hunt. 1992. "Dramaturgy and Social Movements: The Social Construction and Communication of Power." *Sociological Inquiry* 62: 36–55.

Benford, Robert D., and Lester R. Kurtz. 1987. "Performing the Nuclear Ceremony: The Arms Race as a Ritual." *Journal of Applied Behavioral Research* 23: 463–482.

Ben-Yehuda, Nachman. 1980. "The European Witch Craze of the Fourteenth to Seventeenth Centuries: A Sociologist's Perspective." *American Journal of Sociology* 86: 1–31.

———. 1986. "The Sociology of Moral Panics: Toward a New Synthesis." *Sociological Quarterly* 27: 495–513.

———. 1990. *The Politics and Morality of Deviance: Moral Panics, Drug Abuse, Deviant Science, and Reversed Discrimination*. Albany: SUNY Press.

Berger, Peter L. 1970. *A Rumor of Angels: Modern Society and the Rediscovery of the Supernatural*. Garden City, N.Y.: Doubleday.

Berger, Peter L., and Thomas Luckmann. 1966. *The Social Construction of Reality.* New York: Doubleday.

Bernstein, Mary, and James M. Jasper. 1996. "Whistleblowers as Claims-Makers in Technological Controversies." *Social Science Information* 35: 565–589.

Best, Joel. 1987. "Rhetoric in Claims-Making: Constructing the Missing Children Problem." *Social Problems* 34: 101–121.

Blain, Michael. 1976. "The Role of Death in Political Conflict." *Psychoanalytic Review* 63: 249–265.

———. 1988. "Fighting Words: What We Can Learn from Hitler's Hyperbole." *Symbolic Interaction* 11: 257–276.

———. 1991. "Rhetorical Practice in an Anti-Nuclear Weapons Campaign." *Peace and Change* 16: 355–378.

Bloch, Maurice. 1974. "Symbols, Song, Dance, and Features of Articulation: Is Religion an Extreme Form of Traditional Authority?" *Archives Européenes de Sociologie* 15: 55–81.

Blum, Deborah. 1994. *The Monkey Wars.* New York: Oxford University Press.

Blum, Lawrence. 1980. "Compassion." In Amélie Oksenberg Rorty, ed., *Explaining Emotions.* Berkeley: University of California Press.

Blumer, Herbert G. 1939. "Collective Behavior." In Robert E. Park, ed., *An Outline of the Principles of Sociology.* New York: Barnes and Noble.

Bok, Sissela. 1978. *Lying: Moral Choice in Public and Private Life.* New York: Random House.

Bormann, Ernest G. 1972. "Fantasy and Rhetorical Vision: The Rhetorical Criticism of Social Reality." *Quarterly Journal of Speech* 58: 396–407.

Bourdieu, Pierre. 1977. *Outline of a Theory of Practice.* Cambridge: Cambridge University Press.

———. 1984. *Distinction: A Social Critique of the Judgment of Taste.* Cambridge: Harvard University Press.

———. 1984. "L'Opinion Publique N'Existe Pas." In *Questions de Sociologie.* Paris: Les Editions de Minuit.

Bowles, Samuel, and Herbert Gintis. 1986. *Democracy and Capitalism: Property, Community, and the Contradictions of Modern Social Thought.* New York: Basic Books.

Boyer, Paul. 1978. *Urban Masses and Moral Order in America, 1820–1920.* Cambridge: Harvard University Press.

———. 1985. *By the Bomb's Early Light: American Thought and Culture at the Dawn of the Atomic Age.* New York: Pantheon.

Boyte, Harry C. 1980. *The Backyard Revolution: Understanding the New Citizen Movement.* Philadelphia: Temple University Press.

Branch, Taylor. 1988. *Parting the Waters: America in the King Years, 1954–1963.* New York: Simon and Schuster.

Brecher, Jeremy. 1972. *Strike!* Boston: South End Press.

Breines, Wini. 1982. *Community and Organization in the New Left, 1962–1968: The Great Refusal.* South Hadley, Mass.: J. F. Bergin.

Brimelow, Peter. 1995. *Alien Nation: Common Sense about America's Immigration Disaster.* New York: Random House.

Brion, Denis J. 1991. *Essential Industry and the NIMBY Phenomenon*. New York: Quorum Books.

Brown, Jerald Barry. 1972. "The United Farm Workers Grape Strike and Boycott, 1965–1970: An Evaluation of the Culture of Poverty Theory." Ph.D. diss. Ithaca: Cornell University, Latin American Studies Program, Dissertation Series, No. 39.

Brown, Phil, and Edwin J. Mikkelson. 1990. *No Safe Place: Toxic Waste, Leukemia, and Community Action*. Berkeley: University of California Press.

Brown, Richard. 1970. *Revolutionary Politics in Massachusetts*. Cambridge: Harvard University Press.

Brown, Thomas N. 1966. *Irish-American Nationalism, 1870–1890*. Philadelphia: Lippincott.

Brubaker, Rogers. 1992. *Citizenship and Nationhood in France and Germany*. Cambridge: Harvard University Press.

Bruner, Jerome S. 1990. *Acts of Meaning*. Cambridge: Harvard University Press.

Buechler, Steven M. 1990. *Women's Movements in the United States: Woman Suffrage, Equal Rights, and Beyond*. New Brunswick, N.J.: Rutgers University Press.

Burghardt, Gordon M., and Harold A. Herzog, Jr. 1980. "Beyond Conspecifics: Is Brer Rabbit Our Brother?" *BioScience* 30: 763–768.

Burke, Kenneth. 1950. *A Rhetoric of Motives*. New York: Prentice-Hall.

———. 1954 [1934]. *Permanence and Change: An Anatomy of Purpose*. 3d ed. Berkeley: University of California Press.

Burstein, Paul, Rachel L. Einwohner, and Jocelyn A. Hollander. 1995. "The Success of Political Movements: A Bargaining Perspective." In J. Craig Jenkins and Bert Klandermans, eds., *The Politics of Social Protest: Comparative Perspectives on States and Social Movements*. Minneapolis: University of Minnesota Press.

Buttimer, Anne. 1980. "Home, Reach, and the Sense of Place." In Anne Buttimer and David Seamon, eds., *The Human Experience of Space and Place*. New York: St. Martin's Press.

Caldwell, Lynton K., Lynton R. Hayes, and Isabel M. MacWhirter. 1976. *Citizens and the Environment: Case Studies in Popular Action*. Bloomington: Indiana University Press.

Calhoun, Craig Jackson. 1982. *The Question of Class Struggle: Social Foundations of Popular Radicalism during the Industrial Revolution*. Chicago: University of Chicago Press.

———. 1983. "The Radicalism of Tradition: Community Strength or Venerable Disguise and Borrowed Language?" *American Journal of Sociology* 88: 886–914.

———. 1993. "Nationalism and Ethnicity." *Annual Review of Sociology* 19: 211–239.

Cancian, Francesca M. 1987. *Love in America: Gender and Self-Development*. Cambridge: Cambridge University Press.

Candland, Douglas Keith. 1993. *Feral Children and Clever Animals: Reflections on Human Nature*. New York: Oxford University Press.

Caplow, Theodore. 1982. "Christmas Gifts and Kin Networks." *American Sociological Review* 47: 383–392.

———. 1984. "Rule Enforcement without Visible Means: Christmas Gift Giving in Middletown." *American Journal of Sociology* 89: 1306–1323.

Carney, Timothy. 1989. "The Unexpected Victory." In Karl D. Jackson, ed., *Cambodia 1975–1978*. Princeton: Princeton University Press.

Carson, Rachel. 1962. *Silent Spring*. Boston: Houghton Mifflin.

Carter, Dan T. 1995. *The Politics of Rage: George Wallace, the Origins of the New Conservatism, and the Transformation of American Politics*. New York: Simon and Schuster.

Chalk, Frank, and Kurt Jonassohn. 1990. *The History and Sociology of Genocide: Analyses and Case Studies*. New Haven: Yale University Press.

Chandler, David P. 1983. "Seeing Red: Perceptions of Cambodian History in Democratic Kampuchea." In David P. Chandler and Ben Kiernan, eds., *Revolution and Its Aftermath in Kampuchea: Eight Essays*. New Haven: Yale University Southeast Asian Studies.

———. 1991. *The Tragedy of Cambodian History: Politics, War, and Revolution Since 1945*. New Haven: Yale University Press.

———. 1992. *Brother Number One: A Political Biography of Pol Pot*. Boulder, Colo.: Westview Press.

———. 1992. *A History of Cambodia*. 2d ed. Boulder, Colo.: Westview Press.

Chandler, David P., and Ben Kiernan, eds. 1983. *Revolution and Its Aftermath in Kampuchea: Eight Essays*. New Haven: Yale University Southeast Asian Studies.

Chandler, David P., Ben Kiernan, and Chanthou Boua, eds. 1988. *Pol Pot Plans the Future: Confidential Leadership Documents from Democratic Kampuchea, 1976–1977*. New Haven: Yale University Southeast Asia Studies.

Cheney, Dorothy L., and Robert M. Seyfarth. 1990. *How Monkeys See the World*. Chicago: University of Chicago Press.

Chong, Dennis. 1991. *Collective Action and the Civil Rights Movement*. Chicago: University of Chicago Press.

Chute, Carolyn. 1985. *The Beans of Egypt, Maine*. New York: Ticknor and Fields.

Clark, Candace. 1987. "Sympathy Biography and Sympathy Margin." *American Journal of Sociology* 93: 290–321.

Clemens, Elisabeth S. 1996. "Organizational Form as Frame: Collective Identity and Political Strategy in the American Labor Movement, 1880–1920." In Doug McAdam, John McCarthy, and Mayer Zald, eds., *Opportunities, Mobilizing Structures, and Framing: Comparative Applications of Social Movement Theory*. New York: Cambridge University Press.

Clemens, Elisabeth S., and Patrick Ledger. 1994. "Organizational Culture and Careers of Activism in the Woman Suffrage Movement, 1870–1920." Unpublished paper.

Cohen, G. A. 1978. *Karl Marx's Theory of History: A Defense*. Princeton: Princeton University Press.

Cohen, Jean L. 1985. "Strategy or Identity: New Theoretical Paradigms and Contemporary Social Movements." *Social Research* 52: 663–716.

Cohen, Stanley. 1972. *Folk Devils and Moral Panics: The Creation of the Mods and the Rockers*. New York: St. Martin's Press.

Cohn, Norman. 1975. *Europe's Inner Demons: An Enquiry Inspired by the Great Witch-hunt*. New York: Basic Books.

Collins, Randall. 1990. "Stratification, Emotional Energy, and the Transient Emotions." In Theodore D. Kemper, ed., *Research Agendas in the Sociology of Emotions*. Albany: SUNY Press.

———. 1993. "The Rationality of Avoiding Choice." *Rationality and Society* 5: 58–67.

Commoner, Barry. 1989. "Don't Let City Garbage Go Up in Smoke." *New York Times*, 29 January.

Condit, Celeste Michel. 1990. *Decoding Abortion Rhetoric: Communicating Social Change*. Urbana: University of Illinois Press.

Conell, Carol, and Kim Voss. 1990. "Formal Organization and the Fate of Social Movements: Craft Association and Class Alliance in the Knights of Labor." *American Sociological Review* 55: 255–269.

Corfe, T. H. 1964. "The Troubles of Captain Boycott." *History Today* 14: 758–764 (November) and 854–862 (December).

Cotgrove, Stephen. 1982. *Catastrophe or Cornucopia: The Environment, Politics, and the Future*. Chichester and New York: John Wiley and Sons.

Cotgrove, Stephen F., and Andrew Duff. 1980. "Environmentalism, Middle-Class Radicalism and Politics." *Sociological Review*, new series, 28: 333–351.

Couch, Stephen R., and J. Stephen Kroll-Smith. 1985. "The Chronic Technical Disaster: Toward a Social Scientific Perspective." *Social Science Quarterly* 66: 564–575.

Crosby, Faye J. 1993. "Why Complain?" *Journal of Social Issues*. 49: 169–184.

Csikszentmihalyi, Mihaly. 1990. *Flow: The Psychology of Optimal Experience*. New York: Harper and Row.

Cuba, Lee, and David M. Hummon. 1993. "A Place to Call Home: Identification with Dwelling, Community, and Region." *Sociological Quarterly* 34: 111–131.

Dalton, Russell J., Scott Flanagan, and Paul Allen Beck, eds. 1984. *Electoral Change in Advanced Industrial Countries: Realignment or Dealignment?* Princeton: Princeton University Press.

d'Anjou, Leo. 1996. *Social Movements and Cultural Change: The First Abolition Campaign Revisited*. New York: Walter de Gruyter.

Darwin, Charles. 1981 [1871]. *The Descent of Man and Selection in Relation to Sex*. Princeton, N.J.: Princeton University Press.

———. 1896. *The Expression of the Emotions in Man and Animals*. New York: D. Appleton.

Davies, A. F. 1980. *Skills, Outlooks, and Passions: A Psychoanalytic Contribution to the Study of Politics*. Cambridge: Cambridge University Press.

Day, Mark. 1971. *Forty Acres: César Chávez and the Farm Workers*. New York: Praeger.

de Sousa, Ronald. 1987. *The Rationality of Emotion*. Cambridge: MIT Press.

della Porta, Donatella. 1992. "Life Histories in the Analysis of Social Movement Activists." In Mario Diani and Ron Eyerman, eds., *Studying Collective Action*. London: Sage.

Demac, Donna A. 1990. *Liberty Denied: The Current Rise of Censorship in American*. New Brunswick, N.J.: Rutgers University Press.

Denzin, Norman K. 1984. *On Understanding Emotion*. San Francisco: Jossey-Bass Publishers.

Deutsch, Karl Wolfgang. 1963. *The Nerves of Government: Models of Political Communication and Control*. New York: Free Press of Glencoe.

Deutsch, Morton. 1973. *The Resolution of Conflict: Constructive and Destructive Processes*. New Haven: Yale University Press.

Dewey, John. 1929. *Experience and Nature*. La Salle, Ill.: Open Court.

————. 1958. *Art As Experience*. New York: Capricorn Books.

Diani, Mario. 1995. *Green Networks: A Structural Analysis of the Italian Environmental Movement*. Edinburgh: Edinburgh University Press.

DiMaggio, Paul. 1992. "Cultural Boundaries and Structural Change: The Extension of the High Culture Model to Theater, Opera, and the Dance, 1900–1940." In Michèle Lamont and Marcel Fournier, eds., *Cultivating Differences: Symbolic Boundaries and the Making of Inequality*. Chicago: University of Chicago Press.

DiMaggio, Paul J., and Walter W. Powell. 1983. "The Iron Cage Revisited: Institutional Isomorphism and Collective Rationality in Organizational Fields." *American Sociological Review* 48:147–160.

Dizard, Jan E. 1994. *Going Wild: Hunting, Animal Rights, and the Contested Meaning of Nature*. Amherst, Mass.: University of Massachusetts Press.

Dobbin, Frank. 1994. *Forging Industrial Policy: The United States, Britain, and France in the Railway Age*. Cambridge: Cambridge University Press.

Douglas, Mary. 1966. *Purity and Danger: An Analysis of the Concepts of Pollution and Taboo*. London: Routledge and Kegan Paul.

————. 1973. *Natural Symbols: Explorations in Cosmology*. 2d ed. London: Barrie and Jenkins.

————. 1978. "Cultural Bias." London: Royal Anthropological Institute, Occasional Paper 35. Reprinted in Mary Douglas, *In the Active Voice*. London: Routledge and Kegan Paul, 1984.

————. 1986. *How Institutions Think*. Syracuse: Syracuse University Press.

Douglas, Mary, and Aaron Wildavsky. 1982. *Risk and Culture: An Essay on the Selection of Technical and Environmental Dangers*. Berkeley: University of California Press.

Dower, John W. 1986. *War Without Mercy: Race and Power in the Pacific War*. New York: Pantheon.

Dowie, Mark. 1980. "Pinto Madness." In Robert J. Baum, ed., *Ethical Problems in Engineering*. Vol. 2. *Cases*. Troy, New York: The Center for the Study of the Human Dimensions of Science and Technology, Rensselaer Polytechnic.

Downey, Gary L. 1986. "Ideology and the Clamshell Identity: Organizational Dilemmas in the Anti-Nuclear Power Movement." *Social Problems* 33: 357–373.

Drakulić, Slavenka. 1993. "Nazis Among Us." *New York Review of Books*, 27 May.

Duménil, Gérard. 1979. "Energie Nucléaire et Opinion Publique." In Francis Fagnani and Alexandre Nicholon, eds., *Nucléopolis*. Grenoble: Presses Universitaires de Grenoble.

Dunlap, Riley E., and Kent D. Van Liere. 1978. "The 'New Environmental Paradigm': A Proposed Instrument and Preliminary Results." *Journal of Environmental Education* 9: 10–19.

Dunne, John Gregory. 1967. *Delano: The Story of the California Grape Strike.* New York: Farrar, Straus and Giroux.

Durkheim, Emile. 1965. *The Elementary Forms of the Religious Life.* New York: Free Press.

Duster, Troy S. 1970. *The Legislation of Morality: Law, Drugs, and Moral Judgment.* New York: Free Press.

Edelman, Murray. 1964. *The Symbolic Uses of Politics.* Urbana: University of Illinois Press.

———. 1977. *Political Language: Words That Succeed and Policies That Fail.* New York: Academic Press.

———. 1988. *Constructing the Political Spectacle.* Chicago: University of Chicago Press.

Eder, Klaus. 1985. "The 'New Social Movements': Moral Crusades, Political Pressure Groups, or Social Movements?" *Social Research* 52: 869–890.

Edsall, Thomas Byrne, with Mary D. Edsall. 1991. *Chain Reaction: The Impact of Race, Rights, and Taxes on American Politics.* New York: W. W. Norton.

Eisinger, Peter K. 1973. "The Conditions of Protest Behavior in American Cities." *American Political Science Review* 67: 11–28.

Eldredge, Niles. 1985. *Time Frames: The Rethinking of Darwinian Evolution and the Theory of Punctuated Equilibria.* New York: Simon and Schuster.

Elias, Norbert. 1978 [1939]. *The History of Manners.* Vol. 1. *The Civilizing Process.* New York: Pantheon.

Elliston, Frederick, John Keenan, Paula Lockhart, and Jane van Schaick. 1985. *Whistleblowing Research: Methodological and Moral Issues.* New York: Praeger Press.

Elster, Jon. 1985. *Making Sense of Marx.* Cambridge: Cambridge University Press.

———, ed. 1986. *Rational Choice.* New York: New York University Press.

———. 1989. *The Cement of Society: A Study of Social Order.* New York: Cambridge University Press.

———. 1989. *Nuts and Bolts for the Social Sciences.* Cambridge: Cambridge University Press.

Emery, Douglas B. 1993. "Self, Creativity, Political Resistance." *Political Psychology* 14: 347–362.

Emirbayer, Mustafa, and Jeff Goodwin. 1994. "Network Analysis, Culture, and the Problem of Agency." *American Journal of Sociology* 99: 1411–1454.

Emirbayer, Mustafa, and Ann Mische. 1995. "What Is Agency?" Unpublished paper.

Entrikin, J. Nicholas. 1991. *The Betweenness of Place: Towards a Geography of Modernity.* Baltimore: Johns Hopkins University Press.

Epstein, Barbara. 1985. "The Culture of Direct Action: Livermore Action Group and the Peace Movement." *Socialist Review* 82/83: 31–61.

———. 1991. *Political Protest and Cultural Revolution: Nonviolent Direct Action in the 1970s and 1980s.* Berkeley: University of California Press.

Epstein, Steven. 1996. *Impure Science: AIDS, Activism, and the Politics of Knowledge*. Berkeley: University of California Press.

Erikson, Erik H. 1958. *Young Man Luther: A Study in Psychoanalysis and History*. New York: W. W. Norton.

———. 1969. *Gandhi's Truth: On the Origins of Militant Nonviolence*. New York: W. W. Norton.

Erikson, Kai T. 1966. *Wayward Puritans: A Study in the Sociology of Deviance*. New York: Wiley.

———. 1976. *Everything In Its Path: Destruction of Community in the Buffalo Creek Flood*. New York: Simon and Schuster.

———. 1994. *A New Species of Trouble: The Human Experience of Modern Disasters*. New York: W. W. Norton.

Esler, Anthony. 1984. "'The Truest Community': Social Generations as Collective Mentalities." *Journal of Political and Military Sociology* 12: 99–112.

Etzioni, Amitai. 1988. *The Moral Dimension: Toward a New Economics*. New York: Free Press.

Evans, Sara. 1979. *Personal Politics: The Roots of Women's Liberation in the Civil Rights Movement and the New Left*. New York: Alfred A. Knopf.

Everett, Kevin. 1993. "The Growing Legitimacy of Protest in the United States, 1961–1983." Paper presented at the American Sociological Association annual meeting, Miami, Florida.

Everett, Melissa. 1989. *Breaking Ranks*. Philadelphia: New Society Publishers.

Eyerman, Ron, and Andrew Jamison. 1991. *Social Movements: A Cognitive Approach*. University Park, Pa.: Pennsylvania State University Press.

Fantasia, Rick. 1988. *Cultures of Solidarity: Consciousness, Action, and Contemporary American Workers*. Berkeley: University of California Press.

Fantasia, Rick, and Eric L. Hirsch. 1995. "Culture in Rebellion: The Appropriation and Transformation of the Veil in the Algerian Revolution." In Hank Johnston and Bert Klandermans, eds., *Social Movements and Culture*. Minneapolis: University of Minnesota Press.

Farhi, Farideh. 1990. *States and Urban-Based Revolutions: Iran and Nicaragua*. Urbana: University of Illinois Press.

Fendrich, James Max. 1977. "Keeping the Faith or Pursuing the Good Life: A Study in the Consequences of Participation in the Civil Rights Movement." *American Sociological Review* 42: 144–157.

Fendrich, James Max, and Kenneth L. Lovoy. 1988. "Back to the Future: Adult Political Behavior of Former Student Activists." *American Sociological Review* 53: 780–784.

Fendrich, James Max, and Alison T. Tarleau. 1973. "Marching to a Different Drummer: The Occupational and Political Correlates of Former Student Activists." *Social Forces* 52: 245–253.

Ferejohn, John. 1991. "Rationality and Interpretation: Parliamentary Elections in Early Stuart England." In Kristen Renwick Monroe, ed., *The Economic Approach to Politics: A Critical Reassessment of the Theory of Rational Action*. New York: HarperCollins.

Ferree, Myra Marx. 1992. "The Political Context of Rationality." In Aldon D.

Morris and Carol McClurg Mueller, eds., *Frontiers in Social Movement Theory.* New Haven: Yale University Press.

Fine, Gary Alan. 1979. "Small Groups and Culture Creation: The Idioculture of Little League Baseball Teams." *American Sociological Review* 44: 733–745.

Fine, Gary Alan, and Kent Sandstrom. 1993. "Ideology in Action: A Pragmatic Approach to a Contested Concept." *Sociological Theory* 11: 21–38.

Finke, Roger, and Rodney Stark. 1992. *The Churching of America 1776–1990: Winners and Losers in Our Religious Economy.* New Brunswick, N.J.: Rutgers University Press.

Finks, P. David. 1984. *The Radical Vision of Saul Alinsky.* Ramsey, N.J.: Paulist Press.

Fireman, Bruce, and William A. Gamson. 1979. "Utilitarian Logic in the Resource Mobilization Perspective." In Mayer N. Zald and John D. McCarthy, eds., *The Dynamics of Social Movements: Resource Mobilization, Social Control, and Tactics.* Cambridge, Mass: Winthrop.

Fischer, Kurt W., Phillip R. Shaver, and Peter Carnochan. 1990. "How Emotions Develop and How They Organize Development." *Cognition and Emotion* 4: 81–127.

Fischhoff, Baruch, and Don MacGregor. 1983. "Judged Lethality: How Much People Seem to Know Depends Upon How They Are Asked." *Risk Analysis* 3: 229–236.

Fishman, Joshua A. 1972. *The Sociology of Language.* Rowley, Mass.: Newbury House.

Flanagan, Scott C. 1987. "Changing Values in Industrial Societies Revisited: Towards a Resolution of the Values Debate." *American Political Science Review* 81: 1303–1319.

Flax, Jane. 1993. *Disputed Subjects: Essays on Psychoanalysis, Politics, and Philosophy.* New York: Routledge.

Fogelmann, Eva. 1994. *Conscience and Courage: Rescuers of Jews During the Holocaust.* New York: Anchor.

Ford, Daniel F. 1982. *The Cult of the Atom: The Secret Papers of the Atomic Energy Commission.* New York: Simon and Schuster.

Ford, Gary, and James M. Jasper. 1995. "Culture and Rational Choice." Paper presented at the American Sociological Association annual meetings, Washington, D.C., August.

Freeman, Jo. 1973. "The Origins of the Women's Liberation Movement." *American Journal of Sociology* 78: 792–811.

———. 1983. "A Model for Analyzing the Strategic Options of Social Movement Organizations." In Jo Freeman, ed., *Social Movements of the Sixties and Seventies.* New York: Longman.

Freeman, Leslie J. 1981. *Nuclear Witnesses: Insiders Speak Out.* New York: W. W. Norton.

Freud, Sigmund. 1921. *Group Psychology and the Analysis of the Ego.* London: International Psychoanalytical Press.

Freudenberg, Nicholas. 1984. *Not in Our Backyards! Community Action for Health and the Environment.* New York: Monthly Review Press.

Freudenburg, William R., and Robert Gramling. 1994. *Oil in Troubled Waters: Perception, Politics, and the Battle Over Offshore Drilling*. Albany: State University of New York Press.

Fried, Marc. 1963. "Grieving for a Lost Home." In Leonard Duhl, ed., *The Urban Condition: People and Policy in the Metropolis*. New York: Basic Books.

Frijda, Nico H. 1986. *The Emotions*. Cambridge: Cambridge University Press.

Furet, François. 1981. *Interpreting the French Revolution*. Cambridge: Cambridge University Press.

Gadamer, Hans-Georg. 1982 [1960]. *Truth and Method*. New York: Crossroad Publishing.

Gamson, Joshua. 1989. "Silence, Death, and the Invisible Enemy: AIDS Activism and Social Movement 'Newness.'" *Social Problems* 36: 351–367.

———. 1994. *Claims to Fame: Celebrity in Contemporary America*. Berkeley: University of California Press.

———. 1995. "Must Identity Movements Self-Destruct? A Queer Dilemma." *Social Problems* 42: 390–407.

Gamson, William A. 1975. *The Strategy of Social Protest*. Homewood, Ill.: Dorsey Press.

———. 1987. "Introduction." In Mayer N. Zald and John D. McCarthy, eds., *Social Movements in an Organizational Society: Collected Essays*. New Brunswick, N.J.: Transaction

———. 1988. "Political Discourse and Collective Action." *International Social Movement Research* 1: 219–244.

———. 1992. *Talking Politics*. Cambridge: Cambridge University Press.

———. 1992. "The Social Psychology of Collective Action." In Aldon D. Morris and Carol McClurg Mueller, eds., *Frontiers in Social Movement Theory*. New Haven: Yale University Press.

Gamson, William A., Bruce Fireman, and Steven Rytina. 1982. *Encounters with Unjust Authority*. Homewood, Ill.: Dorsey Press.

Gamson, William A., and David S. Meyer. 1996. "Framing Political Opportunity." In Doug McAdam, John D. McCarthy, and Mayer N. Zald, eds., *Comparative Perspectives on Social Movements: Political Opportunities, Mobilizing Structures, and Cultural Framings*. Cambridge: Cambridge University Press.

Gamson, William A., and Andre Modigliani. 1989. "Media Discourse and Public Opinion on Nuclear Power: A Constructionist Approach." *American Journal of Sociology* 95: 1–37.

Gamson, William A., and Gadi Wolfsfeld. 1993. "Movements and Media as Interacting Systems." *Annals of the American Academy of Political and Social Science* 528: 114–125.

Gans, Herbert J. 1979. *Deciding What's News: A Study of CBS Evening News, NBC Nightly News, Newsweek, and Time*. New York: Random House.

Garfinkel, Harold. 1967. *Studies in Ethnomethodology*. Englewood Cliffs, N.J.: Prentice-Hall.

Geertz, Clifford. 1973. *The Interpretation of Cultures*. New York: Basic Books.

———. 1980. *Negara: The Theatre State in Nineteenth-Century Bali*. Princeton: Princeton University Press.

———. 1983. *Local Knowledge: Further Essays in Interpretive Anthropology.* New York: Basic Books.

Gellner, Ernest. 1983. *Nations and Nationalism.* Oxford: Blackwell.

Gerlach, Luther P., and Virginia H. Hine. 1970. *People, Power, and Change: Movements of Social Transformation.* New York: Bobbs-Merrill.

Gibbs, Lois Marie. 1982. As told to Murray Levine. *Love Canal: My Story.* Albany: State University of New York Press.

Giddens, Anthony. 1984. *The Constitution of Society: Outline of the Theory of Structuration.* Berkeley: University of California Press.

———. 1991. *Introduction to Sociology.* New York: W. W. Norton.

———. 1991. *Modernity and Self-Identity: Self and Society in the Late Modern Age.* Stanford: Stanford University Press.

Gilligan, Carol. 1982. *In a Different Voice: Psychological Theory and Women's Development.* Cambridge: Harvard University Press.

Ginsburg, Faye D. 1989. *Contested Lives: The Abortion Debate in an American Community.* Berkeley: University of California Press.

Gitlin, Todd. 1980. *The Whole World Is Watching: Mass Media in the Making and Unmaking of the New Left.* Berkeley: University of California Press.

———. 1987. *The Sixties: Years of Hope, Days of Rage.* New York: Bantam Books.

Glazer, Myron, and Penina Glazer. 1989. *The Whistleblowers: Exposing Corruption in Government and Industry.* New York: Basic Books.

Goffman, Erving. 1959. *The Presentation of Self in Everyday Life.* Garden City, N.Y.: Anchor Books.

———. 1974. *Frame Analysis: An Essay on the Organization of Experience.* Cambridge: Harvard University Press.

Goldstone, Jack A. 1991. *Revolution and Rebellion in the Early Modern World.* Berkeley: University of California Press.

Goode, Erich, and Nachman Ben-Yehuda. 1994. "Moral Panics: Culture, Politics, and Social Construction." *Annual Review of Sociology* 20: 149–171.

———. 1994. *Moral Panics: The Social Construction of Deviance.* Cambridge, Mass.: Blackwell.

Goodwin, Jeff. 1997. "The Libidinal Constitution of a High-Risk Social Movement: Affectual Ties and Solidarity in the Huk Rebellion." *American Sociological Review* 62: 53–69.

Gordon, Cynthia, and James M. Jasper. 1996. "Overcoming the 'NIMBY' Label: Rhetorical and Organizational Links for Local Protestors." *Research in Social Movements, Conflicts, and Change* 19: 159–181.

Gordon, Michael Allen. 1977. "Studies in Irish and Irish-American Thought and Behavior in Gilded Age New York City." Ph.D. diss. University of Rochester.

Gordon, Robert M. 1987. *The Structure of Emotions: Investigations in Cognitive Philosophy.* Cambridge: Cambridge University Press.

Gould, Stephen Jay, and Niles Eldredge. 1972. "Punctuated Equilibria: An Alternative to Phyletic Gradualism." In Thomas J. M. Schopf, ed., *Models in Paleobiology.* San Francisco: Freeman, Cooper, and Company.

———. 1977. "Punctuated Equilibria: The Tempo and Mode of Evolution Reconsidered." *Paleobiology* 3: 115–151.

Graham, Laurie, and Richard Hogan. 1990. "Social Class and Tactics: Neighborhood Opposition to Group Homes." *Sociological Quarterly* 31: 513–529.

Greanville, Patrice. 1988. "In the Name of Humanity." *The Animals' Agenda* 7 (1): 36–37. January–February.

———. 1988. "The Greening of Animal Rights." *The Animals' Agenda* 7 (7): 36–37. September–October.

Green, Donald P., and Ian Shapiro. 1994. *Pathologies of Rational Choice Theory: A Critique of Applications in Political Science.* New Haven: Yale University Press.

Greenstein, Fred I. 1987. *Personality and Politics: Problems of Evidence, Inference, and Conceptualization.* Princeton: Princeton University Press.

Griffin, Donald R. 1984. *Animal Thinking.* Cambridge: Harvard University Press.

———. 1992. *Animal Minds.* Chicago: University of Chicago Press.

Groves, Julian McAllister. 1992. "Animal Rights and Animal Research." Ph.D. diss. Chapel Hill, N.C.: University of North Carolina.

Guedeney, Colette, and Gérard Mendel. 1973. *L'Angoisse Atomique et les Centrales Nucléaires.* Paris: Payot.

Gurvitch, Georges. 1964. *The Spectrum of Social Time.* Dordrecht: D. Reidel.

Gusfield, Joseph R. 1963. *Symbolic Crusade: Status Politics and the American Temperance Movement.* Urbana, Ill.: University of Illinois Press.

———. 1975. *Community: A Critical Response.* New York: Harper and Row.

———. 1981. "Social Movements and Social Change: Perspectives of Linearity and Fluidity." *Research in Social Movements, Conflicts and Change* 4: 317–339.

———. 1981. *The Culture of Public Problems: Drinking-Driving and the Symbolic Order.* Chicago: University of Chicago Press.

———. 1989. "Constructing the Ownership of Social Problems: Fun and Profit in the Welfare State." *Social Problems* 36: 431–441.

———. 1996. *Contested Meanings: The Construction of Alcohol Problems.* Madison: University of Wisconsin Press.

Habermas, Jürgen. 1984. *The Theory of Communicative Action.* Vol. 1. *Reason and the Rationalization of Society.* Boston: Beacon Press.

———. 1987. *The Theory of Communicative Action.* Vol. 2. *Lifeworld and System: A Critique of Functionalist Reason.* Boston: Beacon Press.

Hacker, Andrew. 1978. "Loyalty—and the Whistle Blower." *Across the Board* 15 (11): 4–67.

Haines, Herbert H. 1988. *Black Radicals and the Civil Rights Mainstream, 1954–1970.* Knoxville: University of Tennessee Press.

Hall, Richard H. 1972. "Professionalization and Bureaucracy." In Richard H. Hall, ed., *The Formal Organization.* New York: Basic Books.

Hall, Stuart, with Chas Critcher, Tony Jefferson, John Clarke, and Brian Roberts. 1978. *Policing the Crisis: Mugging, the State, and Law and Order.* London: Macmillan.

Hallie, Philip P. 1979. *Lest Innocent Blood Be Shed: The Story of the Village of Le Chambon and How Goodness Happened There.* New York: Harper and Row.

Hanna, Judith Lynne. 1979. *To Dance Is Human: A Theory of Nonverbal Communication.* Austin: University of Texas Press.

———. 1990. "Dance, Protest, and Women's 'Wars': Cases from Nigeria and the United States." In Guida West and Rhoda Lois Blumberg, eds., *Women and Social Protest*. New York: Oxford University Press.

Hardin, Russell. 1982. *Collective Action*. Baltimore: Johns Hopkins University Press.

Hariman, Robert. 1995. *Political Style: The Artistry of Power.* Chicago: University of Chicago Press.

Harré, Rom, ed. 1986. *The Social Construction of Emotions*. Oxford: Basil Blackwell.

———. 1986. "An Outline of the Social Constructionist Viewpoint." In Rom Harré, ed., *The Social Construction of Emotions*. Oxford: Basil Blackwell.

Harré, Rom, and Grant Gillett. 1994. *The Discursive Mind*. Thousand Oaks, Calif.: Sage Publications.

Harrison, Robert Pogue. 1992. *Forests: The Shadow of Civilization*. Chicago: University of Chicago Press.

Hart, B. H. Liddell. 1967. *Strategy*. 2d ed. New York: Praeger Publishers.

Harvey, David. 1985. "The Geopolitics of Capitalism." In Derek Gregory and John Urry, eds., *Social Relations and Spatial Structures*. New York: St. Martin's Press.

Hatfield, Elaine, John T. Cacciopo, and Richard L. Rapson. 1992. "Emotional Contagion." In M. S. Clark, ed., *Review of Personality and Social Psychology* 14: 153–154.

———. 1994. *Emotional Contagion*. Cambridge: Cambridge University Press.

Hays, Sharon. 1994. "Structure and Agency and the Sticky Problem of Culture." *Sociological Theory* 12: 57–72.

Hayward, D. Geoffrey. 1982. "The Meanings of Home." *Human Ecology Forum* 13: 2–6.

Heirich, Max. 1971. *The Spiral of Conflict: Berkeley, 1964*. New York: Columbia University Press.

Heise, David R. 1979. *Understanding Events: Affect and the Construction of Social Action*. Cambridge: Cambridge University Press.

———. 1988. "Affect Control Theory: Concepts and Model." In Lynn Smith-Lovin and David R. Heise, eds., *Analyzing Social Interaction: Advances in Control Theory*. New York: Gordon and Breach.

Himmelstein, Jerome L. 1983. *The Strange Career of Marijuana*. Westport, Conn.: Greenwood Press.

Hirsch, Eric L. 1986. "The Creation of Political Solidarity in Social Movement Organizations." *Sociological Quarterly* 27: 373–387.

———. 1990. "Sacrifice for the Cause: Group Processes, Recruitment, and Commitment in a Student Social Movement." *American Sociological Review* 55: 243–254.

Hirsch, H. N. 1980. "Clio on the Couch." *World Politics* 32: 406–424.

Hirschman, Albert O. 1982. *Shifting Involvements: Private Interest and Public Action*. Princeton: Princeton University Press.

———. 1986. "Against Parsimony: Three Easy Ways of Complicating Some Categories of Economic Discourse." In Albert O. Hirschman, *Rival Views of Market Society and other Recent Essays*. New York: Viking.

Hoage, R. J., and Larry Goldman, eds. 1986. *Animal Intelligence.* Washington, D.C.: Smithsonian Institution Press.

Hobsbawm, E. J. 1990. *Nations and Nationalism Since 1780: Programme, Myth, Reality.* Cambridge: Cambridge University Press.

Hobsbawm, Eric, and Terence Ranger, eds. 1983. *The Invention of Tradition.* Cambridge: Cambridge University Press.

Hochschild, Arlie Russell. 1975. "The Sociology of Feeling and Emotion: Selected Possibilities." In Marcia Millman and Rosabeth Moss Kanter, eds., *Another Voice: Feminist Perspectives on Social Life and the Social Sciences.* Garden City N.Y.: Anchor Books.

———. 1979. "Emotion Work, Feeling Rules, and Social Structure." *American Journal of Sociology* 85: 551–575.

———. 1983. *The Managed Heart.* Berkeley: University of California Press.

Holusha, John. 1994. "A Whistle-Blower Is Awarded $22.5 Million." *New York Times* 1 April.

Howard, Judith A., and Peter L. Callero, eds. 1991. *The Self- Society Dynamic: Cognition, Emotion, and Action.* Cambridge: Cambridge University Press.

Hunt, Lynn. 1984. *Politics, Culture, and Class in the French Revolution.* Berkeley: University of California Press.

Hunt, Scott A. No date. "Social Movement Organizations and Collective Identities: A Constructionist Approach to Collective Identity Claims-Making." Unpublished paper.

Hunt, Scott A., and Robert D. Benford. 1994. "Identity Talk in the Peace and Justice Movement." *Journal of Contemporary Ethnography* 22: 488–517.

Hyman, Herbert H., and Charles Wright. 1979. *Education's Lasting Influence on Values.* Chicago: University of Chicago Press.

Inglehart, Ronald. 1977. *The Silent Revolution: Changing Values and Political Styles among Western Publics.* Princeton, N.J.: Princeton University Press.

———. 1990. *Culture Shift in Advanced Industrial Society.* Princeton, N.J.: Princeton University Press.

Iser, Wolfgang. 1978. *The Act of Reading: A Theory of Aesthetic Response.* Baltimore: Johns Hopkins University Press.

Isserman, Maurice. 1987. *If I Had a Hammer . . . The Death of the Old Left and the Birth of the New Left.* New York: Basic Books.

Iyengar, Shanto. 1991. *Is Anyone Responsible? How Television Frames Political Issues.* Chicago: University of Chicago Press.

Jackman, Mary R., and Michael J. Muha. 1984. "Education and Intergroup Attitudes: Moral Enlightenment, Superficial Democratic Commitment, or Ideological Refinement?" *American Sociological Review* 49: 751–769.

Jackson, Karl D. 1989. "The Ideology of Total Revolution." In Karl D. Jackson, ed., *Cambodia 1975–1978: Rendezvous with Death.* Princeton: Princeton University Press.

Jasper, James M. 1988. "The Political Life Cycle of Technological Controversies." *Social Forces* 67: 357–377.

———. 1990. *Nuclear Politics: Energy and the State in the United States, Sweden, and France.* Princeton: Princeton University Press.

———. 1992. "The Politics of Abstractions: Instrumental and Moralist Rhetorics in Public Debate." *Social Research* 59: 315–344.

———. 1992. "Rational Reconstructions of Energy Choices in France." In James F. Short Jr. and Lee Clarke, eds., *Organizations, Uncertainties, and Risk*. Boulder, Colo.: Westview Press.

———. 1992. "Three Nuclear Energy Controversies." In Dorothy Nelkin, ed., *Controversy: Politics of Technical Decisions*. Newbury Park, Calif: Sage Publications.

———. Forthcoming. "Sentiments, Ideas, and Animals: Rights Talk and Animal Protection." In Stuart Bruchey, Peter Coclanis, and Joel Colton, eds., *Ideas in Social Movements*. New York: Columbia University Press.

Jasper, James M., and Dorothy Nelkin. 1992. *The Animal Rights Crusade: The Growth of a Moral Protest*. New York: Free Press.

Jasper, James M., and Jane Poulsen. 1993. "Fighting Back: Vulnerabilities, Blunders, and Countermobilization by the Targets in Three Animal Rights Campaigns." *Sociological Forum* 8: 639–657.

———. 1995. "Recruiting Strangers and Friends: Moral Shocks and Social Networks in Animal Rights and Animal Protest." *Social Problems* 42: 493–512.

Jasper, James M., and Scott Sanders. 1995. "Big Institutions in Local Politics: American Universities, the Public, and Animal Protection Efforts." *Social Science Information* 34: 491–509.

Jay, Martin. 1984. *Marxism and Totality: The Adventures of a Concept from Lukács to Habermas*. Berkeley: University of California Press.

Jenkins, J. Craig. 1983. "Resource Mobilization Theory and the Study of Social Movements." *Annual Review of Sociology* 9: 527–553.

———. 1985. *The Politics of Insurgency: The Farm Worker Movement in the 1960s*. New York: Columbia University Press.

Jenkins, J. Craig, and Craig Eckert. 1986. "Elite Patronage and the Channeling of Social Protest." *American Sociological Review* 51: 812–829.

Jenkins, J. Craig, and Bert Klandermans. 1995. "The Politics of Social Protest." In J. Craig Jenkins and Bert Klandermans, eds., *The Politics of Social Protest: Comparative Perspectives on States and Social Movements*. Minneapolis: University of Minnesota Press.

Jenkins, J. Craig, and Charles Perrow. 1977. "Insurgency of the Powerless: Farm Worker Movements (1946–1972)." *American Sociological Review* 42: 249–268.

Jenkins, Philip. 1992. *Intimate Enemies: Moral Panics in Contemporary Great Britain*. New York: Aldine de Gruyter.

Jennings, M. Kent. 1987. "Residues of a Movement: The Aging of the American Protest Generation." *American Political Science Review* 81: 367–382.

Jensen, J. Vernon. 1987. "Ethical Tension Points in Whistleblowing." *Journal of Business Ethics* 6: 321–328.

Jenson, Jane. 1995. "What's In a Name? Nationalist Movements and Public Discourse." In Hank Johnston and Bert Klandermans, eds., *Social Movements and Culture*. Minneapolis: University of Minnesota Press.

Johnson, Paul E. 1978. *A Shopkeeper's Millennium: Society and Revivals in Rochester, New York, 1815–1837*. New York: Hill and Wang.

Johnston, Hank. 1995. "A Methodology for Frame Analysis: From Discourse to Cognitive Schema." In Hank Johnston and Bert Klandermans, eds., *Social Movements and Culture*. Minneapolis: University of Minnesota Press.

Johnston, Hank, Enrique Laraña, and Joseph R. Gusfield. 1994. "Identities, Grievances, and New Social Movements." In Enrique Laraña, Hank Johnston, and Joseph R. Gusfield, eds., *New Social Movements: From Ideology to Identity*. Philadelphia: Temple University Press.

Joppke, Christian. 1993. *Mobilizing Against Nuclear Energy: A Comparison of Germany and the United States*. Berkeley: University of California Press.

Kahneman, Daniel, Paul Slovic, and Amos Tversky, eds. 1982. *Judgment Under Uncertainty: Heuristics and Biases*. Cambridge: Cambridge University Press.

Kellert, Stephen R. 1983. "Historical Trends in American Animal Use and Perception." *International Journal for the Study of Animal Problems* 4: 133–146.

———. 1989. "Perceptions of Animals in America." In R. J. Hoage, ed., *Perceptions of Animals in American Culture*. Washington, D.C.: Smithsonian Institution Press.

———. 1995. *The Value of Life: Biological Diversity and Human Society*. Washington, D.C.: Island Press.

Kellert, Stephen R., with Miriam O. Westervelt. 1980. "American Attitudes Toward and Knowledge of Animals: An Update." *International Journal for the Study of Animal Problems* 1: 87–119.

Kelly, George A. 1955. *The Psychology of Personal Constructs*. New York: W. W. Norton.

Kemper, Theodore D. 1987. "How Many Emotions Are There? Wedding the Social and the Autonomic Components." *American Journal of Sociology* 93: 263–289.

Kertzer, David I. 1988. *Ritual, Politics, and Power*. New Haven: Yale University Press.

———. 1983. "Generation as a Sociological Problem." *Annual Review of Sociology* 9: 125–149.

Khilnani, Sunil. 1993. *Arguing Revolution: The Intellectual Left in Postwar France*. New Haven: Yale University Press.

Kielbowicz, Richard B., and Clifford Scherer. 1986. "The Role of the Press in the Dynamics of Social Movements." *Research in Social Movements, Conflicts, and Change* 9: 71–96.

Kitschelt, Herbert. 1986. "Political Opportunity Structures and Political Protest: Anti-Nuclear Movements in Four Democracies." *British Journal of Political Science* 16: 57–85.

Klandermans, Bert. 1984. "Mobilization and Participation: Social-Psychological Expansions of Resource Mobilization Theory." *American Sociological Review* 49: 583–600.

Klandermans, Bert, and Dirk Oegema. 1987. "Potentials, Networks, Motivations, and Barriers: Steps towards Participation in Social Movements." *American Sociological Review* 52: 519–531.

Knoke, David. 1984. "Conceptual and Measurement Aspects in the Study of Political Generations." *Journal of Political and Military Sociology* 12: 191–201.

————. 1990. *Political Networks: The Structural Perspective.* Cambridge: Cambridge University Press.

Knoke, David, and James R. Wood. 1981. *Organized for Action: Commitment in Voluntary Associations.* New Brunswick, N.J.: Rutgers University Press.

Kohut, Heinz. 1978. *The Search for the Self.* Edited by Paul Ornstein. Madison, Wisc.: International Universities Press.

Koopmans, Ruud, and Jan Willem Duyvendak. 1995. "The Political Construction of the Nuclear Energy Issue and Its Impact on the Mobilization of Anti-Nuclear Movements in Western Europe." *Social Problems* 42: 235–251.

Kornhauser, William. 1959. *The Politics of Mass Society.* New York: Free Press.

Krauss, Celene. 1989. "Community Struggles and the Shaping of Democratic Consciousness." *Sociological Forum* 4: 227–239.

Kriesi, Hanspeter. 1988. "Local Mobilization for the People's Social Petition of the Dutch Peace Movement." *International Social Movement Research* 1: 41–81.

————. 1989. "New Social Movements and the New Class in the Netherlands." *American Journal of Sociology* 94: 1078–1116.

————. 1995. "The Political Opportunity Structure of New Social Movements: Its Impact on Their Mobilization." In J. Craig Jenkins and Bert Klandermans, eds., *The Politics of Social Protest: Comparative Perspectives on States and Social Movements.* Minneapolis: University of Minnesota Press.

Kriesi, Hanspeter, Ruud Koopmans, Jan Willem Duyvendak, and Marco G. Guigni. 1992. "New Social Movements and Political Opportunities in Western Europe," *European Journal of Political Research* 22: 219–244.

Kroll-Smith, J. Stephen, and Stephen R. Couch. 1990. *The Real Disaster Is Above Ground: A Mine Fire and Social Conflict.* Lexington, Ken.: University of Kentucky Press.

————. 1991. "What Is a Disaster? An Ecological-Symbolic Approach to Resolving the Definitional Debate." *International Journal of Mass Emergencies and Disasters* 9: 355–366.

Kuhn, Thomas S. 1962. *The Structure of Scientific Revolutions.* Chicago: University of Chicago Press.

Kymlicka, Will. 1989. *Liberalism, Community, and Culture.* Oxford: Oxford University Press.

Laclau, Ernesto, and Chantal Mouffe. 1985. *Hegemony and Socialist Strategy: Towards a Radical Democratic Politics.* London: Verso.

Ladd, Anthony E., Thomas C. Hood, and Kent D. Van Liere. 1983. "Ideological Themes in the Antinuclear Movement: Consensus and Diversity." *Sociological Inquiry* 53: 252–272.

Lane, Robert E. 1959. *Political Life: Why People Get Involved in Politics.* Glencoe, Ill.: Free Press.

————. 1962. *Political Ideology: Why the American Common Man Believes What He Does.* New York: Free Press of Glencoe.

Lanouette, William, with Bela Silard. 1992. *Genius in the Shadows: A Biography of Leo Szilard: The Man Behind the Bomb.* New York: C. Scribner's Sons.

Larner, Christina. 1984. *Witchcraft and Religion: The Politics of Popular Belief.* New York: Basil Blackwell.

Lasch, Christopher. 1991. *The True and Only Heaven: Progress and Its Critics.* New York: W. W. Norton.

Lasswell, Harold D. 1930. *Psychopathology and Politics.* Chicago: University of Chicago Press.

Latour, Bruno, and Steven Woolgar. 1979. *Laboratory Life: The Social Construction of Scientific Facts.* Beverly Hills: Sage Publications.

Laumann, Edward O., and David Knoke. 1987. *The Organizational State: Social Choice in National Policy Domains.* Madison: University of Wisconsin Press.

Law, Kim S., and Edward J. Walsh. 1983. "The Interaction of Grievances and Structures in Social Movement Analysis: The Case of JUST." *Sociological Quarterly* 24: 123–136.

Lazarus, Richard S. 1991. *Emotion and Adaptation.* New York: Oxford University Press.

Le Bon, Gustave. 1960 [1895]. *The Crowd: A Study of the Popular Mind.* New York: Viking Press.

Leclerc, George Louis, Comte de Buffon. 1812. *Natural History, General and Particular.* London: T. Cadell and W. Davies.

Lesher, Stephan. 1993. *George Wallace: American Populist.* Reading, Mass.: Addison-Wesley.

Levine, Adeline Gordon. 1982. *Love Canal: Science, Politics, and People.* Lexington, Mass.: D.C. Heath.

Lévi-Strauss, Claude. 1963 [1958]. *Structural Anthropology.* New York: Basic Books.

———. 1966 [1962]. *The Savage Mind.* London: George Weidenfeld and Nicolson.

Lichbach, Mark I. 1994. "Rethinking Rationality and Rebellion: Theories of Collective Action and Problems of Collective Dissent." *Rationality and Society* 6: 8–39.

Lichterman, Paul. 1995. "Piecing Together Multicultural Community: Cultural Differences in Community Building Among Grass-Roots Environmentalists." *Social Problems* 42: 513–534.

Lifton, Robert Jay. 1968. *Revolutionary Immortality: Mao Tse-tung and the Chinese Cultural Revolution.* New York: Random House.

———. 1986. *The Nazi Doctors: Medical Killing and the Psychology of Genocide.* New York: Basic Books.

Linden, Eugene. 1974. *Apes, Men, and Language.* New York: Saturday Review Press.

———. 1986. *Silent Partners: The Legacy of the Ape Language Experiments.* New York: Times Books.

Lindholm, Charles. 1990. *Charisma.* Oxford: Blackwell.

Lipset, Seymour Martin. 1960. *Political Man: The Social Bases of Politics.* Garden City, N.J.: Anchor.

Lipset, Seymour Martin, and Earl Raab. 1978. *The Politics of Unreason: Right-Wing Extremism in America, 1790–1977,* 2d ed. Chicago: University of Chicago Press.

Lipsky, Michael. 1968. "Protest as a Political Resource." *American Political Science Review* 62: 1114–1158.

Lo, Clarence Y. H. 1992. "Communities of Challengers in Social Movement Theory." In Aldon D. Morris and Carol McClurg Mueller, eds., *Frontiers in Social Movement Theory*. New Haven: Yale University Press.

Lofland, John. 1966. *Doomsday Cult*. Englewood Cliffs, N.J.: Prentice-Hall.

———. 1985. *Protest: Studies of Collective Behavior and Social Movements*. New Brunswick, N.J.: Transaction.

———. 1993. *Polite Protesters: The American Peace Movement of the 1980s*. Syracuse, N.Y.: Syracuse University Press.

———. 1993. "Theory-Bashing and Answer-Improving in the Study of Social Movements." *American Sociologist* 24: 37–58.

———. 1995. "Charting Degrees of Movement Culture: Tasks of the Cultural Cartographer." In Hank Johnston and Bert Klandermans, eds., *Social Movements and Culture*. Minneapolis: University of Minnesota Press.

———. 1996. *Social Movement Organizations: Guide to Research on Insurgent Realities*. New York: Walter de Gruyter.

Lofland, John, and Michael Fink. 1982. *Symbolic Sit-Ins: Protest Occupations at the California Capitol*. Lanham, Md.: University Press of America.

Lofland, John, and Lyn H. Lofland. 1969. *Deviance and Identity*. Englewood Cliffs, N.J.: Prentice-Hall.

Lofland, John, and Rodney Stark. 1965. "Becoming a World Saver: A Theory of Conversion to a Deviant Perspective." *American Sociological Review* 30: 863–74.

Lofland, Lyn H. 1985. "The Social Shaping of Emotion: The Case of Grief." *Symbolic Interaction* 8: 171–190.

Lukács, Georg. 1963 [1937]. *The Historical Novel*. Boston: Beacon Press.

———. 1964. *Studies in European Realism*. New York: Grosset and Dunlap.

Luker, Kristin. 1984. *Abortion and the Politics of Motherhood*. Berkeley: University of California Press.

Lutz, Catherine A. 1988. *Unnatural Emotions: Everyday Sentiments on a Micronesian Atoll and Their Challenge to Western Theory*. Chicago: University of Chicago Press.

Macfarlane, Alan. 1970. *Witchcraft in Tudor and Stuart England: A Regional and Comparative Study*. London: Routledge.

MacIntyre, Alasdair. 1981. *After Virtue: A Study in Moral Theory*. Notre Dame, Ind.: University of Notre Dame Press.

Mack, John E. 1976. *A Prince of Our Disorder: The Life of T. E. Lawrence*. Boston: Little, Brown.

Macy, Michael W. 1990. "Learning Theory and the Logic of Critical Mass." *American Sociological Review* 55: 809–826.

Madsen, Richard. 1991. "Contentless Consensus: The Political Discourse of a Segmented Society." In Alan Wolfe, ed., *America at Century's End*. Berkeley: University of California Press.

Mann, Michael. 1973. *Consciousness and Action Among the Western Working Class*. London: Macmillan.

———. 1970. "The Social Cohesion of Liberal Democracy." *American Sociological Review* 35: 423–439.

Mannheim, Karl. 1952 [1928]. "The Problem of Generations." In Paul Kecskemeti, ed., *Essays on the Sociology of Knowledge*. London: Routledge and Kegan
Paul.

Mansbridge, Jane J. 1986. *Why We Lost the ERA*. Chicago: University of Chicago Press.

Marchetti, Victor, and John D. Marks. 1980. *The CIA and the Cult of Intelligence*.
New York: Alfred A. Knopf.

Marcus, George E., and Michael B. Mackuen. 1993. "Anxiety, Enthusiasm, and
the Vote: The Emotional Underpinnings of Learning and Involvement During Presidential Campaigns." *American Political Science Review* 87: 672–685.

Marlow, Joyce. 1973 *Captain Boycott and the Irish*. New York: Saturday Review
Press.

Marsh, Alan. 1977. *Protest and Political Consciousness*. Beverly Hills, Calif.:
Sage Publications.

Martin, Brian. 1986. "Nuclear Suppression." *Science and Public Policy* 13:
312–320.

Martin, Brian, C. M. Ann Baker, Clyde Manwell, and Cedric Pugh, eds. 1986.
Intellectual Suppression: Australian Case Histories, Analysis, and Responses.
North Ryde, NSW, Australia: Angus and Robertson.

Martin, Linda, and Kerry Segrave. 1988. *Anti-Rock: The Opposition to Rock 'n'
Roll*. Hamden, Conn.: Archon.

Marwell, Gerald, Michael T. Aiken, and N.J. Demerath III. 1987. "The Persistence of Political Attitudes Among 1960s Civil Rights Activists." *Public Opinion Quarterly* 51: 359–375.

Marwell, Gerald, and Pamela Oliver. 1993. *The Critical Mass in Collective Action:
A Micro-Social Theory*. Cambridge: Cambridge University Press.

Mauer, Richard. 1991. "Pipeline Company, Stung by Critic, Goes After Whistle-
Blowers." *New York Times* 23 September.

McAdam, Doug. 1982. *Political Process and the Development of Black Insurgency,
1930–1970*. Chicago: University of Chicago Press.

———. 1983. "Tactical Innovation and the Pace of Insurgency." *American Sociological Review* 48: 735–754.

———. 1986. "Recruitment to High-Risk Activism: The Case of Freedom Summer." *American Journal of Sociology* 92: 64–90.

———. 1988. *Freedom Summer*. New York: Oxford University Press.

———. 1996. "The Framing Function of Movement Tactics: Strategic Dramaturgy in the American Civil Rights Movement." In Doug McAdam, John D.
McCarthy, and Mayer N. Zald, eds., *Comparative Perspectives on Social Movements: Political Opportunities, Mobilizing Structures, and Cultural Framings*.
Cambridge: Cambridge University Press.

McAdam, Doug, John D. McCarthy, and Mayer N. Zald. 1988. "Social Movements." In Neil J. Smelser, ed., *Handbook of Sociology*. Beverly Hills, Calif.:
Sage.

———, eds. 1996. *Comparative Perspectives on Social Movements: Political Opportunities, Mobilizing Structures, and Cultural Framings*. Cambridge: Cambridge
University Press.

McAdam, Doug, and Ronnelle Paulsen. 1993. "Specifying the Relationship between Social Ties and Activism." *American Journal of Sociology* 99: 640–667.

McCarthy, John D. 1987. "Pro-Life and Pro-Choice Mobilization: Infrastructure Deficits and New Technologies." In Mayer N. Zald and John D. McCarthy, eds., *Social Movements in an Organizational Society: Collected Essays*. New Brunswick, N.J.: Transaction.

———. 1994. "Activists, Authorities, and Media Framing of Drunk Driving." In Enrique Laraña, Hank Johnston, and Joseph R. Gusfield, eds., *New Social Movements: From Ideology to Identity*. Philadelphia: Temple University Press.

McCarthy, John D., and Mayer N. Zald. 1973. *The Trend of Social Movements in America: Professionalization and Resource Mobilization*. Morristown, N.J.: General Learning Press. Reprinted in Mayer N. Zald and John D. McCarthy, *Social Movements in an Organizational Society: Collected Essays*. New Brunswick, N.J.: Transaction, 1987.

———. 1977. "Resource Mobilization and Social Movements: A Partial Theory." *American Journal of Sociology* 82: 1212–1241. Reprinted in Mayer N. Zald and John D. McCarthy, *Social Movements in an Organizational Society: Collected Essays*. New Brunswick, N.J.: Transaction, 1987.

McCarthy, John D., Jackie Smith, and Mayer N. Zald. 1996. "Accessing Public, Media, Electoral, and Governmental Agendas." In Doug McAdam, John D. McCarthy, and Mayer N. Zald, eds., *Comparative Perspectives on Social Movements: Political Opportunities, Mobilizing Structures, and Cultural Framings*. Cambridge: Cambridge University Press.

McNeill, William H. 1995. *Keeping Together in Time: Dance and Drill in Human History*. Cambridge: Harvard University Press.

McPhail, Clark. 1991. *The Myth of the Madding Crowd*. New York: Aldine de Gruyter.

Meehan, Richard L. 1984. *The Atom and the Fault: Experts, Earthquakes, and Nuclear Power*. Cambridge: MIT Press.

Meier, August, and Elliott Rudwick. 1969. "The Boycott Movement Against Jim Crow Streetcars in the South, 1900–1906." *The Journal of American History* 55: 756–775.

Meiksins, Peter F., and James M. Watson. 1989. "Professional Autonomy and Organization Constraint: The Case of Engineers." *Sociological Quarterly* 30: 561–585.

Melucci, Alberto. 1980. "The New Social Movements: A Theoretical Approach." *Social Science Information* 19: 199–226.

———. 1985. "The Symbolic Challenge of Contemporary Movements." *Social Research* 52: 789–816.

———. 1988. "Getting Involved: Identity and Mobilization in Social Movements." *International Social Movement Research* 1: 329–348.

———. 1989. *Nomads of the Present: Social Movements and Individual Needs in Contemporary Society*. Philadelphia: Temple University Press.

———. 1995. "The New Social Movements: Reflections on a Sociological Misunderstanding." In Louis Maheu, ed., *Social Movements and Social Classes: The Future of Collective Action*. London: Sage Publications.

————. 1995. "The Process of Collective Identity." In Hank Johnston and Bert Klandermans, eds., *Social Movements and Culture*. Minneapolis: University of Minnesota Press.

————. 1996. *Challenging Codes: Collective Action in the Information Age*. Cambridge: Cambridge University Press.

Meyer, David S. 1990. *A Winter of Discontent: The Nuclear Freeze and American Politics*. New York: Praeger Publishers.

Meyer, David S., and Joshua Gamson. 1995. "The Challenge of Cultural Elites: Celebrities and Social Movements." *Sociological Inquiry* 65: 181–206.

Meyer, David S., and Nancy Whittier. 1994. "Social Movement Spillover." *Social Problems* 41: 277–298.

Meyer, John W. 1977. "The Effects of Education as an Institution." *American Journal of Sociology* 83: 53–77.

Meyer, John W., and Brian Rowan. 1977. "Institutionalized Organizations: Formal Structure as Myth and Ceremony." *American Journal of Sociology* 83: 340–363.

Meyer, John W., and W. Richard Scott, with B. Rowan and T. Deal. 1983. *Organizational Environments: Ritual and Rationality*. Beverly Hills: Sage Publications.

MHB Technical Associates. 1990. *Advanced Reactor Designs*. Prepared for the Union of Concerned Scientists. Washington, D.C.: Union of Concerned Scientists.

Midgley, Mary. 1991. *Can't We Make Moral Judgements?* New York: St. Martin's Press.

Milbrath, Lester W. 1984. *Environmentalists: Vanguard for a New Society*. Albany: State University of New York Press.

Mills, C. Wright. 1940. "Situated Actions and Vocabularies of Motive." *American Sociological Review* 5: 904–913.

————. 1959. *The Sociological Imagination*. New York: Oxford University Press.

Minow, Martha. 1980. *Making All the Difference: Inclusion, Exclusion, and American Law*. Ithaca, N.Y.: Cornell University Press.

Mintzberg, Henry, and Alexandra McHugh. 1985. "Strategy Formation in an Adhocracy." *Administrative Science Quarterly* 30: 160–197.

Molotch, Harvey. 1970. "Oil in Santa Barbara and Power in America." *Sociological Inquiry* 40: 131–144.

————. 1979. "Media and Movements." In Mayer N. Zald and John D. McCarthy, eds., *The Dynamics of Social Movements*. Cambridge, Mass.: Winthrop Publishers.

Monroe, Kristin Renwick. 1996. *The Heart of Altruism: Perceptions of a Common Humanity*. Princeton: Princeton University Press.

Monroe, Kristin R., Michael C. Barton, and Ute Klingemann. 1991. "Altruism and the Theory of Rational Action: An Analysis of Rescuers of Jews in Nazi Europe." In Kristin Renwick Monroe, ed., *The Economic Approach to Politics: A Critical Reassessment of the Theory of Rational Action*. New York: HarperCollins, 1991.

Moore, R. I. 1987. *The Formation of a Persecuting Society: Power and Deviance in Western Europe, 950–1250*. Oxford: Basil Blackwell.

Moore, R. Laurence. 1986. *Religious Outsiders and the Making of Americans*. New York: Oxford University Press.

Morgan, Patricia. 1980. "The State as Mediator: Alcohol Problem Management in the Postwar Period." *Contemporary Drug Problems* 9: 107–140.

Morris, Aldon D. 1984. *The Origins of the Civil Rights Movement: Black Communities Organizing for Change*. New York: Free Press.

Morris, Aldon D., and Carol McClurg Mueller, eds. 1992. *Frontiers in Social Movement Theory*. New Haven: Yale University Press.

Morrison, Toni. 1992. *Playing in the Dark: Whiteness and the Literary Imagination*. Cambridge: Harvard University Press.

Moscovici, Serge. 1981. *L'Age des Foules*. Paris: Fayard.

Mottl, Tahi L. 1980. "The Analysis of Countermovements." *Social Problems* 27: 620–635.

Nader, Ralph, Peter J. Petkas, and Kate Blackwell, eds. 1972. *Whistle Blowing: The Report of the Conference on Professional Responsibility*. New York: Grossman.

Nash, Roderick. 1982. *Wilderness and the American Mind*. 3d ed. New Haven: Yale University Press.

Nelkin, Dorothy. 1971. *Nuclear Power and Its Critics: The Cayuga Lake Controversy*. Ithaca, N.Y.: Cornell University Press.

New York Observer. 1992. "Wise Guys. Smearing the Whistle Blowers." 23 March.

New York Times. 1994. "Report of $1 Million Offer to Whistle- Blower to Keep Quiet." 27 June.

Oakley, Justin. 1992. *Morality and the Emotions*. London: Routledge.

Oates, Joyce Carol. 1991. "Capital Punishment." In *Heat and Other Stories*. New York: Dutton.

Oberschall, Anthony. 1973. *Social Conflict and Social Movements*. Englewood Cliffs, N.J.: Prentice-Hall.

———. 1978. "Theories of Social Conflict." In Ralph Turner, James Coleman, and Renée C. Fox, eds., *Annual Review of Sociology* 4: 291–315.

———. 1980. "Loosely Structured Collective Conflict: A Theory and an Application." *Research in Social Movements, Conflicts, and Change* 3: 45–68.

———. 1993. *Social Movements: Ideologies, Interests, and Identities*. New Brunswick, N.J.: Transaction.

Oelschlager, Max. 1991. *The Idea of Wilderness from Prehistory to the Age of Ecology*. New Haven: Yale University Press.

Offe, Claus. 1985. "New Social Movements: Challenging the Boundaries of Institutional Politics." *Social Research* 52: 817–868.

———. 1985. "Two Logics of Collective Action." In *Disorganized Capitalism: Contemporary Transformations of Work and Politics*. Cambridge: MIT University Press.

Oliner, Samuel P., and Pearl M. Oliner. 1988. *The Altruistic Personality: Rescuers of Jews in Nazi Europe*. New York: Free Press.

Olson, Mancur Jr. 1965. *The Logic of Collective Action: Public Goods and the Theory of Groups*. Cambridge: Harvard University Press.

Olzak, Susan. 1992. *The Dynamics of Ethnic Competition and Conflict*. Stanford: Stanford University Press.

Opp, Karl-Dieter. 1989. *The Rationality of Political Protest: A Comparative Analysis of Rational Choice Theory*. Boulder, Colo.: Westview Press.

Orwell, George. 1958 [1937]. *The Road to Wigan Pier*. New York: Harcourt Brace Jovanovich.

Ozouf, Mona. 1988. *Festivals and the French Revolution*. Cambridge: Harvard University Press.

Paehlke, Robert C. 1989. *Environmentalism and the Future of Progressive Politics*. New Haven: Yale University Press.

Park, Robert E. 1982 [1904]. *The Crowd and the Public*. Chicago: University of Chicago Press.

Parks, Tim. 1993. *Shear*. New York: Grove Press.

Parmerlee, Marcia A., Janet P. Near, and Tamila C. Jensen. 1982. "Correlates of Whistle-Blowers' Perceptions of Organizational Retaliation." *Administrative Science Quarterly* 27: 17–34.

Parsons, Talcott. 1939. "The Professions and Social Structure." *Social Forces* 17: 457–467.

PBS. 1986. *Eyes on the Prize: America's Civil Rights Years*. Video series.

Perrow, Charles. 1979. "The Sixties Observed." In Mayer N. Zald and John D. McCarthy, eds., *The Dynamics of Social Movements*. Cambridge, Mass.: Winthrop.

———. 1984. *Normal Accidents: Living with High-Risk Technologies*. New York: Basic Books.

Perrucci, Robert, Robert M. Anderson, Dan E. Schendel, and Leon E. Trachtman. 1980. "Whistle-Blowing: Professionals' Resistance to Organizational Authority." *Social Problems* 28: 149–164.

Peters, Charles, and Taylor Branch. 1972. *Blowing the Whistle: Dissent in the Public Interest*. New York: Praeger.

Peters, Edward. 1978. *The Magician, the Witch, and the Law*. Philadelphia: University of Pennsylvania Press.

Phelan, Jo, Bruce G. Link, Ann Stueve, and Robert E. Moore. 1995. "Education, Social Liberalism, and Economic Conservatism: Attitudes Toward Homeless People." *American Sociological Review* 60: 126–140.

Piller, Charles. 1991. *The Fail-Safe Society: Community Defiance and the End of American Technological Optimism*. New York: Basic Books.

Piven, Frances Fox, and Richard A. Cloward. 1977. *Poor People's Movements: Why They Succeed, How They Fail*. New York: Vintage.

———. 1992. "Normalizing Collective Protest." In Aldon D. Morris and Carol McClurg Mueller, eds., *Frontiers in Social Movement Theory*. New Haven: Yale University Press.

Pizzorno, Allesandro. 1978. "Political Exchange and Collective Identity in Industrial Conflict." In Colin Crouch and Allesandro Pizzorno, eds., *The Resurgence of Class Conflict in Western Europe Since 1968*. New York: Holmes and Meier.

———. 1986. "Some Other Kinds of Otherness: A Critique of 'Rational Choice' Theories." In Alejandro Foxley, Michael S. McPherson, and Guillermo O'Donnell, eds., *Development, Democracy, and the Art of Trespassing: Essays in Honor of Albert O. Hirschman.* Notre Dame, Ind.: University of Notre Dame Press.

Polletta, Francesca A. 1994. "Strategy and Identity in 1960s Black Protest: Activism of the Student Nonviolent Coordinating Committee, 1960–1967." Ph.D. diss. New Haven: Yale University.

Ponchaud, François. 1989. "Social Change in the Vortex of Revolution." In Karl D. Jackson, ed., *Cambodia 1975–1978.* Princeton: Princeton University Press.

Popper, Karl. 1974 [1945]. *The Open Society and Its Enemies.* London: Routledge and Keagan Paul.

Powell, Walter W., and Paul J. DiMaggio, eds. 1991. *The New Institutionalism in Organizational Analysis.* Chicago: University of Chicago Press.

Pring, George W., and Penelope Canan. 1996. *SLAPPS: Getting Sued for Speaking Out.* Philadelphia: Temple University Press.

Proietto, Rosa. 1995. "New Social Movements: Issues for Sociology." *Social Science Information* 34: 355–388.

Quarantelli, E. L. 1979. "Consequences of Disasters for Mental Health: Conflicting Views." Preliminary Paper 62, Disaster Research Center.

Rabe, Barry G. 1994. *Beyond NIMBY: Hazardous Waste Siting in Canada and the United States.* Washington, D.C.: The Brookings Institution.

Rambo, Eric, and Elaine Chan. 1990. "Text, Structure, and Action in Cultural Sociology." *Theory and Society* 19: 635–648.

Rapoport, Anatol. 1992. "Game Theory Defined: What It Is and Is Not." *Rationality and Society* 4: 74–82.

Rapoport, Anatol, and Melvin Guyer. 1966. "A Taxonomy of 2 x 2 Games." *General Systems: Yearbook of the Society for General Systems Research* 11: 203–214.

Regan, Tom. 1983. *The Case for Animal Rights.* Berkeley: University of California Press.

Reinarman, Craig, and Harry Gene Levine. 1989. "Crack in Context: Politics and Media in the Making of a Drug Scare." *Contemporary Drug Problems* 16: 535–577.

Rieder, Jonathan. 1985. *Canarsie: The Jews and Italians of Brooklyn against Liberalism.* Cambridge: Harvard University Press.

Ritvo, Harriet. 1987. *The Animal Estate.* Cambridge: Harvard University Press.

Rorty, Amélie Oksenberg, ed. 1980. *Explaining Emotions.* Berkeley: University of California Press.

Rorty, Richard. 1979. *Philosophy and the Mirror of Nature.* Princeton, N.J.: Princeton University Press.

Rosenberg, M. J. 1956. "Cognitive Structure and Attitudinal Affect." *Journal of Abnormal Social Psychology* 53: 367–372.

Rothschild, Joyce, and J. Allen Whitt. 1986. *The Cooperative Workplace: Potentials and Dilemmas of Organizational Democracy and Participation.* Cambridge: Cambridge University Press.

Rothschild-Whitt, Joyce. 1979. "The Collectivist Organization: An Alternative to Rational-Bureaucratic Models." *American Sociological Review* 44: 509–527.

Rowles, Graham D. 1983. "Place and Personal Identity in Old Age: Observations from Appalachia." *Journal of Environmental Psychology* 3: 299–313.

Ruddick, Sara. 1989. *Maternal Thinking: Toward a Politics of Peace.* Boston: Beacon Press.

Rudé, George F. E. 1959. *The Crowd and the French Revolution.* New York: Oxford University Press.

Rule, James B. 1988. *Theories of Civil Violence.* Berkeley: University of California Press.

Russell, Jeffrey. 1980. *A History of Witchcraft, Sorcerers, Heretics, and Pagans.* London: Thames and Hudson.

Ryan, Charlotte. 1991. *Prime Time Activism: Media Strategies for Grassroots Organizing.* Boston: South End Press.

Salisbury, Joyce E. 1994. *The Beast Within: Animals in the Middle Ages.* New York: Routledge.

Sanders, Scott, and James M. Jasper. 1994. "Civil Politics in the Animal Rights Conflict: God Terms versus Casuistry in Cambridge, Massachusetts." *Science, Technology & Human Values* 19: 169–188.

Sapir, Edward. 1935. "Symbolism." *Encyclopaedia of the Social Sciences* 14: 492–495.

Sartori, Giovanni. 1970. "Conceptual Misinformation in Comparative Politics." *American Political Science Review* 66: 1033–1053.

Sartre, Jean-Paul. 1946. *Portrait of the Anti-Semite.* New York: Partisan Review.

———. 1972. *The Psychology of Imagination.* London: Methuen.

Sayer, Derek. 1987. *The Violence of Abstraction: The Analytic Foundations of Historical Materialism.* Oxford: Basil Blackwell.

Scaminaci, James III, and Riley E. Dunlap. 1986. "No Nukes! A Comparison of Participants in Two National Antinuclear Demonstrations." *Sociological Inquiry* 56: 272–282.

Schacter, Stanley, and Jerome Singer. 1962. "Cognitive, Social, and Physiological Determinants of Emotional States." *Psychological Review* 69: 379–399.

Scheff, Thomas J. 1983. "Toward Integration in the Social Psychology of Emotions." *Annual Review of Sociology* 9: 333–354.

———. 1990. *Microsociology: Discourse, Emotion, and Social Structure.* Chicago: University of Chicago Press.

———. 1994. *Bloody Revenge: Emotions, Nationalism, and War.* Boulder, Colo.: Westview Press.

Scheler, Max. 1992. *On Feeling, Knowing, and Valuing.* Chicago: University of Chicago Press.

Schelling, Thomas C. 1960. *The Strategy of Conflict.* Cambridge: Harvard University Press.

———. 1984. "What Is Game Theory" In *Choice and Consequence: Perspectives on an Errant Economist.* Cambridge: Harvard University Press.

Schmitt, Carl. 1976. *The Concept of the Political.* New Brunswick, N.J.: Rutgers University Press.

Schudson, Michael. 1978. *Discovering the News: A Social History of American Newspapers*. New York: Basic Books.

Schuman, Howard, and Jacqueline Scott. 1989. "Generations and Collective Memory." *American Sociological Review* 54: 359–381.

Schwartz, Barry. 1981. *Vertical Classification: A Study in Structuralism and the Sociology of Knowledge*. Chicago: University of Chicago Press.

Scott, Alan. 1990. *Ideology and the New Social Movements*. London: Unwin Hyman.

Scott, James C. 1985. *Weapons of the Weak: Everyday Forms of Peasant Resistance*. New Haven: Yale University Press.

———. 1990. *Domination and the Arts of Resistance: Hidden Transcripts*. New Haven: Yale University Press.

Scott, W. Richard. 1966. "Professionals in Bureaucracies—Areas of Conflict." In Howard M. Vollner and Donald L. Mills, eds., *Professionalization*. Englewood Cliffs, N.J.: Prentice-Hall.

———. 1987. *Organizations: Rational, Natural, and Open Systems*. 2d ed. Englewood Cliffs, N.J.: Prentice-Hall.

Serpell, James. 1986. *In the Company of Animals*. Oxford: Basil Blackwell.

Sewell, William H. Jr. 1980. *Work and Revolution in France: The Language of Labor from the Old Regime to 1848*. Cambridge: Cambridge University Press.

———. 1990. "Collective Violence and Collective Loyalties in France: Why the French Revolution Made a Difference." *Politics and Society* 18: 527–552.

———. 1992. "A Theory of Structure: Duality, Agency, and Transformation." *American Journal of Sociology* 98: 1–29.

———. 1996. "Three Temporalities: Toward an Eventful Sociology." In Terrence J. McDonald, ed., *The Historic Turn in the Human Sciences*. Ann Arbor: University of Michigan Press.

Shearing, Clifford D., and Richard V. Ericson. 1991. "Culture as Figurative Action." *British Journal of Sociology* 42: 481–506.

Shibutani, Tamotsu. 1955. "Reference Groups as Perspectives." *American Journal of Sociology* 60: 562–569.

Shils, Edward. 1981. *Tradition*. Chicago: University of Chicago Press.

Shin, Gi-Wook. 1994. "The Historical Analysis of Collective Action: The Korean Peasant Uprisings of 1946." *American Journal of Sociology* 99: 1596–1624.

Shorter, Edward. 1975. *The Making of the Modern Family*. New York: Basic Books.

Shorter, Edward, and Charles Tilly. 1974. *Strikes in France, 1830–1968*. London: Cambridge University Press.

Shott, Susan. 1979. "Emotion and Social Life: A Symbolic Interactionist Analysis." *American Journal of Sociology* 84: 1317–1334.

Sihanouk, Norodom. 1980. *War and Hope: The Case for Cambodia*. New York: Pantheon.

Silver, Morris. 1974. "Political Revolution and Repression: An Economic Approach." *Public Choice* 17: 63–71.

Singer, Peter. 1975. *Animal Liberation: A New Ethics for Our Treatment of Animals*. New York: New York Review of Books.

Slater, Philip. 1963. "On Social Regression." *American Sociological Review* 28: 339–364.

Slovic, Paul, Baruch Fischhoff, and Sarah Lichtenstein. 1980. "Facts and Fear: Understanding Perceived Risk." In Richard C. Schwing and Walter A. Albers Jr., eds., *Societal Risk Assessment: How Safe Is Safe Enough?* New York: Plenum.

Smelser, Neil J. 1962. *Theory of Collective Behavior.* New York: Free Press.

Smith, Anthony D. 1983. *Theories of Nationalism.* 2d ed. New York: Holmes and Meier.

———. 1986. *The Ethnic Origins of Nations.* Oxford: Blackwell.

———. 1991. *National Identity.* London: Penguin.

———, ed. 1992. *Ethnicity and Nationalism.* New York: E. J. Brill.

Smith, Christian. 1996. *Resisting Reagan: The U.S. Central America Peace Movement.* Chicago: University of Chicago Press.

Smith, Christian S., ed. 1996. *Disruptive Religion: The Force of Faith in Social Movement Activism.* New York: Routledge.

Smith, Jonathan Z. 1987. *To Take Place: Toward Theory in Ritual.* Chicago: University of Chicago Press.

Snepp, Frank. 1977. *Decent Interval: An Insider's Account of Saigon's Indecent End.* New York: Random House.

Snow, David A., and Robert D. Benford. 1988. "Ideology, Frame Resonance, and Participant Mobilization." *International Social Movement Research* 1: 197–217.

———. 1992. "Master Frames and Cycles of Protest." In Aldon D. Morris and Carol McClurg Mueller, eds., *Frontiers in Social Movement Theory.* New Haven: Yale University Press.

Snow, David, and C. L. Phillips. 1980. "The Lofland-Stark Conversion Model: A Critical Reassessment." *Social Problems* 27: 430–437.

Snow, David A., E. Burke Rochford, Jr., Steven K. Worden, and Robert D. Benford. 1986. "Frame Alignment Processes, Micromobilization, and Movement Participation." *American Sociological Review* 51: 464–481.

Snow, David A., Louis A. Zurcher, Jr., and Sheldon Ekland-Olson. 1980. "Social Networks and Social Movement: A Microstructural Approach to Differential Recruitment." *American Sociological Review* 45: 787–801.

———. 1983. "Further Thoughts on Social Networks and Movement Recruitment." *Sociology* 17: 112–120.

Soeken, Karen L., and Donald R. Soeken. 1987. "A Survey of Whistleblowers: Their Stressors and Coping Strategies." Unpublished paper, Laurel, Maryland.

Solomon, Robert C. 1976. *The Passions.* New York: Doubleday- Anchor.

Solomon, Susan D., Elizabeth M. Smith, Lee N. Robins, and Ruth L. Fischbach. 1987. "Social Involvement as a Mediator of Disaster-Induced Stress." *Journal of Applied Social Psychology* 17: 1092–1112.

Sontag, Susan. 1977. *On Photography.* New York: Farrar, Straus and Giroux.

———. 1978. *Illness as Metaphor.* New York: Farrar, Straus and Giroux.

Spector, Malcolm, and John I. Kitsuse. 1987. *Constructing Social Problems.* New York: Aldine de Gruyter.

Sperling, Susan. 1988. *Animal Liberators: Research and Morality.* Berkeley and Los Angeles: University of California Press.

Staggenborg, Suzanne. 1991. *The Pro-Choice Movement: Organization and Activism in the Abortion Conflict.* New York: Oxford University Press.

Starhawk. 1988. *Dreaming the Dark: Magic, Sex, and Politics.* Boston: Beacon Press.

Stearns, Carol Zisowitz, and Peter N. Stearns. 1986. *Anger: The Struggle for Emotional Control in America's History.* Chicago: University of Chicago Press.

Stephens, Mitchell. 1988. *A History of News.* New York: Penguin Books.

Stockwell, John. 1978. *In Search of Enemies: A CIA Story.* New York: W. W. Norton.

Stromberg, Peter G. 1993. *Language and Self-Transformation: A Study of the Christian Conversion Narrative.* Cambridge: Cambridge University Press.

Stults, Karen. 1989. "Women Movers: Reflections on a Movement By Some of Its Leaders." *Everyone's Backyard* 7. Published by the Citizens' Clearinghouse for Hazardous Waste, Arlington, Virginia.

Sullins, Ellen. 1991. "Emotional Contagion Revisited: Effects of Social Comparison and Expressive Style on Mood Convergence." *Personality and Social Psychology Bulletin* 17: 166–174.

Svensson, Frances. 1979. "Liberal Democracy and Group Rights: The Legacy of Individualism and Its Impact on American Indian Tribes." *Political Studies* 27: 421–439.

Swanson, Guy E. 1988. *Ego Defenses and the Legitimation of Behavior.* Cambridge: Cambridge University Press.

Swidler, Ann. 1986. "Culture in Action: Symbols and Strategies." *American Sociological Review* 51: 273–286.

———. 1995. "Cultural Power and Social Movements." In Hank Johnston and Bert Klandermans, eds., *Social Movements and Culture.* Minneapolis: University of Minnesota Press.

Szasz, Andrew. 1994. *EcoPopulism: Toxic Waste and the Movement for Environmental Justice.* Minneapolis: University of Minnesota Press.

Talmon, Jacob Leib. 1952. *The Origins of Totalitarian Democracy.* London: Secker and Warburg.

———. 1967. *Romanticism and Revolt.* New York: Harcourt, Brace and World.

Tarrow, Sidney. 1983. "Struggling to Reform: Social Movement and Policy Change During Cycles of Protest." Western Societies Occasional Paper 15. Ithaca, N.Y.: Cornell University.

———. 1994. *Power in Movement: Social Movements, Collective Action, and Politics.* Cambridge: Cambridge University Press.

Taylor, Charles. 1985. *Philosophy and the Human Sciences.* Cambridge: Cambridge University Press.

———. 1985. "Understanding and Ethnocentricity." In *Philosophy and the Human Sciences.* Cambridge: Cambridge University Press.

———. 1989. *Sources of the Self: The Making of the Modern Identity.* Cambridge: Harvard University Press.

Taylor, Michael. 1987. *The Possibility of Cooperation.* Cambridge: Cambridge University Press.

————. 1988. "Rationality and Revolutionary Collective Action." In Michael Taylor, ed., *Rationality and Revolution*. Cambridge: Cambridge University Press.

Taylor, Verta, and Nancy E. Whittier. 1992. "Collective Identity in Social Movement Communities: Lesbian Feminist Mobilization." In Aldon D. Morris and Carol McClurg Mueller, eds., *Frontiers in Social Movement Theory*. New Haven: Yale University Press.

————. 1995. "Analytical Approaches to Social Movement Culture: The Culture of the Women's Movement." In Hank Johnston and Bert Klandermans, eds., *Social Movements and Culture*. Minneapolis: University of Minnesota Press.

Tec, Nechama. 1986. *When Light Pierced the Darkness: Christian Rescue of Jews in Nazi-Occupied Poland*. New York: Oxford University Press.

Thelen, David. 1986. *Paths of Resistance: Tradition and Dignity in Industrializing Missouri*. New York: Clarendon Press.

Thoits, Peggy A. 1985. "Self-Labeling Processes in Mental Illness: The Role of Emotional Deviance." *American Journal of Sociology* 92: 221–249.

————. 1989. "The Sociology of Emotions." *Annual Review of Sociology* 15: 317–342.

————. 1990. "Emotional Deviance: Research Agendas." In Theodore D. Kemper, ed., *Research Agendas in the Sociology of Emotions*. Albany: SUNY Press.

Thomas, Keith. 1971. *Religion and the Decline of Magic*. New York: Scribner's.

————. 1983. *Man and the Natural World*. New York: Pantheon.

Thompson, E. P. 1966. *The Making of the English Working Class*. New York: Vintage.

Tilly, Charles. 1964. *The Vendée*. Cambridge: Harvard University Press.

————. 1978. *From Mobilization to Revolution*. Reading, Mass: Addison-Wesley.

————. 1986. *The Contentious French: Four Centuries of Popular Struggle*. Cambridge: Harvard University Press.

————. 1988. "Social Movements, Old and New." *Research in Social Movements, Conflicts, and Change* 10: 1–18.

————. 1993. *European Revolutions, 1492–1992*. Oxford: Basil Blackwell.

————. 1995. *Popular Contention in Great Britain, 1758–1834*. Cambridge: Harvard University Press.

Tilly, Charles, and Lynn. H. Lees. 1975. "The People of June, 1848." In Roger Price, ed., *Revolution and Reaction: 1848 and the Second French Republic*. New York: Barnes and Noble.

Tilly, Charles, Louise Tilly, and Richard Tilly. 1975. *The Rebellious Century, 1830–1930*. Cambridge: Harvard University Press.

Touraine, Alain. 1971. *The Post-Industrial Society: Tomorrow's Social History: Classes, Conflicts and Culture in the Programmed Society*. Translated by Leonard F. X. Mayhew. New York: Random House.

————. 1977. *The Self-Production of Society*. Chicago: University of Chicago Press.

————. 1981. *The Voice and the Eye: An Analysis of Social Movements*. New York: Cambridge University Press.

———. 1988. *Return of the Actor: Social Theory in Postindustrial Society*. Translated by Myrna Godzich. Minneapolis: University of Minnesota Press.

———. 1995. *Critique of Modernity*. Cambridge, Mass.: Blackwell.

Touraine, Alain, François Dubet, Michel Wieviorka, and Jan Strzelecki. 1983. *Solidarity: Poland 1980–1981*. New York: Cambridge University Press.

Touraine, Alain, Zsuzsa Hegedüs, François Dubet, and Michel Wieviorka. 1983. *Anti-Nuclear Protest: The Opposition to Nuclear Energy in France*. Translated by Peter Fawcett. New York: Cambridge University Press.

Touraine, Alain, Michel Wieviorka, and François Dubet. 1987. *The Workers' Movement*. Translated by Ian Patterson. New York: Cambridge University Press.

Traugott, Mark. 1980. "Determinants of Political Organization: Class and Organization in the Parisian Insurrection of June 1848." *American Journal of Sociology* 86: 32–49.

Tuan, Yi-Fu. 1982. *Segmented Worlds and Self*. Minneapolis: University of Minnesota Press.

———. 1984. *Dominance and Affection: The Making of Pets*. New Haven: Yale University Press.

Tucker, Robert C. 1973. *Stalin as Revolutionary, 1879–1919: A Study in History and Personality*. New York: W. W. Norton.

Tullock, Gordon. 1971. "The Paradox of Revolution." *Public Choice* 11: 89–99.

Turner, James. 1980. *Reckoning with the Beast: Animals, Pain, and Humanity in the Victorian Mind*. Baltimore: Johns Hopkins University Press.

Turner, Ralph H. 1996. "The Moral Issue in Collective Behavior and Collective Action." *Mobilization* 1: 1–15.

Turner, Ralph H., and Lewis M. Killian. 1987. *Collective Behavior*. 3d ed. Englewood Cliffs, N.J.: Prentice-Hall.

Turner, Victor. 1967. *The Forest of Symbols: Aspects of Ndembu Ritual*. Ithaca, N.Y.: Cornell University Press.

———. 1969. *The Ritual Process: Structure and Anti-Structure*. Ithaca, N.Y.: Cornell University Press.

———. 1974. "Pilgrimages as Social Processes." In *Dramas, Fields, and Metaphors*. Ithaca, N.Y.: Cornell University Press.

Turner, Victor, and Edith Turner. 1978. *Image and Pilgrimage in Christian Culture: Anthropological Perspectives*. New York: Columbia University Press.

United States Congress. 1976. "Investigation of Charges Relating to Nuclear Reactor Safety: Hearings Before the Joint Committee on Atomic Energy, 94th Congress, Second Session, February 18 to March 4, 1976." Washington, D.C.: U.S. Government Printing Office.

Vaillant, George E. 1993. *The Wisdom of the Ego: Sources of Resilience in Adult Life*. Cambridge: Harvard University Press.

Valien, Preston. 1961. "The Montgomery Bus Protest as a Social Movement." In Jitsuichi Masuoka and Preston Valien, eds., *Race Relations: Problems and Theory*. Chapel Hill: University of North Carolina Press.

Vanderford, Marsha L. 1989. "Vilification and Social Movements: A Case Study of Pro-Life and Pro-Choice Rhetoric." *Quarterly Journal of Speech* 75: 166–182.

van Ginneken, Jaap. 1991. *Crowds, Psychology, and Politics, 1871–1899.* New York: Cambridge University Press.

van der Pligt, Joop. 1992. *Nuclear Energy and the Public.* Oxford: Basil Blackwell.

van der Pligt, Joop, J. Richard Eiser, and Russell Spears. 1986. "Attitudes Toward Nuclear Energy: Familiarity and Salience." *Environment and Behavior* 18: 75–93.

Vaughan, Diane. 1990. "Autonomy, Interdependence, and Social Control: NASA and the Space Shuttle Challenger." *Administrative Science Quarterly* 35: 225–257.

———. 1996. *The Challenger Launch Decision: Risky Technology, Culture, and Deviance at NASA.* Chicago: University of Chicago Press.

Vickery, Michael. 1984. *Cambodia: 1975–1982.* Boston: South End Press.

Waddington, David, Karen Jones, and Chas Critcher. 1989. *Flashpoints: Studies in Disorder.* London: Routledge.

Wald, Matthew L. 1989. "Energy Department to Pay $73 Million to Settle Uranium Case in Ohio." *New York Times* 1 July.

Walker, J. Samuel. 1992. *Containing the Atom: Nuclear Regulation in a Changing Environment 1963–1971.* Berkeley: University of California Press.

Walker, Stephen F. 1983. *Animal Thought.* London: Routledge and Kegan Paul.

Wallerstein, Immanuel. 1989. *The Modern World System, III: The Second Era of Great Expansion of the Capitalist World- Economy.* New York: Academic Press.

Walsh, Edward J. 1981. "Resource Mobilization and Citizen Protest in Communities Around Three Mile Island." *Social Problems* 29: 1–21.

———. 1986. "The Role of Target Vulnerabilities in High- Technology Protest Movements: The Nuclear Establishment at Three Mile Island." *Sociological Forum* 1: 199–218.

———. 1988. *Democracy in the Shadows: Citizen Mobilization in the Wake of the Accident at Three Mile Island.* New York: Greenwood Press.

———. 1988. "New Dimensions of Social Movement: The High-Level Waste-Siting Controversy." *Sociological Forum* 3: 586–605.

Walsh, Edward J., Rex Warland, and D. Clayton Smith. 1993. "Backyards, NIMBYs, and Incinerator Sitings: Implications for Social Movement Theory." *Social Problems* 40: 25–38.

———. Forthcoming. *The Environmental Justice Movement: Eight Grassroots Challenges to Modern Incinerator Projects.* University Park: Pennsylvania State University Press.

Walzer, Michael. 1965. *The Revolution of the Saints: A Study in the Origins of Radical Politics.* Cambridge: Harvard University Press.

———. 1983. *Spheres of Justice: A Defense of Pluralism and Equality.* New York: Basic Books.

Wasielewski, Patricia L. 1985. "The Emotional Basis of Charisma." *Symbolic Interaction* 8: 207–222.

Watters, Pat. 1971. *Down to Now: Reflections on the Southern Civil Rights Movement.* New York: Pantheon.

Weart, Spencer R. 1988. *Nuclear Fear: A History of Images.* Cambridge: Harvard University Press.

Weinstein, Deena. 1991. *Heavy Metal: A Cultural Sociology*. New York: Lexington Books.

Weller, J. M., and E. L. Quarantelli. 1974. "Neglected Characteristics of Collective Behavior." *American Journal of Sociology* 79: 665–683.

Westin, Alan F., ed. 1981. *Whistle Blowing! Loyalty and Dissent in the Corporation*. New York: McGraw-Hill.

Whalen, Jack, and Richard Flacks. 1984. "Echoes of Rebellion: The Liberated Generation Grows Up." *Journal of Political and Military Sociology* 12: 61–78.

Whittier, Nancy. 1995. *Feminist Generations: The Persistence of the Radical Women's Movement*. Philadelphia: Temple University Press.

Whorf, Benjamin Lee. 1956. *Language, Thought, and Reality*. Cambridge: MIT Press.

Wiley, Norbert. 1994. *The Semiotic Self*. Chicago: University of Chicago Press.

Williams, Raymond. 1973. *The Country and the City*. New York: Oxford University Press.

———. 1977. *Marxism and Literature*. Oxford: Oxford University Press.

Williams, Rhys H. 1995. "Constructing the Public Good: Social Movements and Cultural Resources." *Social Problems* 42: 124–144.

Winch, Peter. 1970. "Understanding a Primitive Society." In Bryan R. Wilson, ed., *Rationality*. Oxford: Basil Blackwell.

Wittgenstein, Ludwig. 1980. *Remarks on the Philosophy of Psychology*. Vol. 1. Oxford: Basil Blackwell.

Wolfe, Alan. 1989. *Whose Keeper? Social Science and Moral Obligation*. Berkeley: University of California Press.

Worrell, Dan L., Wallace N. Davidson III, and Abuzar El-Jelly. 1993. "Do Boycotts and Divestitures Work? A Stock Market Based Test." Unpublished manuscript.

Wuthnow, Robert, and Marsha Witten. 1988. "New Directions in the Study of Culture." *Annual Review of Sociology* 14: 49–67.

Yack, Bernard. 1986. *The Longing for Total Revolution: Philosophical Sources of Social Discontent from Rousseau to Marx and Nietzsche*. Princeton: Princeton University Press.

Zablocki, Benjamin. 1971. *The Joyful Community: An Account of the Bruderhof, a Communal Movement Now in Its Third Generation*. Baltimore: Penguin.

Zajonc, Robert B. 1980. "Feeling and Thinking: Preferences Need No Inferences." *American Psychologist* 35: 151–175.

Zald, Mayer N., and Roberta Ash. 1966. "Social Movement Organizations: Growth, Decay, and Change." *Social Forces* 44: 327–40. Reprinted in Mayer N. Zald and John D. McCarthy, *Social Movements in an Organizational Society: Collected Essays*. New Brunswick, N.J.: Transaction.

Zald, Mayer N., and John D. McCarthy, eds. 1987. *Social Movements in an Organizational Society: Collected Essays*. New Brunswick, N.J.: Transaction.

———. 1979. *The Dynamics of Social Movements: Resource Mobilization, Social Control, and Tactics*. Cambridge, Mass: Winthrop.

Zald, Mayer N., and Bert Useem. 1987. "Movement and Countermovement Interaction: Mobilization, Tactics, and State Involvement." In Mayer N. Zald and John D. McCarthy, eds., *Social Movements in an Organizational Society: Collected Essays*. New Brunswick, N.J.: Transaction.

Zeigler, Joseph Wesley. 1973. *Regional Theatre: The Revolutionary Stage*. Minneapolis: University of Minnesota Press.

Zelizer, Viviana A. 1985. *Pricing the Priceless Child: The Changing Social Value of Children*. New York: Basic Books.

————. 1994. *The Social Meaning of Money*. New York: Basic Books.

Zerubavel, Eviatar. 1991. *The Fine Line: Making Distinctions in Everyday Life*. New York: Free Press.

Zolberg, Aristide R. 1972. "Moments of Madness." *Politics and Society* 2: 183–207.

Zonabend, Françoise. 1993. *The Nuclear Peninsula*. Cambridge: Cambridge University Press.

Zuboff, Shoshana. 1988. *In the Age of the Smart Machine: The Future of Work and Power*. New York: Basic Books.

Zurcher, Louis, and David Snow. 1981. "Collective Behavior: Social Movements." In Ralph H. Turner and Morris Rosenberg, eds., *Social Psychology: Sociological Perspectives*. New York: Basic Books.

Zucker, Lynne G. 1987. "Institutional Theories of Organizations." *Annual Review of Sociology* 13: 443–464.

Index

Abalone Alliance, 188–92; activist identities in, 185; affinity groups in, 190; community sense in, 192; emotions as resources for, 203–5; expanding into other issues, 231; formal leadership lacking in, 203; and formal organizations, 376; *It's About Times* newsletter, 171, 178, 203; member solidarity in, 191; and Mothers for Peace, 200, 229, 233–34; movement identity in, 89–90; singing and dancing in, 192, 193–94; social networks of, 233; solidarity in, 194; staff fires itself, 211; taste in tactics, 229, 233, 238, 239

abolition movement, 395n.60

abortion: cognitive understandings regarding, 135; fetuses, 176, 373; as life passage, 448n.8; pro-choice movement, 307, 421n.9; *Roe v. Wade*, 177; the two sides characterizing each other, 121; worldviews of the two sides, 156. *See also* anti-abortion movement

abstract systems, 352–56, 363, 366, 377

action: cognitive belief reinforced by, 207; communicative, 43–44, 351; culture channeling political, 12–13; expressive, 43; strategic, 43–44, 219, 160, 271, 351. *See also* collective action; direct action; ends (goals) of action; means of action

activist identity, 197–200; in Abalone Alliance, 185; components of, 197; as designed for political work, 328; of Diablo Canyon protestors, 195; in infiltrators, 141; jail time in, 197; in Mothers for Peace, 105; as movement identity, 87; as property of individuals, 215; as proxy for many specific characteristics,

214–15; and radicalization, 245; tactical identities diverging within, 237–38; tactical taste in, 246; whistleblowers developing, 146

activist networks: activist identity supported by, 197–98; California direct-action subculture as, 194

acts of god, 118–19

ACT UP, 6, 95, 119–20, 387n.4

Adelson, Kathryn Pyne, 406n.68

admiration, 112

AEC. *See* Atomic Energy Commission

affect: as building block of protest movement, 154; as central component of social life, 111; and emotion, 409n.21; in familial and friendship bonds, 62; in moral shock, 107; for place, 93; possible effects of, 114; and rationality, 58. *See also* affective bonds; emotions

affect control theory, 111

affective bonds: in activist networks, 197; creation of, 80, 191–92; as psychological universal, 55; in recruitment, 401n.11; as resources, 204; and revolutionary discipline, 218

affinity groups, 190, 202, 203, 242

African-American churches, 38, 173, 193, 256, 427n.16, 434n.9

African-Americans: black nationalism, 433n.25; black power, 11, 85; Canarsie integration protest, 281–85, 289–92; images of, 282; young black men as stigmatized, 362. *See also* civil rights movement

agency, 11, 65, 93, 398n.41

AIDS, 119–20

Albany, Georgia, 301–2

ments, 323; people rewriting their own, 382; place as carrier of, 93; punctuated equilibria in, 22; for revolutionaries, 362; single narrative for rejected, 54; visions of as differing, 12. *See also* events

Hochschild, Arlie, 186, 396n.17

Hoffman, Abbie, 6

Holifield, Chester Earl, 222, 225

Hollander, Jocelyn, 316, 318

home: construction of sense of, 93–94, 406n.59; natural disasters destroying, 123; and ontological security, 124; pilgrimage contrasted with, 202; symbolic meaning of, 11; threats to as cause of protest, 107

home domain of a paradigm, 20, 388n.2

homemakers (housewives), 105, 307, 358, 407n.1

homosexual rights movement. *See* gay and lesbian rights movement

Hooker Chemical, 418n.28

hope, 114, 128

hostility, 114

housewives (homemakers), 105, 307, 358, 407n.1

Hubbard, Richard, 144, 145, 146

Huk rebellion, 218, 221

humane movement, 153, 164, 246–47

Humane Society of the United States, 246

Humphrey, Hubert, 260

Hunt, Scott, 89

hypergoods, 220, 226

ideas: changing, 333; defined, 155; in social movements, 157; transmitted from movement to movement, 57

identity: cultural concepts ignoring, 98; emotions giving power to motivate, 127; kinds of, 85–90, 328; as labels for shared visions and beliefs, 328; moral obligations carried by, 136; Nazi definition of German, 355; participation in movements as crafting, 84; place in forming, 93; as a product, 74; public identity, 405n.50. *See also* collective identity; movement identity; personal identity

identity theory: cultural movements giving rise to, 20; new social movement

theorists and, 71, 404n.47; overextension in, 40; as post-industrial theory, 71

ideological radicalization, 433n.23

ideologies: and animal rights movement, 167; defined, 155; emotion in, 127, 408n.6; enemies made by abstract, 356–58; marxist interpretation of, 419n.6; and moral shock, 140; and organizations, 289; poets compared with ideologists, 159; resources used to promulgate, 291; sensibilities limiting, 353; simplifying ideologies, 356, 446n.34; in social movements, 157; as source of moral resistance, 150; totalizing ideologies, 354, 363; universalistic ideologies, 289; value-free ideologies, 135; worldviews compared with, 157

iiFAR (incurably ill for Animal Research), 313

immigrants, 348, 368, 361

incinerators, Brooklyn campaign against, 278–81, 289–92

indignation, 114

individualism, 4, 350

individual protest: border with organized movements, 104; in boycotts, 253; emergence of, 325; as form of moral protest, 5, 387n.1; scholars ignoring, 5, 387n.1

individuals: activist identity as property of, 215; as artfully crafting their lives, 367; change in, 354; culture linking through symbols, 50; and formal organizations, 215–16, 382; groups as work of, 216–17; ideas transmitted from movement to movement by, 57; innovation starting with, 66; practices in lives of, 338–39; protest's benefit for, 367; symbolic power of, 92; as troublesome for social science, 216. *See also* biography; self; individual protest

infiltrators, 137–38, 141

Inglehart, Ronald, 423n.37

injustice frames, 120–21; belief that others are shaping the world in, 357; components of, 49; defined, 78; the media and, 288; negative emotions in, 126, 179; resources used to promulgate, 291

innocent victims, 118, 120, 156, 166, 176, 282

innovation, 66, 369, 375